13th International Conference on Strategic Management and Its Support by Information Systems 2019

Ostrava, Czech Republic
21-22 May 2019

Editors:

Radek Nemec
Lucie Chytilova

ISBN: 978-1-5108-8872-2

Printed from e-media with permission by:

Curran Associates, Inc.
57 Morehouse Lane
Red Hook, NY 12571

VŠB - Technical University of Ostrava
17. Listopadu 15/2172
708 33 Ostrava - Poruba
Czech Republic

Phone: +420 597 325 278
Fax: +420 596 918 507

university@vsb.cz

Additional copies of this publication are available from:

Curran Associates, Inc.
57 Morehouse Lane
Red Hook, NY 12571 USA
Phone: 845-758-0400
Fax: 845-758-2633
Email: curran@proceedings.com
Web: www.proceedings.com

VŠB - Technical University of Ostrava, Faculty of Economics

SMSIS

Proceedings of the

13th International Conference

on

Strategic Management and its Support by Information Systems

Radek Němec
Lucie Chytilová
(Eds.)

May 21st - 22nd
Ostrava
Czech Republic

2019

DESIGN Radek Nemec *(title background graphic is a free vector art designed by Starline / Freepik and downloaded from the URL: http://www.freepik.com/)*

EDITORS Radek Nemec, Lucie Chytilova

PUBLISHER VŠB – Technical University of Ostrava
Faculty of Economics
Department of Systems Engineering

PUBLICATION YEAR 2019

NUMBER OF PAGES 425

PAPER CITATION EXAMPLE:

Author, A. (2019). 'Title of the paper'. In: Nemec, R. and Chytilova, L. (eds.) *Proceedings of the 13th International Conference on Strategic Management and its Support by Information Systems 2019*, May 21-22, 2019, Ostrava, Czech Republic, pp. x-y.

All papers published in the proceedings have been peer-reviewed by 2 independent reviewers. Editors are not responsible for the grammar and language used in papers.

VSB TECHNICAL UNIVERSITY OF OSTRAVA | FACULTY OF ECONOMICS

ČSSI

MEMBERS OF THE PROGRAMME COMMITTEE

Members of the Organizing Committee

Chair **Lucie Chytilová**

VŠB – Technical University of Ostrava, Czech Republic

Members

Blanka Bazsová

VŠB – Technical University of Ostrava, Czech Republic

Radek Němec

VŠB – Technical University of Ostrava, Czech Republic

František Zapletal

VŠB – Technical University of Ostrava, Czech Republic

Conference website

http://www.ekf.vsb.cz/smsis/

PREFACE

Two years have passed and, once again, we are here with our international meeting of academics and professionals – the conference on Strategic Management and its Support by Information Systems (SMSIS). This year, the conference is held for the 13th consecutive year and, again, we are glad for the support from the dean of the Faculty of Economics, VŠB – Technical University of Ostrava, prof. Zdeněk Zmeškal.

The first SMSIS conference has been held in 1995 and, to this day, it continues as a traditionally bi-annual platform for professional discussions and exchange of experiences between research teams from various countries and institutions around the world, namely from the Czech Republic, Hungary, Iran, Spain, Slovakia and the United Kingdom. The conference focuses on a relatively broad scale of topics that are associated with:

- strategic management,
- quantitative methods and their applications in management issues,
- trends and issues in information systems design, management and security,
- and applications of new media and intelligent tools in the Digital Economy.

This year, several new hot topics are presented and discussed, namely, social dimension of strategic management, benchmarking in supply chain management, spatial econometrics, cybersecurity for industry 4.0, or artificial neural network and machine-learning with human-in-the-loop.

The SMSIS 2019 conference is organized in cooperation with the Czech Society for Systems Integration (CSSI) and three Czech universities: VŠB – Technical University of Ostrava (Faculty of Economics), University of Economics in Prague (Faculty of Informatics and Statistics) and Masaryk University in Brno (Faculty of Informatics).

The SMSIS conference proceedings usually contains about 50 carefully selected scholarly and professional papers, which are double-blind reviewed by members of the programme committee, who certainly deserve thanks for their devoted work. I would like to thank the members of the organizing committee as well, for their dedication and hard-work during the preparation and organization of the SMSIS 2019 conference event.

I wish all of us to be successful in the presentation of our work, our contributions to be beneficial to conference participants and that the event will meet everyone's expectations.

To a successful conference!

Jana Hančlová

May 2019

TABLE OF CONTENTS

KEYNOTE SPEECHES (ABSTRACTS)

REGULAR PAPERS

SECTION A

STRATEGIC MANAGEMENT

SECTION B

QUANTITATIVE METHODS IN MANAGEMENT

SECTION C

CURRENT TRENDS AND ISSUES IN INFORMATION SYSTEMS DESIGN, MANAGEMENT AND SECURITY

SECTION D

APPLICATIONS OF NEW MEDIA AND INTELLIGENT TOOLS IN THE DIGITAL ECONOMY AND MODELLING

KEYNOTE SPEECHES

(ABSTRACTS)

Industry 4.0 and its Impact on the Labour Market: an Opportunity or a Threat?

Jakub Fischer [1]

Abstract. Several studies and discussions focus on automation and digitisation which are parts of the forthcoming process called Industry 4.0. Their authors analyse the impact of Industry 4.0 on the economy and the labour market in particular. In their conclusions, they warn against the future situation on the labour market and the employment destruction.
The speech aims to present the analysis of the impact of structural changes on production, gross value added and employment. The effect of change in the total demand sharply differs across specific industries. While an increase in demand for oil extraction of 1 mil. CZK leads to an increase in employment of 200 hours per year, the same increase in demand for security and investigation services causes an increase in work of 4,912 hours. Using the input-output analysis, we present different scenarios of the Czech economic development in the overall context of the current Czech economy.

Jakub Fischer graduated at the University of Economics, Prague, in 2001 (Statistics and Insurance) and attained a PhD degree in statistics in 2005. In 2008 he became an associate professor of statistics, in 2018 he has been appointed as the professor of economic policy. Since 2018, he serves as the Dean of the Faculty of Informatics and Statistics of the University of Economics, Prague.

He focuses his research on the field of social and economic statistics and national accounting. As the key research results, he co-authored articles containing historical time series of the Czech GDP 1970-1989 estimated according to the ESA95 methodology, estimates of the efficiency of the Czech higher education institutions, estimates of internal rates of return on human capital investment differenced by study fields, sex and regions and some interdisciplinary papers related to connections between ICT and economy.

He has been the principal investigator or co-investigator of several research projects funded by the Czech Science Foundation and the Technology Agency of the Czech Republic. He is a member of the International Statistical Institute, Czech Statistical Society, Czech Demographic Society, a member of the Board of the Czech Economic Society and a member of the Academic Assembly of the Czech Academy of Science. Jakub Fischer is an author or co-author of 9 monographs, 54 peer-reviewed articles and 120 conference papers. H-index=8.

[1] University of Economics, Prague, Faculty of Informatics and Statistics, nam. W. Churchilla 4, 130 67 Prague 3, Czech Republic, fischerj@vse.cz.

Benchmarking in Supply Chain management Using Data Envelopment analysis

Adel Hatami-Marbini [2]

Abstract. During recent years, supply chain management has become an overriding subject for research in production and operations management. Supply chain performance measurement is often restricted to the key performance indicators to evaluate the success of a centralized organization- whether in the private or public sector- with multiple stages (tiers). However, this approach suffers from several intrinsic limitations (e.g. partial evaluations and Fox's Paradox). This paper explores a general model for supply chain performance assessment where the decomposition of productive efficiency is introduced in the entire supply chain vs chain level effects. Moreover, we provide a synopsis and constructive guidance on the type of models that could be appropriate for supply chain management. We also study a real application of performance assessment to a multi-national supply chain in the paper and pulp sector.

Adel Hatami-Marbini is a Professor in Business and Management, Faculty of Business and Law and his research revolves around operations research, performance measurement, and operations and supply chain management. He holds a BSC and an MSc in Industrial Engineering and received his PhD in Economics and Management Sciences from Louvain School of Management of Université catholique de Louvain (UCL), Belgium. Adel also visited Aston Business School, Technical University of Ostrava, University of Seville, American University of Beirut and Virginia Tech.

His research interests primarily cover two areas. First, he explores the performance measurement and management processes within organizations when uncertainty matters, particularly stochastic and subjective uncertainty. This research area is intrinsically interdisciplinary in the sense that the activities and processes of public or private sectors -R&D, education, transportation, banking, health care, and hospital- are obliged to continuously monitor, analyse and review their performances and productivity. Second, he focuses on operations and supply chain management, with the particular emphasis on centralized decision making in supply chains, transportation and logistics, resource allocation, supplier relationship management and the impact of environmental issues on supply chain management. Research methodologies largely embrace optimisation methods with emphasis on linear, multi-objective programming, multi-criteria decision analysis (MCDA) and frontier analysis.

He has published over 55 research papers in a variety of scholarly academic journals including European Journal of Operational Research (ABS List 4), Omega (ABS List 3), Expert Systems with Applications (ABS List 3) and Journal of the Operational Research Society (ABS List 3), among others and has regularly presented his work at various national and international conferences.

---

[2] De Montfort University, Leicester Castle Business School, Department of Strategic Management and Marketing, Hugh Aston Building, The Gateway, Leicester LE1 9BH, United Kingdom, adel.hatamimarbini@dmu.ac.uk.

Fitting disjunctive functions to the information retrieval and decision making tasks

Miroslav Hudec [3]

Abstract. Disjunction is formalized by any aggregation function bounded by the maximal value of atomic predicates (the overall score cannot be smaller than the maximum of all atomic predicates often expressed by fuzzy sets) and value 1. A convenient way to model disjunction is by t-conorms, which convey variety of algebraic properties and therefore are able to solve diverse tasks. The MAX function, although often used, is not suitable for a large scale of tasks. For instance, adding a piece of positive evidence should cause increased value of the overall score (e.g., belief about something). Further, even though not a single piece of evidence reached its maximal intensity, the solution should be equal to 1 (indicating the full concern), or the solution should be limited by a certain degree. The next class are tasks, where people consider OR operator as the left-right order of predicates (alternatives), i.e. the first predicate is a full alternative, whereas the other are less relevant ones. This requirement is managed by the asymmetric disjunction, an aggregation of disjunctive and averaging functions.

Diverse tasks require disjunctive functions of the desired properties. We should be aware of properties and limitations to recognize suitable functions and their parameters when fitting to the users' requirements, which are often expressed linguistically. The next perspective is fitting function to the available sets of input-output data. The synergy of both approaches is an important topic for the explainable machine learning with human-in-the-loop.

Miroslav Hudec is an associate professor at the University of Economics in Bratislava (Slovakia), Faculty of Economic Informatics. He received the Master and PhD degrees from the University of Belgrade (Serbia) in information science and operations research, respectively. His work is mainly focused on fuzzy logic, aggregation functions, knowledge discovery, and information systems. He is a member of program committees of several international conferences and serves as an editorial board member in several journals including Applied Soft Computing (IF 3.907). He has published more than 50 articles including monograph in Springer. In the FP7 project Blue-ETS focused on the modernizing official statistics, he was leader of two working packages.

---

[3] University of Economics in Bratislava, Faculty of Economic Informatics, Dolnozemska cesta 1/b, 852 35 Bratislava 5, Slovakia, miroslav.hudec@euba.sk.

SECTION

A

STRATEGIC MANAGEMENT

Responsible Employment as a Strategic Issue

Károly Balaton[1], Dóra Diána Horváth[2]

Abstract. Companies have become important players in the development of society and their responsibilities exceed economic functions and the legal requirements. By practicing corporate social responsibility, companies can be conscious of the impact they are having on all aspects of society, including economic, social, and environmental aspects.

The internal dimension of CSR is basically the responsibility towards the employees. They should be involved in the company's CSR activities in order to engage and motivate them. Studies have shown that employee engagement may have a positive effect on their work, including decreased absenteeism and turnover, as well as increased customer satisfaction and loyalty. Also, it can lead to increased productivity and revenue growth in the long run, creating a win-win situation for the company and both parties. The authors intend to make empirical research to confirm it in the future, for which this paper gives the theoretical base to explore the topic of strategic CSR.

Keywords: Corporate Social Responsibility; responsible employment; CSR strategy; internal CSR; employee engagement.

JEL Classification: M14

1 Introduction and aim of the paper

Corporate Social Responsibility (or CSR) has become a well-known and widely used term during the last two decades. Not only papers and studies have been written about it but also companies have been taking CSR issues into consideration during their everyday operation. However, much misunderstanding and misleading information exist around the approach, while the opinion of practitioners differ about many elements of the definition and implementation of CSR.

In this paper, after a general introduction to the CSR approach, we highlight the importance of the CSR strategy by incorporating it to a company's corporate strategy. Many enterprises at low level of CSR consciousness think that carrying out ad-hoc, single projects (e.g. donations) is enough. We believe that if a company intends to reach a higher level of CSR application, they must consider it as a strategic question. We deal particularly with the theoretical background, our aim is only to clarify the issue of CSR on the theoretical base. We intend to make further, empirical research in the future after we explored the main concepts and doctrines of the topic thoroughly.

Here we discuss the internal type of CSR, as in our opinion a company should start acting responsibly 'within its own walls', in its activities towards its own employees. Responsible corporate behavior could mean many different things; we try to enumerate the ones that we consider the most important. We would like to show the main interrelations and interdependence of the different phenomena, emphasizing the importance of the strategic thinking.

[1] Institute of Management Sciences, University of Miskolc, szvbk@uni-miskolc.hu

[2] Institute of Management Sciences, University of Miskolc, horvath.dora@uni-miskolc.hu

2 The concept of Corporate Social Responsibility (CSR)

Stakeholders have many expectations towards the organization, so the company makes social, environmental and ethical commitments to satisfy these expected issues. These issues can be related to environmental quality, employee rights, community development, and diversity management, and all make claims on the attention of today's business manager.

In its broadest sense, CSR refers to "the firm's consideration of, and response to, issues beyond the narrow economic, technical, and legal requirements of the firm… (to) accomplish social benefits along with the traditional economic gains which the firms seek" (Davis, 1973, p. 312).

A considerable amount of literature has been published and much research has been carried out on the topic of CSR so far. The different interpretations and approaches that have emerged are shown below (Table 1):

Period	Name of Concept	Description	Literature
1950s-1960	Social Responsibility of businessmen	The obligations of businessmen to pursue policies, to make decisions or to follow lines of action which are desirable in terms of the objectives and values of society.	Bowen (1953)
		Some socially responsible business decisions can be justified by the long-run economic gain of the firm, thus paying back for its socially responsible behavior.	Davis (1960)
		Private contribution to society's economic and human resources and a willingness on the part of business to see that those resources were utilized for broad social ends.	Frederick (1960)
1960s-1970s	Stakeholder Approach	Instead of striving only for larger returns to its shareholders, a responsible enterprise takes into account the interests of employees, suppliers, dealers, local communities and the nation as a whole.	Johnson (1971)
	Three Dimensional Model	The concept consists of corporate responsibilities (i.e., economic, legal, ethical and philanthropic), social issues of business (e.g., labor standards, human rights, environment protection and anticorruption) and corporate actions (e.g., reactive, defensive, accommodative and proactive).	Carroll (1979)
1980s-1990s	Three-dimensional model of principles, policies and processes	Integration of the principles of corporate responsibility, the policies of social issue management and the process of action into an evolving system.	Wartick and Cochran (1985)
	Institutional Framework and extended corporate actions	Four types of corporate responsibilities (i.e., economic, legal, ethical and philanthropic) were linked to three institutional levels (i.e., legal, organizational and individual), while corporate actions are extended to assessment, stockholder management and implementation management.	Wood (1991)

2000s	Three-domains approach	Three domains of corporate responsibilities: economic, legal and ethical.	Schwartz and Carroll (2003)
	New Concept	A process to integrate social, environmental, ethical, human rights and consumer concerns into business operations and core strategy in close corporation with the stakeholders.	European Commission (2011)

Table 1 Development of CSR concepts [Jhawar and Gupta, 2017]

The first serious discussions of it emerged during the 1950s, when Bowen introduced the concept of social responsibility of a businessman in a much wider sphere than pure profit seeking (Bonsón and Bednárová, 2015).

According to Business for Social Responsibility (BSR), corporate social responsibility is defined as "achieving commercial success in ways that honour ethical values and respect people, communities, and the natural environment" (White, 2006, p. 6). McWilliams and Siegel (2000) describe CSR as actions that appeal to further some social good, beyond the interest of the firm and that which is required by law.

Based on these definitions and explanations we can conclude that CSR goes beyond just following the laws and legal regulations. It means much more than that. According to some practitioners of the 'stricter' approach, only those initiatives of the company belong to CSR which are truly voluntary, philanthropic activities.

3 CSR strategy

According to Krainz (2015), Corporate Social Responsibility (CSR) as a comprehensive concept incorporated into organization strategy increases competitiveness.

Every company differs in the way it implements CSR. "The differences depend on such factors as the specific company's size, the particular industry involved, the firm's business culture, stakeholder demands, and how historically progressive the company is in engaging CSR. For successful implementation, it is crucial that the CSR principles are part of the corporations' values and strategic planning, and that both management and employees are committed to them. Furthermore, it is important that the CSR strategy is aligned with the company's specific corporate objectives and core competencies." (Tsoutsoura, 2004, pp. 3-4)

How to develop a well-established and well-functioning CSR strategy and how to build it into the company strategy is an important issue for an organization today. A CSR strategy operates as a 'road map' for moving ahead on CSR issues. It sets the company's direction for and scope of CSR over the long term. It also allows the company to be successful by using its resources within its unique environment to meet market needs and fulfill stakeholder expectations.

As Hohnen and Potts (2007, p. 33) puts it, "following a CSR strategy helps to ensure that a firm builds, maintains and continually strengthens its identity, its market, and its relationships". A good CSR strategy identifies and consists of the following elements (Hohnen and Potts, 2007):

- overall direction for where the company wants to take its CSR work (planning phase);

- the stakeholders and their specific perspectives, interests and expectations (key players of the company's environment);
- a basic approach for moving ahead (showing orientation for the future);
- specific priority areas (list and ranking of those initiatives that the company intends to participate in);
- a time line for action, responsible staff, and immediate next steps (project-oriented approach);
- a process for reviewing and assuring outcomes (control and feedback phase).

There could be many different ways of making CSR strategy part of the global company strategy. In the paper we show a simple, obvious, three-step method that can serve as a frame for the future implementation and realization phase.

According to Guadamillas-Gómez et al. (2010) the integration of CSR into company strategy could be established through the development of the following stages:

1) *Introduction.* In this stage, the fundamental issue is the transmission of ethical principles and their integration into the culture which is shared by the organizational members. From this starting point, formal plans are elaborated in order to reach specific goals. Also, it is necessary to develop an effective communication plan so that the employees and other stakeholders have a clear perception that CSR is an aspect of strategic importance for the company.
2) *Implementation of the CSR plan.* In this stage certain factors become important when CSR formal plans are implemented, which are mainly related to HR practices, capabilities development and certain changes in order to adapt the organizational structure to the new situation, for which knowledge management systems and organizational culture are essential aspects.
3) *Generalization of CSR.* CSR integration into the company strategy is only possible to achieve if the previous stages have been successfully completed. It means a global change for the company, as CSR will be incorporated into the company's culture, mission and values. This third and last stage is completed with reports in order to measure advances in CSR and benefits for the stakeholders.

3.1 The types of CSR

Corporate Social Responsibility can have internal and external dimensions (Ludian, 2004). The internal dimension is basically the responsibility for the operations of employees and the company, while the external dimension covers the broader, "non-corporate" social responsibility (e.g. to the local community, consumers, NGOs, but ultimately the environment or the developing world).

The CSR for employees is undoubtedly at the heart of the company's sphere of influence, and as such, it is the primary focus of the CSR. In practice, corporate human rights programs and policies also start with the topic of employee rights. Obviously, the closer the company is to the concerned stakeholder, the greater the responsibility is in their direction.

However, it is not uncommon for companies to emphasize the external side of CSR because of its higher PR value (Barnard et al., 2004). At the same time, international CSR literature and initiatives seek to focus on the internal dimensions of CSR, i.e. the concept of responsible treatment of employees (Gatto, 2002).

3.2 Importance of internal CSR as the source of employee satisfaction and wellbeing

The importance of internal CSR can be explained by a very simple reason. An important prerequisite for an organization's ethical operation is to act responsibly towards those who produce its products or provide its services. So the most important internal concern of the organization is the employees themselves. According to Gross (2011), employers want employees who will do their best work to help the company achieve its objectives. Employees want good jobs that are challenging and meaningful.

William Kahn (1990) of the Boston University School of Management defined the concept of work engagement as "the harnessing of organizational members' selves to their work roles." An engaged workforce can create a win-win situation that has benefits for both employers and employees and result in an efficient and productive work environment. Studies have shown that employee engagement may lead to a number of positive business outcomes, including decreased absenteeism and turnover, increased customer satisfaction and loyalty, increased productivity and increased revenue growth. (Sorenson, 2013)

Fulfilling the expectations of employees is an opportunity not only to improve their or the company's efficiency but it also affects employee satisfaction with their work (Biesok and Wyrod-Wrobel, 2014).

Indeed, there are many factors influencing employee satisfaction. We may mention, among others, the identification with the company, communication, perception by superiors, motivation, staff development, interpersonal relations, and working conditions (Turon, 2016).

4 Responsible employment

Employees, being considered as one of the most important internal resources, require special attention because of their key role. In order to achieve a competitive advantage, organizations should invest in intellectual human capital, ensuring safe and healthy working conditions for their employees and thus contributing to their wellbeing. All of the aspects of employees' wellbeing form a constituent part of internal dimension of CSR (Krainz, 2015).

According to Kisil (2013), the key actions associated with good labor practices are the following:

- compliance with the principles of diversity;
- providing voluntary work;
- fair relationships between co-workers;
- opportunity to express views and ratings by employees;
- ensuring safety in the workplace;
- providing employees with information about any activities that are associated with them;
- providing medical care;
- ensuring an appropriate structure for work and fair wages;

- ensuring satisfactory conditions of employment;
- encouraging the development of employees;
- respecting the private and family life of employees;
- supporting employees in unexpected circumstances;
- implementation of outplacement programs.

4.1 Legal sources of responsible behavior

The international regulation of the social responsibility of multinational companies is now basically not through traditional legal instruments, but mainly through soft law. Soft law is only a moral force, its punishment is only the 'shame of non-compliance'. This also means that soft law is largely based on a mature, informed, conscious social environment.

At the same time, soft law is not to be underestimated in the system of international law, as it can become a positive law over time with a broad consensus. Many say that it is not a question that soft law CSR regulations will be replaced by codified legislation, the question is only when and how it will happen. Moreover, soft law itself is always a strong indication of the importance of the topic (Kun, 2009). Meanwhile, the ethical expectation of these principles is increasingly growing among the internal and external, market and non-market stakeholders of the company (Szegedi and Mélypataki, 2016).

We would like to highlight some of the most important legal sources of responsible behavior:

- OECD Guidelines for Multinational Enterprises (1994);
- The UN Global Compact (2000);
- Universal Declaration of Human Rights (1948);
- The Voluntary Principles on Security and Human Rights (2000);
- International Labor Organization: Tripartite Declaration of Principles on Multinational Enterprises and Social Policy (1977);
- Fair Labor Association Workplace Code of Conduct (1996);
- The Rio Declaration on Environment and Development (1992);
- Coalition for Environmentally Responsible Economies – The CERES Principles (1989);
- Organisation for Economic Co-operation and Development Principles of Corporate Governance (1999);
- The Sustainability: Integrated Guidelines for Management – SIGMA – Project (1999)
- UN Declaration of Women's Rights (1995);
- Green Paper Promoting a European Framework for Corporate Social Responsibility (2001) EU COM 366;
- Communication from the Commission concerning Corporate Social Responsibility (2002) EU COM 347.

4.2 A good example of employee engagement – Community volunteer work

Last but not least, we would like to mention a 'best practice' as a general example, a good way of an employer to engage an employee in the company and its objectives with the help of CSR. Today every employer must consider introducing the system of community volunteer work as it may lead to major benefits.

According to Kotler and Lee (2005), community volunteering is an activity in which the company encourages its employees to carry out voluntary work; by their expertise, talents, ideas and/or physical strength to serve local community goals. Corporate volunteering is easy to distinguish from other CSR initiatives, as it is the only program in which employees of a company personally volunteer for local organizations and local initiatives.

Many benefits of these initiatives reflect the unique ability to build strong and genuine relationships with local communities and to recruit employees. It can help the company achieve its business goals, strengthen the corporate image, and enable the company's products and services to be displayed.

Beneficiaries of volunteering recognize the spirit of commitment as company volunteers appear in person to help non-profit organizations. Volunteers with sincere enthusiasm are the strongest community builders, and this virtue is the most prominent of all CSR initiatives. There is a need for real commitment and care to give employees time to leave work in order to act for the community, or to encourage them to spend their free time for a good cause.

Typical community volunteer programs:

- Promoting ethical behavior through corporate communication that encourages employees to engage in voluntary community work, so they can get information on the resources available to take advantage of volunteering opportunities;
- Demonstration of specific social affairs and foundations for the employee to consider; detailed information on how to get involved in these programs;
- Organizing volunteer groups for specific goals or events;
- Help the employees choose the options that suit individual interests and current community needs, with company-based coordinators or special software;
- Providing employees with the opportunity to do volunteer work on company time; typically 2–5 days a year as paid absence to much longer absence for more serious commitments, such as one year of volunteer work in a developing country covered by the company;
- Allocating donations to charitable organizations where employees work voluntarily; often the amount for donation is adjusted to the number of hours of volunteering;
- Recognition of exemplary volunteers such as mentioning them in internal newsletters, awarding badges, or giving awards at annual corporate meetings.

5 Conclusion

In our opinion, employers should understand one important thing. If employees are properly involved in the CSR activities of the company, they can identify more easily with the company's goals, values, vision or mission. This is a good method to reduce fluctuations and increase efficiency and productivity. This is obviously in line with the company's primary, most important goal of profit-making.

We are certain that the employee-employer relationship is like a two-way process, as both players influence each other. Thus, it is crucial for the employer to engage and motivate employees by acting responsibly and involving them in the CSR activities and strategy of the company. This way a mutually beneficial relation can be created with the cooperation of both parties. Based on these findings we will carry out an empirical research among Hungarian companies analyzing the relationship between the level of their internal CSR activities and the motivation of their employees. Hopefully we will verify the assumption that more conscious and strategically built CSR projects can lead to better engaged employees.

Acknowledgements

This research was supported by the project no. EFOP-3.6.2-16-2017-00007, titled Aspects on the development of intelligent, sustainable and inclusive society: social, technological, innovation networks in employment and digital economy. The project has been supported by the European Union, co-financed by the European Social Fund and the budget of Hungary.

References

Barnard, C., Deakin, S. and Hobbs, R. (2004). 'Reflexive law, CSR and the Evolution of Labour Standards: The Case of Working Time.' *ESRC Centre for Business Research, University of Cambridge, Working Paper,* 294, CBR research Programme on Corporate Governance.

Biesok, G. and Wyrod-Wrobel, J. (2014). 'Wybrane aspekty satysfakcji pracownikow'. *Etyka, kultura organizacyjna i społeczna odpowiedzialność biznesu w kształtowaniu potrzeb i relacji z klientami Wydawnictwo Naukowe Akademii Techniczno-Humanistycznej*, Bielsko-Biała, pp. 147–162.

Bonsón, E. and Bednárová, M. (2015). 'CSR Reporting Practices of Eurozone companies'. *Revista de Contabilidad – Spanish Accounting Review*, 18 (2), pp. 182–193.

Coalition for Environmentally Responsible Economies – The CERES Principles (1989).

Davis, K. (1973). 'The case for and against businesss assumption of social responsibilities'. *Academy of Management Journal,* 16, pp. 312–322.

European Commission (2001). 'Green Paper Promoting a European Framework for Corporate Social Responsibility', COM (2001) 366.

European Commission (2002). 'Communication from the Commission concerning Corporate Social Responsibility: A business contribution to Sustainable Development', COM(2002) 347 Final (Brussels, 2nd July 2002).

Gatto, A. (2002). 'The European Union and CSR: Can the European Union contribute to the accountability of multinational enterprises for human rights?' Master's Thesis, *European Master's Degree in Human Rights and Democratisation*

Gross, R. (2011). 'Corporate Social Responsibility and Employee Engagement: Making the Connection'. *CR Strategies.*

Guadamillas-Gómez, F. Donate-Manzanares, M.J. and Skerlavaj, M (2010). 'The integration of corporate social responsibility into the strategy of technology-intensive firms: a case study.' *Zbornik Radova Ekonomskog Fakulteta u Rijeci.* (2010) 28, pp. 9–34.

Hohnen, P. and Potts, J. (2007). 'Corporate Social Responsibility – An Implementation Guide for Business.' International Institute for Sustainable Development, *IISD Publisher.*

International Labour Organization: Fair Labor Association Workplace Code of Conduct (1996).

International Labour Organization. Tripartite Declaration of Principles on Multinational Enterprises and Social Policy (1977).

Jhawar, N. and Gupta, S. (2017). 'Understanding CSR – Its History and the Recent Developments'. *IOSR Journal of Business Management*, (19) 5, pp. 105-109.

Kahn, William (1990). ‘Psychological conditions of personal engagement and disengagement at work.’ *Academy of Management Journal,* (33) 4, pp. 692-724.

Kisil, A. (2013). ’Zarządzanie przez odpowiedzialność: Podstawa odpowiedzialnego biznesu’, *Difin, Warszawa.*

Kotler, P. and Lee, N. (2005). *Corporate Social Responsibility.* John Wiley & Sons, Inc.

Krainz, K.D. (2015). ’Enhancing wellbeing of employees through corporate social responsibility context.’ *Megatrend Review*, (12) 2, pp. 137–154.

Kun, A. (2009). ’A multinacionális vállalatok szociális felelőssége’. *Ad Librum Kft*, Budapest.

Ludian, U. (2004). ’What social responsibility for the enterprise?’ *The Polish Perspective, Conference Paper – International Seminar on Comparative Labour Law, Industrial Relations and Social Security*, 5-16 July, 2004, Bordeaux, France.

McWilliams, A. and Siegel, D. (2000). ’Corporate social responsibility and financial performance: Correlation or misspecification?’ *Strategic Management Journal*, 21 (5), pp. 603-609.

OECD Guidelines for Multinational Enterprises (1994), [Online]. Available at: https://heinonline.org/HOL/LandingPage?handle=hein.journals/envlnw24&div=10&id=&page=&t=1557216225 [Cited 2019-02-05].

OECD Principles of Corporate Governance (1999), [Online]. Available at: http://bestpractices.cz/wp-content/uploads/2013/09/Etika-podnik%C3%A1n%C3%AD-OECD-principles-of-corporate-govemance.pdf [Cited 2019-02-05].

SIGMA Project - The Sustainability: Integrated Guidelines for Management (1999).

Sorenson, S. (2013). How Employee Engagement Drives Growth, [Online]. Available at: www.gallup.com/workplace/236927/employee-engagement-drives-growth.aspx [Cited 2019-02-05].

Szegedi, K. and Mélypataki, G. (2016). ’A vállalati társadalmi felelősségvállalás (CSR) és a jog kapcsolata.’ *Miskolci Jogi Szemle: A Miskolci Egyetem Állam- És Jogtudományi Karának Folyóirata,* 2016 (1), pp. 51-70.

The Voluntary Principles on Security and Human Rights (2000).

Tsoutsoura, M. (2004). ’Corporate Social Responsibility and Financial Performance.’ *Haas School of Business, University of California at Berkeley.*

Turon, K. (2016). ’Corporate Social Responsibility to Employees: The Best Labour Practices in Transport and Logistics Companies.’ *Journal of Corporate Responsibility and Leadership*. 2016, (3) 1, pp. 37-47.

United Nations. Declaration of Women’s Rights (1995).

United Nations: The Rio Declaration on Environment and Development (1992).

United Nations. The UN Global Compact (2000).

United Nations. Universal Declaration of Human Rights (1948).

White, A. L. (2006). ’Business Brief: Intangibles and CSR’. *Business for Social Responsibility*, [Online]. Available at: https://www.tellus.org/pub/Business%20Brief%20-%20Intangibles%20and%20CSR.pdf. [Cited 2019-02-05].

A Central European approach to the typology of social enterprises

Sándor Bozsik[1], Zoltán Musinszki[2], Judit Szemán[3]

Abstract Our research's aim is to create a new Balance Scorecard Model for Social Enterprises. This paper represents the beginning phase of a longer research programme. We focus on how to describe the concept of social enterprise in the current Central-European environment with special regard to social co-operatives. We use the classic Gui model (Gui, 1991) and extend and partly modify the General Interest part separating the Government Interest and the Regional Interest. The proper identification of interest-holders is vital for our research, because the viewpoint of the Balance Scorecard should be justified to the requirements of the interest-holders.

Keywords: social enterprises, Gui model, social co-operatives.

JEL Classification: L31

1 Introduction

This paper represents the beginning phase of a longer research programme. The aim of this research programme is to create a new Balance Scorecard Model for Social Enterprises (further SE). In this model we want to create indicators and view-points based on the available data stock of Social Enterprises. We plan to collect best practice examples (case studies), by which this concept can be further developed.

The goal of this paper is to clarify the concept of Social Enterprises in Central-European context. We collect the major theoretical approaches of the social enterprises, introduce the main types of them, and rethink the interest-holders of SEs compared to Gui's model (Gui, 1991). The proper identification of interest-holders is vital for our research, because the viewpoint of the Balance Scorecard should be justified to the requirements of the interest-holders.

2 Typology of social enterprises

This section is devoted to defining and classifying the concept of social enterprises. The task is difficult due to the great variety of objectives, legal forms, organisational types, and activities of social enterprises. To work out our definition, the overview of previous research findings is required (Defourny et al., 2016).

The economic role of social enterprises is not negligible. According to the European Commission, the social economy includes 2 million enterprises which means 10 % of all

[1] Institute of Finance and Accounting, University of Miskolc, 3515 Miskolc Egyetemváros Hungary, pzbozsi@uni-miskolc.hu

[2] Institute of Finance and Accounting, University of Miskolc, 3515 Miskolc Egyetemváros Hungary, stmusiz@uni-miskolc.hu

[3] Institute of Finance and Accounting, University of Miskolc, 3515 Miskolc Egyetemváros Hungary, pzszeman@uni-miskolc.hu

European businesses and employs over 11 million employees, 6 % of the EU working population in 2011. (Cecop, 2014)

Social enterprises have been studied both widely and in depth but have no clear and unique definition. The lowest common denominator of the definitions is organisations which trade to achieve their social objectives (Peattie and Morley, 2008). But the problem of a very general definition is that it does not say us too much about the origin of these organisation, the nature of their objectives, their governance form or their funding; consequently, it gives small help in understanding the deep nature of social enterprises (Kocziszky et al., 2017).

A lot of papers have attempted to create more specific definitions. Some of these terms are the following:

Social purpose businesses which primarily reinvest surpluses in the business or community rather than generating profits for shareholders or owners (OECD, 1999); the definition narrows the concept of SE to social businesses but excludes those enterprises which run public services but are out of direct control of the state.

SEs are third system organisations (based on citizen collaboration, mutuality and self-help to address social needs) that are most engaged in trading within a three-system model of the economy (Pearce, 2003); the definition is hardly understandable without the whole concept of the author.

SEs are organisations that use business methods to achieve social goals (Meadows and Pike, 2010). By this definition the SEs have social goals, but the tools achieving their goal are business-like. They raise (partly) private funding, their income is generated mostly from the private market. The operation efficiency is crucially important so market-based controlling methods for their special circumstances should be adapted.

SEs are those enterprises that bridge the non-profit sector and the social economy and tend towards non-prescriptive but archetypal indicators (distinguishing various economic and social criteria), thereby placing initiatives differentially within a spectrum of social enterprises (Defourny et al., 2006). The definition is a tautology because the definition contains the defined object.

The common social enterprise characteristics are multi-agency environments, enterprise orientation, social aims, and social ownership (Shaw and Carter, 2007). This definition reflects the most important features of a social enterprises, but does not tell us, whether all elements are required in an organisation to identify it as a social enterprise, or if not, how many.

Kerlin adopted Salamon's institutional perspective model (Salamon et al., 2000) to compare the size and profile of the non-profit sector across countries: she identified some macro-institutional key factors. She stated that the social enterprises' objectives and organisational features are the function of historical traditions, values, existing legal frameworks and discourses with strong national characteristics (Kerlin, 2013, 2015).

3 Groups of social enterprises

Spear identified four types of social enterprise in the United Kingdom:

- mutual - which forms to meet the needs of a special group through trading activities;
- trading charity, which develops commercial activities to fulfil their primary mission;
- public sector spin-off, which takes over the operation of services previously provided by the state;
- and finally, new social enterprise, which creates a new business (Spear at al., 2009).

Gordon rethought the categorisation and identified six types of social enterprises:

- mutual (based on cooperation and mutuality),
- community (based on community solidarity),
- altruistic (based on charity and philanthropy),
- ethical (based on sustainability and radicalism),
- private market (based on private business),
- public statist (providing a public service) (Gordon, 2015).

Teasdale focuses on the different actors that participate in the life of a social enterprise. He differentiated five types:

- earned income social enterprise, which are voluntary organizations selling goods and services;
- public services provider which simply replaces the budgeted institutions to fulfil some tasks;
- social business entity which applies market-based strategies to achieve a social or environmental goal;
- community enterprise, which works to create or retain wealth for the targeted community;
- co-operative, which means a special way of doing business due to its special structure of ownership (Teasdale, 2012).

Teasdale's second achievement was to identify six reasons for establishing social enterprises (Teasdale, 2010).

1) State/market failure means if the market actors hesitate to finance public services due to the long (or infinite) payback period and the state being unable to provide them in a proper way, social enterprises can fill the niche,
2) Resource dependence theory argues if the public service providers are dependent on declining government funding, they are willing to find new sources of funding elsewhere and try to increase their commercial activity,
3) Institutional theory states that non-profit organisations are formed as being definitely different from business organisations, but some activities cannot distinctively be made by just one type of organisation, so social enterprises are becoming increasingly hybrid, straddling the borders among non-profit organisations and for-profit business units,
4) Social origins theory says that the modern Western societies are becoming more and more multicultural and inherit social activities with various cultural sources. Social enterprises offer a flexible organisational way to express and manage these differences,
5) Political expediency supposes that the government wants to source out some traditional public services to the more flexible and more efficient social enterprises. In

this way the public authorities can also shift the responsibility for providing public services to these social enterprises,

6) Interdependence theory states that there can be considerable potential for interdependence and collaboration between the public and third sectors. Similarly, in addition to the market and state failure there are "voluntary failures" (due to the inability to generate sufficient resources, due to the tendency of voluntary organisations to focus on particular sub-groups, due to undemocratic management or due to the lack of professional staff). The creative combination of government and non-profit organisation can be the answer to these problems (Teasdale, 2010).

4 The original Gui model

Gui (1991) separated three types of interest and gave the ruling form of funding. In his categorisation there are three major drivers or interests that can be found in the overall economy: the general interest (GI) represented by the state will, mutual interest (MI), which comes from the common interest of the participants and the capital interest (CI), which is determined by profit achievement. The approach is demonstrated by Figure 1 below.

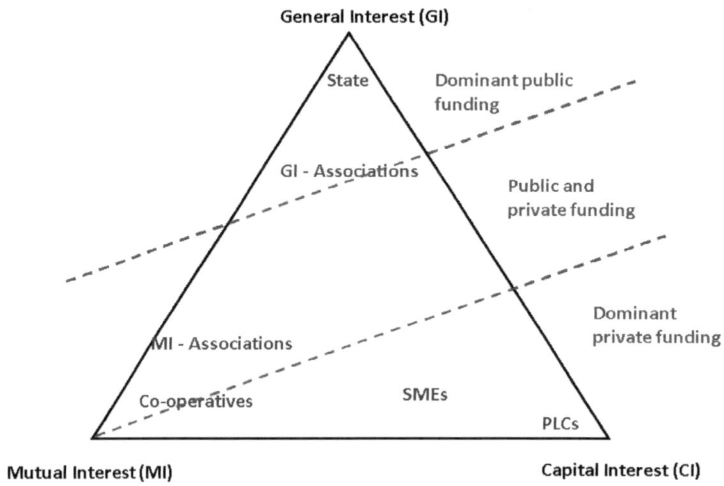

Figure 1 Interest principles and resource mix [Gui, 1991; p. 561]

If we see Figure 1 from top to bottom, we can detect the "classic" organisations. The state represents the budget institutions like the police, parliament and ministries. The GI Associations are partly financed from private sources, but the public interest dominates. Examples for these institutions are hospitals and universities. The Mutual Interest Associations are formed by individuals with a common interest – like church societies, angling & hunting companies or hiking clubs. The co-operatives have a unique ownership structure, but mostly work for the members' economic interest. Small and Medium-sized Enterprises (SMEs) and Public Limited Companies (PLC) are examples of the smaller and larger version of private companies.

The untraditional social enterprises can originate in two ways:

- by an "upward" move of mutual or capital interest organisations (MI-Assoc., Coops, SMEs and PLCs) towards an organization with a social or societal mission. Such evolution is marked by green;

- or by "downward" move of a general interest organization towards more market-oriented activities in order to complement their existing resources. This evolution is represented by brown.

These institutional changes lead to various social enterprise models marked by yellow (see Figure 2).

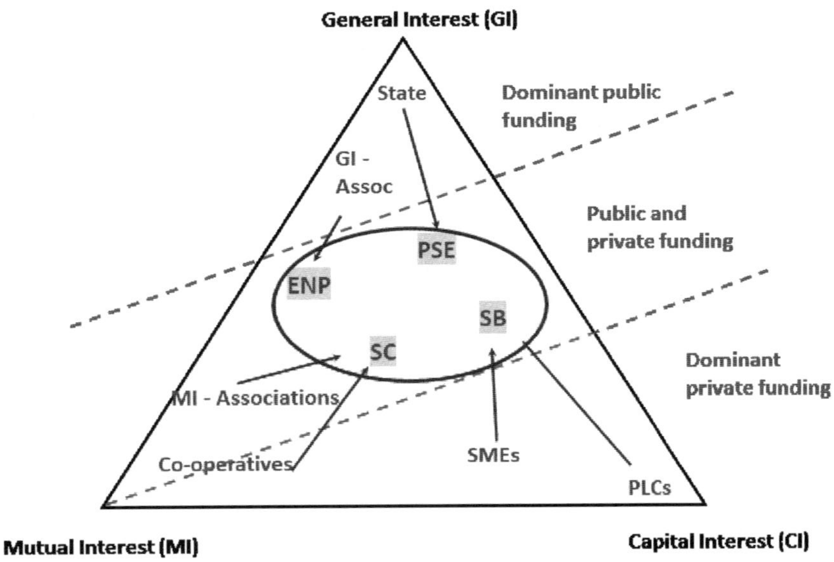

Figure 2 Creation of social enterprise models [Gui, 1991, p. 563]

The four created social enterprise models are the following:

The entrepreneurial non-profit (ENP) model runs an income generating activity to sponsor a social mission. Typical examples are charity activities or non-profit work integration social enterprises which sell their goods or services and train unskilled workers.

The social cooperative (SC) model keeps the organisation form of a traditional co-operative – i.e. equal voting and limitation of capital shares' remuneration – but it combines the private interest with the interest of the whole community or of a specific target group.

The social business (SB) model develops business activities for a social purpose or mission. The typical social businesses focus their activities on a "social or societal field" such as personal services (for instance elderly care), environmental protection or fair trade. They are non-profit organisations but also market-based companies with a very strong social mission.

The public-sector social enterprise (PSE) model aims to decrease the expenses of public service provision and/or to reach higher efficiency. Local entities take over the job of public authorities in fields of public transport, elderly care or adult education. Their funding, as opposed to social businesses, is mostly public.

5 The result of our research – the extended Gui model adapted to Central-Europe

The Gui model has three pillars, one of which is the General Interest (further GI). However, in Central Europe, especially in Hungary, the power of the GI to establish a social enterprise is much bigger than in an Anglo-Saxon culture. And not only the power is larger, but the actors of a GI have different and sometimes conflicting interests.

That is the reason why we separated the GI into two parts. The Governmental Interest (GOI) incorporates the will of the Central Government, while the Regional Interest (RI) expresses the will of local governments (local municipalities and regional entities). Figure 3 shows the modified Gui model, in which Gui's triangle has become a rhombus.

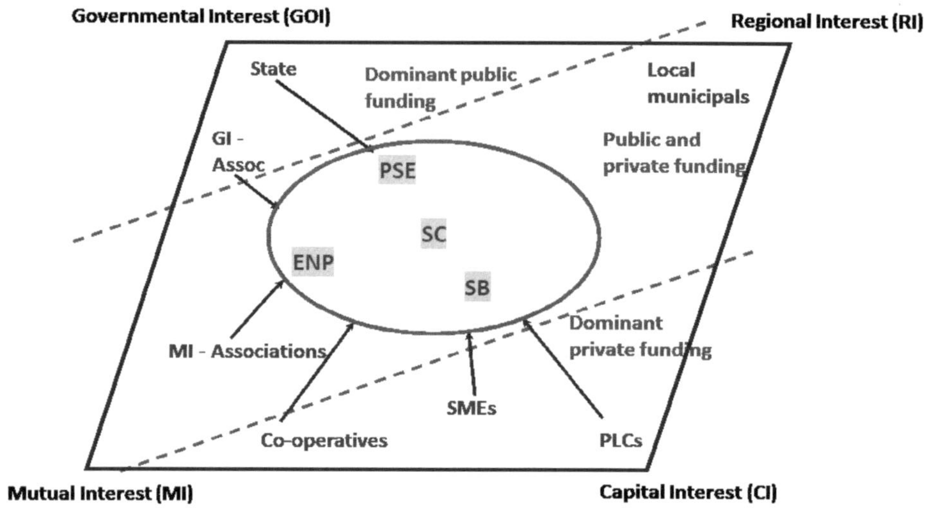

Figure 3 A Central-European extension to the Gui model [own contribution from Gui 1991]

Let's take the example of Hungarian social co-operatives. The major reason to create social enterprises from mostly central budget financing (including European Union funding) was to offer a way for former public workers to the labour market. In contrast to the public work programmes, the social co-operatives are working in the market, achieving market revenues, and can earn profit. Their activities are heavily subsidised by the central government, but the local municipalities have compulsory membership in this type of organisation. This membership benefits the central government because:

- this offers a kind of guarantee for proper working;
- they can help with the management of social cooperatives in administrative processes;
- they act as an internal control;
- they partly ensure the objective conditions of operation (by leasing some equipment).

But the GOI and the RI have got different goals, different roles and also can have conflicting interests. Table 1 shows the main points of the comparison of these two interests.

Interests	Governmental	Regional
Goal	marketable employment, regional cohesion, sustainability of operation	increase of quality of life in local settlements, economic development of the local community
Role	funding, regulation, external control	management, internal control, guarantor
Conflicting interest (maybe)	effective usage of public wealth, budget constraint	high cash payment for beneficiaries, permanent source of funding

Table 1 Comparison of Governmental and Regional Interests [own contribution]

From the government's perspective the social enterprises can be considered as a bridge from the public work programme toward marketable employment. Besides this, the vital social enterprises can accelerate the economic development of the rural regions, where the number of jobs is limited. The government is also interested in the efficiency and effectiveness of these programmes (i.e. creating the bigger number of jobs from a given public fund, and later these enterprises can operate without public assistance). The local governments want to increase the quality of life in the local settlements and encourage economic development in their region. The Governmental and Regional interests can be easily harmonized.

The job sharing in the current situation is the following. The government funds the creation and operation (mostly from EU sources), regulates the operation and externally controls the implementation. The representative of the regional government actually helps to manage the enterprise, internally control the operation and may guarantee the proper usage of public funds.

The main tension occurs if the public funds are limited and only occasionally available. Without constant funding these enterprises suspend their operation up to the arrival of the next funding shot. But in this case the effectiveness of the whole operation becomes limited.

6 Summary

The major contribution of this paper to extend the original Gui model and adapt it to the specific needs of Central-European SEs.

Facing the problem of creating a model for Central-European social enterprises, we believe that the traditional Gui model should be extended. The General Interest pillar was split into two parts. The Government Interest incorporates the will of the Central Government, and the Regional Interest expresses the will of local governments (local municipalities and regional entities). The new rhombus model better describes the current situation due to the conflicting interests of the two bodies representing the public interest. The main problem is the tension between the intermittently available public funding and the sustainability of the social enterprises.

A potential solution to this conflict could be to include private funds in the financing of social enterprises. These private funds can come from private customers or suppliers of the social enterprise or some external partner can be also involved in the frame of their own corporate social responsibility programme.

Acknowledgement

This research was supported by the project no. EFOP-3.6.2-16-2017-00007, titled Aspects on the development of intelligent, sustainable and inclusive society: social, technological, innovation networks in employment and digital economy. The project has been supported by the European Union, co-financed by the European Social Fund and the budget of Hungary.

References

Cecop (2014). Social cooperatives at the high-level debate during the European Commission conference on social enterprises, [Online]. Available at: http://www.cecop.coop/European-Policymakers-agree-on-the [cited 2014-01-20]

Defourny, J. and Nyssens, M. (2006). 'Introduction: Defining Social Enterprise', *Social Enterprise: At the Crossroads of Market, Public Policies and Civil Society*, Abingdon, Routledge.

Defourny, J. and Nyssens, M. (2016). 'Fundamentals for an International Typology of Social Enterprise Models', *ICSEM Working Papers*, (33).

Gordon, M. (2015). 'A Typology of Social Enterprise 'Traditions', *ICSEM Working Papers*, (18).

Gui, B. (1991). 'The Economic Rationale for the Third Sector', *Annals of Public and Cooperative Economics*, (62) 4, pp. 551-72.

Kerlin, J. (2013). 'Defining Social Enterprise across Different Contexts: A Conceptual Framework Based on Institutional factors', *Nonprofit and Voluntary Sector Quarterly*, (12) 1, pp. 84-108.

Kerlin, J. (2015). 'Kerlin's Macro-Institutional Framework', *Social Enterprise Journal*, (11) 2, pp.178-194.

Kocziszky, Gy., Veresné, S.M. and Balaton, K. (2017). A társadalmi innováció vizsgálatának tapasztalatai és fejlesztési lehetőségei, *Vezetéstudomány*, (18) 6-7, pp. 15-19.

Meadows, M. and Pike, M. (2010). 'Performance management for social enterprises'. *Systemic MPractice and Action Research*, (23) 2, pp. 127–141. DOI: 10.1007/s11213-009-9149-5.

Organisation for Economic Co-operation and Development (OECD) (1999). Social Enterprises, Paris: OECD (Report by Noya, A. and Lecamp, G. for the OECD).

Pearce, J. (2003). *Social Enterprise in Anytown*, London: Calouste Gulbenkian Foundation.

Peattie, K. and Morley, A. (2008). 'Social Enterprises: Diversity & Dynamics, Contexts and Contributions', *A Research Monograph, ESRC Monograph, March.*

Salamon, L., Sokolowski, W. and Anheier, H. (2000). 'Social Origins of Civil Society: An Overview', *Working Paper of the Johns Hopkins Comparative Nonprofit Sector Project*, 38, Baltimore.

Spear, R., Cornforth, C. and Aiken, M. (2009). 'The Governance Challenges of Social Enterprises: Evidence from a UK Empirical Study', *Annals of Public and Cooperative Economics*, (80) 2, pp. 247-73.

Teasdale, S. (2010). 'Social enterprise: discourses, definitions and (research) dilemmas'. *TSRC paper to 3rd Social Enterprise Research Colloquium, University of Oxford*, [Online]. Available at: http://tsrc.ac.uk/LinkClick.aspx?fileticket=K8QJkLRdnL0%3d&tabid=527 [cited 2019-06-01].

Teasdale, S. (2012). 'What's in a Name? Making Sense of Social Enterprise Discourses', *Public Policy and Administration*, (27) 2, pp. 99-119.

External Analysis for the Purpose of Strategic Decision-Making of Heating Company

Jakub Chlopecký[1], Ladislav Moravec[2], Roman Danel[3], Omar Ameir[4]

Abstract. This paper summarizes the outputs of an external analysis for strategic decision-making in the company Havířovská teplárenská společnost, a. s. and it sets out proposals for other individual strategies. Since the company lacks any strategic document for the period of 2019-2022, the paper primarily focuses on an external analysis of the environment outside the company itself. The following methods were used for the external analyses: Porter's Five Forces model and a SWOT analysis. The practical importance and impact of this paper rests in presenting the analyses results to the company's management and the members of the board of directors. The analyses are carried out by the authors in such a way that it is possible to also use theirs methods, procedures and results for other heating companies of similar scope.

Keywords: Havířovská teplárenská společnost, a. s., Porter's Five Forces model, SWOT analysis, strategy decision making.

JEL Classification: L10, L100

1 Introduction

The authors (Chlopecký, Rolčíková, and Kratochvíl, 2015) state that today's turbulent world is characterized by a high degree of globalization. From the physical, and especially business point of view, the limits to trade are virtually absent and any competitive organization must now take into consideration factors that were once less important (Rolstadås, 1998, Kozel et al, 2018). One such factor may be the social responsibility of companies (Katsoulacos, 2007). Entrepreneurship is subject to the specific dynamics (Skokan, Pawliczek, 2013, 2014) and the life cycle of an enterprise can be greatly extended by appropriate strategic planning. It is no great exaggeration to claim that company management and its success in business in a market environment depends above all on timely forecasting in various business sectors and resolving potential strategic threats (Jurkasová, Cehlár, and Khouri 2016).

Company strategy is defined in (Rothaermel, 2008, and Somosi and Kocziszky, 2017) as a procedure to gain and maintain competitive potential and advantage. M. E. Porter is regarded as the father of the theory of competitive advantage. He defined sustainable competitive advantage as the "*basis of above-average performance over the long-term*" (Porter, 1985). The main objective of this paper is to present an external analysis of the company Havířovská teplárenská společnost (hereinafter referred to as HTS, a. s.) and how it might best employ strategic management. The results of this analysis will be incorporated into the strategic document of

[1] Moravská vysoká škola Olomouc, o.p.s., třída Kosmonautů 1288/1, 779 00 Olomouc, Ústav managementu a marketingu, jakub.chlopecky@mvso.cz.
[2] VŠB-Technická univerzita v Ostravě/Hornicko-geologická fakulta, Institut ekonomiky a systémů řízení, 17. listopadu 2172/15, 708 33 Ostrava-Poruba. Havířovská teplárenská společnost, a.s., Konzumní 298/6a, Šumbark, 736 01 Havířov, moravec@htsas.cz
[3] Vysoká škola technická a ekonomická v Českých Budějovicích/Katedra strojírenství, Ústav technicko-technologický, Okružní 517/10, 370 01 České Budějovice, rdanel@mail.vstecb.cz.
[4] Moravská vysoká škola Olomouc, o.p.s., třída Kosmonautů 1288/1, 779 00 Olomouc, Ústav managementu a marketingu, omar.ameir@mvso.cz.

HTS, a. s. for the period 2019–2022. The paper's intermediate objective is to prepare a proposal for possible HTS, a. s. strategies.

The reason for selecting this field of research was the fact that one of the authors has long been active in the top management and supervisory board of HTS, a. s., as well as the lack of any company conceptual strategy for the period 2019–2022.

2 Characteristics of HTS, a.s.

HTS, a.s. is a company whose priority is to deliver quality and reliable supply of thermal current in Havířov. Distribution and heat production accounted for 91 % of the company´s revenues in 2018. The primary customers are the inhabitants of Havířov, where thermal energy is supplied to more than 20 thousand households (approx. 90 % of the city´s territory) and to as well as thousand m^2 of non-residential premises. In addition to heat distribution, HTS, a. s. also produces thermal energy which is supplied by 9 local 0.779 MW gas boilers. Producing 2,865 GJ of thermal energy. The company has no solid fuel source. Primary heat supplies were provided by Veolia Energie, ČR, a. s., which produces thermal energy by burning fossil fuels outside Havířov. HTS, a. s. supplies more than 90 % of the city´s households thermal energy. Veolia Energie ČR, a. s. supplies more than 728 ths. GJ of thermal energy, which makes up 99 % of the energy used in Havířov. HTS, a. s. and Veolia Energie, a. s. cooperate on long-term heat supply contracts. The majority position of the thermal energy producer leads to potential threats to HTS, a. s. Veolia Energie, a. s. may also jeopardize HTS, a.s. within alternative energy sources (heat pumps, etc.) Additional information about the company can be found at www.htsas.cz

3 Selected Methods and Methodology Applied

The authors (Kozel and Chuchrová, 2015) state that in strategic management it is absolutely necessary to also evaluate the factors of a company's external environment. These factors may include the behaviour of competitors, technological progress, macroeconomic developments, social and demographic developments, etc. However, factors inside the company cannot be overlooked (Porter 2008, Matthyssens and Vandenbempt, 1998, Chlopecký, Rolčíková and Kratochvíl, 2015). This analysis defines new strategic objectives for the heating company by drawing on selected methods of strategic management. The authors have focused on effective management methods, specifically relying on Porter's analysis and SWOT analysis. These methods build upon earlier research published under the title "PESTLE Analysis of the Heating Company as a Strategic Tool" at the QUAREE conference (Chlopecký, et al, 2018). The methodology used is defined in Figure 1.

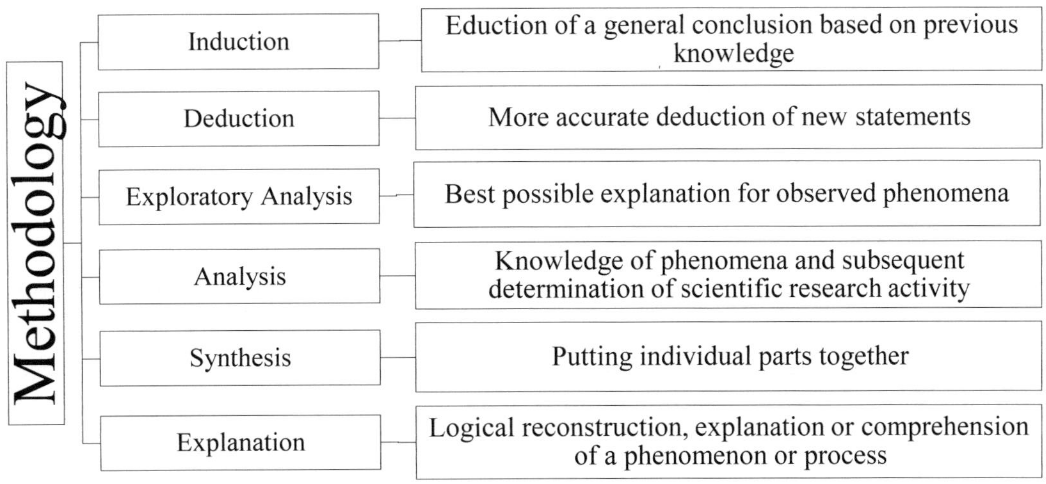

Figure 1 Methodology selected for analysing the external environment of HTS, a. s. [Chlopecký, 2017]

The details for preparing the paper were obtained from the following sources:

- studying specialized Czech and foreign literature;
- Czech Statistical Office, Eurostat;
- consultations with experts (selected expert group);
- Czech and foreign expert studies and papers in databases (EBSCO, WOS, SC).

3.1 Selected Expert Group

For reasons of objectivity and to ensure the relevance of the study results and their usability in practice, an expert group was established at the beginning of the research. The group is closely involved in the company's operation and is logically therefore has the greatest possible interaction with the routine operation of the organization. This expert group of engaged persons was supplemented with relevant academics from Czech universities as recommended by the authors Ministr and Pitner (2015) – see Table 1.

Academics	Academic employees from Moravská vysoká škola Olomouc, o.p.s., Institute of Management and Marketing; VSB – Technical University of Ostrava, Faculty of Mining and Geology, Department of Economics and Control Systems and Institute of Technology and Bussines in České Budějovice, Department of Mechanical Engineering.
Management of HTS, a.s.	Chairman and Vice-Chairman of the Board of Directors of HTS, a.s.
	Chairman and Member of the Supervisory Board of HTS, a.s.

Table 1 Selected expert group

3.2 Methodology of Survey

Source data were discovered through the use of the orientation survey of the issue. The aim of the orientation survey was to identify key parameters of the analysis to obtain a basic overview of the issue and formulate further procedures of the research work. The acquired data was amended of the information about the status of the initial situation. This amendment was realized by brainstorming in an expert group using diagnostic (descriptive) research. The aim of the diagnostic research was to monitor selected aspects of effects and to verify whether the data are valid and reliable. The aim of the explanatory methodology used in the brainstorming was to explain the effects and finding the solution of this effects.

The contribution of the authors themselves led to new ideas and streamlining the practical view of practitioners. Academics have brought the theoretical background to the issue. This foundation will be extended by another narrow profile of managers on the issue. These results, as indicated, will further be useful for further strategic direction of HTS, a.s.

The director of company led the brainstorming formally, but he did not participate in the debate. Brainstorming took place in several rounds according to the basic rules of brainstorming (preparatory phase, session, evaluation and implementation of results). Questions were processed electronically. In each subsequent round, the results were refined. There were six rounds of session and two rounds of evaluation and performance. Numerical expression is the product of the probability and impact of a given factor.

The aim was to solve the problem of managers and the "unbiased" view of academics on the issue. Brainstorming was focused on PESTLE analysis, see description above, Porter analysis and SWOT analysis. The results of PESTLE and Porter analysis were decisive for the SWOT analysis. The distinctive features for the analysis were slight differences in the views of academics and managers on the same problem. However, these were not major fluctuations that changed.

The estimates of the expert group were the rate of the strength of the individual factors. These expert estimates were obtained pursuant to discussions. The results were processed using the MS Excel. The particular factors were scored by force of an expert estimation on the basis of a product of probability and impact. The formulation of the expert responses corresponds with the complexity of the issue.

4 Results

The authors of the paper have drawn upon the results of a PESTLE analysis of HTS, a. s. (Chlopecký, et al, 2018). For an overview, an abridged list of individual factors of the PESTLE analysis is shown in Table 2.

Political factors	Sector regulation – Energy Regulatory Office
	Support for renewable energy
	Political aspects of the company's owner
Economic factors	Low dependence on basic macroeconomic indicators
	High dependency on the price of energy raw materials
	Influence of monetary indicators (exchange rates)
Social factors	Decreasing demographic curve
	Ageing population in the city
	Generally adverse public opinion
	Bounded local range
Technological factors	Technological development of alternative resources

	Thermal insulation of buildings
	Absence of own resource
	Advantage of combined power and heat generation
Legislative factors	Licensing of the sector
	Price regulation
	Substantial power of the State Energy Inspection
Environmental factors	Resource dislocation
	System centralization

Table 2 Summary of the PESTLE analysis results

HTS, a. s. is most negatively affected by political and legislative interventions in the heat production industry, and further by the price of energy commodities, the technological development of alternative sources and demographic development of the population of Havířov (Moravec, Danel, and Chlopecký, 2018). The main positive factors in the business of HTS, a. s. are resource dislocation and system centralization as environmental factors. Advantages in terms of technological factors are conferred by combined power and heat generation.

4.1 Porter's Five Forces Model

The results of Porter's Five Forces model and how the individual effects of the model are oriented are shown in Table 3.

Porter's model effects	Score estimates/2019	Score estimates/2022
Existing competitors in the sector	2.99	4.69
Threat of entry of new competitors	1.35	2.83
Threat of substitutes	4.30	4.74
Bargaining effect of suppliers	2.25	4.82
Bargaining effect of customers	4.47	3.31

Table 3 Summary of the results of Porter's Five Forces competitive model

The model in Table 3 indicates the fact that the threat of entry of new competitors into CHS (central heat supply) is the least probable risk for competitiveness. More significant appears to be the risk of the existing competitor in the sector, which is the multinational Veolia. HTS a. s. has a long-term contract with Veolia until 2020. Successful trade negotiations on extending the contract are crucial for the future of HTS. The bargaining effect of customers will not change significantly in the years 2019–2022. In contrast, a significant reinforcement of the bargaining position of the supplier will occur: the figure is more than double in 2022 compared to 2019. From Porter's Five Forces model, the authors evaluate the threats posed by substitutes as having the greatest effect on the company's competitiveness. These are also related to the bargaining effect of customers, since in the case of customer dissatisfaction, possible transfer to a substitutive alternative source of heating acts as an important lever. In addition, regarding the threat of substitutes, it is apparent from the high score for 2019 (4.30 points) that the expert group estimates a trend of increasing threat in 2022. The phenomenon is amplified by the structure of customers, where the transfer of just the three most significant customers could cause the absolute liquidation of HTS, a. s. due to a loss of up to two thirds of revenue.

4.2 SWOT Analysis of HTS, a.s.

A combination of input data was applied to construct the SWOT analysis. The results of the PESTLE analysis and Porter's analysis in the chapters above were assessed by the expert team. Their intersection comprises part of the opportunity and a part of the threat. The company's strengths and weaknesses were added to make the SWOT analysis complete. They were identified by brainstorming and controlled talks with the expert group. Kotler's method was applied to evaluate the SWOT analysis (Anton, 2015 and Abdel Basset et al, 2018). The arithmetic product of the evaluating criteria generates the result of that item for a value comparison (Acuña et al, 2019). To make the SWOT analysis results clearer, a graph of the individual quadrants of the SWOT analysis has been created figure 2 therefore indicates the following: the most significant strengths of HTS, a. s. relate to its capital, including human capital. The company's three largest weaknesses relate to the monopoly position of the heat supplier to the CHS. Opportunities for HTS, a. s. are represented by factors that would increase its effect on the heat production market in that locality. The largest threat for the company is the decentralization of heating for alternative sources.

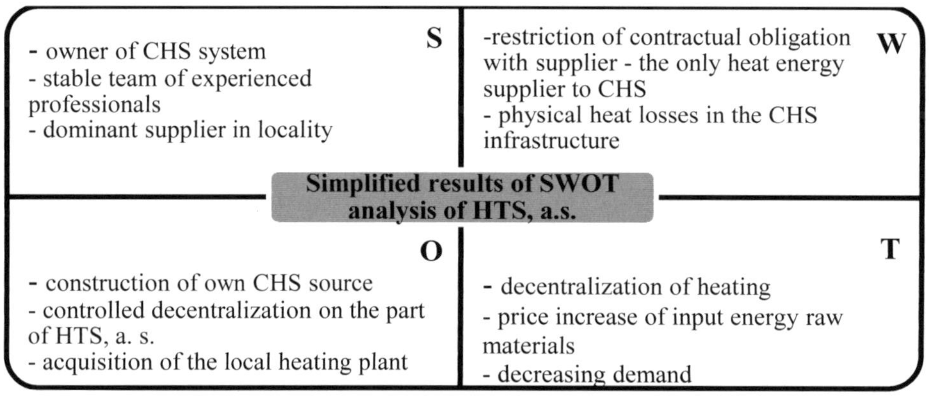

Figure 2 Simplified results of SWOT analysis

The authors of the article defined the monopoly heat supplier as a major threat for the company, (transition to alternative heating was defined as a second threat). An experienced team of experts can deal with controlled decentralization of heating already.

5 Suggestion of strategy

With regard to the scope of the article, one strategy proposal was chosen, which emerged from the results of the analyzes, namely the proposal of the strategy of removing the weaknesses by eliminating the impact of the threats.

WT strategy – removing weaknesses by eliminating the impact of threats

The SWOT analysis shows significant risks associated with having a single heat energy supplier to the CHS network. The WT strategy therefore tackles this issue, which undoubtedly will be demanding in terms of time and investment. However, it is the only cost-effective strategy which will gradually decrease dependence on the monopoly supplier of heat energy to the CHS system.

WT strategic objective: Controlled gradual decentralization of CHS by HTS, a. s. in the form of diversifying heat sources. Description of how the objective would be implemented: When implementing this objective it is possible to eliminate the identified weakness in the form of one monopoly supplier to CHS by gradually installing powerful cogeneration units at topologically suitable sites. The controlled decentralization will also prevent the competitors' efforts from disturbing the network at sites where inclusion of a cogeneration unit in the portfolio of sources will be cost-effective to gain potential in loss reduction, which is the synergic effect of a locally closer source.

6 Discussion of the results

Significant risks can be observed from the results of the external analyses; moreover, Porter's analysis shows a rising level of threat over time. The most pressing threat, with a score of 4.47 points, is the current "bargaining effect of customers". However, its intensity will not increase over time. Conversely, in the group: "threat of substitutes", which reached a score of 4.30 points in 2019, the trend is expected to increase to 4.74 points (from a maximum of 5). The threat of "bargaining effect of suppliers" will develop most dynamically – from 2.25 points presently to a predicted 4.82 points. By comparing the results of the PESTLE analysis, which evaluated the effects of the macro-environment of HTS, a. s., with the results of Porter's analysis tool, the expert estimate of the expert group selected a portfolio of the most significant threats and opportunities for a SWOT analysis. To ensure that every angle was covered, the expert group additionally supplemented this portfolio by brainstorming the company's strengths and weaknesses. The SWOT analysis pointed out significant threats. In particular, these involved increasing prices of input energy raw materials owing to reduced extraction and, especially, as a result of the decentralization of heating through the use of alternative sources. Currently, HTS, a. s. enjoys a superiority of strengths over weaknesses, and indeed the SWOT analysis also identified some promising opportunities.

7 Conclusion

The energy sector is associated with a specific set of business conditions, mainly in terms of high investment costs with concurrent strict price regulation by the state. In addition, these significant factors are reinforced in the heat production sector by a certain physical disadvantage inherent in the fact heat energy is difficult to store, unlike resources in the gas or water in supply sectors. Despite inhabitants frequently regarding the heat production sector as a public service, the level of support for developed centralized systems from the state does not correspond to such a view in the long run. This combined set of facts should be impulse enough for the senior management of heating companies to conduct intensive analytical activity with the aim of long-term strategic planning. The results of this paper will be discussed at the next meeting of the company's board of directors, and will be presented as the basis for strategic planning and managerial decision-making in the medium-term and long-term. Also, in the spirit of good business relations, these results will be shared with heating companies of a similar scope, particularly with members of the Association for District Heating of the Czech Republic.

8 References

Acuña-Carvajal, F., Pinto-Tarazona, L., López-Ospina, H., Barros-Castro, R., Quezada, L. and Palacio, K. (2019). 'An integrated method to plan, structure and validate a business strategy using fuzzy DEMATEL and the balanced scorecard'. *Expert Systems with Applications*, 122, pp. 351-368.

Anton, R. (2015). 'An Integrated Strategy Framework (ISF) for Combining Porter's 5-Forces, Diamond, PESTEL and SWOT Analysis'. *Open Science*, 4 (1), (2016), pp. 21-26.

Basset, M., Mohamed, M., Sangaiah, A. and Jain, V. (2018) 'An integrated neutrosophic AHP and SWOT method for strategic planning methodology selection'. *Benchmarking: An International Journal*, 25 (7), pp. 2546-2564.

Chlopecký, J. (2017). 'Stanovení závislosti exploatace vybraných nerostných surovin na vnějších podmínkách', [Online]. Dissertation thesis, Ostrava, VŠB-Technical university of Ostrava. Available at: http://hdl.handle.net/10084/127408 [cited 2019-01-26].

Chlopecký, J., Moravec, L., Rössler, M., Navrátilová, D. and Ameir, O. (2018). 'PESTLE analysis of the heating company as a strategic tool'. *Proceedings of Magnanimitas 2018*, Hradec Králové, Czech Republic.

Chlopecký, J., Rolčíková, M. and Kratochvíl, M. (2015). 'Decision making influence of some macroeconomic factors concerning prospective sales of fine silicon carbide'. *Proceedings of 15th International Multidisciplinary Scientific GeoConference SGEM*, Albena, Bulgaria, pp. 171-178.

Jurkasová, Z., Cehlár, M. and Khouri, S. (2016). 'Tools for organizational changes managing in companies with high qualified employees', *Production Management and Engineering Sciences - Scientific Publication of the International Conference on Engineering Science and Production Management*, ESPM 2015, pp. 409-412.

Katsoulacos, T. and Katsoulakos, Y. (2007). 'Integrating corporate responsibility principles and stakeholder approaches into mainstream strategy: a stakeholder-oriented and integrative strategic management framework'. *The international Journal of Business in Society*, 7 (4), pp. 355-369.

Kozel, R. and Chuchrová, K. (2015). 'Creation of System Support for Decision-Making Processes of Managers'. *Proceedings of IDIMT-2015: Information Technology and Society - Interaction and Interdependence: 23rd Interdisciplinary Information Management Talks,* Poděbrady, Czech Republic, pp. 163-170.

Kozel, R., Podlasová, A., Šikýř, P. and Smelik, R. (2018). 'Innovations in Waste Management'. *Proceedings of IDIMT-2018: Strategic Modeling in Management, Economy and Society: 26th Interdisciplinary Information Management Talks*, Kutná Hora, Czech Republic, pp. 119-126.

Matthyssens, P. and Vandenbempt, K., (1998). 'Creating competitive advantage in industrial services', *Journal of Business & Industrial Marketing*, 13 (4/5), pp. 339-355.

Ministr, J. and Pitner, T. (2015). 'Use of Non-investment Subsidies in Academic and Business Co-operation'. *Proceedings of IDIMT-2015: 23rd Interdisciplinary Information Management Talks*. Poděbrady, Czech Republic, pp. 141-146.

Moravec, L., Danel, R., Řepka, M. and Chlopecký, J. (2018). 'Innovative method of the correction in heat distribution against the actual status using thermovision'. *Proceedings of IDIMT 2018: 26th Interdisciplinary Information Management Talks*, Poděbrady, Czech Republic, pp. 137-144.

Porter, M. (1985). *The Competitive Advantage: Creating and Sustaining Superior Performance*. NY: Free Press.

Porter, M. (2008). 'The five competitive forces that shape strategy'. *Harvard Business Review*, Harvard University, 86 (1), pp. 79-93.

Rolstadås, A. (1998). 'Enterprise performance measurement'. *International Journal of Operations & Production Management*, 18 (9/10), pp. 989-999.

Rothaermel, F. (2008). 'Competitive advantage in technology intensive industries', Chapter 7 in *Technological Innovation: Generating Economic Results (Advances in the Study of Entrepreneurship, Innovation & Economic Growth, Volume 18)*, Emerald Group Publishing Limited, pp. 201-225.

Skokan, K. and Pawliczek, A. (2014). 'Lifecycle dynamics of Czech and Slovak enterprises in selected regions'. *Ekonomický časopis (EKON CAS) Ekonomický ústav SAV a Prognostický ústav SAV Bratislava*, 62 (7), pp. 728-742.

Skokan, K. and Pawliczek, A. (2013). 'Lifecycle of enterprises and its dynamics on the basis of annual turnover: an empirical study of Czech and Slovak enterprises'. *Proceedings of 22th IBIMA Conference Rome*, Norristown, pp. 268-280.

Somosi, M. and Kocziszky, G. (2017). 'Performance-based management of public utility organizations'. *Proceedings of the 12th International Conference on Strategic Management and its Support by Information Systems 2017*, Ostrava, Czech Republic, pp. 105-111.

Performance management features in the light of social innovation in the public sector

Daniella Kucsma[1]

Abstract. My research focuses primarily on the public service sector, as many expectations have to be met in this area, both when examining organization interests and customer needs. Nowadays, social innovation activities also play a significant role, as every public service company wants to provide a service that meets the expectations of society and implements developments that represent public interest. I am looking for the answer to the question why it is good for a public service organization to carry out social innovation and how this can affect the organization's performance management system. The answer is simple, as it leads to competitiveness, efficiency, cheaper service and social cohesion. However, it is also worth examining not only how to integrate these elements, but how to focus on the measurability of the organization, and the contribution to the performance measurability. In my work, it shows what performance management methods are and what is being used in practice by the examined health care organization.

Keywords: Performance Management, Public Sector, Social Innovation, Healthcare, Balanced Scorecard.

JEL Classification: H83, L25, L32, M10

1 Introduction

Numerous publications deal with the important role of a performance management system in the life of an organization. Nowadays, this area is not only present in the business sphere but public service organizations also use their methods and approaches. However, the public sector has specifications that make performance management work in a different field and way than the private sector. (Kaplan and Norton, 2002, Horvath, 2016). Performance management is one of the key elements of management toolbox, so it should be not only dealt with in the business sector but also among public service organizations. In this article I summarize some of the results of my research in the public sector and use logical elements to analyze the potential of social innovation in this sector. Additionally, I propose the use of a general strategic map as a framework for both the objective operation of performance management and the utilization of social innovation opportunities. The purpose of this article is to illustrate how well-chosen performance management contributes to achieve the target hierarchy described at the beginning of this paper. Furthermore, I consider it important to highlight the social innovation focus of the research, as I assume that this can contribute to the success of the research.

2 Characteristics of performance management characteristics in the public sector

The first task of each system is to define one or more goals to be achieved during the operation, so it is important to focus on what the particular organization needs to pay attention when examining and evaluating a public service organization. Primarily, based on the literature

[1] University of Miskolc / Institute of Management Science, H-3515 Miskolc- Egyetemvaros, Hungary, szvkd@uni-miskolc.hu

examination, I present the aims of the operation of a public service organization and the possible methods of its performance evaluation system. In the second place, I conducted in-depth interviews with the leaders of the investigated institutions, which helped me to get a clear picture of the performance rating system that health institutions favour.

During the literature research I examined numerous definitions and it can be concluded that they highlighted and formulated elements and as the main goal of organizational efficiency and effectiveness within performance. However, these goals should be interpreted in terms of what they mean and how they can achieve and measure these two factors. So I set up a general target hierarchy illustrated in Figure 1.

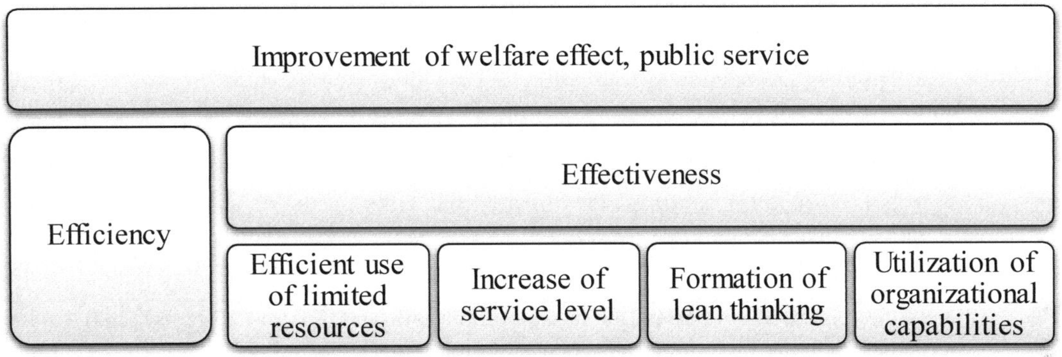

Figure 1 Target hierarchy of performance management of public service organizations [Kocziszky and Veres-Somosi, 2016]

In Figure 1 it can be seen that the top level is improvement of the welfare effect, since in the case of a public service organization this is the main goal, regardless of the sector. (Kocziszky and Veres-Somosi, 2016). So this priority should be given in case of performance management system also. At the second level, efficiency and efficiency are at stake. We are talking about non-competitive sector but performance indicators need to focus on these elements. At the third level, there are elements that promote the above-mentioned higher-level goals, and it is necessary to focus on the following elements:

- Use of limited resources: limited term is intentionally introduced here, as in the case of a public service organization economic, human and physical assets are limited. Health sector is a very good example for this, as hospitals have a cost control system, so their financial resources are limited within specific facilities. It is also worth mentioning that in this sector profit maximization is not the ultimate goal, but as it manages public finance, must concentrate on efficient and cost-effective operation. (Csath, 2016).
- Increase of service level: Although we are talking about a public service organization but one of the features of this kind of organizations is that its customer base is the entire population. Therefore, services need to be provided not only for a certain layer, but also in some way almost everyone is in contact with this type of organization throughout their lives.
- Developing Lean Approach or Process Approach: since the structure of the organization also shows that it is not a simple one-line organization, the coordination and development of the processes should be taken care of. The lean approach basically targets the loss-making operation of services as much as possible. International

literature has reported a large number of health related best practices in this field (Molnar and Kerchner, 2016).

- Utilization of organizational capabilities: as performance management systems focus on these elements primarily, so it needs to be highlighted, as it is important in defining the vision and achieving the elements at the first two levels.

The first task of an organization is to define the strategy in each case, since the alignment of the individual areas can be linked to the strategy and can be achieved based on the goals set out in the strategy. In the life of public service organizations, this is a priority process, as each sector has not only different goals, but also has a different value system. I have already mentioned that performance management system should be applied in the public sector. For the selection, this method helps the target hierarchy described above. Important to emphasize that the recommendation is to choice a system that proposes an objective evaluation and, in particular, it has a crucial role to pay attention to risk reduction as well. Because of the special nature of public sector, as it has a much wider range of customers it is characterized by risk aversion.

In my research I collected the most commonly used methods in these areas and in the following part, these methods are introduced.

3 Performance evaluation methods applied by public service organizations

Since, performance management system is primary match to the target hierarchy; there are features that can be applied to all methods. The first column of Table 1 contains these elements. However, the characteristics of each organization are heterogeneous (size, resources, geographic location), so the appropriate method must be associated with this. In addition, each procedure has novelty content, so in the last column of the table contains those differences that represent an advantage for the organization when selecting a system.

Characteristics	Methods	Novelties
Future oriented Effectiveness	BSC	Breakdown of organizational strategy to individual level
Efficiency Main element is strategy	EFQM/CAF	Cyclical innovation projects can be developed
Relationship between organization and individual	SZTÉR	Framework model applied in the public sector / administration
High level of compliance	HOSHIN Management	Focuses on critical processes, system development PDCA cycle
Show multiple areas at one time	Performance Prizm	Ability to multi-purpose optimization
Simultaneous use of qualitative and quantitative indicators	10 probes	Qualified criteria system

Table 1 Introduction of performance evaluation methods with special regard to the public sector [Own edition, based on Veres-Somosi and Hogya (2011), Czegledi (2011) and Wimmer (2000)]

By collecting the methodologies, my goal was to examine the methods applied in the public sector. In addition, I also came up with the novelty content, that should contribute as much as possible to the goals defined in the Figure 1.

It can be stated that the application of all methods has advantages and disadvantages, so no one can be said to be the best, but there are special sectors that prefer a particular method. My research is in the health sector and within the hospitals, therefore, in order to substantiate my hypothesis, I sought the answer to the question of how some hospitals prefer to use performance assessment methods in Hungary. The importance of this can only be measured by what is best suited to objectively measure the results of the health sector. Perhaps this is the sector where many factors need to be taken into account, as variables may vary from patient to patient. There are factors that need to be tackeld with highest priority and quantified in a later research (Govindarajan and St Gupta, 1985).

Human capital: Here we can express the quantity and qualification of employees that are needed for an institution to achive effective services Human capital is a priority because without this factor there are no services. So, if we examine the contribution of performance management methods the best is the BSC because strategy appears on individual levels, so an organization is also split into levels and linking to it is much more easier.

Capital is also important, but a public service provider works with a specific framework and here the main target is not the profit maximization but the economical operation. It should be mentioned that there are costs for the introduction and maintenance of each system, so it would be difficult to generate comparability based on this factor (Davis and Albright, 2003).

Time: The last is the time, because in every process a kind of optimization has to be carried out, especially in a health care unit, because in many cases life can also depend on this factor. BSC also focuses on this element, but in this respect, the cyclicity of EFQM can also be effective (Whitley, 1999).

I examined the performance management systems of seven Hungarian hospitals through web content analysis and interviews. I was primarily looking for the performance management and methods used by each institution. The results of this research supported the information in Table 2. The health care institutions were very heterogeneous, as I also used the methodology applied in the county town and in the institutions of smaller cities. The size and location of the institution is significant because it has priority in setting goals, since it is important how many people use the service. (Musinszki, 2016). My sample was a small sample, the results are shown in Table 2. Research finds that Balance Score Card is the most commonly used method of health care institutions, as it can break down the organization to individual levels so that it can create both a quality and quantity indicator system that provides a true picture of the institution and the developments based on them.

Hospital	Size	Method presented and applied in the strategy
Miskolc	County hospital	Balance Scorecard base
Zirci Hospital	Small town hospital	Individual performance reviews, there is no specific data on organizational evaluation

Csornai Margit Hospital	Small town hospital	Balance Scorecard base
Szent Raffael	County hospital	Balance Scorecard base
Szent Pantelon	Surgery institute	Balance Scorecard base
Bugát Pál	City hospital	Balance Scorecard base
Szent János	Joint hospital	There is no public interest information, but its nature shows Balance Scorecard base

Table 2 Methodology applied to the examined institutions [Own edition based on websites and strategic statements of institutions]

It is worth mentioning that during the international outlook, I met a strategic statement by many institutions that prefer this method. Balance Scorecard has typically been used in the public service sector since the turn of the millennium, its success being a management tool that takes into account the company's non-financial performance alongside financial indicators. In addition, it focuses on engaging with customers and considers the pursuit of internal operations and development as essential. It also focuses not only on past events, but also on future opportunities (Voelker, Rakich and French, 2001).

It is worthwhile to support the 4 pillars of BSC with indicators that can help us in designing an institution's performance management system and address the three elements mentioned above, such as human capital, capital and time. I defined this as the next milestone in my research, where I will name the metrics and work out an effective index system.

4 The appearance of social innovation in a public service organization

It can be stated that every healthcare institution is trying to adapt to the environment, it also appears in its performance management. However, there are limitations, and there are a number of areas that are not only significant in the life of an organization, but also in meeting social needs. The role of social innovation is also significant, so the next matrix presents the practical use of social innovation in the sphere. It should be noted, that the definition background of social innovation is very diverse, so it is also important to clarify it. Figure 2 shows this.

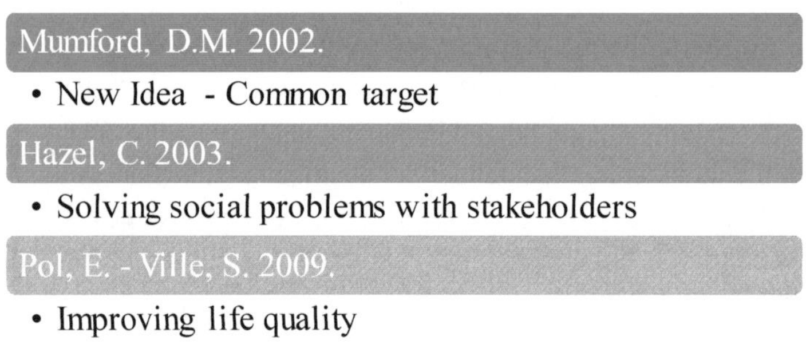

Figure 2 Elements of Social Innovation [Own edition based on Pol (2009), URBACT (2015) and Kelly (2008)]

This conceptual structure is well suited to the target hierarchy described earlier. We can highlight three areas that a public service organization may be affected by social innovation activities (social compliance, efficiency of operating conditions, learning and development), and formulated five elements to help develop these areas and introduce social innovation processes. and its organization. In the next relationship matrix (Figure 3), we can see which area is displayed.

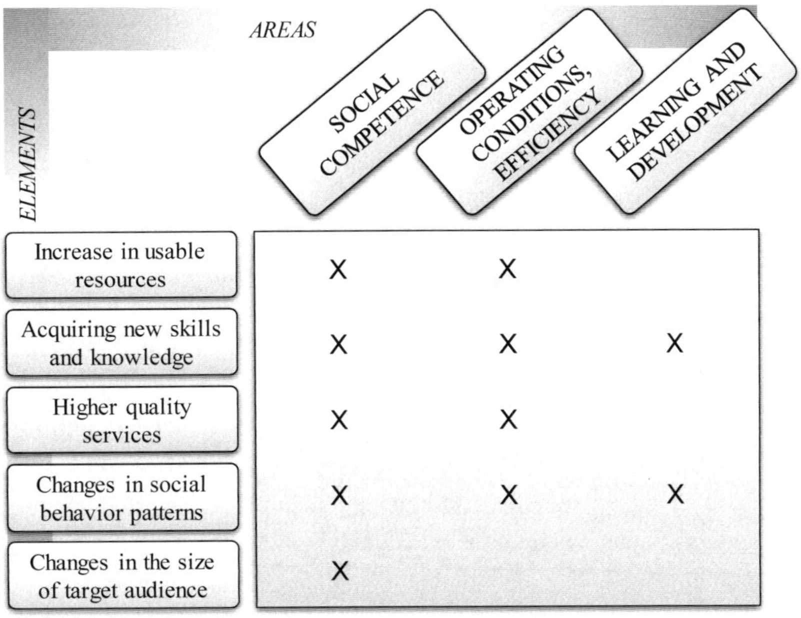

Figure 3 Matrix of social innovation exploitation in the public sector [Own edition based on Kocziszky, Veres-Somosi and Balaton (2015)]

Measuring social innovation is difficult because this process is reflected in the activities of each organization. However, if I want to find indicators in a health care facility where measurability can be defined, the five elements mentioned above can be used. I think the most important goal, as shown in Figure 3, is social compliance, as these activities are created for the sake of social well-being and satisfaction, but if we carry out a more detailed study, many indicators and elements can also affect this area not shown in Figure 3 (Kattel et al, 2013 and Kazmer, 2018).

5 Summary, results

Since there is no unified performance management system, I consider it worthwhile to develop an integrated system that will help to effectively evaluate the healthcare sector. There are also differences between institutions within the sectors but I consider that such a model provides an opportunity to integrate these individual features. Based on research the four aspects of Balance Scorecard system have proven its effectiveness in evaluating these institutions. I believe that the basics of the method are good, but there are elements that can be inserted based on previous gathered knowledge and defined target hierarchy.

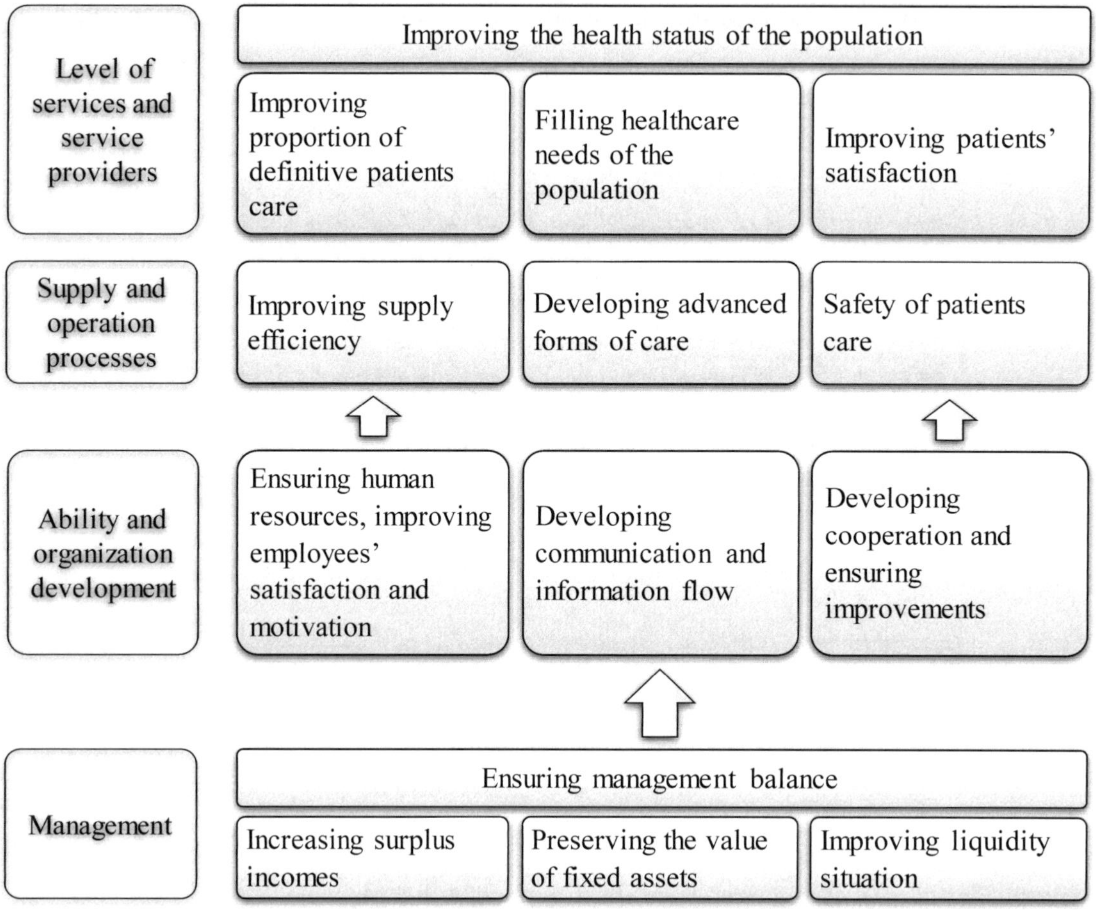

Figure 4 Strategy map of health care institution [Own edition based on websites and strategic statements of institutions (Bugat 2019, Mészaros2014, Nagy 2015, Winiczai 2017, Versmes2015)]

Additionally, I consider it useful to design strategy maps as this information can contribute to the formulation and implementation of successful application of integrated systems. Based on the aforementioned, I have prepared a strategy map on the basis of investigated institutions', which is intended to facilitate my further research. This shows that it is very difficult to plan in such a specific sector and how many elements need to be taken into account in order for an institution to operate efficiently and effectively, while also meeting social needs.

My research presents results that contribute to the development of a single indicator system, which can be said to be effective in the performance management of a public service organization. It is important to pair the factors outlined in the Figure 1 with the selected power management system. Balance Scorecard-based performance management takes place in the institutions I examined. It can be stated that this is good because it keeps in mind the organizational strategy. In the process of strategy planning, the organization can prioritize the organization, including the aforementioned time, human resource planning, and the time of the processes. I believe that by comparing this information, the link between the target hierarchy and the introduction of the BSC system is significant, as the introduction of this system will make the service more efficient. The lean approach helps in the process development and process time reduction, can utilize the organizational capabilities in the right way, and can manage economically limited resources. In my further research, based on the strategy map shown above, I would like to focus on the development of a system that, despite the specificity of the organization, will be effective and will be a replacement in this area.

Acknowledgement

This research was supported by the project nr. EFOP-3.6.2-16-2017-00007, titled Aspects on the development of intelligent, sustainable and inclusive society: social, technological, innovation networks in employment and digital economy. The project has been supported by the European Union, co-financed by the European Social Fund and the budget of Hungary.

References

Bugat, P. K. (2019). Quality Policy and Mission Statement (In Hungarian: Minőségpolitika és küldetésnyilatkozat), [Online]. Available at http://www.bugatpal.hu/index.php/magunkrol/minosegpolitika-es-kuldetesi-nyilatkozat [cited 19-02-2019].

Csath, M. (2016). 'Közintézmények stratégiai menedzsmentje'. *Államtudományi Műhelytanulmányok*, 14, pp. 2-9.

Czegled, L. (2011). Minőségmenedzsment, [Online]. Available at: http://www.tankonyvtar.hu/hu [cited 20-10-2018].

Davis, S. and Albright, T. (2004). 'An investigation of the effect of Balanced Scorecard implementation on financial performance'. *Management Accounting Research*, 15 (2), pp. 135-153.

Govindarajan, V. and St Gupta, A. K. (1985). 'Linking Control Systems to Business Unit Strategy: Impact on Performance'. *Accounting, Organizations and Society,* 10 (1), pp. 5 l-66.

Horvath, L. (2016). *'Az innováció-kutatás általános tudáshátterének áttekintése'*. Budapest: ELTE PPK. pp. 6-22.

Kaplan, R. S. and Norton, D. (2002). *A Stratégia Központú Szervezet – Hogyan lesznek sikeresek a Balanced Scorecard vállalatok az új üzleti környezetben?* Budapest: Panem.

Kattel, R., Cepilovs, A., Drechsler, W., Kalvet, T., Lember, V. and Tonurist, P. (2013). 'Can we measure public sector innovation?' *LIPSE Project paper. WP 6 Social innovation indicators,* pp. 1-15.

Kazmer, T. (2018). Szent Janos Hospital and North-Buda Joint Hospitals – Organizational and Operational Ruls (In Hungarian: Szent János Kórház és Észak-budai Egyesített Kórházak – Szervezeti és Működési Szabályzat), [Online]. Available at: http://www.janoskorhaz.hu/assets/2_1_szmsz.pd [cited 06-11-2018].

Kelly, A. E., Lesh, R. A. and Baek, J. Y. (2008). *Handbook of Design Research Methods in Education. Innovations in Science, Technology, Engineering and Mathematics Learning and Teaching*. New York: Taylor & Francis.

Kocziszky, G., Veres-Somosi, M. and Balaton, K. (2015). 'Characteristics of Measuring Social Innovation (In Hungarian: Társadalmi innováció mérésének sajátosságai)'. *Proceedings of 'Balance and Challenges' 9th International Scientific Conference'*, Miskolc, Hungary, pp. 288-302.

Kocziszky, G. and Veres-Somosi, M. (2016). 'Közszolgálattó szervezetek hatékonyság növelésének lehetőségei'. *Észak- Magyarországi Stratégiai Füzetek*, 13 (2), pp. 41-56.

Meszaros, L. (2014). Szent Pantaleon Hospital / Clinic Dunaujvaros – Organizational and Operational Rules (In Hungarian: Szent Pantaleon Kórház- Rendelőintézet Dunaújváros – Szervezeti És Működési Szabályzat), [Online]. Available at http://www.pantaleon.hu/kozerdeku/SZMSZ%20-%202014.pdf [cited 10-02-2019].

Molnar, V. and Kerchner, A. (2016). 'Application Possibilities of Mean Management in the Public Sector (In Hungarian: 'A lean menedzsment alkalmazási lehetőségei a közszférában')'. *Proceedings of the conference 'Technical Science in the Nothern Hungarian Region,* Miskolc, Hungary, pp.425-432.

Musinszki, Z. (2016). 'Innovations and cost systems trends and ways in the cost accounting'. *Organizational and economic mechanisms of development of the financial system*. Riga, Latvia: ISMA University, pp. 209-219.

Nagy, L. (2015). The Dr. Albert Kenessey Clinic – Strategic Document 2016-2022 (In Hungarian: A Dr. Kenessey Albert Rendelőintézet – stratégiai dokumentum 2016-2022), [Online]. Available at: http://kenessey.hu/kozadatok/strategia [cited 15-10-2018].

Pol, E. and Ville, S. (2009). 'Social innovation: buzz word or enduring term?' *The Journal of Socio-Economics*, 38 (6), pp. 878-885.

State Audit Office of Hungary. (2015). Jelentés a központi alrendszer egyes intézményei pénzügyi és vagyongazdálkodásának ellenőrzéséről – Zala Megyei Kórház, [Online]. Available at http://www.zmkorhaz.hu/doc/nyilvadat/aszellenorzes2015.pdf [cited 21-10-2018]

State Audit Office of Hungary. (2011). Jelentés Miskolc Megyei Jogú város Önkormányzata pénzügyi helyzetének ellenőrzéséről (43/3), [Online]. Available at: https://asz.hu/storage/files/files/%C3%96sszes%20jelent%C3%A9s/2011/1139j000.pdf?ctid=730 [cited 16-10-2018].

URBACT II Capitalisation (2015). *Social innovation in cities*. Apr. 2015.

Veres-Somosi, M. and Hogya, O. (2011). '*Teljesítménymenedzsment.*' Budapest: Nemzeti Tankönyvkiadó.

Vermes, T., Varsanyi, A., Valler, I. and Horvath, S. (2015). Zirc Erzsebet Hospital / Clinic – Development Plan 2015-2020 (In Hungarian: Zirci Erzsébet Kórház / Rendelőintézet – Fejlesztési terv 2015-2020), [Online]. Available at https://www.zirckorhaz.hu/?page_id=1000 [cited 12-10-2018].

Voelker, K. E. , Rakich. J. S. and French, G. R. (2001). 'The Balanced Scorecard in Healthcare Organizations: A Performance Measurement and Strategic Planning Methodology'. *Hospital Topics*, 79 (3), pp. 13-24.

Winiczai, Z., Abraham, P. and Nemeth-Borsodi, I. (2017). Strategic Goals for the Year 2018 in the Csornai Margit Hospital (In Hungarian: 2018. évi stratégiai célok a Csornai Margit Kórházban), [Online]. Available at: http://www.margitkorhaz.hu/pdf/2018_evi%20strategia_terv.pdf [cited 16-10-2018].

Wimmer, A. (2000). 'A vállalati teljesítménymérés az értékteremtés szolgálatában, a működési és a pénzügyi teljesítmény kapcsolatának vizsgálatában', [Online]. Available at: http://unipub.lib.uni-corvinus.hu/32/1/10_mht_wimmer.pdf [cited 25-05-2018].

Whitley, R. (1999). 'Firms, institutions and management control: the comparative analysis of coordination and control systems'. *Accounting, Organisations and Society*, 24 (5/6), pp. 507–524.

Investigating the Process of Social Innovation – A Social Learning Based Approach

Gabriella Metszosy[1]

Abstract: A number of challenges are requiring more and more involvement from the humanity, and solutions are hardly possible without wider participation in social innovation and social learning. The characteristics that are essential factors for implementing social innovation need to be further developed. In this paper, social innovation is presented in the aspect of social learning with its influential indicators, possible success and failure factors. In every phase of the process of social innovation, different tools and techniques can be applied to investigate the available resources and supporting decisions. In this paper a short illustrative case demonstrates a decision support method which can be applied in the process to choose the orientation of the social innovation practice to be accomplished. Based on the available factors and the weighting of decision maker, the result of the method shows the best alternative which worth to implement.

Keywords: social innovation, social learning, social innovation process, social innovation factors, decision support method.

JEL Classification: O35

1 Introduction

Nowadays social innovation phenomena are found in every aspect of life (e.g. new educational forms, movements, crowdfunding). Uncountable social innovations have appeared in the last decades. These changes have occurred due to individuals, organizations, foundations and movements in a wider area.

In most of the social innovations new combinations or a hybrid form of existing elements are created – rather than something entirely new – and they are cross-border (Sanders et al., 2007). This results in new social relationships between earlier separated individuals and groups and it promotes the spread and apperception of innovation, which opens the door to other innovations.

There are many definitions to describe social innovation, because so far there is no final version of it. The internationally accepted concept contains the following elements (Reeder et al., 2012):

- new organizational environment,
- new idea,
- new arrangements,
- new scope of activities,
- new relationships and interactions,
- which give satisfaction to a social need.

Social innovation differs from the traditional approach to innovation. It does not satisfy realized needs with the focus on the market; here, the primary focus is on people (Secco et al.,

[1] University of Miskolc, Faculty of Economics, szvmg@uni-miskolc.hu

2016). With the help of social innovation processes, products, services, new approaches can be created in the wider area of different organizations, for example in a co-op, joint business, a for-profit or non-profit corporation. These organizations can be profitable and effective for the whole society, if the created values mean something important for the target group, which is the society and the community (Marshall and Dolley, 2019).

The role of social innovation is very important in economic growth, because of its cross-border and self-exciter attributes. In the opinion of Murray, Mulgan and Caulier-Grice (2010) there are four critical areas in implementing and supporting social innovations, which contain the following elements:

- Public economy: community financing, labour force, organizational forms, measuring and rating, information circulation.
- Donations: innovative projects, finance, support packages, innovation tools, platforms, protocols, government and accountability, regularisation, legal and other conditions for expanding social innovation.
- Market economy: value creation, finance, organizations, information, regularisation, legal and other conditions for generating social innovation.
- Household economics: public grounds, appreciation of time, mutuality, social movements.

Arising the social innovation in these fields to be supported by causation with different decision support methods. To determine the applicability framework, it is necessary to investigate the decision support techniques in various levels of complexity and to determine the possible decision points, which supports to draw the inference the applicability of decision support methods in the social innovation process.

2 The process of social innovation

The social innovation may trend towards a particular technology, policy, institution, organization, culture, population, target group, etc. The focus – social need – is the most critical point. All types of social innovation processes go through the following steps (Sanders et al., 2007; Tohidi and Jabbari, 2012; Rajapathirana and Hui, 2018; Soma et al., 2018).

Phases of the innovation process:

- Preparation: define the range, develop the common knowledge of the process of social innovation and the innovation ground. Strengthen the common understanding with informative tools, configuration of the innovation ground (define the goals, values of key performance indexes (KPI) to support and monitor the innovation), and recruitment (promoting, recruitment of the participants).
- Directives: define the challenge (what is the challenge, what can be optimized), Understanding, especially on the part of the target group. Define the benefits and the efforts of participation. Generate ideas to understand the needs and to determine the potential solutions. The starting point of the social innovation is an unsatisfied need, and an idea for helping to meet this need.

- Concept: value proposition, highlighting of the effects and feasibility, selection of concepts. Feasibility assessments with stakeholder and possible collaborator involvement with the usage of proper communication tools.
- Prototyping: start the project and recruit members (design the project team), optimize the value proposition and define the goal of the iteration period (how can the solution create value for the target group and how can it decrease the limitations of the development of the society, optimize the value proposition with the help of these data, develop and rate the prototype – including the members of the target group, who takes part in the processes and the rating and redefine the goals using the results).
- Maintenance: business model, legal form, strategy (determine the clear goals and actions to reach the goals), realization and rating (with the help of monitoring and feedback).
- Equalization, measurement: strategy, people, realization (measure the performance of the organization and the society), finance (from different sources, venture capital, support, donations, common finance, benefit).
- Systematic changes: balanced approach – top-down, bottom-up, define goals and measurable indicators. Mobilize the stakeholders because of the development of the social movements.
- Learning and development.

The process of social learning is connected to the process of social innovation with the context of social change. In both processes there are different learning phases where new knowledge and networks will be essential for the long-term sustainability of the implemented action. Since social learning is in evidence from the initial phase of the social innovation, it is

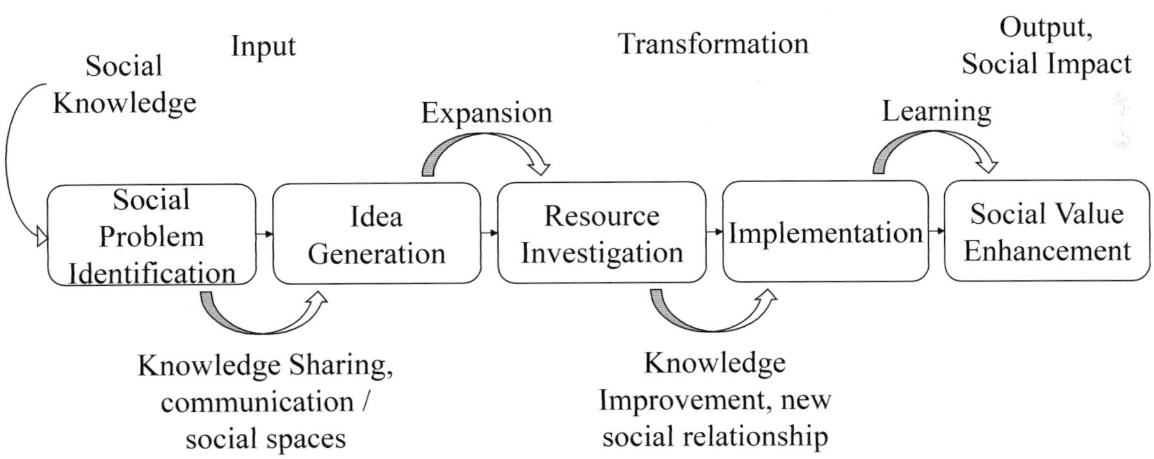

necessary to integrate its elements into the process of social innovation (Figure 1).

Figure 1 Social Innovation process with a focus on social learning [Own edition]

Each stage of the process is described in more detail:

Input phase:

- The identification of the social problem can be done by individuals, groups, campaigns, political movements, religious movements, volunteers, attitudes, demographic changes.

Personal motivation is also a critical factor, when somebody is concerned in the problem and he/she would like to deal with it.

- Ideas can come from various sources: theories, crises, experiences, specifications, new knowledge from the social spaces.

Transformation phase:

- The evaluation of ideas is based on feasibility and available resources. Analysis of the present and required conditions is essential.
- Ideally, before implementation the chosen idea needs to be tested or prototyped. The test phase might happen in a small sample, community, process, etc.
- With all the necessary resources in place, and if testing is successful, the implementation is begun in cooperation with the partners involved in the process. New knowledge is created, which helps to maintain and circulate the process of innovation.

Output, social impact phase:

- Sustainable practice requires the commitment of the target group; for value enhancement of the implemented social innovation idea, it is necessary for it to take root in the common knowledge.

Measurable indicators need to be specified for rating the phases of social innovation. in this way the special results can be ranked, and it can be decided which approach could be useful to take. Measurable improvement can be factors such as quality, satisfaction, acceptance, understanding, cost reduction and other characteristics.

According to Kaderabkova and Saman (2013), the main dimensions for evaluating social innovation are:

- new value of innovation,
- taking part in the process of social innovation,
- creativity or techniques to develop the new concepts,
- learning mechanism and rating,
- the mechanism of collecting information and knowledge sharing,
- types of co-operation,
- source(s) of finance.

Based on these dimensions, indicators of the social innovation are collected and characterised with potential success and failure factors in Table 1.

Social Innovation Indicator	**Success Factors**	**Failure Factors**
Previous activities	Successful social activities, former best practice	No former activities
Stakeholders	Acceptance, support, relationships, reinvestment, social responsiveness, participation	Lack of support, quickening, conflicts
Social contribution	Employment, increasing the quality of life, self-help, mentoring, financial stability, transparency	Lack of interest among target group, lack of confidence, underemployment

Social Innovation Indicator	Success Factors	Failure Factors
Local abilities	Participation, supportive atmosphere, infrastructure, active local government, collaboration, local organizations, positive perception, social responsiveness	Conflicts, lack of local government support, difficulties with transportation
Financial aspect	Reinvestment, alternative financial opportunity, crowdfunding, self-financing, voluntary-financing, contingency fund	Underfunding, lack of grants to apply for, incapability of self-preservation, over-assessment, lack of financial feasibility
Legal	Support system, regulatory environment, legal knowledge	Barriers, lack of demandable support
Communication	Active communication, knowledge sharing, externalisation, internalisation, involvement	Infrequent, missing communication, top-down approach without bottom-up
Education	Mentoring, self-learning, training	Lack of learning process
Applied techniques	IT, sustainable technology, low consumption, design thinking	Timing, obsolete technology, lack of optimization, adaptation without testing
Expectations	Supportive approach, reasonable expectations	High expectations without support
Novelty	Competitiveness, successful implementation in another place with similar attributes	Imitation without similar conditions
Networks	Collaboration, voluntariness, supply chain, regular customers with occasional buyers	Competitors
Focus of the social innovation can be:	– disadvantages – unemployment – migration – ethnics – education – art – culture – holiday – health – poverty – homelessness – indebtedness – family – youth chances	– psychosocial damages – local development – regional development – violence – addictions – criminals – justice

Table 1. Social innovation indicators and its potential factors [Own edition based on Dainienė and Dagilienė (2015), Dziallas and Blind (2018), Smith et al. (2016) and Tohidi and Jabbari (2012)]

3 Decision support potential for the social innovation process

Each phases of the social innovation process contain decision points what require the application of different decision support techniques. Due to the diversity of the problem and the range of available data, it is not practical to rely on a unique best practice in different social innovation decisions. The complexity of the problem, the range of stakeholders involved in the decision and the existence of influential conditions will be the basis for selecting the adequate decision support method:

- voting procedures,
- elementary decision methods (decision matrices, decision trees),
- complex methods (ELECTRE, POMETHEE, TOPSIS),
- evaluation functions,
- utility functions,
- AHP,
- game theory,
- linear programming,
- artificial intelligence.

3.1 Case study

The application steps of Analytic Hierarchy Process (AHP) as a potential decision support method are presented in the case study. The methodology and framework of AHP are described by Saaty (1987). Choosing the method is explained by the fact that it can be applied in case of both well- and ill-structured problems (Forman, 1993), and for estimating the actual abilities of the place where the social innovation will be implemented.

The aim of the adaptation is to choose the orientation of a social innovation solution which can be applied with the available level of social innovation indicators. It can be applied in the transformation phase of the process. The decision maker - who provides the information needed to select the orientation - is a group or individual who initiate the innovation. In addition, the available resources and experiences from former practices with similar characteristics play an important part to define the criteria (C_1-C_3) which exert influence on the objective. The criteria can be broken down to sub-criteria at second (C_{11}-C_{33}) and third (C_{221}-C_{332}) level because of the deeper structure. The structure of the decision tree is shown in Figure 2.

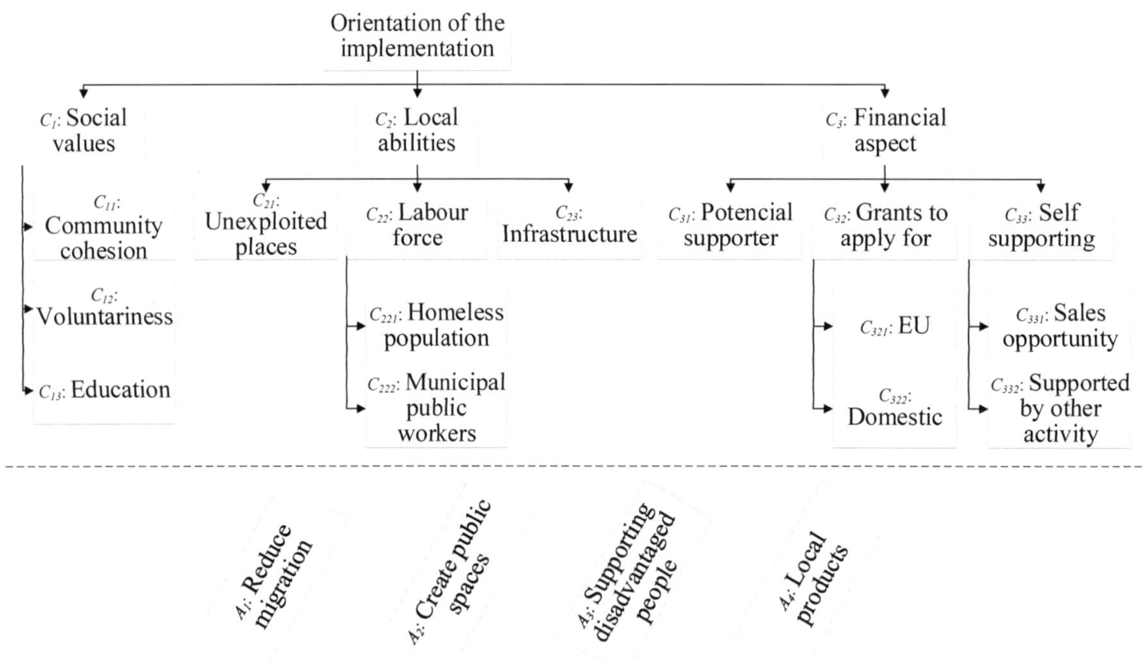

Figure 1. Decision hierarchy [Own edition]

The pairwise comparison have to be done by the decision maker, where the criteria are compared with the scale defined by Saaty (1987). The matrices are constructed by the right of pairwise comparison, and the weight vectors (**w**) of the alternatives (A_1-A_4) are calculated from them. Based on the weight vectors and the aggregated values of bottom criteria, the aggregated sums of weights (S(A_i)) can be calculated. The calculated results are shown in Table 2.

Based on the calculation of AHP method, the preference order of the alternatives as: $A_4 \succ A_2 \succ A_3 \succ A_1$. The fourth alternative – local products – can be considered the most useful in the described case. This is a source of income to people who work on it if the sales opportunities are initiated. Producing local products require local particularity or raw material which can be adapted, and the collective work helps strengthening the community cohesion. The first alternative is the worst in the analysed case, its relative performance is 48% of the fourth one.

	C_{11}	C_{12}	C_{13}	C_{21}	C_{221}	C_{222}	C_{23}	C_{31}	C_{321}	C_{322}	C_{331}	C_{332}	
A_i	0.11250	0.02500	0.11250	0.14000	0.15600	0.08400	0.02000	0.05250	0.10500	0.07000	0.08575	0.03675	S(A_i)
A_1	0.300	0.100	0.025	0.100	0.020	0.030	0.160	0.310	0.400	0.500	0.020	0.200	0.1642
A_2	0.500	0.300	0.300	0.550	0.130	0.180	0.730	0.015	0.100	0.030	0.120	0.700	0.2739
A_3	0.050	0.400	0.025	0,100	0.750	0.160	0.010	0.005	0.400	0.200	0.010	0.050	0.2221
A_4	0.150	0.200	0.650	0.250	0.100	0.630	0.100	0.670	0.100	0.270	0.850	0.050	0.3398

Table 2. Assessment of the alternatives [Own edition]

4 Conclusion

Linking social innovation to social learning is essential for the proper understanding of how the entire process works. This paper provides a brief overview of the connection between social innovation and social learning. Social innovation formulates a constant demand to improve people's well-being, which is also part of the framework for social progress. Accordingly, achieving the intentions of social innovation contributes to leaps in social progress.

In every phase of the social innovation process is essential to applying various tools and decision support techniques to choose the appropriate option. The investigation of available resources and future possibilities is indispensable to rank the alternatives. In early phases using elementary tools are proposed for the survey, such as SWOT, and cause and effect analysis. With the progress of the process, the complexity of applied methods can be risen. Selecting the new social innovation implementation is the most critical part of the process, and adequate decision-making and applied methods are needed for the right choice. An adaptable framework construction is essential to choose a suitable and sufficiently complex decision-making method.

A case study was described the application of AHP, a decision support method which can be applied after the resource investigation phase of the social innovation process. This method is useful when the decision maker is capable of weighting consistently the criteria, the adequate knowledge is essential. It should be noted that AHP method can be applied without biases, if interaction cannot be suspected. If supposedly it is, other method, such as Analytic Network Process – ANP, or the reorganization of the criteria is required (Molnar and Horvath, 2017).

Acknowledgements

This research was supported by project no. EFOP-3.6.2-16-2017-00007, titled 'Aspects on the development of intelligent, sustainable and inclusive society: social, technological, innovation networks in employment and digital economy'. The project has been supported by the European Union, co-financed by the European Social Fund and the budget of Hungary.

References

Dainienė, R. and Dagilienė, L. (2015). 'A TBL Approach Based Theoretical Framework for Measuring Social Innovations'. *Procedia – Social and Behavioral Sciences*, 213 (1), pp. 275-280.

Dziallas, M. and Blind, K. (2018). 'Innovation indicators throughout the innovation process: An extensive literature analysis'. *Technovation*, In Press, Corrected Proof, 27 p.

Forman, E. H. (1993). 'Facts and fictions about the Analytic Hierarchy Process'. *Mathematical and Computer Modelling*, 17 (4/5), pp. 19-26.

Kaderabkova, A. and Saman, S. M. (2013). 'Evaluations of social innovations: their characteristics and impacts, cross country comparisons and implications for policy support'. *(Paper presented at the international conference Social Frontiers: The next edge of social innovation research, at GCU's London Campus on 14th and 15th November 2013).*

Marshall, F. and Dolley, J. (2019). 'Transformative innovation in peri-urban Asia'. *Research Policy*, 48 (4), pp. 983-992.

Molnar, V. and Horvath, D. D. (2017). 'Determination of Coefficients of Multi-Attribute Utility Function with Attribute Breakdown'. *Proceedings of the 12th International Conference on Strategic Management and its Support by Information Systems*, pp. 312-319.

Murray, R., Mulgan, G., and Caulier-Grice, J. (2010). *The Open Book of Social Innovation*. The Young Foundation, NESTA Innovating Public Services

Rajapathirana, J. and Hui, Y. (2018). 'Relationship between innovation capability, innovation type, and firm performance'. *Journal of Innovation & Knowledge*, 3 (1), pp. 44-55.

Reeder, N., O'Sullivan, C., Tucker, S., Ramsden, P. and Mulgan, G. (2012). 'Strengthening social innovation in Europe. Journey to effective assessment and metrics'. *Enterprise and Industry*. European Commission, Brussels, Belgium.

Saaty, T. L. (1987). 'The analytic hierarchy process—what it is and how it is used'. *Mathematical Modelling*, 9 (3–5), pp. 161-176.

Sanders, B., Mulgan, G., Ali, R. and Tucker, S. (2007). 'Social Innovation: what it is, why it matters and how can be accelerated'. *Working Paper*, Oxford Business School, UK,

Secco, L., Pisani E., Burlando, C., Da Re, R., Pettenella D., Nijnik, M., Miller, D., Slee, B., Gezik, V. and Kluvankova, T. (2016). *Social Innovation in Marginalised Rural Areas.* Work Programme: Topic ISIB-03-2015. Report D4.1.

Smith, C., Rassia, S., Delioglanis, I., Bougliouklis, M., Gilbert, N., Penn, A., Poggio, D., Kerckow, B. and Piedra-Garcia, D. (2016). 'Social Innovation and Community Energy best practices, methods and tools across Europe' in Triggering Sustainable Biogas Energy Communities through Social Innovation project, *ISABEL Consortium*. EC, HORIZON 2020 Programme for Research and Innovation.

Soma, K., van den Burg, S. W. K., Hoefnagel, E. W. J., Stuiver, M. and van der Heide, M. (2018). 'Social innovation – A future pathway for Blue growth?'. *Marine Policy*, 87, pp. 363-370.

Tohidi, H. and Jabbari, M. M. (2012). 'The Effective Factors on Formation of Innovation Processes'. *Procedia Technology*, 1, pp.524-527.

Comparison of supply-chain coordinating contract types

Viktor Molnar[1], Tamas Faludi [2]

Abstract. Contract types as hard coordinating tools of supply chains have become an important focus point in the strategic issues of enterprises in recent decades. The market mechanisms connected to simple or even complex chains can be analyzed on the basis of mathematical formulation of coordination models This study, through a quantitative example, investigates how strong a coordinating power certain contract types (wholesale pricing and quantity discount) have; that is, among the applied contract types which can be considered as more profitable from a coordinating point of view. The aim of this study is comparing the basic wholesale pricing contracts in centralized and decentralized settings and the widely applied quantity discount type contract in order to get clear information about their advantages or disadvantages. Both the centralized and the quantity discount type is recommended to apply in supply chains where possible.

Keywords: Supply-Chain Coordination, Quantity discount; Wholesale Price; Contract Type.

JEL Classification: D21, L11, L14, M10

1 Introduction

Supply chain management appeared for the first time in the literature in the 1980s. In that period globalization was evolving and as a result supply chains were widening. The number of cooperating enterprises increased and the sudden development of information technology tools increasingly affected the operation of enterprises (Juhasz and Banyai, 2018a). This development process is still continuing nowadays. This is why supply chain management is one of the most important research areas today.

The chains have formed complicated networks in the 21st century. There are many suppliers, raw material manufacturers and distribution centers within the supply networks. They have to cooperate in an efficient manner in order that all of the customers' needs be satisfied (Tamas and Illes, 2017). These processes have to be operated in a way that the members of the network are able to earn profits. This is the reason for the increased scientific interest in the coordination of supply chains.Two groups of coordination possibilities can be distinguished. One is the group of soft factors, which attempt to increase coordinating efficiency through the behavioral aspect (Singh and Benyoucef, 2013). The other is the group of hard factors that facilitate coordination through financing. Many believe that the potentially best hard factor is the set of contract types (Gomez-Padilla and Mishina, 2009).

To analyze supply chain coordination mechanisms, the detailed study of basic elements or basic processes of production or providing service is necessary. In manufacturing, for example, one of the most elementary solutions, sufficiently accurate cutting tool management in mass

[1] Institute of Management Science / University of Miskolc, H-3515 Miskolc-Egyetemvaros, Hungary, szvmv@uni-miskolc.hu

[2] Institute of Management Science / University of Miskolc, H-3515 Miskolc-Egyetemvaros, Hungary, szvft@uni-miskolc.hu

production can result in a significant saving of cost annually (Vasvari et al., 1994; Mamalis, Kundrak and Horvath, 2005). In another example, the proper formation of surface topography of the produced parts can significantly influence the scrap rate and therefore the customers' satisfaction (Felho and Kundrak, 2012). However, these elements, which seem to be minor, have significant effects on costs, particularly if the development level of calculation procedures and systems at a given enterprise is high enough (Musinszki, 2014, 2016a).

In the time of Industry 4.0, the in-depth analysis of complex organizational systems requires relatively quick processing and analysis of great amounts of data (Musinszki, 2016b; Juhasz and Banyai, 2018b). The reason for success of cooperation between companies is not simply their bargaining power but also the elements determining the efficiency of activities defined within the basic processes of an organization. Another important issue is that a strategic step that may profitable in the short term does not necessarily lead to long-term success, and vice versa.

According to the state-of-the-art the aims of contract types are to ensure a legal framework for the cooperation of companies and determining responsibilities and rates of costs and profits (Coltman et al., 2009). These ensure clear rules, therefore conflicts can be avoided. Another definition points out that contracts are used mainly to increase the performance of supply chain. At the same time most of the contracts are applied on the basis of their coordinating capability and the resulting advantages (Wang, Wang and Su, 2013; Tilson, 2008).

There are many contract types in practice that are used by companies to make agreements. Researchers intensified their interest in this topic around the year 2000. There are traditional contracts, e.g. wholesale contracts, hybrid ones (Molnar, Musinszki and Faludi, 2018), and relatively new types as well, e.g. the trade credit type (Luo and Zhang, 2012). Choosing the most suitable contract type for a certain operation and contact system of a company could be a potential coordinating factor. The wholesale contract type can be used in both centralized and decentralized supply chains. In the latter case companies maximize their profits individually on the basis of previously determined prices. In a centralized setting there is a chain member who manages the rest of the members due to its bargaining power, and they all intend to maximize the profit of the whole supply chain. This means that the profit maximizing variable is the quantity to be sold (Chakraborty, Shauhan and Vidyarthi, 2015). The quantity discount type contract is also an option that can be applied in supply chains operating either in centralized or decentralized settings. The main goal of this type is that the seller motivates the customer to buy as great an amount of product as possible. Here the price and quantity sold are in inverse relationship, that is the larger the lot the customer buys, the greater discount it obtains.

In our study the above mentioned contract types are compared. The methodology of the analysis consists of a supply chain model formulation and an analysis through an illustrative mathematical example. The model consists of two supply chain members and it can be generalized to a sequential chain by several members.

2 Model formulation

The coordination powers of the two contract types (wholesale pricing and quantity discount) are demonstrated through a quantitative example when centralized and decentralized settings are applied. The analysis is carried out with the use of a simple supply chain model with two members (Fig. 1).

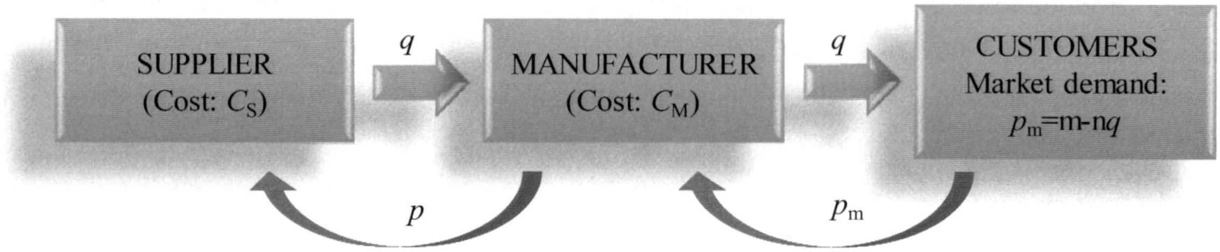

Figure 1 The supply chain structure of the model

The two members are the supplier and the manufacturer. They serve the market and therefore the customers. The notations applied in the model are summarized in Table 1.

Symbol	Description
S	supplier
M	manufacturer
p	supplier's price
p_m	market price
q_{DC}	quantity – decentralized setting
q_C	quantity – centralized setting
π_{DC}	profit – decentralized setting
π_C	profit – centralized setting
π_{QD}	profit – quantity discount
m; n	constants of market demand function
C	total cost of the SC members
α_M	manufacturer's revenue rate

Table 1 Notations applied in the model

3 Analysis

The objective of this case study is to demonstrate the difference between the centralized and decentralized settings of supply chains by emphasizing the applied prices, sold quantities, total profit of the chain and the individual profits of chain members. In the case study two contract types – wholesale pricing and quantity discount – are analyzed.

Parameter	pm	C_S	C_M	α_M
Value	$100–1.5q$	EUR 15	EUR 25	0.7

Table 2 Economic parameters

The simplified market demand function ($p_m(q)$) and the given process are valid in the case of durable consumer goods that are not strongly seasonal. Data necessary for calculations are summarized in Table 2.

In wholesale pricing when the decentralized setting is applied, profit values can be calculated by the formulas below. Eq. (1) is the supplier's profit, Eq. (2) is the manufacturer's profit. The manufacturer maximizes its profit on the basis of the sold quantity, i.e. it choses q_{DC} on the basis of market demand. Therefore $\pi_{DC,M}$ has to be partially derived by quantity. When this expression is equal to zero, quantity q_{DC} can be expressed (Eq. (3)).

$$\pi_{DC,S} = (p - C_S)q_{DC} \tag{1}$$

$$\pi_{DC,M} = (p_m - p - C_M)q_{DC} \tag{2}$$

$$\frac{\partial \pi_{DC,M}}{\partial q_{DC}} = 0 \rightarrow q_{DC}(p) = \frac{m - p - C_M}{2n} \tag{3}$$

The supplier determines the price to be charged to the manufacturer (p) if it orders quantity q_{DC}. The supplier's profit and the supplier's price determined by the profit maximum criteria can be calculated by Eqs. (4) and (5).

$$\pi_{DC,S} = (p - C_S)\frac{m - p - C_M}{2n} \tag{4}$$

$$\frac{\partial \pi_{DC,S}}{\partial p} = 0 \rightarrow p = \frac{m - C_M + C_S}{2} \tag{5}$$

The quantity q_{DC} (Eq. (6)) can be determined using Eqs. (3) and (5). Substituting this in the demand function provides the market price (Eq. (7)).

$$q_{DC} = \frac{m - C}{4n} \tag{6}$$

$$p_m = \frac{3m + C}{4} \tag{7}$$

Profits of the supply chain members and the whole chain are calculated by Eqs. (8)–(10). They incorporate only the known costs and constants that describe market demand.

$$\pi_{DC,S} = \frac{(m - C)^2}{8n} \tag{8}$$

$$\pi_{DC,M} = \frac{(m - C)^2}{16n} \tag{9}$$

$$\pi_{DC} = \frac{3(m - C)^2}{16n} \tag{10}$$

In the centralized setting the chain members maximize the total profit of the supply chain (Eq. (11)) on the basis of the market demand q_C (Eq. (12)). Substituting q_C quantity in the marked demand function, the market price can be determined (Eq. (13)).

$$\pi_C = (p_m - C)q_C \tag{11}$$

$$\frac{\partial \pi_C}{\partial q_C} = 0 \rightarrow q_C = \frac{m - C}{2n} \tag{12}$$

$$p_{\mathrm{m}} = \frac{m + C}{2} \tag{13}$$

Profits of the supply chain members and the whole chain are calculated by Eqs. (14)–(16) They incorporate only the known costs, the constants that describe market demand and the price charged by the supplier. In the centralized setting the supplier's price, which splits the total profit of the chain equally, can be calculated (Eq. (17)).

$$\pi_{\mathrm{C,S}} = (p - C_{\mathrm{S}})\frac{m - C}{2n} \tag{14}$$

$$\pi_{\mathrm{C,M}} = (p_{\mathrm{m}} - p - C_{\mathrm{M}})\frac{m - C}{2n} \tag{15}$$

$$\pi_{\mathrm{C}} = \frac{(m - C)^2}{4n} \tag{16}$$

$$\pi_{\mathrm{C,S}} = \pi_{\mathrm{C,M}} \to p^* = \frac{m - C_{\mathrm{M}} + 3C_{\mathrm{S}}}{4} \tag{17}$$

In the case of a quantity discount type contract the supplier charges the manufacturer price $p(q_{\mathrm{C}})$, which depends on the quantity q_{C}. It is assumed that the price is the declining continuous function of the quantity. The profit of the manufacturer is the difference between its revenue ($R(q_{\mathrm{C}})$) and costs (Eq. (18)). In this contract type the centralized setting of the wholesale pricing contract is considered optimal. In such a situation the quantity is identical to q_{C} and by applying this quantity the profit of the whole chain is identical to the profit of the centralized setting. This means that the profit of the manufacturer is an α_{M} portion of the total profit (Eqs. (19) and (20)). The price $p(q_{\mathrm{C}})$ can be expressed from these (Eq. (21)). Using the resulting formulas, the profit of the supplier can be calculated by Eq. (22).

$$\pi_{\mathrm{QD,M}} = R(q_{\mathrm{C}}) - [p(q_{\mathrm{C}}) + C_{\mathrm{M}}]q_{\mathrm{C}} \tag{18}$$

$$\pi_{\mathrm{QD,M}} = \alpha_{\mathrm{M}}\pi_{\mathrm{C}} \tag{19}$$

$$R(q_{\mathrm{C}}) - [p(q_{\mathrm{C}}) + C_{\mathrm{M}}]q_{\mathrm{C}} = \alpha_{\mathrm{M}}[R(q_{\mathrm{C}}) - Cq_{\mathrm{C}}] \tag{20}$$

$$p(q_{\mathrm{C}}) = (1 - \alpha_{\mathrm{M}})\frac{R(q_{\mathrm{C}})}{q_{\mathrm{C}}} - C_{\mathrm{M}} + \alpha_{\mathrm{M}}C \tag{21}$$

$$\pi_{\mathrm{QD,S}} = [p(q_{\mathrm{C}}) - C_{\mathrm{S}}]q_{\mathrm{C}} = (1 - \alpha_{\mathrm{M}})\pi_{\mathrm{C}} \tag{22}$$

For the quantity discount type it was also analyzed how the studied economic parameters change when the quantity is lower or higher than the optimum sold quantity (q_{C}). The reason for this is to gain more realistic insight into the market and to simulate a situation where the quantity sold not always remains the optimum expected by the market. In the first case the sold quantity is identical to that of the centralized setting, in the second it is lower and in the third it is higher. Table 3 summarizes the results of applying the formulas above and the data of Table 2.

Parameter	Wholesale pricing		Quantity discount		
	decentralized	**centralized**	$q=q_C$	$q<q_C$	$q>q_C$
quantity, q [1000 pcs]	10	20	20	17	25
market price, p_m [EUR]	85	70	70	74.5	62.5
supplier's price, p [EUR]	45	30	24	25.35	21.75
supplier's profit, π_S [EUR 1000]	300	300	180	175.95	168.75
manufacturer's profit, π_M [1000 EUR]	150	300	420	410.55	393.75
total profit, π [1000 EUR]	450	600	600	586.5	562.5

Table 3 Results of the calculation

From the numerical results it can be stated that each company that applies wholesale pricing earns a higher profit in the centralized setting than in the decentralized setting. This means that the total profit of the whole supply chain is also higher. It is recommended to apply the centralized setting because this statement is valid not only in case of two but more members too.

In quantity discount any alteration in the optimal centralized quantity results in the decrease of profit values: in case of lower quantity the prices increase; in case of higher quantity the prices decrease but the marginal revenue decreases to a higher extent. Due to the share rate the share of profits between the members is relatively unequal. The reason for this is the preliminary given α_M rate, whose value in practice depends on the bargaining powers of the members. This value highlights the connection between the quantity discount type and the revenue sharing type: In the latter model the supplier always earns (1-α) part of the total profit of supply chain while when a quantity discount is applied, the profit of retailer depends on the p price determined by q_C quantity. Therefore, in an uncertain market situation the risk is borne completely by the retailer. If a quantity discount can be applied in the transactions between the members, the q_C quantity is worth to be bought because of the highest profit. Of course; it is not always possible because the quantity is determined by the market but endeavoring to that could be useful. However; the lower or higher quantities also result in higher profits than that in the decentralized setting of wholesale pricing.

4 Summary

One of the most important questions in supply chain management is how the operation efficiency and profitability of supply chains or networks can be increased. Supply chain coordination solutions can be considered as the greatest help in meeting this aim. Applying soft and hard coordinating factors, the operation of supply chains can become more efficient. Hard factors, namely the supply chain coordination by contracts, were the focus of this study. Two relatively frequently applied contract types were compared in supply chains operating in either centralized or decentralized settings. The comparison was demonstrated in a case study. It was found that the centralized setting ensures more advantageous conditions with the wholesale pricing type of contract than the decentralized one. When quantity discount is applied, it is worth selling the same quantity of products as determined in centralized setting because this allows a maximum profit. The profitability of supply chains can be increased by altering the present contracts between the members to a more profitable one. In this paper it was demonstrated that the widely applied decentralized wholesale pricing contract can be substituted by more profitable ones. The most important step in this modification is the development of ability for a more efficient communication process and trust between the partners. It can be reached only by the change of attitude of managers. It is recommended to apply additional variables in order to make revenue sharing fairer. This issue can be a direction for further research.

Acknowledgements

This research was supported by the project no. EFOP-3.6.2-16-2017-00007, titled "Aspects on the development of intelligent, sustainable and inclusive society: social, technological, innovation networks in employment and digital economy". The project has been supported by the European Union, co-financed by the European Social Fund and the budget of Hungary.

References

Chakraborty, T., Shauhan, S.S. and Vidyarthi, N. (2015). 'Coordination and competition in a common retailer channel: Wholesale price versus revenue-sharing mechanisms'. *International Journal of Production Economics*, 166, pp. 103–118.

Coltman, T., Bru, K., Perm-Ajchariyawong, N., Devinney, T. M. and Benito, G. R. (2009). 'Supply Chain Contract Evolution', GR, Supply Chain Contract Evolution. *European Management Journal*, pp. 1–30.

Felho, C. and Kundrak, J. (2012). 'Characterization of topography of cut surface based on theoretical roughness indexes'. *Key Engineering Materials*, 496, pp. 194–199.

Gomez-Padilla, A. and Mishina, T. (2009). 'Supply contract with options'. *International Journal of Production Economics*, 122 (1), pp. 312–318

Juhasz, J. and Banyai, T. (2018a). 'Last mile logistics: an integrated view'. *Proceeding of IOP Conference Series: Materials Science and Engineering*, Kecskemét, Hungary, pp. 448

Juhasz, J. and Banyai, T. (2018b). 'What industry 4.0 means for just-in-sequence supply in automotive industry?'. *Lecture Notes in Mechanical Engineering*, pp. 226–240.

Luo, J. and Zhang, Q. (2012). 'Trade credit: A new mechanism to coordinate supply chain'. *Operations Research Letters*, 40, pp. 378–384.

Mamalis, A.G., Kundrak, J. and Horvath, M. (2005). 'On a novel tool life relation for precision cutting tools'. *Journal of manufacturing science and engineering*, 127 (2), pp. 328–332.

Molnar, V., Musinszki, Z. and Faludi, T. (2018). 'Profit allocation in supply chains on the basis of revenue-sharing rates'. *International Journal of Economics and Management Systems*, 2, pp. 47–52.

Musinszki, Z. (2014). 'Cost to be a cost? Cost in the management accounting', *Controller Info Studies Budapest, Copy & Consulting Ltd.*, pp. 134–138.

Musinszki, Z. (2016a). 'Innovations and cost systems trends and ways in the cost accounting'. *Proceedings of Organizational and economic mechanisms of development of the financial system*, Riga, Latvia, pp. 209–219.

Musinszki, Z. (2016b). 'Ipar 4.0 – költségrendszer 4.0?: Innovációk a költségrendszerekben'. *Controller Info*, 4 (3), pp. 2–9.

Singh, R.K. and Benyoucef, L. (2013). 'A consensus based group decision making methodology for strategic selection problems of supply chain coordination'. *Engineering Applications of Artificial Intelligence*, 26, pp. 122–134.

Tamas, P. and Illes, B. (2017). 'Novel trends in improvement of warehouse management systems for manfacturing companies'. *Academic Journal of Manufacturing Engineering*, 15 (3), pp. 23–28.

Tilson, V. (2008). 'Monotonicity properties of wholesale price contracts'. *Mathematical Social Sciences*, 56 (1), pp. 127–143.

Vasvary, L., Ditroi, F., Takacs, S., Szabo ,Z., Szucs, J., Kundrak, J. and Mahunka, I. (1994). 'Wear measurement of the cutting edge of superhard turning tools using TLA technique'. *Nuclear Inst. and Methods in Physics Research*, 85, pp. 255–259.

Wang, X., Wang, X. and Su, Y. (2013). 'Wholesale-price contract of supply chain with information gathering'. *Applied Mathematical Modelling*, 37 (6), pp. 3848–3860.

The influence of reviews and new media reputation on film box office revenues

Antonín Pavlíček[1], Ladislav Luc[2]

Abstract. Reviews can play an important role in consumer decision making in general, and film choice in particular. The paper examines the influence of reviews on box office revenues in the course of the years 1926 to 2016. It attempts to answer the question of whether or not such an influence exists and how its strength depends on the length of a period the film had been on in cinemas, high production budgets, genres and famous actors.
This work follow correlation between box office revenue and film budget, user reviews, Facebook likes for film, 3 main actors and director. Study shows these variables have the impact on box office revenue.

Keywords: film review, IMDb rating, box office revenue, actor, influence.

JEL Classification: D83, L86

1 Introduction

Cinema is a relatively young, but extremely rapidly growing area of art. More than a thousand films are released annually. About 800 films are released annually only in India, which is four times more than the Hollywood production. Reviews can play an important role in consumer decision making in general, and film choice in particular, and by proxy also affect the box office results.

2 Literature review

2.1 Critics

Critics play a significant role in consumers decisions in many industries (Austin 1984; Cameron 1995; Caves 2000; Einhorn and Koelb 1982; Eliashberg and Shugan 1997; Greco 1997; Holbrook 1999; Vogel 2001; Walker 1995). For example, investors closely follow the opinion of financial analysts before deciding which stocks to buy or sell, readers often defer to literary reviews before deciding on a book to buy. However, the role of critics may be most prominent in the film industry. For example, in the USA more than one-third of Americans actively seek the advice of film critics (The Wall Street Journal, 2001), and approximately one of every three filmgoers say they choose films because of favorable reviews. Realizing the importance of reviews to films box office success, studios often strategically manage the review process by excerpting positive reviews in their advertising and delaying of forgoing advance screenings if they anticipate bad reviews (The Wall Street Journal, 2001).

2.2 Users rating

Individual viewers' ratings are another significant measure, effectively summarizing consumer satisfaction in the movie industry. All registered IMDb users can submit a single rating – a

[1] University of Economics, Prague, Department of System Analysis, 4 W. Churchill sq., pavlant@vse.cz
[2] University of Economics, Prague, Department of System Analysis, 4 W. Churchill sq., ladislav.luc@vse.cz

number between one and ten – for any film on the website. These votes are then re-jigged so that certain demographics (newly-registered users, for example) don't disproportionately influence the overall ranking of the film. Other web-site, Metacritic.com gathers critics' reviews from a variety of sources, and translates written comments to numerical scores. (The Michigan Journal of Business)

2.3 Starpower

Starpower has received considerable attention in the literature (De Silva 1998; De Vany and Walls 1999). Hollywood seems to favor films with stars (e.g., award-winning actors and directors), and it is almost axiomatic that stars are key to a film's success. However, empirical results of star power on box office performance have produced conflicting evidence. Litman and Kohl (1989) find that stars' presence in a film's cast has a significant effect on that film's revenue.

The popularity of the actors most of all affects the financial success of the film during the hire. Then the influence of popularity diminishes and the further success of the film is influenced equally by both the popularity of the actors and their professional recognition. Whether to cast a movie star or not is a classical question for movie makers; however, the answers for this question are mixed (Suman Basuroy, Subimal Chatterjee and S. Abraham Ravid, 2014) We study effects of star power on the movie revenue.

2.4 Facebook likes

We live in a world where mostly everyone has a Facebook profile and also give likes to pictures, posts, music band, actors, brands, famous people, etc. (Smutny, 2014, Vondra, 2015, Sigmund, 2014) So for our analysis, we were interested in the relationship between Facebook likes for films, 3 main actors and director and relationship with movie's box office revenue.

Facebook like count on movie pages, motivated by a recent study which illustrates that Facebook is probably the most disruptive context in which we can see the pages, statuses etc. powered by the Like button. Theories of social influence suggest that the like count might influence people's decision making, in our case the decision to buy a ticket to watch movie in theater (Karniouchina, 2011).

3 Hypothesis

We assume, that there is a relationship between box office revenue and reviews of audience and that reviews of public have a strong influence over film box office.

This paper examines the influence of reviews on box office revenues in the course of the years 1926 to 2016. It attempts to answer the question of whether or not such an influence exists and how its strength depends on the length of a period the film had been on in cinemas, high production budgets, genres and famous actors. Then this work follow correlation between box office revenue and film budget, user reviews, Facebook likes for film, 3 main actors and director. Study shows which of these variables have the biggest impact on box office revenue.

4 Methodology

In our work, the idea is to find correlation between box office ratings and critical reviews. We have analyzed the data from Data World, with 5000+ movies from IMDB - we were able to obtain all needed variables for 5043 movies and 4096 posters. Overall, they span across 100 years in 66 countries. There are 2399 unique director names, and 30K actors/actresses.

The image below shows all the 28 variables that we have. Roughly speaking, half of the variables is directly related to movies themselves, such as title, year, duration, etc. Another half is related to the people who involved in the production of the movies, eg. director names, director facebook popularity, movie rating from critics, etc. In our work we use only part of this datas such as gross, budget, actor likes, film likes, director likes, etc.

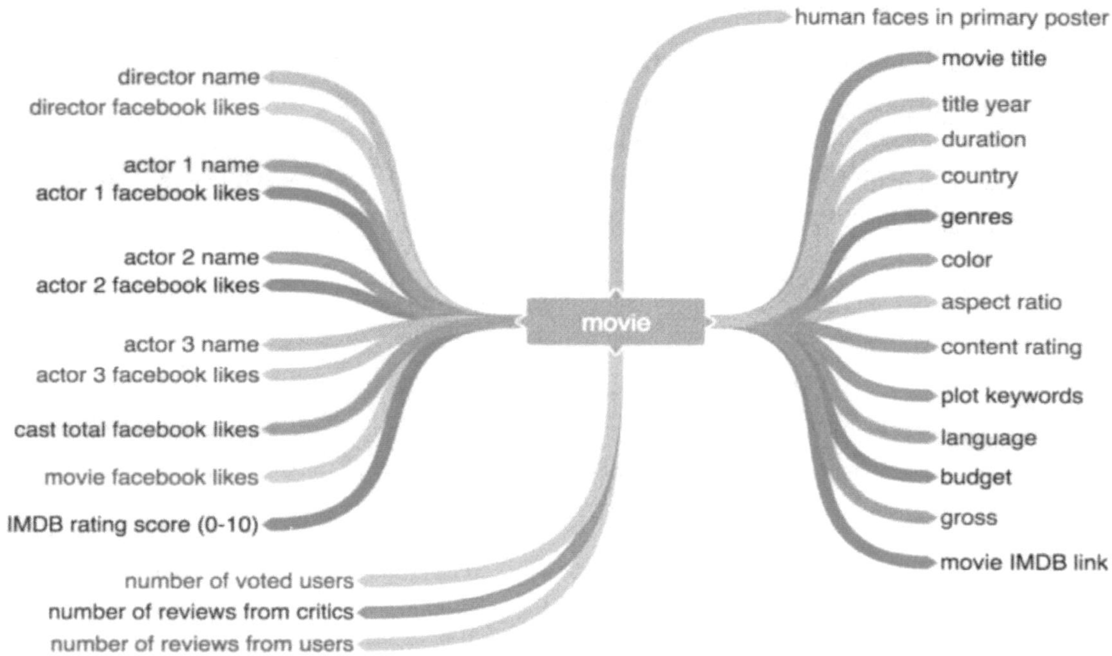

Figure 1 Structure of dates [Data.world]

4.1 Definition and description of variables

IMDb score - We examined box office and film quality data from the past century until 2016, using our favorite proxy for film quality: IMDb rating. Internet Movie Database (IMDb) is an online database of information related to films, television programs, home videos and video games, and internet streams, including cast, production crew and personnel biographies, plot summaries, trivia, and fan reviews and ratings. As of October 2018, IMDb has approximately 5.3 million titles (including episodes) and 9.3 million personalities in its database as well as 83 million registered users. The IMDb offers a rating scale that allows users to rate films on a scale of one to ten

Number of critic reviews on IMDb

This is the number of critics who left their reviews on the server. The value varies from 1 review to 813 according to data for year 2016.

Number of registered votes on IMDb
This is the number of IMDB users who cast votes to rate a movie. It reflects how many users watched a movie.

IMDb registered users can cast a vote (from 1 to 10) on every released title in the database. Individual votes are then aggregated and summarized as a single IMDb rating, visible on the title's main page. By 'released title' server means that the movie (or TV show) must have been shown publicly at least once (including festival screening)

Users can update their votes as often as they'd like, but any new vote on the same title will overwrite the previous one, so it is one vote per title per user.

Production budget
Production budget determines how much money will be spent on the entire film project. It involves the identification and estimation of cost items for each phase of filmmaking (development, pre-production, production, post-production and distribution).

Star-power
Star-power expresses how the star cast is capable of attracting viewers to cinemas. We divided star power into several parts – actors star-power and director star-power. In our world people often measure success in likes on Facebook. We examined number of likes of actor 1, actor 2 and actor 3. The same way we measured director star-power.

Likes on Facebook
This is the number of likes of the official movie page received on Facebook.

Box office revenues gross
It's the total revenues of all the ticket sales, added together. There are numerous websites that monitor box-office receipts, such as Boxoffice, Box Office India, Box Office Mojo, Koimoi, ShowBIZ Data and The Numbers which provide detailed information for many movies but have less and incomplete data for older movies due to the history of how box office reporting evolved, especially in the U.S., and the availability of this information prior to the introduction of the internet.

5 Results

After running the analysis, it is interesting to note that many of the variables are significant and that all have positive signs. The results are presented in graphs. The most significant variables are budget, number of votes and number of reviews.

Box office revenues according to IMDb rating and number of votes

Correlation coefficient = 0.63 (for number of votes)

Correlation coefficient = 0.21(for IMDb rating)

The Internet Movie Database (IMDb) is one of the most-visited websites in the world and the premier source for information on films. Similar to Wikipedia, much of IMDb's information is user contributed. IMDb also allows users to voice their opinion on the quality of films through voting. We investigate whether there is a connection between user voting data and box office revenues.

We examined if there is possible connection between IMDb rating and box office revenues. Do IMDb rating correlate with a film's popularity and its box office revenues? Yes. As you can see below, the higher the IMDb rating, the higher box office revenues. Our correlation coefficient of these 2 variables equals + 0.21, so we can see a weak positive linear relationship.

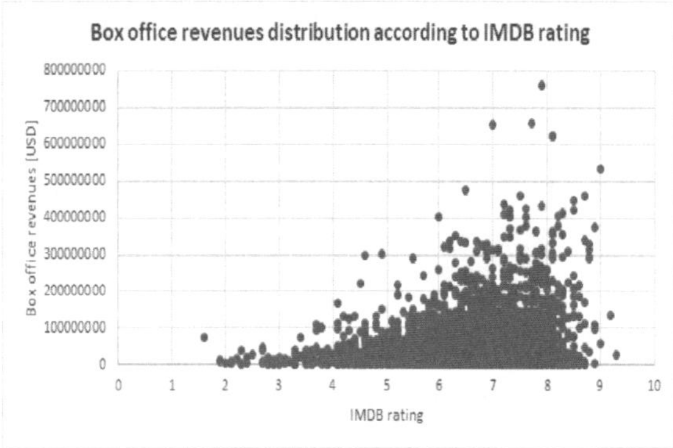

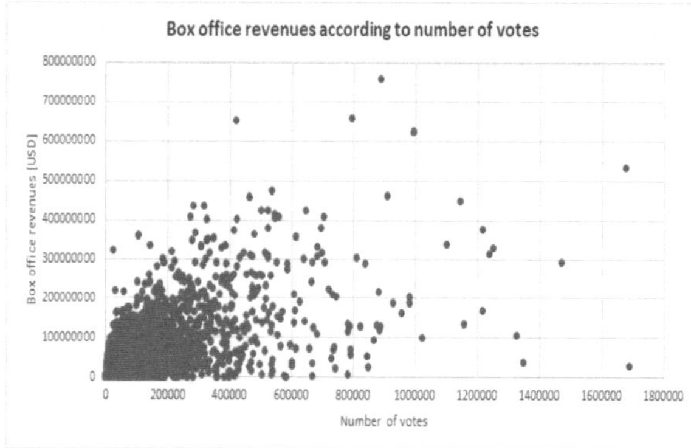

Graph 1 Box office revenues distribution according to IMDb rating [authors]

Graph 2 Box office revenues according to number of votes [authors]

From the correction analysis, we find that box office revenues correlate strongly with total number of user votes. Correlation coefficient equals +0.63 and as you can see below, the higher number of votes, the higher box office revenues.

Our result suggests that the number of user votes is an indicator of a film's fame. After all, a person is more likely to enter a rating for a film if he or she has viewed it, regardless of whether he or she found the film to be good or bad. However, fame is not necessarily tied to box office success, as many films become notable for other reasons such as major award nominations. Films also can become notable for especially poor performances at the box office.

Box office revenues according to number of votes and number of critics reviews

Correlation coefficient = 0.48 (critics reviews)

Correlation coefficient between film gross and user votes is 0.63 and between film gross and critics reviews is 0.48.

If we compare correlation between critics reviews and user reviews, we`ll see that critics review is smaller than user reviews on 0.16. This means that people trust consumer reviews to give them more accurate information than critics. This could be because they see consumers more similar to themselves, in terms of taste and knowledge. They may feel that critics write longer and more complex reviews that are too inconvenient to read. This also has to do with the ease at which they feel positive reviews allow them to make a decision. They are more inclined to trust the reviewer's opinion, and a mixed review simply makes it more difficult and time consuming to reach a conclusion.

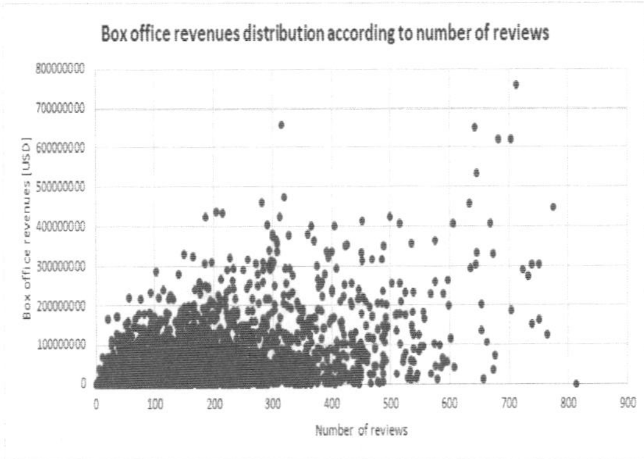

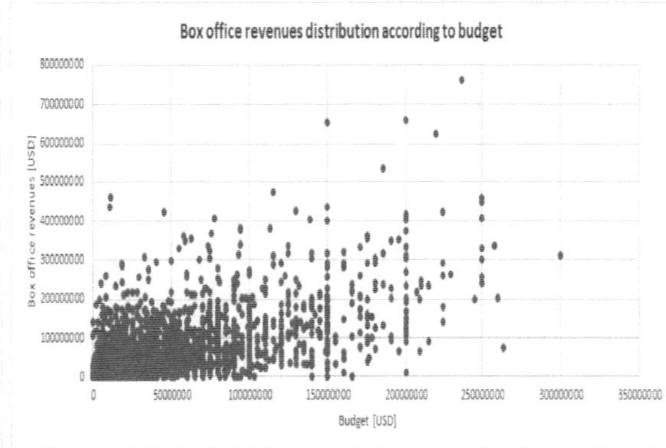

Graph 3 Box office revenues distribution according to number of reviews [authors]

Graph 4 Box office revenues distribution according to budget [authors]

Box office revenues according to production budget

Correlation coefficient = 0.65

Box office revenues correlates more strongly with budget than with IMDb rating or number of votes. We assume budget is directly related to the amount spent on a film's promotion, which increases its prominence. Moreover, budget is overwhelmingly the most relevant factor in determining a film's ultimate prominence and higher box office revenues. To make a film more notable Hollywood just needs to spend more money. Correlation coefficient is + 0.65, the most positive in our analysis, as you can see it below.

Star power

Results of correlation analyses comparing box office revenues distribution and number of Facebook likes for 3 main actors. The study shows that the Facebook popularity of the top 3 actors/actresses is not so important. The average correlation coefficient for three main actors is 0.2627.

Box office revenues distribution according to number of likes of actor 1

A weak positive linear relationship between box office revenues and number of likes of actor 1. That fact that an actor is popular in social network does not mean that a movie has high box office revenue because he is the leading actor.

Correlation coefficient = 0.19223

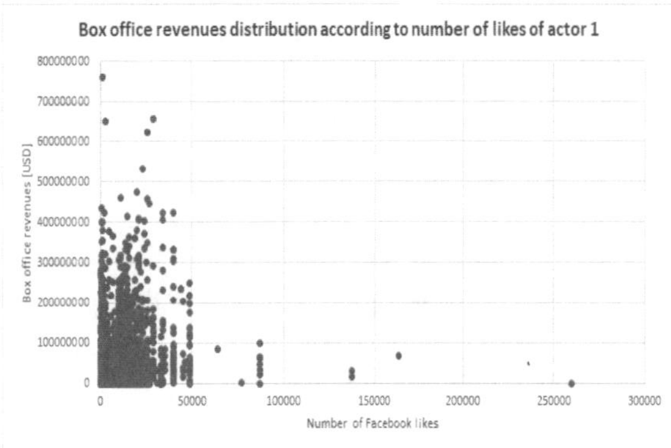

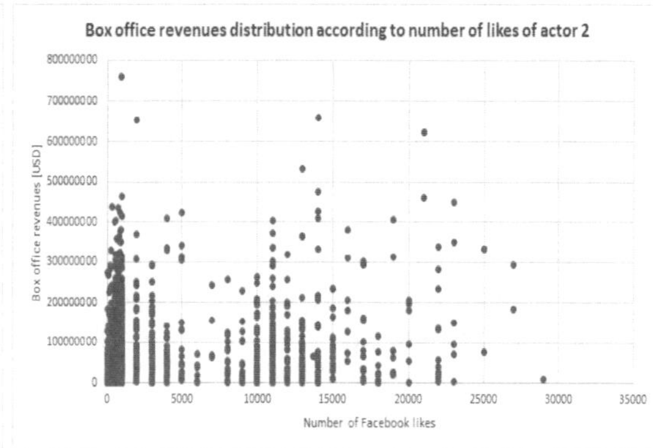

Graph 5 Box office revenues distribution according to number of likes of actor 1 [authors]

Graph 6 Box office revenues distribution according to number of likes of actor 2 [authors]

Box office revenues distribution according to number of likes of actor 2

Correlation coefficient = 0.29203

Correlation for 2 actor is a little bit bigger. That meant number of likes for second actor have bigger impact on film gross then number of likes for actor 1. What can seem strange, but we can explain it in this way: director choose new main actor (actor 1), who is not as popular as other actor in the film.

Box office revenues distribution according to number of likes of actor 3

Same situation as is with actor 2. Actor 3 has slightly bigger impact on box office revenue then actor 2.

Correlation coefficient = 0.30385

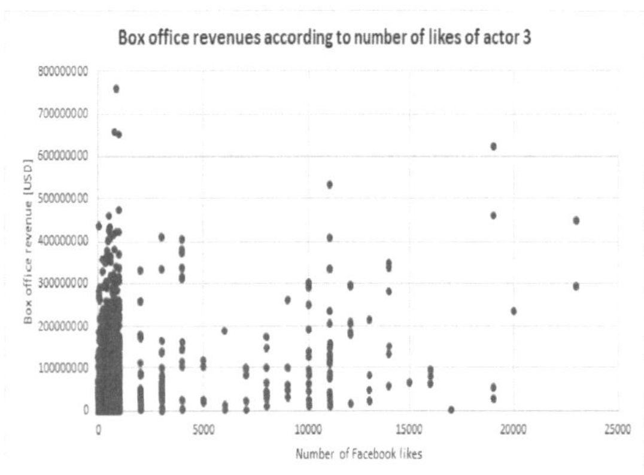

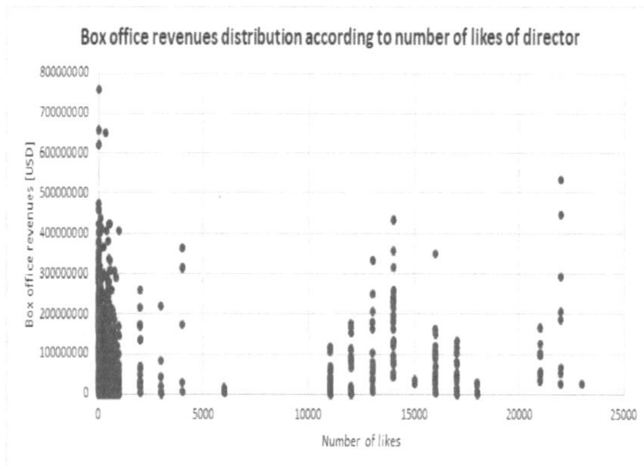

Graph 7 Box office revenues distribution according to number of likes of actor 3 [authors]

Graph 8 Box office revenues distribution according to number of likes of director [authors]

Of course, none of these estimates guarantee that a particular star will make a movie successful. In fact, they assure that no star can guarantee any outcome because there is infinite variance in the distribution every star has a sizable probability of making a bomb. Moreover, it would be an error to attribute causality to what is only a correlation between stars and movie outcome. Also it could even go in the other direction and star might just be someone who is good enough to give a fine performance in a terrific movie and get a lot of likes.

Box office revenues distribution according to number of likes of director

The results show really small positive linear relationship between box office revenues distribution according to number of Facebook likes of director, meaning a popular director does not necessarily mean his directed movie is great.

Correlation coefficient=0.14288

Box office revenues distribution according to number of likes of the movie

The results of this regression analysis showed that there was minimal relationship between box office revenues and number of likes of the movie. That's mean that there is a small relationship between number of Facebook likes and box office revenue. So only ⅓ part of people are going to watch film in the cinema because other people liked it. Overall, considering the positive correlations discussed above, and the linear relationships between Facebook and box office sales visualized in the graphs, it appears that increased social media engagement does in fact relate to box office sales.The flaw in this study, however, is that it is nearly impossible to imply causation for correlation.

Correlation coefficient =0.37575

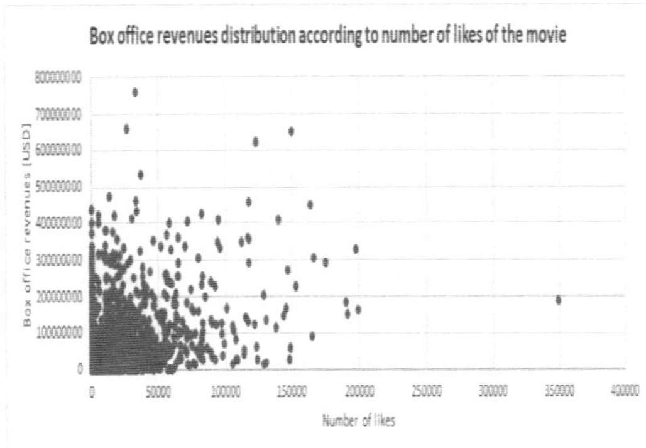

Graph 9 Box office revenues distribution according to number of likes of the movie [authors]

Discussion

The data were analyzed to find connection between box office revenues and nine other attributes. The highest correlation was found between box office revenues and budget of the movie. There is quite high possibility that movies with high budget will be more successful = earn more money.

On the other hand the lowest correlation was found between the box office revenues and number of Facebook likes of the director. Especially the correlation between the box office revenues and Facebook likes are not damning. Not everyone is using Facebook and even if they do, there is no guarantee that the people will like the official profile of the movie/actor/director.

Connection can be considered between box office revenues and number of reviews, number of votes and budget. Other attributes have inconclusive connection which is in some cases surprising. Missing clear connection between box office revenues and IMDb rating is one of those cases. Movies with higher rating are not automatically more profitable.

6 Conclusion

The box office revenue is an important source of income to the movie industry as a way for extending profits or minimizing losses. This study examines the determinants of box office revenue for the years 1926-2016. The most important result of the study is the observation that box office revenues positively depend on film budgets and number of Facebook votes. We found strong support for the view that popular star participation indeed positively affects movies' revenues, but not as much as films reviews.

Box office revenue, the amount of money generated through movie ticket sales, remains one of the motion picture industry's most important measures of a film's commercial success.

References

Austin, B. A. (1984). 'Portrait of an Art Film Audience', *Journal of Communications*.

Cameron, S. (1995). 'On the Role of Critics in the Culture Industry', *Journal of Cultural Economics*.

Caves, R. E. (2000). *Creative Industries*, Cambridge, MA: Harvard University Press.

De Silva, I. (1998). 'Consumer Selection of Motion Pictures' in: *The Motion Picture Mega-Industry*, Barry R. Litman, ed. Needham Heights, MA.

De Vany, A. and Walls, D. (1999), 'Uncertainty in the Movies: Can Star Power Reduce the Terror of the Box Office?' *Journal of Cultural Economics*.

Greco, A. N. (1997). '*The Book Publishing Industry*', Needham Heights, MA: Allyn Bacon.

Holbrook, M. B. (1999). 'Popular Appeal Versus Expert Judgments of Motion Pictures,' *Journal of Consumer Research*.

Jeon, J. and Jiao, L. (2012). *The Influence Effect of Critics, Reviews on Foreign and Domestic Movies*, Duke University.

Karniouchina, E. (2011). 'Impact of star and movie buzz on motion picture distribution and box office revenue', *International Journal of Research in Marketing*, 28, pp 62-74.

Litman B. and Kohl, L.S. (1989). 'Predicting Financial Success of Motion Pictures: The '80s Experience,' *Journal of Media Economics*.

Reinstein, D. A. and Snyder, Ch. M. (2005). 'The influence of expert reviews on consumer demand for experience goods: a case study of movie critics', *The Journal of Industrial Economics*, 53, pp 27-51.

Sigmund, T. (2014). 'Privacy in the Information Society: How to Deal with Its Ambiguity?', *IDIMT-2014: Networking Societies - Cooperation and Conflict,* pp. 191–201, Czech Republic.

Smutny, Z. (2014). 'The use of social media for marketing purposes by Czech companies doing business in the environment of services on the internet: a national survey'. *IDIMT-2014: Networking Societies - Cooperation and Conflict*, pp. 145–151, Czech Republic.

Basuroy, S., Chatterjee, S. and Ravid, S. A. (2014). 'How Critical Are Critical Reviews? The Box Office Effects of Film Critics, Star Power, and Budgets', *Journal of Marketing*, 67 (4).

The Wall Street Journal (2001). ''Town & Country' Publicity Proves an Awkward Act'.

Vogel, H. L. (2001). *Entertainment Industry Economics*, 5th ed. Cambridge, UK: Cambridge University Press.

Vondra, Z. (2015). 'Explanation of Multimedia Communication Using Catwoe Analysis'. *IDIMT-2015: Information Technology and Society Interaction and Interdependence*, pp. 311–318, Czech Republic.

Walker, Ch. (1995). 'Word of Mouth,' *American Demographics*.

SECTION

B

QUANTITATIVE METHODS IN MANAGEMENT

Efficiency of the Agrarian Sector in the NUTS II regions in V4 countries

Helena Brožová[1], Ivana Boháčková [2]

Abstract. This contribution analyses the development of the efficiency of the agrarian sector in the NUTS 2 regions of the four Visegrad countries using Data Envelopment Analysis and Malmquist index. The agrarian sector is characterized by three inputs (agricultural land, annual work units and gross fixed capital formation) and one output (gross value added). The panel data refers to periods 2005 - 2013.

Malmquist index shows very unstable development agrarian sector in the Slovak regions, there is a significant growth and decline. Contrary similar slightly positive development of efficiency is seen in the Czech Republic and Hungary. In Poland there are much less changes in the efficiency of agrarian sector, there are practically no changes in the long run. This shows the high degree of agriculture permanence.

Keywords: Visegrad countries, agrarian sector, efficiency, DEA model, Malmquist index.

JEL Classification: C44, C61, D24, Q10

1 Introduction

The Visegrad Groups is a cultural and political alliance of four Central European states having the historically common roots, tradition, culture relations and similar economic development. The economies of the Visegrad Group (V4) as the European Union (EU) members have reached a comparable level of development. However, the accession to the European Union, the Common Agricultural Policy (CAP) and the World financial crises influence the development and the performance of the agrarian sector in the Visegrad countries. Therefore, the objective of this paper is to investigate and compare the relative technical efficiency of the agrarian sector and its changes in the Visegrad regions.

A number of methods have been developed for this and similar analysis and evaluation of individual units, elements, Except the multiple criteria decision methods (MCDM) there are methods evaluating efficiency divided into two groups, the parametric approaches, using the regression analysis, and the non-parametric approaches, connected with the mathematical programming techniques. The Data Envelopment Analysis (DEA) is the mostly used one from the non-parametric methods. Starting from work of Clark (1940) and Bhattacharjee (1955), a number of studies use non-parametric DEA to analyse the cross-country differences in efficiency of agrarian sector and its development, efficiency of agriculture as a whole in the individual countries, regions or evaluation of the efficiency of a particular type of agricultural production, agricultural enterprises and so on (for instance Błażejczyk-Majka, Kala, Maciejewski, 2011, Bojnec et al., 2014, Kočišová, 2015, Nowak, Kijek, Domanska, 2015, Záhorský, Pokryvčák,

[1] Dept. of Systems Engineering, Faculty of Economics, Czech University of Life Sciences, 165 00 Praha – Suchdol, e-mail: brozova@pef.czu.cz.

[2] Dep. of Economics, Faculty of Economics, Czech University of Life Sciences, 165 00 Praha -Suchdol, e-mail: bohackiv@pef.czu.cz.

2016, Fandel, Bartova, 2018). The analysis of the efficiency development over time is possible using Malmquist index.

In this paper, the agrarian sector is seen as defined by European Union documents, where the agrarian sector includes, besides own agriculture also forestry and possibly fishery. The regions are monitored at NUTS II level in the period 2005-2013. We start in 2005 when the V4 countries became a full member of the Union and involved in the Common Agrarian Policy (CAP). To analyse the development of the agrarian sector in V4 regions, we attempted to answer the following research questions:

1) What is the development of the agrarian sector efficiency in the V4 regions in this period?
2) Is the development of the agrarian sector efficiency similar in all the V4 countries and regions in this period?
3) Is it possible to see here the influence of the crisis in 2008?

The DEA approach, Malmquist index and the panel data about the V4 regions are shortly described in the Section 2. The efficiency of the agrarian sector and its changes using the MI in the selected years are described in the Section 3. In the Conclusions, the findings are summarized.

2 Material and Methods

2.1 Data

The panel data was gathered from the EUROSTAT databases. The data describes the monitored agrarian sector in regions of V4 countries at NUTS II level, in the Czech Republic there are 8 regions, in Poland 16, in Hungary again 7 and in Slovak Republic there are 4 regions. Given that agriculture almost does not exist in the Praha Region, only the other seven Czech regions are included in further analyses. So, totally 34 NUTS II regions are analysed (Table 1).

Czech Republic	Slovak Republic	Hungary	Poland	
Stredni Cechy	Bratislavsky kraj	Kozep-Magyarorszag	Lodzkie	Wielkopolskie
Jihozapad	Zapadne Slovensko	Kozep-Dunantul	Mazowieckie	Lubuskie
Severozapad	Stredne Slovensko	Nyugat-Dunantul	Malopolskie	Dolnoslaskie
Severovychod	Vychodne Slovensko	Del-Dunantul	Slaskie	Opolskie
Jihovychod		Eszag-Magyarorszag	Lubelskie	Kujawsko-Pomorskie
Stredni Morava		Eszag-Alfold	Podkarpackie	Pomorskie
Moravskoslezko		Del-Alfold	Swietokrzyskie	Zachodniopomorskie
			Podlaskie	Warminsko-Mazurskie

Table 1 Analysed V4 regions at NUTS II level

Panel data comprises of the years 2005, 2010, 2011, 2012 and 2013. These years were selected, because the countries have already joined the European Union and the world economic crisis occurred between years 2007 and 2010. The latest reference year is 2013 due to the availability of data, later data are no longer comparable due to the methodology change. As the inputs the Utilized agricultural area (UAA, thousand ha), the labour costs as Annual Work Units (AWU, EUR million/ha), the Gross fixed capital formation (GFCF, EUR million/ha), and the Gross value added (GVA, EUR million) as the output are used.

2.2 Data Envelopment Analysis Methods

DEA methodology defines the efficiency as a ratio of weighted sum of outputs to a weighted sum of inputs, where the weights structure is calculated by means of mathematical programming. The simplest input oriented CCR DEA model (Charnes, Cooper, Rhodes, 1978) evaluates the efficiency of DMU in time t under the assumption of constant returns to scale (CRS) as the distance from the efficient frontier solving optimization model (1):

$$\Phi_H^t(\boldsymbol{x}^t, \boldsymbol{y}^t) = \sum_{j=1}^{n} u_{jH} y_{jH}^t \rightarrow MAX \quad \text{subject to} \quad \begin{aligned} &\sum_{i=1}^{m} v_{iH} x_{iH}^t = 1 \\ -&\sum_{i=1}^{m} v_{iH} x_{ik}^t + \sum_{j=1}^{n} u_{jH} y_{jk}^t \leq 0, k = 1, 2, \dots, p \\ &u_{jH} \geq 0,\ j = 1, 2, \dots, n, v_{iH} \geq 0,\ i = 1, 2, \dots, m \end{aligned} \tag{1}$$

where $\boldsymbol{\Phi}_H^t$ is efficiency of DMU H, u_{jk} and v_{ik} are weights of outputs and inputs, y_{jk}^t is the amount of jth output from unit k, and x_{ik}^t is the amount of input to i^{th} unit in time t, H is index of the evaluated DMU (this notation is used through the whole paper). The efficient DMU lies on the efficient frontier and its efficiency is equal to 1. If the DMU is inefficient, the efficiency ratio can be interpreted as an estimation of the necessary input reduction with the same amount of output to make this DMU efficient.

The dynamics of the DMU efficiency between two periods, the growth or decline of productivity efficiency can be evaluated by Malmquist productivity index (Malmquist, 1953, Caves, Christensen, Diewert, 1982). The Malmquist index M_H (MI) could be decomposed into two partial indices, the first one quantifying the DMU technical efficiency change E_H between two periods, and the second one representing the technological change P_H, the shift of the efficiency frontier between two periods (Färe et al., 1994). MI and its decomposition are calculated using the formula (2)

$$M_H(\boldsymbol{x}^{t+1}, \boldsymbol{y}^{t+1}, \boldsymbol{x}^t, \boldsymbol{y}^t) = E_H P_H = \frac{\Phi_H^{t+1}(\boldsymbol{x}^{t+1}, \boldsymbol{y}^{t+1})}{\Phi_H^t(\boldsymbol{x}^t, \boldsymbol{y}^t)} \times \left(\frac{\Phi_H^t(\boldsymbol{x}^{t+1}, \boldsymbol{y}^{t+1}) \Phi_H^t(\boldsymbol{x}^t, \boldsymbol{y}^t)}{\Phi_H^{t+1}(\boldsymbol{x}^{t+1}, \boldsymbol{y}^{t+1}) \Phi_H^{t+1}(\boldsymbol{x}^t, \boldsymbol{y}^t)} \right)^{1/2} \tag{2}$$

where $\boldsymbol{y}^t$ is the output and $\boldsymbol{x}^t$ is the input in time t and $\boldsymbol{y}^{t+1}$ is the output and $\boldsymbol{x}^{t+1}$ is the input in time t+1 of the decision-making unit H. The graphical representation of MI is much clearer, if they are adapted by the following formulas (Zbranek, 2015)

$$\begin{aligned} &\text{If } M_H < 1 \text{ than } \bar{M}_H = 1 - \frac{1}{M_H} \\ &\text{If } M_H = 1 \text{ than } \bar{M}_H = 0 \\ &\text{If } M_H > 1 \text{ than } \bar{M}_H = M_H - 1 \end{aligned} \tag{3}$$

If value of corrected MI is equal to 0, there is no efficiency change. If corrected MI value is greater than 0, there is efficiency increasing, and if it is lower than 0, there is efficiency decreasing.

The long-term development of the DMU H efficiency over all monitored periods can be evaluated using cumulated MI and its cumulated components. Because these indices have multiplicative character, their summaries are calculated as the sequential multiplicative sums (Färe et al., 1994) by the following formula

$$CM_H(1) = 1 \text{ and } CM_H(t) = CM_H(t-1)M_H(t), t = 2, \dots, n \tag{4}$$

The graphical representation of the cumulated indices shows the efficiency development in relation to the initial period.

3 Results

3.1 Analysis of inputs and outputs

Utilized agricultural area is an essential factor of production in agriculture and forestry. The agricultural area is generally decreasing over the years but the changes are really small as the average change indices show (Table 2). The Figure 1 shows the basic data on size of agricultural land in regions of each country.

	Average						**Average change over periods**
	2005	**2007**	**2010**	**2011**	**2012**	**2013**	
Czech Republic	503.35	497.99	496.06	496.20	497.61	496.89	99.73%
Poland	940.18	985.63	908.64	906.88	900.13	901.74	99.21%
Slovakia	469.87	484.16	473.88	475.63	474.69	475.40	100.28%
Hungary	836.40	829.57	763.13	762.46	762.57	748.81	97.87%

Table 2 Basic data on size of UAA in V4 regions (thousand ha)

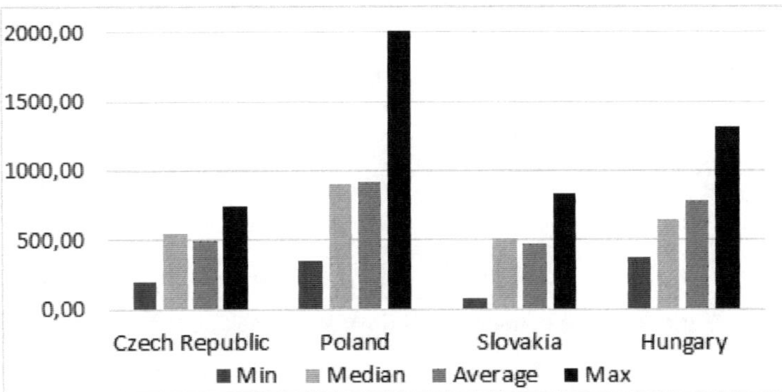

Figure 1 Descriptive statistics of the data set on size of UAA in V4 regions (thousand ha)

The labour consumption as Annual Work Units represents the second input factor. The amount of AWU increase slightly (approximately 10% per year) and overall remains without significant changes (Table 3). Czech and Slovak agrarian sector show the highest average labour costs per hectare UAA and conversely the lower labour cost is in most Polish regions. Min value in Figure 2 represents situation in 10 Polish regions. It can be explained by the different methodology of its calculation; the work of family members is not counted in Poland.

	Average 2005	2007	2010	2011	2012	2013	Average change over periods
Czech Republic	0.21	0.24	0.26	0.27	0.28	0.29	106.46%
Poland	0.11	0.13	0.19	0.20	0.23	0.23	114.81%
Slovakia	0.20	0.24	0.26	0.29	0.31	0.31	109.81%
Hungary	0.12	0.13	0.14	0.14	0.17	0.18	109.16%

Table 3 Basic data on AWU in V4 regions (EUR million/ha)

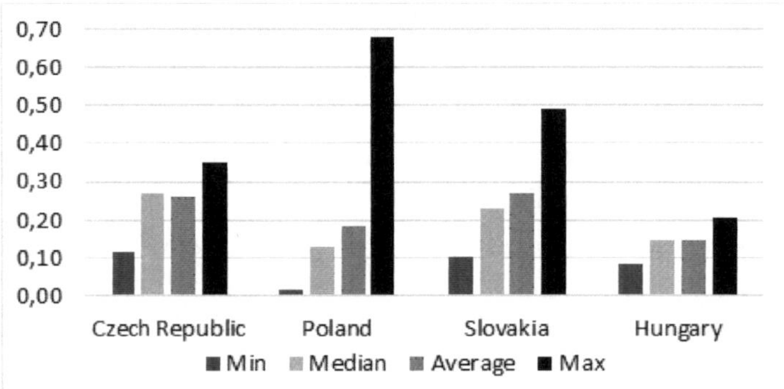

Figure 2 Descriptive statistics of the data set on AWU in V4 regions (EUR million/ha)

Gross fixed capital formation is selected as input representing machine and technology costs and innovation, although these costs need not be reflected only in the period in which they were incurred. The reason of this usage is the data availability. The GFCF shows a similar growth rate as AWU. The Czech and Hungarian agrarian sector show the highest average GFCF per hectare UAA (Table 4, Figure 3). The lowest average GFCF per hectare UAA is in Poland.

	Average 2005	2007	2010	2011	2012	2013	Average change over periods
Czech Republic	0.13	0.15	0.12	0.19	0.20	0.19	112.56%
Poland	0.05	0.05	0.06	0.07	0.07	0.08	114.84%
Slovakia	0.08	0.09	0.10	0.14	0.09	0.07	109.75%
Hungary	0.12	0.12	0.14	0.15	0.15	0.16	107.10%

Table 4 Basic data on GFCF in V4 regions (EUR million/ha)

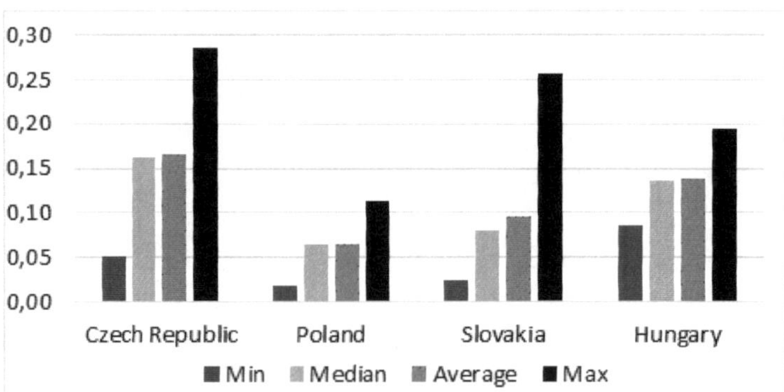

Figure 3 Descriptive statistics of the data set on GFCF in V4 regions (EUR million/ha)

The Gross value added is often used output indicator. Polish agrarian sector shows the highest GVA per hectare UAA (Table 5, Figure 4). The decreasing of the GVA down to 71% between 2007 and 2010 as the impact of the global crisis is seen in the Czech Republic only. In Poland and Hungary, GVA increases slightly without significant changes in the whole period (in average 15 % and 7 % per year). Development of GVA in Slovakia is very unstable.

	Average						Average change over periods
	2005	**2007**	**2010**	**2011**	**2012**	**2013**	
Czech Republic	0.28	0.34	0.26	0.39	0.38	0.39	110.68%
Poland	0.42	0.54	0.51	0.61	0.58	0.63	111.30%
Slovakia	0.24	0.25	0.23	0.34	0.43	0.34	112.07%
Hungary	0.37	0.36	0.37	0.50	0.47	0.53	110.28%

Table 5 Basic data on GVA in V4 regions (EUR million/ha)

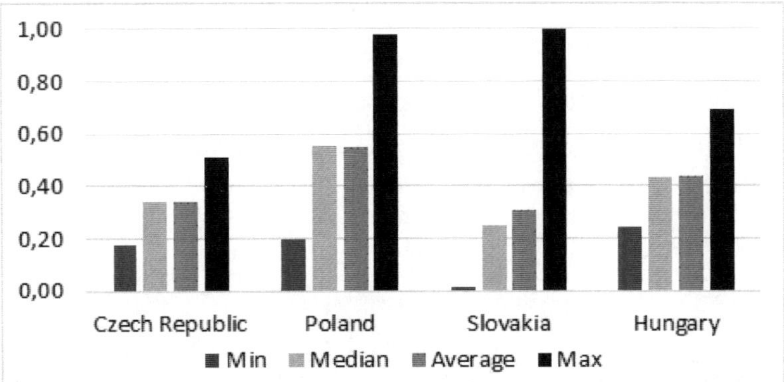

Figure 4 Descriptive statistics of the data set on GVA in V4 regions (EUR million/ha)

3.2 Efficiency of agrarian sector

The efficiency of NUTS II regions in V4 countries shows that the agrarian sector of 13 regions in Poland is evaluated better than in 70 % of all regions. Only Podkarpackie, Zachodniopomorskie and Warminsko-Mazurskie regions did not reach the enough high efficiency. The agrarian sector in the other three countries is significantly worse. The worst is the agrarian sector in Slovakia, then in the Czech Republic (Table 6, Figure 5).

The fall in agrarian sector efficiency is visible between the years 2007 and 2010, the highest decreasing is in the Czech Republic. This is the direct consequence of the economic crisis.

	2005	**2007**	**2010**	**2011**	**2012**	**2013**	**Average efficiency**
Czech Republic	42.89	48.68	34.42	46.00	44.24	39.86	42.68
Poland	75.41	88.36	79.71	78.85	81.14	73.93	79.56
Slovakia	37.17	37.84	29.38	39.92	50.17	37.43	38.65
Hungary	57.93	53.98	52.19	59.48	59.33	55.56	56.41

Table 6 Average CCR efficiency of agrarian sector in V4 countries

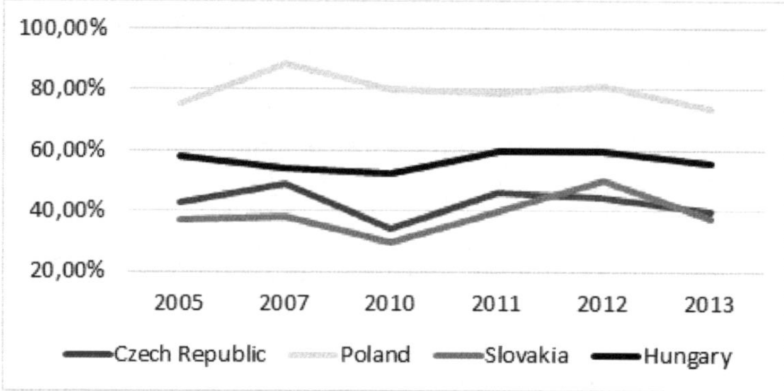

Figure 5 Average CCR efficiency of agrarian sector in V4 countries

A more detailed description of changes in the efficiency of the agricultural sector can be seen through the adapted Malmquist index and the cumulative MI. The adapted MI shows the changes proportionally and comparatively, positive value represents increasing and negative decreasing. The cumulative MI describe the overall trend.

The adapted MI shows very similar development in the Czech Republic, Hungary and Poland, although the changes in Poland are smaller. On the contrary, there is a great instability in Slovakia, high positive and negative changes.

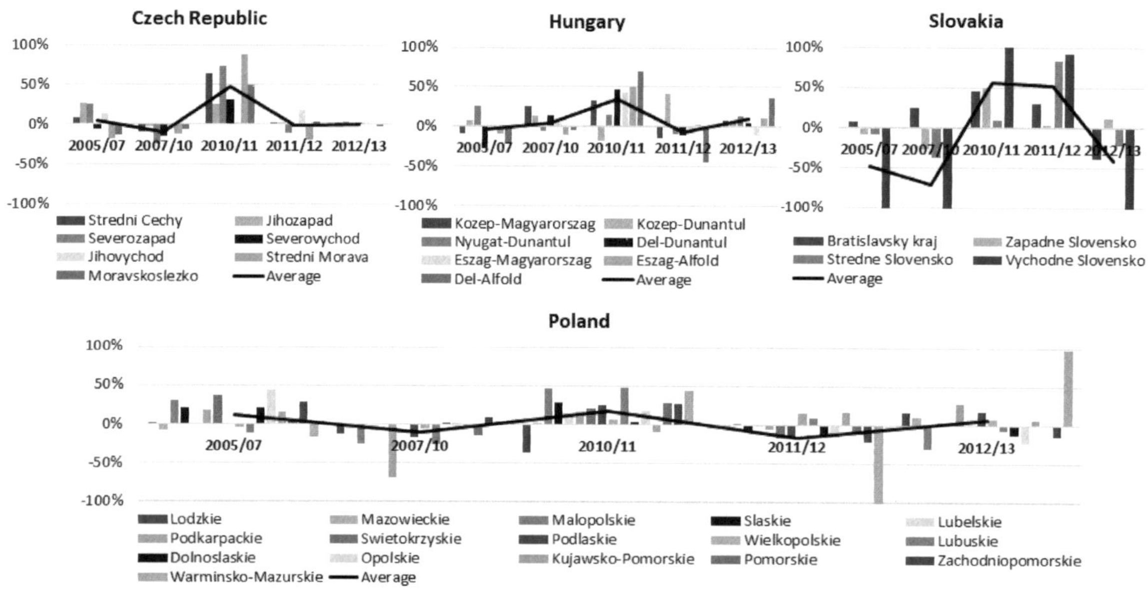

Figure 6 Values of adapted MI - Change of productivity efficiency of V4 regions

Cumulative MI shows the situation similarly. It does not show absolute changes between periods, but the overall trend of development. From graphs of the cumulative MI (Figure 7), there is seen a slow growth in the efficiency of the agricultural sector more or less in all V4 countries. Again, the worst situation is in Slovakia, where there is a great instability and at least agrarian sector in Vychodne Slovensko is getting worse.

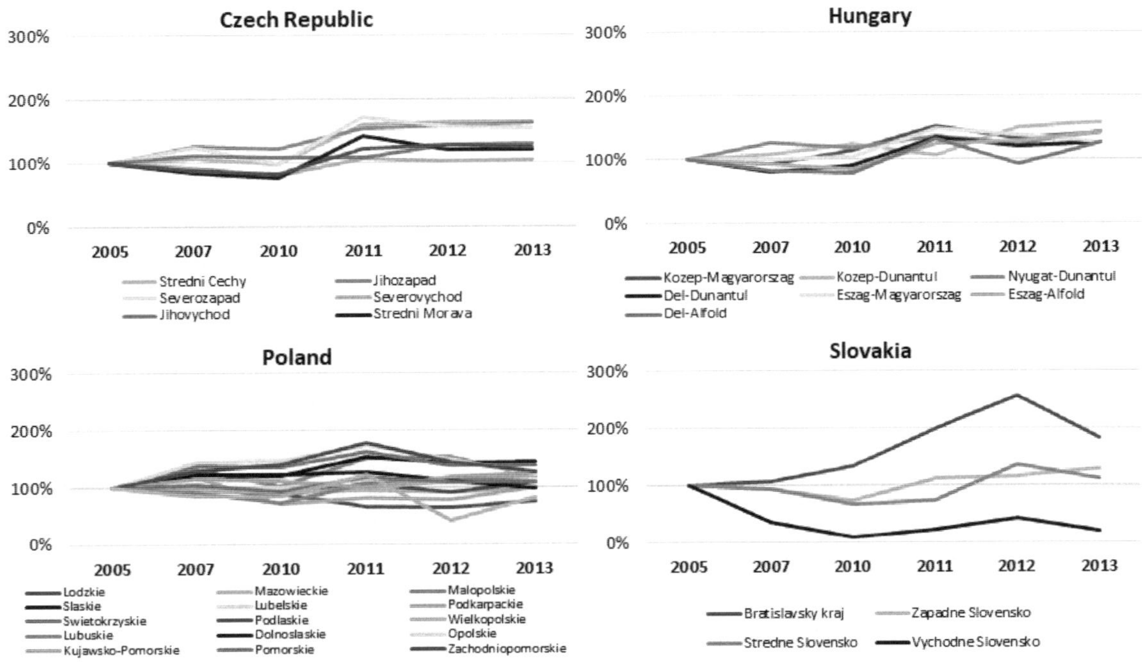

Figure 7 Values of adapted MI - Change of productivity efficiency of V4 regions

4 Conclusion

We showed the most efficient agrarian sector in regions in Poland, then in Hungary, in the Czech Republic and finally in the Slovak Republic as least efficient. The Polish regions were least affected and among the Slovak regions reflected significantly large unevenness.

This article follows up our analysis of the efficiency of the agrarian sector in NUTS III regions in the Czech Republic (Brožová, Boháčková, 2016). Here we showed that the development of efficiency of agrarian sector has similar behaviour in the regions of all V4 countries.

The agricultural sector shows efficiency decreasing during crisis, efficiency increasing immediately after the crisis followed by little efficiency changes after 2011. Also Dombi (2013) shows that the Central Eastern European countries with the exception of Poland were hit by the global economic crisis in 2008 varying degrees and the recovery in these regions appears to be much slower.

The highest efficiency of the Polish regions results from a small number of AWU and low GFCF and a high level of GVA. This is in acordance with results of Střeleček, Losová, Zdeněk (2009). Nowak and Kaminska (2016) also showed the highest competitiveness of agriculture in Poland compared to other V4 states.

From theoretical point of view we showed the possibility and advatages of application of adapted and cumulative MI. The adapted MI shows proportionally the increasing and decreasing of efficiency, the cumulative MI shows overall development trend.

The question may be to use GFCF as input for DEA models.The GFCF is the cost of future production, but since it is not consumed only in a particular year, it can cause inefficiency in this year. However, high GFCF rate can also be seen as an output because large investments are only possible with very good economic results. Therefore, in our future research, we will test the calculation of efficiency using DEA models with dual role factors and we will compare these and new results.

References

Błażejczyk-Majka, L., Kala, R. and Maciejewski, K. (2011). 'Data Envelopment Analysis in Estimation of Technical Efficiency Change of Regional Agriculture Production EU, 1989–2007'. *Journal of Mathematics and System Science*, 1 (1), pp. 43–51.

Bhattacharjee, J. (1955). 'Resource Use and Productivity in World Agriculture'. *Journal of Farm Economics*, 37 (1), pp. 57-71.

Bojnec, Š., Fertő, I., Jámbor, A. and Tóth, J. (2014). 'Determinants of Technical Efficiency in Agriculture in New EU Member States from Central and Eastern Europe'. *Acta Oeconomica*, 64 (2), pp. 197–217.

Brožová, H. and Boháčková, I. (2016). 'Post-crisis Development in the Agricultural Sector in the CR – Evidence by Malmquist Index and its Decomposition'. *Proceedingd of the 34th international conference on Mathematical Methods in Economics 2016*, Liberec,Czech Republic, pp. 73-78.

Caves, D. W., Christensen, L. R. and Diewert, W. E. (1982). 'The Economic Theory of Index Numbers and the Measurement of Input, Output and Productivity'. *Econometrica*, 50 (6), pp. 1393-1414.

Charnes, A., Cooper, W. and Rhodes, E. (1978). 'Measuring the Efficiency of Decision-making Units'. *European Journal of Operational Research*, 2 (6), pp. 429–444.

Clark, C. (1940). '*The Conditions of Economic Progress*'. Macmillan & Co.: London.

Dombi, A. (2013). 'Economic Growth and Development in Central and Eastern Europe after the Transformation'. *Public Finance Quarterly*, 58 (4), pp. 452-468.

Fandel, P. and Bartova, L. (2018). 'Eco-Efficiency Using Directional Distance Functions with Undesirable Outputs'. *Proceedings of the conference on Quantitative Methods in Economics - Multiple Criteria Decision Making XIX*, Bratislava, Slovakia, pp. 87-95.

Färe, R., Grosskopf, S., Norris, M. and Zhang, Z. (1994). 'Productivity Growth, Technical Progress, and Efficiency Change in Industrialized Countries'. *The American Economic Review*, 84 (1), pp. 66-83.

Kočišová, K. (2015). 'Application of the DEA on the Measurement of Efficiency in the EU Countries', *Agricultural Economics – Czech*, 61 (2), pp. 51–62.

Malmquist, S. (1953). 'Index Numbers and Indifference Surfaces'. *Trabajos de Estadistica*, 4 (2), pp. 209–242.

Nowak, A. and Kaminska, A. (2016). 'Agricultural competitiveness: The case of the European Union countries' *Agricultural Economics - Czech*, 62 (11), pp. 507–516.

Nowak, A., Kijek, T. and Domanska, K. (2015). 'Technical Efficiency and its Determinants in the European Union Agriculture'. *Agricultural Economics - Czech*, 61 (6), pp. 275–283.

Střeleček, F., Losová, J. and Zdeněk, R. (2009). 'Comparison of subsidies in the Visegrad Group after the EU accession'. *Agricultural Economics - Czech*, 55 (9), pp. 415–423.

Záhorský, T. and Pokrivčák, J. (2016). 'Determinants of Efficiency in Agriculture in CEE Countries'. *Proceedings of the International Scientific Days 2016*, Nitra, Slovakia, pp. 994-1001.

Zbranek, P. (2015). '*Spoločná polnohospodárská politika a jej dopad na výkonnosť polnohospodárských podnikov: Aplikácia Malmquistových indexov a Luenbergerových indikátorov*'. Ph.D. thesis, Slovak University of Agriculture in Nitra.

Productivity and efficiency of automotive companies in the Czech Republic: a DEA approach

Jiří Franek[1], Ondřej Svoboda[2]

Abstract. Current issues of the Czech automotive manufacturing resonate among several topics including EU emission legislation, development of alternative fuels and propulsion, support of R&D, preparation for the upcoming trends like autonomous cars and renewal of vehicles. Automotive industry is viewed as an engine of the Czech industry. The production is close to 1.5 million vehicles per year making up about 1200 billion CZK in revenues. This industry consist of many companies that are interlinked in a supplier network. The goal of this paper is to investigate efficiency of automotive companies in the Czech Republic and to compare regions and identify those with relative low efficiency. To achieve this, we employed data envelopment analysis (DEA) which is a non-parametric approach to measure efficiency of a finite number of decision-making units (DMUs). This approach is very sensitive to the choice of measures. We applied a selecting model, which could also help to identify the optimal number of inputs and outputs from a group that make economic sense. Using selected inputs and outputs, we performed analysis of efficiency with CCR and BCC models. Results suggest relatively concentrated efficiency with large differences among automotive firms across NUTS2 regions.

Keywords: data envelopment analysis; efficiency; productivity; automotive industry; inputs; outputs.

JEL Classification: C44, M20

1 Introduction

The automotive manufacturing industry comprises the production of trucks, passenger's cars and motorcycles. The truck manufacturers market consists of the production of light commercial vehicles (LCVs), heavy trucks, and buses & coaches. According to the MarketLine report, (2014) poor industry performance in years after the global financial crisis has increased the severity of rivalry, which is assessed as strong overall. Buyer power in this industry is weakened by the high switching costs faced by dealerships and customer loyalty with respect to dominant brands. Amongst the suppliers there are providers of commodity items such as metals, and their power is boosted due to their large size, consolidation of the industry and the fact that automotive manufacturers account for only a small proportion of their revenues. For new entrants to the industry, setting up a production facility involves large capital outlay thus constituting a significant entry barrier and high fixed cost. Furthermore, the global tightening of emission standards is ramping up costs further. Substitutes exist for manufacturers in the form of other companies' products being stocked by dealerships, but this is often negated by contractual agreements and difficulty of changing stock. Rivalry is boosted by the presence of large incumbents. The Eastern European automotive manufacturing industry has produced some excellent

[1] VSB – Technical University of Ostrava, Faculty of Economics, Sokolská třída 33, 702 00, Ostrava, Czech Republic, jiri.franek@vsb.cz
[2] University of Pardubice, Institute of Regional and Security Sciences, Studentská 95, 532 10, Pardubice, Czech Republic, ondrej.svoboda@upce.cz.

levels of growth, before it decelerated sharply in 2012 and 2013. The market picked up again and produced good growth through to the end of the period in 2018. The Eastern European automotive manufacturing industry had total revenues of $75.1bn in 2013, representing a compound annual growth rate (CAGR) of 15.5% between 2009 and 2013. In comparison, the Polish industry declined with a compound annual rate of change (CARC) of -7.1%, and the Czech industry increased with a CAGR of 4.8%, over the same period, to reach respective values of $8.9bn and $13.9bn in 2013. Industry production volume increased with a CAGR of 10.1% between 2009 and 2013, to reach 4,377.1 thousand units in 2013. According to the MarketLine report (2018) the industry's volume has risen to 5 million units by the end of 2018, representing a CAGR of 2.6% for the 2013-2018 period. The performance of the industry is forecast to decelerate, with an anticipated CAGR of 7.3%. Current industry value is about $106.8bn at the end of 2018. Comparatively, the Polish and Czech industries have grown with CAGRs of 5.7% and 4.8% respectively, over the same period, to reach respective values of $11.8bn and $17.6bn in 2018.

Currently the Czech automotive manufacturing faces several challenges including stiffening EU emission legislation, development of alternative propulsion including hybrid and electric engines, rising focus on creating more value added jobs and spending more on R&D and preparation for the upcoming trends like autonomous cars and IoT (Petzl, 2018). Automotive industry is viewed as an engine of the Czech industry, which has its positives and negatives. Yearly production reaches close to 1.5 million vehicles including cars, lorries, busses, motorcycles and other accessories with total revenue about 1 200 billion CZK. This industry comprises of many suppliers in form of global firms, foreign subsidiaries and Czech based SMEs (SAP, 2017).

The goal of this paper is to investigate productivity in the form of efficiency of automotive companies in the Czech Republic and to compare NUTS 2 regions and identify those with relative low efficiency. Staníčková, Melecký and Navrátil (2013), Staníčková (2015) published similar studies focusing on DEA method or DEA method with regional point of view. To achieve this, we employed data envelopment analysis (DEA) which is a non-parametric approach to measure efficiency of a finite number of decision-making units (DMUs). This approach is very sensitive to the choice of measures. Traditionally the rule of thumb has been used for initial decision about number of inputs and outputs. To mitigate this we applied selecting model proposed by Toloo and Tichy (2015) that uses extension of the multiplier form of the BCC model and multiplier form of selecting model to deal with selective measures. Then we applied both CCR and BCC input-oriented models to compare and investigate the efficiency of automotive manufacturing firms based on their results from the year 2017. The paper is structured as follows: the second section deals with introduction to the productivity and efficiency measurement and includes short summaries of used methods. The third section includes description of the dataset and preliminary statistical analysis. Results and discussion can be found in the fourth section. Conclusion deals with the limitation of our study and further research agenda.

2 Productivity and efficiency measurement with DEA

A general definition of productivity can be summed up as the relationship between an output generated by a production or service system and an input provided to create this output. It can be said that productivity is the efficient use of resources (labour, capital, land, materials, energy and information) in the production of various goods and services (Prokopenko, 1998). Manufacturing productivity is a finite measurement that encompasses the performance level of production machinery as well as utilization of that machinery (Smith, 1981). Fenske (1968) defined productivity from five different perspectives: (i) productivity is a form of efficiency; (ii) productivity is the utilization of resources or effectiveness of utilization of resources; (iii) productivity is a ratio; (iv) productivity is a measure of some kind and in monetary terms, (v) productivity is a rate of return. Also using well-known decomposition of return on equity (ROE), we can distinguish three part of the company performance: the effectiveness measured by return on assets (ROA), efficiency measured by assets turnover. The remaining ratio of assets and equity represents financial risk (Selucky, Ho and Hsu, 2011).

The concept of efficiency dates to the industrial revolution. The term manufacturing efficiency can be described as a measure that determines the proportion of value-added operational time to the total amount of time required to convert raw materials into finished goods (Bragg, 2010). In general, manufacturing efficiency is internal measure that is factory focused and relates to the utilization of resources (namely assets, materials, energy and people). On the other hand, manufacturing effectiveness is external, customer-focused and relates to quality, delivery and environment (Basu and Wright, 2005). Chytilová and Hančlová (2017a, 2017b) apply similar approach in recent studies in the bank industry. Two approaches are commonly used to measure efficiency: the parametric approach, which relies on statistical techniques to estimate the parameters of a production function (e.g. Kolková, 2018), and the non-parametric approach, which com-pares the observed inputs and outputs of each firm with that of the most performing firms in the information set. Data envelopment analysis is a non-parametric method, which does not assume any specific production function. Parametric models do assume a particular a priori specification on the production process, non-parametric models estimate the relationship between inputs and outputs with minimal assumptions (Charnes et al., 1985). The DEA model is based on a linear programming technique, which evaluates the efficiency of entities relative to best practice observations (Charnes, Cooper and Rhodes, 1978). Instead, it uses linear programming to identify points on a convex hull defined by the inputs and outputs of the most efficient firms.

2.1 Selected DEA models

Modelling efficiency with non-parametric tools was first introduced as an extension of activity analysis. The CCR model (Charnes, Cooper and Rhodes, 1978) formally introduced the linear programming to measure technical efficiency with the assumption of constant returns to scale. In the CCR model, DMUs adjust either their use of inputs or their outputs to reach the production frontier. The BCC model (Banker, Cooper and Charnes, 1984) removed the assumption of constant returns to scale, and proposed the additive DEA model, where both inputs and outputs can be adjusted simultaneously (Cooper, Seiford and Tone, 2007). All models use the distance to one of the facets of the production or cost frontier to generate an efficiency index. The DEA approach also has also earned its own set of criticisms, centred on two points: (i) measures of technical efficiency are very sensitive to the omission of variables from the production function and (ii) efficiency scores are biased if the degree of freedom is not uniform for all DMUs. One of the other problems was to deal with the ratio of the number of measures and DMUs. The problem of selection of appropriate number of outputs and inputs is frequently based on so called rule of thumb. A rough rule of thumb expresses the relation between the number of DMUs and the number of performance measures (see Cook et al., 2017):

$$n \geq \max\{3(m+s), m \times s\}. \tag{1}$$

Exhaustive review of studies and used numbers of measures and DMUs can be found in Toloo, Barat and Masoumzadeh (2015). However, in this paper we concentrate on application and validation of a lately proposed selective model based on BCC model of efficiency on empirical data.

2.2 The CCR model

The efficiency measure for DMUo is defined as following (Amirteimoori and Tabar, 2010):

$$\theta_0 = \frac{\sum_{r=1}^{s} u_r y_{ro}}{\sum_{i=1}^{m} v_i x_{io}} \tag{2}$$

u_r and v_i are positive. When estimating the DEA efficiency of DMUo, we solve the following DEA model (Charnes, Cooper and Rhodes, 1978):

$$\begin{aligned} Max \quad \theta_o = \sum_{r=1}^{s} \bar{u}_r\, y_{ro} \quad , \\ s.t. \quad \sum_{i=1}^{m} \bar{v}_i x_{io} = 1\,, \\ \sum_{r=1}^{s} \bar{u}_r\, y_{rj} - \sum_{i=1}^{m} \bar{v}_i x_{ij} \leq 0\,, \quad j = 1, \dots, n, \\ \bar{u}_r\,, \bar{v}_i \geq \bar{\varepsilon}\,, \quad \text{for all } r \text{ and } i. \end{aligned} \tag{3}$$

DMUs efficiency ratios changes between 0 and 1. DMU_o is being considered efficient relatively if the ratio receives a score of "1".

2.3 The BCC model

Suppose that, we have *n DMUs*, where each *DMU* is utilizing *m* inputs $x_{1,j}, x_{2,j}, \dots, x_{n,m}$ (all positive) to produce *s* outputs $y_{1,j}, y_{2,j}, \dots, y_{n,s}$ (all positive). The BCC model as introduced by Banker, Charnes and Cooper (1984) for evaluation efficiency of a specific DMU_o assumes that the returns to scale can be variable is presented as follows

$$\begin{aligned} Max \quad & Y_o^T v + u_o \\ s.t \quad & X_o^T\, v = 1 \\ & -Xv + Y_o^{\,T} u + u_o \leq 0 \\ & u \geq 0, \\ & v \geq 0, \end{aligned} \tag{4}$$

In above formulation Y is a $s \times n$ sample output matrix and X is a $n \times m$ sample input matrix, u, v are multipliers that imputed output and input, respectively.

2.4 The DEA input and output selective model

In practice, it is hardly possible to increase the number of DMUs and consequently we resort to formulate some models, which optimally decrease the number of performance measures. In some cases, the decision maker believes that some performance measures are more important than others are and can use MCDM approach to decide which measures are important or not. Multiplier form of selecting model proposed by Toloo and Tichy (2015) uses extension of the multiplier form of the BCC model and multiplier form of selecting model to deal with selective measures:

$$\begin{aligned}
&\max z_3 = \sum_{r=1}^{s} u_r y_{ro} + u_0 \\
&\text{s.t.} \\
&\sum_{i=1}^{m} v_i x_{io} = 1 \\
&\sum_{r=1}^{s} u_r y_{rj} + u_0 - \sum_{i=1}^{m} v_i x_{ij} \leqslant 0 \qquad j = 1, \ldots, n \\
&\sum_{r \in s_2} b_r^y + \sum_{i \in m_2} b_i^x \leqslant \min\left\{ \left\lceil \frac{m}{3} \right\rceil, 2\sqrt{n} \right\} - (|m_1| + |s_1|) \\
&\varepsilon b_i^x \leqslant v_i \leqslant M b_i^x \qquad i \in m_2 \\
&\varepsilon b_r^y \leqslant u_r \leqslant M b_r^y \qquad r \in s_2 \\
&b_i^x, b_r^y \in \{0, 1\} \qquad i \in m_2, r \in s_2 \\
&v_i, u_r \geqslant \varepsilon \qquad i \in m_1, r \in s_1
\end{aligned} \tag{5}$$

In the next section, we utilize a real data set of automotive firms from the Czech Republic in order to show the applicability of the proposed approach to measure efficiency.

3 Efficiency measurement of automotive firms in the Czech Republic

Aforementioned approaches to efficiency require specific dataset that has to have a certain homogeneity among the DMUs (firms). Also, it is important to note that selection of inputs and outputs is another crucial step for making valid evaluation. Transformation processes in manufacturing involve number of different type of inputs and outputs. They differ in units and information value. Traditionally manufacturing productivity is measured in labour productivity, return on assets, cost of equity and other business ratios (Klečka and Čámská, 2013) or economic value added (MIT, 2018). However, some studies help to identify inputs and outputs for the global evaluation of efficiency.

The goal of the evaluation is to find appropriate input and output measures, apply CCR and BBC DEA models to investigate efficiency of firms in three categories according to their size: more than 250 employees, from 100 to 250 employees and less than 100 employees. Finding appropriate inputs and outputs in case of industrial firms is not a straight forward. Some previous studies that applied data envelopment analysis have used different measures. In some previous studies, (see Düzakin and Düzakin, 2007) assets and equity were used as inputs and sales with profits as outputs. Selucky, Ho and Hsu (2011) applied number of employees, total assets, total equity and R&D spending as inputs and revenue and profit as outputs. Rath (2017) identified outputs as gross sales and inputs as labour, capital expenditure, consumption. Li, Liu and Liu et al. (2017) used in general as gross output and export. As inputs, they considered employment fixed assets and R&D spending. However, we found high correlation among financial measures. Thus, we applied our own correlation analysis and then a selecting model to confirm which inputs and outputs are appropriate.

3.1 Description of the dataset

In this case, we will focus on inputs and outputs available to us for a global evaluation and comparison of automotive firms. These variables will come in form of monetary units namely from the balance sheet and P/L statement. This is a first limitation of this study. The dataset characteristics is presented on the Table 1. Where the *LTA represents long term assets; inventory represents sum of all inventories; AP represents account payables; OC are operation costs; PC represent personal costs; E represents employees; Cash represents cash equivalents; EBIT represents operations profit.* The dataset is comprised of 200 firms from the automotive industry categorized by the NUTS 2 regions. These firms are represented by several measures that are from the balanced sheet and profit and loss statement from the year 2017.

	Input 1	**Input 2**	**Input 3**	**Input 4**	**Input 5**	**Input 6**	**Input 7**	**Output 1**	**Output 2**
	LTA	*Inventory*	*Equity*	*AP*	*OC*	*PC*	*E*	*Cash*	*EBIT*
MAX	17449568	3242453	42837335	11421835	121287973	3056890	4007	32011528	10064626
MIN	85	0.001	969	1630	1487	3552	11	0.001	650
Std	1592651	408531	3230910	1523541	9677406	412633	634	2277839	751537
Avg.	703948	256239	941179	803057	3253918	297989	544	243767	190525
DMUs	200								

Table 1 Descriptive statistics of selected automotive firms from the Czech Republic (in thousand CZK, besides no. of employees)

Another assumption we must make is to relate the dataset to a certain homogeneity. Firstly, all firms are based in the Czech Republic. They are part of the vast supply chain on automotive parts and products. Efficiency of firms was evaluated within categories according to their sizes.

3.2 Selection of inputs and outputs

The first step of the evaluation is the selection of inputs and outputs. This can be done using experience, literature review, decision-making models and even DEA approach. We have selected to use the literature review and selecting DEA model developed by Toloo and Tichy (2015) see (5). We have selected variables that are related to the production function of manufacturing firms based on aforementioned literature and correlation analysis. Those are variables registered in the balance sheet and profit and loss statement (see Table 1). This selecting model (5) was applied on data from large firms (more than 250 employees), medium sized firms (between 100 and 250) and small firms with up 100 employees. This enabled us to find inputs and outputs that have the best explanatory value to find efficient scores. In the Table 2 we show how many times particular input or output was selected by the selecting model (5).

Types of firms	Input 1 *LTA*	Input 2 *Inventory*	Input 3 *Equity*	Input 4 *AP*	Input 5 *OC*	Input 6 *PC*	Input 7 *E*	No. of DMUs
Large	79	48	19	1	2	5	78	116
Medium-sized	24	15	9	3	1	3	27	41
Small	11	16	6	21	10	4	18	43

Table 2 Results from application of the selecting model for inputs

Based on the results shown in the Table 2, we can see difference between large, medium and small firms. Whereas we should select LTA, Inventory and employees as clear inputs. In the case of small firms, this indicates AP (accounts payable), inventory and employees. The selecting model has confirmed selection of outputs where for all types of firms it has identified both variables e.g. EBIT and Cash.

3.3 Results of efficiency evaluation using CCR and BCC input-oriented models

Identified inputs and outputs were used for evaluation of efficiency using selected input-oriented models. In this case, we suppose that firms can influence their inputs in order to reach higher levels of efficiency. We used both models to see difference between results under the constant and variable returns to scale (CCR and BCC models respectively). In the Table 3 we can see results for the group of large firms (250+ employees). Results show difference in evaluation under different assumption regarding returns to scale.

Code	CCR(I)	BCC(I)	Code	CCR(I)	BCC(I)	Code	CCR(I)	BCC(I)
DMU_JV10	1	1	DMU_SV43	0.3372	0.4712	DMU_JZ34	0.1344	0.1352
DMU_MS15	1	1	DMU_SM08	0.3273	0.3679	DMU_SV28	0.1341	0.5323
DMU_MS23	1	1	DMU_JZ37	0.3237	0.3746	DMU_ST22	0.1327	0.3871
DMU_ST14	1	1	DMU_JV17	0.322	0.7635	DMU_MS08	0.1292	0.3679
DMU_ST33	1	1	DMU_SZ09	0.3065	0.4815	DMU_SV19	0.128	0.7461
DMU_SV22	1	1	DMU_JZ21	0.2969	0.4049	DMU_SV27	0.1269	0.4452
DMU_SZ08	1	1	DMU_SZ17	0.2899	0.7147	DMU_PH05	0.1261	0.4154
DMU_SZ13	1	1	DMU_JZ12	0.2743	0.4485	DMU_JZ36	0.1258	0.5428
DMU_SZ19	1	1	DMU_ST16	0.2742	0.6855	DMU_MS26	0.1254	0.9755
DMU_JZ24	0.7646	0.9894	DMU_SV18	0.2671	0.333	DMU_MS30	0.1251	0.2001
DMU_MS02	0.7236	0.7262	DMU_SV38	0.2624	0.3701	DMU_SV32	0.125	0.3663
DMU_SV14	0.6922	0.7155	DMU_SZ14	0.2608	0.5953	DMU_JZ20	0.1203	0.3529
DMU_MS09	0.6854	1	DMU_MS31	0.2574	0.2999	DMU_JZ06	0.1139	0.4794
DMU_JV16	0.6586	0.7198	DMU_JZ25	0.2419	0.5563	DMU_SV25	0.1073	0.6741
DMU_ST19	0.6481	0.8237	DMU_JZ10	0.2374	0.4784	DMU_SV17	0.097	0.3607
DMU_MS16	0.6212	0.6486	DMU_SV02	0.2348	0.2479	DMU_MS22	0.0962	0.3471
DMU_SM10	0.5864	0.8763	DMU_ST15	0.2344	0.7605	DMU_JZ08	0.0891	0.4567
DMU_MS14	0.5829	0.6045	DMU_JZ07	0.2324	0.2339	DMU_ST07	0.0739	0.3416
DMU_SV09	0.5703	1	DMU_JZ17	0.223	0.2318	DMU_ST06	0.0737	0.3293
DMU_SV46	0.4849	1	DMU_JZ23	0.2162	0.4784	DMU_JV04	0.0693	0.0906
DMU_SV48	0.4766	0.5112	DMU_ST09	0.2134	0.587	DMU_JZ32	0.0679	0.4927
DMU_MS05	0.4728	1	DMU_MS03	0.2053	0.3409	DMU_MS27	0.0659	0.2568
DMU_JZ33	0.4614	0.7529	DMU_JZ18	0.1987	0.2	DMU_SZ02	0.0578	0.249

DMU_JZ31	0.4554	0.7685	DMU_SV05	0.1947	0.4033	DMU_JV21	0.0531	0.1196
DMU_ST39	0.4417	0.443	DMU_SM16	0.1912	0.5928	DMU_SV07	0.0515	0.1757
DMU_JV09	0.4336	0.5385	DMU_MS04	0.1885	0.1927	DMU_MS18	0.0493	0.6551
DMU_ST10	0.4279	0.4749	DMU_SV04	0.1844	0.3699	DMU_SV20	0.049	0.9363
DMU_SZ07	0.4113	0.5074	DMU_JZ28	0.1818	0.5298	DMU_MS12	0.0468	0.1431
DMU_SM19	0.4058	0.4075	DMU_SV13	0.1804	1	DMU_ST08	0.0446	0.3952
DMU_SM15	0.4026	0.9003	DMU_SZ16	0.1804	0.2333	DMU_SZ25	0.0391	0.2276
DMU_SV37	0.3994	0.7614	DMU_MS32	0.1784	0.3654	DMU_JZ22	0.037	0.6238
DMU_ST43	0.3974	0.4113	DMU_MS17	0.1763	0.2272	DMU_SV16	0.0366	0.436
DMU_ST27	0.3906	0.4688	DMU_ST03	0.1696	0.6387	DMU_SV30	0.0317	0.6208
DMU_MS06	0.3848	0.8495	DMU_MS21	0.161	0.2663	DMU_ST32	0.0282	0.2593
DMU_SV31	0.382	0.3825	DMU_JZ11	0.1446	0.6055	DMU_ST11	0.0281	0.3514
DMU_JV06	0.3704	0.3812	DMU_ST41	0.142	0.5131	DMU_ST26	0.0237	0.362
DMU_ST05	0.3473	0.4887	DMU_MS11	0.141	0.9047	DMU_MS07	0.0179	0.5696
DMU_JZ15	0.3411	0.7064	DMU_MS10	0.1398	0.6634	DMU_ST35	0.0148	0.6181
DMU_SV50	0.339	0.532	DMU_ST23	0.1364	0.2216			

Table 3 Results from application of the selecting model for inputs

Results for BCC model indicate more efficient DMUs than CCR model. There is also number of firms (DMUs) that have relatively low efficiency. In the Table 4 we can see results for the group of medium-sized firms (100 to 250 employees). Similarly, to the results for large firms results from CCR model show a smaller number of efficient DMUs that from the BCC one. Efficiency levels of from the BCC model are on average higher.

Code	CCR(I)	BCC(I)	Code	CCR(I)	BCC(I)
DMU_PH03	1	1	DMU_PH04	0.3223	0.6323
DMU_JV11	1	1	DMU_SM07	0.3139	0.5667
DMU_JZ26	1	1	DMU_SM13	0.2742	1
DMU_SV49	1	1	DMU_SZ26	0.2439	0.6737
DMU_PH13	1	1	DMU_JV22	0.2277	0.5594
DMU_ST17	0.7752	1	DMU_MS28	0.2243	0.9045
DMU_JZ39	0.7151	0.9047	DMU_PH09	0.222	0.8204
DMU_SM09	0.6493	1	DMU_MS29	0.2087	0.5097
DMU_SM20	0.6129	0.8115	DMU_SV33	0.1944	0.7707
DMU_SV10	0.5867	0.7716	DMU_ST21	0.1903	0.483
DMU_SZ24	0.5753	0.8085	DMU_SM03	0.1833	0.9574
DMU_MS25	0.4843	0.8634	DMU_SM01	0.1317	0.7886
DMU_ST04	0.459	0.9763	DMU_ST28	0.1209	0.5923
DMU_JV01	0.436	0.6292	DMU_SV15	0.1153	0.6137
DMU_ST37	0.4346	0.5979	DMU_JZ27	0.1003	0.4815
DMU_SZ12	0.4157	0.8606	DMU_JV24	0.0813	0.9656
DMU_SV12	0.4008	0.6535	DMU_SV42	0.0669	0.4649
DMU_SV39	0.3862	1	DMU_SM11	0.0654	0.4603

DMU_ST45	0.3782	0.5647	DMU_MS24	0.0629	0.479
DMU_JV18	0.3733	0.855	DMU_ST02	0.0183	0.6887
DMU_JZ29	0.3268	0.7383			

Table 4 Results from application of the selecting model for inputs

In the Table 5 we can see results for the group of medium-sized firms (up to 100 employees). In the case of small firms, results from the BCC and CCR are more coherent. However, models produce large number of efficient DMUs.

4 Results and discussion

According to results from the CCR and BCC input oriented model following large firms were found efficient: ELCATEC, s.r.o.; Hyundai Motor Manufacturing Czech s.r.o.; Mobis Automotive Czech s.r.o.; HBPO Czech s.r.o.; SAS Autosystemtechnik s.r.o.; Iveco Czech Republic, a. s.; Elektromodul s.r.o.; K W L, s.r.o.; Pierburg s.r.o.. In general, when comparing regional (NUTS2) differences we can see that Southwest (JZ) has lowest average efficiency but also low variability. Thus, we can say that the automotive firms in that region show relative low efficiency. Similar results have occurred in the Northeast (SV) region and Central Bohemia (ST). On the other hand, largely, efficient firms can be found in the Central Moravia (SM), however a lower number of firms in the sample can influence this and the variability is low too. Firms in the Southeast (JV) and Northwest (SZ) regions are on average more efficient, but several highly efficient firms influence the results and thus the variability is high. In the case of medium-sized firms, results show lower overall variability among regions. Low efficiency and low variability can be found in Central Bohemia and Moravian-Silesian (MS) regions. Higher efficiency can be found among firms from the Prague (PH) region and Southwest. EMS-PATVAG s.r.o.; Megatech Industries Plzeň s.r.o.; C.I.E.B. Kahovec, spol. s r.o.; Zanini CZ, s.r.o.; VAPOS, spol. s r.o. were found the most efficient.

Code	CCR(I)	BCC(I)	Code	CCR(I)	BCC(I)
DMU_JZ04	1	1	DMU_ST25	0.3902	0.556
DMU_SV44	1	1	DMU_JV13	0.3709	0.918
DMU_SV34	1	1	DMU_JZ02	0.3647	0.3689
DMU_SZ11	1	1	DMU_MS19	0.3105	0.6476
DMU_JV25	1	1	DMU_PH08	0.3001	0.7251
DMU_JZ03	1	1	DMU_SV01	0.295	0.6402
DMU_JV03	1	1	DMU_SZ21	0.2914	0.4945
DMU_PH12	1	1	DMU_SV29	0.2851	0.6706
DMU_ST34	1	1	DMU_ST20	0.2368	0.5303
DMU_ST40	1	1	DMU_SM06	0.2112	0.5341
DMU_SZ22	1	1	DMU_ST31	0.194	0.4609
DMU_PH11	1	1	DMU_JV02	0.1921	0.7462
DMU_JV05	0.8832	1	DMU_PH02	0.1906	0.3361
DMU_SV03	0.8613	0.8616	DMU_SV06	0.1819	0.6168
DMU_ST38	0.7434	0.9376	DMU_SZ23	0.1651	0.4952

DMU_JV12	0.7168	0.9247	DMU_JZ30	0.1599	0.6057
DMU_JV15	0.7122	0.7579	DMU_PH10	0.1127	0.6313
DMU_JV08	0.6132	0.6144	DMU_ST44	0.1082	0.6938
DMU_JZ09	0.583	0.5835	DMU_JV23	0.0882	0.6214
DMU_JZ35	0.4874	0.6316	DMU_PH01	0.0877	0.4119
DMU_MS01	0.4573	0.7955	DMU_JZ16	0.052	0.4128
DMU_ST01	0.4315	0.5854			

Table 5 Results from application of the selecting model for inputs

Results for the last group of firms that have less than 100 employees. Firms from the Southeast and Northeast have relatively high efficiency and low variability. On the other hand, firms from Prague and Southwest are relatively less efficient. Firms that were evaluated as efficient using both DEA models are ZPSHelp, s.r.o.; ASN HAKR Brno s.r.o.; BANES, spol. s r.o.; AMI AUTOINTERIER, s.r.o.; Rastr elektro s.r.o.; PRODUCTION AUTOMOTIVE spol. s r.o.; SCHEDL Automotive System Service, s.r.o.; Trelleborg Boots Mladá Boleslav s.r.o.; SVOS, spol. s r.o.; MEDTEC - VOP, spol. s r.o.; Hitachi Cable Europe, s.r.o.; Schlaeger M-Tech s.r.o. Some comparable results can be found in Selucky, Ho and Hsu (2011) were the larger firms tend to have better efficiency. Klečka and Čámská (2013) have compared productivity of automotive industry in Northwest and Central Bohemia regions in 2006 to 2011, concluding that there are specific difference among regions that may influence their productivity levels. They found that the Central Bohemian region was more influenced by the crisis in 2009 – 2010 than the Northwest region.

There are some limitations to this analysis. The homogeneity of firms can be questionable since there are difference in the type of production (mass, batch or job production). This analysis of efficiency is a first step in finding an approach to understand the development in automotive industry and its productivity changes. Authors are going to create larger database including past results of investigated firms and will perform analysis focused on annual changes to produce time series of theirs efficiency fluctuations.

5 Conclusion

This paper is one among vast number of studies in application of DEA models. Its goal was to investigate possibilities of efficiency evaluation of the automotive industry in the Czech Republic. The main motivation is to see, which types of companies are more efficient. The main contribution can be seen in the selection of inputs and outputs based on relatively publicly available data from a large sample of companies. The main concern can be found in the application of basic DEA models and use of data only from one year. Overall, efficiency evaluated by the BCC model tends to be higher than that calculated by using CCR model. Further analysis would be possible using superefficiency models (Lovell and Rouse, 2003), finding other input-output relations. More insight would be possible using Malmquist index (Pastor and Lovell, 2005). The model can be extended using approach to nonhomogeneous set of DMUs as presented by Cook et al. (2013).

Further research will be focused on number of topics stemming from this research. Primarily authors will in the future investigate annual changes using Malmquist indices, use of ratio data, differences among regions with possible effects coming from main manufactures in those areas and their supply chains. It would be interesting to see difference in efficiency of various supply chains.

Acknowledgements

The first author research was supported by the Czech Science Foundation project GACR 17-23495S. All support is greatly acknowledged.

References

Amirteimoori, A. and Tabar, M.M. (2010). 'Resource allocation and target setting in data envelopment analysis'. *Expert Systems with Applications,* 37 (4), pp. 3036-3039.

Banker, R.D., Charnes, A. and Cooper, W.W. (1984). 'Models for estimation of technical and scale inefficiencies in data envelopment analysis'. *Management Science*, 30, pp. 1078–1092.

Basu, R. and Wright, J. N. (2005). *Total operations solutions,* [Online]. Amsterdam, Elsevier Butterworth-Heinemann. Available at: http://site.ebrary.com/id/10138617.

Bragg, S. M. (2010). *Business Ratios and Formulas: a Comprehensive Guide*. Somerset: Wiley.

Charnes, A., Cooper, W. W., Lewin, A. Y., Morey, R. C., Rousseau, J. (1985). 'Sensitivity and stability analysis in DEA'. *Annals of Operations Research*, 2, pp. 139-156

Charnes, A., Cooper, W.W. and Rhodes, E. (1978). 'Measuring the efficiency of decision making units'. *European Journal of Operations Research,* 2, pp. 429–444.

Chytilová, L. and Hanclova, J. (2017a). 'Comparison of efficiency results for financial institutions using different DEA models'. *Proceedings of Mathematical Methods in Economics (MME 2017)*, pp. 271-276.

Chytilová, L. and Hanclova, J. (2017b). 'An application of convex nonparametric least squares to estimation banks (in)efficiency in the Visegrad countries'. *Proceedings of the 12th International Conference on Strategic Management and its Support by Information Systems (SMSIS) 2017*, pp. 231-238.

Cook, W. D., Ruiz, J. L., Sirvent, I. and Zhu, J. (2017). 'Within-group common benchmarking using DEA'. *European Journal of Operational Research*, 256 (3), pp. 901–910.

Cook, W., Harrison, J., Imanirad, R., Rouse, P. and Zhu, J. (2013). 'Data Envelopment Analysis with Nonhomogeneous DMUs'. *Operations Research*, 61 (3), pp. 666–676.

Cooper, W.W., Seiford, L. M. and Tone, K. (2007). *Data Envelopment Analysis: A Comprehensive Text with Models, Applications, References and DEA-Solver Software*, 2nd ed. Springe: Berlin.

Düzakın, E. and Düzakın, H. (2007). 'Measuring the performance of manufacturing firms with super slacks based model of data envelopment analysis: An application of 500 major industrial enterprises in Turkey'. *European Journal of Operational Research*, 182 (3), pp. 1412-1432.

Fenske, R. W. (1968). 'A Method To Determine Whether or Not To Backhaul Inbound Merchandise'. *Journal of Purchasing*, 4, pp. 70-88. DOI: 10.1111/j.1745-493X.1968.tb00595.x.

Klečka, J. and Čámská, D. (2013). 'Development of Value Productivity in Automotive Industry'. *WASET International Journal of Economics and Management Engineering*, 7 (11), pp. 2957 – 2962.

Kolková, A. (2018). 'Indicators of Technical Analysis on the Basis of Moving Averages as Prognostic Methods in the Food Industry'. *Journal of Competitiveness*, 10 (4), pp. 102-119.

Li, L., Liu, B., Liu, W. and Chiu, Y.-H. (2017). 'Efficiency evaluation of the regional high-tech industry in China: A new framework based on meta-frontier dynamic DEA analysis'. *Socio-Economic Planning Sciences*, 60, pp. 24–33.

Lovell, C.A.K. and Rouse, A.P.B. (2003). 'Equivalent standard DEA models to provide superefficiency scores'. *Journal of The Operational Research Society*, 54 (1), pp. 101-108.

MarkerLine (2014). MarketLine Industry Profile: Automotive Manufacturing in Eastern Europe, September 2014.

MarkerLine (2017). MarketLine Industry Profile: New Cars in the Czech Republic, September 2017.

MarkerLine (2018). MarketLine Industry Profile: Automotive Manufacturing in Eastern Europe, September 2018.

Ministry of Industry and Trade (MIT) (2018). Panorama of the Manufacturing Industry of the Czech Republic 2017, [Online]. Available at: https://www.mpo.cz/assets/en/industry/manufacturing-industry/panorama-of-the-manufacturing-industry/2018/9/Panorama-2017-en.pdf [cited 2019-01-10].

Pastor, J.T. and Lovell, C.A.K. (2005). 'A global Malmquist productivity index'. *Economic Letters*, 88 (2), pp. 266-271.

Petzl, Z. (2018). Autoprůmysl v roce 2018 - na prahu změn, [Online]. Available at: https://www.cma.cz/wp-content/uploads/2018/01/180118-vecer_CMA-vyzvy_automotive.pdf [cited 2019-01-10].

Prokopenko, J. (1998). *Productivity management: a practical handbook*. Geneva: International Labour Office.

Rath, B. N. (2017). 'Productivity growth and efficiency change: Comparing manufacturing- and service-based firms in India'. *Economic Modelling*, 70 (C), pp. 447-457.

SAP (2017). Automobilový průmysl v ČR 2017, [Online]. Available at: https://www.khkkk.cz/files/uploads/2018/10/Analyza_AutoSAP_2017_prehled_%C4%8CJ.pdf [cited 2019-01-10].

Selucky, J., Chien-Ta Ho, B. and Hsu, H-J. (2011). 'Measuring Performance and Risk of Automotive Industry in Czech Republic'. *Proceedings of the XV International Scientific Conference on Industrial Systems (IS'11)*, pp. 313-319.

Smith, M. R. (1981). *Manufacturing controls: how the manufacturing manager can improve profitability*. New York, Van Nostrand Reinhold.

Staníčková, M. (2014). 'Classifying The EU Competitiveness Factors using Multivariate Statistical Methods'. *Conference Proceeding of 2nd Global Conference on Business, Economics and Management and Tourism. Book Series: Procedia Economics and Finance*, 23, pp: 313-320.

Staníčková, M., Melecký, L. and Navrátil, B. (2013). 'Measuring the Student Research Projects' Efficiency Using Dea Method'. *Conference Proceeding of 10th International Conference on Efficiency and Responsibility in Education 2013*, Prague, Czech Republic, pp: 573-580.

Toloo, M and Tichý, T. (2015). 'Two alternative approaches for selecting performance measures in data envelopment analysis'. *Measurement*, 65, pp. 29-40.

Toloo, M., Barat, M. and Masoumzadeh, A. (2015). 'Selective measures in data envelopment analysis'. *Annals of Operations Research*, 226, pp. 623-642.

Performance Evaluation of Printed Media in Online Social Media Using Data Envelopment Analysis

Hourieh Haghighinia[1], Mohsen Rostamy-Malkhalifeh[2]

Abstract. We are in the golden age of content and media. Today, media companies invest a huge amount of their money in non-traditional media for new messaging options. The center for business innovation reported that technology is one of the indicators of value creation that is used to evaluate the performance of companies. Social media are technological phenomena that have been grown in recent years. The advanced combination of this new interactive technology can be of various benefits to businesses.

This paper employs the data envelopment analysis method to evaluate Iranian printed newspapers and utilizes the Malmquist Productivity Index (MPI) in order to evaluate the productivity change of each unit between two time periods (2015-2016). In order to investigate the impact of online social media on the performance of Iranian printed newspapers, we include the social media indicators into consideration and recalculate the effectiveness of each newspaper. The obtained results point out that the social media indicators significantly affect the performance of the printed newspapers in Iran.

Keywords: Data Envelopment Analysis, Malmquist Index, Efficiency, Printed Newspapers, Social Media Analysis.

JEL Classification: C00, C60, L82

1 Introduction

Today, global competition has caused markets to change. New technologies have introduced new tools towards creating value in the form of quality. "The rate at which technology has been advancing in the last two decades has forced media organizations to constantly address the need for adaptation with such developments and revolutions (Farhangi and Danayi, 2013). Such organizations are increasingly becoming more and more complex, and in order to optimize their potential, they require solutions in the fields of Production Management and Digital Media Content Production in order for their products to be shared and distributed on a global scale. Newspapers are the most popular of the printed media. They are often delivered to houses or widely available in newsstand, they are also the least expensive form of news being delivered to masses. Additionally, as different kinds of newspaper are helpful to specific groups, they can be targeted at diverse groups (Lad, 2018). According to the Center for Business Innovation (CBI), technology is an indicator for value which is used for benchmarking organizational company performance (Kalafut and Low, 2001). In addition, according to Daft and Lengel's theory (1986), "Media which has the capacity of transferring multidimensional signals, namely auditory, visual, kinesthetic, interpersonal interactions, etc. is the richest kind of media for conveying messages" (Daft and Lengel, 1986). As a result, online social media are considered as rich

[1] Science and Research Branch, Islamic Azad University, Department of Media Management, Faculty of Management and Economics, Simon Bulivar Blvd, Tehran, Iran, Haghighinia_h@yahoo.com.

[2] Science and Research Branch, Islamic Azad University, Department of Applied Mathematics, Faculty of Basic Sciences, Simon Bulivar Blvd, Tehran, Iran, mohsen_rostamy@yahoo.com.

media which generate value as invisible assets of organizations and will be effective in the value chain of the organization. Online social media are indeed a new philosophy found in user-oriented websites, which grow increasingly important for businesses. Indeed, such networks, websites, and applications are user-oriented, i.e. they allow their users to contribute to its content production. This modern combination of interactive technology holds a number of advantages for businesses (Martinez and Perez, 2014).

The current study focuses on online social media, such as Twitter, Instagram, and Telegram as interactive technological resources. In addition, we aim to evaluate the amount of activity and presence of Iranian newspaper on online social media through Data Envelopment Analysis (DEA). We are also aiming to propose a new model as a means to optimizing the use of online social media.

2 Background

Social media are useful tools which bring customers closer and increases competition among businesses (Agnihotri et al, 2016; McCann and Barlow, 2015; He, Wang, and Zha, 2014; Durkin, Mcgowan and Mckeown, 2013). Majumdar and Venkataraman (1998) evaluated the application and effects of technological resources, e.g. ICT in combination with other tangible and human resources in the Information and Communication Technology in the USA (Majumdar and Venkataraman, 1998), and Fernandez-Menendez et al (2009) investigated the impact of accepting new technologies (Fernandez-Menendez and et al, 2009). "In 2010, Data Envelopment Analysis (DEA) was used for in analysis of technological resources in the markets. Similarly, Emrouznejad and Cabanda (2010) proposed a method of evaluating the use of ICT in 183 industrialized countries (Emrouznejad, Cabanda, and Gholami, 2010), and Ceccobelli and Gitto (2012) studied the correlation between the implementation and application of information and communication Technology with a leverage boost in 14 OECD countries (Ceccobelli, Gitto and Mancuso, 2012). In addition, Martinez and Perez (2014) evaluated the online social media in a Spanish telecommunication firms with the help of DEA (Martinez and Perez, 2014). Mariani and Visani (2019) Ranked the performance of hotels by evaluating online customers in Rome with the help of DEA (Mariani and Visani, 2019). Also, Ahmad and Abu Bakar (2018) showed that the effect of using Facebook, Twitter, YouTube, and Instagram among SMEs (Small and Medium-sized Enterprises) leads to an increased brand awareness, loyalty and reputation, reduced communication and marketing costs, Attracted new customers and competitive advantage, and increased customer clientele and revenue generation for the company (Ahmad and Abu Bakar, 2018). Fortunati and O'Sullivan (2019) have investigated whether print-based communication model remains sustainable with complimenting the digital media and online social media (Fortunati and O'Sullivan, 2019). In Iran, extensive research has been conducted using the DEA, however, there are few articles or papers relevant to investigating the capacity of information and communication technology, particularly in the field of online social media in the media industry. Despite this, there are two relevant papers which used DEA, namely Farzipoor Saen (2011), analyzed Media selection in the Steel industry (Farzipoor Saen, 2011), and Mousavi Kashi and Hojaji (2016), the efficiency of the organizational social media (particularly the SharePoint Software Platform) in the Social Security Investment Co (Mousavi Kashi, Hojaji and Hassanzadeh, 2016).

3 Methodology

The approach used in this study is based on mathematics and the analysis of performance using DEA. DEA is considered as a Non-Parametric Frontier Approach and with its help, a rough judgment on relative efficiency can be determined through analyzing the input and output of the decision making units versus the input and output of other decision making units. As a result, a point on the frontier of efficiency is reached to be the compared with the decision making unit (DMU). The frontier point is determined by less input or more output compared to the input and output under question (Jahanshahloo, Hosseinzadeh Lotfi and Nikomaram, 2008). DEA models have been developing ever since they were first introduced. Farrell (1957) set the move to measure efficiency in a manufacturing unit using the procedure of efficiency measurement in engineering fields (Seydel, 2006). Building on the ideas of Farrell (1957), the seminal work measuring the efficiency of decision making units by Charns, Cooper, and Rhodes (1978) proposed a model which allowed the efficiency measurement to be done with multi-input and multi-output. This model was coined DEA and the method is commonly known as CCR Model (1) (an abbreviation of the initial letters of its developers, Charns, Cooper, and Rhodes):

$$max \frac{\sum_{r=1}^{s} u_r \, y_{ro}}{\sum_{i=1}^{m} v_i \, x_{io}}$$

$$s.t. \quad \frac{\sum_{r=1}^{s} u_r \, y_{rj}}{\sum_{i=1}^{m} v_i \, x_{ij}} \leq 1, j = 1, 2, \ldots, n \qquad (1)$$

$$u_r \geq 0, r = 1, \ldots, s \qquad v_i \geq 0, i = 1, \ldots, m,$$

where, u_r: r th output weight, v_i: i th input weight, o: Subscript of decision-making unit ($o \in \{1,2,\ldots,n\}$), y_{ro} and x_{io}: values of r th output and i th input for o unit, y_{ri} and x_{ij}: values of r th output and i th input for j th unit, s: number of output, m: number of input, n: number of units. It is worth mentioning that definition of efficiency in CCR model is the result of dividing output weight combination into input weight combination. As suggested by Charnes and Cooper (1978), this model has changed into linear planning (2) (Charns, Cooper, and Rhodes, 1978):

$$max \sum_{r=1}^{s} u_r \, y_{ro}$$

$$s.t. \sum_{i=1}^{m} v_i \, x_{io} = 1 \qquad (2)$$

$$\sum_{r=1}^{s} u_r \, y_{rj} - \sum_{i=1}^{m} v_i \, x_{ij} \leq 0, j = 1, 2, \ldots, n$$

$$u_r \geq 0, r = 1, \ldots, s \qquad v_i \geq 0, i = 1, \ldots, m,$$

In this study, Multiplier CCR model with weight restriction is used. CCR models are considered as Constant Returns to scale and are useful in conditions where all units of measurement are performing at an optimum. DEA has been developing by the course of time and is currently regarded as a useful method for organization design for decision making output efficiency (Lee,

Lee and Kang, 2005). The main reason for selecting the DEA for this study is that it evaluates each unit at its optimum and determines the best weight for it. The researcher does not intervene in the weight selection and the model makes the selection for the optimization of the most efficient frontier selection. If there are any restrictions in weight selection, the restrictions can be added to the model and evaluate the optimum weight accordingly. Also, Malmquist Productivity Index (MPI) is used to evaluate the printed newspaper efficiency in two periods (2015-2016). MPI is a very useful approach in DEA, which was coined by Professor Sten Malmquist and introduced by Caves et al (1982). This index estimates the relative performance of DMUs in different periods using a base course technology. The most accredited method was proposed by Fare et al (1992) which estimates geometric mean of MPI of two base periods (Jafari, 2014). In this study, for calculating the Malmquist Productivity Index, first we solve the following four models (Wang and Lan, 2011):

Model (3): the evaluated unit (x_0 and y_0) and other units (PPS frontiers) are all in time *t*:

$$\begin{aligned} &\theta_t^t = Min\ \theta \\ &s.t. \sum_{j=1}^{n} \lambda_j x_j^t \le \theta x_o^t \\ &\sum_{j=1}^{n} \lambda_j y_j^t \ge y_o^t \\ &\lambda_j \ge 0 \qquad j = 1, 2, \ldots, n. \end{aligned} \tag{3}$$

Model (4): the evaluated unit in time *(t+1)* and other units (PPS frontiers) are all in time *t*:

$$\begin{aligned} &\theta_t^{t+1} = Min\ \theta \\ &s.t. \sum_{j=1}^{n} \lambda_j x_j^t \le \theta x_o^{t+1} \\ &\sum_{j=1}^{n} \lambda_j y_j^t \ge y_o^{t+1} \\ &\lambda_j \ge 0 \qquad j = 1, 2, \ldots, n. \end{aligned} \tag{4}$$

Model (5): the evaluated unit in time *t* and other units (PPS frontiers) are all in time *(t+1)*:

$$\begin{aligned} &\theta_{t+1}^t = Min\ \theta \\ &s.t. \sum_{j=1}^{n} \lambda_j x_j^{t+1} \le \theta x_o^t \\ &\sum_{j=1}^{n} \lambda_j y_j^{t+1} \ge y_o^t \\ &\lambda_j \ge 0 \qquad j = 1, 2, \ldots, n. \end{aligned} \tag{5}$$

Model (6): the evaluated unit and the frontiers are both in time *(t+1)*:

$$\theta_{t+1}^{t+1} = Min\ \theta$$

$$s.t. \sum_{j=1}^{n} \lambda_j\, x_j^{t+1} \leq \theta x_o^{t+1} \tag{6}$$

$$\sum_{j=1}^{n} \lambda_j\, y_j^{t+1} \geq y_o^{t+1}$$

$$\lambda_j \geq 0 \qquad j= 1, 2, \ldots, n.$$

The θ, which is calculated after solving the four models presented, is afterwards inserted into the formula below to produce MPI (7):

$$MPI_o = \frac{\theta_{t+1}^{t+1}}{\theta_t^t} \times \sqrt{\frac{\theta_t^t \times \theta_{t+1}^t}{\theta_{t+1}^{t+1} \times \theta_{t+1}^{t+1}}} \tag{7}$$

The decision making units in this paper include 87 titles among Iranian newspapers, whether national, provincial, regional, and local, which are printed media that use similar input and output in the evaluation process. Consequently, homogeneity is assumed among the DMUs. Also, purposive sampling is done with concentration on newspapers with an active presence on online social media. The printed newspapers selected as the decision making units are presented in Table 1.

Sub-sector	The number of DMUs	%
National	67	77.011
Regional	7	8.045
Provincial	11	12.643
Local	2	0.311
Total	87	100

Table 1 Classification of the selected printed newspapers

The effective input and output indicators for printed newspapers and the input and output indicators for each social media were identified with the help of a group of experts working in the printed media and are shown in Table 2.

Input[3]	Newspapers	Instagram	Telegram	Twitter
Skills of writers	*			
Insured Employees	*			
Newspaper experience	*			
Governmental subsidies	*			
Following		*		*
Tweets/Posts/Shared Media		*	*	*
Stories		*		
Likes				*
Output[4]				
Circulation	*			
Number of pages	*			
Graphic quality	*			
Ratio of advertising to content	*			
Score of rating	*			
Followers/Subscribers		*	*	*
Comments		*		
Likes		*		
Views			*	

Table 2 Variables selected for each model

Also, the weight restrictions of every social media were identified with the help of a group of experts. The necessary measurements of the DMUs analysis are performed by GAMS software. The General Algebraic Modeling System (GAMS) is a high-level modeling system for mathematical programming and optimization. GAMS software is tailored for complex, large scale modeling applications, and is specifically designed for modeling linear, nonlinear and mixed integer optimization problems[5].

[3] The description of input variables is: Skills of writers: Scientific levels and ranks of the authors of each newspaper. Insured Employees: The number of insured employees working in each newspaper. Newspaper experience: The number of years of work experience of each newspaper. Governmental subsidies: The amount of subsidy received annually by each of the newspapers from Ministry of Culture and Guidance Press Office in Iran. Following: The number of people who followed by each newspaper. Tweets/Posts/Shared Media: The number of content such as text, photo, video and music which is shared on the newspaper's social media page. Stories: The number of stories on the Instagram page of each newspaper. Likes: The number of newspaper's like on the Twitter page of each newspaper.

[4] Circulation: The circulation of each newspaper. Number of pages: the number of the pages each newspaper prints. Graphics quality: The quality of the newspaper graphics. Ratio of advertising to content: The amount of space the newspapers devote to advertising. Score of rating: The annual rankings each newspaper receives from the Press Office of the Ministry of Culture and Guidance in Iran. Followers/Subscribers: The number of members on the newspaper's social media page. Comments: The number of comments made by the audience on the Instagram page of each newspaper. Likes: The number of likes by the audience on the Instagram page of each newspaper. Views: The number of audience's visits on the Telegram page of each newspaper.

[5] https://www.gams.com/products/introduction/

4 Results

Nowadays, due to the ability to attract more audience, subscribe to social media play a significant role in improving the performance of printed media such as newspapers and magazines. Therefore, in this paper, we have been selected some Iranian newspapers in four categories (National, Regional, Provincial, and Local) by considering three social media (Instagram, Telegram and Twitter) in 2019. The results of the evaluation of productivity changes of 87 titles of Iranian newspapers by using Malmquist Productivity Index (MPI) in two time periods (2015-2016), i.e. before adding the social media indexes, are shown in Table 3. The results show that 33.33% of the newspapers have progressed and 66.66% of them have regressed. The lowest amount of progress belongs to DMU14 and the highest amount of progress belongs to DMU 51.

Productivity change	The number of DMUs	%	Min	Max	Average	St. Dev.
Progress	29	33.33	1.0236	2.4295	1.4205	O.3144
Regress	58	66.66	1.1429	0.9422	0.5196	0.2350
Total	**87**	**100**				

Table 3 Result of productivity changes between 2015 and 2016

Since we would like to compare the impact of each social media in performance of newspapers, the efficiency of DMUs is measured in two phase. At first we have been evaluated efficiency of each DMUs regardless considering social media and after that by applying those factors. The factors are obtained by interviews with managers and experts[6]. In this study, three factors as inputs and three factors as output are considered for *Instagram*. Also, one input and two output for *Telegram* and three input and one output for *Twitter* are assumed[7]. Finally, comparison of efficiency has been given in figure 1 and the effects of social media factors are visible. Due to the large amount of data, it cannot be provided a detailed description here so the results of the evaluation of each social media are shown in Figure 1. the figure indicates some information regarding effect of Instagram, Telegram and Twitter as social media. According to the result it can be found that there is a significant improvement in DMUs performance in presence social media. For instance, the efficiency score of DMU16 has been 0.8682 regardless any social media but after adding them its efficiency score increase to 1.0000, 1.0000 and 0.9929 in presence Instagram, Telegram and Twitter respectively. Before entering the social media indicators there were five efficient units while after adding them, the number of efficient units increased to twelve, ten and eleven DMUs in presence Instagram, Telegram and Twitter respectively.

5 Discussion

After the initial research, it became clear that the selected newspapers in this study were more likely to be active in the three social media (Instagram, Telegram and Twitter) than in other

[6] The weight restrictions added to newspaper indicators are: $U_1 \geq U_2, U_2 \geq U_3, U_3 \geq U_4, U_1 \geq V_3, V_3 \geq V_1, V_1 \geq V_2$, and $V_2 \geq V_4$.
7 The weight restrictions added to social media indicators are: Instagram: $U_2 \geq U_3, U_3 \geq U_1, U_2 \geq V_2, V_2 \geq V_3$, and $V_3 \geq V_1$. Telegram: $U_2 \geq U_1$, and $U_1 \geq V_1$. Twitter: $U_1 \geq V_2, V_2 \geq V_3$, and $V_3 \geq V_1$.

social media. The data needed for each of these social media was extracted on a particular day [Instagram: 22 Jan 2019, Telegram: 24 Jan 2019, and Twitter: 25 Jan 2019]. 31 decision making units out of the 87 newspapers surveyed were are active in all three social media (Instagram, Telegram, and Twitter). The results of adding the indicators of each social media to newspaper indicators reveal that, in most cases, there is a direct relationship between an increased efficiency and the use of online social media. Overall, the use of online social media capacity has been instrumental in improving the efficiency of decision making units.

6 Future research

It is suggested that considering the weights obtained from each model, we can find the best indicator in each social media and then present the model. Also, given that the number of effective DMUs is more than one, we can rank them. It is suggested that an overall study is done with equal input and output indicators. In addition, future research can compare the activities of different industries in online social media. Although assuming the limitations of the DEA in homogeneity of the sample is necessary.

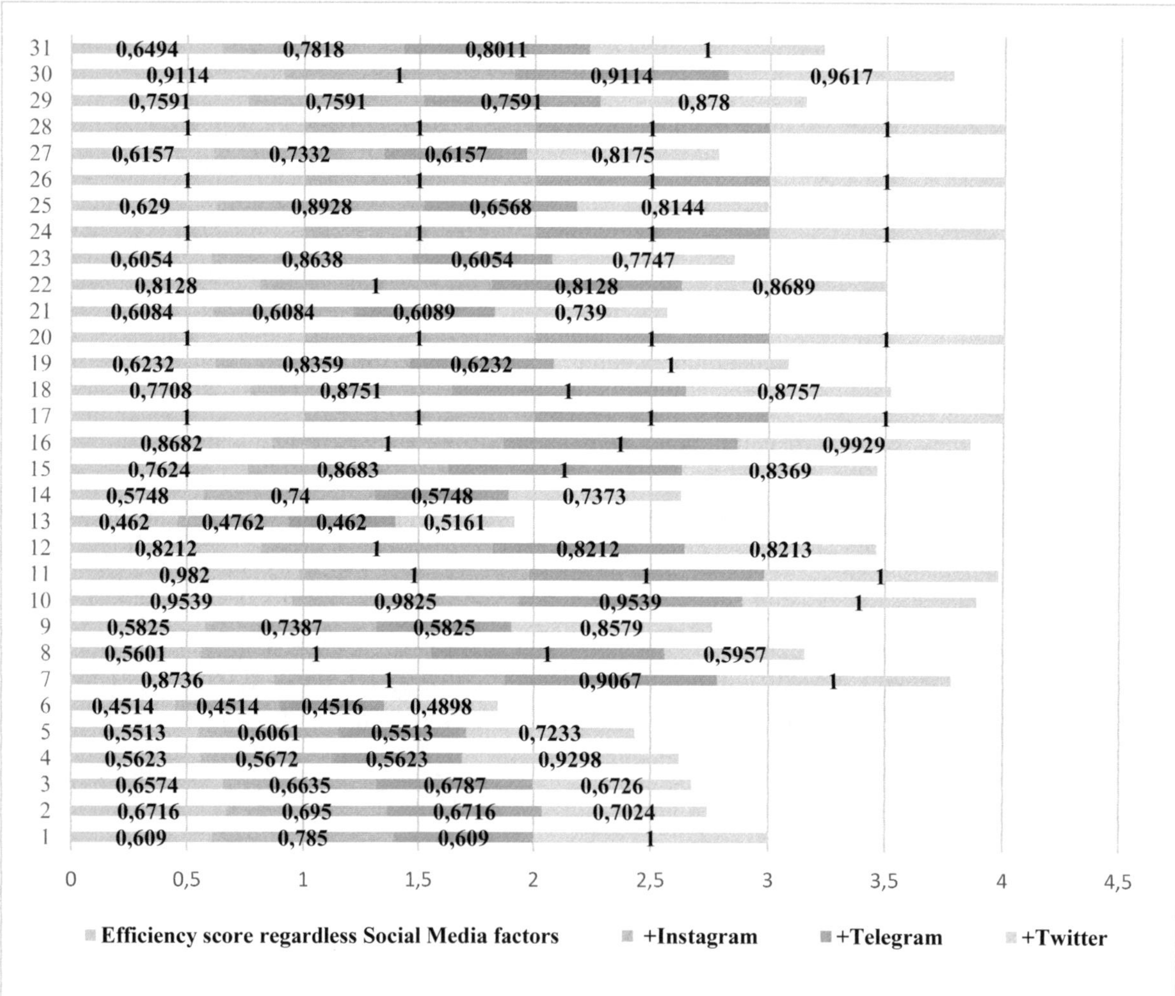

Figure 1 Evaluation of Social Media efficiency

References

Agnihotri, R., Dingus, R., Hu, M. Y. and Krush, M. T. (2016). 'Social media: Influencing customer satisfaction in B2B sales'. *Industrial Marketing Management,* 53, pp. 172-180.

Ahmad, S. Z., Ahmad, N. and Abu Bakar, A. R. (2018). 'Reflections of entrepreneurs of small and medium-sized enterprises concerning the adoption of social media and its impact on performance outcomes: Evidence from the UAE'. *Telematics and Informatics,* 35, pp. 6-17.

Ceccobelli, M., Gitto, S. and Mancuso, P. (2012). 'ICT capital and labour productivity growth: A non-parametric analysis of 14 OECD countries'. *Telecommunications Policy,* 36, pp. 282-292.

Charnes, A., Cooper, W. W. and Rhodes, E. (1978). 'Measuring the efficiency of decision making units'. *European Journal of Operational Research,* 2, pp. 429-444.

Daft, R. L. and Lengel, R. H. (1986). 'Organizational information requirements, media richness and structural design'. *Management Science,* 32, pp. 554-571.

Durkin, M., Mcgowan, P. and Mckeown, N. (2013). 'Exploring social media adoption in small to medium-sized enterprises in ireland'. *Journal of Small Business and Enterprise Development,* 20, pp. 716-734.

Emrouznejad, A., Cabanda, E. and Gholami, R. (2010). 'An alternative measure of the ICT opportunity index'. *Information & Management,* 47, pp. 246-254.

Farhangi, A. A. and Danaei, A. (2013). *Development and Implementation of System through Balanced Performance in Media Organization,* Iran: Max Nazar.

Farzipoor Saen, R. (2011). 'Media selection in the presence of flexible factors and imprecise data'. *Journal of The Operational Research Society,* 62, pp. 1695–1703.

Fernandez-Menendez, J., Lopez-Sanchez, J. I., Rodriguez-Duarte, A. and Sandulli, F. D. (2009). 'Technical efficiency and use of information and communication technology in spanish firms'. *Telecommunications Policy,* 33, pp. 348-359.

Fortunati, L. and O'sullivan, J. (2019). 'Situating the social sustainability of print media in a world of digital alternatives'. *Telematics and Informatics,* 37, pp. 137-145.

He, W., Wang, F.K. and Zha, S. (2014). 'Enhancing social media competitiveness of small businesses: Insights from small pizzerias'. *New Review in Hypermedia and Multimedia,* 20, pp. 225 –250.

Jafari, Y. (2014). 'Malmquist productivity index for multi time periods'. *International Journal of Data Envelopment Analysis,* 2, pp. 315-322.

Jahanshahloo, G. R., Hosseinzadeh Lotfi, F. and Nikomaram, H. (2008). *Data envelopment analysis and its applications,* Iran: Nafis.

Kalafut, P. C. and Low, J. (2001). 'The value creation index: Quantifying intangible value'. *Strategy & Leadership,* 29, pp. 9-15.

Lad, K. (2018). Different types of print media: All effective in their own ways, [Online]. Available at: https://www.marketingwit.com/Types-Of-Print-Media [cited 2018-04-09].

Lee, S., Lee, K. and Kang, I. W. (2005). 'Efficiency analysis of controls in edi applications'. *Information & Management,* 42, pp. 425-439.

Majumdar, S. K. and Venkataraman, S. (1998). 'Networks effects and the adoption of new technology: Evidence from the U.S. telecommunications industry'. *Strategic Management Journal,* 19, pp. 1045–1062.

Mariani, M. M. and Visani, F. (2019). 'Embedding ewom into efficiency DEA modelling: An application to the hospitality sector'. *International Journal of Hospitality Management,* 80, pp. 1-12.

Martinez-Nunez, M. and Perez-Aguiar, W. S. (2014). 'Efficiency analysis of information technology and online social networks management: An integrated DEA-Model assessment'. *Information & Management,* 51, pp. 712-725.

Mccann, M. and Barlow, A. (2015). 'Use and measurement of social media for SMEs'. *Journal of Small Business and Enterprise Development,* 22, pp. 273-287.

Mousavi Kashi, Z., Hojaji, H. and Hassanzadeh, A. (2016). *Proceedings of Third International Conference on Accounting and Management with Applied Approaches and New Research,* Tehran, Iran.

Seydel, J. (2006). 'Data envelopment analysis for decision support'. *Industrial Management & Data Systems,* 106, pp. 81-95.

Oliveira, L. and Figueira, A. (2017), 'Improving the benchmarking of social media content strategies using clustering and KPI', *International Conference on Project Management*, *Procardia Computer Science*, 121, pp. 826–834.

Wang, Y. M. and Lan, Y. X. (2011). 'Measuring Malmquist productivity index: A new approach based on double frontiers data envelopment analysis'. *Mathematical and Computer Modelling,* 54, pp. 2760-2771.

Estimating the effects of contextual variables on Spanish banks efficiency

Jana Hanclova [1] , Lucie Chytilova [2] , Lorena Caridad [3]

Abstract. Evaluation of banks efficiency is an important research topic during past 40 years. There is a number of review articles. Currently, nonparametric methods as data envelopment analysis (DEA) or parametric method as stochastic boundary (SFA) are used to measure efficiency. This article examines the impact of the contextual variables into the production function of commercial banks with an application for 22 selected Spanish banks for time period 2014-2016. The efficiency assessment follows the methodological gap between DEA and SFA methods. The Convex Least Squares (CNLS) models are used in both additive and multiplicative forms with the possibility of introducing the contextual variables. The obtained results show the influence of contextual variables from the perspective of efficiency development, the number of effective banks, the number of production functions with constant yield from the range, and the influence of input factors on the production level (loans).

Keywords: convex nonparametric least squares, contextual variables, production efficiency, Spanish banks.

JEL classification: D24, G20, C14, C51

1 Introduction

Measuring and evaluating the bank's efficiency is an integral part of comparing banks' performance from a macroeconomic and microeconomic perspective. The main role of retail banks is to arrange financial services for private individuals as well as corporate clients, especially from the macroeconomic point of view of regulators or economic policy makers. Also, each commercial bank creates production plans and allocates economic resources to maximize profits under certain conditions and risk levels.

A number of researchers and practitioners are evaluating the efficiency of banks. The number of citations over the past 40 years has grown significantly, as summarized below. Technical efficiency is seen as a production capacity that does not allow waste. The given level of outputs is achieved by minimum costs of input (input-oriented approach) or vice versa. The basic methods for measuring the technical efficiency are non-parametric data envelopmnet analysis (DEA), which uses optimization models, and parametric analysis of stochastic frontier (SFA), using econometric prayer. The gap between axiomatic DEA and stochastic SFA is completed by the convex nonparametric least squares (CNLS) founded by Kuosmanen (2007), Kuosmanen and Johnson (2010) and Kuosmanen and Kortelainen (2012).

The paper Liu, Lu and Lu (2013) is a review article. It focuses on DEA methods and applications listed in the articles of the Web of Science (WOS) database. The banking industry is in

[1]VSB-Technical University of Ostrava, Faculty of Economics, Department of Systems Engineering, Sokolska tr. 2416/33, 702 00 Ostrava, Czech Republic, jana.hanclova@vsb.cz.

[2]VSB-Technical University of Ostrava, Faculty of Economics, Department of Systems Engineering, Sokolska tr. 2416/33, 702 00 Ostrava, Czech Republic, lucie.chytilova@vsb.cz.

[3]University of Cordoba, Faculty of Law and Business Sciences, Department of Statistics, Econometrics and Applied Economics, Plaza de Puerta Nueva, s/n, 14002 Crdoba, lorena.caridad@uco.es.

the top-five applications, as well as finance. The article also shows that the recent trends will be the use of two-step contextual analysis. Another review study, Lampe and Hilgers (2015), shows the increasing research in efficiency and performance measurement using bibliometric literature analysis, namely DEA and SFA using the WOS database during years 1978 - 2012. The results document that banking is also the most influential application area using co-citation analysis. DEA analysis in financial services are seen in Kaffash and Marra (2017). The authors examined 620 papers with the DEA application in financial services from 1985 to April 2016 from the WOS database. Citation analysis identified 3 groups of applications - banking groups, money market funds and insurance group. Research articles are dominated by innovation DEA methodology. A systematic review of bank performance literature analysis is documented by Bhatia, Basu, Mitra and et al. (2018). The key topic of the articles were the discussion of approaches to optimizing inputs and outputs and the ideal technique to measure the banks performance.

The aim of this paper is to compare the effect of introducing contextual variables in estimating Farrell output efficiency. The application is for 22 selected banks from Spain in 2014, 2015 and 2016. The additive and multiplicative convex nonparametric least squares models are used.

The second chapter deals with the methodological definition of CNLS models in additive and multiplicative forms and the introduction of contextual variables. The third chapter deals with the selection of input, output and contextual variables and data description. Subsequently, the effective frontier is estimated by four used models. The final chapter summarizes the results and presents the possibilities for further research.

2 Convex Least Squares Methods

Let's evaluate the efficiency of $i = 1, 2, , n$ production units (banks). Let's have $j = 1, 2, , m$ inputs for the $i-$th bank given by the vector $\mathbf{x}_i' = (x_{1i}, x_{2i}, ..., x_{mi})$ and one output y_i. For the deterministic form of production frontier f with one output y_i and multiple inputs can be formulated using the axiomatic approach by streaming function in additive form $y_i = f(\mathbf{x}_i) + \epsilon_i$ or multiplicative form $y_i = f(\mathbf{x}_i) \cdot \exp(\epsilon_i)$, where f is monotonic increasing and concave production function and ϵ_i is residual error.

Now we can formulate a DEA model as a sign-constrained Convex Nonparametric Least Squares model (Kuosmanen, 2007) in additive form, which we note **ACNLS model**:

$$\min_{\alpha,\beta,\epsilon} \left\{ \sum_{i=1}^{n} \epsilon_i^2 \left| \begin{array}{ll} y_i = \alpha_i + \beta_i' \mathbf{x}_i + \epsilon_i & \forall i = 1, 2, ..., n \\ \alpha_i + \beta_i' \mathbf{x}_i \leq \alpha_h + \beta_h' \mathbf{x}_i & \forall i, h = 1, 2, ..., n \text{ and } i \neq h \\ \beta_i \geq \mathbf{0} & \forall i = 1, 2, ..., n \\ \epsilon_i \leq 0 & \forall i = 1, 2, ..., n \end{array} \right. \right\}, \quad (1)$$

where α_i and vector β_i express the intercept and slope parameters of the tangent hyperplanes for i-th bank in point x_i. For $\alpha_i = 0 \; \forall \; i$ we can define constant return to scale (CRS). In equation (1) the condition CRS is not specified and therefore we will only deal with model with condition of variable return to scale (VRS). The model ACNLS contains a quadratic objective function and condition constrains are in form of linear equations and inequality. So this is a quadratic programming. The second constraints are Afriat inequalities (Afriat, 1972) and Kuosmanen

(2018) has defined this key condition for concavity modeling in the general multiple regression. The third condition imposes imposes monotonicity and the last condition is sign constrain for inefficiency. It should be noted that the inefficiency estimates ϵ_i are nonnegative with the value zero indicating efficient bank (Hanclova and Chytilova, 2017). The inefficiency measures can be converted to Farrell (1957) output efficiency scores $EF\_ACNLS_i = \frac{y_i}{\hat{y}_i}$, where $\hat{y}_i = y_i + \epsilon_i$.

To eliminate the heteroskedasticity caused by the size of the bank, it is advisable to use the CNLS model in multiplicative form, which corresponds to the classic Cobb-Douglas or translog production function. Applying the log-transfomation we can define **MCNLS model** (sign-constrained CNLS multiplicative model) using equation (2):

$$\min_{\alpha,\beta,\phi,\epsilon} \left\{ \sum_{i=1}^{n} \epsilon_i^2 \left| \begin{array}{ll} \ln y_i = \ln(\phi_i + 1) + \epsilon_i & \forall i = 1,2,...,n \\ (\phi_i + 1) = \alpha_i + \beta_{\mathbf{i}}'\mathbf{x_i} + \epsilon_i & \forall i = 1,2,...,n \\ \alpha_i + \beta_{\mathbf{i}}'\mathbf{x_i} \leq \alpha_h + \beta_{\mathbf{h}}'\mathbf{x_i} & \forall i,h = 1,2,...,n \text{ and } i \neq h \\ \beta_{\mathbf{i}} \geq \mathbf{0} & \forall i = 1,2,...,n \\ \epsilon_i \leq 0 & \forall i = 1,2,...,n \end{array} \right. \right\} \tag{2}$$

The first condition is the log-linear transformation regression equation, $(\phi_i + 1)$ is definition, the third condition is convexity constraint using Afriat inequalities, the forth condition imposes monotonicity and last is sign constrain for inefficiency. The Farrell output efficiency score is $EF\_MCNLS_i = \exp(\epsilon_i)$.

ACNLS and MCNLS models can be extended with contextual variables. These variables may monitor not only the best practice, but also different operational conditions when evaluating production efficiency. The formerly used two-stage DEA (2-DEA) method (Ray, 1988) came from the first stage, where the technical efficiency coefficients were estimated, and in the second stage these scores were regressed on contextual variables. Johnson and Kuosmanen (2012) confirmed that the finite sample of 2-DEA in the first stage is transmitted to the second stage and also causes bias to estimate the coefficients of contextual variables, especially when contextual variables are correlated with inputs. Thus, the authors proposed a one-stage DEA (1-DEA) method that estimates efficiency in a jointly model with contextual variables. This 1-DEA approach will be used in an additive and mutually exclusive form for assessing the technical efficiency of banks under the input-oriented and VRS model conditions.

Model ACNLSZ is noted as ACNLS model with contextual variables:

$$\min_{\alpha,\beta,\delta,\epsilon} \left\{ \sum_{i=1}^{n} \epsilon_i^2 \left| \begin{array}{ll} y_i = \alpha_i + \beta_{\mathbf{i}}'\mathbf{x_i} + \delta'\mathbf{z_i} + \epsilon_i & \forall i = 1,2,...,n \\ \alpha_i + \beta_{\mathbf{i}}'\mathbf{x_i} \leq \alpha_h + \beta_{\mathbf{h}}'\mathbf{x_i} & \forall i,h = 1,2,...,n \text{ and } i \neq h \\ \beta_{\mathbf{i}} \geq \mathbf{0} & \forall i = 1,2,...,n \\ \epsilon_i \leq 0 & \forall i = 1,2,...,n \end{array} \right. \right\} \tag{3}$$

where δ is vector of coefficients of the contextual variables z_i. Technical efficiency of 1-DEA model under VRS condition is define as $EF\_ACNLSZ_i = \frac{y_i}{\alpha_i + \beta_{\mathbf{i}}'\mathbf{x_i} + \delta'\mathbf{z_i}}$.

Model MCNLSZ also introduces the contextual variable into multiplicative form of production function (2):

$$\min_{\alpha,\beta,\phi,\epsilon,\delta} \left\{ \sum_{i=1}^{n} \epsilon_i^2 \left| \begin{array}{ll} \ln y_i = \ln(\phi_i + 1) + \delta' \mathbf{z_i} + \epsilon_i & \forall i = 1, 2, ..., n \\ (\phi_i + 1) = \alpha_i + \beta_i' \mathbf{x_i} + \epsilon_i & \forall i = 1, 2, ..., n \\ \alpha_i + \beta_i' \mathbf{x_i} \leq \alpha_h + \beta_h' \mathbf{x_i} & \forall i, h = 1, 2, ..., n \text{ and } i \neq h \\ \beta_\mathbf{i} \geq \mathbf{0} & \forall i = 1, 2, ..., n \\ \epsilon_i \leq 0 & \forall i = 1, 2, ..., n \end{array} \right. \right\} \quad (4)$$

Bank's efficiency is measured by the relationship $EF\_MCNLSZ_i = \exp(\epsilon_i)$.

3 Data and application

The examination of the impact of contextual variables on efficiency evaluation will be applied to 22 selected Spanish domestic and foreign banks in the years 2014, 2015 and 2016.

The original **data** are from Bloomberg and included 37 banks. Some banks were excluded because of missing values. The list of 22 selected are available on request.

There are many ways to select variables. This article is based on method for commercial banks based on surveys by Berger and Humphrey (1997) or Paradi and Zhu (2013). We use the intermediation approach defined by Hancock (1991). The commercial banks perform financial intermediary transformations of deposits (inputs) into loans (outputs). There are other applications, for example Melecky and Stanickova (2017) used the cost efficiency.

There are two input variables - x_1 (number of employees), x_2 (total deposits in millions of EUR). One output variable is y (total deposits in millions of EUR). Contextual variables were divided into 3 groups: *capital strength* - z_1 (total equity / total assets), *operations ratios and bank's profitability* - z_2 (net interest margin), z_3 (return on assets) and *liquidity ratios* as loans risk ratios - z_4 (liquid assets / (total deposits + borrowings & repos). The size of the bank is represented by the variable z_6 , which were set as the quartile of the total asset (1 = small bank (Q1),, 4 = large banks for Q4). Descriptive statistics of all variables is in Table 1 for each year.

year		x_1	x_2	y	z_1	z_2	z_3	z_4	z_5
2014	Mean	70382	296292	315604	0.061	1.456	0.333	0.476	0.415
	SD	71936	278863	252138	0.018	0.637	0.232	0.162	0.183
2015	Mean	72067	324918	337321	0.064	1.523	0.418	0.499	0.463
	SD	74043	301391	269875	0.019	0.564	0.241	0.160	0.290
2016	Mean	70423	321232	325267	0.065	1.504	0.315	0.499	0.499
	SD	70672	297921	255638	0.018	0.544	0.617	0.159	0.251

Table 1 Descriptive statistics of input and output variables

Bank's efficiency estimation for additive models

The results of additive models ACNLS and ACNLSZ are presented in Figure 1 and Table 2. The mean of technical bank's efficiency model without contextual variables ACNLS decreases from 0.812 in 2014 to 0.790 in 2016. Also, the classic standard deviation (SD) decreases from 0.235 to 0.212. It is evident that the inclusion of contextual variables in the additive model ACNLSZ brings a higher level of efficiency to banks, which from 0.986 in 2014 declines to 0.962 in 2016.

The analysis of the estimated parameters α_1, β_1 and β_2 in the ACNLS model confirms that the majority of production functions have declining range returns except for two Spanish Bankiter banks in all years and at Liberbank in 2015-6.

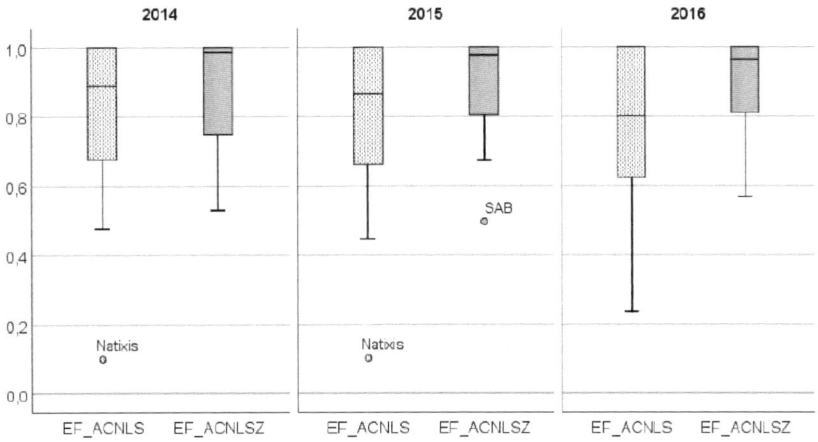

Figure 1 Distribution of efficient bank for additive models in 2014-2016

		year 2014			year 2015			year 2016	
model	**Mean**	**Median**	**SD**	**Mean**	**Median**	**SD**	**Mean**	**Median**	**SD**
EF_ACNLS	0.812	0.886	0.235	0.799	0.865	0.236	0.790	0.799	0.212
EF_ACNLSZ	0.830	0.902	0.194	0.847	0.917	0.177	0.882	0.915	0.123

Table 2 Descriptive statistics for efficient bank and additive models

Bank's efficiency estimation for additive models

The results of multiplicative models MCNLS and MCNLSZ are shown in Figure 2 and Table 3. Mean bank's efficiency model without contextual variables MCNLS decreases from 0.812 to 0.790 in 2016 with a slightly decreasing SD as well as additive model. However, for a contextual variable model, the average efficiency of banks in years rises from 0.830 to 0.915, with a decreasing average SD of 0.194 to 0.123. It is also true that the average bank efficiency is higher for the multiplicative model with contextual variables. These variables contribute to the explanation of bank's efficiency.

The analysis of the estimated parameters α_1, β_1 and β_2 in the MCNLS model confirms that the majority of production functions have declining range revenues except for two Spanish Bankiter banks in all years and at Liberbank in 2016.

		year 2014			year 2015			year 2016	
model	**Mean**	**Median**	**SD**	**Mean**	**Median**	**SD**	**Mean**	**Median**	**SD**
EF_ACNLS	0.812	0.887	0.235	0.799	0.865	0.236	0.790	0.800	0.212
EF_ACNLSZ	0.878	0.984	0.160	0.895	0.976	0.142	0.889	0.962	0.140

Table 3 Descriptive statistics for efficient bank and multiplicative models

4 Conclusions

The presented paper dealt with the influence of contextual variables on the development of efficiency banks in time period from 2014 to 2016 for 22 selected local and foreign commercial

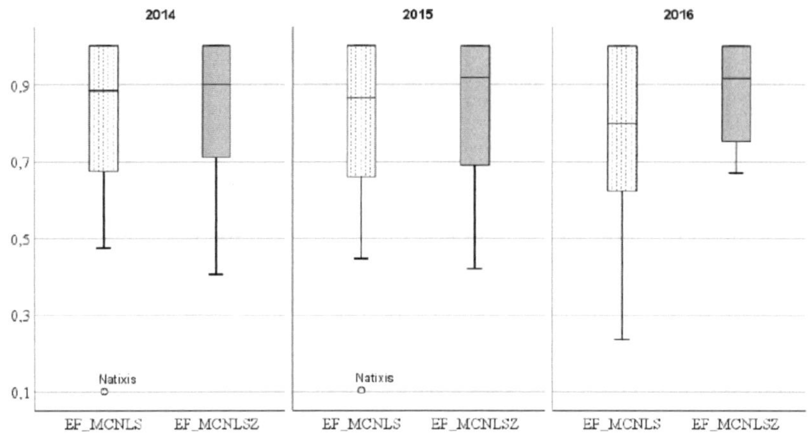

Figure 2 Distribution of efficient bank for multiplicative models in 2014-2016

banks operating in Spain. The obtained results confirm that:

- the average efficiency of the investigated banks in both additive and multiplicative models decreases in 2014 - 2016 when contextual variables are not included. Models with contextual variables have growing trend. In both cases, the standard deviation decreases.
- the number of efficient banks for both additive and multiplicative models without contextual variables decreases in 2014-2016. The number of efficient banks for additive models with contextual variables also decreases, but in multiplicative form there is an increase and a subsequent decline.
- the additive model ACNLS has consistently 5 effective banks throughout the period - DNB, HSBA, ING, Mediobanca, Nordea bank. The last two banks are also efficient for both versions of the multiplier model in 2014-2016. In general, it may be said that models involving contextual variables have less stable efficient banks in 2014-2016. This is due, among other things, to the possibility of including the heterogeneity of these banks.
- the least efficient banks have models without contextual variables in both additive and multiplicative forms - Natixis, Spanish Liberbank and UBS.
- the introduction of contextual variables causes a different evaluation of the least efficient banks. Investigating the revenues from the range of bank production functions shows that the number of banks with declining revenues is increasing when contextual variables are introduced.
- the analysis of the influence of the number of workers on the variability of the production function in 2014-2016 showed that for the multiplicative models without and with contextual variables, the average influence of the input factor of labor on the production of banks increases over time. When investigating the effect of the second input factor - deposit, it was not possible to identify unambiguously increasing or decreasing tendencies except for the multiplicative contextual model model, where the average elasticity of production relative to this factor increased. A positive effect on the increase in production was recorded for contextual variables, return on assets, loans risk ratios and negative effects on net interest margin.

Further research can be focused on adequately eliminating missing data values, expanding the number of banks and adding additional time series, examining the right choice of contextual variables, expanding panel data models.

Acknowledgements

This article was supported by European Social Fund within the project CZ.1.07/2.3.00/20.0296 and also through the Czech Science Foundation GACR 19-13946S.

References

Afriat, S. N. (1972). 'Efficiency estimation of production functions'. *International Economic Review*, 13 (3), pp. 568-598.

Berger, A. N. and Humphrey, D. B. (1997). 'Efficiency of financial institutions: international survey and directions for future research'. *European Journal of Operational Research*, 98 (2), pp. 175-212.

Bhatia, V., Basu, S., Miltra S. K. et al. (2018). 'A review of bank efficiency and productivity'. *OPSEARCH*, 55 (3-4), pp. 557-600.

Farrell, M. J. (1957). 'The measurement of productive efficiency'. *Journal of the Royal Statistical Society Series A-General*, 120 (3), pp. 253-290.

Hanclova, J. and Chytilova, L. (2017). 'An application of convex nonparametric least squares to esti-mation banks (in)efficiency in the Visegrad countries'. *Proceedings of 12th International Conference SMSIS*. Ostrava, Czech Republic, VB TU of Ostrava, 2017, pp. 231-238.

Hancock, D. (1991). *A theory of production for the financial firm*. NY: Springer Science.

Johnson, A. L. and Kuosmanen, T. (2012). 'One-stage and two-stage DEA estimation of the effects of contextual variables'. *EJOR*, 220 (2012), pp. 559-570.

Kaffash, S. and Marra, M. (2017). 'Data envelopment analysis in financial services: a citations network analysis of banks, insurance companies and money market funds'. *Annals of Operations Research*, 253 (1), pp. 307-344.

Kuosmanen, T. (2008). 'Representation theorem for convex nonparametric least squares'. *Econometric Journal*, 11 (3), pp. 308-325.

Kuosmanen, T. and Johnson, A. L. (2010). 'Data envelopment analysis as nonparametric least-squares regression'. *Operations Research*, 58 (1), pp. 149-160.

Kuosmanen, T. and Kortelainen, M. (2012). 'Stochastic non-smooth envelopment of data: Semi-para-metric frontier estimation subject to shape constraints'. *Journal of Productivity Analysis*, 38 (1), pp. 11-28.

Lampe, H. W. and Hilgers, D. (2015). 'Trajectories of efficiency measurement: A bibliometric analysis of DEA and SFA'. *European Journal of Operational Research*, 240 (1), pp. 1-21.

Melecky, L. and Stanickova, M. (2017). 'Cost Efficiency of EU Funded Projects: Case of Selected SMEs in the Moravian-Silesian Region'. *Proceedings of 12th International Conference SMSIS*. Ostrava, Czech Republic, VB TU of Ostrava, pp. 293-302.

Paradi, J. C. and Zhu, J. (2013). 'A survey on bank branch efficiency and performance research with data envelopment analysis'. *Omega*, 41(3), pp. 61-79.

Ray, S. C. (1988). 'Data envelopment analysis, nondiscretionary inputs and efficiency: an alternative interpretation'. *Socio-Economic Planning Sciences*, 22 (4), pp. 167-176.

Spatial Component in Regression Modelling of Unemployment in Czechia

Jiří Horák[1], Lucie Orlíková[2]

Abstract. Unemployment is influenced by many factors. Some of them vary geographically in intensity or form of relationship. Spatial regression modelling enables integration of spatial factors (spatial autocorrelation as well as spatial heterogeneity). The model tested 13 social and economic indicators influencing unemployment rate in Czech municipalities. The spatial error model improves adjusted R^2 by 0.2 compared with OLS. GWR with 15 km bandwidth reaches R2 0.5 (increasing by 0.1). The GWR model improves understanding of local differences in elasticity of the labour market and highlights divergent local behaviour of selected factors. Spatial regression modelling brings new ideas for interpretation despite the usual issues with local multicollinearity and insufficient explanation of variability.

Keywords: unemployment; municipality; SAR; GWR.

JEL Classification: J23, C31

1 Introduction

Unemployment is a variable phenomenon influenced by many well-known global factors (i.e. Niebuhr 2003, Hančlová et al. 2012, Johnson et al. 2017, Demidova et al. 2018). The labour market may also be affected by local factors (Simionescu, 2015), which may worsen or improve the situation. The main local changes are usually not driven by specific local additional factors but are given by changes in the intensity of global factors' influences, or in the form of influence. Some of the changes may be real and some may only reflect the changes of the data carrier which is known as a modified area unit problem (MAUP) (Openshaw, 1984). For an extreme manifestation of these influences we can discuss the Simpson paradox where the relationship at the local level is inversed to those at the regional level (when the partial relationships are stronger than the basic relationship) (Spurná, 2008). We can also anticipate that these changes will not appear suddenly, but usually with some level of spatial continuity where neighbouring localities share similar conditions. Among various approaches to explore these factors, spatial regression modelling offers appropriate tools.

The following examples document several spatial econometric studies aiming to explain the level of unemployment by a set of spatially related determinants (explanatory variables). Simple regression models with logistic function were originally applied to the labour market where the inclusion of the spatial factor was done by substituting the constant parameter for linear variables as follows a=a1+a2d where d refers a distance (Nijkamp, Rietveld, 1987). Fieldhouse and Tranmer (2001) proved the relative importance of the neighbourhood and the local labour market in explaining variations in unemployment risk. The relationship between spatial distribution and unemployment rate (UR) has been studied in the context of performance indicators by Patuelli (2007) and Cracolici, Cuffaro and Nijkamp (2007). Spatial correlations re-

[1] VSB-TU Ostrava, dep. of geoinformatics, 17.listopadu 2172/15, jiri.horak@vsb.cz.
[2] VSB-TU Ostrava, dep. of geoinformatics, 17.listopadu 2172/15, lucie.orlikova@vsb.cz.

lated to the labour market were analyzed for Germany's regions by Niebuhr (2003), Elhorst (2010) and Longhi, Nijkamp (2007). Patuelli et al. (2011) used a semi-parametric approach to eliminate the spatial patterns observed in the UR of German regions. Spatial filtering and a spatial vector autoregressive model for unemployment rate forecasts in Spain and Switzerland were applied by Patuelli and Mayor (2012). The spatial autoregressive model (SAR), including random effects, was utilized to forecast the UR in 42 counties in Romania and to improve a national UR prediction by Simionescu (2015). Deller (2011) found a significant spatial heterogeneity in the unemployment elasticity of pay for US counties using geographically weighted regression (GWR). In Poland, Muller-Frazek and Pietrzak (2011) applied SAR with a linear spatial trend and found two important exogenous variables: investments and economic entities. Later Pietrzak, and Balcerzak (2016) utilized a spatial SAR model for NUTS3 level and confirmed the positive impact of entrepreneurship and investments. Lewandowska-Gwarda (2018a, 2018b) preferred a GWR model for LAU1 (Local Administrative Units ranked below regions, i.e. districts) and discovered that determinants of unemployment are diverse in the geographic space and do not have a significant impact on UR in all spatial units.

The successful implementation of spatial regression modelling is not confined only to the labour market. In many economical as well as sociological studies the UR plays the role of an explanatory variable in spatial regression modelling. LeSage (1998) proved the better performance of spatial regression modelling for crime estimation using income and dwelling assessment. Kouba (2007) explored spatial differences in voting preferences in the Czech elections using GWR. Spurná (2008) proved the strong variability of the relationship between flat cost and density of population in the surroundings. Weisent et al. (2012) applied GWR to identify socioeconomic determinants of the geographic disparities of campylobacteriosis risk and to investigate related associations with socioeconomic factors including unemployment on a municipal level. Yildirim and Ocal (2013) found significant differences in the provincial effects of per capita income, unemployment and education to reduce the average provincial level of terrorism using GWR. Benassi and Naccarato (2018) studied a foreign population in Italy using GWR for the NUTS3 level and confirmed that the dependent variable is significantly affected by the provincial variability of the unemployment rate of Italians. Similarly, Jivraj et al. (2013) used GWR to model family out-migration from neighborhoods in England and the influence of worklessness. Ma and Gopal (2018) used the standard GWR and Mixed GWR (MGWR incorporates both classic linear regression and the GWR where global parameters are modelled with a constant while local parameters by GWR) models to analyze the effects of spatial non-stationarity to assess the significance of key spatial determinants of median home price in towns in Massachusetts.

The aim of this paper is to demonstrate a contribution of spatial regression methods in exploring unemployment determinants on a municipal level, and to evaluate the role of the spatial component in such regression analysis.

2 Methodology and data

2.1 Spatial regression

Spatial regression methods extend the classic regression models by taking into account the spatial structure of data, in particular the lack of independence that typically exists between measurements made at nearby locations. Different spatial regression models exist. Usually two different approaches in spatial regression analysis are applied; spatial dependency is solved on the global level using an explicit form of spatial autocorrelation (i.e. SAR), and on the local level by enabling spatially variable model parameters (i.e. GWR). SAR directly evaluates a spatial component (typically as an independent variable) and includes into the model's design. The theory and detailed discussion about spatial regression models may be found in Cressie (1993), Bailey and Gatrell (1995), Anselin (1988), LeSage, 1998, Anselin and Bera (1998), Anselin (2002) and Haining (2003). Although the pure spatial autoregressive model (SAR) means autoregression of a dependent variable (LeSage, 1998), other authors emphasize common autoregressive features in other models including a spatial error model (Smith et al., 2018). Links between models are explained, and the unified concept of global spatial dependence models is introduced by Elhorst (2010). The Manski model is the most complex model including endogenous interaction effects among the dependent variables, exogenous interaction effects among the independent variables, and the interaction effects among the disturbance terms of the different spatial units. The Kelejian-Prucha model eliminates the spatial dependency of interaction among independent variables. The Spatial Durban model deals with spatial influence of independent and dependent variables, but no spatial autocorrelation of errors is included. The Spatial Durban Error model integrates influences of spatial autocorrelation of independent variables and spatial autocorrelation of errors. The most simple and most often utilized are spatial lag and spatial error models. The spatial lag model (or mixed regressive spatial autoregressive model according to Smith et al., 2018) contains components of a standard regression model $\mathbf{X}\beta$ (where $\mathbf{X}$ is a vector of independent variables and β regression coefficients) and a spatially lagged version of the dependent variable y (eq. 1) with a vector of spatial autoregression parameters ρ, weight matrix W (see later) and an error vector $\boldsymbol{\varepsilon}$.

$$y = \mathbf{X}\beta + \rho \mathrm{W} y + \varepsilon \tag{1}$$

The spatial error model (SEM) is defined by eq. 2 with spatial autoregressive parameters λ for errors and a vector of unit errors (Smith et al., 2018). The spatial autocorrelation does not enter as an additional variable in the model, but instead affects the covariance structure of random disturbance terms (Anselin, 2006).

$$y = \mathbf{X}\beta + \varepsilon\,, \qquad where\ \varepsilon = \lambda \mathrm{W}\varepsilon + u \tag{2}$$

The spatial error model is applied when there appears to be significant spatial autocorrelation, but tests for spatial lag effects do not suggest that inclusion of the latter would provide a significant improvement. Simionescu (2015) explains that a spatial lag model is better in the case of insignificant unobserved variables while a spatial error model is applied if the unobserved variables have a relevant effect. Nevertheless, all such models are criticized for their one-size-fits-all approach (Weisent et al., 2012).

GWR was introduced by Brundson et al. (1996) for regression models in which the coefficients β are allowed to vary spatially. The coefficients $\beta(t)$ are evaluated at each target point (i.e. polygon centroid) using a spatially weighted least squares regression (Smith et al., 2018) for a set of points within radius r. Instead of using a fixed value for r, it is replaced by a distance-decay function, $f(d)$ (i.e. Gaussian, bi-square, tri-cube). Optimization of the result is reached with a modification of bandwidth. Among various methods for optimization, a minimization of the Akaike Information Criterion (AIC) is usually applied (Weisent et al., 2012; Ma, Gopal 2018). The result is a model of the form (Smith et al., 2018):

$$y = \mathbf{X}\beta(t) + \varepsilon \tag{3}$$

To verify spatial influence and contribution of spatial factors, the OLS linear regression model is usually used as a benchmark. It enables evaluation of the overall performance of the model to indicate the spatial influence (heteroscedascity, non-stationarity, spatial autocorrelation of residuals etc.) and to discover explanatory variables with global multicollinearity or information redundancy. To evaluate the global multicollinearity, a variance inflation factor VIF is usually used. Many authors apply some limits to the VIF to eliminate serious multicollinearity (i.e. quite often 10, but 7.5 according to Ma, Gopal (2018), and 5 according to Akinwande et al. (2015)). But multicollinearity is as such critical an issue as these authors describe. As explained by O'Brien (2007) VIF cannot be interpreted in isolation and has to be understood within the context. There are other factors (besides multicollinearity) that affect the stability of regression coefficients including the sample size, the proportion of the variance in the dependent variable associated with the independent variables and the variance of the independent variable. Such factors can ameliorate or exacerbate the effects of multicollinearity.

All of these models contain W as a spatial weighting matrix; it gives weights for all combinations of spatial units. Obviously, the weights for nearby locations are higher. Usually some a simple scheme is used (i.e. all topological neighbours obtain 1 otherwise 0; queen or rook cases). Nevertheless, such a simple scheme has significant weaknesses in the interpretation of the spatial structure with especially worse behaviour in irregular lattices (polygonal scheme like municipalities) (Wall, 2004). This is why we have tested several possibilities - different numbers of neighbourhoods and bandwidths (maximal distance) for GWR and SAR, and queen neighbourhoods of the 1st and 2nd order for SAR. We have optimized the spatial scheme of weights, and the bandwidth setting respectively. Finally, the bandwidth of 15 km was selected.

SAR and GWR models were modelled in GeoDa v. 1.8 and ArcGIS 10.4 software, and statistical processing was performed in IBM Statistics SPSS v.25.

2.2 Data

To evaluate the role of the spatial component in the regression analysis of unemployment, we have selected data from census 2011 to have the most complete list of potential determinants which may influence unemployment. To evaluate unemployment, the UR from the Labour Office data was selected for the closest day (end of March 2011). Despite many other analyses using large spatial units (NUTS2, NUTS3, LAU1), we decided to use the municipal level to reach a profound understanding of spatial trends and relationships. Obviously, such models demonstrate many more issues due to a higher variability of values and quite different sizes of municipalities.

Explanatory (independent) variables cover both social and economic indicators. The social variables express demographic factors directly influencing local unemployment (i.e. the share of older people usually staying out of the labour market), factors related to expectations about increasing personal value on the labour market (i.e. education) and factors linked with social status (mainly approximated by housing conditions). The economic variables are expressed by the number of occupied and currently unoccupied positions and by the share of people commuting to work. The entire list contains: the share of population aged 65 and more (Age6500), the share of people with primary and lower education (EduLow), the share of people with tertiary education (EduUniv), the share of the religious people (Relig), the share of foreigners (FOREIGN), the share of people born in the same municipality (NATIVE), the share of undesired cohabitation meaning two and more households in one flat (TooHousH), the share of occupied flats in residential houses with decreased quality (PoorFlat), the share of households in flats with 5 and more persons (LargeFam), the share of people commuting to work daily (Commute), share of people commuting to work not daily (commuteD), the number of occupied positions (ratios to 1000 inhabitants) (EMPLO) and currently unoccupied positions (ratios to 1000 inhabitants) (VACANT).

Variables	Mean	Median	Variance	Skewness	Kurtosis
AGE6500	15.928	15.483	19.110	1.311	5.491
EDULOW	18.559	17.939	25.237	1.064	3.657
EDUUNIV	6.242	5.723	10.942	1.382	3.745
RELIG	17.381	13.650	162.896	1.268	1.391
FOREIGN	0.382	0.112	1.406	20.295	663.602
NATIVE	43.967	44.161	96.942	-0.169	0.187
POORFLAT	6.231	5.682	11.576	1.403	4.206
LARGEFAM	8.889	8.356	15.479	1.117	3.053
COMMUTED	34.599	32.864	210.212	1.167	3.007
EMPLO	196.067	134.450	74024	8.936	134.427
VACANT	1.991	0.000	66.585	16.850	450.973

Table 1 Summary statistics of all explanatory variables

First of all, an ESDA for all variables was performed to check the statistical (tab. 1) and spatial distribution of values (fig.1), especially statistical variability of values and spatial clustering using LISA. If the variable demonstrates spatial clustering of close values (concentration of high values or low values), it is recommended to remove this variable from the model (Smith et al. 2018). Extreme skewness and kurtosis occur for FOREIGN, EMPLOY and VA-

CANT (tab.1). The next important step is to check the correlation of all explanatory variables. Wheeler, Tiefelsdorf (2005) provide thorough explanation of influence of such correlation in GWR where moderate to strong correlation of two explanatory variables makes their associated local parameters almost completely interdependent. Smith et al. (2018) recommend eliminating variables with correlation higher than 0.8, but Weisent et al. (2012) applied the limit of 0.6. Pairwise correlations between independent variables were calculated and checked. The only pair, COMMUTE and COMMUTED, exhibits a high correlation of 0.985. To remove this dependency we designed a new independent variable "non-daily commuting to work" (COMMUTEND).

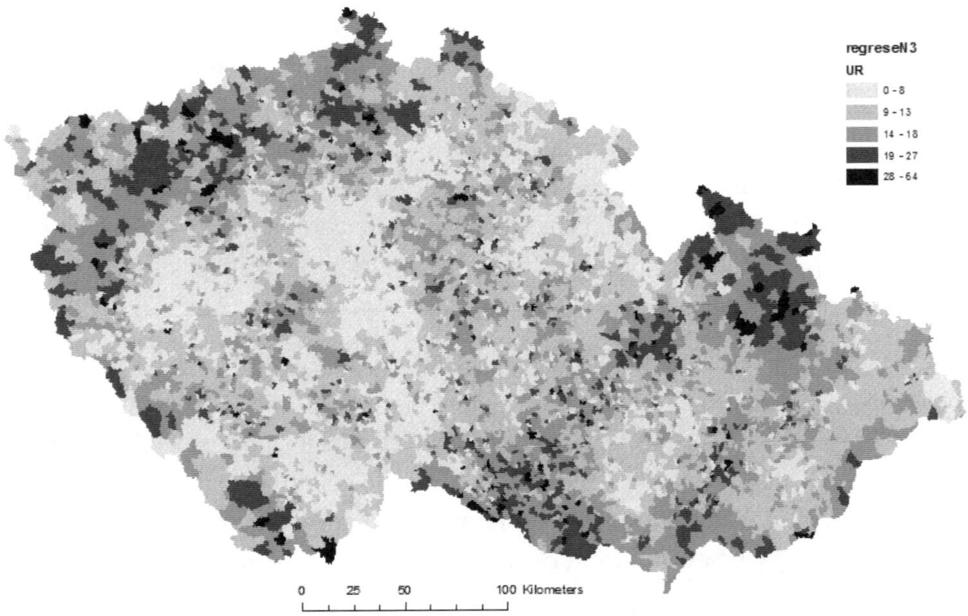

Figure 1 Unemployment rate in Czech municipalities (31.3.2011)

3 Results and discussion

3.1 OLS modelling results

The OLS model was built iteratively according to the significance of variables. Two variables were excluded due to their low significance - TOOHOUSH (p=0.167) and COMMUTEND (*p*=0.143).

Variables	Coefficient	Std. error	*t*-stat	*p*	Robust_t	Robust_P	VIF
Intercept	13.058520	0.669	19.53	0.000*	15.1	0.000*	----
AGE6500	-0.215940	0.016	-13.32	0.000*	-9.9	0.000*	1.27
EDULOW	0.328725	0.016	20.20	0.000*	13.6	0.000*	1.69
EDUUNIV	-0.152825	0.025	-6.18	0.000*	-5.5	0.000*	1.69
RELIG	0.057473	0.007	7.89	0.000*	6.9	0.000*	2.18
FOREIGN	-0.107717	0.054	-1.98	0.048*	-2.7	0.006*	1.04

NATIVE	-0.099488	0.009	-10.68	0.000*	-8.6	0.000*	2.11
POORFLAT	0.234455	0.019	12.04	0.000*	8.7	0.000*	1.10
LARGEFAM	0.106314	0.019	5.58	0.000*	4.2	0.000*	1.42
COMMUTED	-0.042991	0.005	-8.43	0.000*	-7.1	0.000*	1.39
EMPLO	-0.001496	0.000	-5.87	0.000*	-3.5	0.000*	1.21
VACANT	-0.019269	0.008	-2.35	0.019*	-2.3	0.018*	1.13

Table 2 Explanatory variables in the OLS model

The influences of explanatory variables (table 1) correspond to expectations. UR is positively influenced mainly by low education, but also by bad living conditions (POORFLAT), and social conditions (large families). It is negatively influenced by tertiary education, and by the share of older people. Surprisingly, a relatively low influence from job opportunities (number of positions and vacant positions) was observed. According to the Joint Wald Statistic (1094.7 $p<0.001$), the model is significant, however, it explains only part of the variability (adjusted R^2 is only 0.22). Akaike's Information Criterion (AICc) is 38490. All VIF values are sufficiently low and indicate no problems of global multicollinearity and no redundant information from explanatory variables.

Nevertheless, the model is not satisfactory. The multicollinearity is not fully reduced (a condition number CN=35), the errors are not normally distributed (Jarque-Bera Statistic is 5077, $p<0.001$), and the model suffers from heteroscedasticity (Breusch-Pagan test is 1573, DF=10, $p<0.001$; Koenker-Bassett test is 528.7, DF=10, $p<0.001$). The result of the Koenker (BP) Statistic is statistically significant (458.9, $p<0.001$) and it means the modelled relationships are not consistent (either due to non-stationarity or heteroscedasticity). Results also indicate an occurrence of the spatial autocorrelation of the residuals.

According to the results of OLS, only the reduced set of explanatory variables is used in SAR and GWR models to assure elimination of the global multicollinearity.

3.2 SAR modelling results

The SAR model is iteratively developed from the set of variables selected according to the OLS results and to the testing of different spatial neighbourhood scheme. The diagnostics for spatial dependence for the given weight matrix (Euclidean distances below 15 km) were calculated in GeoDa. Values for the Lagrange Multiplier are higher for the spatial error model SEM (5432, $p<0.001$) than for the spatial lag model SLM (4158.9, $p<0.001$) and we found similar behaviour for Robust LM values (1704.4, $p<0.001$ for SEM while 431.1, $p<0.001$ for SLM). Thus, we decided to create a spatial regression model based on SEM.

During the iterative optimization of SEM variables FOREIGN, COMMUTED and VACANT were excluded due to their low significance (p=0.232, p=0.289, and p=0.358 respectively).

The final model provides AIC 37073, Schwarz criterion 37133.8 and R^2=0.396. We can see the AICc is decreased by 1300 units and R^2 is higher by 0.2 which documents substantial improvement of the model due to the spatial factor. The parameters for the variables are in table 3. In this model the role of POORFLAT is higher than EDULOW. The influence of variables is similar to the OLS model except for RELIG (but the impact is small due to low values). The important role of the spatial autocorrelation factor λ can be seen from its coefficient, 0.9 (table 3), which is 4 times higher than the coefficient for the next independent variable (POORFLAT). This means the UR value is driven mainly by the autocorrelation of errors (indicating an existence of unknown explanatory variables).

The spatial error dependence is significant (Likelihood Ratio Test is 1487.7, $p<0.001$). Nevertheless, the model is again not satisfactory because it indicates problems of heteroscedasticity (Breusch-Pagan test is 1853, $p<0.001$). The errors of predictions have very low spatial autocorrelation (Moran's I = -0.0058 and several small isolated clusters are evenly distributed). The residuals (fig. 2) are quite high, especially in the eastern part of Czechia.

Variables	Coefficient	Std. error	*z*-value	Probability
CONSTANT	13.964	0.7925	17.61931	0.00000
AGE6500	-0.128	0.0157	-8.178051	0.00000
EDULOW	0.207	0.0154	13.4538	0.00000
EDUUNIV	-0.120	0.0238	-5.051099	0.00000
RELIG	-0.030	0.0088	-3.42988	0.00060
NATIVE	-0.097	0.0087	-11.14488	0.00000
POORFLAT	0.229	0.0176	12.99703	0.00000
LARGEFAM	0.088	0.0171	5.155249	0.00000
EMPLO	-0.0014	0.0002	-6.751055	0.00000
LAMBDA	0.8969	0.0156	57.60186	0.00000

Table 3 Explanatory variables in the spatial error model

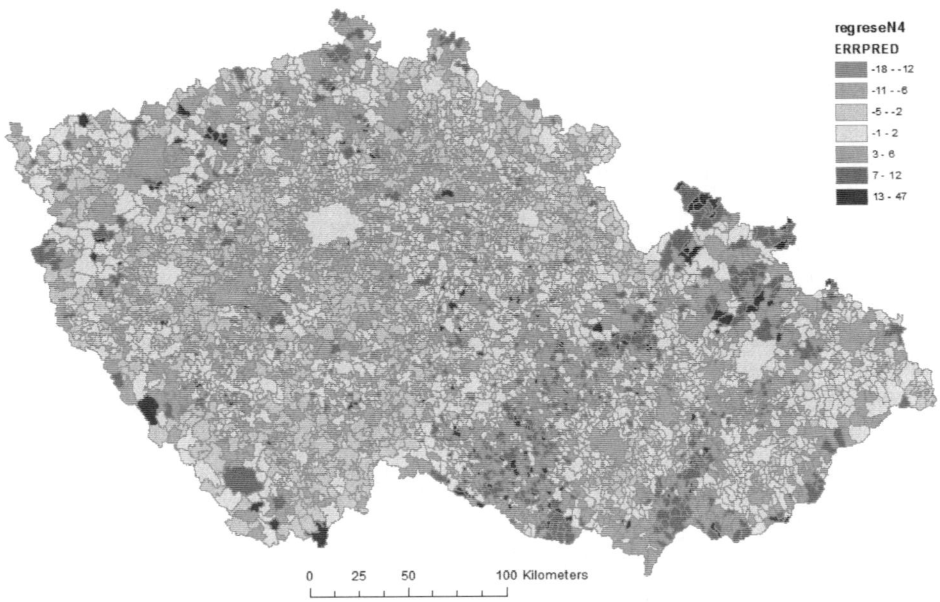

Figure 2 Prediction errors in the spatial error model

The SEM approach proves the importance of a spatial factor in improving models; nevertheless, the result is not fully satisfactory.

3.3 GWR modelling results

The results of the GWR modelling (table 4) show the continually decreasing AICc with larger bandwidth. The results for bandwidths above 15 km show an unusual drop of AICc values and negative adjusted R^2 which indicates a failed model (the model does not correspond to the linear trend, Motulsky, 2014). After exclusion of the (RELIG) variable, the models provide more reliable results and indicate a substantial increase of AICc and decrease of adjusted R^2. Nevertheless, the spatial structures revealed by GWR modelling with different bandwidths are similar (obviously with different levels of smoothing) which proves the occurrence of spatial heterogeneity and the real existence of discovered relationships. In all tested cases we did not obtain a fully satisfactory model with appropriate statistics. Models indicate problems with a local multicollinearity (high CN) and normality of residuals. The main reason could be a low carrier of the data (municipality); this means we explore small numbers which are quite variable and highly influenced by random effects. The second reason is that some other important explanatory variables are missing in the model.

No	Model	BW [km]	*Y*	X_i	AICc	Adj R^2	RS
1	OLS		UR	all	38490	0.22	
2	GWR	10	UR	all	298	0.41	679
3	GWR	13	UR	all	243	0.43	723
4	GWR	15	UR	all	226	0.50	829
5	GWR	17	UR	all	146	-0.21	447
6	GWR	17	UR	Without RELIG	630	0.40	2476
7	GWR	20	UR	all	-6.1	-0.51	8
8	GWR	20	UR	Without RELIG	1025	0.37	4420

Table 4 Parameters of different models in the optimization process

Notes: All=AGE6500, EDULOW, EDUUNIV, RELIG, FOREIGN, NATIVE, POORFLAT, LARGEFAM, COMMUTED, EMPLO, VACANT; RS - ResidualSquares, BW - Bandwidth, X_i - independent variable, Y - dependent variable.

The model with a 15 km fixed bandwidth (No. 4) was selected as the best solution due to the highest adjusted R^2 and relatively low AICc. It was verified that the residuals are not spatially autocorrelated. Parameters of the model are in table 5.

Variables	min	median	max	% of negative	% of positive
Intercept	-16.32	14.16	44.89	2.38	97.62
AGE6500	-0.84	-0.10	0.83	74.07	25.93
EDULOW	-0.43	0.2	1.34	9.16	90.84
EDUUNIV	-1.41	-0.16	1.10	74.00	26.00
RELIG	-0.91	-0.02	0.93	55.44	44.56
FOREIGN	-3.72	0.00	6.52	49.88	50.12

NATIVE	-0.44	-0.11	0.19	89.23	10.77
POORFLAT	-0.46	0.19	1.15	8.49	91.51
LARGEFAM	-0.58	0.06	1.13	33.92	66.08
COMMUTED	-0.44	-0.01	0.21	60.20	39.80
EMPLO	-0.04	-0.002	0.02	89.34	10.66
VACANT	-0.67	-0.002	1.34	50.92	49.08

Table 5 Explanatory variables in the model n.4

Large changes in R^2 show substantial differences in the model performance. R^2 is high namely close to borders where there are less geographical neighbours and higher CN values. The best model performance is anticipated in northern Moravia and Silesia and in western Bohemia.

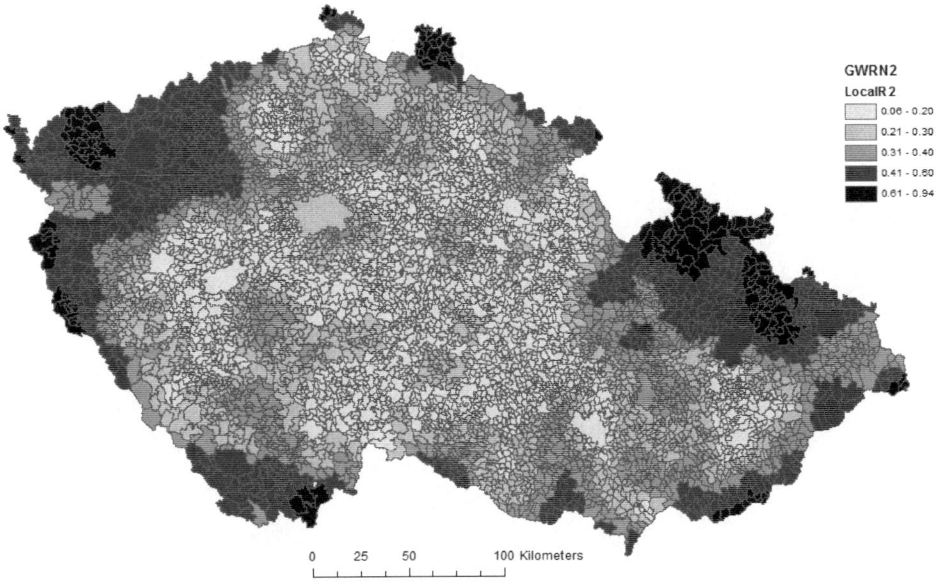

Figure 3 Local R^2 in the GWR model n.4

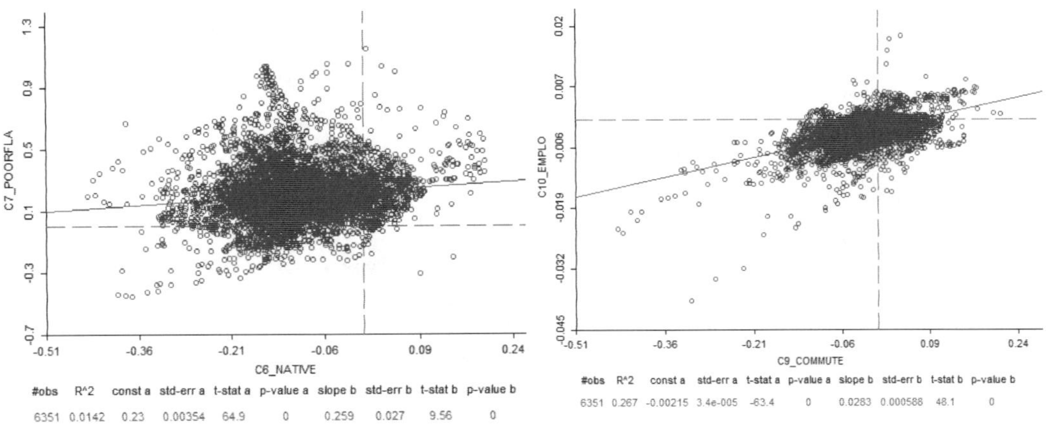

Figure 4 Local GWR coefficients' correlations at prediction location i between POORFLAT and NATIVE (left), EMPLOY and COMMUTEND (right)

The local multicollinearity was examined using explanatory spatial data analysis (ESDA) (Wheeler, Tiefelsdorf 2005). The correlation between local GWR coefficients for all pairs of explanatory variables in municipalities is low. Typical values of R^2 range between 0 and 0.05, and only the correlation between EMPLOY and COMMUTEND provides a value above 0.1 (R^2=0.267). Also scatter diagrams (fig. 4) do not show any significant relationship.

To demonstrate the advantages of the GWR model to explore geographical disparities we provide maps of local GWR coefficients for 2 explanatory variables (EDULOW and LARGMEFA). To improve the interpretation, the significances (*p*-values) for all local coefficients were calculated to distinguish places where the model provides highly confident results.

According to our assumptions, low education positively correlates with the UR almost everywhere. The most important influence of low education is in the Jeseniky area, around Poběžovice and Nový Jičín. Those are the places where uneducated people have low chances of being employed due to lack of appropriate working positions or to low accessibility of such positions (unattractive workplaces with low salaries and people preferring to stay unemployed due to the small difference between potential salaries and social allowances). Exceptions from this relationship are local and unreliable according to the high *p*-values in these places.

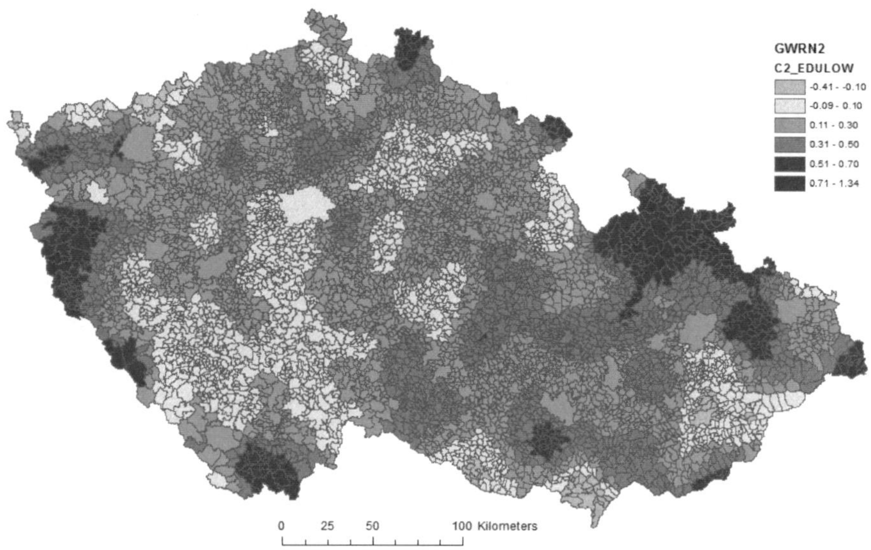

Figure 5 Local coefficients of the low educated population proportion

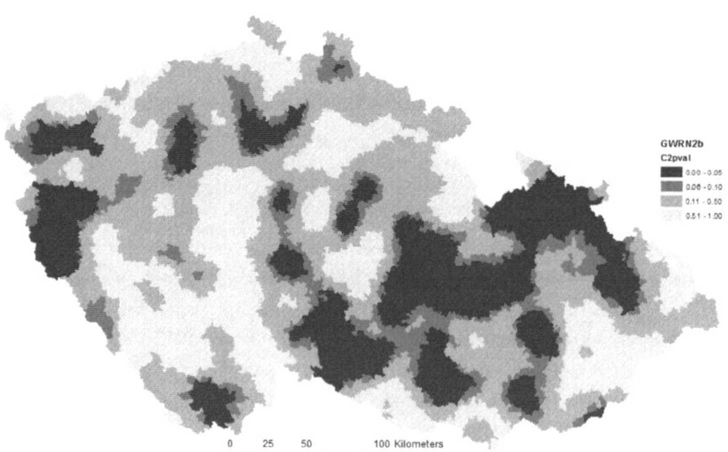

Figure 6 *p*-values for the local coefficients of the low educated population proportion

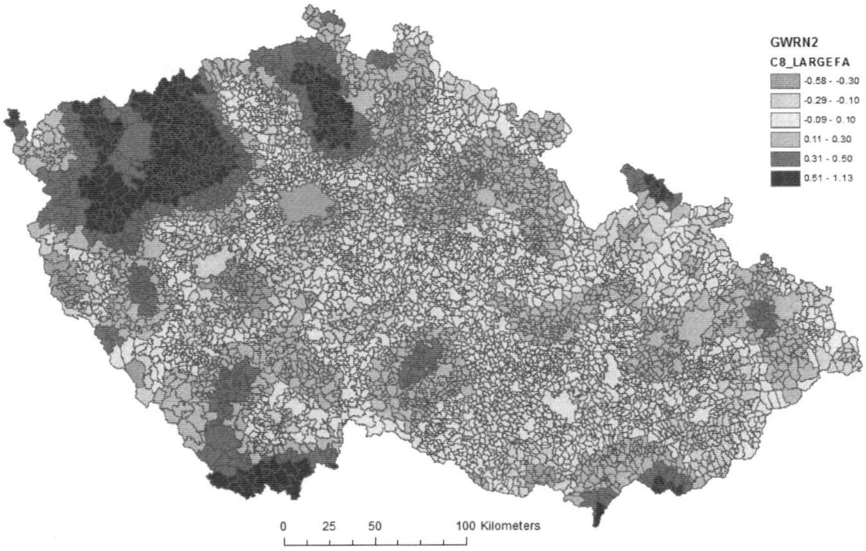

Figure 7 Local coefficients of the large families proportion

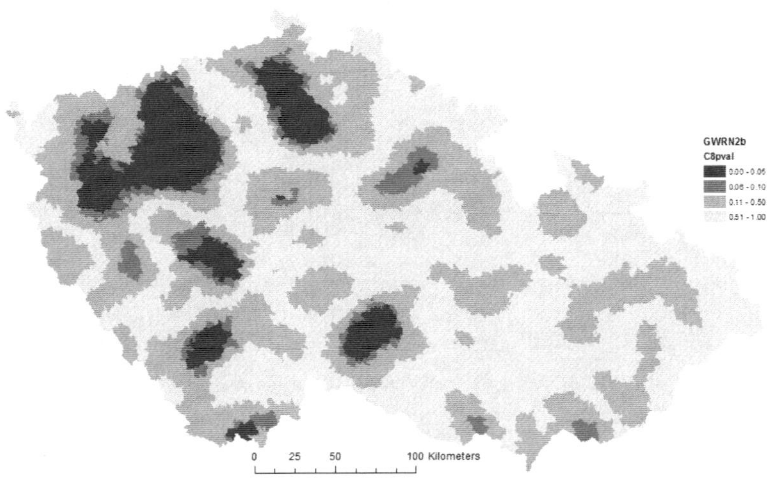

Figure 8 *p*-values for the local coefficients of the large families proportion

The proportion of large families prevails to negatively influence the labour market situation by increasing the UR. An especially strong impact can be seen in Western Bohemia – between Most and Marianske Spa, a belt between Děčín and Doksy, a small area around Horní Dvořiště (fig. 7). Contrarily, a positive influence of large families on the labour market by decreasing UR can be seen around Příbram and Znojmo. Other places are not statistically significant (fig. 8). This example nicely demonstrates the contribution of GWR modelling. Despite the global slightly positive effect of large families on UR (0.08-0.10 for the global coefficient in OLS or SEM), GWR shows big regional differences with very high positive correlation and with the opposite relationship.

4 Conclusion

The study proves the significant effect of spatial factors on regression modelling of the unemployment rate. The model has tested 13 social and economic indicators originating from census 2011, statistics of the Czech Ministry of Finance and Labour offices. The spatial regression models provide better statistical parameters (improved AICc, R^2 etc.). The spatial error model improves adjusted R^2 by 0.2 (from 0.22 to 0.40). Nevertheless, the model is not fully satisfactory because it indicates problems with heteroscedasticity and unevenly distributed high residuals.

Several geographically weighted regression models were developed to optimize a spatial neighbouring effect. The best model was found with a 15 km bandwidth where the adjusted R^2 reached 0.5. The maps of local GWR coefficients for explanatory variables show the heterogeneity of the relationships between these exogenous factors and unemployment. We can find areas with different intensities of influence of the selected factor (i.e. low education), but also factors oscillating locally between positive and negative influences (i.e. share of large families). These findings show the usefulness and contribution of spatial regression models in exploring the determinants of unemployment.

Further work should be oriented on the utilization of mixed GWR models to distinguish better geographically stationary and non-stationary independent variables and to extend the set of explanatory variables to increase the model performance.

5 Acknowledgements

The authors gratefully acknowledge the financial support from the grant RPP42/2019. Data provided by the courtesy of the Czech Statistical Office, Ministry of Finance, and Labour Offices.

References

Akinwande, M. O., Dikko, H. G. and Samson, A. (2015). 'Variance inflation factor: as a condition for the inclusion of suppressor variable(s) in regression analysis'. *Open Journal of Statistics,* 5 (7). DOI: 10.4236/ojs.2015.57075.

Anselin L. (1988). *Spatial Econometrics: Methods and Models*. London: Kluwer.

Anselin, L. (2002). 'Under the Hood: Issues in the Specification and Interpretation of Spatial Regression Models'. *Agricultural Economics,* 27 (3), pp. 247-267. DOI: 10.1111/j.1574-0862.2002.tb00120.x

Anselin, L. and Bera, A. K. (1998). 'Spatial Dependence in Linear Regression Models with an Introduction to Spatial Econometrics'. *Statistics: Textbooks and Monographs*, 155, pp. 237-289.

Bailey, T. and Gatrell, A. (1995). *Interactive spatial data analysis*. Essex, Longman Scientific & Technical.

Benassi, F. and Naccarato, A. (2018). 'Foreign Citizens Working in Italy: Does Space Matter?' *Spatial Demography*, 6(1), pp.1-16. DOI: 10.1007/s40980-016-0023-7.

Brunsdon, C., Fotheringham, A. S. and Charlton, M. (1996). 'Geographically weighted regression: A method for exploring spatial nonstationarity'. *Geogr Anal,* 28 (4), pp. 281–298.

Cracolici, M. F., Cuffaro, M. and Nijkamp, P. (2007). 'Geographical distribution of unemployment: an analysis of provincial differences in Italy'. *Growth and Change,* 38 (4), p. 649.

Cressie, N. (1993). *Statistics for spatial data*. USA, Wiley.

Deller, S. (2011). 'Spatial heterogeneity in the wage curve'. *ECONOMICS LETTERS*, 113 (3), pp. 231-233. DOI: 10.1016/j.econlet.2011.04.015.

Demidova, O., Daddi, P., Medvedeva, E. and Signorelli, M. (2018). 'Modeling the employment rate in Russia: a spatial-econometric approach!'. *EKONOMIKA REGIONA-ECONOMY OF REGION*, 14 (4), pp. 1383-1398. DOI: 10.17059/2018-4-25.

Elhorst, J. P. (2010). 'Spatial Panel Data Models'. Fischer, M.M. and Getis, A., Eds., *Handbook of Applied Spatial Analysis: Software Tools, Methods and Applications*, Springer Berlin Heidelberg, Berlin, pp. 377-407. DOI: http://dx.doi.org/10.1007/978-3-642-03647-7_19.

Elhorst, J. P. and Zeilstra, A. S. (2007). 'Labour force participation rates at the regional and national levels of the European Union: An integrated analysis'. *Papers in Regional Science,* 86, pp. 525.

Fieldhouse, E. and Tranmer, M. (2001). 'Concentration effects, spatial mismatch, or neighborhood selection? Exploring labor market and neighborhood variations in male unemployment risk using census microdata from Great Britain'. *Geographical Analysis*, 33 (4), pp. 353-369.

Fotheringham, A. S., Charlton, M. and Brunsdon, C. (1997). 'Measuring spatial variations in relationships with geographically weighted regression'. *M. Fischer & A. Getis (Eds.). Recent developments in spatial analysis*. London: Springer Verlag.

Fotheringham, A. S., Charlton, M., Brunsdon, C. and Nakaya, T. (2005). 'Model selection issues in Geographically Weighted Regression'. *Proc. of Geocomputation 2005 Conference*, Ann Arbor, Mi. USA.

Hančlová, J., Šimek, M. and Horák, J. (2012). 'Factors influencing the long-term unemployment level and development in the European Union'. *Proceedings of 30th International Conference Mathematical Methods in Economics*, pp. 249-254.

Hančlová, J. and Šimek, M. (2003). 'The Possibilities of the Usage of Multicriterial Analysis for Local Labour Market Research'. *ECON03,* 10 (1), pp. 133-142.

Haining, R. (2003). *Spatial Data Analysis Theory and Practice*. Cambridge University Press, Cambridge.

Jivraj, S., Brown, M. and Finney, N. (2013). 'Modelling Spatial Variation in the Determinants of Neighbourhood Family Migration in England with Geographically Weighted Regression'. *Applied Spatial Analysis and Policy*, 6 (4), pp. 285-304.

Johnson, D., Ercolani, M. and Mackie, P. (2017). 'Econometric analysis of the link between public transport accessibility and employment'. *Transport Policy*, 60, pp. 1-9. DOI: https://doi.org/10.1016/j.tranpol.2017.08.001.

Kouba, K. (2007). 'Prostorová analýza českého stranického systému. Institucionalizace a prostorové režimy'. *Sociologický časopis*, 43 (5), pp. 1017-1037.

LeSage, J. P. (1998). *Spatial Econometrics*.

Lewandowska-Gwarda, K. (2018a). 'Geographically Weighted Regression in the Analysis of Unemployment in Poland'. *ISPRS International Journal of Geo-Information* 7 (1), Article Number 17. DOI: 10.3390/ijgi7010017.

Lewandowska-Gwarda, K. (2018b). 'Female unemployment and its determinants in Poland in 2016 from the spatial perspective'. *Oeconomia Copernicana*, 9 (2), pp. 183–204. DOI: 10.24136/oc.2018.010.

Longhi, S. and Nijkamp, P. (2007). 'Forecasting regional labor market developments under spatial autocorrelation'. *International Regional Science Review, 30* (2), pp. 100-119.

Ma, Y. and Gopal, S. (2018). 'Geographically Weighted Regression Models in Estimating Median Home Prices in Towns of Massachusetts Based on an Urban Sustainability Framework'. *SUSTAINABILITY* 10 (4), Article Number 1026, DOI: 10.3390/su10041026.

Motulsky, H. (2014). When is R2 negative?, [Online]. Available at: https://stats.stackexchange.com/questions/12900/when-is-r-squared-negative.

Muller-Frazek, I. and Pietrzak, M. (2011). 'Spatial analysis of the unemployment rate in Poland in 2004-2008'. *Proceedings of 9th International Conference on Hradec Economic Days 2011* - *Economic Development and Management of Regions,* Hradec Kralove, Czech Republic, pp. 205-209.

Niebuhr, A. (2003). Spatial interaction and regional unemployment in Europe.*European Journal of Spatial Development*, 5, pp. 26.

Nijkamp, P. and Rietveld, P. (1987). 'Technological development and regional labour markets'. *Fischer, M., Nijkamp, P. (ed.): Regional Labour Markets,* Elsevier Science Publishers, pp. 117-138.

O'Brian (2007). 'A Caution Regarding Rules of Thumb for Variance Inflation Factors'. *Quality & Quantity,* 41, pp. 673–690. DOI 10.1007/s11135-006-9018-6.

Openshaw, S. (1984). 'The modifiable areal unit problem'. *CATMOG* (38).

Patuelli, R. (2007). *Regional labour markets in Germany: statistical analysis of spatio-temporal disparities and network structures*, PhD thesis.

Patuelli, R., Griffith, D. A., Tiefelsdorf, M. and Nijkamp, P. (2011). ,Spatial filtering and eigenvector stability: space-time models for German unemployment data'. *International Regional Science Review*, 34 (2), pp. 253.

Patuelli, R. and Mayor, M. (2012). 'Short-Run Regional Forecasts: Spatial Models Through Varying Cross-Sectional and Temporal Dimensions'.

Pietrzak, M. and Balcerzak, A. (2016). 'A Spatial SAR Model in Evaluating Influence of Entrepreneurship and Investments on Unemployment in Poland'. *Proceedings of the International Conference: Quantitative Methods in Economics: Multiple Criteria Decision Making XVIII*, pp. 303-308.

Simionescu, M. (2014). 'Predicting the National Unemployment Rate in Romania using a Spatial Auto-Regressive Model that includes Random Effects'. *Proceedings of 2nd International Conference Economic Scientific Research - Theoretical, Empirical and Practical Approaches (ESPERA). Procedia Economics and Finance*, 22, pp. 663-671. DOI: 10.1016/S2212-5671(15)00281-6.

Smith M. J., Goodchild M. F. and Longley P. A. (2018). *Geospatial Analysis*. [Online]. Available at: http://www.spatialanalysisonline.com.

Spurná, P. (2008). 'Geograficky vážená regrese: metoda analýzy prostorové nestacionarity geografických jevů'. *Geografie*, 113 (2), pp. 125-139.

Wall, M. M. (2004). 'A close look at the spatial structure implied by the CAR and SAR models'. *J of Statistical Planning and Inference*, 121, pp. 311-324.

Wheller D. and Tiefelsdorf, M. (2005). 'Multicollinearity and correlation among local regression coefficients in geographically weighted regression'. *J Geograph Syst,* 7, pp. 161–187. DOI: 10.1007/s10109-005-0155-6.

Weisent, J., Rohrbach, B., Dunn, J. and Odoi, A. (2012). 'Socioeconomic determinants of geographic disparities in campylobacteriosis risk: a comparison of global and local modeling approaches'. *International Journal of Health, Geographics*, 11, article Number 45. DOI: 10.1186/1476-072X-11-45.

Yildirim, J. and Ocal, N. (2013). 'Analysing the Determinants of Terrorism in Turkey using Geographically Weighted Regression'. *Defence and Peace Economics*, 24 (3), pp. 195-209. DOI: 10.1080/10242694.2012.695034.

Beta-convergence of the EU Regions, 2004-2014: the GWR Approach

Michaela Chocholatá[1]

Abstract. This paper analyses the beta-convergence hypothesis for the 249 NUTS 2 EU regions over the period 2004-2014. Besides the classic global regression model, the main concentration is given on estimation of the locally different coefficients from the geographically weighted regression (GWR). GWR thus enables to analyse the beta-convergence concept for individual regions and to estimate locally different speeds of convergence. The results revealed huge spatial differences in parameter values and indicated that there are both the regions which are diverging as well as regions which are converging. Furthermore, it was proved that the local GWR model taking into account the local characteristics of the analysed regions describes the data set significantly better than the global regression model supposing the single relationship across the group of analysed regions.

Keywords: convergence, European union (EU), region, geographically weighted regression (GWR).

JEL Classification: R12, O47

1 Introduction

For the last few decades, the issue of convergence on various regional levels has been attractive for researchers as well as for policy makers almost from every part of the world. Traditionally two concepts of convergence can be distinguished – the beta-convergence and the sigma-convergence (Barro and Sala-i-Martin, 2004; Hančlová et al., 2010). While the beta-convergence concept answers the question whether poor economies catch-up to wealthier economies, the validity of the sigma-convergence concept requires the declining dispersion of regional per capita income over the analysed time period.

Since the majority of early studies had a tendency to omit the topic of space (Szomolányi, Lukáčiková and Lukáčik, 2011), with the huge development of the spatial econometrics during the last years the researchers have recognized the necessity to consider the spatial dimension while analysing the beta-convergence hypothesis (Abreu, De Groot and Florax, 2005; Rey and Janikas, 2005; Arbia, 2006; Fingleton and López-Bazo, 2006, Battisti and DiVaio, 2009; Chocholatá and Furková, 2017). Two categories of the spatial effects can be distinguished, the spatial autocorrelation and the spatial heterogeneity. While the first spatial effect – spatial autocorrelation (reflecting the spatial dependence of the observations) is considered in empirical spatial studies quite often, the incorporation of the second effect – spatial heterogeneity is scarce. On one hand, Ertur and Le Gallo (2008) pointed out that majority of beta-convergence studies is based on the assumption of homogeneity, i.e. on the assumption that the model parameters do not vary across the space. On the other hand, many authors (Temple, 1999; Eckey, Kosfeld and Türck, 2007; Curran 2009; Ertur and Le Gallo, 2008; Farahmand, Sameti and Sasan, 2014 and Chocholatá, 2018a) presented that the beta-convergence models should assume

[1] University of Economics in Bratislava, Faculty of Economic Informatics, Department of Operations Research and Econometrics, Dolnozemská cesta 1/b, 852 35 Bratislava, michaela.chocholata@euba.sk.

the parameter heterogeneity across the regions. Geographically weighted regression (GWR) developed by Brunsdon, Charlton and Fotheringham (see e.g. Fotheringham, Brunsdon and Charlton, 2002) represents a useful tool enabling to capture the spatial heterogeneity across analysed regions.

Eckey, Kosfeld and Türck (2007) analysed the regional convergence of the German labour market using the GWR technique and proved the different speed of convergence across the analysed regions. Curran (2009) studied the British regional growth and sectoral trends based both on global and local spatial analysis. Regarding the GWR approach he was able to identify and to confirm regional differences in convergence and divergence trends. Farahmand, Sameti and Sasan (2014) applying the GWR approach for the convergence analysis of the Asian countries pointed out the spatial variations of beta-convergence parameters across these countries as well as different convergence or divergence speed. Chocholatá (2018a) dealt with the spatial analysis of convergence in the selected regions of Central Europe. Besides the global spatial econometric methods also the local spatial econometric methods based on the GWR approach were employed. It was confirmed the huge difference in the speed of convergence and half-life period across the tested regions. Since, as it was already mentioned above, the effect of the spatial heterogeneity is often a neglected issue in empirical studies, the main aim of this paper is oriented on testing of the beta-convergence hypothesis for the 249 NUTS[2] 2 EU regions over the period 2004-2014 based on the GWR approach.

The paper is organized as follows: section 2 deals with the methodology, section 3 is devoted to the data description and the empirical results of the analysis and section 4 concludes and presents some directions for the further research.

2 Methodology

The analysis of the beta-convergence concept for n regions is traditionally based on estimation of the following cross-sectional linear regression model (see e.g. Barro and Sala-i-Martin, 2004; Arbia, 2006):

$$\frac{1}{T}\ln\left(\frac{y_{i,T}}{y_{i,0}}\right)=\alpha+\beta\ln\left(y_{i,0}\right)+\varepsilon_i \qquad (1)$$

where the left side of model (1) denotes the average annual income growth in the region i during the period $(0, T)$, symbols α and β denote unknown regression parameters and ε_i is a disturbance term. To confirm the beta-convergence hypothesis, the estimated parameter β must be statistically significant and have a negative sign. Since it is unrealistic to suppose the same parameter values across individual regions, the effect of spatial heterogeneity should be considered. In general, we can either expect the different values of parameters for some groups of regions or we can estimate the parameter values for each individual region (Furková, 2018). In accordance with the aim of the paper, as well as with Eckey, Kosfeld and Türck (2007) and Curran (2009), we will further present the geographically weighted regression to calculate the

[2] Nomenclature of Units for Territorial Statistics

different speed of convergence for each analysed region. The GWR augmentation of model (1) is as follows:

$$\frac{1}{T}\ln\left(\frac{y_{i,T}}{y_{i,0}}\right)=\alpha_i+\beta_i\ln\left(y_{i,0}\right)+\varepsilon_i \tag{2}$$

Local estimates of the regression parameters α_i, β_i are functions of region i and can be calculated by weighted least squares (for formula see e.g. Wheeler and Páez, 2010; Ertur and Le Gallo, 2008; Furková, 2018). In GWR the weights are presented by $n \times n$ diagonal matrix specific to each region i. The local weight matrix for the region i is calculated based on a spatial kernel function giving higher weight to the nearby regions in comparison to regions more distant in space (Fotheringham, Brunsdon and Charlton, 2002; Wheeler and Páez, 2010). The first step of the GWR approach is the choice of the kernel function and its bandwidth parameter. We can distinguish two types of kernel functions, fixed and adaptive. While the fixed kernel function is based on the same spatial range in each local kernel (e.g. Gaussian decay function), the adaptive kernel function is characterized by the same number of observations in each local kernel (e.g. bi-square kernel based on nearest neighbours)[3].

The estimation of local regression parameters should be followed by testing if the GWR local model (2) describes the data significantly better than a traditional global model (1) and by testing of spatial variation of the estimated local regression coefficients (Leung, Mei and Zhang, 2000; Fotheringham, Brunsdon and Charlton, 2002; Nakaya, 2016; Chocholatá, 2018a).

3 Data and Empirical Results

The analysed data set comprises the regional data for the 249 NUTS 2 regions of the EU countries[4] retrieved from the regional database of the Eurostat (http://ec.europa.eu/eurostat/)[5]. The analysis of the beta-convergence is based on the development of the net disposable income of households (in Euro per capita) observed over the period 2004-2014. Analyses were provided in the softwares GeoDa, GeoDaSpace and GWR4. The shapefile for analyses was obtained from the web page of Eurostat (http://ec.europa.eu/eurostat/web/gisco/geodata/reference-data/administrative-units-statistical-units) and correspondingly reduced in the GeoDa software.

Quartile maps of the average annual income growth values for 2004-2014 period (calculated using the formula from the left side of model (1)) as well as the levels of the initial net disposable income in 2004 are depicted in Figure 1. Based on the Figure 1 there is a visible tendency of the beta-convergence especially for the regions of the post-communist countries since these regions with low initial levels of the net disposable income have substantially higher growth rates than regions with high initial income values. On the other hand, there are regions with both the low initial values and low growth rates (e.g. some Portuguese and Greek regions) which is in contradiction with the beta-convergence concept.

[3] For more information, see Wheeler and Páez (2010) who present also the possibilities how to choose the optimal kernel bandwidth parameter.
[4] The original data set of 272 regions was reduced by 20 isolated regions and 3 regions with no available data.
[5] The empirical part of the analysis is based on the same data set as used in Chocholatá (2018b).

This initial visual preliminary analysis was followed by the ordinary least squares (OLS) estimation of the global model (1) – see Table 1. The estimated β parameter has an expected negative sign confirming the beta-convergence hypothesis with the speed of convergence of 3.41% which implies the 20.345 years' half-life period of the convergence process. Since the global model (1) was estimated for the spatial data, testing for the spatial autocorrelation in residuals is a usual procedure. Moran's *I* statistic of the OLS residuals based on an inverse distance weight matrix was 0.4966 indicating the presence of the statistically significant positive spatial autocorrelation.[6] As pointed out by Fotheringham (2009), the spatial autocorrelation among residuals can by caused by the spatial non-stationarity and in such cases it seems to be useful to apply the local approach.[7]

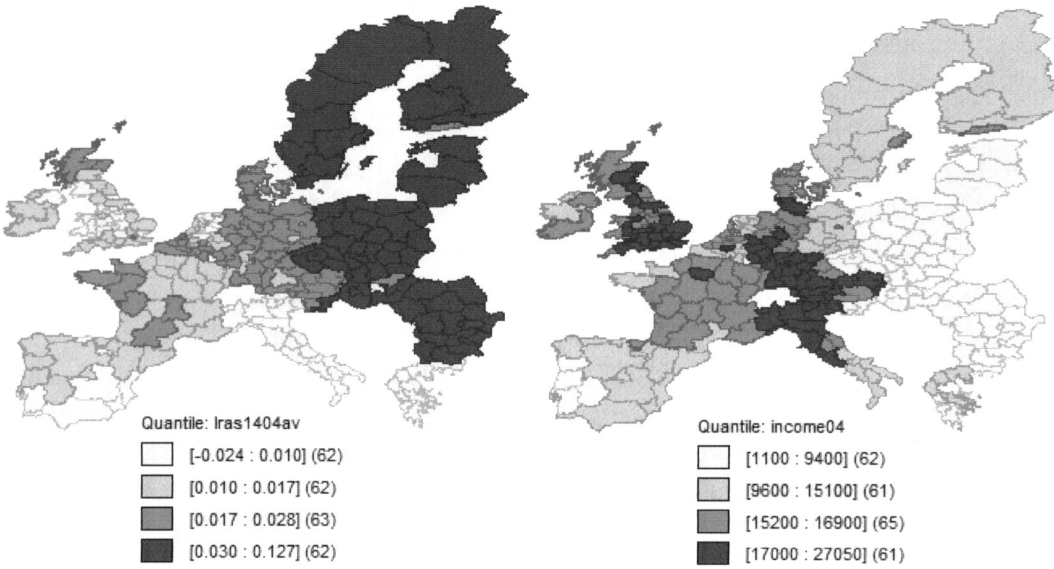

Figure 1 Quartile maps of the annual income growth over the period 2004-2014 (*lras1404av*) and for initial level of the net disposable income of households in 2004 (expressed in Euro per capita, *income04*) [own calculations]

In order to capture the spatial heterogeneity, the local model (2) was estimated based on the GWR approach using the adaptive bi-square kernel based on 44 nearest neighbours (Nakaya, 2016, Chocholatá, 2018a). Selected results of the GWR estimation are gathered in Table 1. The both local GWR parameters, i.e. α_i and β_i, have changing signs indicating different relationship across analysed regions. Concerning the beta-convergence hypothesis, the local slope parameters β_i, varying between -0.0633 and 0.0204 (with the median value of -0.0157), do not enable to confirm the beta-convergence concept for all regions, since there are both the regions which converge as well as regions which are diverging. The convergence characteristics corresponding to median values indicate the speed of convergence of 1.71% and the half-life of 40.622 years. More detailed information about half-life periods as well as about different model

6 For more information about testing for spatial autocorrelation see e.g., Arbia (2006).

7 In this context Fortheringham (2009, p.403) highlights the fact, that "other causes of spatially autocorrelated residuals exist. What is unknown is the extent to which commonly observed residual autocorrelation is caused by the incorrect application of global models." From the other researchers dealing with this methodological problem related to the links between the spatial dependence and spatial heterogeneity can be mentioned e.g., Bivand and Brunstadt (2003), Ertur and Le Gallo (2008).

performance in individual regions is available based on the colour-coded maps for the GWR fit in Figure 2.

Mapping the half-life values indicates huge differences across the space. Since majority of regions is characterized by the convergence process, there are 78 regions (all Spanish, Portuguese and UK regions, 2 French regions, 1 Irish region, 7 Netherland regions and 11 German regions) which are diverging. With regard to converging regions, the shortest half-life values were calculated mainly for eastern and south-eastern regions (Polish, Slovak, Hungarian, Bulgarian, Romanian and Greek regions) as well as for some other regions (3 French, single Danish, German and Austrian regions). Some more time is needed for the half of the initial gap in the per capita income to be eliminated in case of the central European regions. For the remaining regions located e.g., in France, Italy, Germany and Sweden it will last more than 35 years for half of the distance between the initial income level and the steady-state to be vanished. In accordance with Eckey, Kosfeld and Türck (2007) it is possible to find some linkages between the spatial structure of the initial income values and the length of the half-life period of converging regions. Regions with low initial income values (especially eastern and south-eastern regions) are characterized by short half-life periods. On the other hand, e.g. north Italian and German regions with high initial income levels have a long half-life period. The values of local coefficients of determination R_i^2 for the GWR fit ranging between 0.027 and 0.951 reflect huge differences in the model performance for individual regions.

Parameter	**OLS**	**GWR**				
		Minimum	**Lower Quartile**	**Median**	**Upper Quartile**	**Maximum**
α or α_i	0.2933***	-0.1861	-0.0417	0.1621	0.2379	0.5721
β or β_i	-0.0289***	-0.0633	-0.0221	-0.0157	0.0058	0.0204
AICc	-1380.6919			-1563.2153		
Adjusted R^2	0.6603			0.8477		
		Convergence characteristics				
Speed of convergence	0.0341	0.1003	0.0250	0.0171	-	-
Half-life	20.345	6.907	27.743	40.622	-	-

Table 1 Estimation results of the beta-convergence models. Note: *** denotes the statistical significance at 1% level of significance[8]. [own calculations]

[8] The significance tests for the local coefficients from the GWR fit will not be handled in this paper, since, as it was pointed out by Charlton and Fotheringham (2009) and Furková (2018), there is a problem of multiple significance testing.

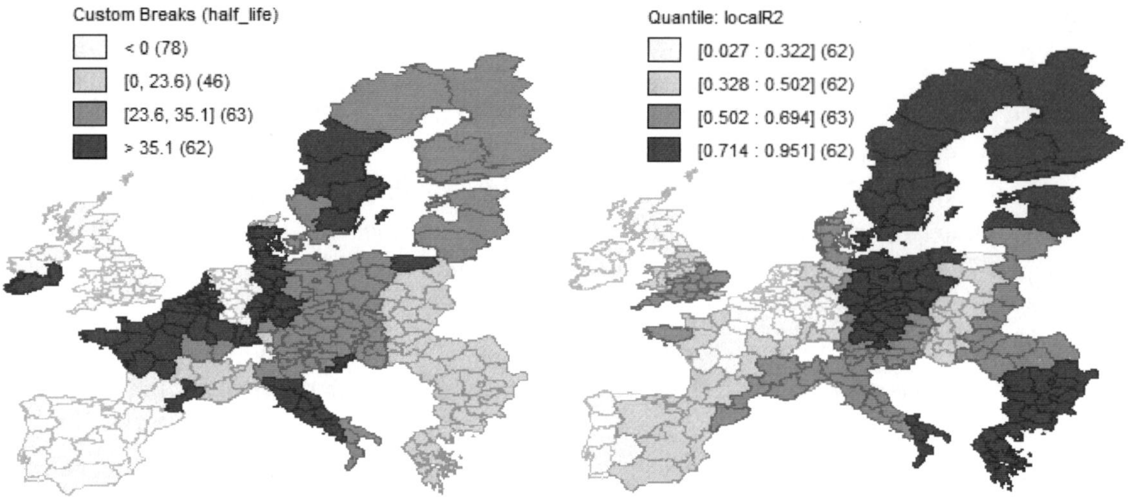

Figure 2 Half-life period of the convergence process 2004-2014 and local coefficients of determination for the GWR fit [own calculations]

Following Charlton and Fotheringham (2009), the goodness-of-fit based on values of the adjusted R^2 and corrected Akaike Information Criterion (AICc) for the global OLS model (1) and local GWR model (2), respectively, indicate the clear evidence of improvement in the model performance. Residuals from the GWR fit exhibited substantially lower degree of spatial autocorrelation (Moran's I of 0.108) than it was in case of the OLS residuals. The statistically significant improvement in the GWR model performance over the global OLS model was confirmed by the GWR ANOVA test with the test statistic $F = 11.384$. Testing the geographical variability of local coefficients proved statistically significant spatial variations in their values. Our results are in accordance with those of e.g. Eckey, Kosfeld and Türck (2007), Curran (2009), Farahmand, Sameti and Sasan (2014) and Chocholatá (2018a) analysing the convergence process across the different groups of regions since all these studies confirmed the different local parameter values and thus different convergence or divergence speed of individual regions.

4 Conclusion

This paper analysed the beta-convergence process of the EU regions considering the location of individual regions in space. From the two spatial effects (spatial autocorrelation and spatial heterogeneity) the main attention was given to the spatial heterogeneity. Besides the traditional global OLS beta-convergence model, the local model based on GWR approach was specified and estimated. The results show that although the global OLS model strongly confirms the beta-convergence hypothesis, the spatial dimension of the analysis should be taken into account as well. The estimates of the local β_i parameters together with the diagnostic checking of the local GWR model strongly confirm that the GW model describes the analysed data set significantly better than the global OLS model. Furthermore, the local analysis enabled to identify that although the majority of the regions was converging with different speed of convergence, there were 78 regions which were diverging. Based on these results it was not possible to confirm the beta-convergence hypothesis for all analysed regions.

However, open remains the methodological issue of links between spatial autocorrelation and spatial heterogeneity. The simultaneous incorporation of both these spatial effects using the generalized version of GWR in beta-convergence analysis is an inspiring challenge for the further author's research.

Acknowledgements

This work was supported by the Grant Agency of Slovak Republic – VEGA grant No. 1/0248/17 "Analysis of Regional Disparities in the EU based on Spatial Econometric Approaches".

References

Abreu, M., De Groot, H. L. F. and Florax, R. J. G. M. (2005). 'Space and Growth: A Survey of Empirical Evidence and Methods'. *Région et Développement*, 21, pp. 13-44.

Arbia, G. (2006). *Spatial Econometrics. Statistical Foundations and Applications to Regional Convergence.* Berlin Heidelberg: Springer-Verlag.

Barro, R. J. and Sala-i-Martin, X. (2004). *Economic growth.* Cambridge, Massachusetts, London: The MIT Press.

Battisti, M. and Di Vaio, G. (2009). 'A spatially filtered mixture of β-convergence regressions for EU regions, 1980–2002'. *Arbia, G. and Baltagi, B.H. Spatial Econometrics. Methods and Applications.* Heidelberg: Physica-Verlag, pp. 105-122.

Bivand, R. S. and Brunstad, R. J. (2003). 'Regional Growth in Western Europe: An Empirical Exploration of Interactions with Agriculture and Agricultural Policy'. *Fingleton, B. European Regional Growth.* Berlin Heidelberg: Springer-Verlag, pp. 351-374.

Charlton, M. and Fotheringham, A. S. (2009). Geographically Weighted Regression. A Tutorial on using GWR in ArcGIS 9.3, [Online]. Available at: https://www.geos.ed.ac.uk/~gisteac/fspat/gwr/gwr_arcgis/GWR_Tutorial.pdf [cited 2019-01-30].

Chocholatá, M. and Furková, A. (2017). 'Does the location and the institutional background matter in convergence modelling of the EU regions?' *Central European Journal of Operations Research*, 25 (3), pp.679-697.

Chocholatá, M. (2018a). 'Spatial Analysis of Convergence in the Selected Regions of Central Europe'. *Proceedings of the 18th International Scientific Conference „AIESA – BUILDING OF SOCIETY BASED ON KNOWLEDGE"*. Bratislava, Slovakia, pp. 19-30.

Chocholatá, M. (2018b). 'Analysis of income convergence based on different specification of spatial weights: Evidence from NUTS 2 EU regions'. *Proceedings of the International Scientific Conference Quantitative Methods in Economics: Multiple Criteria Decision Making XIX.* Bratislava, Slovakia, pp. 32-40.

Curran, D. (2009). British Regional Growth and Sectoral Trends – Global and Local Spatial Econometric Approaches, [Online]. Available at: https://www.researchgate.net/publication/277826233 [cited 2019-01-30].

Eckey, H., Kosfeld, R., and Türck, M. (2007). 'Regional Convergence in Germany: A Geographically Weighted Regression Approach'. *Spatial Economic Analysis*, 2 (1), pp. 45-64.

Ertur, C. and Le Gallo, J. (2008). Regional Growth and Convergence: Heterogenous reaction versus interaction in spatial econometric approaches, [Online]. Available at: https://hal.archives-ouvertes.fr/hal-00463274/document [cited 2019-01-30].

Farahmand, S., Sameti, M. and Sasan, S. S. (2014). 'Spatial Variations of β-Convergence Coefficient in Asia (The GWR Approach)'. *Iranian Economic Review*, 18 (1), pp. 81-101.

Fingleton, B. and López-Bazo, E. (2006). 'Empirical growth models with spatial effects'. *Papers in Regional Science*, 85 (2), pp.177-198.

Fotheringham, A. S., Brunsdon, C. and Charlton, M. E. (2002). *Geographically Weighted Regression. The Analysis of Spatial Varying Relationships*. Chichester: Wiley.

Fotheringham, A. S. (2009). 'The problem of spatial autocorrelation and local spatial statistics'. *Geographical Analysis*, 41 (4), pp. 398-403.

Furková, A. (2018). 'Spatial Heterogeneity of Regional Innovation Processes: Geographically Weighted Regression Approach'. *Proceedings of the International Scientific Conference Quantitative Methods in Economics: Multiple Criteria Decision Making XIX. Bratislava*, Slovakia, pp. 127-134.

Hančlová, J., Kubicová, I., Macháček, M., Melecký, A., Melecký, L., Melecký, M., Nevima, J. and Ramík, J. (2010). *Makroekonometrické modelování České ekonomiky a vybraných ekonomik EU*. Ostrava: VŠB- Technical University of Ostrava.

Leung, Y., Mei, C. and Zhang, W. (2000). 'Statistical Tests for Spatial Nonstationarity Based on the Geographically Weighted Regression Model'. *Environment and Planning A*, 32 (1), pp. 9-32.

Nakaya, T. (2016). GWR4.09 User Manual. GWR4 Windows Application for Geographically Weighted Regression Modelling, [Online]. Available at: https://gwrtools.github.io/gwr4-downloads.html [cited 2019-01-30].

Rey, S. J. and Janikas, M. V. (2005). 'Regional Convergence, Inequality, and Space'. *Journal of Economic Geography*, 5 (2), pp. 155-176.

Szomolányi, K., Lukáčiková, A. and Lukáčik, M. (2011). 'The β convergence of the EU27 countries'. *Proceedings of 29th International Conference on Mathematical Methods in Economics 2011*, Praha, Czech Republic, pp. 287-291.

Temple, J. (1999). 'The New Growth Evidence'. *Journal of Economic Literature*, 37 (March 1999), pp. 112-156.

Wheeler, D. C. and Páez, A. (2010). 'Geographically Weighted Regression'. *Fischer, M. and Getis, A. Handbook of Applied Spatial Analysis. Software Tools, Methods and Applications*. Berlin Heidelberg: Springer-Verlag, pp. 461-486.

http://ec.europa.eu/eurostat/ [cited 2017-01-05].

http://ec.europa.eu/eurostat/web/gisco/geodata/reference-data/administrative-units-statistical-units [cited 2017-01-05].

Multi-Level Stackelberg Game in Emergency Service System Reengineering

Jaroslav Janáček[1]

Abstract. An emergency service system is a public service system designed for satisfaction of public randomly emerging demands. The system consists of service centers, which are run by private service providers, whose profit is proportional to transportation performance expended on the service provision. The original positions of the centers were suggested by a system administrator to minimize expected response time of individual system users asking for service. After some time, the center positions cease to suit changed distribution of the public demands and thus reengineering of the system must be done to face the new situation. In this paper, we study a special form of reengineering, when two main providers play so called Stackelberg's game and compete about profit following from the service provision.

Keywords: Emergency service system, reengineering, competition of service providers, Stackelberg's game.

JEL Classification: C61, C63

1 Introduction

An emergency service system design problem is often presented as the weighted p-median problem (Brotcorne, Laporte and Semet, 2003), (Doerner et al, 2005), (Jánošíková and Žarnay, 2014), (García, Labbé and Marín, 2011), (Janáček and Kvet, 2013), (Elloumi, Labbé and Pochet, 2004), (Sayah and Irnich, 2016). This problem consists in determination of p-center locations so that sum of user's distances to the nearest service center weighted by an expected number of the user demands is minimal. This approach is based on the assumption, that the system administrator assigns the emerging demands for service to the nearest service center (Kvet, 2014), (Kvet, 2015).

The centers equipped with emergency vehicles are usually run by private service providers, and profit of these providers depends on transportation performance expended in satisfying all assigned demands (Matiaško and Kvet, 2017).

This paper deals with the case of reengineering, when the service providers are allowed to change their center locations under some rules imposed by the system administrator, what enables them to improve their profit. This case of reengineering has been applied in the emergency health care system of the Slovak Republic, contrary to some other national or local emerging systems (Reuter-Oppermann, van den Berg and Vile, 2017), (Guerriero, Miglionico and Olivito, 2016).

We study the case of reengineering, when only two providers called the leader and the follower are considered and their competition about profit has form of Stackelberg's game (von Stackelberg, 1952), (Karakitsu, 2010), (Kvet and Janáček, 2018c).

[1] Prof. RNDr. Jaroslav Janáček, CSc., University of Žilina, Faculty of Management Science and Informatics, Univerzitná 8215/1, 010 26 Žilina, Slovakia, e-mail: jaroslav.janacek@fri.uniza.sk

We will study so called multi-level Stackelberg's game, which consists of a sequence of steps (levels), where one level consists of the leader's move followed by the follower's move. Each move is represented by solving one-participant profit optimization problem. In this paper, we focus on trend of profit partition, when the Stackelberg's game is played in several levels.

The remainder of the paper is organized as follows. The next section presents the one-participation's profit optimization problem. The third section contains description of multi-level Stackelberg's game. The fourth section is devoted to numerical experiments and to presentation of the obtained results. The last section summarizes obtained findings.

2 Participant's profit optimization in reengineering

The one-participation's profit optimization problem is defined here as the problem, where one participant e.g. leader, maximizes his profit by changing a portion w_L of his center locations taking into account the set I_F of fixed locations of the competing provider called follower. The original set of p_L leader's locations is denoted by I_L. The set of all possible center locations is denoted by I. and symbol J denotes a finite set of all users (dwelling places), where b_j denotes a volume of expected demand of user $j \in J$. Let symbol d_{ij} denote the integer network time distance between locations i and j, where $i, j \in I \cup J$ and the maximal relevant distance be m. The profit coefficients c_{ij} of the leader's center at location $i \in I\text{-}I_F$ from servicing a user $j \in J$ are defined so that $c_{ij} = 0$ if $d_{ij} \geq \min\{d_{tj}: t \in I_F\}$ and $c_{ij} = b_j d_{ij}$ otherwise. This definition of c_{ij} ensures that the profit from servicing a user j belongs to the provider, which placed his center closer to the user. Nevertheless, we have to notice that it does not prevent the maximization process from assigning a user demand to a more distant service center. This defect must be treated by other constraints as shown below.

The administrator's rules imposed on leader's reengineering are given by the maximal distance D of the length of center move and by maximal number of w_L of centers, which can be moved. In addition, the public interests must be taken into account. This can be expressed by the constraint that the average user disutility must not be worsen by the system reengineering. The value of the original transportation performance is further denoted by F_0 and it is assumed that this value is proportional to the original average user disutility.

To model all the conditions, we introduce coefficients a^s_{ij} for each pair i, j $i \in I$ and $j \in J$, where $a^s_{ij} = 1$ if and only if $d_{ij} \leq s$ and $a^s_{ij} = 0$ otherwise for $s = 0, 1, \ldots, m\text{-}1$.

Next, we introduce series of decision variables, where binary variable y_i defined for each $i \in I\text{-}I_F$ takes the value of one, if a service center is to be located at i and it takes the value of zero otherwise. To express the total transportation performance necessary for user demand satisfaction, we introduce auxiliary zero-one variables x_{js} for $j \in J$, $s \in 0, \ldots, m\text{-}1$ to model the distance of the nearest service center to the user j. The variable x_{js} takes the value of 1 if the distance from the nearest service center to the customer $j \in J$ is greater than s and it takes the value of 0 otherwise. Then the sum $x_{j0} + x_{j1} + \ldots + x_{jm-1}$ corresponds to the smallest distance from the user j to a located center.

We define the sets N_t and S_i for the problem so that $N_t=\{i\in I\text{-}I_F: d_{ti} \le D\}$ for $t\in I_L$ and $S_i=\{t\in I_L: i\in N_t\}$ for $i \in I\text{-}I_L$. Together with the sets N_t and S_i, we introduce series of decision reallocation variables. The variable $u_{ti}\in\{0, 1\}$ for $t\in I_L$ and $i\in N_t$ takes the value of one, if the service center at t is to be moved to i and it takes the value of zero otherwise.

The last two auxiliary structures are denoted as $\{P_j\}$ and $\{R_j\}$, where $j\in J$ corresponds to a user location. The first of them is a system of ordered lists of possible center location subscripts of $i\in I\text{-}I_F$, where list P_j is ordered so that the following inequalities hold: $d_{Pj(1),j}\le d_{Pj(2),j}\le \dots d_{Pj(q),j}$, where $q = |I\text{-}I_F|$. An element R_j of the second structure is an ordered list of possible service center subscripts from range 1, …, q, where $R_j(r)$ gives the minimal subscript, for which $d_{Pj(r),j}< d_{Pj(Rj(r)),j}$ holds.

The location variables y_i are defined for each $i\in I\text{-}I_L$ and each of them takes the value of one, if a service center is located at i and it takes the value of zero otherwise.

Newly, we introduce series of allocation variables $z_{ij}\in\{0, 1\}$ for $i\in I$ and $j\in J$, where $z_{ij} = 1$ if user demand located to j is serviced from center location i.

Using the above introduced structures and decision variables, we can formulate the model:

$$Maximize \sum_{j\in J}\sum_{i\in I-I_F} c_{ij} z_{ij} \tag{1}$$

$$Subject\ to \sum_{i\in I-I_F} y_i = p_L \tag{2}$$

$$\sum_{i\in I_F} y_i \ge p_L - w_L \tag{3}$$

$$\sum_{i\in N_t} u_{ti} = 1 \quad for\ t\in I_L \tag{4}$$

$$\sum_{t\in S_i} u_{ti} \le y_i \quad for\ i\in I - I_F,\ S_i \ne \emptyset \tag{5}$$

$$\sum_{i\in I-I_F} z_{ij} = 1 \quad for\ j\in J \tag{6}$$

$$z_{ij} \le y_i \quad for\ j\in J, i\in I - I_F \tag{7}$$

$$1 - y_{P_j(k)} \ge \sum_{r=R_j(k)}^{q} z_{P_j(r)j} \quad for\ j\in J,\ k = 1, \dots, q-1 \tag{8}$$

$$x_{js} + \sum_{i\in I_R} a_{ij}^s y_i + \sum_{i\in I_F} a_{ij}^s \ge 1 \quad for\ j\in J,\ s = 0,\dots,m-1 \tag{9}$$

$$\sum_{j\in J} b_j \sum_{s=0}^{m-1} x_{js} \le F_0 \tag{10}$$

$$y_i \in \{0, 1\} \quad for\ \ i\in I - I_F \tag{11}$$

$$z_{ij} \in \{0, 1\} \quad for\ i\in I - I_L,\ j\in J \tag{12}$$

$$u_{ti} \in \{0, 1\} \quad for\ t\in I_F,\ i\in N_t^F \tag{13}$$

$$x_{js} \in \{0, 1\} \quad for\ j\in J,\ s\in 0,\ \dots,\ m-1 \tag{14}$$

The objective function (1) expresses the value of transportation performance allocated to the considered provider (provider's profit). If a user is nearer to a center of other providers, the contribution to the considered provider is zero. The misallocation of a user to a more distant center of the considered provider is prevented by constraints (8).

Constraint (2) gives number of centers belonging to the considered provider under reengineering and constraints (3) allow to move only limited number of leader's centers.

Constraints (4) allow moving the leader's center from the current location t to at most one other possible location in the radius D. Constraints (5) enable to locate at most one center to a location i subject to condition that the original location of the moved center lies in the radius D. These constraints also connect decisions on move with decisions on center location.

Constraints (6) assure that each user demand is allocated to exactly one center belonging to the considered provider - leader.

Link-up constraints (7) give relation between allocation variables z_{ij} and the location variables y_i, which model the decisions on locating service centers operated by considered provider. Constraints (8) forbid misallocating a demand to a more distant service center than the nearest one. The constraint formulated for location $P_j(k)$ and user j forbids allocation of user's j demand to every service center $P_j(r)$, which is more distant from the location j than the center location $P_j(k)$.

Constraints (9) are the constraints, which link-up location variables y_i to the variables x_{js} so that the variable x_{js} takes the value of 1 if the distance from the nearest service center to the customer $j \in J$ is greater than s. The constraint (10) ensures that the current transportation performance does not exceed the original value F_0.

The optimal set of the provider's center locations obtained by solving the integer linear problem (1) – (14) for a set I_F of fixed centers and for a given matrix $\mathbf{c}$ of cost coefficients will be denoted as $I_P(\mathbf{c}, I_F)$.

3 Multi-level Stackelberg's game

Let us formulate the problem of a leading provider according to (Kvet and Janáček, 2018c). The leader begins his game with a rearrangement of the set I_L of his service center locations. The leader's move is followed by the follower's move, which also consists of changes of the follower's service center locations. The leader's profit from a given user j for the current leader's and follower's sets I_L and I_F respectively can be expressed by (15).

$$\begin{aligned}&\textit{If } \min\{d_{ij} : i \in I_L\} > \min\{d_{ij} : i \in I_F\}\\ &\quad \textit{then } C_j(I_L, I_F) = 0\\ &\quad \textit{else } C_j(I_L, I_F) = b_j \min\{d_{ij} : i \in I_L\}\end{aligned} \tag{15}$$

Then, the total leader's profit can be expressed by (16).

$$\sum_{j \in J} C_j(I_L, I_F) \tag{16}$$

The leader's problem of one-level Stackelberg's game can be described as maximization of the profit (1) by changing set I_L taking into account the subsequent follower's move. The existing approaches to this problem made use of heuristics and their authors tried to obtain a good solution of (17) by a searching process, where a heuristics for $I_I(\mathbf{c}, I_L)$ determination was embedded into heuristic process searching for I_L (Doerner et al, 2005), (Guerriero, Miglionico and Olivito, 2016), (Karakitsu, 2010).

$$\max\{\sum_{j\in J} C_j(I_L, I_P(\mathbf{c}, I_L)) : I_L \subset I - I_F,\ |I_L| = p\} \quad (17)$$

A different approach was used in (Kvet and Janáček, 2018c). The approach makes use of the exact solving technique for $I_P(\mathbf{c}, I_L)$ mentioned in (Kvet and Janáček, 2018b) and uses modified profit coefficients, which reflect the possibility that the follower places his center so that it will be nearer to the user than a leader's center. It is based on the hypothesis that the original contribution $b_j d_{ij}$ of a user j to the leader's center located at i will decrease proportionally to the number n_{ij} of possible center locations, which distance from the user location j is less than or equal to the distance between locations i and j. Following the hyphothesis, the modified coefficients $\underline{c}_{ij}$ are determined by (18).

$$\text{If } d_{ij} \geq \min\{d_{tj} : t \in I_F\} \text{ then } \underline{c}_{ij} = 0 \text{ else } \underline{c}_{ij} = b_j d_{ij} / (n_{ij})^{\alpha} \quad (18)$$

The exponent $\alpha > 0$ in (18) is a parameter of this strategy. The leader's solution, can be denoted as $I_P(\underline{\mathbf{c}}, I_F)$ and it corresponds to the result of the leader's move and this result can be used in the optimization process to obtain the result $I_P(\mathbf{c}, I_P(\underline{\mathbf{c}}, I_F))$ of the follower's move. Then, the resulting profit of the leader, after the both steps of the one-level game have been performed, can be expressed by (19).

$$\sum_{j\in J} C_j(I_P(\underline{\mathbf{c}}, I_F), I_P(\mathbf{c}, I_P(\underline{\mathbf{c}}, I_F))) \quad (19)$$

The M-level Stackelberg's can be played according to the following algorithm, for which the original sets I_L and I_F represent input.

1) Set $I_{FF} = I_F$, l=1.
2) If l>M terminate, otherwise go to 2.
3) Define $\underline{\mathbf{c}}$ for I_{FF} and set $I_{LL} = I_P(\underline{\mathbf{c}}, I_{FF})$.
4) Define $\mathbf{c}$ for I_{LL} and set $I_{FF} = I_P(\mathbf{c}, I_{LL})$, set l=l+1 and go to 1.

The final leader's profit is computed according to (16) for the resulting sets I_{LL} and I_{FF}.

4 Numerical experiments

The computational study of leader's profit development during multilevel Stackelberg's game was performed by numerical experiments with ten instances. A background of the instances was based on the current emergency service system in the self-governing region of Žilina of the Slovak Republic. The base of the benchmarks is the road transportation network, which connects 315 dwelling places (cities and villages) of the region. Each of the dwelling places is taken as an aggregate user with location j and with the rate of demands proportional to the number b_j of population. Each user location is considered to be a possible service center location. Original set of 29 emergency service centers is also taken into account. The completion of the benchmarks consists only in random partitioning of the set of original center locations into two leader's and follower's sets I_L and I_F. The original transportation performance was F_0= 31955.

Parameters of the individual instances are described in Table 1, where $|I_L|$ and $|I_F|$ denote the numbers of leader's and follower's centers respectively. The numbers w_L and w_F of the original locations, which can be changed, were set at half of the number $|I_L|$ of the centers, which belong to the leader. The partition of the original transportation performance between the leader and follower is presented in columns Leader's TP and Follower's TP. Our preliminary experiments with solving Stackelberg game yielded good setting of α for each considered instance (Kvet and Janáček, 2018a). These values are also plotted in Table 1.

Benchmark	|IL|	|IF|	wL(wF)	Leader's TP	Follower's TP	α
1	15	14	7	15437	16518	0.7
2	13	16	6	12802	19153	0.3
3	12	17	6	9923	22032	0.1
4	16	13	8	14634	17321	0.65
5	14	15	7	17986	13969	0.25
6	13	16	6	14622	17333	0.75
7	14	15	7	18207	13748	0.15
8	18	11	9	17477	14478	0.65
9	15	14	7	14565	17390	0.1
10	15	14	6	13939	18016	0.1

Table 1 Description of the instances

The 15-level Stackelberg's game has been played with each of the ten instances and the results have been processed in the Table 2, where each benchmark corresponds to one row. The columns of the table correspond to the resulting leader's profit at the end of the level presented in the head of the column. Due to lack of space, only odd levels are reported in the table.

Level: Benchmark	1	3	5	7	9	11	13	15
1	14856	9904	10587	12266	11447	10815	10321	11671
2	10606	9338	8745	9055	9415	9977	11186	10146
3	8057	11135	11177	9477	9161	8350	8896	8009
4	13718	12084	14630	14073	12361	12926	13696	13762
5	16221	16175	15461	14800	13666	13595	16431	15161
6	12150	10248	10301	11751	10372	11201	10971	11548
7	16751	15955	16015	15495	15250	16846	13669	15051
8	15155	13495	13798	13492	15858	14795	14540	14444
9	12913	12363	11952	13894	15537	15282	15282	15282
10	12367	12867	13376	12817	11140	12416	11699	12052

Table 2 Leader's profit development during the 15-level Stackelberg's game

Solutions of $I_P(\underline{\mathbf{c}}, I_{FF})$ and $I_P(\mathbf{c}, I_{LL})$ were found by the optimization software FICO Xpress 8.3 (64-bit, release 2017) and the experiments were run on a PC equipped with the Intel® Core™ i7 3610QM processor with the parameters: 2.3 GHz and 8 GB RAM.

5 Conclusions

Observation of the leader's profit values connected with the individual levels confirms our hypothesis that the competition is considerably disadvantageous for the leader, if compared with the original profit. Even if the sequences of the profit values oscillate and they equalize the starting drop in some benchmarks, they do not reach the original values in no case. Generally, we can observe that the trend of the leader's profit values is decreasing. That is why, we can formulate the conclusion that this way of emergency system reengineering is unsuitable.

Acknowledgements

This work was supported by the research grants VEGA 1/0342/18 "Optimal dimensioning of service systems" and APVV-15-0179 "Reliability of emergency systems on infrastructure with uncertain functionality of critical elements" and VEGA1/0089/19 "Data analysis methods and decisions support tools for service systems supporting electric vehicles".

References

Brotcorne, L., Laporte, G.and Semet, F. (2003). 'Ambulance location and relocation models'. *European Journal of Operational Research,* 147, pp. 451–463.

Doerner, K. F., Gutjahr, W. J., Hartl, R. F., Karall, M. and Reimann, M. (2005). 'Heuristic Solution of an Extended Double-Coverage Ambulance Location Problem for Austria'. *Central European Journal of Operations Research*, 13 (4), pp. 325-340.

Elloumi, S., Labbé, M. and Pochet, Y. (2004). 'A new formulation and resolution method for the p-center problem'. *INFORMS Journal on Computing,* 16, pp. 84-94.

García, S., Labbé, M. and Marín, A. (2011). 'Solving large p-median problems with a radius formulation'. *INFORMS Journal on Computing*, vol. 23, no 4, pp. 546-556.

Guerriero, F., Miglionico, G. and Olivito, F. (2016). 'Location and reorganization problems: The Calabrian health care system case'. *European Journal of Operational Research,* 250, pp. 939-954.

Janáček, J. and Kvet, M. (2013). 'Public service system design with disutility relevance estimation'. *Proceedings of Mathematical Methods in Economics* 2013, Jihlava, Czech Republic, pp. 332-337.

Janáček, J.and Kvet, M. (2018a). 'Online Learning Search for Stackelberg Game Strategy'. *Proceedings of 2018 IEEE Workshop on Complexity in Engineering (COMPENG 2018)*, Florence, Italy, October 10-12, pp. 109-112.

Janáček, J. and Kvet, M. (2018b). 'Reengineering of the Emergency Service System from the Point of Service Provider'. *Proceedings of the ICORES* 2018: *7th International Conference on Operations Research and Enterprise Systems*, Madeira, Portugal, pp. 224-231.

Janáček, J. and Kvet, M. (2018c). 'Stackelberg game in emergency service system reengineering'. *Proceedings of the Conference Mathematical methods in Economics*, Jindřichův Hradec, Czech Republic, pp. 186-191.

Jánošíková, Ľ. and Žarnay, M. (2014). 'Location of emergency stations as the capacitated p-median problem'. *International scientific conference: Quantitative Methods in Economics-Multiple Criteria Decision Making* XVII, Virt, Slovakia.

Karakitsu, A. (2010). *Modeling Discrete Competitive Facility Location*, Heidelberg, Springer.

Kvet, M. (2014). 'Computational Study of Radial Approach to Public Service System Design with Generalized Utility'. *Digital Technologies 2014: Proceedings of the 10th International IEEE Conference*, pp. 198-208.

Kvet, M. (2015). 'Advanced Radial Approach to Resource Location Problems'. *Studies in Computational Intelligence: Developments and Advances in Intelligent Systems and Applications*, Springer, pp. 29-48.

Kvet, M. and Janáček, J. (2018). 'Reengineering of the emergency service system under generalized disutility'. *Proceedings of the ICORES 2018: 7th International Conference on Operations Research and Enterprise Systems*, Madeira, Portugal, pp. 85-93.

Matiaško, K. and Kvet, M. (2017). 'Medical data management'. *Proceedings of IEEE conference Informatics 2017*, Poprad, Slovakia, pp. 253-258.

Reuter-Oppermann, M., van den Berg, P. L. and Vile, J. L. (2017). 'Logistics for Emergency Medical Service Systems'. *Health Systems*, (6) 3, pp 187-208.

Sayah, D. and Irnich, S. (2016). 'A new compact formulation for the discrete p-dispersion problem'. *European Journal of Operational Research*, (256) 1, pp. 62-67.

Von Stackelberg, H. (1952). *The Theory of the Market Economy*. London: William Hodge.

Economic Evaluation of LTPD variable plans without memory

Nikola Kaspříková [1]

Abstract. In this paper we calculate the rectifying LTPD sampling plan minimizing the mean inspection cost per lot of the average process quality for the inspection by variables which uses just the information from the current lot and compare the economic efficiency of the plan with the corresponding attributes sampling plan using a cost model considering differences in variable and fixed cost. The free R software extension package LTPDvar is used for the calculation and evaluation of the plans.

Keywords: Acceptance sampling, LTPD, cost optimization, inspection by variables.

JEL classification: C44

1 Introduction

The paper (Kasprikova, 2017) has shown an economic evaluation of the recently proposed rectifying lot tolerance percent defective (LTPD) plans for the sampling inspection by variables based on the exponentially weighted moving average (EWMA) statistic. Such plans, designed in (Kasprikova, 2017a), actually use not only the information from the current lot, but also the information obtained from the previous lots and are a sort of plans with memory. The analysis has been performed for the known standard deviation case and the economic efficiency of the plans has been compared with the attributes sampling plan using a simple cost model considering the differences in variable and fixed cost. It has been shown that in many situations in the business practice the EWMA based plans bring significant economic advantage over the corresponding attribute sampling plans. Nevertheless in many cases it may be efficient even to use the plans without memory, i. e. working only with the information from the current lot, which may be easier to design and implement. In this paper we calculate the no-memory LTPD sampling plan for the inspection by variables and compare the economic efficiency of the plan with the corresponding attributes sampling plan using a cost model considering differences in variable and fixed cost. The LTPDvar software (Kasprikova, 2019) is used for the calculation and evaluation of the plans.

The LTPDvar software (Kasprikova, 2019) which has been published on the Comprehensive R Archive Network is an extension package for R computing environment (R Core Team, 2019) developed for the computation and evaluation of optimal plans for statistical acceptance sampling. It is a free software and it can be used for the calculation of the LTPD and AOQL variable sampling plans minimizing the mean inspection cost per lot of the average process quality when the remainder of the rejected lots is inspected.

The LTPD sampling plans minimizing the mean inspection cost per lot of process average quality when the remainder of rejected lots is inspected were originally designed by Dodge and Romig for the inspection by attributes - see (Dodge and Romig, 1998). Plans for the inspection

[1] University of Economics in Prague, Department of Mathematics, Nám. W. Churchilla 4, Praha, Czech Republic, nb33@tulipany.cz.

by variables and for the inspection by variables and attributes (all items from the sample are inspected by variables, the remainder of rejected lots is inspected by attributes) were then proposed and it was shown that these plans are in many situations more economical than the corresponding Dodge-Romig attribute sampling plans, see (Kasprikova and Klufa, 2015). The LTPD plans for the inspection by variables and attributes have been introduced in (Klufa, 1994), using an approximate calculation of the plans. Exact plans, using non-central t distribution in the calculation of the operating characteristic, have been reported in (Klufa, 2010) and implemented in the LTPDvar R package (Kasprikova, 2019). It has been shown that these plans are in many situations superior to the original attribute sampling plans and similar results have been obtained for the AOQL plans – the analysis is provided in (Kasprikova and Klufa, 2015). An economic model considering difference in variable cost is used in (Kasprikova and Klufa, 2015).

The rectifying variable sampling LTPD plans without memory minimizing the mean inspection cost per lot of process average quality are addressed in the present paper and the discussion of the economic performance of such plans is provided. The case of the unknown standard deviation is considered in this paper. The structure of the paper is as follows: the LTPD plans for the inspection by attributes minimizing the mean inspection cost per lot of the process average quality when the remainder of the rejected lots is inspected are recalled first, then the rectifying LTPD plans for the inspection by variables and attributes are calculated using the LTPDvar package and the evaluation of the comparative economic efficiency is shown, using a simple economic model which considers differences in both variable and fixed costs.

1.1 LTPD attribute sampling plans

First we recall the attribute sampling plans, as introduced by Dodge and Romig, see e. g. (Dodge and Romig, 1998). Dodge and Romig consider the case, where each inspected item is to be classified as either good or non-conforming (acceptance sampling by attributes) and they search for the sampling plans which minimize the mean number of the items inspected per lot of the process average quality

$$I_s = N - (N - n) \cdot L(\bar{p}; n; c) \tag{1}$$

under the condition

$$L(p_t; n; c) \leq \beta, \tag{2}$$

where $L(p, n, c)$ is the operating characteristic (the probability of accepting a submitted lot with the proportion defective p when using the plan (n, c) for acceptance sampling),
N is the number of the items in the lot (an input parameter),
$\bar{p}$ is the process average proportion defective (an input parameter),
p_t is the lot tolerance proportion defective (an input parameter, $P_t = 100p_t$ is the lot tolerance per cent defective, denoted LTPD),
n is the number of items in the sample $(n < N)$,
c is the acceptance number (the lot is rejected when the number of defective items in the sample is greater than c).

Condition (2) provides a guarantee for the consumer that the lots of the unsatisfactory quality level, with the proportion defective p_t are going to be accepted only with the specified probability β at most (the so-called consumer's risk). The standard value 0.1 is used for the consumer's risk in (Dodge and Romig, 1998).

1.2 Sampling plans for the inspection by variables

We recall the LTPD plans for the inspection by variables and attributes designed in (Klufa, 2010) and implemented in (Kasprikova, 2019). The plans have been designed under the following assumptions: The measurements of a single quality characteristic X are independent and identically distributed normal random variables with parameters μ and σ^2. We consider the unknown σ case. For the quality characteristic X, either an upper specification limit U (the item is defective if its measurement exceeds U), or a lower specification limit L (the item is defective if its measurement is smaller than L), is given.

For the design of the rectifying LTPD plans minimizing the mean inspection cost per lot of the process average quality we shall use the following procedure: draw a random sample of n items from the lot and compute the sample mean $\bar{x}$ and the sample standard deviation s.

Accept the lot if

$$\frac{U - \bar{x}}{s} \geq k, \quad \text{or} \quad \frac{\bar{x} - L}{s} \geq k. \tag{3}$$

The operating characteristic is (e.g. (Klufa, 2010))

$$L(p; n, k) = \int_{k\sqrt{n}}^{\infty} g(t; n-1, u_{1-p}\sqrt{n})\, dt, \tag{4}$$

where

$$g(t; n-1, u_{1-p}\sqrt{n}) \tag{5}$$

is the probability density function of the non-central t distribution with $(n-1)$ degrees of freedom and noncentrality parameter $u_{1-p}\sqrt{n}$.

The plan parameters (n, k) are to be determined so that the plan has optimal economic characteristics and satisfies the requirement (2), when (4) is used as the operating characteristic.

Regarding the economic optimality, Klufa in (Klufa, 1994) uses the economic model, described in more detail in (Kasprikova and Klufa, 2015) and searches for the acceptance plan (n, k), minimizing the mean inspection cost per lot of the process average quality C_{ms} under the condition (2). We are going to use this model for the design of the plans too. The inspection cost per lot, assuming that the remainder of the rejected lots is inspected by attributes (the inspection by variables and attributes), is $n\, c_m^*$, with the probability $L(p; n, k)$, and $[n\, c_m^* + (N-n)\, c_s^*]$ with the probability $[1 - L(p; n, k)]$, where c_s^* is the cost of the inspection of one item by attributes, and c_m^* is the cost of the inspection of one item by variables. The mean inspection cost per lot of the process average quality is then

$$C_{ms} = n \cdot c_m^* + (N - n) \cdot c_s^* \cdot [1 - L(\bar{p}; n, k)]. \tag{6}$$

Let us denote

$$c_m = \frac{c_m^*}{c_s^*}. \tag{7}$$

Instead of C_{ms} we shall look for the acceptance plan (n, k) minimizing

$$I_{ms} = n \cdot c_m + (N - n) \cdot [1 - L(\bar{p}; n, k)] \tag{8}$$

(both functions C_{ms} and I_{ms} have a minimum for the same acceptance plan ($C_{ms} = I_{ms} \cdot c_s^*$)) under the condition (2).

For the discussion of the c_m parameter, see (Kasprikova and Klufa, 2015). The value of this parameter must be estimated based on the real cost calculation in practice. Usually it is $c_m > 1$.

2 Calculation and evaluation of the plans with LTPDvar package

The LTPD acceptance sampling plan for the sampling inspection by variables without memory when the remainder of rejected lots is inspected by attributes, as implemented in (Kasprikova, 2015) will be calculated in the example below. The solution for the unknown σ case will be searched for, using the operating characteristic given by (4). The resulting sampling plan will then be evaluated with regard to the economic characteristics and compared with the corresponding LTPD attributes sampling plan as discussed in (Dodge and Romig, 1998), using the model which considers differences both in the variable cost and the fixed cost.

Example 1. A lot with $N = 1000$ items is considered in the acceptance procedure. The lot tolerance proportion defective is given to be $p_t = 0.01$, and the process average quality is $\bar{p} = 0.001$. It is known that the cost of the inspection of one item by variables is 1.5 times higher than the cost of the inspection of one item by attributes, so the parameter c_m equals 1.5. Find the LTPD acceptance sampling plan for sampling inspection by variables when remainder of rejected lots is inspected by attributes.

The plan can be calculated using the functions available in the LTPDvar package for the R software (R Core Team, 2019), see the documentation of the package for a more detailed description. The implementation is based on the following principles: the k corresponding to particular sample size n is obtained using the condition (2) and the cost-optimizing n is searched for using numerical methods, where the approximate solution, which is calculated first, is used for setting the bounds of the intervals to be searched in.

The resulting plan may be obtained using the following call in the LTPDvar package:

```
planLTPD(N=1000, pbar=0.001, pt=0.01,cm=1.5,method="exact")
```

and the output of the calculation is as follows.

```
An object of class "ACSPlan"
Slot "n":
[1] 77

Slot "k":
[1] 2.644489
```

Which presents the solution $n = 77, k = 2.644489$.

The corresponding Dodge-Romig attributes sampling plan is $n = 250, c = 0$.

For the comparison of these two plans - the plan for inspection by variables and attributes ($n = 77$, $k = 2.644489$) and Dodge-Romig plan ($n = 250$, $c = 0$) from an economic point of view we use a simple economic model of cost difference (measured in the c_s^* units) in which we consider the difference of the mean inspection costs per lot of the process average quality of the particular plans and the effect of the difference in fixed costs:

$$c = I_{ms}(77, 2.644489) - I_s(250, 0) + f, \tag{9}$$

where f is the increase in fixed cost (measured in c_s^*) in case that we opt for the plan for the inspection by variables and attributes. The decision to implement the plan for the inspection by variables and attributes may bring higher fixed cost in some cases in practice in comparison with performing just the attribute inspection due to presumably more difficult preparation of the inspection procedure.

The I_{ms} function is implemented in the LTPDvar package too and (for plan $n = 77$, $k = 2.644489$) may be called as shown below.

```
Ims(n= 77, k=2.644489, N= 1000, pbar=0.001, cm=1.5, type="exact")
```

In this case we obtain $I_{ms} = 145.1232$. The cost measure c then represents the cost difference (measured in the c_s^* units) in the mean inspection cost per lot of the process average quality in case that the plan for the inspection by variables and attributes is used in place of the corresponding attribute sampling plan. The guidelines for the application and interpretation of the measure are as follows: in case that the resulting c value is negative, then one should preferably choose the plan for the inspection by variables and attributes.

Let's suppose that in our example situation $f = 120c_s^*$, then we get $c = -102.9$, which shows that there can be expected savings in the mean inspection cost per lot of the process average quality if the variables sampling plan is used in place of the corresponding attribute inspection plan.

3 Conclusion

It has been shown, considering the unknown standard deviation case and working with the economic model with differences in variable and fixed cost, that the LTPD plans for the sampling inspection by variables when the remainder of the rejected lots is inspected by attributes minimizing the mean inspection cost per lot of the process average quality in many cases bring significant economic advantages over the corresponding attribute inspection plans. The calculation of the optimal acceptance sampling plan and its economic evaluation can be easily performed in the LTPDvar package for the R computing environment.

Acknowledgements

This paper has been produced with contribution of long term institutional support of research activities by Faculty of Informatics and Statistics, University of Economics, Prague.

References

Dodge, H. F. and Romig, H. G. (1998). *Sampling Inspection Tables: Single and Double Sampling*. New York: John Wiley.

Kasprikova, N. (2019). *LTPDvar: LTPD and AOQL plans for acceptance sampling inspection by variables*. R package, [Online]. Available at: http://CRAN.R-project.org/package=-LTPDvar.

Kasprikova, N. (2017). 'LTPDvar: A decision support tool for LTPD sampling plans'. *Strategic Management and its Support by Information Systems (SMSIS)*, Ostrava, Czech Republic, pp. 261-266.

Kasprikova, N. (2017a). 'Rectifying LTPD Plans Minimizing Mean Inspection Cost Per Lot of Process Average Quality Using EWMA Statistics'. *Journal of Testing and Evaluation*, 45 (4), DOI: 10.1520/JTE20150259.

Kasprikova, N. and Klufa, J. (2015). 'AOQL sampling plans for inspection by variables and attributes versus the plans for inspection by attributes'. *Quality technology and quantitative management*, 12 (2), pp. 133-142.

Klufa, J. (1994). 'Acceptance sampling by variables when the remainder of rejected lots is inspected'. *Statistical Papers*, 35, pp. 337-349.

Klufa, J. (2010). 'Exact calculation of the Dodge-Romig LTPD single sampling plans for inspection by variables'. *Statistical Papers*, 51 (2), pp. 297-305.

R Core Team. (2019). R: A language and environment for statistical computing. R Foundation for Statistical Computing, Vienna, Austria, [Online]. Available at: http://www.R-project.org.

Comparison of two different approaches to capture volatility developments of gold returns

Stanislav Kováč[1]

Abstract. Currently, there are many scientific ways to capture the volatility. The goal of this paper is to analyze the developments of gold returns standard deviation over the subsample using two approaches. Firstly, we apply widely used GARCH model and secondly it is Nadaraya-Watson kernel estimation of a non-parametric regression. We find out that simulation over the whole sample made by GARCH leads to underestimate the volatility, while a non-parametric simulation captures the volatility relatively trustworthy. Since a non-parametric estimation does not involve any dynamics, we cannot conclude its superiority over GARCH. We also provide a short- and a long-run forecast.

Keywords: GARCH, non-parametric regression, simulation, volatility, forecast.

JEL Classification: C14, C58, G17

1 Introduction

Financial time series such as stocks, exchange rates, interest rates, commodities, exhibits certain pattern which are defined as *stylized facts*. A good survey of these facts is offered by Knight and Satchell (2007). Let us introduce the most important ones:

- nonstationarity: time series of prices are nonstationary and carry a local trend at least;
- heavy tails: returns have a leptokurtic distribution;
- white noise: return process is white noise which is not independent since the sample autocorrelations of absolute and squared returns are greater than zero;
- volatility clustering: large (small) volatility movements is followed by further large (small) movements which is an indication of shock persistence;
- leverage effects: asymmetric impact of previous volatility on actual volatility;
- long memory: volatility is highly persistent;
- seasonality: non-tradable days tend to increase volatility;
- volatility comovements: big movements in time series is matched by big movements in another which expresses cross-correlations in different markets.

Econometric methods offer many ways to measure, capture and analyze the volatility developments in financial markets, such as ARCH models, ARMA models, stochastic volatility models, structural breaks models, threshold models. We focus on ARCH (Autoregressive Conditional Heteroskedasticity) models and compare an outcome with a non-parametric regression.

An important feature of ARCH models is the ability to capture already presented stylized facts. Engle (1982) proposed a model which takes into account fact that volatility is a time-varying, positive and measurable function. Engle used ARCH to model an inflation in the United Kingdom.

[1] University of Economics in Bratislava, Faculty of Economic Informatics, Department of Operations Research and Econometrics, Dolnozemská cesta 1, 852 35 Bratislava, Slovakia, stanislav.kovac@euba.sk.

Generalized ARCH (GARCH) model was proposed independently by Bollerslev (1986) and Taylor (1986). In case of GARCH(*p,q*), the unconditional variance depends on the *p*-lagged innovations and the *q*-lagged conditional variances. Harvey (1981) showed if the summation of the estimated parameters is less then one, the model is stationary and so is white noise. In most of the empirical implementations, GARCH(*1,1*) is sufficient to model the volatility. The review of GARCH models can be found in the work of Bollerslev (2009). There are many successful applications of univariate and multivariate GARCH models, e.g. Chocholatá (2015), Kováč (2018).

Starica (2003) used parametric ARCH modelling embodied by the GARCH(*1,1*) to capture the dynamics of returns of the Standard & Poors 500. Before the paper was revealed, there were no differences between GARCH(*1,1*) modelling and non-parametric regression to capture and predict next-day volatility. Starica showed that GARCH(*1,1*) model overestimated the unconditional variance of returns which led to a poor volatility forecast. He also pointed out that GARCH(*1,1*) failed during significantly long period to provide a good local description. In general, estimated parameters of GARCH(*1,1*) changes significantly over time which brings some doubts to the using of GARCH for volatility forecasting over longer horizons. Starica was not the only one who used non-parametric regression, Engle and Gonzalez-Rivera (1991) used semi-parametric approach to examine returns, also Pagan and Schwert (1990), Gallant and Tauchen (1989).

In this paper we follow the structure of Starica's work in the case of gold returns. There is a plenty of studies that have attempted to model the determinants of gold prices. According to Levin, Montagnoli and Wright (2006) these studies focus on modeling the variation in the gold price in terms of variation in main macroeconomic variable, modeling with speculation and the rationality of gold price movements and modeling gold as hedge against inflation, political and financial risk. The main and only explanatory variable in our analysis is the lagged value of returns because it carries the necessary information about macroeconomic situation as well as financial evolution that have been accumulated by the immediately previous time period.

The aim of this paper is to compare GARCH(*1,1*) and non-parametric approaches to model gold returns volatility. The rest of the paper is organized as follows: section 2 deals with methodology, section 3 presents empirical results and final section concludes.

2 Methodology

In the following section we describe GARCH(*p,q*) model and Nadaraya-Watson estimation.

2.1 GARCH(*p,q*) model

Let X_t be a discrete stochastic process, then a relative change (continuously compounded return) can be expressed

$$r_t = \ln(X_t/X_{t-1}) \tag{1}$$

and let $\mathcal{F}_t$ denotes the information set at time t, which encompasses X_t and all the past realizations of the process X_t. In general, we have (mean equation)

$$r_t = \mu_t + \varepsilon_t \tag{2}$$

with $\mathrm{E}[\varepsilon_t|\mathcal{F}_{t-1}] = 0$. Here μ_t represents the risk premium and ε_t is the stochastic error.

The process $(\varepsilon_t), t \in \mathbb{Z}$ is GARCH(*p,q*) if $\mathrm{E}[\varepsilon_t|\mathcal{F}_{t-1}] = 0$ and (variance equation)

$$\sigma_t^2 = \omega + \sum_{i=1}^{q} a_i \varepsilon_{t-i}^2 + \sum_{j=1}^{p} \beta_j \sigma_{t-j}^2, \tag{3}$$

where σ_t^2 is the conditional variance of ε_t. ω; $a_i, i = 1, \dots, q$; $\beta_j, j = 1, \dots, p$ are estimated parameters. For $\mathrm{P}[\sigma_t^2 > 0] = 1$ to hold, we impose some restrictions on parameters: $\omega > 0$; $a_i \geq 0, i = 1, \dots, q$; $\beta_j \geq 0, j = 1, \dots, p$.

Unconditional variance of a GARCH(*p,q*) process can be defined

$$\sigma^2 = \omega / \left(1 - \sum_{i=1}^{q} a_i - \sum_{j=1}^{p} \beta_j\right), \quad \sum_{i=1}^{q} a_i + \sum_{j=1}^{p} \beta_j < 1. \tag{4}$$

The likelihood function of GARCH(*p,q*) is

$$l^b(\boldsymbol{\theta}) = -\frac{n-1}{2}\ln(2\pi) - \frac{1}{2}\sum_{t=2}^{n} \ln(\sigma_t^2) - \frac{1}{2}\sum_{t=q+1}^{n} \frac{\varepsilon_t^q + 1}{\sigma_t^2}, \tag{5}$$

where $\boldsymbol{\theta} = (\omega, a_1, \dots, a_q, \beta_1, \dots, \beta_p)^T$ is a vector of parameters. Maximization of function (5) is a nonlinear optimization problem which can be solved by using numerical methods, e.g. Fisher algorithm. Let $Z_t = \varepsilon_t/\sigma_t$ and we also assume it is leptokurtic which often occurs in financial data, then maximum of (5) is still consistent but no longer efficient then we talk about quasi-maximum likelihood estimation.

If data follows GARCH(*1,1*) with $a_1 + \beta_1 < 1$, the *p*-step ahead conditional variance forecast is given by

$$\sigma_{t+p}^{2,GARCH} = \sigma^2 + (a_1 + \beta_1)^p (\sigma_t^2 - \sigma^2). \tag{6}$$

2.2 Nadaraya-Watson estimation

Nadaraya (1964) and Watson (1964) independently came with the estimation of a non-parametric regression for variables $\{X_t, Y_t\}_{t=1}^n$

$$Y_t = m(X_t) \tag{7}$$

with $m(\cdot)$ being an arbitrary function. Nadaraya-Watson regression concur with a local constant least square fit. Taylor expansion of the unknown function $m(X_t)$ is

$$m(X_t) \approx m(x) + m'(x)(X_t - x) + \dots + m^{(p)}(x)(X_t - x)^p (1/p!) \tag{8}$$

for X_t being in the neighborhood of a point x. The neighborhood is realized by including kernel weights into the minimization problem

$$\min_{\boldsymbol{\beta}} \sum_{t=1}^{n} \{Y_t - \beta_0 - \beta_1(X_t - x) - \dots - \beta_p(X_t - x)^p\}^2 K_h(x - X_t), \tag{9}$$

where $\boldsymbol{\beta} = (\beta_0, \dots, \beta_p)^T$ represents a vector of coefficients, K is a kernel and h is a bandwidth. The result is a weighted least squares estimator with weights $K_h(x - X_t)$.

The problem occurs in the identifying kernel and bandwidth. Kernel can obtain several functional forms, such as uniform, Gaussian, Epanechnikov. We use a quadratic kernel in form

$$K_h(u) = (15/16)(1-u^2)^2 I(|u| \leq 1), \tag{10}$$

where $I(\cdot)$ is an identification function which defines the value of kernel to zero or otherwise.

In vector-matrix form we have

$$\boldsymbol{X}_{n\times(p+1)} = \left((X_t - x)^j\right), \qquad t = 1, \dots, n; j = 0, \dots p, \tag{11}$$

$$\boldsymbol{Y}_{n\times 1} = (Y_t), \qquad t = 1, \dots, n, \tag{12}$$

$$\boldsymbol{W}_{n\times n} = \operatorname{diag}(K_h(x - X_t)), \qquad t = 1, \dots, n, \tag{13}$$

then the optimal vector of coefficient $\widehat{\boldsymbol{\beta}}$ which minimizes (9) is

$$\widehat{\boldsymbol{\beta}}(x) = (\boldsymbol{X}^T\boldsymbol{W}\boldsymbol{X})^{-1}\boldsymbol{X}^T\boldsymbol{W}\boldsymbol{Y}. \tag{14}$$

The main difference to a parametric least square method is the fact that the estimates are varying based on chosen x. We choose x to be a sequence $\{x_i\}$ form the smallest returns to the highest where difference q is set to be

$$q = ((\max r_t - \min r_t)/100). \tag{15}$$

A non-parametric alternative for variance equation is a zero-degree local polynomial (Wand and Jones, 1995)

$$\sigma^2_{r_t;h} = \sum_{t=1}^{n} W_t(r_t; h) r_t^2, \tag{16}$$

where $W_t(r_t; h)$ is a function of weights

$$W_t(r_t; h) = K\left(\frac{r_t - x_t}{h}\right) \Big/ \sum_{t=1}^{n} K\left(\frac{r_t - x_t}{h}\right). \tag{17}$$

A non-parametric regression does not define any dynamics, so the p-step prediction of the future unconditional variance is a simple moving average in form

$$\sigma^2_{t,p} = \frac{p}{\tau}\sum_{i=1}^{\tau} r^2_{t-i+1} \tag{18}$$

where τ stands for the number of included past observations, which carry the information about the evolution in time series.

3 Empirical results

The analyzed time series, the daily closing prices of gold during the period March 6, 1969 to December 28, 2018, were retrieved from the website www.stooq.com. The analysis in this paper was carried out in the econometric software EViews.

In Figure 1 we can see the evolution of gold prices and their returns. The evolution depicts presented statistical features of financial data. The higher volatility in the early 1980s tends to cluster as well as in the time of the global financial crisis in 2008, in the same matter, the lower volatility clusters in relatively calm period 1995-2000. We also include the descriptive statistics of time series in Table 1. The prefix 'dl' identifies returns.

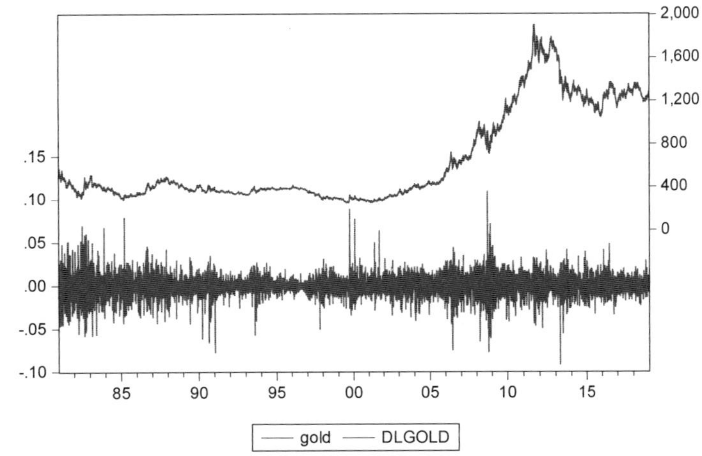

Figure 1 Gold prices (right axes) and their returns (left axis) [own calculation]

Variable	Mean	St. deviation	Skewness	Kurtosis	Jarque-Bera (Prob)
$gold_t$	648.65	427.6751	1.0910	2.7222	1 930.893 (0.00)
$dlgold_t$	7.85×10^{-5}	0.0111	-0.0797	9.8309	18 631.66 (0.00)

Table 1 Descriptive statistics of variables

We have tested stationarity of time series by examining the results of individual unit root tests with augmented Dickey-Fuller test (ADF) on the levels of each series with an intercept and trend (ADF has the unit root null hypothesis):

$$ADF_{gold_t} = -2.1212, \qquad Prob = 0.53, \tag{19}$$

$$ADF_{dlgold_t} = -100.0460, \qquad Prob = 0.00. \tag{20}$$

While the time series of prices are non-stationary, continuously compounded returns are stationary therefore they are used in the following analysis.

3.1 GARCH simulation

We assume that GARCH(*1,1*) model generates a real data process. In general, the estimation based on a reasonable long subsample should provide a good model for the entire sample. Our subsample consists of 1 477 observation over the period March 28, 2013 to December 28, 2018.

The estimated mean equation has the form (standard deviations in the brackets)

$$\widehat{dlgold}_t = \underset{(-0.63)}{-0.0002} - \underset{(-0.56)}{0.0146} dlgold_{t-1}. \tag{21}$$

The estimated parameters of mean equation are irrelevant at this point so is their statistical significance because the model exhibits conditional heteroscedasticity which we tested with ARCH LM test (the null hypothesis says there is no conditional heteroscedasticity)

$$F_{\hat{\varepsilon}_t^2} = 49.2193, \qquad \text{Prob} = 0.00. \tag{22}$$

The estimated variance equation has the form

$$\hat{\sigma}_t^2 = 3.9 \times 10^{-7} + 0.0174\varepsilon_{t-1}^2 + 0.9764\sigma_{t-1}^2. \quad (23)$$
$$(1.2 \times 10^{-7}) \; (0.0024) \qquad (0.0032)$$

It is obvious that stationarity condition defined in (4) holds. For a confidence level 1 % there is no residual heteroscedasticity in (23). Figure 2 portrays the development of the conditional volatility which was simulated with model (23) for the whole sample.

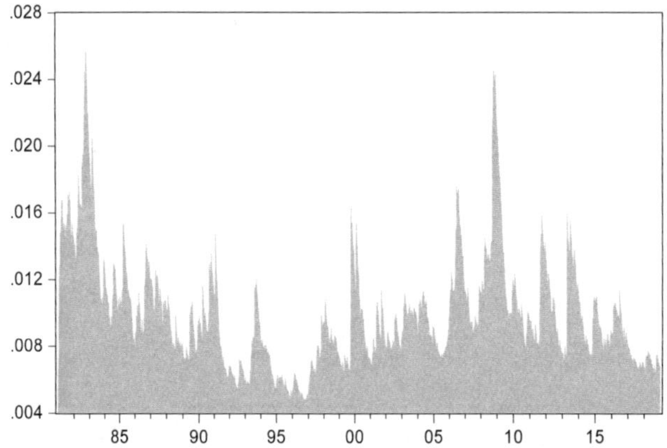

Figure 2 GARCH(*1,1*) simulation [own calculation]

As we can see in Figure 1, from the global perspective the development appears to be relatively stable till 2005 when the prices slightly varied around 370 $/troy ounce. The Figure 2 disproves this naïve assertion. The mean of simulated conditional standard deviations is 0.0098. The range of the values is $\langle 0.0047; 0.0256 \rangle$. According to the simulation, the highest volatility was reached in October 1982 (2. - 3. 10.) when the price fell about 4.96 % or 20.50 $/troy ounce. Higher volatility can be seen again in October 2008 (21. - 22. 10) when the price fell about 5.78 % or 44.60 $/troy ounce. Even though the relative and absolute change in 2008 is higher than in 1982, model attributes higher volatility to the beginning of 1980s due to the cluster. This fact can refer to the end of Breton-Wood system and the implementation of flexible exchange rates besides other factors.

Using the formula (4) we calculate unconditional volatility which has the value 0.0079. If we compare it with standard deviation presented in Table 1 for $dlgold_t$, we do not confirm the Starica's findings. In the case of gold, GARCH(*1,1*) under-estimates volatility.

3.2 Non-parametric simulation

A non-parametric simulation of volatility based on Nadaraya-Watson estimation of a zero-degree polynomial and quadratic kernel is presented in Figure 3.

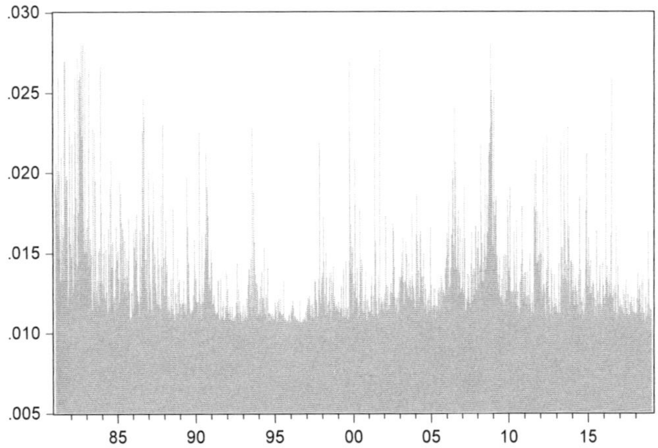

Figure 3 Non-parametric simulation [own calculation]

The volatility range in the case of non-parametric simulation is $\langle 0.0053; 0.0280\rangle$. Volatility clustering can also be seen in Octobers, 1982 and 2008. The mean of simulated unconditional standard deviations is 0.0113 which is in consensus with the true standard deviation. Due to this fact, one is motivated to believe that non-parametric regression is a trustworthy and real data generating process. It cannot be said because a non-parametric estimation does not involve any dynamics as it was already implied that volatility of financial data exhibits some kind of dynamics. In the non-parametric estimation, we assume that volatility is controlled by nonstructural exogenous factors. Therefore, in a non-parametric framework we predict a future volatility to be the same as a current one. On the other hand, GARCH(*1,1*) involves endogenous mechanism for capturing volatility.

3.3 Forecast

We performed a prediction of volatility for 250 days, using formulas (6) and (18), which is presented in Figure 4.

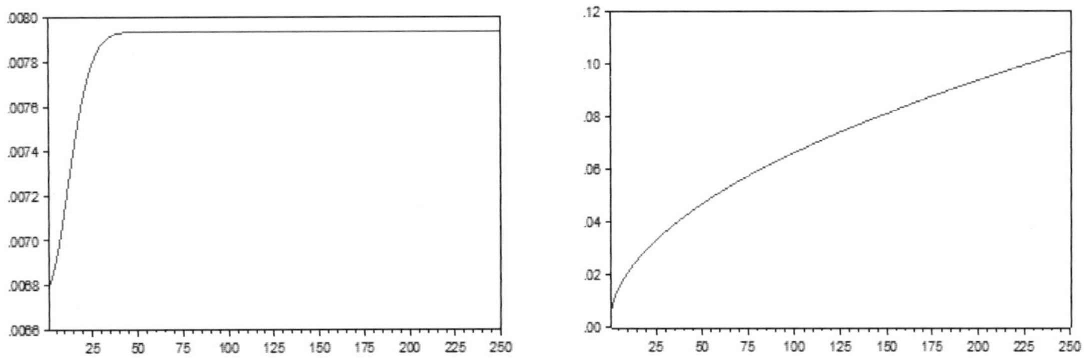

Figure 4 Volatility forecast with GARCH (left) and non-parametric (right) approaches [own calculation]

Although a non-parametric approach seemed to be sufficient for analyzing volatility developments, from Figure 4 it is obvious that volatility forecast accelerates faster and it is not stable. GARCH forecast stays in the unconditional standard deviation after 50. observation. This is an obvious consequence of formula (6) and stationarity property. However, the prediction of the next-day volatility is similar: GARCH model predicts 0.0068 and non-parametric model 0.0066. The lower value of mean square root error is achieved with GARCH model.

4 Conclusion

Starica claimed in his work that GARCH(*1,1*) tended to over-estimate conditional volatility. We showed that this was not the case for gold returns. We also pointed out that forecast of next-day volatility did not significantly differ. We also provided an example of replacement widely used GARCH model by non-parametric regression.

Correctly specified volatility developments and forecast are necessary for rational decisions of investors, portfolio management and they also can give a clue about possible crisis and the reaction of financial markets to them.

Acknowledgements

This work was supported by the Grant Agency of Slovak Republic - Vega grant No. 1/0294/18 "Short-run and long-run dynamic analysis of economic development of European post-communist countries and regions" and Vega grant No. 1/0248/17 "Analysis of Regional Disparities in the EU based on Spatial Econometric Approaches".

References

Bollerslev, T. (1986). 'Generalized autoregressive conditional heteroskedasticity'. *Journal of Econometrics*, 31 (3), pp. 307-327.

Bollerslev, T. (2009). Glossary to ARCH (GARCH), [Online]. Available at: https://pdfs.semanticscholar.org/ea8e/a53721fbc28efec73e509259b00a9193ba12.pdf [cited 2019-01-14].

Chocholatá, M. (2015). 'Dynamic interactions between stock returns and exchange rate returns in the Czech Republic'. *Proceedings of 11th International Conference on Strategic Management and Its Support by Information Systems 2015,* Ostrava, Czech Republic, pp. 229-236.

Engle, R. F. (1982). 'Autoregressive conditional heteroscedasticity with estimates of the variance of United Kingdom inflation'. *Econometrica*, 50 (4), pp. 987-1007.

Engle, R. F. and Gonzalez-Rivera, G. (1991). 'Semi-parametric ARCH models'. *Journal of Business and Economic Statistics,* 9 (4), pp. 345-360.

Gallant, A. R. and Nychka, D. W. (1989). 'Semi-non-parametric estimation of conditionally constrained heterogeneous processes: Asset Pricing Applications'. *Econometrica*, 57 (5), pp. 1091-1120.

Harvey, A. (1981). *The Econometric Analysis of Time Series*. New York: Wiley.

Knight, J. and Satchell, S. (2007). *Forecasting Volatility in the Financial Markets*, 3rd ed. Oxford: Elsevier.

Kováč, S. (2018). 'Analysis of interactions between the United Kingdom and Germany stock markets based on DVECH model'. *Proceedings of 18th International Scientific Conference, AIESA - Building of Society Based on Knowledge*, Bratislava, Slovakia, pp. 459-465.

Levin, E. J. and Montagnoli, A. and Wright, R. E. (2006). Short-run and long-run determinants of the price of gold, [Online]. Available at: https://strathprints.strath.ac.uk/7215/6/strathprints007215.pdf [cited 2019-01-14].

Nadaraya, E. A. (1964). 'On estimating regression'. *Theory of Probability and its Applications*, 9 (1), pp. 141-142.

Pagan, A. R. and Schwert, G. W. (1990). 'Alternative models for conditional stock volatility'. *Journal of Econometrics*, 45 (1), pp. 267-290.

Starica, C. (2003). *Is GARCH(1,1) as good a model as the accolades of the nobel prize would imply?* Working Paper.

Taylor, S. J. (1986). *Modelling Financial Time Series*. Chichester: John Wiley.

Wand, M. P. and Jones, M. C. (1995). *Kernel Smoothing*. London: Chapman and Hall.

Watson, G. S. (1964). 'Smooth regression analysis'. *Sankhyā: The Indian Journal of Statistics, Series A*, 26 (4), pp. 359-372.

www.stooq.com [cited 2019-01-14].

Optimization Model for the Personnel Scheduling Problem

Martina Kuncová[1], Lucie Beranová[2]

Abstract. Planning shifts and rostering workers is a routine activity of most businesses, but not everyone realizes how the way of planning can affect the efficiency of the entire business. Usually, simple methods based on the managers' knowledge are implemented. Optimization model applied in this situation can help not only to create the rosters but also to simplify and improve the process at all. This paper describes the creation of the optimization model for the employees' shifts schedule in one shop of the T-mobile company. Based on the real data the model was created and solved via LINGO solver connected with the MS Excel tool.

Keywords: Optimization model, shift work, scheduling, rosters, MS Excel, LINGO.

JEL Classification: C44, M12

1 Introduction

Scheduling of workers into shifts is a common manager's activity and is not always perceived as a difficult problem. The difficulty increases with the higher number of requirements on both employees' and employers' side. In such a situation, the manager gets into complicated bargaining with employees or is forced to set up a shift order by order, which can cause a variety of problems at the workplace. That is why a mathematical model and solution can be helpful.

Literature offers several ways to classify the tasks of this type. According to Van den Bergh et al. (2013), shift scheduling problems can be sorted by many criteria, such as:

- Characteristics of workers (contract type and length, team or individual work necessary, abilities of workers);
- Types of shifts (fixed, variable);
- Types and number of limitations (soft and hard constraints);
- Solution models with uncertainty elements (deterministic or stochastic models);
- Application area:
  - Crew scheduling - air, rail and bus services - examples in Dowling et al. (1997) or Graf et al. (2018);
  - Health care systems - as in Azaiez and Al Sharif (2005);
  - Protection and rescue services - fire and security services, ambulances and police;
  - Call centers - example in Robbins and Harrison (2010);
  - Retail – frequently solved, for example in Kuncová and Picková (2017);

Scheduling problems - usually called shift scheduling problems, rostering problems (Dowling et al., 1997), personnel scheduling problems (Van den Bergh et al., 2013) or timetabling problems (that are slightly different and connected with the time slots more than shifts (Skočdopolová, 2015)) - belong to the problems that can be solved via various technics of

[1] University of Economics, Dpt. of Econometrics, W.Churchill Sq. 4, 130 67 Prague 3, kuncovam@vse.cz.
[2] University Economics, Dpt. of Econometrics, W.Churchill Sq. 4, 130 67 Prague 3, beranova7@seznam.cz

operational research. Managers often use the Gantt chart only to add a person to an activity and to see the working hours for each person or to display the roster graphically (Dowling et al., 1997). But with a rising number of persons and different shifts or shift lengths and with other conditions being met it is better to use an optimization model. Usually these models are based on linear programming (LP), integer (ILP) or mixed-integer linear programming (MILP), combination of queuing model and integer programming (Green et al, 2001), stochastic programming (Robbins and Harrison, 2010), non-linear programming or goal programming (Azaiez and Al Sharif, 2005; Skočdopolová, 2015) but also other solution methods are possible such as demand modeling, metaheuristics (Dowling et al., 1997), constructive and improvement heuristics (Van den Bergh et al., 2013) or heuristics based on the combination of several linear programming models (Graf et al., 2018).

Due to the complexity of the problem with a lot of variables and constraints, the help of optimization software is necessary. Several software packages are available to help with staff scheduling but they are usually connected with the given type of the problem or with the given application area and cannot be easily transferred to another industry or company (Dowling et al., 1997; Robbins and Harrison, 2010). That is why it is always necessary to create a model for the given conditions. The rostering process can be separated into 6 phases (sometimes not all of them are necessary) (Dowling et al., 1997):

- demand modeling – setting the number of staff necessary for each shift;
- days-off scheduling – description of the rest days for workers;
- shift scheduling - an assignment of the number of employees to each shift to meet demand;
- a line of work construction – work schedule for each staff member;
- task assignment – if necessary, assignment of a task to the shifts;
- staff assignment - assignment of employees to the lines of work.

The application area also influences the type of the model concerning the number of days and hours - some are aimed at 5 workdays and 2 consecutive off-days, some at 5-7 days with limited workdays (airline crew, bus crew, call centers, restaurants staff etc.) and some at 7 workdays operating 24 hours a day like hospitals, manufacturing plants or retail stores (Musliu et al, 2002). Sometimes also the type of the work contract (full-time, part-time) is important to create a roster (Van den Bergh et al, 2013).

The aim of this work is to propose a more efficient way of solving the scheduling of shift employees at selected T-mobile store using selected methods of operational research, which would speed up the existing scheduling and optimize the timetable.

2 Data and methods

For this paper, data from the year 2016 from the T-Mobile system, which monitors people's passes through the store, was used (Beranová, 2018). Since passes include employee movements, it is necessary to use the so-called actual customer ratio, which has been set by managers at 0.6 for the given store. Currently, shift plans are manually set up, and the manager of a given branch uses the MS Excel file with a pre-arranged shift table. Two types of input data are taken into account when planning: the attendance of a store to estimate staff numbers for a certain amount of time and employee availability. Every employee can make a holiday request for a maximum of 4 days in a month, the remaining days will be taken a leave and must notify these requirements by the 20th of the month at the latest. Because of the uneven distribution of shifts, there is no fixed number of hours worked per week, but the hours are set based on the annual fund, with an average of 40 hours per week in all 12 months. In fact, the number of hours worked usually varies from 35h per week to 50h per week.

The company tries to count the required number of employees in advance - daily and for every hour and every month. The calculation is based on the attendance of the given store. Expected traffic is estimated from the hourly traffic during last year and the total number of visitors in the previous month of the current year. The use of these estimated data is very inefficient, the manager sees it in the graphs, but it is up to him/her to use this data in his/her planning. In practice, managers often did not respect charts, as it is very time-consuming to plan employees shifts based on twelve graphs while respecting many other limitations.

The schedule of shifts is always drawn for the entire month in advance, and the individual shifts are written into the schedule in the form of the start and end of the given shift. Six types of shifts are usually used (Table 1). Based on the information in Table 1, four time slots, 9-11hr, 11-15h, 15-19h, and 19-21hrs can be created.

Shift No.	Shift length in hours	Shift start	Shift end
1	12	9:00	21:00
2	6	9:00	15:00
3	10	9:00	19:00
4	8	11:00	19:00
5	10	11:00	21:00
6	6	15:00	21:00

Table 1 Types of the shifts

A total of 11 employees work in the shop, of which 1 employee works half-time, the remaining employees are full-time employees. Representatives have the task not only to supervise the processes in the shop, but at least 1 of them must unlock and lock the shop. Furthermore, each newcomer has an assigned mentor during the first three months of his/her work. Therefore, the mentor must always have a shift with the newcomer. The manager is also responsible for dealing with emergencies, such as a worker's illness. In this case, the manager is required to obtain an alternate. On one shift a maximum of 6 employees can be used because of the workspace.

For the analysis of the input data the knowledge and expert estimates of the employee of the shop were used and on this basis the queuing theory models were used to determine the intervals between the customer's arrival with the individual requirements (for details see Beranová, 2018). The required number of shift workers depends on the number of entry requirements to the system. Too many employees increase the company's costs and vice versa lack of staff leads to queues and customer dissatisfaction. Concerning the fact that data on staff costs was not available, the objective function will maximize the number of employees for a given period with respect to other conditions. In similar models, the objective function minimizing the number of employees is usually used. However, in this case the objective function was not the key one, since the number of employees is already given by the constraint (5) in which the number of employees necessary for each time slot is defined by matrix **A** (calculated before on the basis of real data using queuing theory model) and by the time period *d*. For example the number of employees necessary for the time slot 3 (15:00-19:00) is 5 which is the highest one, that is why minimal and maximal number of employees' time slots for 7 days should be 35. Based on the results of the models tested, where maximization has given more diverse shifts to employees compared with the minimization type, we decided to use the maximization type of the objective function.

The model should optimize the employees' schedule for one week. First, the input data table was prepared in MS Excel to know who out of 11 employees is available on a given day (Monday to Sunday) and a given shift 1-6.

According to the previous information we define the mathematical model for the personnel scheduling to shifts. We suppose the set of employees $B = \{B_1, B_2, \dots, B_n\}$, $n=11$ and the set of shifts $S = \{S_1, S_2, \dots, S_s\}$, $s = 6$. The aim is to assign the employees to the shifts to cover all shifts and with respect to other conditions given by managers of the company. Each employee who is available for the given week must work for a minimum of 35 hours and a maximum of 50 hours per week (if he/she works for the whole week). An employee should not have more than 3 twelve-hour shifts and he/she can work maximally 5 days a week.

The mathematical model of the problem can be formulated as follows:

$$z = \sum_{l=1}^{d} \sum_{k=1}^{s} \sum_{i=1}^{n} y_{lki} \to max \tag{1}$$

Subject to:

$$x_{lji} = \sum_{k=1}^{s} z_{jk} y_{lki}, \quad l = 1,2, \dots, d; j = 1,2, \dots, t; i = 1, 2, \dots, n \tag{2}$$

$$\sum_{k=1}^{s} y_{lki} \leq 1, \quad l = 1,2, \dots, d; i = 1, 2, \dots, n \tag{3}$$

$$y_{lki} \leq p_{lki}, \quad l = 1,2, \dots, d; k = 1, 2, \dots, s; \; i = 1, 2, \dots, n \tag{4}$$

$$\sum_{i=1}^{n} x_{lji} = a_{lj}, \quad l = 1,2, \dots, d; j = 1, 2, \dots, t \tag{5}$$

$$\sum_{l=1}^{w} \sum_{k=1}^{s} h_{lk} y_{lki} \geq minw_i, \quad i = 1, 2, \dots, n \tag{6}$$

$$\sum_{l=1}^{w} \sum_{k=1}^{s} h_{lk} y_{lki} \leq maxw_i, \quad i = 1, 2, \dots, n \tag{7}$$

$$y_{l1i} + y_{(l+1)1i} + y_{(l+2)1i} + y_{(l+3)1i} \leq 3, \quad l = 1, 2, \dots, d;\ i = 1, 2, \dots, n \tag{8}$$

$$y_{l1i} + y_{l2i} + y_{l3i} + y_{l4i} + y_{l5i} + y_{l6i} \leq 5, \quad l = 1, 2, \dots, d;\ i = 1, 2, \dots, n \tag{9}$$

$$x_{lji} \in \{0,1\}, \quad l = 1, 2, \dots, d;\ j = 1,2, \dots, t;\ i = 1, 2, \dots, n \tag{10}$$

$$y_{lki} \in \{0,1\}, \quad l = 1, 2, \dots, d;\ k = 1,2, \dots, s;\ i = 1, 2, \dots, n \tag{11}$$

where:

d is the number of working days in a week (d=7),

n is the number of employees (in the given case n=11),

s is the number of shifts (s=6),

t is the number of time slots (t=4),

y_{lki} is a binary variable that is equal to 1 if the i-th worker is assigned to the k-th shift in the l-th day, 0 in other cases,

x_{lji} is a binary variable that is equal to 1 if the i-th worker is assigned to the j-th time slot in in the l-th day, 0 in other cases,

z_{jk} is the value from the matrix Z which connects shifts and time slots (Table 2),

p_{lki} is the parameter of the input matrix P that defines the workers availability in the day l

a_{lj} indicates the number of workers to be assigned to the j-th time period of day l

h_{lk} indicates the lengths of the k-th shift in the day l

$minw_i$ is the minimum number of working hours per week for the worker i (in our model $minw_i$=35 for each worker)

$maxw_i$ is the maximum number of working hours per week for the worker i (in our model $maxw_i$=50 for each worker)

			shift					
		z_{jk}	**1**	**2**	**3**	**4**	**5**	**6**
time slot	**9:00**	1	1	1	1	0	0	0
	11:00	2	1	1	1	1	1	0
	15:00	3	1	0	1	1	1	1
	19:00	4	1	0	0	0	1	1

Table 2 Z matrix – connections of the time slots and shifts

The objective function (1) maximizes the number of employees assigned to the given shift in a whole week. The equation (2) guarantees the interconnection of shifts and time slots with the Z-matrix. The matrix determines what shift covers the time slots during the day. The constraint (3) stipulates that employees may not be assigned more than 1 shift per day. The condition (4) will guarantee that employees will be assigned a shift on a given day only if they can come to work on that day (they set it in the input data table). The equation (5) guarantees that an optimal number of employees will be assigned within a given time period, given by the queuing theory model. The constraints (6) and (7) regulate the minimum and maximum hours worked per worker per week. Furthermore, the worker should not work more than 3 twelve-hour shifts consecutively, which is the condition (8) and for a whole week the twelve-hour shifts should not exceed 5, see the condition (9).

3 Results and discussion

The solution to the personnel scheduling problem is based on two phases. In the first phase, it is necessary to enter the input data for the given week for all workers and the expected customer arrival data (table were created in MS Excel – see Beranová, 2018). Based on this, the optimal number of shop staff for each shift is estimated using the queuing theory model (Beranová, 2018). This data then enters the linear optimization model. The main result of the model is determining which worker should work on which shift. Due to the number of integer variables, the optimization model cannot be solved in MS Excel (it is possible to solve the problem with max. 200 variables), so the data was transferred to LINGO solver and the optimization results were then written back to the tables in MS Excel. There is also, by means of other tables, checked that all the parameters entered by the manager are met.

According to the LINGO solver results (LINGO 12.0, 2019) the model has 770 variables and 953 constraints. The solution time was 0.41 seconds after 6621 iterations. LINGO classify this problem as PILP, it means pure integer linear problem where "*all expressions are linear, and all variables are restricted to integer values*" (LINGO-Solver Status Window, 2019).

Figure 1 describes the results of the model for one tested case with 11 employees where 2 employees cannot work during the week (for this article the rows and columns were renamed into English names, the original design prepared for T-Mobile is in Czech). The table shows the results for the matrix Y (on the left) and the other two control matrices.

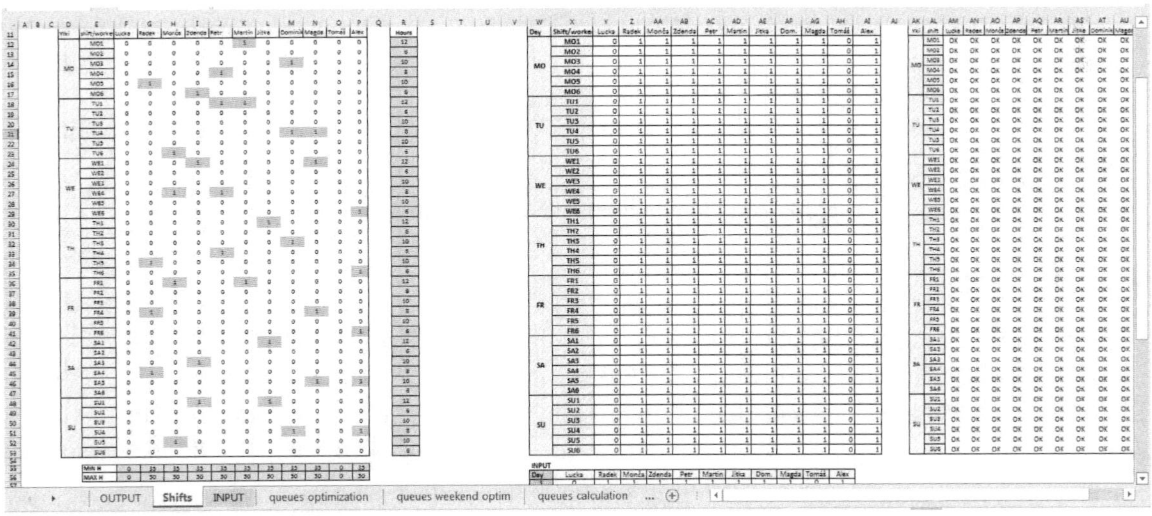

Figure 1 Results of the model in MS Excel [customized by the data from Beranová, 2018]

Other results (matrix X – Figure 2) indicate the layout of the employees at time slots according to the pre-set requirements of the manager.

X_{ij}	slot	Lucka	Radek	Monča	Zdenda	Petr	Martin	Jitka	Dom.	Magda	Tomáš	Alex	a_{ij}	contr.
MO	MON1	0	0	0	0	0	1	0	1	0	0	0	2	OK
	MON2	0	1	0	0	1	1	0	1	0	0	0	4	OK
	MON3	0	1	0	1	1	1	0	1	0	0	0	5	OK
	MON4	0	1	0	1	0	1	0	0	0	0	0	3	OK
TU	TUE1	0	0	0	0	1	1	0	0	0	0	0	2	OK
	TUE2	0	0	0	0	1	1	0	1	1	0	0	4	OK
	TUE3	0	0	1	0	1	1	0	1	1	0	0	5	OK
	TUE4	0	0	1	0	1	1	0	0	0	0	0	3	OK
WE	WED1	0	0	0	1	0	0	0	0	1	0	0	2	OK
	WED2	0	0	1	1	1	0	0	0	1	0	0	4	OK
	WED3	0	0	1	1	1	0	0	0	1	0	1	5	OK
	WED4	0	0	0	1	0	0	0	0	1	0	1	3	OK
TH	THU1	0	0	0	0	0	0	1	1	0	0	0	2	OK
	THU2	0	1	0	0	1	0	1	1	0	0	0	4	OK
	THU3	0	1	0	0	1	0	1	1	0	0	1	5	OK
	THU4	0	1	0	0	0	0	1	0	0	0	1	3	OK
FR	FRI1	0	0	1	0	0	1	0	0	0	0	0	2	OK
	FRI2	0	1	1	0	0	1	0	0	1	0	0	4	OK
	FRI3	0	1	1	0	0	1	0	0	1	0	1	5	OK
	FRI4	0	0	1	0	0	1	0	0	0	0	1	3	OK
SA	SAT1	0	0	0	1	0	0	1	0	0	0	0	2	OK
	SAT2	0	1	0	1	0	0	1	0	1	0	1	5	OK
	SAT3	0	1	0	1	0	0	1	0	1	0	1	5	OK
	SAT4	0	0	0	0	0	0	1	0	1	0	1	3	OK
SU	SUN1	0	0	0	1	0	0	1	0	0	0	0	2	OK
	SUN2	0	0	1	1	0	0	1	1	0	0	1	5	OK
	SUN3	0	0	1	1	0	0	1	1	0	0	1	5	OK
	SUN4	0	0	1	1	0	0	1	0	0	0	0	3	OK

Figure 2 Results of the model in MS Excel – matrix X [customized by the data from Beranová, 2018]

The results recorded in matrices may be confusing for the manager, so the resulting form has been modified to the final statement of assignment of shift workers (Table 3).

Data	Lucka	Radek	Monča	Zdenda	Petr	Martin	Jitka	Dominik	Magda	Tomáš	Alex
MO	free day	11:00-21:00		15:00-21:00	11:00-19:00	11:00-21:00		09:00-19:00		free day	
TU	free day		15:00-21:00		09:00-21:00	11:00-21:00		11:00-19:00	11:00-19:00	free day	
WE	free day		11:00-19:00	09:00-21:00	11:00-19:00				09:00-21:00	free day	15:00-21:00
TH	free day	11:00-21:00			11:00-19:00		09:00-21:00	09:00-19:00		free day	15:00-21:00
FR	holi-day	11:00-19:00	09:00-21:00			11:00-21:00			11:00-19:00	holiday	15:00-21:00
SA	holi-day	11:00-19:00		09:00-19:00			09:00-21:00		11:00-21:00	holiday	11:00-21:00
SU	holi-day		11:00-21:00	09:00-21:00			09:00-21:00	11:00-19:00		holiday	11:00-19:00

Table 3 Results – description of the shifts assigned to each worker

4 Conclusions

Personnel scheduling of employees into shifts is made in many companies rather randomly and based on managers' ability to create the right roster. The use of operational research methods could be helpful in the situation. One of the possible approaches for assigning workers on shifts was presented in this paper. The created optimization model is based on defined inputs and data entered by the manager, part of the input is also obtained from the queuing theory model. By linking MS Excel and LINGO, the resulting shift schedule for workers is obtained. The model has been tested for a schedule within 1 week. It would be appropriate to assign employees for a longer period of time, but it means both further extension of the model in terms of number of variables and addition of new constraints arising from the nature of work at the shop (as the model do not cover the types of employees – if it is a newcomer or not). As the input data can be entered into tables in MS Excel, it would not be necessary for the manager to have knowledge of the linear models' creation. The problem, however, lies in the solvability of the model, where Solver in MS Excel cannot be used, and it is necessary to obtain the solution elsewhere (here in LINGO solver). The company would have to invest in appropriate optimization software, which also implies the need to extend the knowledge of managers or one of the staff members in the field of operational research or the need for long-term cooperation with the school/company that would manage the models. But finally, the model and results could help both managers and employees.

Acknowledgements

This work was supported by grant IGA F4/66/2019 of the Faculty of Informatics and Statistics, University of Economics, Prague.

References

Azaiez, M.N. and Al Sharif, S.S. (2005). 'A 0-1 goal programming model for nurse scheduling'. *Computers & Operations Research*, 32 (2005), pp. 491–507.

Beranová, L. (2018). 'Nástroj pro optimalizaci směn ve společnosti T-Mobile'. Master theses, University of Economics, Prague, 2018.

Dowling, D., Krishnamoorthy, M., Mackenzie, H. and Sier, D. (1997). 'Staff rostering at a large international airport'. *Annals of Operations Research*, 72 (1997), pp. 125–147.

Graf, V., Teichmann, D. and Dorda, M. (2018). 'Contribution to Crew Rostering in Air Transport'. *Proceedings of the International Scientific Conference Quantitative Methods in Economics – Multiple Criteria Decision Making XIX,* Trenčianske Teplice, Slovakia, pp. 135-143.

Green, L.V., Kolesar, P.J. and Soares, J. (2001). 'Improving the SIPP approach for staffing service systems that have cyclic demands'. *Operations Research,* 49 (4), pp. 549–564.

Kuncová, M. and Picková, V. (2017). 'Optimization Model for the Employees' Shifts Schedule'. *Proceedings of 35th International Conference Mathematical Methods in Economics*, Hradec Králové, Czech Republic, pp. 390-395.

LINGO 12.0 (2019). Optimization Modeling Software for Linear, Nonlinear, and Integer Programming. Lindo Systems Inc.

LINGO (2019). Solver Status Window, [Online]. Available at: https://www.lindo.com/doc/online_help/lingo15_0/solver_status_window.htm [cited 2019-03-14].

Musliu, N., Gartner, J. and Slany, W. (2002). 'Efficient generation of rotating workforce schedules'. *Discrete Applied Mathematics* 118 (1-2), pp. 85-98.

Robbins, T.R. and Harrison, T.P. (2010). 'A stochastic programming model for scheduling call centers with global Service Level Agreements'. *European Journal of Operational Research,* 207 (2010), pp. 1608-1619.

Skočdopolová, V. (2015). 'Optimisation of University Timetable via Complex Goal Programming Model'. *Proceedings of 33rd International Conference Mathematical Methods in Economics*, Cheb, Czech Republic, pp. 725-730.

Van den Bergh, Beliën, J.J., De Bruecker, P., Demeulemeester, E. and de Boeck, L. (2013). 'Personnel scheduling: A literature review'. *European Journal of Operational Research,* 226 (3), pp. 367-385, [Online]. Available at: http://linkinghub.elsevier.com/retrieve/pii/S0377221712008776 [cited 2019-01-21].

Identifying Factors Affecting Visitor Attendance in a City Building – Case Study of Brno Market

Martina Langhammerová [1], Vlastimil Reichel[2]

Abstract: This research investigates the factors that could affect the visitor attendance of a public city building. Specifically, it describes the most common factors and trends affecting visitor attendance of Brno Market building. The study is looking at aspects such as weather and outside temperature, events inside the building, other events in Brno city centre, public holidays, school holidays, day of a week, day of a month, month and precipitations. Data for this study was gathered from a camera system installed in the building of Brno Market specially for needs of this study. This paper provides partial results of the whole study and depicts predictions for the final results. The whole study will be published in May 2019 when longer observation of visitor attendance will be provided.

Keywords: linear regression, visitor monitoring, visitor attendance, Brno Market.

JEL Classification: C1, M37, M210

1 Introduction

The building of Brno Market[3] has an unique position in Brno city center. This location naturally makes it necessary to think about its use in a broader context. Brno Market complements the traditional epicenter of Brno social life at Zelný trh. Thanks to traditional outdoor markets, national theatre Reduta and theatre Husa na provázku, Brno underground labyrinth, many coffee shops and three important Brno hotels, Zelný trh became the gastronomic and cultural center of Brno.

Brno Market offers to its visitors not only the possibility of buying local products but also non-commercial activities such as degustation, presentation of exotic food, workshops and diverse cultural events.

The building of Brno Market should primarily ensure the possibility of selling products that cannot be offered in the open market areas at Zelný trh for hygienic reasons, such as cheese or meat. The second purpose of roofed market place in Brno should be demonstration of various foreign cuisines to Brno citizens and that is why there are also bistros and cafés in the building.

This kind of building with its unique position have undoubtedly a big potential to become a significant attribute of the whole city and should be visited not only by Brno citizens but also by many tourists.

[1] Masaryk University, Lipová 41a, Brno, Czech Republic, 421196@mail.muni.cz
[2] Masaryk University, Lipová 41a, Brno, Czech Republic, reichel.v@mail.muni.cz
[3] More info at Brno Market official web page (Brno Market (2018))

1.1 Statement of Problem

The building of Brno Market has not always been used as a marketplace. The history of the building started in 1951 when the city let built "Dům potravin" (Foodstuff House) in the late functionalist style. In 1990's very insensitive reconstruction took place and the statics of the building were disturbed. The building was then rented out and served as Vietnamese market hall where mainly clothes were sold and then finally closed due to critical statics issues.

After several years of non-functioning, the leadership of Brno-center district, at that time headed by the ODS political party, decided to undertake a new reconstruction and return such an important building to the city life. This should have led also to returning Brno citizens back to the city center which became an increasing problem after development of big shopping malls and multifunctional buildings on the Brno outskirts (Padilla, Hermosilla and Ozores (2017)). This last reconstruction costed 70 million CZK of public finance and was completed in July 2017 when today's Brno Market building started to operate.

One and half year after its reopening, the building does not seem to fulfill its potential which has been predicted not only by leadership of the Brno-center district but also by public.

1.2 Purpose of Study

The main reason why this study is carried out is to identify the main factors affecting visitor attendance in the building of Brno Market and to recommend possible solutions for an increase in use of the building potential. There are many studies which examine visitor attendance for further marketing purposes such as Ploner and Brandenburg (2003), Pettebone, Newman and Lawson (2010) or þórhallsdóttir and Ólafsson (2017). This research emphasizes the aspect of organizing events in the building which was inspired also by already carried out studies such as Connell, Page and Meyer (2014). However, majority of previous studies focused much attention to mega events and civic events but events organized by profit-making organizations such as shopping centers or markets were not examined properly (Wu and Lo, (2018)). The consumer preferences for visitors and their motivation to visit the business centers (markets) was thoroughly elaborated by Blommenstein, Nijkamp and Van Veenendaal, (1980). Our research will provide Brno market management with an inside look at visitors' motivation to visit the building and to carry out a purchase inside the building.

The results of the study will be helpful not only for the management of the building as handy recommendations how to increase visitor attendance, which might be subsequently transformed into higher number of purchases carried out by visitors inside the building, but also for the leadership of Brno-center district as a research for improving use of public places (buildings) and returning social life to Brno city center. This might be very beneficial as the partnership between the private (mainly shops and retailers) and the public (local authority) sectors became accepted as a crucial aspect for vitality and viability (Whyatt, 2004). In the final consequence, this study could help to allocate public finance more effectively.

The study will identify factors affecting the visitor attendance in a city building and it will also assess the weights of particular factors. In this manner the study will determine the factor with the biggest influence (however, the partial results presented in this paper will answer only the question about all significant factors, not the biggest one). The study will also answer a question, if there is any difference in visitor attendance in a public building when cultural event takes place in it. Also, the study will detect a correlation between visitor attendance in a public building and number of purchases inside the building, if there is any.

2 Data

The quantitative data was gathered (1) from camera system installed in Brno Market building exclusively for needs of this study (see Camea (2018), Cognitechna (2018)), (2) from record sheets concerning number of purchases per day from businesses placed inside the building and (3) from the Internet sources containing information on outside temperature, weather, public and school holidays (E-Pocasi (2018)).

Variable	Shortcut	Description
total visits	t_visit	Number of total visits in Brno Market
women visits	w_visit	Number of total visits of women in Brno Market
men visits	m_visit	Number of total visits of men in Brno Market
total purchases	purch	Number of total purchases made in Brno Market per day
average temperature	avg_temp	Average outside temperature over three days
temperature difference	dif_temp	Change in outside temperature over three days
event	event	Event organized in Brno Market
public holiday	p_holi	Day of public holiday
school holiday	s_holi	Day of school holiday
day of week	day	Day of a week (Monday – Sunday)
month	month	Month (August – December)
august	aug	Month of August
september	sept	Month of September
october	octo	Month of October
november	novem	Month of November
december	decem	Month of December
very small event	vs_event	Event with up to 100 expected participants
small event	s_event	Event with 101 – 499 expected participants
medium event	m_event	Event with 500 – 2499 expected participants
large event	l_event	Event with more than 2500 expected participants
monday to wednesday	mo_we	Beginning of a week (Monday – Wednesday)
thursday to friday	th_fr	Middle of a week (Thursday – Friday)
weekend	weend	Weekend (Saturday – Sunday)
monday to wednesday with very small event	mw_vse	Day in the beginning of a week when very small event is organized
monday to wednesday with small event	mw_se	Day in the beginning of a week when small event is organized

monday to wednesday with medium event	mw_me	Day in the beginning of a week when medium event is organized
monday to wednesday with large event	mw_le	Day in the beginning of a week when large event is organized
thursday to friday with very small event	tf_vse	Day in the middle of a week when very small event is organized
thursday to friday with small event	tf_se	Day in the middle of a week when small event is organized
thursday to friday with medium event	tf_me	Day in the middle of a week when medium event is organized
thursday to friday with large event	tf_le	Day in the middle of a week when large event is organized
weekend with very small event	w_vse	Weekend day when very small event is organized
weekend with small event	w_se	Weekend day when small event is organized
weekend with medium event	w_me	Weekend day when medium event is organized
weekend with large event	w_le	Weekend day when large event is organized
precipitation	rain	Precipitation per day

Table 1 Description of dataset

The data was gathered between August 2018 and December 2018. During that period, permanent time-lapse video recording systems were installed at 3 main entrances points to Brno Market during all its opening hours. To be able to guarantee anonymity of visitors, the video system installed was not able to identify individual persons, but it was able to determine sex and approximate age.

The video system registered date, exact time of a visit, video station, estimated sex and age and direction of movement of a visitor. Complete data sets were obtained only for 73 days when all installed cameras operated without failure.

The record sheets concerning number of purchases per day were obtained from 10 gastronomic businesses placed inside the building (out of 17 businesses in total in August and September and out of 15 businesses in total from October to December).

Meteorological data was gathered from Czech Internet web page providing information about average day temperature and amount of precipitation per day (E-Pocasi (2018)).

In Table 1 we describe the dataset with all variables considered. The first six variables are numeric, and all other variables are dummy. Not all the variables from Table 1 are used later in the models (see results in Table 3) due to their statistical characteristics. However, Table 1 provides summary of all collected variables for potential needs of any further research in the future.

3 Methods

Three groups of variables are used for the identification of determinants of the visitor attendance. We chose the variables according to a research made by Ploner and Brandenburg (2003).

The function describing relationship between the visitor attendance and individual group of variables can be defined by the following equation (1):

$$V = f(FOT, FNTR, FNTN) \tag{1}$$

where *V* stands for the visitor attendance, *FOT* stands for the factors that can be influenced by Brno Market such as events organized inside the building, *FNTR* stands for accidental factors affecting the visitor attendance in Brno Market such as weather, *FNTN* stands for factors affecting the visitor attendance in Brno Market that are not accidental and Brno Market is not able to influence them but they can be predicted, such as day of week, event organized in neighbourhood etc.

The visitor attendance in Brno Market is modelled using linear regression model (see Pindyck and Rubinfeld, (1997)). The specific form of the model can be described by following equation (2):

$$V = \alpha + \sum_{i=1}^{j} \beta_i \, FOT_i + \sum_{i=1+j}^{k} \beta_i \, FNTR_i + \sum_{i=1+k}^{n} \beta_i \, FNTN_i + \varepsilon_i \tag{2}$$

where α stands for a level constant, β_i denotes the marginal effects for each parameter belonging to the individual group of variables affecting Brno Market visitor attendance, ε_i denote errors.

Estimation of linear regression model was obtained by the ordinary least squares method. The estimation of the model was executed in the Gretl program. The correctness of the estimation results was verified by the selected model selection criteria, Heteroskedasticity test (White test) and Normality test (Doornik and Hansen test). For more information about model selection criteria and tests see Gretl User's Guide, Cottrell and Lucchetti (2019).

4 Results

In this section we provide partial results of provisional data analysis (using linear regression model) of the whole study.

The first question that can be already answered is whether there is a positive relationship between number of total visits of Brno Market and number of total purchases carried out in the building. The Table 2 describes the calculated correlation coefficients between number of total visits (divided into three observed groups - the total number of visits, the number of visits of men and the number of visits of women) and number of total purchases per day. We further consider three more groups of variables– all days, days with an event organized inside the building, days where there is no event in the building).

Correlation	**M+W**	**M**	**W**
All days	0.778	0.612	0.780
Event	0.771	0.607	0.759
No Event	0.850	0.789	0.858

Table 2 Correlation coefficients between number of total visits and purchases per day

The Table 2 clearly shows the positive correlation between number of total purchases per day and number of total visits. From the Table 1 it can be also seen that the correlation between the men and women visitor attendance differs when days with an event and days with no event are taken into account. In the case when there is an event organized inside the building there is a lower correlation for both men and women.

The interpretation of the estimated models is following. In total, three models were estimated (Model A-C) and they differ only in use of dependent variables. One by one was used the number of total visits, number of visits of women and number of visits of men as a dependent variable. The results of each model are shown in Table 3. The quality of the model (Model A-C) was assessed using various statistical tests. The F-test confirmed that the whole model is statistically significant. According to the White test there is no problem with heteroscedasticity of residuals and Doornik and Hansen test also showed that the residuals are normally distributed.

We can interpret the level constant in all three models in a similar way. The level constant includes a reference group which denotes the average visitor attendance during a weekend in the month of December in the case when all other explanatory variables equaled zero. We can conclude from the level constants of model A-C that during weekends in December women (model B) visited Brno Market more often than men (model C). If marginal effects of other months are taken into account (octo, novem), we can observe that the same is true for October and November. The only month when men were estimated to visit Brno Market during weekends as often as women is September. This finding might be explained by higher frequency of events organized specifically for men (for example Octoberfest, beer tap takeovers etc.). In Table 3, the standard deviations of the parameter estimate are given in the brackets.

We also decided to examine whether the visitor attendance differs significantly from the weekend in the case when it is a beginning of a week (mo_we) and a middle of a week (th_fr). Both variables were statistically insignificant in all estimated models (A-C). However, if the point estimates are observed, then it is found that the visitor attendance should be lower in a beginning of a week and gradually increase.

The effects of events organized inside Brno Market building on its visitor attendance are following. Very small events, small events and medium events do not significantly increase the visitor attendance in Brno Market. From the point estimates it follows that there is an increase in total visits when a very small event (increase especially in women visits) and medium event (increase especially in men visits) is organized. This finding might be explained by the typical character of very small events that are organized in Brno Market, it is usually about handcraft workshops, yoga classes or cooking sessions. These kinds of events are, by nature, attended mostly by women. On the contrary, any large event organized in a beginning of a week significantly increases Brno Market visitor attendance.

Small and medium events organized in the middle of a week has insignificant influence on the visitor attendance. What we find interesting, it is the interpretation of the difference between the marginal influence of a small event organized on Thursdays or Fridays on the men and women visitor attendance. Those small events on Thursdays are craft beer events ("tap takeovers" when all taps are overtaken by only one brewery, typically with the presence of a representant of the brewery) that are aimed at men and this might explain the mentioned difference.

Small events at weekends have positive, but statistically insignificant, effect only on the visitor attendance by women. Medium and large events organized at weekends have positive and significant effect on the visitor attendance by both men and women.

Another group of variables are public holidays and school holidays that were also examined. We assumed that the visitor attendance in Brno Market would decrease for both of those variables. When the variable of public holiday was taken into account, there was a significant decrease in the total visits of men and contrarily insignificant increase in the total visits of women. Considering the variable of school holiday did not provide any convincing results.

Last group of variables are variables containing weather. The variable dif_temp includes a change in temperature over the last three days. The variable rain, which gains value 1 when it rains and interaction variable dif_temp*rain. The point estimates of those variables came out as it was expected. In the case that it rains, the visitor attendance in Brno Market is lower. As the temperature rises, Brno Market visitor attendance increases, but not when the temperature rises and it simultaneously rains. The interesting finding is the fact, that those variables are statistically significant only for the total visits of women.

Variable	Model A	Model B	Model C
nst	2653.2	1778.0	874.1
	(322.4)***	(246.0)***	(133.2)***
sept	-1101.0	-1083.2	-31.2
	(348.1)***	(265.7)***	(143.0)
octo	-1247.2	-744.0	-516.7
	(299.3)***	(228.4)***	(123.7)***
novem	-1173.1	-702.4	-482.9
	(223.0)	(170.2)***	(92.2)***
mo_we	-607.6	-368.0	-237.3
	(372.2)	(284.0)	(153.0)
th_fr	22.7	76.5	-53.6
	(357.6)	(272.1)	(147.8)
mw_vse	-156.7	-118.1	-46.4
	(210.5)	(160.6)	(87.0)
mw_se	200.1	144.5	56.3
	(202.6)	(154.6)	(83.8)
mw_me	119.4	-4.2	127.9
	(356.5)	(272.1)	(147.4)
mw_le	3754.2	1808.6	1953.3
	(559.9)***	(427.2)***	(231.4)***
tf_se	-121.0	-288.1	175.3
	(322.6)	(246.1)	(133.4)
tf_me	-161.4	-125.2	-35.2
	(205.01)	(156.4)	(87.7)

w_se	239.8	541.8	-299.331
	(483.0)	(368.6)	(199.7)
w_me	899.2	602.6	296.909
	(388.5)**	(296.5)**	(160.6)*
w_le	2506.0	1329.9	1180.43
	(422.5)***	(322.1)***	(174.0)***
p_holi	-586.7	204.1	-784.028
	(604.8)	(461.6)	(250.0)***
s_holi	-14.0	-66.1	50.0276
	(304.5)	(232.1)	(125.9)
ZT_market	40.5	-59.0	114.247
	(245.3)	(187.3)	(101.4)
dif_temp	56.4	47.9	9.67186
	(36.1)	(27.5)*	(14.9)
rain	-224.1	-221.2	-2.65882
	(49.1)	(113.8)*	(61.6)
rain*dif_temp	-75.9	-44.6	-32.6642
	(65.3)	(49.88)	(27.0)
Adjusted R^2	0.81	0.71	0.86
F test	0.00***	0.00***	0.00***
Heteroscedasticity test	0.24***	0.14***	0.06**
Normality test	0.03*	0.16***	0.07**

Table 3 Results of models A-C. Note: The standard deviations of the parameter estimate are given in the brackets; *, **, *** denote level of importance 10%, 5%, 1%.

5 Conclusion

This paper provides discussion only of partial results of the "Identifying factors affecting the visitor attendance in a city building – case study of Brno Market" study due to shorter observation of visitor attendance in the building. The whole study will be published in May 2019 when there will be longer observed period available. However, there are interesting findings so far as well. The positive correlation between number of total purchases per day and number of total visits was found as well as the fact that the correlation between the total visits of women and men differs if we consider days with an event and days with no event.

In this paper we presented three estimated models (A-C) that differ only in the use of dependent variables (total visits, number of visits of women and number of visits of men). We found out that women visited Brno Market more often than men in all months except September. Very small events, small events and medium events proved to have insignificant effect on the visitor attendance in Brno Market. On the other hand, there is a significant increase in the visitor attendance when large event is organized in the beginning of a week. In the models we also consider public holidays, school holidays and weather. There is a significant decrease in the total visits of men and insignificant increase in the total visits of women when we include public holiday in the model. When considering temperature and precipitation, the visitor attendance in Brno Market increases as the temperature rises but not in the case when it rains at the same time.

Acknowledgements

This work was supported by funding of specific research at Faculty of Economics and Administration, Masaryk University, project MUNI/A/0966/2017.

References

Brno Market (2018). http://www.trznicebrno.cz/historie-trznice/.

Blommenstein, H., Nijkamp, P. and Van Veenendaal, W. (1980). 'Shopping Perceptions and Preferences: A Multidimensional Attractiveness Analysis of Consumer and Entrepreneurial Attitudes'. *Economic Geography*, 56 (2), pp. 155-174.

Camea (2018). https://www.camea.cz/cz/.

Cognitechna (2018). http://cognitechna.cz/.

Connell, J., Page, S. and Meyer, J. (2014). 'Visitor attractions and events: Responding to seasonality'. *Tourism Management*, 46 (2015), pp. 283-298.

E-Pocasi (2018). http://www.e-pocasi.cz/archiv-pocasi/2018/.

Cottrell, A. and Lucchetti R. (2019). Gretl User's Guide, [Online]. Available at: http://gretl.sourceforge.net/gretl-help/gretl-guide.pdf.

Padilla. A., Hermosilla, A. and Ozores, O. (2017). 'The impact of out-of-town shopping centres on town-centre retailers and employment: The case of the Region of Murcia'. *Land Use Policy*, 65 (2017), pp. 277-286.

Pettebone, D., Newman, P. and Lawson, S.R. (2010). 'Estimating visitor use at attraction sites and trailheads in Yosemite National Park using automated visitor counters'. *Landsc. Plann.*, 97, pp. 229-238.

Pindyck, S. and Rubinfeld, L. (1997). *Econometric models and economic forecasts*. 4th ed. Boston: Irwin.

Ploner, A. and Brandenburg, Ch. (2003). 'Modelling visitor attendance levels subject to day of the week and weather: a comparison between linear regression models and regression trees'. *J. Nat. Conserv.*, 11 (4), pp. 297-308.

þórhallsdóttir, G. and Ólafsson, R. (2017). 'A method to analyse seasonality in the distribution of tourists in Iceland'. *Journal of Outdoor Recreation and Tourism*, 19 (2017), pp. 17-24.

Whyatt, G. (2004). 'Town centre management: how theory informs a strategic approach'. International *Journal of Retail & Distribution Management*, 32 (7) (2004), pp. 346-353.

Wu, S. and Lo. S. (2018). 'Events as community function of shopping centres: A case study of Hong Kong'. *Cities*, 72 (2018), pp. 130-140.

The forecast of unemployment in Hungary and the role of social innovation in employment expansion

Katalin Lipták[1]

Abstract. The aim of the study is to analyse unemployment in the Hungarian labour market using the ARIMA (autoregressive-integrated-moving-average) model. According to my opinion, knowing the unemployment forecast is very useful and important for the decision makers and researchers. If the forecast is well known, the employment policies and directions can be formulated easier. I prepare a 12-month prognosis for the data of Hungarian unemployment (number of registered job-seekers). Such forecasts can be useful for decision makers and managers. Next, I introduce an example of social innovation at the settlement level. It is my belief that social innovation can be a good solution to the problem of unemployment. Any interpretation of social innovation so far can also be assigned the specific feature of employment expansion.

Keywords: unemployment, forecast, social innovation.

JEL Classification: C53, J21

1 Introduction

The forecast of unemployment is very important tool. The aim of my paper is to give new results of forecast of unemployment in Hungary (national level) and define what is the social innovation. Nowadays the unemployment rate is not so high in Hungary (3.7% in 2018), but some years ago (in 2010) it was 12% or higher (Central Statistical Office). The reasons for the decrease are a very strong employment policy and some new solutions in the public employment; it cannot be attributed, however, to the spread of atypical forms of employment. The transition from the traditional employment model to a new model, requires a change in the attitude of labour market participants. In this situation, successful examples of social innovations play a key role; these can be observed in local development or in employment expansion. My hypothesis is that Hungary is performing less strongly in the area of labour market participation, because atypical employment is not widespread, and there is some social innovation, but not enough. More good examples and best practices are needed.

2 Methodology - the forecast of unemployment

We distinguish two types of time series: theoretical and empirical (observed) timelines. Empirical time lines always contains a finite number of n-element members and contain observation error, while theoretical time lines in principle can be infinite and free of observation error (Hunyadi et al., 1997). The monthly unemployment data is suitable for stochastic time line analysis, as I wish to deal with the analysis of the short-term effects, primarily. The decomposition models include the most popular time line analysis methods. The principles of these time lines are that they consist of four well separated components (additive models as in the case of ARIMA):

[1] Department of Labour Market and Employment Policy, Faculty of Economics, University of Miskolc, liptak.katalin@uni-miskolc.hu

$$Y(t) = X_T(t) + X_S(t) + X_C(t) + X_\xi(t) \quad (1)$$

where:

$Y(t)$ – the factual data of the examined time lines,

$X_T(t)$ – trend (permanently prevailing tendency, is a long-term basis tendency),

$X_S(t)$ – seasonal component (differing from the trend, the measure of a periodic fluctuation),

$X_C(t)$ – cyclic component (the long-term fluctuation),

$X_\xi(t)$ – irregular component (stationery, Gauss – distribution random effect).

The application of the ARIMA (autoregressive-integrated-moving-average) model in the literature is known as Box-Jenkins methodology, which was first developed in the 1930s (Box and Jenkins, 1976). Auto-regression is a form of regression in which the dependent variable relates to its own different delayed values of the past instead of to other variables.

$$Y_t = \varphi_1 Y_{t-1} + \ldots + \varphi_p Y_{t-p} + \varepsilon_t \quad (2)$$

where p indicates the order of auto-regression.

The moving average (MA) model expresses the current value of the time lines in the function of the present and past random variables. Thus the moving average means that the value of the timelines at a time t affects the current term and the weighted combination of the past error terms.

$$Y_t = \varepsilon_t + \theta_1 \varepsilon_{t-1} + \ldots + \theta_q \varepsilon_{t-q} \quad (3)$$

where q indicates the order of the moving average (Kehl and Sipos, 2011).

The model is stationary transformed with difference formation, called d-rate integral written to *[I(d)]* time series ARIMA model. We can give the ARIMA model's dimensions in the following way: *ARIMA (p, d, q)* (Kehl and Sipos, 2011). ARIMA models in every case relate to linear contexts. The equation for estimating the explanatory variables of the result variable can be divided into two groups: the auto-regressive (AR) and the moving averaged (MA) model variables. In the case of the auto-regressive model the indicators are explained with its past values. If the value of maximum delay is p, thus the values are included at least p-term in the explanatory variables; we can talk about p-order AR model, and the sign of it: *AR (p)*. For the analysis of the monthly unemployment data line, I use a so-called seasonal ARIMA model, whose general marking is: $ARIMA\ (p, d, q)\ (P, D, Q)_S$. We mean under seasonal fluctuation the same wavelength and regular amplitude, repeated regularly with short-term fluctuations (Hunyadi et al., 1997). The starting point of modelling is to determine whether the desired timeline to be examined is stationary, and if it is not, whether it can be done to stationary with appropriate transformation. Stationary means temporal stability of the variables of the time lines, the expected values of certain variables, its variance, and the relationship variables belonging to different times expressing auto-covariance are constant in time (Rédey, 1991).

A stationary time line is the $Y_1, Y_2, \ldots, Y_t, \ldots, Y_T$ theoretical time line if:

$$1.\ E\,(Y_t) = \mu$$

$$2.\ Var\,(Y_t) = \sigma^2$$

$$3.\ \rho_k = \frac{Cov\,(Y_t, Y_{t-k})}{\sigma^2} \qquad k = 1, 2, \ldots \tag{4}$$

where $Cov\,(Y_t, Y_{t-k}) = E\left[(Y_t - \mu)(Y_{t-k} - \mu)\right]$ and

$$\sigma^2 = \sigma_t \times \sigma_{t-k}\,, \quad \sigma_t = \sigma_{t-k} = \sigma$$

Stationary time lines do not contain trend effect, as the values of the time line fluctuate around an average level of constant with constant scattering. The constant scattering means that the intensity of fluctuations in time does not change (either increase or decrease) (Kehl and Sipos, 2011).

Determining the existing contexts between the consecutive observations means the description of the correlation structure of the time lines, which happens with calculation of the auto-correlation and partial auto-correlation coefficient method.

$$r_k = \frac{\sum_{t=1}^{n-k}(y_t - \bar{y})(y_{t-k} - \bar{y})}{\sum_{t=1}^{n}(y_t - \bar{y})^2} \quad k = 1,2,\ldots,K \tag{5}$$

The autocorrelation coefficients' estimated values measure the tightness between the values of the time line delayed with time unit k and the linear correlation contact. The r_1 means the consecutive relationship and r_2 means the intensity of the relationship between the values being from each other in two time units. The coefficients in the function of delaying (k=1, 2, ..., K) form the autocorrelation function (ACF). The partial autocorrelation coefficients measures the tightness of the linear correlation contact between the k time unit delayed values of the time line in such way that the intermediate effect of 1, 2, ..., k-1 delays are filtered out. The coefficients form the partial autocorrelation function (PACF) in the function of retardation (k=i, 2, ..., K). The type of the stochastic process can be identified on the basis of ACF and PACF values of an experiential time line, which also appoints the model to be elected (Chatfield, 2004).

It is necessary to define what kind of ARMA model we could try and what the order of the auto-aggressively (p) and/or the moving average (q) would be. It can be defined on the basis of experimental or transformed ACF and PACF values. We call this phase of modelling identification. We have to examine the adequacy of matching so that the selected model characterizes the data well. Either Akaike information criteria (AIT) or the Bayes – criteria of the Schwartz-type – is suitable for testing, but the application of the two leads to misinformation, thus I apply the Akaike-type criterion.

$$AIC(p) = n \log \hat{\sigma}_p^2 + 2p \tag{6}$$

where n – the size of the sample; p – the number of the estimated parameters; σ - the size of residuum.

We choose the model where the value of the Akaike criterion is the smallest. After that, it is necessary to check that there is no auto-correlation between the residuum, which was carried out by the testing of the normality of error members (Maddala, 2004).

Many researchers use the ARIMA model, because this is a well-known estimation instrument. One of the main advantages of ARIMA models is that they perform quite well in forecasting based only on past observations of the series (Mayor Fernández et al., 2007). According to Wilson and Perry (2004), the results of spectral analysis need to be compared with model forecasts other than ARIMA, given that the results of spectral analysis are indeed a worthy contender. Mayor Fernández et al. (2007) used the quarterly information provided by the Spanish Economically Active Population Survey, finding that a dynamic ARIMA model gave better results. Knudsen (2000) used shift-share analysis to get forecast results by regional level. According to Barnichon and Garda (2016), forecasting the unemployment rate is an important and difficult task for policymakers. Despite decades of research on the topic, policymakers often rely on simple time series models, such as ARIMA models, to forecast unemployment. The unemployment flow data underlying our approach have already been calculated for as many as 70 developed and developing countries (Viegelahn and Wieser, 2013).

3 The evaluation of the results – The empirical results of the forecasts for Hungary

For the forecast I took as a basis of the monthly data line of the registered number of the job seekers in the period January 2000–December 2018 for Hungary from the database of the National Employment Service.

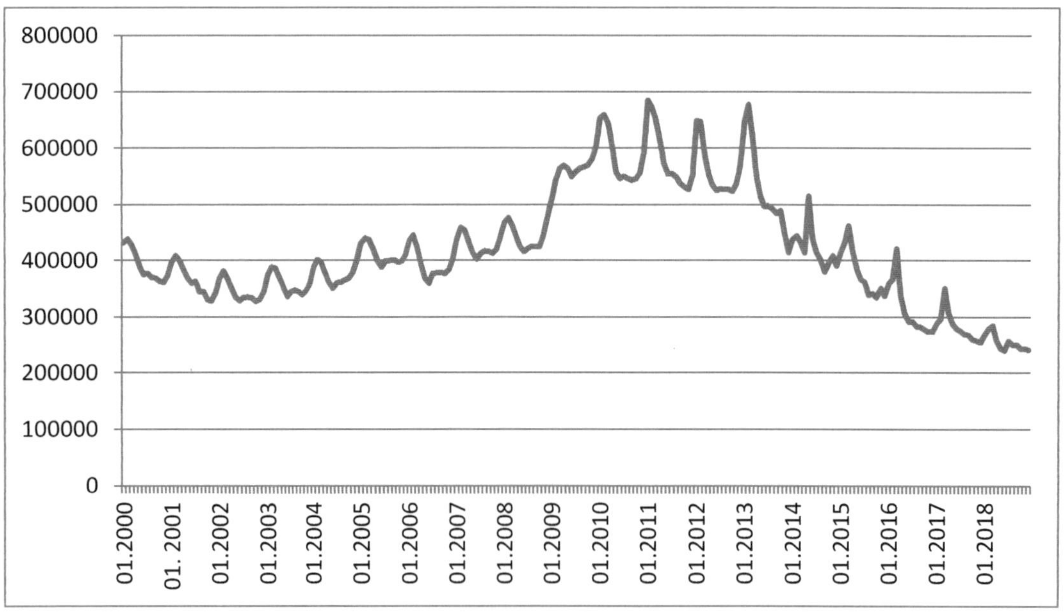

Figure 1 The number of registered job-seekers in Hungary (January 2000–December 2018) [Own compilation]

I used Gretl software for the calculations. First I examined whether the data line of unemployment is stationary. The time line is not stationary on the basis of the smallest squares' method (OLS), so I checked it with the Dickey-Fuller test. I examined the fitting with constant, constant and trend, and with constant, trend and square. The null hypothesis can be rejected at the level of 1% significance in all three cases, which means that the time line contains unity of root (Herman et al, 1994).

Because of the presence of the unit root, it is not possible to fit the ARIMA model to the time line, the time line has to be changed to a stationary time line. For transformation the seasonal differenced values of the data have to be accounted for (we call this differentiation: the deviation happening in a discrete time). The time line in which first differences are stationary are called a first-order integrated *I(1)* time line. Then, I looked again at the results of the ADF test.

According to the ADF test, because of the low p-values there is no unit root in the time line (the delay is 1). The next step is choosing the right ARIMA model, for which we have to examine the correlogram. Just from the correlogram we cannot clearly define the exact model which will be used, thus ARIMA models have to be formed in which there is first-order differentiation, thus the model variants *ARIMA (1,1,1) (1,1,1)* $_{12}$, *ARIMA (1,1,0) (1,1,0)* $_{12}$ and the *ARIMA (0,1,1) (0,1,1)* $_{12}$ were constituted.

It is necessary to examine which of these models can be used best for forecasts. Among the known model selection procedures I compared the Akaike criteria (that model type is the best where the value is the smallest one). Based on this indicator the *ARIMA (0,1,1) (0,1,1)* $_{12}$ model can be applied. In order to be able to use the model for forecasts, we need to determine whether the error members are normally distributed or autocorrelated. As the correlogram shows a minimal autocorrelation, let us try a forecast with the *ARIMA (0,1,1) (0,1,1)* $_{12}$ model (Table 1).

Period	Forecast (number of job-seekers)
2019 January	240 571
2019 February	239 737
2019 March	238 902
2019 April	238 068
2019 May	237 233
2019 June	236 399
2019 July	235 565
2019 August	234 730
2019 September	233 896
2019 October	233 061
2019 November	232 227
2019 December	231 393

Table 1 The values of the forecast at 95% reliability level to the data line

I demonstrated the results also graphically with the help of the software (Fig. 2).

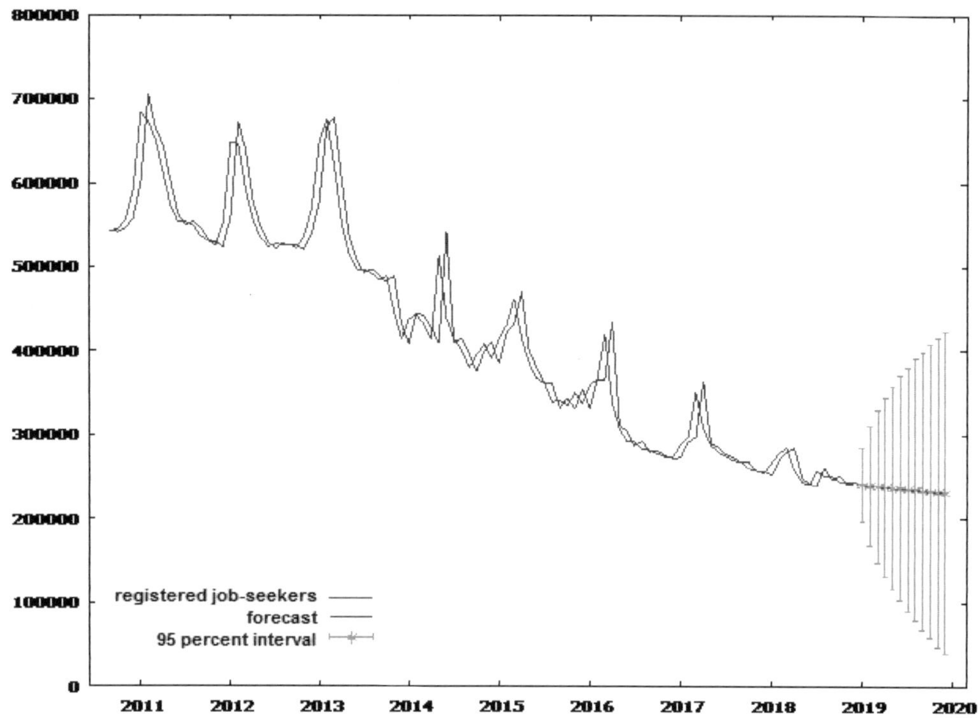

Figure 2 The forecast of the number of registered job-seekers in Hungary [Own compilation]

It can be seen well that the number of registered job-seekers in Hungary shows a slight decrease for 2019. It is interesting that there is no seasonal fluctuation. Overall, the Hungarian processes point in a favourable direction, but the number of unemployed is high (230,000). We must solve this problem in the Hungarian labour market.

I made a further unemployment estimation using the ARIMA model by gender. The projected value shows that women are expected to have higher unemployment rates than men. The main reason for this is that women with families are bound to a place and sometimes women with young children do not find easily a new job. It is necessary to seek the improvement of the women's labour market participation, and the application of the active policy employment forms would be a great help for Hungarian women. Increasing the number of women working in part-time job or distance work is really justified, and is a primary help for mothers with young children. In my opinion, we can solve this problem of unemployment if we use social innovations. This is a new direction, but active employment policy instruments have not solved the high unemployment situation in Hungary. In the next paragraph I will show the different definitions of social innovation and an example.

4 The interpretation of social innovation and an example (innovative management approach in Nemesvámos)

The definition of social innovation in the literature is not yet uniform (Benedek et al, 2015; Benedek et al, 2016; G.Fekete, 2015; Kocziszky et al, 2015; Kocziszky et al, 2017; Varga, 2017) at the same time all novel and innovative ideas to overcome existing social problems can be considered as social innovation.

I would like to introduce an example of social innovation in Hungary which led to employment expansion and decreased the high unemployment rate on a settlement level. The settlement of Nemesvámos is not far from Lake Balaton, and has a population of 2,500 people based on the latest census data. After the change of the regime (from 1989), there was a very high unemployment rate. After some years not only the successful grants had a big impact on the settlement, but multinational companies had also located in the region. Alcoa–Köfém Ltd. is based in Székesfehérvár, and one of its sites can be found in Nemesvámos. It currently employs 1,700 people, of whom 120 employees work at the Nemesvámos site. In August 2000, a 23,000 m^3HARIBO factory was built in a green field investment. In 2006, the two-shift work schedule was expanded to three shifts, with a workforce of 160 people. In almost four years, the factory increased its production volume six-fold and the number of employees tripled. Nemesvámos has attracted more and more businesses, thanks to its favourable business environment and local government regulations, including free utilities transfer and the implementation of road construction without a company contribution. Initially, the local trade tax was only one or two thousandths, which over the years has been increased with the developmental rate of the enterprises.

Nemesvámos ascribes an important role to other development alongside the local economic development. During the local authorities emphasized it among other things that such implementations will be accomplished that residential source is not needed. As a result, the household savings can remain or can be increased, so local incomes can be spent locally. In 2010, a new mayor was elected. The biggest change was caused by the fact that the new mayor started his work with a management approach, he considered Nemesvámos as an enterprise. This is a new point of view. Continuing the previous work, new ideas were formulated; the establishment and the maintenance of the financial independence of the village received a central role. Furthermore, there was a focus on creation and the retention of independent decision-making possibilities. Thanks to the local needs local products have emerged, enabling a local market to appear. Employment has started to grow. I think this is a good example of social innovation at the level of a settlement.

5 Conclusions and proposals

Since the development of a coordinated strategy for employment is one of the main goals of the European Union, the building of forecasts under alternative scenarios could be very useful. As we have seen above, forecasting unemployment is relatively easy to calculate, which gives good results for decision makers or managers. High unemployment is not a big problem at the national level in Hungary, but on micro-regional or settlement level it can be a major problem (due to the large regional differences). The limited labour catchment area is replaced by the cross-country international market. Due to the expanding labour market, career opportunities are broadening and the mobility of labour is increasing. Despite this, mothers with young children are at a disadvantage in the labour market because their mobility and career chances are worse than men's. It appear that the social innovations are playing an increasingly important role in employment expansion, as for the minimizing of the existing problems. The active involvement of citizens and civil service organizations is also necessary.

Acknowledgement

This research was supported by the project no. EFOP-3.6.2-16-2017-00007, titled *Aspects on the development of intelligent, sustainable and inclusive society: social, technological, innovation networks in employment and digital economy*. The project has been supported by the European Union, co-financed by the European Social Fund and the budget of Hungary.

References

Barnichon, R. and Garda, P. (2016). 'Forecasting unemployment across countries: The ins and outs'. *European Economic Review*, 84 (1), pp. 165-183.

Benedek, J., Kocziszky, Gy. and Veresné Somosi, M. (2015). 'Új innovációs paradigma? Regionális társadalmi innovációs potenciál javításának lehetősége szakértői rendszer segítségével, lehetőségek és korlátok'. *Veresné Somosi, M. (ed.) Mérleg és Kihívások IX. Nemzetközi Tudományos Konferencia*, Miskolc: Miskolci Egyetem Gazdaságtudományi Kar.

Benedek, J., Kocziszky, Gy., Veresné Somosi, M. and Balaton. K. (2016). 'Generating and Measuring Regional Social Innovation'. *Theory Methodology Practice: Club of Economics in Miskolc,* 12 (special issue), pp. 14-25.

Box, G. and G. Jenkins (1976). *Time Series Analysis: Forecasting and Control.* Revised Edition. San Francisco: Holden Day.

Chatfield, C. (2004). *The Analysis of Time Series: An Introduction*. Sixth Edition. London: Chapman and Hall.

G. Fekete É. (ed.) (2015): *Társadalmi innovációk a felzárkóztatás szolgálatában: Dél-Cserehát - Nyitás a jövőre.* Miskolc: Miskolci Egyetem Gazdaságtudományi Kar.

Herman, S., Pintér, J., Rappai, G. and Rédey, K. (1994). *Statisztika II.* Pécs: JPTE Kiadó.

Hunyadi, L., Mundruczó, G. and Vita, L. (1997). *Statisztika*. Budapest: Aula Kiadó.

Kehl, D. and Sipos, B. (2011). *Excel parancsfájlok felhasználása a statisztikai elemzésekben*. Pécs.

Knudsen D.C. (2000). 'Shift-share analysis: further examination of models for the description of economic change'. *Socio-Economic Planning Sciences,* 34, pp. 177-198.

Kocziszky, Gy., Benedek, J., Veresné Somosi, M. and Balaton, K. (2015). 'Regionális társadalmi innováció generálása szakértői rendszer segítségével'. *Észak-magyarországi Stratégiai Füzetek,* 12 (2), pp. 4-22.

Kocziszky, Gy., Veresné Somosi, M. and Balaton, K. (2017). 'A társadalmi innováció vizsgálatának tapasztalatai és fejlesztési lehetősége'. *Vezetéstudomány*, 48 (6-7), pp. 15-19.

Maddala, G. (2004). *Bevezetés az ökonometriába.* Budapest: Nemzeti Tankönyvkiadó.

Mayor Fernández, M., López, A. J. and Pérez, R. (2007). 'Forecasting Regional Employment with Shift–Share and ARIMA Modelling'. *Regional Studies*, 41 (4), pp. 543-551.

Rédey, K. (1991). *Sztochasztikus idősori modellek (ARIMA modellek).* OTKA tanulmány, p. 130

Varga, K. (2017). 'A regionális társadalmi innováció kérdése'. *International Journal of Engineering and Management Sciences*, 2 (4), pp. 602-616.

Viegelahn, C. and Wieser, C. (2014). The ILO Estimates on Unemployment Flows. In: ILO (2014). *Key Indicators of the Labour Market*. Eighth edition. Geneva. pp. 21-27.

Wilson, P.G. and Perry L.J. (2004). 'Forecasting Australian Unemployment Rates Using Spectral Analysis'. *Australian Journal of Labour Economics*, 7 (4), pp. 459-480.

Travel and Tourism Competitiveness Index 2017 – Quantile Regression Approach of Enabling Environment Pillars

Eva Litavcová [1], Petra Vašaničová [2], Sylvia Jenčová[3], Martina Košíková [4]

Abstract. The aim of the paper is to examine how much five pillars of Travel and Tourism Competitiveness Index (TTCI) sub-index Enabling Environment contributes to the overall TTCI and ranking among 136 countries. To meet the goal, we use quantile regression. We have obtained some findings through the analysis. Firstly, results show that pillars such as Business Environment, Safety and Security, Health and Hygiene have almost no effect on the overall TTCI score or TTCI rank. Secondly, the most important pillars are Human Resources and Labour Market, and ICT Readiness. Thirdly, we compared the results of multiple regression analysis with simple ordinary least squares, and we recognized that the results of the mentioned methods do not differ greatly, taking into account our dataset. The reason for its use is justified only because of the restrictive OLS assumptions that quantile regression does not require. This paper contributes to the existing literature connected with tourism competitiveness. As tourism represents a significant part of the total economy of the country, at the end of this paper, we suggest some recommendations for tourism policymakers, mainly in the areas of information-communication technologies, human resources, and labour market.

Keywords: Travel and Tourism Competitiveness Index, tourism, competitiveness, quantile regression.

JEL Classification: C31, L83, Z32

1 Introduction

As tourism represents a significant part of the total economy of the country and creates many jobs, tourism competitiveness is a focal point for many tourism policymakers. An international comparison of the main components of the competitiveness of the tourism sector can provide us valuable information connected with accumulation of investment in potential destinations suitable for the development and promotion of tourism (Vašaničová et al, 2017). The application of competitiveness indicators in international tourism research determined relevant entry attributes, provided the ranking of destinations and opened a discussion on the adequacy of the current definitions and the adequacy of measuring the competitiveness of destinations (Mendola and Volo, 2017).

Current literature covers a wide range of research on competitiveness subject. For example, tourism destination competitiveness was studied in Leung and Baloglu (2013), Aguas, Veiga

[1] University of Presov, Faculty of Management, Department of Mathematical Methods and Managerial Informatics, Konstantinova 16, 080 01 Presov, Slovakia, eva.litavcova@unipo.sk.

[2] University of Presov, Faculty of Management, Department of Mathematical Methods and Managerial Informatics, Konstantinova 16, 080 01 Presov, Slovakia, petra.vasanicova@unipo.sk.

[3] University of Presov, Faculty of Management, Department of Finance, Konstantinova 16, 080 01 Presov, Slovakia, sylvia.jencova@unipo.sk.

[4] University of Presov, Faculty of Management, Department of Mathematical Methods and Managerial Informatics, Konstantinova 16, 080 01 Presov, Slovakia, martina.kosikova@smail.unipo.sk.

and Reis (2010), Cracolici and Nijkamp (2009). Since 2007 Travel and Tourism (T&T) Competitiveness Index (Blanke and Chiesa, 2007) provides the opportunity to compare countries within the T&T competitiveness. It means that through this index are explored factors and policies driving T&T competitiveness in nations worldwide. T&T Competitiveness Report has been published seven times up to the year 2018 but the composition of the index has been changed over the years. We can find publications that focus on the methodological improvement of tourism competitiveness indicators (see Lopes, Muñoz and Alarcón-Urbistondo, 2018; Dias, 2017; Pulido-Fernández and Rodríguez-Díaz, 2016; Wu, Lan and Lee, 2012; Wu, 2011). Some authors examine relationships between selected indicators of T&T Competitiveness Index (Vašaničová et al, 2017; Kalina, Vašaničová and Litavcová, 2019; Cîrstea, 2014), or their impact on international inbound and outbound tourism (Khan et al, 2017). In some cases, data of T&T Competitiveness Index was used for the other analysis (see Ivanov and Ivanova, 2016).

2 Data

Travel and Tourism (T&T) Competitiveness Index provides a comprehensive strategic benchmarking tool and contributes to the development and competitiveness of a given country. For 2017, the main index was divided into 4 subindexes, which were made up by 14 pillars (in total), and 90 individual indicators. A composition of T&T Competitiveness Index in 2017 presents Table 1.

Year	2017
Subindex I.	**Enabling Environment**
Pillars of subindex I.	1. Business Environment (BE) 2. Safety and Security (SS) 3. Health and Hygiene (HH) 4. Human Resources and Labour Market (HRL) 5. ICT Readiness (ICT)
Subindex II.	**T&T Policy and Enabling Conditions**
Pillars of subindex II.	6. Prioritization of Travel and Tourism (TT) 7. International Openness (IO) 8. Price Competitiveness (PC) 9. Environmental Sustainability (ES)
Subindex III.	**Infrastructure**
Pillars of subindex III.	10. Air Transport Infrastructure (ATI) 11. Ground and Port Infrastructure (GPI) 12. Tourist Service Infrastructure (TSI)
Subindex IV.	**Natural and Cultural Resources**
Pillars of subindex IV.	13. Natural Resources (NR) 14. Cultural Resources and Business Travel (CRB)

Table 1 Composition of T&T Competitiveness Index in 2017 [Own processing]

The five pillars, which form the first subindex Enabling Environment, are directly linked to economic growth. The second subindex Prioritization of T&T is consist of four pillars which can direct measure of observable T&T policies (Prioritization of Travel and Tourism), which can directly impact tourists' decision to select a destination (International Openness, Price Competitiveness) and which indicates to what extent natural capital is being conserved (Environmental Sustainability). The third subindex Infrastructure is isolated from 2015 because connectivity and hospitality infrastructure which is assessed more clearly, will allow accurate information to policymakers. Last subindex Natural and Cultural Resources was also isolated because these two heritages can constitute the main reason to visit a country (Crotti and Misrahi, 2017).

Our dataset consist of values of Travel and Tourism Competitiveness Index (TTCI) and its pillars among 136 economies from the year 2017. The question is, how much each pillar contributes to the overall index or ranking in 136 countries. This article aims to answer that question in the context of the five pillars that form first subindex by using quantile regression.

Subindex Enabling Environment is composed by pillars, which are directly linked to economic growth and relevant for business development (not only for the T&T sector) (Crotti and Misrahi, 2015). The first pillar indicates whether the political environment is business-friendly. It incorporates factors important for all sectors, including T&T, namely property rights, impact of rules on FDI, efficiency of legal framework in settings disputes and in challenging regulations, time required and cost to deal with construction permits, extent of market dominance, time required and cost to start a business, extent and effect of taxation on incentives to work and to invest, total tax rate.

In general, it is assumed that tourists do not like to travel to dangerous countries. Therefore, the second pillar that determines the country's T&T competitiveness is Safety and Security. Business costs of crime and violence, reliability of police services, business costs of terrorism, index of terrorism incidence, homicide rate are evaluated within this area.

As is stated in Vašaničová, Litavcová, Jenčová (2018), tourists may appear to travel to countries that provide simple health care. Therefore, in determining the competitiveness of tourism destinations, the third pillar – Health and Hygiene – is also determining. Pillar is composed by six subpillars, such as physician density, access to improved sanitation and to improved drinking water, hospital beds, HIV prevalence, and malaria incidence.

Human capital also has a significant impact on the economic activity of tourism businesses. Knowledge is an important tool for achieving the competitive advantage of tourism businesses. Therefore, next important pillar that composes TTCI is Human Resources and Labour Market, which put together indicators such as primary and secondary education enrolment rate, extent of staff training, treatment of customers, hiring and firing practices, ease of finding skilled employees, ease of hiring foreign labour, pay and productivity, and finally, female labour force participation.

The need for innovation has become a precondition for the survival, sustainability and future growth of tourism in a highly competitive environment (Divisekera and Nguyen, 2018). Unconventional communication tools can also bring a competitive advantage of a destination (Štefko and Pollák, 2016; Bačík et al., 2014). The development and innovation of information and communication technologies are therefore involved in tourism, travel experience and the overall functioning of the tourism sector. Into the fifth pillar – ICT Readiness – are involved following sub-pillars: ICT use for business-to-business transactions, internet use for business-to-consumer transactions, individuals using the internet, broadband internet subscribers, mobile telephone subscriptions, mobile broadband subscriptions, mobile network coverage, and quality of electricity supply.

3 Methodology

The effect of a change in the TTCI score and in the TTCI rank of the country among 136 countries depending on the five pillars of Enabling Environment would be tested by using simple ordinary least squares method, which describes conditional mean of response variable as a linear function of the explanatory variable. In addition, we can use other procedures and methods (see Kalina and Peštová, 2017; Jurczyk, 2012). In our study, we focus on mentioned relationships of investigated variables by using quantile regression. According to Agresti (2015), quantile regression models quantiles of a response variable as a function of explanatory variables. This method can be less severely affected by outliers than ordinary least squares. When the response conditional distributions are highly skewed with possibly highly non-constant variance, the method can describe the relationship better than a simple normal model with constant variance. Quantile regression model fitting minimizes of a weighted sum of absolute residuals, formulated as a linear programming problem. However, when the normal linear model truly holds, the least squares estimators are much more efficient.

Koenker and Bassett (1978) specified the τ-th regression quantile function as $Q(\tau \mid x) = x^T \beta(\tau)$ and consider of $\hat{\beta}(\tau)$ solving

$$\min_{\beta \in R^p} \sum_{i=1}^{n} \rho_\tau \left(y_i - x_i^T \beta\right) \tag{1}$$

with check function $\rho_\tau(u) = u\tau$ for $u \geq 0$ and $\rho_\tau(u) = u(\tau - 1)$ for $u < 0$. Quantile regression problem may be reformulated as a linear program. As reported by Fenske (2012), founded quantile regression parameter $\beta_{\tau 1}$, for example, can be interpreted as the change of the conditional quantile function when x_{i1} changes to $x_{i1} + 1$, given all other covariates remain constant.

4 Results

Table 2 shows the coefficients of the TTCI score and the TTCI rank among 136 countries as dependent variable, which were estimated at the 15th, 20th, 25th, 30th, 40th, 50th, 60th, 70th, 75th, 80th and 85th quantile levels using multiple quantile regression on the five pillars of the first sub-index. The tests of significance were based on the robust bootstrap estimations of standard errors (Koenker and Hallock, 2001). There can be seen in detail the relationship of each selected quantiles of the dependent variable on the chosen five variables.

Dependent: TTCI Rank					
τ	BE	SS	HH	HRLM	ICT
0.15	19.569[b]	3.457	1.230	-22.255[b]	-30.053[d]
0.2	15.039	2.078	-0.562	-21.819[b]	-26.952[d]
0.25	6.145	4.231	-0.629	-23.760[c]	-22.162[d]
0.3	2.210	4.417	-0.663	-22.632[c]	-20.895[d]
0.4	3.166	4.299[a]	-0.848	-20.418[c]	-21.544[d]
0.5	-1.336	2.472	0.148	-19.654[b]	-20.080[d]
0.6	-1.060	4.347	0.917	-25.001[c]	-18.429[d]
0.7	1.060	2.761	0.751	-26.191[c]	-17.444[d]
0.75	2.279	2.226	4.408	-27.451[c]	-21.124[d]
0.8	-7.795	2.847	2.607	-22.432[c]	-18.972[d]
0.85	-11.185	3.758	0.364	-21.784[c]	-15.208[c]
Dependent: TTCI Score					
τ	**BE**	**SS**	**HH**	**HRLM**	**ICT**
0.15	0.091	-0.021	-0.022	0.395[c]	0.234[c]
0.2	-0.017	-0.012	-0.023	0.440[d]	0.274[d]
0.25	0.020	-0.009	-0.014	0.339[b]	0.291[d]
0.3	0.019	-0.009	-0.027	0.295[b]	0.324[d]
0.4	-0.022	-0.004	0.001	0.334[b]	0.317[d]
0.5	0.052	-0.016	0.031	0.230	0.340[d]
0.6	0.022	-0.024	0.029	0.255	0.341[d]
0.7	-0.192	-0.038	0.003	0.319[b]	0.475[d]
0.75	-0.135	-0.024	0.031	0.324[b]	0.443[d]
0.8	-0.181	-0.072	0.031	0.379[b]	0.477[d]
0.85	-0.225[a]	-0.054	0.015	0.410[c]	0.496[d]

Table 2 Estimated parameters as a results of 2 multiple quantile regressions [own calculations in R]
Notes: "*a*", "*b*", "*c*", "*d*" denotes 10%, 5%, 1%, and 0.1% significance level.

It is clear from Table 2 that the first three pillars (*Business Environment*, *Safety and Security*, *Health and Hygiene*) have almost no effect on the overall TTCI score or TTCI rank. On the contrary, the pillars *Human Resources and Labour Market*, and *ICT Readiness* influence significantly both of the examined dependent variables, the other of them much more significantly. Dependent variable TTCI Score often has the same value for two to three countries, but the value of TTCI Rank was determined for each country ambiguously. Therefore, the results of these two multiple regressions differ slightly in the significance of the individual coefficients. The following figures (Figure 1, Figure 2) provide a more detailed and moderate overview of the examined dependencies.

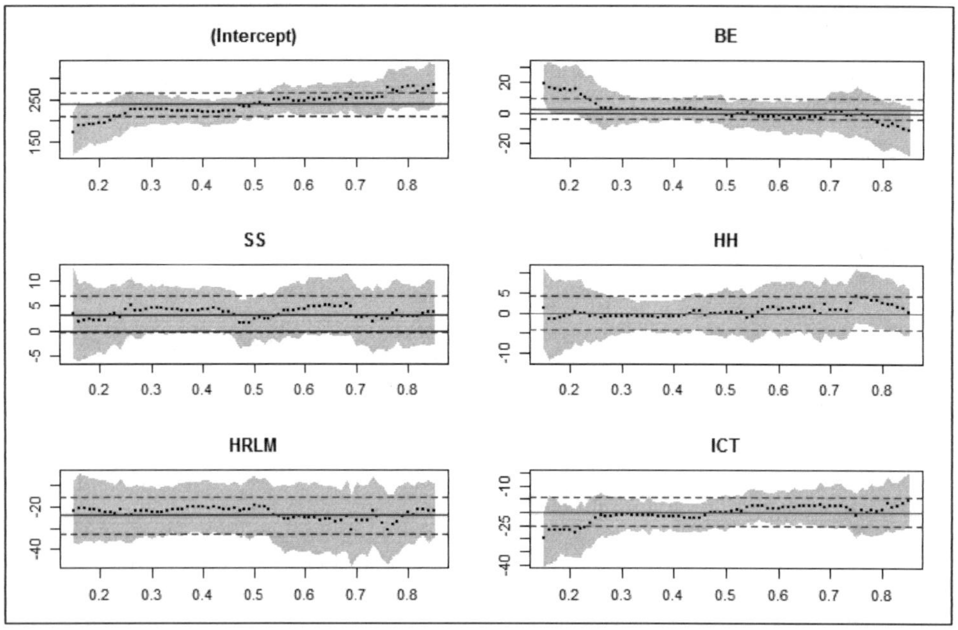

Figure 1 Comparison of estimated parameters at various quantile levels as a result of quantile regression with dependent variable *TTCI Rank* [own processing in R]. Notes: CIs are based on bootstrap estimates of standard errors.

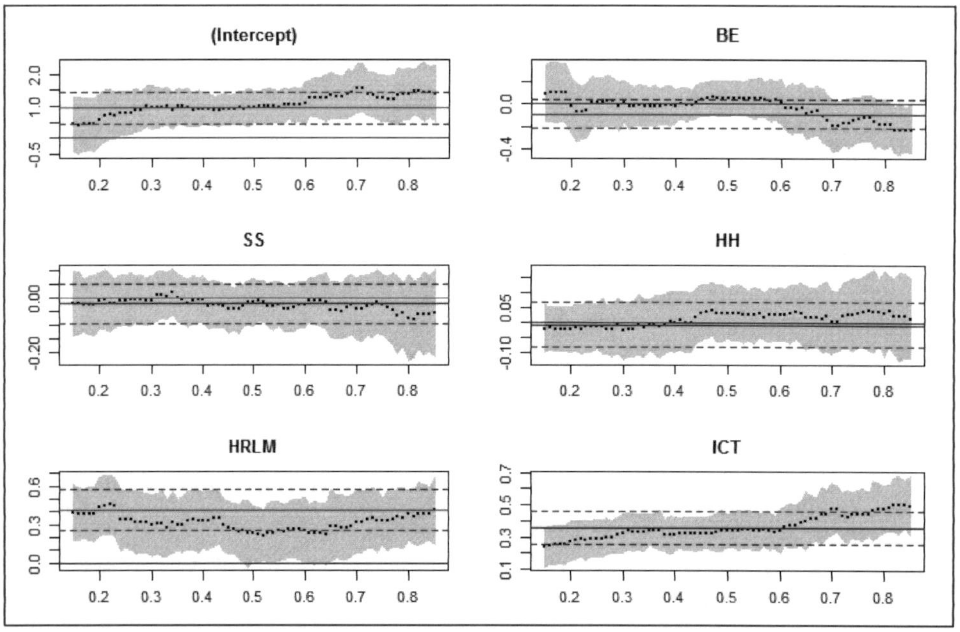

Figure 2 Comparison of estimated parameters at various quantile levels as a result of quantile regression with dependent variable *TTCI Score* [own processing in R]. Notes: CIs are based on bootstrap estimates of standard errors.

5 Conclusion

The difference of the most significant *ICT Readiness* pillar impact between the various quantile levels is more noticeable in the TTCI Score than in the TTCI Rank. With increasing quantile level, this effect is higher. However, this difference does not deviate from the framework of

OLS confidence intervals (CI) at any of the examined quantile levels. It does not deviate within the second significant pillar (Human Resources and Labour Market), too, where the lowest influence on the TTCI Score dependent variable was found at the quantile level in the right vicinity of the median. Surprisingly, we found that the first three pillars (Business Environment, Safety and Security, and Health and Hygiene) of Enabling Environment sub-index had almost no impact on the overall TTCI score and rank. Quantile regression has allowed us to examine dependencies in more detail, but its results do not differ greatly from the OLS results within the data we use. The reason for its use is justified only because of the restrictive OLS assumptions that quantile regression does not require.

There exist researches that also used the composition of TTCI in the analysis. For comparison, in the article of Kalina, Vašaničová, Litavcová (2019) that test the impact of 12 pillars on the Tourist Service Infrastructure pillar, the relevant variables turn out to be Health and Hygiene, Information and Communication Technologies Readiness, Prioritization of Travel and Tourism, and Air Transport Infrastructure. Vašaničová et al. (2017) explored the interrelationships between all pillars of TTCI. On the other hand, Jovanović, Janković–Milić and Ilić (2015) looked only at the impact of health and hygiene components on the total value of the Health and Hygiene pillar. However, this article provides insight into the impact of Enabling Environment components on the overall TTCI. Based on our results, countries wishing to improve their competitive advantage in tourism sector should focus in particular on significant indicators, namely Human Resources and Labour Market, and ICT Readiness. In our future research, we would like to examine how other pillars of TTCI contribute to the overall TTCI index and ranking among studied countries.

We can conclude that tourism policymakers should focus on the area of information and communication technologies. Several authors have already pointed out ICT importance in the tourism area (see Štefko et al, 2018; Gajdošíková 2017; Conrady and Buck, 2008), and our results confirmed this. Other important areas in this context are human resources and the labor market. This area has also become the focus of several studies (see Ungureni, Kaçmazb and Kahvecic, 2014; Vašaničová, Litavcová and Jenčová, 2016). In many cases, it is claimed that one of the tools for increasing tourism development of a given country is to increase the readiness of human resources. It includes raising the level of qualification, language skills, information and communication skills and motivation of these workers. The starting point is to create professionally targeted and affordable educational programs that take into account the needs and specificities of the tourism sector. It will achieve a synergistic effect and allow development to increase the employability of people in this sector by increasing their competitiveness.

Acknowledgements

This contribution was supported by research grant VEGA No. 1/0470/18 "Economic activity of tourism in the European area". This work was supported by the Slovak Research and Development Agency under the contract no. APVV-17-0166.

References

Agresti, A. (2015). *Foundations of Linear and Generalized Linear Models*. Hoboken, New Jersey: John Wiley & Sons.

Aguas, P., Veiga, C. and Reis, H. (2010). 'Competitive Destination Analysis in Southern European Countries'. *Worldwide Hospitality and Tourism Themes,* 2 (4), pp. 364-375.

Bačík, R. et al. (2016). 'Analysis of Tourism Travel Trends after 2014'. *Journal of Environmental Management and Tourism*, 7 (1), pp. 88-93.

Blanke, J. and Chiesa, T. (2007). *The Travel & Tourism Competitiveness Report 2007: Furthering the Process of Economic Development*. Geneva: The World Economic Forum.

Cîrstea, Ş. D. (2014). 'Travel & Tourism Competitiveness: A Study of World's Top Economic Competitive Countries'. *Procedia Economics and Finance*, 15, pp. 1273-1280.

Conrady, R. and Buck, M. (2008). *Trends and Issues in Global Tourism*. Berlin: Springer.

Cracolici, M. F. and Nijkamp, P. (2009). 'The Attractiveness and Competitiveness of Tourist Destinations: A Study of Southern Italian Regions'. *Tourism Management*, 30 (3), pp. 336-344.

Crotti, R. and Misrahi, T. (2015). *The Travel & Tourism Competitiveness Report 2015: Growth through Shocks*. Geneva: The World Economic Forum.

Crotti, R. and Misrahi, T. (2017). *The Travel & Tourism Competitiveness Report 2017: Paving the way for a more sustainable and inclusive future*. Geneva: The World Economic Forum.

Dias, J. G. (2017). 'Environmental sustainability measurement in the Travel & Tourism Competitiveness Index: An empirical analysis of its reliability'. *Ecological Indicators*, 73, pp. 589-596.

Divisekera, S. and Nguyen, V. K. (2018). 'Determinants of Innovation in Tourism Evidence from Australia'. *Tourism Management*, 67, pp. 157-167.

Fenske, N. (2012). *Structured additive quantile regression with applications to modelling undernutrition and obesity of children*. Dissertation thesis. Munchen.

Gajdošíková, Z. (2017). *Inovácie v cestovnom ruchu*. Banská Bystrica: Belianum.

Ivanov, S. and Ivanova, M. (2016). 'Do hotel chains improve destination's competitiveness?'. *Tourism Management Perspectives*, 19, pp. 74-79.

Jovanović, S., Janković–Milić, V. and Ilić, I. (2015). 'Health and hygiene importance for the improvement of tourism sector competitiveness in Serbia and the South-Eastern Europe countries'. *Procedia Economics and Finance*, 19, pp. 373-382.

Jurczyk, T. (2012). 'Outlier Detection under Multicollinearity'. *Journal of Statistical Computation and Simulation*, 82 (2), pp. 261-278.

Kalina, J. and Peštová, B. (2017). 'Exact Inference in Robust Econometrics under Heteroscedasticity'. *Proceedings of 11th International Days of Statistics and Economics MSED 2017*, Prague, Czech Republic, pp. 636-645.

Kalina, J., Vašaničová P. and Litavcová, E. (2019). 'Regression Quantiles under Heteroscedasticity and Multicollinearity: Analysis of Travel and Tourism Competitiveness'. *Ekonomický časopis*, 67 (1), pp. 69-85.

Khan, S. A. R. et al. (2017). 'Travel and tourism competitiveness index: The impact of air transportation, railways transportation, travel and transport services on international inbound and outbound tourism'. *Journal of Air Transport Management*, 58, pp. 125-134.

Koenker, R. and Bassett, G. (1978). 'Regression Quantiles'. *Econometrica*, 46 (1), pp. 33-50.

Koenker, R. and Hallock, K. F. (2001). 'Quantile regression'. *The Journal of Economic Perspectives*, 15 (4), pp. 43-56.

Leung, X. Y. and Baloglu, S. (2013). 'Tourism Competitiveness of Asia Pacific Destinations'. *Tourism Analysis*, 18 (4), pp. 371-384.

Lopes, A. P. F., Muñoz M. M. and Alarcón-Urbistondo, P. (2018). 'Regional tourism competitiveness using the PROMETHEE approach'. *Annals of Tourism Research*. 73, pp. 1-13.

Mendola, D. and Volo, S. (2017). 'Building Composite Indicators in Tourism Studies: Measurements and Applications in Tourism Destination Competitiveness'. *Tourism Management*, 59, pp. 541-553.

Pulido-Fernández, J. I. and Rodríguez-Díaz, B. (2016). 'Reinterpreting the World Economic Forum's global tourism competitiveness index'. *Tourism Management Perspectives*, 20, pp. 131-140.

Štefko, R., and Pollák, F. (2016). 'Multifactor analysis of online reputation as a tool for enhancing competitiveness of selected Slovak towns'. *European Journal of Science and Theology*, 12 (5), pp. 195-204.

Štefko, R. et al. (2018). 'New Possibilities for Evaluating Tourist Facilities in Slovakia from the Point of View of Employees'. *Proceedings of 7th International Scientific Conference Management 2018: Management and the World in Motion, Challenges, Opportunities and Threats*, Nový Smokovec, Slovakia, pp. 488-493.

Üngüren, E., Kaçmaz, Y. Y. and Kahveci, A. (2015). 'Accommodation Business Management's Attitudes towards Employees Received Vocational Tourism Education'. *Procedia - Social and Behavioral Sciences*, 174, pp. 2767-2776.

Wu, W. W. (2011). 'Beyond Travel & Tourism competitiveness ranking using DEA, GST, ANN and Borda count'. *Expert Systems with Applications*, 38 (10), pp. 12974-12982.

Wu, W. W., Lan, L. W. and Lee, Y. T. (2012). 'Critiquing the World Economic Forum's concept of destination competitiveness: A further analysis'. *Tourism Management Perspectives*, 4, pp. 198-206.

Vašaničová, P., Litavcová, E. and Jenčová, S. (2016). 'On Modelling of the Development of Share of Inbound Tourism on GDP in Slovakia'. *Proceedings of the 10th International Days of Statistics and Economics*, Prague, Czech Republic, pp. 1938-1947.

Vašaničová, P., Litavcová, E. and Jenčová, S. (2018). 'Evaluation of health and hygiene subindex of travel and tourism competitiveness index within V4 countries'. *Proceedings of the 5th International Multidisciplinary Scientific Conference on Social Sciences and Arts SGEM 2018*, Sofia, Bulgaria, pp. 283-290.

Vašaničová, P. et al. (2017). 'Dependencies between Travel and Tourism Competitiveness Subindexes: The Robust Quantile Regression Approach'. *Proceedings of the 11th International Days of Statistics and Economics*, Prague, Czech Republic, pp. 1729-1739.

How to evaluate the efficiency of projects in the context of business performance? Review of possible approaches and choice of relevant method

Lukáš Melecký[1], Michaela Staníčková[2]

Abstract. The realisation of structural changes in the globalised economy requires an evaluation of the efficiency of taken decisions. Measuring the relative efficiency of similar units have been open research for years. The assessment of efficiency is an integral part of the management of every company, which allows determining the impact of business management decisions on the project results, as well as the direction of the decisions that need to be made to improve them. In today's dynamic environment the appropriate control of the performance is crucial. The article aims to investigate and compare the modern methods for project efficiency evaluation. The research is carried out using a systematic analysis of scientific literature, comparison, and aggregation methods. The comparative study confirms that modern performance evaluation methods, combining financial and non-financial performance indicators and allowing the performance to be evaluated both quantitatively and qualitatively, should be used.

Keywords: Efficiency, Evaluation, Method, Project, Project Management.

JEL Classification: C67, H43, M11, O22.

1 Introduction

Making the connection between business strategy and project management isn't easy, but it is necessary if projects are going to serve a purpose and meet basic business needs. The foundation for overall business success and project initiatives starts by having company and project leadership in lockstep, project success ratios are more likely to increase, and in turn, stand a better chance of supporting company-wide objectives. Project management can be a powerful tool for enabling business strategy and creating sustainable wins. The modern means of project management include management by projects meaning a set of activities such as planning, decision making, organisation and leadership, used with the intention of achieving the objectives of various projects efficiently and effectively. Management by projects has become today a trendy management tool used in organisations. By using this concept, managers help the company to adapt better to changing operating conditions and uncertain environment, especially during its dynamic change. However, merely executing projects can become an excessive drain on company resources, time and productivity. It's imperative that companies draw a direct line between project activities, resources, time and effort and "how" it helps the overall company-wide business goals. Creating a project strategy that works can help give the organisation a competitive position on the market. It becomes difficult to accurately assess the real impact of projects on objectives of the company, and even more problematic to find the best way of performance evaluation.

[1] VŠB-Technical University of Ostrava/ Faculty of Economics, Department of European Integration, Sokolská třída 33, 702 00 Ostrava 1, Czech Republic, lukas.melecky@vsb.cz.

[2] VŠB-Technical University of Ostrava/ Faculty of Economics, Department of European Integration, Sokolská třída 33, 702 00 Ostrava 1, Czech Republic, michaela.stanickova@vsb.cz.

Business performance evaluation is an integral management part of a company without which it would be difficult to define the impact of business management decisions, the direction of its activity results and the conclusions that must be taken to improve the outcomes. Traditionally, business results are evaluated following the company's financial data that are given in the financial reports. However, it can be noted that the company's financial information is insufficient for more and more companies and, striving to better unfold causal relationships between management decisions and final activity results, considerable attention is drawn on a company's non-financial performance indicators.

Before taking certain decisions, it is essential that business managers, who intend to pursue strategic goals, foresee the impact that the decisions will have on the future results and timely make corrections when noticing that performance results tend to go to the wrong direction. Since non-financial indicators are more sensitive for the impact of today's decisions, it is expected that decision impact will be reflected earlier in non-financial results than in financial indicators. Research shows that non-financial performance indicators positively affect financial performance results and non-financial indicators are better indicators for future financial results than historical financial data. Moreover, non-financial indicators reflect the company's economic position and growth possibilities better than financial company performance indicators provided in the reports (Kotane, 2015).

As well, it is worth noting that financial results depend not only on how the company performs its activity, but they are also responsive to the impact of external factors. To achieve the best performance results, managers must know how much of success is impacted by their actions, and whereto they must add more efforts to improve outcomes. Since non-financial indicators are less sensitive to external factors, they do better reflect the impact of the actions, which are taken in the company, on its success and can provide more detailed information about the effect of taken decisions on final results (Ittner and Larcker, 2000).

The paper aims to review and compare modern company performance evaluation methods. This research is conducted using the methods of scientific research literature analysis, comparison and aggregation of research information.

2 The Context of Performance Evaluation

Efficiency is one of the main components of measuring organisational business performance. Efficiency is measured with a target to the organisation's goals for example maximisation outputs, maximisation of profits or minimisation of costs. The efficiency measurement deals with the way how an organisation uses the resources in the best way to produce output. The optimisation of resources can amplify the efficiency and competitiveness of the organisation.

Performance evaluation is defined ambiguously in the research literature. Some authors (Najmi and Kehoe, 2001; Neely et al, 2002) perceive performance evaluation as a process, where the company's results are evaluated quantitatively by analysing specific indicators. On the other hand, the authors of the latter decade (Moullin, 2007) note that performance evaluation should not necessarily be quantitative. Managing quality evaluation, defining customer value and value created for other interested parties, the disclosure of common business situation, and raising further goals for improvement is significant. Out of a list of definitions in research literature, the most presumptive and exact perception of performance evaluation is provided by Narkunienė and Ulbinaitė (2018): it is a broad and multifunctional process that combines the key performance indicators which help to evaluate performance, guarantees company management process, value creation, adjustment, speedy reaction, and enables improvement and growth of a company.

Under a dynamic business environment, performance control plays an especially significant role, thanks to which one can observe ongoing changes and timely react to them. For a long time, performance evaluation has been conducted based on financial activity information by analysing indicators of profitability, liquidity, solvency and other financial ones. Such an assessment has formed a traditional view that is as well followed by businesses nowadays. On the other hand, under the modern economic environment, it is more and more often than the traditional performance evaluation methods receive criticism. Narkunienė and Ulbinaitė (2018) state that the traditional performance evaluation systems do not help to solve managerial problems that arise under the context of dynamic business conditions; these systems are not capable of evaluating real factors that create value. For this reason, the modern performance evaluation methods have a higher and higher demand in business performance evaluation.

3 Review of Possible Approaches and Choice of Relevant Method

At the beginning of the 21st century, the formation of strategies and rising of goals for implementation of the plan has become an inseparable part of strategic business management. Indeed, business strategies are not restricted to barely profit increase. Therefore, the evaluation of performance results cannot be limited to traditional evaluation methods based on the analysis of financial performance indicators. As a counterbalance for the conventional performance evaluations systems, striving to join internal and external indicators, financial and non-financial indicators, long-term and short-term performance indicators, modern performance evaluation systems were created (Adomavičiūtė, 2011). According to Kučinskienė and Fominienė (2015), complex viewpoint towards adapting strategic management principles in a company's performance processes under the period of dynamic and heavily forecasted changes should help companies prepare management decisions and guarantee the successful continuation of performance.

De Toni and Toncia (2001) distinguished the essential differences between traditional and modern performance evaluation systems. According to these authors, the conventional performance evaluation systems are oriented to profit and based on performance cost and efficiency analysis. With these systems, one strives to evaluate the results of the period in the past by calculating individual financial indicators and comparing them to the defined standard values. Differently, from the traditional systems, the modern performance evaluation systems are oriented to consumers and satisfaction of their needs and are based on the company's created value. With these systems, one has an intention not only to evaluate results of the period in the past but also to define reasons that led to these results and to foresee steps to improve the future outcomes. For this purpose, not individual indicators, but sets of critical indicators that include various crosscuts of performance are evaluated.

3.1 Possible techniques to evaluate the performance

Organisational performance is a critical requirement for an organisation to survive in the market. One of the approaches to determining organisational performance is through performance measurement. Measuring business performance and presenting the resulting information for action is one aspect of achieving business success. Several techniques exist to measure the efficiency of an organisation. After conducting research literature analysis on the topic of business evaluation systems (Tangen, 2004; Gimžauskienė, 2007; Cardinals and van Veen-Dirks, 2010; Adomavičiūtė, 2011; Kučinskienė and Fominienė, 2015; Bhasin, 2017; Chouhan et al, 2017), the authors suggest the classification of performance evaluation methods, where the methods are classified into smaller groups according to method contents and performance evaluation purpose. According to this scheme, performance evaluation methods are first of all classified into traditional and modern ones. Traditional performance evaluation methods, as it was mentioned earlier, include analysis of financial performance results and their relative values. In the opinion of the authors of this paper, modern evaluation methods have to be split up into the following six groups of methods:

1) *performance record (accounting) methods*, i.e. accounting data-based performance evaluation methods that calculate the financial value created by performance;
2) *quality management concept methods*, i.e. performance evaluation methods that are based on the conception of total quality management. The purpose of these methods is to evaluate how the companies keep up with the requirements, what progress they do when improving their performance, and similar;
3) *causal relationship theory models*, i.e. performance evaluation models that distinguish the main factors which affect the successful performance;
4) *business process evaluation models*, i.e. models that emphasise processes during performance evaluation. The purpose of these models is to evaluate the economy of performance and efficacy during the separate steps of the process;
5) *balanced system models*, i.e. overall models of performance evaluation that are strictly related to the company's vision and strategy. They involve both financial and non-financial performance evaluation indicators and reflect the results in different performance perspectives;
6) *multicriteria methods*, i.e. complex performance evaluation methods that join many relevant performance indicators into a single summarising performance estimator.

Following the above-mentioned research papers, it is observed that out of all performance evaluation methods that are distinguished in the classification scheme, the most popular and most widely employed are the following ones: economic value added, balanced scorecard, performance prism, performance pyramid, six sigma, and multicriteria performance measurement (e.g. Franek, 2017), as stated the review made by Narkunienė and Ulbinaitė (2018).

3.2 DEA as a suitable method to evaluate the efficiency of projects

For a project manager to become truly successful, they must have the ability to align the project within the greater context of the company. Understanding the core business strategy is the key to reaching a positive outcome. Business strategy is about stepping back and looking at the ultimate goal. The modern means of project management ask a professional to consider the business strategy as a whole and what exactly will happen with the output of the project after it leaves your hands. And for these reasons, efficiency measurement of projects is one of the main components of measuring organisational performance. The theory of efficiency is related to the association between resources used and results achieved (Hančlová and Chytilová, 2017). Parametric and non-parametric are two approaches that can be used to measure performances. Parametric approaches specify the functional form and take into account the residual term in the analysis. Non-parametric approaches put less structure on the specification of the best practice frontier and assume no random error (Huth and Pokorna, 2004). The main difference between both of the approaches is the distribution of data. Parametric approaches concern with the normality of the data distribution while non-parametric methods do not.

Efficiency measurement using a non-parametric approach had originated from the attempt to evaluate the efficiency of units that produce multiple outputs with multiple inputs in a situation where input and output prices were hardly available. Several types of non-parametric approach are available and among them, is *Data envelopment analysis* (DEA). DEA has been widely used among researchers for efficiency measurement. DEA uses different inputs/outputs to measure the relative efficiency of one unit compared with other similar units. This part presents a comprehensive review of recent applications of DEA techniques on measuring the relative efficiency of project management units. For years, there have been significant efforts to implement DEA for measuring the relative efficiency of similar units (Charnes et al, 1978; Banker et al, 1984). DEA has been commonly applied when input/output are not measurable by applying financial figures. For example, in educational systems, one may be interested in promoting schools with students who reach academic excellence.

Orouji (2016) made an overview of measuring the relative efficiency of project management using data envelopment analysis, based on this review, DEA technique has been used in measuring the efficiency of project management methods, as confirmed following applications. Trindade et al (2015) used the DEA method for measuring project management efficiency of a Portuguese electricity distribution utility. Kwon et al (2017) proposed an innovative three-stage model using DEA and backpropagation neural network for supporting 'better practice' benchmarking as contrasted with the traditional 'best practice' benchmarking. They reported that DEA models could provide the capability of setting optimal objectives, but the drawback of standard DEA was its inability to give actionable targets necessary for incremental improvement.

Enterprise Resource Planning (ERP) packages developed by ERP vendors are intended not only to standardise the existing business processes of the using organisation but also to offer some of the best practices of the industry. There are different studies on the assessment of the efficiency of standard ERP projects. Evaluating the efficiency of customised ERP packages is necessary for benchmarking best customisation practices. Parthasarathy and Sharma (2016) investigated the efficiency of customised ERP software packages based on DEA. They also studied the relationship between the degree of customisation of ERP packages and efficiency. The results implied that customisation adversely influenced the efficiency of ERP packages. Sudhaman and Thangavel (2015) analysed the efficiency of ERP projects based on their quality measures (defect counts) using the DEA model and identified the most efficient ERP projects.

Research and Development (R&D) project teams are concerned with efficiency under limited resources must cohesively coordinate cooperation, interactions, and the exchange of ideas to sustain innovation. Hung (2017) studied the management of social networks, technology ties, and gatekeeper functionality from a networking perspective and investigated their contribution to R&D performance, which was assessed using the DEA method. El-Mashaleh et al (2010) utilised DEA to benchmark safety performance of construction contractors. Vitner et al (2006) studied the possibility of applying the DEA method for assessing the performances of different projects in a multi-project environment. Karasakal and Aker (2017) applied multiple criteria sorting methods based on DEA to evaluate R&D projects. Lu et al (2016) implemented a network DEA model called network slacks-based measure to investigate the R&D efficiency and socio-economic efficiency of Taiwan's technology development programs.

Application of DEA in *construction projects* represent, e.g. Nazarko and Chodakowska (2015), they applied DEA and Tobit regression for analysing the productivity of the construction industry in Europe and measured labour productivity using with DEA method. Shuqiang and Qiankun (2012) proposed the engineerization management method, discussed the connotation and main contents of engineerization management and implemented the DEA method in performance evaluation of engineerization management. Sánchez (2015) developed a framework to learn whether or not an organisation is working on the right projects to gain its a business strategy and stakeholders demands.

Therefore, an organisation's performance can be measured not only by analysing the organisation's business units but also by examining the projects produced by each business unit.

4 Conclusion

Measuring business performance and presenting the resulting information for action is one aspect of achieving business success. Performance is the results of the organisation's effort to achieve its goals or objectives. In the research literature, a company's performance evaluation is defined as a comprehensive and multifunctional process which joins all its significant performance indicators in a way that allows it is evaluating performance, enables a constant company management process, value creation, adjustment, and fast reaction that leads to improvement and growth of the company.

Measuring the relative efficiency of similar units have been open research for years. Despite this fact, no single method would be appropriate for all companies, so further work can be targeted at establishing a multi-criteria performance evaluation method that would satisfy the needs of a particular business' activity and targets for evaluation. A company's performance evaluation methods can be grouped into two categories: traditional methods that are justified only by the analysis of financial indicators and modern ones that combine the company's financial and non-financial performance information and allow evaluating its activity both quantitatively and qualitatively. No single performance evaluation method would be appropriate for all companies; the method should be chosen individually considering the aim of the evaluation and the needs of the company.

Acknowledgements

This paper was created under Operational Programme Education for Competitiveness – Project CZ.1.07/2.3.00/20.0296.

References

Adomavičiūtė, D. (2011). *Customs Audit Model for Evaluation of Business Activities*. Vilnius: Vilniaus universitetas.

Banker, R. D., Charnes, A. and Cooper, W. W. (1984). 'Some models for estimating technical and scale inefficiencies in data envelopment analysis'. *Management science*, 30 (9), pp. 1078-1092.

Bhasin, M. (2017). 'A study of economic value added disclosures in the annual reports: is EVA a superior measure of corporate performance?' *East Asian Journal of Business Economics*, 5 (1), pp. 10-26.

Cardinaels E. and van Veen-Dirks, P. M. G. (2010). 'Financial versus non-financial information: The impact of information organization and presentation in a Balanced Scorecard'. *Accounting, Organizations and Society*, 35, pp. 565-578.

Charnes, A., Cooper, W. W. and Rhodes, E. (1978). 'Measuring the efficiency of decision making units'. *European Journal of Operational Research*, 2 (6), pp. 429-444.

Chouhan, V., Soral, G. and Chandra, B. (2017). 'Activity based costing model for inventory valuation'. *Management Science Letters*, 7 (3), pp. 135-144.

De Toni, A. and Tonchia, S. (2001). 'Performance measurement systems – Models, characteristics and measures'. *International Journal of Operations & Production Management*, 21 (1/2), pp. 46-71.

Franek, J. (2017). 'Hybrid OWA COPRAS-G approach to startup evaluation using BLUES tool'. *International Conference on Strategic Management and its Support by Information Systems*, Ostrava, Czech Republic, pp. 209-218.

Gimžauskienė, E. (2007). *Organizations' evaluation systems*. Kaunas: Technologija.

Hančlová, J. and L. Chytilová (2017). 'An application of convex nonparametric least squares to estimation banks (in)efficiency in the Visegrad countries'. *International Conference on Strategic Management and its Support by Information Systems 2017*, Ostrava, Czech Republic, pp. 231-238.

Hung, C. L. (2017). 'Social networks, technology ties, and gatekeeper functionality: Implications for the performance management of R&D projects'. *Research Policy*, 46 (1), pp. 305-315.

Huth, R. and Pokorna, L. (2004). 'Parametric versus non-parametric estimates of climate trends'. *Theoretical and Applied Climatology*, 77, pp. 107-112.

Ittner, C. and Larcker, D. (2000). Non-financial performance measures: what works and what doesn't. The Wharton School, University of Pennsylvania, [Online]. Available at: http://knowledge.wharton.upenn.edu/article/non-financial-performance-measures-what-works-and-what-doesnt/.

Karasakal, E. and Aker, P. (2017). 'A multicriteria sorting approach based on data envelopment analysis for R&D project selection problem'. *Omega*, 73, pp. 79-92.

Kotane, I. (2015). 'Evaluating the importance of financial and non-financial indicators for the evaluation of company's performance'. *Management Theory and Studies for Rural Business and Infrastructure Development*, 37 (1), pp. 80-94.

Kučinskienė, M. and Fominienė, A. (2015). *Complex approach to evaluation of activity of public organizations*. Vilnius: Vilniaus universiteto leidykla

Kwon, H. B., Marvel, J. H. and Roh, J. J. (2017). 'Three-stage performance modeling using DEA–BPNN for better practice benchmarking'. *Expert Systems with Applications*, 71, pp. 429-441.

Lu, W. M., Kweh, Q. L., Nourani, M. and Huang, F. W. (2016). ‘Evaluating the efficiency of dual-use technology development programs from the R&D and socio-economic perspectives‘. *Omega*, 62, pp. 82-92.

Najmi, M. and Kehoe, D. F. (2001). ‘The role of performance measurement system in promoting quality development beyond ISO 9000‘. *International Journal of Operations & Production Management*, 21 (1/2), pp. 159-172.

Narkunienė, J. and Ulbinaitė, A. (2018). ‘Comparative Analysis of Company Performance Evaluation Methods‘. *The International Journal Entrepreneurship and Sustainability Issues*, 6 (1), pp. 125-138.

Nazarko, J. and Chodakowska, E. (2015). ‘Measuring productivity of construction industry in Europe with Data Envelopment Analysis‘. *Procedia Engineering*, 122, pp. 204-212.

El-Mashaleh, M. S., Rababeh, S. M. and Hyari, K. H. (2010). ‘Utilizing data envelopment analysis to benchmark safety performance of construction contractors‘. *International Journal of Project Management*, 28 (1), pp. 61-67.

Moullin, M. (2007). ‘Performance measurement definitions: Linking performance measurement and organisational excellence‘. *International Journal of Health Care Quality Assurance*, 20 (3), pp. 181-183.

Neely, A., Adams, C. and Kennerley, M. (2002). *The performance prism: the scorecard for measuring and managing business success*. New Jersey: Financial Times Prentice Hall.

Orouji, S. (2016). ‘Measuring the relative efficiency of project management using data envelopment analysis‘. *Journal of Project Management*, 1 (2016), pp. 1-6.

Parthasarathy, S. and Sharma, S. (2016). ‘Efficiency analysis of ERP packages – A customization perspective‘. *Computers in Industry*, 82, pp. 19-27.

Sánchez, M. A. (2015). ‘Integrating sustainability issues into project management‘. *Journal of Cleaner Production*, 96, pp. 319-330.

Shuqiang, W. and Qiankun, W. (2012). ‘Effect evaluation of construction engineerization management for military projects‘. *Systems Engineering Procedia*, 3, pp. 351-356.

Sudhaman, P. and Thangavel, C. (2015). ‘Efficiency analysis of ERP projects—software quality perspective‘. International Journal of Project Management, 33 (4), pp. 961-970.

Tangen, S. (2004). ‘Performance measurement: from philosophy to practice‘. *International Journal of Productivity and Performance Management*, 53 (8), pp. 726-737.

Trindade, D., Barroso, A. P. and Machado, V. H. (2015). ‘Project management efficiency of a Portuguese electricity distribution utility using data envelopment analysis‘. *Procedia Computer Science*, 64, pp. 674-682.

Vitner, G., Rozenes, S. and Spraggett, S. (2006). ‘Using data envelope analysis to compare project efficiency in a multi-project environment‘. *International Journal of Project Management*, 24 (4), pp. 323-329.

Application of AHP Method for Choosing of Suitable Airplane in Air Cargo Transport

Ivana Olivková[1], Lenka Kontriková[2]

Abstract. This article focuses on selecting a suitable airplane to ensure that a particular cargo is transported. An Analytic Hierarchy Process (AHP) was chosen to select an airplane. AHP is a multi-criteria decision-making method that divides the main decision target into smaller and more detailed elements. After compiling a set of criteria and creating a hierarchical structure, different variants are compared at each level of evaluation through the selected criteria. The result is given by weight on the relative scale for variants and criteria. At the conclusion of the article the advantages and disadvantages of the AHP method and the consequent suitability of its use in air transport are presented.

Keywords: air cargo transport, selecting of suitable airplane, AHP method, multi-criteria decision-making.

JEL Classification: C44

1 Introduction

The air transport which including air freight, is a dynamically developing industry and is so much more in demand today than it was in the past. The amount of cargo transported is constantly increasing every year. The main reasons are the speed, availability and reliability of air transport. The goods can be transported both in the cargo bay of passengers and in special aircraft intended solely for the carriage of goods. The problem is well-known (Průša et al, 2010).

Due to economic costs, competition and customer requirements, airlines need to make the most efficient and productive decision regarding the choice of the appropriate type of airplane for a particular shipment. For a good decision, a sufficient amount of accurate information is needed on the variations that enter the decision-making process. For this reason, it is an effort to obtain information about its essential properties that are important for decision making. This means that they are judged by certain selected evaluation criteria.

Multi-criteria decision-making depends on the choice of the appropriate method. It should be a method that makes it possible to quantify the usefulness of variants entering the decision-making process. The resulting decision affects the importance of the evaluation criteria and therefore it is necessary to consider the procedures that allow the weighting of the evaluation criteria to be determined.

[1] VŠB-Technical University of Ostrava, Institute of Transport, 17. listopadu 2172/15, 708 00 Ostrava-Poruba, e-mail: ivana.olivkova@vsb.cz

[2] VŠB-Technical University of Ostrava, Institute of Transport, 17. listopadu 2172/15, 708 00 Ostrava-Poruba, Czech Technical University in Prague/ Department of Logistics and Management of Transport, Konviktská 20, 110 00 Praha, Czech Republic, e-mail: lenka.kontrikova@vsb.cz

One suitable means of multi-criteria decision-making is the AHP (Analytic Hierarchy Process) method. (Dožić and Kalić, 2014) propose to solve aircraft type(s) selection problem for hypothetical airline example and forecasted air travel demand by using the Analytic Hierarchy Process (AHP). The aim of this paper is to apply AHP method in the aviation industry when selecting a suitable airplane for the transport of a particular cargo.

2 Methodology

This article describes how to use the Analytical Hierarchy Process (AHP). The method for analyzing decision problems using hierarchical representation (AHP method) was designed by prof. Saaty in the 1980s. (Saaty, 1980). The method was significantly improved (Saaty, 1999). The basic procedure for solving the decision-making problem by this method takes place in three steps.

2.1 The first step of AHP method

The first step is to create a hierarchical structure. The AHP method is based on a hierarchy in which k-criteria and p-variants are defined. This hierarchy is presented in Figure 1.

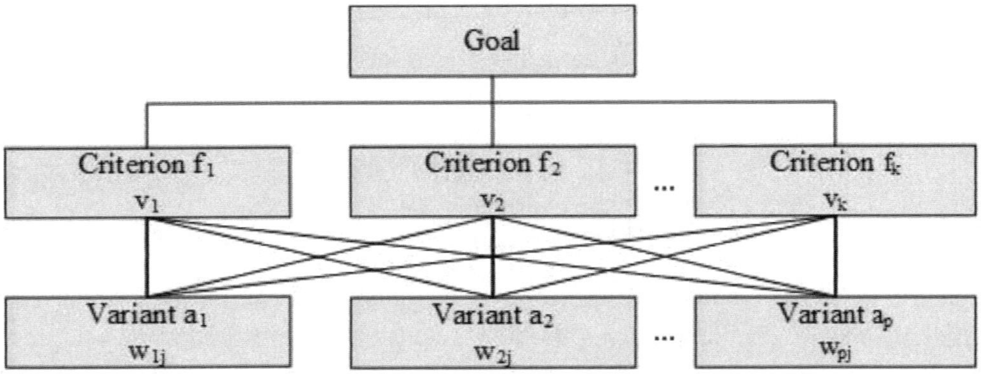

Figure 1 Hierarchy of multi-criteria evaluation of variants [Fiala, Jablonský and Maňas, 1994]

At the first level of the hierarchy, the goal of evaluation is defined - the arrangement of variants. This goal depends primarily on what evaluation criteria are used. Therefore, the criteria are in the hierarchy immediately at the next, second level. At the last level of the hierarchy are said the considered variants. Their arrangement depends on their relationship to the evaluation criteria.

The fundamental question is how a user can determine the intensity of the relationships between the elements of the hierarchy. If the necessary information is not available in the detailed structure but the evaluation is carried out by an expert, his evaluation can be objectivized. The AHP method is very suitable for solving such type of task. This method offers a relatively accessible procedure for the user. The expert does not have to enter absolute values of weight of criteria, preference indexes of variants. The expert only gives information about the relationship between each criterion and evaluates variants through these criteria.

2.2 The second step of AHP method

The second step of the solution is to create a pair of matched comparisons at each level of the hierarchy. (Fiala, Jablonský and Maňas, 1994) pointed out the problem. Suppose that the number of elements of m is defined at each level of the hierarchy. By comparing these elements with each other, the evaluator (expert) builds a pair of matched comparisons (Saaty's matrix) S=(s_{ij}), i,j=1, 2,..., m. The matrix of paired comparison S contains quantified information from the expert on the relationship of the individual pairs of elements:

- *1*-one element is as significant as the second;
- *3*-one element is slightly more significant than the second element;
- *5*-one element is more significant than the second element;
- *7*-one element is demonstrably more significant than the second element;
- *9*-one element is absolutely more significant than the second element.

In addition to these five basic steps for expressing preferences, the expert also has an intermediate stage, which corresponds to numerical values 2, 4, 6 and 8. The element s_{ij} of this matrix can be interpreted as the ratio of importance of elements i and j. From this determination are the properties of the elements of this matrix result:

- elements on the diagonal $s_{ii}=1$, $i=1, 2, \ldots, m$;
- the matrix A is a reciprocal matrix; $s_{ij} = 1/s_{ji}$. Thus the matrix S, we can define:

$$\begin{array}{cc} & \begin{array}{ccc} f_1 & \cdots & f_m \end{array} \\ S = \begin{array}{c} f_1 \\ \vdots \\ f_m \end{array} & \begin{bmatrix} 1 & \cdots & s_{1m} \\ \vdots & \ddots & \vdots \\ 1/s_{1m} & \cdots & 1 \end{bmatrix}. \end{array} \tag{1}$$

The geometric mean method is often used to estimate elements of the vector v (weights, preferential indexes of elements). This method determines the estimates of weights, as the normalized geometric diameter of the rows of the S matrix. (Fotr and Švecová, 2016) provide the solution. The G_i values can be calculated as the geometric mean rows of the Saaty matrix

$$G_i = \sqrt[m]{\prod_{j=1}^{m} s_{ij}} \qquad , i = 1, 2, \ldots, m. \tag{2}$$

The elements of the vector v are then calculated by normalization of the vector v

$$v_i = \frac{G_i}{\sum_{j=1}^{m} G_i}. \tag{3}$$

The matrix of paired comparison S = (s_{ij}) must be consistent. The consistency of a matrix of paired comparison S = (s_{ij}) can be defined as follows: if the element x_i is s_{iq} - times more important than the element s_q and the element s_q is s_{qj} - times more important than the element x_j, then the element x_i is $s_{ij} = s_{iq} \bullet s_{qj}$ - times more important than the element x_j. The matrix of paired comparison S = (s_{ij}) is consistent if

$$S_{ji} = \frac{v_i}{v_j} \tag{4}$$

is true for the elements of the paired comparison matrix. If this relation is true, the matrix S = (s_{ij}) is reciprocal and consistent (Ramík, 2000).

The consistency index is important for the success of the AHP method. It is true that the maximum eigenvalue of a square matrix of paired comparison S = (s_{ij}) of the type $m \times m$, which is always reciprocal, but have not to be consistent, λ_{max} is greater than or equal to m. If the matrix S = (s_{ij}) is consistent, it is always true that $\lambda_{max} = m$. The consistency index is called the C_I number calculated from the relationship

$$C_I = \frac{\lambda_{max} - 1}{m - 1}. \quad (5)$$

The consistency index C_I is therefore equal to 1 for a consistent matrix. The inconsistency of the matrix expresses the magnitude of the deviation C_I from 1 (Ramík, 2000).

2.3 The third step of AHP method

The third step of the solution is to determine the weights using quantitative paired comparison for all levels. This paired comparison and calculation of the preferential indices of the variants are the same. If $v = (v_1, v_2, \ldots, v_k)$ are the weight of the criteria and w_{ij} are the preferential indices of the variants a_i evaluated according to the criteria f_j, then the global preferential indices of the variants a_i in terms of all criteria is calculated (Fiala, Jablonský and Maňas, 1994):

$$u(a_i) = \sum_{j=1}^{n} v_j w_{ij} \;, i = 1, 2, \ldots, p. \quad (6)$$

The global preferential indices of the variants represent the utility of variants. The best variant is the variant with the highest global preferential index of the variant. The variants are possible to arrange by falling values of the global preferential indices of the variants.

3 Application of the AHP method

The AHP method is applied to select the most suitable airplane for the transport of a particular cargo. This is a requirement to transport cargo on a regular KLM flight from Amsterdam to Mumbai. Total weight of 5000 kg is transported in 10 pallets. The distance from the flight is 7918 km.

Based on the previous analysis, we are selected 5 airplane variants for this flight. These are airplanes for the transport of persons whose cargo spaces are designed to carry pallets:

1) Boeing B777-200ER - is a long-range, wide-body, twin-engine jet airplane. With the length 63.7 m, wingspan 60.9 m and height 18.5 m. The total capacity of the cargo is 163 m^3.
2) Boeing B787-9 – is a long-range, wide-body, twin-engine jet airplane. With the length 63 m, wingspan 60.1 m and height 17.2 m. The total capacity of the cargo is 124.6 m^3.
3) Airbus A330-200 - is a medium-to-long-range, wide-body, twin-engine jet airplane. With the length 58.8 m, wingspan 60.3 m and height 17.4 m. The total capacity of the cargo is 132.4 m^3.
4) Airbus A340-300 - is a long-range, wide-body, four-engine jet airplane. With the length 63.6 m, wingspan 60.3 m and height 16.85 m. The total capacity of the cargo is 162.8 m^3.

5) Airbus A380-800 - is a double-deck, wide-body, four-engine jet airplane. With the length 72.72 m, wingspan 79.75 m and height 24.09 m. The total capacity of the cargo is 184 m^3.

The individual airplane variants are evaluated by six criteria: size of cargo space [m^3], capacity of cargo [t], maximum range [km], maximum cruise speed [km/h], maximum takeoff weight [kg] and maximum fuel capacity [l].

The aim is to select a variant of the airplane, which achieves the best evaluation in terms of all the criteria, or to arrange these variants. This problem is solved by using the AHP method.

3.1 The first step of solution

The first step is to create a hierarchical structure. Similar solution already exists (Olivková, 2018). The hierarchy structure is shown in Figure 2.

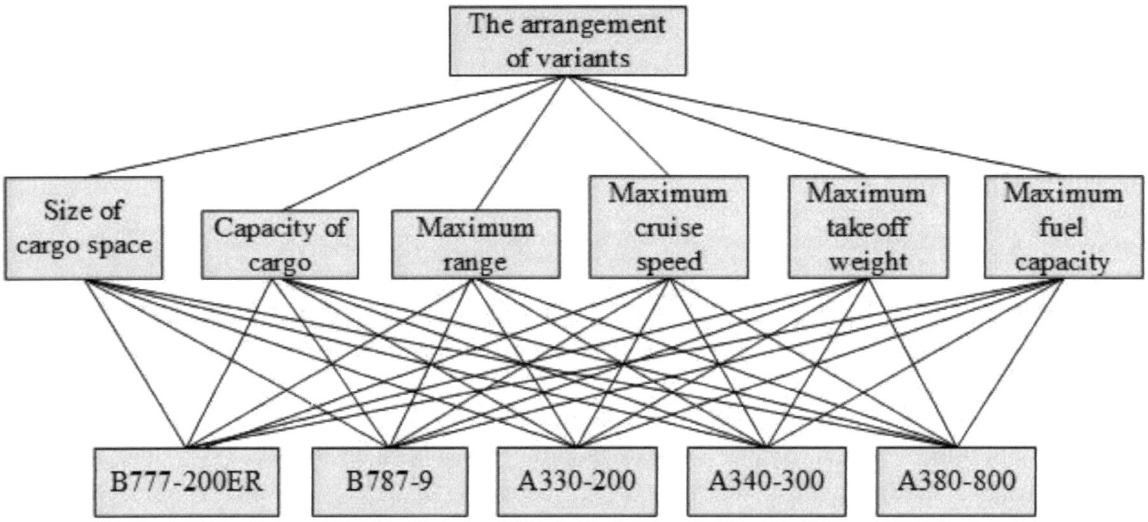

Figure 2 Hierarchical structure of the problem

The data for the evaluation was obtained by a survey of the evaluator (expert on air transport). The evaluator was informed about the variants of the airplanes and based on his expertise he evaluated variants through criteria.

3.2 The second step of solution

The second step of the solution is to determine the weight of the individual criteria. The weights of the evaluated criteria numerically express their importance, importance from the point of view of the evaluator (expert). The Saaty method was used to determine the weight.

Saaty's method is a method of quantitative paired comparison of criteria. The evaluator (expert) via mutual comparing the criteria has created Saaty matrix. Based on formula (2) was calculated the geometric mean of the rows of Saaty matrix G_i and formula (3) was calculated the weights of criteria v_i (Table 1).

Criteria	Size of cargo space	Capacity of cargo	Max. range	Max. cruise speed	Max. takeoff weight	Max. fuel capacity	G_i	v_i
Size of cargo space	1	1/3	1/2	3	4	5	1.47	0.18
Capacity of cargo	3	1	2	4	5	6	2.99	0.37
Max. range	2	1/2	1	3	4	5	1.98	0.24
Max. cruise speed	1/3	1/4	1/3	1	5	6	0.97	0.12
Max. takeoff weight	1/4	1/5	1/4	1/5	1	2	0.41	0.05
Max. fuel capacity	1/5	1/6	1/5	1/6	1/2	1	0.29	0.04

Table 1 The weights of criteria

The Saaty matrix was verified and is consistent. The Saaty matrix contains quantified information from the evaluator (expert) about the relation of the individual pairs of criteria. The highest weight (importance) has the criterion of capacity of cargo.

3.3 The third step of solution

The third step of the solution is to determine preferential indices of the variants by using the paired comparison for each criterion. For example, the criterion size of cargo space was selected for this article (Table 2). The elements of this matrix express the relationship of the pair of variants to the relevant criterion. We obtained the preferential indices of the variants w_{ij}, which represent the evaluation of i-th variant in terms of j-th criterion.

Size of cargo space	B777-200ER	B787-9	A330-200	A340-300	A380-800	G_i	w_{ij}
B777-200ER	1	4	1/7	1/2	1/3	0.6248	0.0807
B787-9	1/4	1	1/9	1/4	1/6	0.2586	0.0334
A330-200	7	9	1	6	5	4.5216	0.5842
A340-300	2	4	1/6	1	1/3	0.8503	0.1099
A380-800	2	6	1/5	3	1	1.4841	0.1918

Table 2 The matrix of paired comparison and the preferential indices of the variants

Similarly, we calculated the preferential indices of the variants for other criteria. The matrixes were verified and are consistent. The preferential indices of all variants and the weighs of all criteria are the basis for calculating the global preferential indices of the variants. Table 3 shows the calculation of the global preferential indices of the variants and the resulting order of the variants.

Variants / Criteria	B777-200ER	B787-9	A330-200	A340-300	A380-800
Size of cargo space	0.0807	0.0334	0.5842	0.1099	0.1918
Capacity of cargo	0.1082	0.6156	0.0413	0.1835	0.0515
Max. range	0.1970	0.1493	0.0266	0.0829	0.5441

Max. cruise speed	0.2899	0.2899	0.1499	0.1499	0.1204
Max. takeoff weight	0.1804	0.0617	0.0403	0.1042	0.6133
Max. fuel capacity	0.1943	0.0400	0.0613	0.0954	0.6090
$u(a_i)$	0.1939	0.3089	0.1496	0.1345	0.2536
Order	**3.**	**1.**	**4.**	**5.**	**2.**

Table 3 Table of resulting values

In the resulting order of the variants, B787-9 was evaluated as the best airplane, the second was A380-800 and the third was B777-200ER.

4 Conclusions

The aim of this article was to apply AHP method in the aviation industry for selecting a suitable airplane for the transport of a particular cargo. The Boeing B787-9 is the best airplane evaluated by the evaluator (expert) via using the AHP method, the second airplane is the Airbus A380-800 and the third airplane is the Boeing B777-200ER.

The analytical hierarchical process has some advantages and disadvantages as the same as other methods. One of the advantages of AHP over other multi-criteria evaluation methods is the division of the decision-making problem into a hierarchy. Thus, the decision-making problem becomes clearer because the hierarchy will give the evaluator a structure that allows a complex view of the problem. It is possible to determine if the model is including all the important aspects. The breakdown of criteria and variants into the hierarchies is advantageous from a mathematical point of view. The pairwise comparison, that the evaluator must make, is a direct and intuitive method. The evaluator always works with only two elements, making it easy for him to say which element he prefers.

One of the disadvantages of the AHP method is the total number of paired comparisons to be made. Is necessary to compare all criteria on the same hierarchical level as well as all variants with respect to each criterion. A large number of paired comparisons can be time-consuming to calculate. The evaluator can lose the attention and then he can start to do inconsistent decisions. One way to simplify the method for the user in this regard is to group the criteria and group them into other hierarchical levels.

Despite the disadvantages described above it is possible to use the AHP method also in other areas of the airline's decision-making process. For example, this method may be used to apply to choose the most appropriate destination. The decision to which destination the air carrier will fly is based on a comparison of business, operational and economic criteria. This decision can be made by using more evaluators (experts) to determine the weighting of the criteria either in a team manner or individually and independently.

References

Dožić, S., Kalić, M. (2014). 'An AHP Approach to Aircraft Selection Process'. *Transportation Research Procedia,* 3, pp. 165-174.

Fiala, P., Jablonský, J. and Maňas M. (1994). *Multi-criterial decision-making.* Prague: University of Economics, Prague.

Fotr, J. and Švecová, L. (2016). *Managerial decision making: procedures, methods and tools*, 3rd ed. Prague: Ekopress, s. r. o.

Olivková, I. (2018). 'Methodology for Assessment of Electronic Payment Systems in Transport Using AHP Method'. *Reliability and Statistics in Transportation and Communication, RelStat 2017. Lecture Notes in Networks and Systems*, 36, pp. 290-299.

Průša, J. et al (2016). *The world of air transport*, 2nd ed. Prague: Galileo.

Ramík, J. (2000). *Analytical hierarchical process (AHP) and its use in small and medium enterprises*, Opava: Silesian University in Opava.

Saaty, T. L. (1999). 'The seven pillars of the analytic hierarchy process'. *Multiple Criteria Decision Making in the New Millennium. Lecture Notes in Economics and Mathematical Systems*, 507.

Saaty, T. L. (1980). *The Analytic Hierarchy Process,* New York: Mc Graw Hill.

Node subset heuristic for non-split delivery VRP

Jan Pelikán [1] , Petr Štourač [2] , Michal Černý [3]

Abstrakt. The paper proposes a new heuristic for a non-split delivery modification of VRP (VRPPC). There are two types of carriers. A private carrier has a fleet of vehicles with known capacities. His fleet can be used in the TSP-style and the price of delivery is proportional to the sum of distances traveled. Common carrier has no capacity limit and costs are proportional to the quantity of transported goods only. The goods and vehicles for both carriers are located in the same depot. A set of customers with given demand are known. The goal is to minimize the overall costs. The model, modified insert heuristic and a new type of heuristic have been tested on instances from testing dataset. The performance of the mathematical model and both heuristics has been compared.

Keywords: vehicle routing, integer programming, insert heuristic, non-split delivery model.

JEL classification: C61

1 Introduction

Solving vehicle routing problems by using specific models and methods belong to the core of operations research. The vehicle routing problem (VRP) addresses distribution of goods from a central depot to customers. This problem was originally formulated by Clark and Wright (1964). Over the years, many modifications of this problem have been studied this problem (VRP with heterogenous fleet of vehicles, VRP with the pick and delivery problem, VRP with time windows and many others). There are a lot of heuristics for such modifications. One of the theme is used in Chu (2005) to solve the so called truckload and less-than-truckload problem. A heuristic proposed by Plevný (2013) selects customers according the distance from depot. Pelikán (2016) described a modified insert heuristic for solving split and non-split demand with a uniform and heterogeneous fleet of vehicles.

We consider a modification of VRP known as non-split delivery VRP with private and common carriers (VRPPC). The goods can be transported as a complex from the depot to the customers by private carrier's fleet with limited capacity or by common carrier.

To formalize the problem more precisely, assume that we obtain customers demands with known quantity. The customers are represented as nodes on a given graph with weighted edges, where weights correspond to distances. The goods are placed in the depot where also the fleets of both carriers are located. The private carrier has a fleet of vehicles with known capacities. This fleet can be used in the TSP-style and the price of delivery is proportional to the sum of distances traveled by the vehicles. The common carrier has no capacity limit and costs are proportional to the quantity of transported goods only. The goal is to minimize the overall costs.

[1]University of Economics, Department of Econometrics, nám. W. Churchilla 1938/4, Prague, Czech Republic, jan.pelikan@vse.cz.
[2]University of Economics, Department of Econometrics, nám. W. Churchilla 1938/4, Prague, Czech Republic, stop02@vse.cz.
[3]University of Economics, Department of Econometrics, nám. W. Churchilla 1938/4, Prague, Czech Republic, cernym@vse.cz.

A new kind of a heuristic is designed in Sect. 3. Before that, in Sect. 2, we give a description of the problem as an integer program.

2 Mathematical model

Non-split delivery model (VRPPC) contains a binary variable z_i which is equal 1 if common carrier assures whole demand q_i of node i. This model can be formulated as integer programing problem. Let $G = \{V, E\}$ be an undirected complete graph, $V = \{1, 2, \ldots, n\}$, node 1 is the depot and nodes $2, 3, \ldots, n$ are customers.

Parameters of the model are:

- d_{ij} = distance between nodes i, j,
- q_i = demand in node i,
- W = capacity of private carrier's vehicles,
- c_c = costs of transport of a unit of goods by the common carrier,
- S = number of vehicles of private carrier,
- p = costs per km of private carrier vehicles.

Variables of the model are:

- $x_{ij}^{\mathrm{s}} \in \{0, 1\}$, $x_{ij}^{\mathrm{s}} = 1$ if the vehicle s of the private carrier travels from node i to node j, $x_{ij}^{\mathrm{s}} = 0$ otherwise,
- $z_i \in \{0, 1\}$, $z_i = 1$ if the common carrier serves whole demand q_i of node i, $z_i = 0$ otherwise,
- u_i^{s} are auxiliary variables in anti-cyclic constraints, s $= \{1, 2, \ldots, S\}$.

ILP model of VRPPC

$$p \sum_{s=1}^{S} \sum_{i=1}^{n} \sum_{j=1}^{n} d_{ij} x_{ij}^{s} + c_c \sum_{i=1}^{n} z_i q_i \rightarrow min \tag{1}$$

$$\sum_{i=1}^{n} x_{ij}^{s} = \sum_{i=1}^{n} x_{ji}^{s} \qquad s = 1, \ldots, S, j = 1, \ldots, n \tag{2}$$

$$\sum_{s=1}^{S} \sum_{j=1}^{n} x_{ij}^{s} = 1 - z_i \qquad i = 1, \ldots, n \tag{3}$$

$$u_i^{s} \leq W \qquad s = 1, \ldots, S, \quad i = 1, \ldots, n \tag{4}$$

$$\sum_{j=1}^{n} x_{1j}^{s} \leq 1 \qquad s = 1, \ldots, S \tag{5}$$

$$u_i^{s} + q_j - W(1 - x_{ij}^{s}) \leq u_j^{s} \qquad s = 1, \ldots, S, \quad i = 1, \ldots, n, \quad j = 2, \ldots, n, i \neq j \tag{6}$$

The objective function (1) minimizes the sum of costs of vehicles of the private carrier and the common carrier. Constraint (2) states that a vehicle must enter and leave a node. Equation (3) means that a node not served by the common carrier has to be served by avehicle of the private carrier. Inequality (4) assures that capacity of the s-th vehicle is not exceeded. Inequality (5) means that a vehicle can leave the depot maximum once. Anti-cyclic conditions and defining of load u_i^{s} of the vehicle s entering node i are in (6).

3 Heuristics

We consider two heuristics for VRPPC. The first is the standard insert heuristic. The latter called *node subset heuristic*, is based on sorting of the list of nodes, minimization of the sum of the private carrier's costs for the first ℓ nodes by the Clarke and Wright heuristic and assignment of the remaining demand of the nodes $\ell+1, \ell+2, \ldots, n$ to the common carrier.

The following notation is used for the heuristics:

- the route of sth vehicle is $R^s = \{v_1^s, v_2^s, \ldots, v_{h^s}^s\}$, where $v_1^s = v_{h^s}^s = 1$ and $(v_j^s, v_{j+1}^s), j = 1, 2, \ldots, h^s - 1$ are arcs of route R^s,
- $n =$ number of nodes,
- $S =$ number of vehicles,
- $c_c =$ costs of the transport of unit of goods by the common carrier,
- $p =$ costs per km of private carrier vehicles,
- $q_i =$ demand at the node i,
- $w^s =$ load of the private carrier vehicle s,
- $W =$ capacity of private carrier vehicles,
- $d_{ij} =$ distance between nodes i, j.

3.1 Insert heuristic

The following algorithm is used for insert heuristic:

Step 0: $s := 0$,
Step 1: {**initial route** s} $s := s+1, k := 0, \delta := 0, w^s := 0$,

Repeat for $i = 2, 3, \ldots, n$:
  If $c_c q_i - p(d_{1i} + d_{i1}) > \delta$ and $q_i > 0$ then $k := i, \delta := c_c q_i - p(d_{1i} + d_{i1})$.
If $k = 0$ then go to Step 3
else $v_1^s := v_3^s := 1, v_2^s := k, h_s := 3, w^s := q_k, q_k := 0$.

Step 2: {**insertion**} $\delta := 0, k := 0$,

Repeat for $i := 1, 2, \ldots, n$
If $q_i > 0$ then
Repeat for $j = 1, 2, \ldots, h_s - 1$:
  If $c_c q_i - p(d_{v_j^s i} + d_{i v_{j+1}^s} - d_{v_j^s v_{j+1}^s}) > \delta$ and $w_s + q_i \leq W$
  then $k := i, \bar{j} := j, \delta := c_c q_i - p(d_{v_j^s i} + d_{i v_{j+1}^s} - d_{v_j^s v_{j+1}^s})$
If $k = 0$ then $h^s := h^s + 1, v_{h^s}^s := 1$. Go to Step 1.
Else $(v_{\bar{j},k}^s, v_{k,\bar{j}+1}^s)$ add to the arcs of route R^s, set $w^s := w^s + q_k, q_k := 0, h^s := h^s + 1$, go to Step 2.

Step 3: {**common carriers transport**} The remaining demand $q_i > 0, i = 1, 2, \ldots, n$ is assigned to transport by common carrier.

3.2 Node subset heuristic

The heuristic first sorts the list of nodes (in the descending order) according a particular rule. We consider these rules:

- *dist-1* sorts nodes according to the distance from the depot (node 1),
- *dist-2(m)* sorts nodes according to sum: $d_{1i} + \sum_{k=1}^{m} d_{ij_k}$ where j_k is k-th nearest neighbor of i (the parameter m can be choosen as $2, 3, \ldots, n-1$),
- *km-tons* sorts nodes according to $d_{1i}(\max q_j - q_i + \overline{q_j})$, where $\overline{q_j} = \sum_{i=2}^{n} q_i/(n-1)$,
- *costs-dist* sorts nodes according to the cost difference $p(d_{1i} + d_{i1}) - c_c q_i$.

Then it calculates in the cycle for $\ell = 2, 3, \ldots, n$ the total travel costs as the sum of the private carrier's travel costs TP for the first l nodes calculated by some heuristic or mathematical model and the common carrier travel costs TC for the last $n - \ell + 1$ nodes of sorted list.

The following algorithm is used for all variants:

Step 0: $\ell := 0, T^* := \infty$.
Step 1: $\{$**sorting**$\}$
Create sorted list $(v_1 = 1, v_2, \ldots, v_n)$ of nodes $\{1, 2, \ldots, n\}$ according to the selected rule.
Step 2: $\{$**private and common transportation costs**$\}$
Repeat for $\ell = 2, 3, \ldots, n$
2a) solve VRP for the node subset $(v_1, v_2, \ldots, v_l)$ using ILP or some heuristic method (i.e. nearest neighbor method, savings Clarke Wright heuristic, insert heuristic). Results are a set of routes R and private carrier's costs TP.
2b) The remaining demand $q_i > 0, i = v_{\ell+1}, v_{\ell+2}, \ldots, v_n$ is assigned to the common carrier with costs $TC = \sum_{i=\ell+1}^{n} q_{v_i}$.
2c) If $T^* < TP + TC$ then $T^* := TP + TC, l^* := l, R^* := R$

Results of the heuristic are the set of routes R^* and the total costs T^* . The heuristic can be applied with different values of parameter m, so with different choices of m we can get different values of T^* and take the lovest.

4 Numerical examples

The model and both heuristics were testing on examples *VAL3*, *VAL6* and *E3* published on http://www.uv.es/belengue.carp.html. The ILP model is solved by CPLEX 12.0. The heuristics are written in VBA language. PC (IntelCore2Quad, 2.83GHz) is used for computation. Computation of the model ran for three times and interrupted gradually after 1 minute, 10 minutes and 1 hour. Parameters and computational results are summarized in Table 1.

The columns stand for the tested examples VAL3, VAL6 and E3. The first four rows represents parameters of examples, n = number of nodes, c_c = costs of the transport of unit of goods by the common carrier, W = capacity of private carrier vehicles and p = costs per km of private carrier vehicles. The next three rows contain results for the model (with different time of interuption in brackets in the first column). Result values are followed in parentheses by GAP (difference between best feasible solution found so far and the corresponding best lower bound found so far). In one case (E3/1 hour), the result was not obtained. The remaining rows contain results for Insert heuristic and Node subset heuristic (4 rows for different type of nodes sorting). In case of the dist-2 variant, the number of adjacent nodes whose sum of distances is applied to sorting is written in parentheses.

sample	VAL3	VAL6	E3
n	24	31	77
c_c	10	15	300
W	50	50	50
p	20	20	20
$model$ (1 min)	1200 (31%)	2690 (29%)	151260 (72%)
$model$ (20 mins)	1200 (31%)	2690 (18%)	138020 (71%)
$model$ (1 hour)	1200 (31%)	2540 (14%)	-
insert	1560	3175	155340
dist-1	1340	2950	**136520**
dist-2 (m)	1270 (7)	2630 (7)	**125740 (12)**
km-tons	1230	2735	**128180**
costs dist.	1310	2780	**127360**

Tabulka 1 Summary data for test instances.

5 Conclusion

We consider non-split delivery modification of VRP. ILP of the problem has been presented and a new type of a heuristic approach has been designed. The model, the modified insert heuristic and a new type of heuristic were tested on instances from a benchmark dataset. The results show that the ILP formulation need not be suitable for solving the real problems. The proposed heuristic method gives us good solutions, better than results from the modified insert heuristic.

Acknowledgements

The work was supported by the Czech Science Foundation under grant 19-02773S and by the Internal Grant Agency of University of Economics, Prague under Grant F4/19/2019.

Reference

Chu, Ch-W. (2005). 'A heuristic algorithm for the truckload and less-than-truckload problem'. *European Journal of Operational Research*, 165, pp. 657–667.

Clarke, G. and Wright, J. W. (1964). 'Scheduling of Vehicles from a Central Depot to a Number of Delivery Points'. *Operational Research*, pp. 568–581.

Pelikán, J. (2016). 'Heuristics for VRP with private and common carriers'. *Proceedings of the International Conference on Mathematical Methods in Economics*, Liberec, pp. 658–662.

Plevný, M. (2013). 'Vehicle routing problem with a private eet and common carriers - the variety with a possibility of sharing the satisfaction of demand'. *Mathematical Methods in Economics, 31st International Conference Proceedings*, College of Polytechnics Jihlava, pp. 730–736.

Return and Volatility Spillover Effects in Western European Stock Markets

Petr Seďa[1], Lorena Caridad López del Río [2]

Abstract. Understanding of the linkages between different financial markets has great importance especially for portfolio managers. When considering international stock markets integration, it is important not only investigate linkages of prices, but also measure volatility spillover effects. Volatility is usually understood as a measure of risk of financial assets. This paper deal with modelling and interpreting the return and volatility spillover effect in Western European stock markets with a help of autoregressive conditional volatility models. More precisely, there will be modelled an impact of returns and volatility generated by the US and eurozone stock markets in French, German, British and Swiss stock markets in the period of 2007-2017. All the markets are approximated by their main stock indexes. Achieved results confirmed significant impact of the return and volatility spillover effect coming from the US stock market. This effect is greater after the period of the global financial crisis.

Keywords: AR/EGARCH model, financial market, global financial crisis, return and volatility spillover effect, time series.

JEL Classification: C10

1 Introduction

Recent development of trading technologies and transmission of information lead to the liberalization of capital flows. It resulted in deeper integration of financial markets than before. This empirical fact has been observed both in developed and emerging stock markets. The growth of financial transactions reduced isolation of particular national stock markets. These factors contributed to the ability of stock markets to react to the announcements or shocks generated by other markets (Singh, Kumar, and Pandey, 2010). It has been empirically observed that the stock markets around the world are becoming closer in general. International linkages became significant in assets pricing and international hedging strategies as well (Ng, 2000). The announcements from developed stock markets may affect significantly the stock returns and volatilities in domestic stock markets. This especially applies when the linkages between markets are strong. The degree of linkages may be very important for international portfolio diversification and hedging strategies in general.

Return and volatility spillover effects means that returns and volatility of stock markets may be also affected by the prices and volatility generated by other stock markets apart from own noise (Engle, Ito and Wen-Ling, 1990). Several episodes of turbulence in mature financial markets in the past decade. For instance, the recent global financial crisis that originated in the US stock market spread in other stock markets worldwide and caused great volatility in stock

[1] VSB-Technical University of Ostrava, Faculty of Economics, Department of Mathematical Methods in Economics, Sokolská třída 33, 702 00 Ostrava 1, Czech Republic, petr.seda@vsb.cz.
[2] University of Cordoba, Department of Statistics and Econometrics, Agrifood Campus of International Excellence ceiA3, E-14001 Cordoba, Spain, lcyldr@gmail.com.

returns. That is why, proper and deep analysis of the sources in volatility of returns may be very important, especially in short term.

The number of studies on the extent of Western European stock markets being influenced by shocks coming from developed stock markets is relatively small. Authors usually investigated the spillover effects between developed and emerging markets. For instance, Li and Giles (2015) investigated the linkages of stock markets across the USA, Japan, and six Asian emerging stock markets. Neaime (2012) investigated the transmissions across different markets during a specific event such as a financial crisis. Diebold and Yilmaz (2012) found that the cross-market volatility spillovers increased substantially following the global financial crisis.

The events of 2007-08 suggested that this may be an important gap in the empirical contagion literature. The aim of this paper is to estimate and interpret return and volatility spill-over effect in selected European developed stock markets with a help of extended nonlinear autoregressive conditional volatility models. In particular, there will be modelled an impact of shocks generated by the US and eurozone stock markets. We will utilize daily returns of US, eurozone, German, French, British and Swiss stock markets in the period of 2007-2017. All the markets will be approximated by their main stock indexes. The novelty of this paper consists in comparison of the return and volatility spillover effects in different testing sub-period in order to quantify an impact of the global financial crisis on return and volatility spillover effects in Western stock markets. In other words, we will investigate the time varying patterns of spillover effects and the extent to which shocks transmitted across four major Western European stock markets when economic uncertainties reached high level.

Our paper is organized in the following way. In Introduction, the importance of the return and volatility spillover effect was emphasized, short review of literature provided, and the added value of this paper was stressed. Second chapter delivers a description of return and volatility spillover effect model that is based on the approach defined by Christiansen (2007). This chapter is finished by a brief description of data sample. Third chapter is provides an estimation of return and volatility spillover models. Moreover, the variance ratios will be computed for all Western European stock markets. Further, the results for two different testing sub-period will be compared. Conclusion summarizes this paper. Outcomes of this paper will be also discussed with regard to similar works of other authors.

2 Methodology

In this chapter, the return and volatility spillover model applied in practical part of this paper will be described. Next, the data used to assess the contribution will be analyzed from statistical point of view.

2.1 Return and Volatility Spillover Model

In this paper, there will be utilized a model that is based on the model introduced by Christian-sen (2007) who estimated volatility spillover effect in bond markets. He proposed to estimate the volatility spillover effect that is based on a three steps AR-GARCH model. However, for the purpose of his paper, we will apply a non-linear EGARCH model instead. This model can capture even nonlinear dependencies in the form of asymmetric effect in univariate volatility model (Nelson, 1991). We will modify original model as proposed by Christiansen (2007) in order to be applicable when modelling the return and volatility spillover effects in stock market as well.

In accordance with Christiansen (2007), in the first step the US stock return $R_{US,t}$ approximated by S&P500 index is estimated by AR-EGARCH model:

$$R_{US,t} = C_{0,US} + C_{1,US}R_{US,t-1} + e_{US,t} \tag{1}$$

where $e_{US,t} \sim N(0, \sigma^2_{US,t})$ is the innovation of the US stock market and $C_{1,US}$ measures an impact of lagged value of returns from US stock market $R_{US,t-1}$. The logarithm of conditional variance of the US stock market $\sigma^2_{US,t}$ then follows an equation:

$$\ln \sigma^2_{US,t} = \mu_{US} + \alpha_{1,US}\frac{e_{US,t-1}}{\sigma_{US,t-1}} + \alpha_{2,US}\left[\left|\frac{e_{US,t-1}}{\sigma_{US,t-1}}\right| - \sqrt{\frac{2}{\pi}}\right] + \beta_{US} ln\sigma^2_{US,t-1} \tag{2}$$

where β_{US} measures the persistence in volatility of US stock market, parameter $\alpha_{1,US}$ measures the variance to the shocks. This model allows the asymmetric responses to negative or positive shocks. If the ratio $\frac{e_{US,t-1}}{\sigma_{US,t-1}} > 0$ then the effect of the shock is $(\alpha_{1,US} + \alpha_{2,US})$, and conversely, if the ratio $\frac{e_{US,t-1}}{\sigma_{US,t-1}} < 0$ then the effect of the shock is $(\alpha_{2,US} - \alpha_{1,US})$.

Further, in the second step, the extended version of univariate AR-EGARCH model is utilized to model the aggregated European stock market return that is represented by EURO STOXX 50 index. The return of the eurozone stock market $R_{EUR,t}$ can be expressed as follows:

$$R_{EUR,t} = C_{0,EUR} + C_{1,EUR}R_{EUR,t-1} + \gamma_{EUR}R_{US,t-1} + \varphi_{EUR}e_{US,t} + e_{EUR,t}. \tag{3}$$

The return of the eurozone stock market depends on own lagged return, the lagged value of US return and the US residual term at time *t*. Next, the shocks from the US stock market and from own eurozone market at time *t* influence the return of eurozone stock market. The volatility and return spillover effect from the US stock market to eurozone stock market is then measured by parameters φ_{EUR} and γ_{EUR} respectively. The volatility of the eurozone market is as follows:

$$\ln \sigma^2_{EUR,t} = \mu_{EUR} + \alpha_{1,EUR}\frac{e_{EUR,t-1}}{\sigma_{EUR,t-1}} + \alpha_{2,EUR}\left[\left|\frac{e_{EUR,t-1}}{\sigma_{EUR,t-1}}\right| - \sqrt{\frac{2}{\pi}}\right] + \beta_{EUR} ln\sigma^2_{EUR,t-1} \tag{4}$$

where $\alpha_{1,EUR}$ is a parameter of symmetric response of the variance to eurozone shocks.

In the final step, the extended univariate AR-EGARCH model is utilized when estimating the returns of individual stock markets. This model ensures the residuals from US and eurozone stock markets are orthogonal. One can investigate the impacts of the US and eurozone stock markets on individual country. The individual stock market return is then expressed as follows:

$$R_{i,t} = C_{0,i} + C_{1,i}R_{i,t-1} + \gamma_i R_{US,t-1} + \delta_i R_{EUR,t-1} + \varphi_i e_{US,t} + \psi_i e_{EUR,t} + e_{i,t}. \quad (5)$$

The return of individual country is affected by the lagged returns of the US and eurozone stock market at time *t*-1. The shocks transmitted from the US market, eurozone market and local market as well. The volatility and return spillover effects from the US stock market are estimated by parameters γ_i and φ_i, while the eurozone mean and volatility spillover effects are measured by δ_i and ψ_i. The volatility of individual market is as follows:

$$\ln \sigma_{i,t}^2 = \mu_i + \alpha_{1,i}\frac{e_{i,t-1}}{\sigma_{i,t-1}} + \alpha_{2,i}\left[\left|\frac{e_{i,t-1}}{\sigma_{i,t-1}}\right| - \sqrt{\frac{2}{\pi}}\right] + \beta_i ln\sigma_{i,t-1}^2 \quad (6)$$

where parameter $\boldsymbol{\alpha_{1,i}}$ measures the asymmetric response of the sign of the shocks $\boldsymbol{e_{US,t}}$~N(0, $\boldsymbol{\sigma_{i,t}^2}$). The unexpected returns for each market can be expressed as follows:

$$\varepsilon_{US,t} = e_{US,t}, \quad (7)$$

$$\varepsilon_{EUR,t} = \varphi_{EUR}e_{US,t} + e_{EUR,t}, \quad (8)$$

$$\varepsilon_{i,t} = \varphi_i e_{US,t} + \psi_i e_{EUR,t} + e_{i,t}. \quad (9)$$

The idiosyncratic shocks expressed by $\varepsilon_{US,t}, \varepsilon_{EUR,t}$ and $\varepsilon_{i,t}$ are assumed to be mutually independent. Thus, the conditional variance of the *i*-th country unexpected return is as follows:

$$h_{i,t} = E(\varepsilon_{i,t-1}^2 | I_{t-1}) = \varphi_i^2\sigma_{US,t}^2 + \psi_{i,t}^2\sigma_{EUR,t}^2 + \sigma_{i,t}^2. \quad (10)$$

The conditional variance according to equation (10) therefore depends on the variance of world, eurozone and its own idiosyncratic shocks at time *t*. The variance ratio computed to measure whether the volatility is caused more by the US market or the eurozone market is expressed as follows:

$$VR_{i,t}^{US} = \frac{\varphi_i^2\sigma_{US,t}^2}{h_{i,t}}, \quad (11)$$

$$VR_{i,t}^{EUR} = \frac{\psi_i^2\sigma_{EUR,t}^2}{h_{i,t}}. \quad (12)$$

When considering the US and eurozone stock markets effect, the rest of the volatility must be caused by local factors or individual market itself:

$$VR_{i,t}^{i} = 1 - VR_{i,t}^{US} - VR_{i,t}^{EUR} = \frac{\sigma_{i,t}^2}{h_{i,t}}. \quad (13)$$

The variance ratios can deliver a picture to what extend the local market variance is affected by US, eurozone or local shocks.

2.2 Data Sample Description

Empirical investigation will be done using daily returns of the French, German, British, Swiss, eurozone and US stock market in the period from February 2007 to August 2017. The indexes are DAX for Germany, CAC40 for France, FTSE100 for UK, SMI20 for Switzerland, EURO-STOXX for eurozone and S&P500 for US stock market. This basic data sample includes around 3850 trading days. We get more than 10 years long time series of the closing rates. This period was chosen intentionally to investigate changes of the volatility and return spillover effects. The basic testing period was divided into two sub-periods in order to compare the degree of volatility and return spillover effects. In other words, it would be useful to investigate a potential impact of the global financial crisis. The sub-periods are as follows:

a) 08.02.2007 – 30.06.2009 - the crisis period is characterized by deep economic recession. It includes a shock in the form of the global financial crisis. There has been observed a steady fall of the US stock market. The US National Economic Research Authority officially announced June 30, 2009 the end of the global financial crisis.

b) 01.07.2009 – 22.08.2017 - the post-crisis period follows the previous sub-period. It begins July 1, 2009, when world stock markets recovered from the global financial crisis and started to grow slowly. The end of this sub-period is August 22, 2017.

The descriptive statistics of the daily samples of the 4 Western European countries and 2 benchmarks in both sub-periods are presented in Table 1. The mean values of returns are all negative in crisis period and positive in post-crisis period. US market outperformed eurozone and all regional markets. The standard deviations ranges from 0.0142 to 0.0170 in crisis period, while in post-crisis period, the values of standard deviations were significantly lower. None of the skewness of all six indices is equal to zero and none of the kurtosis follows the value of 3. The negative skewness and excess kurtosis illustrate that negative shocks are more frequent than positive ones in all stock markets in crisis period. The non-normal distribution of these 12 data sets is further confirmed by the values of Jarque-Bera test. All the probabilities to accept the null hypothesis of normality are close to zero.

	USA	**EUR**	**FRA**	**GER**	**UK**	**SWI**
			Crisis period			
Mean	-5.21E-04	-6.53E-04	-6.83E-04	-4.16E-04	-4.63E-04	-6.20E-04
St. dev.	0.0170	0.0164	0.0167	0.0160	0.0155	0.0142
Skewness	-0,1692	0,0832	0.2030	0.3578	-0.0323	0.2323
Kurtosis	11.7073	11.2206	11.8207	12.9931	11.1221	11.5807
Jarq.-Bera	2765.19	2461.95	2839.40	3655.32	2402.50	2689.17
Probability	< 0.00001	< 0.00001	< 0.00001	< 0.00001	< 0.00001	< 0.00001
			Post-crisis period			
Mean	3.27E-04	1.21E-04	1.64E-04	3.12E-04	1.82E-04	1.69E-04
St. dev.	0.0079	0.0112	0.0110	0.0106	0.0082	0.0081
Skewness	-0.4756	-0.1459	-0.1571	-0.2829	-0.1751	-0.7985
Kurtosis	10.4420	9.6708	9.2778	7.5173	7.4072	13.3796
Jarq.-Bera	6977.38	5526.59	4897.47	2569.22	2422.89	13670.93
Probability	< 0.00001	< 0.00001	< 0.00001	< 0.00001	< 0.00001	< 0.00001

Table 1 Descriptive statistics in crisis and post-crisis periods

3 Empirical Results

In this chapter, the main results and findings achieved with respect to the aim of this paper will be described. First the results of basic spillover model in different Western European market in crisis and post-crisis periods will be described. Moreover, the Wald tests for different joint hypotheses will be applied to evaluate the robustness of the results. Finally, the values of variance ratios in all markets will be computed and discussed.

3.1 Basic Spillover Model

Table 2 shows the summary statistics from the spillover model in crisis and post-crisis periods. The first column covers the results from the US stock market. The coefficient of US lagged returns $C_{1,US}$ reached small and negative values, which implies first-order autocorrelation. However, it is significant only in crisis period. The presence of asymmetric conditional volatility is expressed by $\alpha_{1,US}$. The estimated values are negative and statistically significant in both sub-periods. Next, the US returns display a high degree of volatility persistence as confirmed by β_{US}.

	USA	EUR	FRA	GER	UK	SWI
			Crisis period			
$C_{0.i}$	0.00011	-0.00037	-0.00043*	-0.00001	-0.00013	-0.00052*
$C_{1.i}$	-0.12516*	-0.17961*	-0.00479	0.04166	-0.04254	0.01188
γ_i	x	0.26897*	0.02925*	0.02329*	0.05455*	0.06707*
δ_i	x	x	-0.00772	-0.01176	-0.00655	-0.00892
φ_i	x	0.12883*	-0.00101	0.02282*	0.02714*	0.04078*
ψ_i	x	x	0.99153*	0.94487*	0.83891*	0.70370*
ω_i	-0.10832*	-0.16235*	-11.5589	-0.82011*	-11.92646*	-11.83917*
$\alpha_{1.i}$	-0.11138*	-0.12473*	0.01000	0.03039	-0.02609	-0.05999
$\alpha_{2.i}$	0.04167*	0.06766*	0.01000	0.25180*	0.49009*	0.49242*
β_i	0.99100*	0.98739*	0.01000	0.94506*	-0.08798	-0.10344
			Post-crisis period			
$C_{0.i}$	0.00036*	0.00004	0.00001*	0.00023*	0.00015*	0.00017*
$C_{1.i}$	-0.03068	-0.13829*	0.01437	0.04971*	-0.02688	0.00081
γ_i	x	0.23801*	0.24941*	0.23408*	0.24233*	0.20381*
δ_i	x	x	-0.15423*	-0.17070*	-0.11539*	-0.07808*
φ_i	x	0.95454*	0.93941*	0.88516*	0.68204*	0.58326*
ψ_i	x	x	0.95035*	0.88695*	0.55018*	0.53395*
ω_i	-0.27716*	-12.24440*	-15.7555*	-12.3879*	-13.03210*	-12.59789*
$\alpha_{1.i}$	-0.16215*	-0.00442	-0.01602	-0.01294	-0.02218	-0.01999
$\alpha_{2.i}$	0.08078*	0.36115*	0.31335*	0.30110*	0.37934*	0.39877*
β_i	0.97882*	-0.21279*	-0.22586*	-0.03809	-0.1356*	-0.10763*

Table 2 Model estimation in crisis and post-crisis periods

The second column reports the summary statistics for the eurozone stock market. The own lagged returns have negative impact while US return impacts are positive. Both parameters are significant. The coefficients of US residuals are significant and positive with greater value in post-crisis period when explaining the European returns. The volatility spillover effect from the

US market is evident. The asymmetric volatility effect is negative, but significant just in crisis period. The persistence of volatility was higher in crisis period.

Finally, the spillover effects for individual European countries are estimated and reported in the rest four columns. For each stock markets, one-period lagged returns from the US and the eurozone stock markets, and residuals from these two benchmarks are included in the model. This model allows both the mean and volatility from the US and the eurozone stock markets to affect the individual European Western markets. The returns show very small first-order autocorrelation for all four countries. However, this statistics is significant just for Germany in post-crisis period. The asymmetric conditional volatility effect exist. The only exception is France and Germany in crisis period. However estimated parameters are very small and insignificant. The volatility persistence was significant in all markets except in Germany just in post-crisis period. The US lagged returns have greater, positive and significant influence while the eurozone impact on the mean spillover effects was much smaller and negative. In addition, it was significant just in post-crisis period. The parameters for both the US and eurozone volatility spillover effects are positive and significant for all countries. France is the only exception in crisis period. The eurozone volatility had much larger impact than US volatility in crisis period while in post-crisis period, an impact of both markets was very similar.

Table 3 shows results of Wald tests for different spillover effects in all four markets and both testing sub-periods. The robust Wald tests for the null hypothesis of no mean spillover effects: H_0: $\gamma_i = \delta_i = 0$ is strongly rejected. The joint Wald tests for the hypothesis of no volatility spillover effects: H_0: $\varphi_i = \psi_i = 0$ leaves the results unaltered.

		FRA	GER	UK	SWI
Crisis period					
No return spillover effects	*F*-statistic	7.73*	3.61*	11.02*	14.50*
	Chi-square	15.45*	7.21*	22.04*	29.00*
No volatility spillover effects	*F*-statistic	18021.51*	16516.16*	8958.95*	4501.54*
	Chi-square	36043.02*	33032.31*	17917.91*	9003.08*
No US spillover effects	*F*-statistic	9.57*	16.75*	11.11*	14.97*
	Chi-square	19.14*	33.50*	22.21*	29.94*
No eurozone spillover effects	*F*-statistic	18021.51*	8366.17*	4035.01*	1965.21*
	Chi-square	36043.02*	16732.33*	8070.02*	3930.43*
Post-crisis period					
No return spillover effects	*F*-statistic	1208.49*	434.90*	294.41*	177.97*
	Chi-square	2416.99*	869.79*	588.82*	355.94*
No volatility spillover effects	*F*-statistic	95539.16*	31671.48*	10693.08*	8175.62*
	Chi-square	191078.3*	63342.97*	21386.17*	16351.23*
No US spillover effects	*F*-statistic	40615.79*	15117.52*	6139.33*	4028.27*
	Chi-square	81231.58*	30235.05*	12278.66*	8056.54*
No eurozone spillover effects	*F*-statistic	47394.23*	16088.97*	4114.20*	3556.62*
	Chi-square	94788.47*	32177.94*	8228.40*	7113.23*

Table 3 Joint Wald Tests in crisis and post-crisis periods

The robust Wald test results for no US-spillover effects: H_0: $\gamma_i = \varphi_i = 0$, is strongly rejected for all markets in both testing periods as well. Finally, the joint Wald tests results of no eurozone-spillover effects: H_0: $\delta_i = \psi_i = 0$ is also rejected for all countries in both testing periods.

To sum up, the values of F-statistics and Chi-square statistics are greater in post-crisis period. The volatility spillover effects from both the US and eurozone stock are stronger in post-crisis period compared to the period of the global financial crisis. In addition, there is a weak indication of positive mean spillover effects from the US market, and negative and insignificant mean spillover effects from the eurozone stock market in crisis period. On the other hand, the mean spillover effects from both markets reached significantly greater values in the post-crisis period.

3.2 Variance Ratios

Conclusions in subchapter 3.1 can only illustrate the sign and significance of the spillover parameters of the US and eurozone stock markets. In order to get the quantitative extents of the influence from these two stock markets, the variance ratios were estimated. The mean and standard deviation of the variance ratios $VR_{i,t}^{US}, VR_{i,t}^{EUR}$ and $VR_{i,t}^{i}$ from equations (11) to (13) are calculated to investigate the extend of the volatility spillover effects from the US, eurozone and local stock markets on the individual Western European stock markets. Results for crisis and post-crisis periods are reported in Table 4.

In crisis period, most of the conditional variance of the unexpected return for individual i-th country is made up by the US volatility spillover effects, which accounts from 30.3% in Germany up to 39.8% in Switzerland. The average value of the eurozone volatility spillover effects reached relatively small values compared to the US effects. It ranged from 8.4% in France to 19.2% in Switzerland only. France and Germany are mostly influenced by the local volatility. Mean values are 64.4% and 54.0% respectively. On the other hand, in UK and Switzerland the local volatility is less significant. Means are 43.7% and 41%. It is evident that local volatility plays key role in all four markets.

	FRA	**GER**	**UK**	**SWI**
		Crisis period		
VR_US	0.316 (0.396)	0.303 (0,358)	0.385 (0.472)	0.398 (0.509)
VR_EUR	0.084 (0.120)	0.157 (0.241)	0.178 (0.268)	0.192 (0.302)
VR_*i*-th	0.644 (0.862)	0.540 (0.728)	0.437 (0.631)	0.410 (0.617)
		Post-crisis period		
VR_US	0.647 (0.786)	0.605 (0.726)	0.624 (0.758)	0.523 (0.653)
VR_EUR	0.238 (0.228)	0.286 (0.304)	0.215 (0.245)	0.157 (0.189)
VR_*i*-th	0.115 (0.116)	0.109 (0.127)	0.226 (0.274)	0.320 (0.368)

Table 4 Variance ratios in crisis and post-crisis period

In post crisis period, the structure of variance ratios has changed significantly. Local volatility started to be less significant in all four markets, while shocks generated by the US stock market account from 52.3% in Switzerland to 64.7% in France. The average value of eurozone volatility spillover effect increased a little bit and ranges from 15.7% in Switzerland to 28.6% in Germany. There can be identified a clear difference in structure of variance ratios.

France and Germany exhibit similar composition of variance ratios in both testing periods. UK and Switzerland compose another pair with similar variance ratio structure.

4 Concluding Remarks

In this paper, the return and volatility spillover effects transmitted from the US and eurozone stock markets to the four Western European stock markets were empirically investigated. To estimate the both spillover effects from the US, eurozone to the four Western European stock markets, the modified version of the AR-GARCH model was utilized. This model allows to include the both return and volatility from the US and eurozone stock markets into the return regression equation for each single Western European stock market. In this paper, the spillover effects were estimated for French, German, British and Swiss stock markets. Return spillover effects from the US were significant for all countries in both testing sub-periods. The effects generated by the eurozone market are negligible in crisis period and negative and significant in post-crisis period. The significance of the US, eurozone and local effects in all Western European stock markets has changed in both testing sub-periods. The volatility spillover effects are essential from both the US and eurozone stock markets except for France in crisis period. For all these four countries, the European effects are least significant, the local effects are larger than the US effects in crisis period, while the US effects are most significant in post-crisis period according to variance ratios. Our findings are fully consistent with the conclusions of Diebold and Yilmaz (2012).

Acknowledgements

This paper was supported by the Operational Programme Education for Competitiveness – project No. CZ.1.07/2.3.00/20.0296.

References

Christiansen, C. (2007). 'Volatility-Spillover Effects in European Bond Markets'. *European Financial Management*, 13 (5), pp. 923-948.

Diebold, F. X. and Yilmaz, K. (2012). 'Better to give than to receive: Predictive directional measurement of volatility spillovers'. *International Journal of Forecasting*, 28 (1), pp. 57-66.

Engle, R.F., Ito, T. and Wen-Ling, L. (1990). 'Meteor-Showers or Heat Waves? Heteroskedastic Intro-Daily Volatility in the Foreign Exchange Market'. *Econometrica*, 58 (3), pp. 525-542.

Li, Y. and Giles, D. E. (2015). 'Modeling volatility spillover effects between developed stock markets and Asian emerging stock markets'. *International Journal of Finance & Economics*, 20 (2), pp. 155–177.

Neaime, S. (2012). 'The global financial crisis, financial linkages and correlations in returns and volatilities in emerging MENA stock markets'. *Emerging Markets Review,* 13 (3), pp. 268-282.

Nelson, D. B. (1991). 'Conditional heteroskedasticity in asset returns: a new approach'. *Econometrica*, 59 (2), pp. 247-270.

Ng, A. (2000). 'Volatility Spillover effects from Japan and the US to the Pacific-Basin'. *Journal of International Monetary and Finance*, 19 (2), pp. 207-233.

Singh, P., Kumar, B. and Pandey, A. (2010). 'Price and volatility spillovers across North American, European and Asian stock markets'. *International Reviews of Financial Analysis*, 19 (1), pp. 55-64.

Evaluation of an (emergency) situation under uncertainty

Michal Škoda[1], Helena Brožová[2]

Abstract. The importance of taking right and effective decisions is very easy to understand, but usually hard to achieve. Especially in situations where the decision maker has limited time and the consequences of a wrong decision can be disastrous. This article deals with uncertainty in decision making with a focus on emergency management. The approach can be use almost in all areas of human endeavor where decision making takes place. With regards to the limited information that a decision maker has during an emergency situation, the entire approach works with vague input data. First, fuzzy linguistic scales and criteria are set. Then the emergency situation is evaluated. Based on the level of α-cut, the reliability and completeness of information is taken into account. In the end, the defuzzification is done and the situations are sorted.

Keywords: Decision making, fuzzy number, linguistic scale, α-cut, criteria, emergency.

JEL Classification: C44, D70, D80

1 Introduction

A decision is a position or opinion or judgment reached after consideration (The free Dictionary, 2018). During our lives we have to make a lot of decisions. As Vasilescu (2011) claims in his article, it is very important to take right and effective decisions, which can be sometimes hard to achieve especially with regard to a level of uncertainty.

Uncertainty touches most aspects of our lives. It is a huge topic, that causes sleepless nights, not only to scientists. Many papers have been written about uncertainty and many definitions have been proposed. For instance, Klir and Wierman (1999) state that uncertainty itself has many forms and dimensions and may include concepts such as fuzziness or vagueness, disagreement and conflict, imprecision and non-specificity. Another definition is brought by Draper (1995) who frames the definition in the context of unknown quantities y inferred or predicted on the basis of known quantities x. The model M formalizes assumptions about how x and y are related. Uncertainty about predictions, therefore, includes both uncertainty about the form of M (structural uncertainty) and the parameters of M (parametric uncertainty). For the purposes of this paper, it will be sufficient if we define the uncertainty as a situation in which something is not known, or we are not sure if something is not known.

The aim of this paper is to describe a possible approach of making a decision with respect to uncertainty. The main advantage of this approach is high accuracy, variability and simplicity for users. As Medesany, Kim and Krishnapuram (1998) declare the choice of the assessment approach may depend on the kind of the problem and the type of data available. We decided to base the approach on fuzzy set theory introduced by Zadeh (1965), which is widely used in representing uncertain knowledge. Based on the article of Lina and Wu (2008), the fuzzy theory

[1] Czech University of Life Sciences Prague, Department of Systems Engineering, Kamýcká 129, Prague 6, mskoda@pef.czu.cz.

[2] Czech University of Life Sciences Prague, Department of Systems Engineering, Kamýcká 129, Prague 6, brozova@pef.czu.cz.

is very helpful to deal with the vagueness of human thoughts and language in making decisions. Moreover, the fuzzy set theory as Wei (2012) and many others claim is a very useful tool to deal with the uncertainty. The uncertainty in this approach will be illustrated by possible unreliability and incompleteness of information received.

In the case study, an example from emergency environment will be outlined. According to Ye, Dai and Qiu (2008) the use of the fuzzy set theory for emergency response has been proven to be useful. As French et al (2017) stresses, emergencies inevitably involve significant uncertainties.

The structure of the paper is as follows: the second chapter describes the used tools of fuzzy mathematics and other details about them. In the third chapter, the whole approach is described in detail. The fourth chapter provides an example of a specific use of the approach (the case study). In conclusion, the proposed approach and results are evaluated.

2 Tools and Methods Used

The proposed approach is based on the fuzzy set theory, more specifically on fuzzy numbers and α-cuts. In this section, some necessary backgrounds and notions are reviewed.

2.1 Trapezoidal Fuzzy Numbers

Even though the principles of the proposed approach can be applied to nonlinear fuzzy numbers as well, for simplification and clarity the approach will be described with the use of linear fuzzy numbers. More specifically, with a trapezoidal fuzzy number, where $A(x) = (x_1, x_2, x_3, x_4)$, and $x_1 \leq x_2 \leq x_3 \leq x_4$. For the membership function $A(x)$ applies (Klir and Yuan, 1995):

$$A(x) = \begin{cases} 0 & if \quad a < x_1 \\ \dfrac{a - x_1}{x_2 - x_1} & if \quad x_1 \leq a < x_2 \\ 1 & if \quad x_2 \leq a \leq x_3 \\ \dfrac{x_4 - a}{x_4 - x_3} & if \quad x_3 < a \leq x_4 \\ 0 & if \quad a > x_4 \end{cases} \tag{1}$$

2.2 Ranking of Fuzzy Numbers

The defuzzification and subsequent ranking of fuzzy numbers is based on the center of gravity of fuzzy numbers. Suppose $A(x)$ is a trapezoidal fuzzy number that is defined by four elements (x_1, x_2, x_3, x_4). Then for the center of gravity $t_{A(x)}$ of membership function $A(x)$, the following applies:

$$t_{A(x)} = \frac{1}{3} \cdot \frac{x_4^2 + x_3^2 - x_2^2 - x_1^2 + x_4 x_3 - x_2 x_1}{x_4 + x_3 - x_2 - x_1} \tag{2}$$

If A and B are fuzzy numbers and if $t_A \leq t_B$ holds, the fuzzy number A is smaller than fuzzy number B due to their center of gravity, we say that $A \leq B$ (Talašová, 2003).

2.3 Fuzzy Linguistic Scale

For the purposes of the evaluation of an emergency situation under uncertainty, a linguistic fuzzy scale shall be used. There is almost endless number of different linguistic scales. The main classification of linguistic scales is into even scales and uneven scales. Furthermore, the scales can be divided into a two-part scale, three-part scale, etc. (Zemková, 2012). The choice of a suitable scale with the related fuzzy numbers for a specific evaluation depends on many variables as the type of emergency, willingness to take a risk or a level of detail that is sought.

In case that one is making a decision based on not entirely reliable information and do not want to risk that the situation will be underestimated and the linguistic scale is assembled in ascending order, the increasing of the left leg of fuzzy numbers should be bigger than the decreasing of the right leg. Conversely, if one does not want to risk that the situation will be overestimated, then, in the case that the scale is assembled in ascending order, the increasing of the left leg of fuzzy numbers should be smaller than the decreasing of the right leg. The possible example of such scale is described in Figure 1 with corresponding fuzzy numbers in Table 1.

Linguistic term	Fuzzy number
Very Low	(0, 0, 0.1, 0.4)
Low	(0.2, 0.2, 0.3, 0.6)
High	(0.4, 0.4, 0.5, 0.8)
Very High	(0.6, 0.6, 0.7, 1)

Table 1 Four-point scale

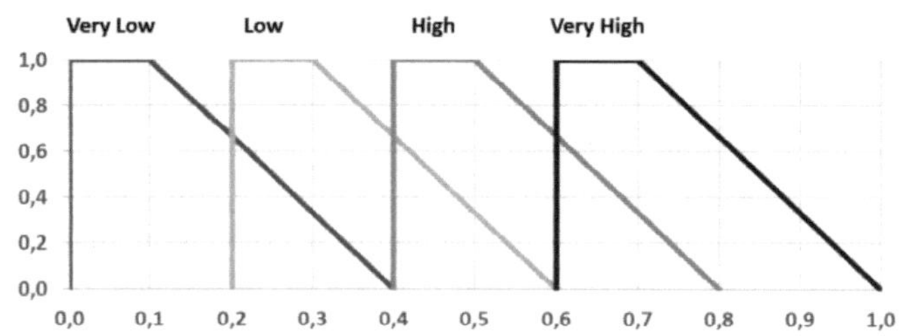

Figure 1 Four-point scale

The degree of slope determines the level of caution. For instance, in case of a scale in ascending order, the greater the leg slope to the left the greater the caution towards underestimation. Also, an uneven scale can be used. Such case can occur when with higher rating the impact of uncertainty should grow, and vice versa.

For the purposes of this paper, the five-part uneven scale assembled in ascending order with the leg slope to the left will be used.

2.4 α-cuts

Let the fuzzy set A be given in the universe U and the real number $\alpha \in \langle 0; 1 \rangle$. Then the α-cut of fuzzy set A is called the sharp set (Talašová, 2003):

$$A_\alpha = \{x \in U | A(x) \geq \alpha\} \tag{3}$$

Li and Yen (1995) in their book wrote, the fuzzy set that contains all elements with a membership of α and above is called the α-cut of the membership function. The higher the value of α the higher the confidence in the parameter.

Suppose now we have a trapezoidal fuzzy number $A(x) = (x_1, x_2, x_3, x_4)$ and α as a measure of the certainty. Let $A(x_{2\alpha}) = A(x_{3\alpha}) = \alpha$. Then for the final parameter estimation is used the fuzzy number $A_\alpha(x) = (x_1, x_{2\alpha}, x_{3\alpha}, x_4)$

2.5 Steps of the Evaluation

In this section, each step of the evaluation of a situation under uncertainty is described.

Determination of Criteria and Fuzzy Linguistic Scales

The first and essential step of this approach is the identification of criteria by which the situation will be evaluated. For instance, an emergency situation can be evaluated for example based on the size of an affected area, based on a number of injured persons etc. For the purposes of this article, criteria by which the situation will be evaluated will be possible threats that can occur as life threat, cyber threat, threat to environment etc.

In the second step, it is necessary to define the linguistic scale and related fuzzy numbers. As it is mentioned in the previous part, the five-part uneven scale assembled in ascending order with the slope to the left will be used.

Classification of a Specific Emergency Situation with Consideration of Uncertainty

In case that an emergency situation takes a place, it has to be evaluated through the identified criteria on the pre-arranged fuzzy linguistic scale. Provided that the information on which the decision should be based may not be entirely reliable (or complete) we will transform the membership function through α-cut. The lower the α-cut, the bigger is the consideration of uncertainty in the final evaluation of the situation.

As Figure 2 shows, by simple arithmetical operations, we will be able to calculate the new fuzzy number based on the chosen level of α-cut. In other words, if we will have a fuzzy number $A(x) = (x_1 x_2 x_3 x_4)$ and the α-cut on a chosen level (based on the reliability of information) will be set, the new fuzzy number will be $A_\alpha(x) = (x_1 x_{2\alpha} x_{3\alpha} x_4)$.

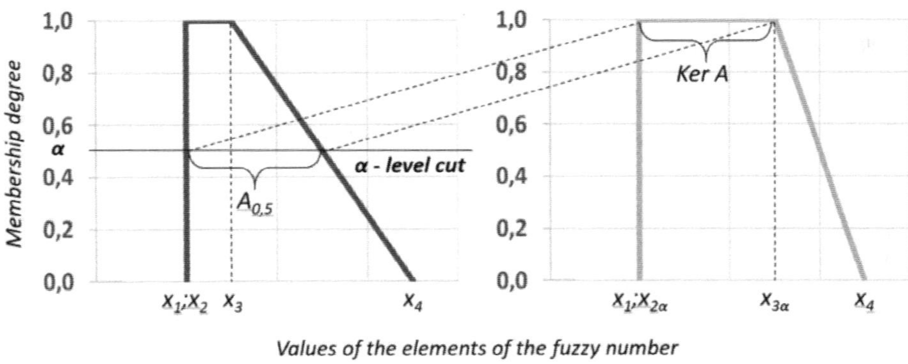

Figure 2 Creation of new trapezoidal fuzzy number

The element x_1 and element x_4 will always remain the same. For the calculation of element x_2 and x_3 the following formulas will be used

$$x_{2\alpha} = x_1 + (x_2 - x_1) \times \alpha \tag{4}$$

$$x_{3\alpha} = x_4 - (x_4 - x_3) \times \alpha \tag{5}$$

Than the new fuzzy number is:

$$A_\alpha(x) = (x_1, x_{2\alpha}, x_{3\alpha}, x_4) = (x_1, x_1 + (x_2 - x_1) \times \alpha, x_4 - (x_4 - x_3) \times \alpha, x_4) \tag{6}$$

Defuzzification and Prioritization

As mentioned in chapter 2.1, the defuzzification will be based on the center of gravity. In the case of the scale based on possible threats, the highest resulting value should be picked as the value of the situation.

For clarity, it is recommended to divide the resulting real number by the possible maximum, so the results will have values from 0 to 1, where 1 is the maximum. However, the interpretation may be different depending on the needs of the decision maker, team or company.

The final prioritization is done by simple sorting of resulting values from the largest to the smallest. The highest the number, the highest the priority. Situations with the same priority are considered to be equivalently important and therefore their order can be determined randomly.

3 Case Study

The designed approach for the evaluation of an emergency situation under uncertainty and its prioritization was applied to the environment of one of the three major gas distributors in the Czech Republic.

Firstly, based on the possible types of emergency situations, six basic types of threats have been identified by employees of the company involved in crisis management:

- Life Threat (LT),
- Health Threat (HT),
- Threat to Gas Supplies (TGS),
- Threat to Property (TP),
- Cyber Threat (CT),
- Enviromental Threat (ET).

Secondly, for the purposes of this case study, the fuzzy linguistic scale described in Table 3 was assigned to the Life threat and Health threat and fuzzy linguistic scale described in Table 4 was assigned to the remaining threats (Threat to Gas Supplies, Threat to Property, Cyber Threat, Environmental Threat).

Linguistic term	Fuzzy number
None	(0, 0, 0, 0)
Very Low	(0.15, 0.15, 0.20, 0.40)
Low	(0.30, 0.30, 0.35, 0.60)
High	(0.45, 0.45, 0.50, 0.80)
Very High	(0.60, 0.60, 0.65, 1)

Table 3 Five-point scale

Linguistic term	Fuzzy number
None	(0, 0, 0, 0)
Very Low	(0, 0, 0.05, 0.25)
Low	(0.15, 0.15, 0.20, 0.45)
High	(0.30, 0.30, 0.35, 0.65)
Very High	(0.45, 0.45, 0.50, 0,85)

Table 4 Five-point scale

Because x_1 and x_2 are equal the only element that will be changing depending on the reliability and completeness of information is element x_3.

Reliability and completeness of information that the decision maker received about the specific emergency situation will be evaluated on the scale described in Table 5.

α	Reliability	Illustrative example
1	Extremely reliable (ER)	Information from a professional on site.
0.8	Reliable (R)	Information reported by more than one person.
0.4	Partially reliable (PR)	Information communicated anonymously.
0.1	Unreliable (UR)	Information from a very drunk person.

Table 5 Scale of reliability and completeness of information

For the purposes of this paper three fictive scenarios were given:

- Someone set an unattended gas control station on fire. Flames already swallowed most of the station including the entrance. The information was received by dispatch center from a confused man who after passing the information hang up immediately.
- A construction company disrupted a high-pressure gas pipeline. The gas started to leak intensively in an inhabited area. Dispatch center received the information from an employee of gas emergency service (a colleague) who was passing by.
- The corporate vehicle transporting odorant and other chemicals had a serious accident. The driver is not in the vehicle and chemicals are leaking. The information was comprehensibly provided to dispatch center by one of the witnesses of the accident.

A decision maker receives information about situations at the same time. The goal is to evaluate the priority of these events and establish their ranking.

Reliability and completeness of information that decision maker received about the specific emergency situations (scenarios) were assessed by the company's employees as follows.

Scenario	Reliability	α-cut
1	partially reliable	0.4
2	extremely reliable	1
3	reliable	0.8

Table 6 Levels of α-cuts

The evaluation of the three fictive scenarios made by employees of the company and the corresponding fuzzy numbers depending on the level of reliability of information are presented in Table 7.

	Scenario 1					Scenario 2					Scenario 3				
Possible threats	**Evaluation**	**Partially reliable, α=0.4**				**Evaluation**	**Extremely reliable, α=1**				**Evaluation**	**Reliable, α=0.8**			
LT	**Low**	0,3	0,3	0,5	0,6	**High**	0,45	0,45	0,5	0,8	**Very Low**	0,15	0,15	0,24	0,4
HT	**High**	0,45	0,45	0,68	0,8	**Very High**	0,6	0,6	0,65	1	**High**	0,45	0,45	0,56	0,8
TGS	**Very High**	0,45	0,45	0,71	0,85	**High**	0,3	0,3	0,35	0,65	**None**	0	0	0	0
TP	**Very High**	0,45	0,45	0,71	0,85	**High**	0,3	0,3	0,35	0,65	**None**	0	0	0	0
CT	**None**	0	0	0	0	**None**	0	0	0	0	**None**	0	0	0	0
ET	**Low**	0,15	0,15	0,35	0,45	**Low**	0,15	0,15	0,2	0,45	**Very High**	0,45	0,45	0,57	0,85

Table 1 The evaluation of fictive scenarios under evaluation of reliability

The defuzzification based on the center of gravity are shown in Table 8. The resulting values were divided according to scenarios and level of reliability and completeness of information received.

Possible threats	Scenario 1	Scenario 2	Scenario 3
LT	0,427	0,569	0,241
HT	0,597	0,735	0,575
TGS	0,617	0,419	0
TP	0,617	0,419	0
CT	0	0	0
ET	0,277	0,252	0,593
Possible max	0,791	0,791	0,791
Results	**0,78**	**0,929**	**0,749**

Table 8 Evaluation after defuzzification

The final (current) evaluation of priority of the three fictive emergency situations based on the calculations above is shown in Table 9.

Order	Emergency situation (scenatio)	Current valuation
1.	2	**0.929**
2.	1	**0.780**
3.	3	**0.749**

Table 9 Final (current) evaluation

Based on the current valuation the emergency situation number 2 would be addressed with the highest priority. Second in the row would be emergency situation number 1 and the last in the row would be emergency situation number 3.

It is important to note, that if we do not take into account the quality of the information the emergency situation 1 and 3 would be evaluated as equal. The clarification was brought after consideration of reliability (or completeness) of information. In case, that we would, for example, have extremely reliable information about emergency situation number 1. The priority of situations would be different. As first in the row would be still situation number 2 but then situation number 3 would follow and the last in priority would be situation number 1.

4 Conclusions

Novák (2000) wrote, that as we increase accuracy, we get to the point where accuracy and relevance become mutually exclusive characteristics. Imagine that when you park your car you will receive instructions as, turn the wheel 8.47° to the left and drive 577 mm back. Such a task would be very difficult to accomplish. The same situation can be observed in the description of an emergency situation. For evaluation at the beginning of an emergency situation you don't need to know the exact amount of gas leaked or the sound that the airplane produced before the impact. Except of special cases, the description based on vague expressions should be sufficient. What is easily forgotten is the completeness and reliability of the information received. Knowledge and assumption are two different things as it is evident, for example, from the work of Sherman and Harman (2011).

The fact that someone is shot does not automatically mean that there is an attacker, it could be an accident. The fact that someone does not cry or does not call for help does not mean that the person is alright and does not need help etc. Not only because of possible mistaken assumptions it is necessary to take into account the possible unreliability or incompleteness of the information received.

The proposed approach has shown that it can take into consideration the unreliability or incompleteness of the information provided, evaluate the situation and create an order of situations. The approach also fulfilled the goal and the expectations of the employees of the company that participated on the case study. The case study has also shown that the whole approach is simple, effective, easy to set and can be useful especially in the early stages of emergency situations. Also, it should be noted that the linear fuzzy numbers do not always have to be sufficient. It would be probably necessary to use nonlinear fuzzy numbers for more complex and accurate evaluations in some cases.

Acknowledgements

This research is supported by the grant No. 2019A0018 "Využití kvantitativních přístupů v oblasti disaster managementu" of the Internal Grant Agency of the University of Life Sciences Prague.

References

Draper, D. (1995). 'Assessment and Propagation of Model Uncertainty (with Discussion)'. *Journal of the Royal Statistical Society Series B*, 57: pp. 45–97.

French, S., Argyris, N., Haywood, S., Hort, M. and Smith, J. Q. (2017). 'Uncertainty Handling during Nuclear Accidents'. *Proceedings of the 14th ISCRAM Conference – Albi, France, May 2017,* CoRe Paper – Analytical Modeling and Simulation.

Klir, G. and Wierman, M. (1999). *Uncertainty-Based Information: Elements of Generalized Information Theory (Studies in Fuzziness and Soft Computing).* 2nd ed. Wurzburg: Physica-Verlag.

Klir, G. and Yuan, Bo. (1995). *Fuzzy sets and fuzzy logic: theory and applications.* Upper Saddle River, N.J.: Prentice Hall PTR.

Li, H.X. and V.C. Yen (1995). *Fuzzy Sets and Fuzzy Decision-Making*. CRC Press.

Lina, Chi-Jen and Wu, Wei-Wen (2008). 'A causal analytical method for group decision-making under fuzzy environment'. *Expert Systems with Applications*, 34 (1), pp. 205-213.

Medasani, S., Kim, J., and Krishnapuram, R. (1998). 'An overview of membership function generation techniques for pattern recognition'. *International Journal of Approximate Reasoning*, 19, pp. 391–417.

Novák, V. (2000). *Základy fuzzy modelování*. Praha: BEN - technická literature.

Sherman, B. and Harman, G. (2011). 'Knowledge and assumption'. *Philosophical Studies,* 156 (1), pp. 131-140.

Talašová, J. (2003). *Fuzzy metody vícekriteriálního hodnocení a rozhodování.* Olomouc: Univerzita Palackého.

Farlex, Inc. The free Dictionary – decision, [Online]. Available at: http://www.thefreedictionary.com/decision [cited 2018-12-31].

Vasilescu, C. (2011). 'Effective Strategic Decision Making'. National Defence University. *Journal of Defense Resources Management*, 2.

Wei, G. (2012). 'Hesitant fuzzy prioritized operators and their application to multiple attribute decision making'. *Knowledge-Based Systems*, 31, pp. 176-182.

Ye, X., Dai, Z. and Qiu, J. (2008). 'A metadata-based flexible function model of decision support system for emergency management'. *Proceedings of 4th International Conference on Wireless Communications, Networking and Mobile Computing: WiCOM '08*; Dalian, China, 12 - 17 October 2008. Piscataway, NJ: IEEE Operations Center, pp. 1-4.

Zadeh, L. A. (1965). 'Fuzzy sets'. *Information and control*, 8, pp. 338–353.

Zemková, B. (2012). *Využití fuzzy množin v oblasti řízení lidských zdrojů.* Olomouc. Ph.D. thesis. Univerzita Palackého v Olomouci. Přírodovědecká fakulta.

Efficiency of small and medium enterprises using Data Envelopment Analysis

Hana Stverkova [1] , Lucie Chytilova [2]

Abstract. The micro, small and medium-sized enterprises (SMEs) are an important segment of every developed economy. They represent 99 % of companies in the European Union and create more value added in the EU. Business performance management, its efficiency, is one of the main means of achieving better results. The aim of this article is to measure technical efficiency of SMEs in the hospitality branch using data envelopment analysis (DEA). Also, the factors affecting the efficiency and performance of SMEs in the hospitality branch are determined and its importance is discussed for some SMEs in the hospitality branch in Ostrava. The results show that SMEs in the hospitality branch may be measured by special DEA models.

Keywords: DEA, SMEs, efficiency.

JEL classification: C67

1 Introduction

In the current competitive environment, companies should focus on assessing aspects that have the ability to increase the impact on long-term business success. It is necessary to take into account the quality of their products, the relationships between managers, employees, customers and focus on manufacturing processes and marketing. These are challenges for all managers who not only struggle to achieve high profits in their company but also to achieve customer, employees and all shareholders satisfaction. For the purpose of quantitative marketing research, the taxonomy of small and medium-sized enterprises according to EU classification[1] - according to the number of employees - was used. The micro enterprise is a company employing up to 9 employees, a small enterprise has between 10 and 49 employees and a medium-sized company from 50 employees up to 249. Large enterprises have not been reflected in the survey as they have in most cases established efficient performance evaluation systems.

In measuring business performance and its efficiency, it has to be borne in mind that new conditions can only be developed by those entities that are able to flexibly respond to changing business conditions, monitor and regularly evaluate the level of business performance and invest in increasing it. Over the past decade, and a broad range of criteria have been developed to express the performance of the business of the owners. Some indicators are the expression of different theoretical concepts that deal with corporate governance and its financial analysis. In modern management concepts, the owners mainly participate in the business, precisely because they have brought their ideas into business, the funds and bear the greatest risk given by business (Pavelkova and Knapkova, 2005). In this article the quantitative method is used for the measuring the efficient.

---

[1]VSB-Technical University of Ostrava, Faculty of Economics, Department of Systems Engineering, Sokolska tr. 2416/33, 702 00 Ostrava, Czech Republic, hana.stverkova@vsb.cz.

[2]VSB-Technical University of Ostrava, Faculty of Economics, Department of Systems Engineering, Sokolska tr. 2416/33, 702 00 Ostrava, Czech Republic, lucie.chytilova@vsb.cz.

[1]EUROSTA

The Data Envelopment Analysis (DEA) has been used in efficiency analysis of many applications - banking industry, insurance industry, health care and so on. The three most known and widely used DEA models are the CCR model by Charnes et al. (1978), the BCC model by Banker et al. (1984) and the Additive model by Charnes et al. (1985). These models were formulated for desirable inputs and outputs. However, in real applications, there are frequently needed undesirable inputs and/or outputs. This problem is also in the application of DEA for SMEs in the hospitality branch. More precisely, it is known that some variables may be undesirable or negative. So, even some non-classical methods of DEA are used and analyzed.

The aim of the article is to map and measure the efficiency of small and medium-sized enterprises in hospitality based on data envelopment analysis (DEA).

The paper is organized as follows. The analysis of the current state of Data Envelopment Analysis in the steel sector is provided in the Chapter 2. The Chapter 3 describes a structure of the problem and corresponding data sets. The results and the close analysis are in the Chapter 4. The final conclusion summarizes the main contributions of this paper and some proposals for a further research are provided in the last Chapter 5.

2 Theoretical principles

Data envelopment analysis (DEA) is non-parametric linear programming based technique for measuring the relative efficiency of a set of similar decision making units (DMUs). Since the work of Charnes et al (1978), DEA has demonstrated an effective technique for measuring the relative efficiency of set homogenous DMUs. In application, DMUs may include banks, hospitals, schools, different types of industries and other. Each DMU allocates its resources into a number of inputs to produce various outputs. The relative technical efficiency of the unit is define as the ratio of its total weighted output to its total weighted input or vice versa. DEA allows each production unit to choose its own weights of inputs and outputs in order to maximize its efficiency score. A technically efficient production unit is able to find such weights that it lies on the production frontier. The production frontier represents the maximum amounts of output that can be produced by given amounts of input in the output maximization model or, alternatively, the minimum amounts of inputs required to produce the given amount of output in the input minimization model. DEA calculates the efficiency score for each production unit and identifies peers for each production unit that is not technically efficient.

2.1 Classic DEA models

As it was mentioned above, the relative technical efficiency of the DMU unit is define as the ratio of its total weighted output to its total weighted input. Mathematically, it can be define as:

$$e_k = \frac{\sum_{j=1}^{S} v_j y_{jk}}{\sum_{i=1}^{R} u_i x_{ik}}, \text{ for } k = 1, ..., T, \tag{1}$$

where we suppose, a set of T DMUs (DMU$_k$ for $k = 1, ..., T$), let input and output variables for be $\mathbf{X} = \{x_{ik}, i = 1, ..., R; k = 1, ..., T\}$ and $\mathbf{Y} = \{y_{jk}, j = 1, ...S; k = 1, ...T\}$, respectively. Also, u_i, for $i = 1, ..., R$ and v_j, for $j = 1, ..., S$ be the weights of i-th input and j-th output, respectively.

The mathematical formulation of the origin DEA model was done by Charmes at al (1978). This model was called CCR model and measures the efficiency score of the under evaluation unit, DMU$_Q$ where $Q \in \{1, ..., T\}$. The mathematical model is following:

$$
\begin{aligned}
& \max\ e_Q = \frac{\sum_{j=1}^{S} v_j y_{jQ}}{\sum_{i=1}^{R} u_i x_{iQ}} & & \\
\text{s.t.}\ & \frac{\sum_{j=1}^{S} v_j y_{jk}}{\sum_{i=1}^{R} u_i x_{ik}} \leq 1, & & k = 1, ..., T, \\
& u_i > 0, & & i = 1, ..., R, \\
& v_j > 0, & & j = 1, ..., S.
\end{aligned}
\tag{2}
$$

However, it is non-linear model, more precisely it is the model of linear-fractional programming. ON the other hand, the model can be transferred by Charmes-Cooper transformation to the standard linear programming problem:

$$
\begin{aligned}
& \max\ e_Q = \sum_{j=1}^{S} v_j y_{jQ} & & \\
\text{s.t.}\ & \sum_{i=1}^{R} u_i x_{iQ} = 1 & & \\
& \sum_{j=1}^{S} v_j y_{jk} - \sum_{i=1}^{R} u_i x_{ik} \leq 0, & & k = 1, ..., T, \\
& u_i > 0, & & i = 1, ..., R, \\
& v_j > 0, & & j = 1, ..., S.
\end{aligned}
\tag{3}
$$

This model must be solved for each DMU. Notice that DMU$_Q$ is CCR-efficient if and only if $e^* = 1$ and there exists at least one optimal solution (u_i^*, v_j^*) with $u_i^* > 0$ and $v_j^* > 0$. Inefficient units have a degree of relative efficiency less than one. The model (3) is called a multiplier input-oriented model.

Banker et al. in (1984) extended the CCR model. The extended model is called the BCC model and considers variable returns to scale assumption. The model has convex envelope of data which leads to more efficient DMUs. The mathematical model of dual multiplier form of input-oriented BCC model is:

$$
\begin{aligned}
& \max\ e_Q = \sum_{j=1}^{S} v_j y_{jQ} - v_0 & & \\
\text{s.t.}\ & \sum_{i=1}^{R} u_i x_{iQ} = 1 & & \\
& \sum_{j=1}^{S} v_j y_{jk} - \sum_{i=1}^{R} u_i x_{ik} - v_0 \leq 0, & & k = 1, ..., T, \\
& u_i > 0, & & i = 1, ..., R, \\
& v_j > 0, & & j = 1, ..., S, \\
& v_0 \in (-\infty, \infty), & &
\end{aligned}
\tag{4}
$$

where v_0 is is the dual variable assigned to the convexity condition of envelopment form of input-oriented BCC model.

2.2 DEA models with zero or negative variables

The models in previous subsection are basic models where the inputs and outputs are desirable or all are non-zero on positive. However, in real applications, there are frequently needed undesirable/negative/zero inputs and / or outputs. In this paper we deal with zero or negative values - labor costs, revenues and profit.

There are many ways of handling the aforementioned type of nonstandard variables in a DEA framework. The simplest is to either perform a frequently unjustified change of variables or to reduce the sample of units by eliminating those with negative values in some variable (see, for example, Charnes et al, 1989). There are also some new methods - priori approach for dealing with interval scale variables (Halme et al, 1998) and so on.

This paper is the first type of this analysis for this type of industry in this are. So we will start with the easiest way. We will manege to do model CCR and BCC to see what is the best variable return to scale. Plus, we will do two types of the models for both models. CCR and BCC model with eliminated data and CCR and BCC model with changed variables. Si there will be four models, noted as following:

- CCR_E - CCR model with eliminated data (there are no DMUs with zero or negative values because these DMUs had been eliminated),
- BCC_E - BCC model with eliminated data (there are no DMUs with zero or negative values because these DMUs had been eliminated),
- CCR_C - CCR model with changed data (there are no DMUs with zero or negative values because these variables had been changed - adding a proper value),
- BCC_C - BCC model with changed data (there are no DMUs with zero or negative values because these variables had been changed - adding a proper value).

3 Data and application

Table 1 is providing the descriptive statistics of four variables. These variables are for 21 SMEs of the hospitality branches from Ostrava. These data had been taken from justice.cz. The four variables are define as two input variables and two output variables. Labor costs and supplies should be minimized and these variables are define as input variables. Revenues and profit should be maximised and these variables are defined as output variables.

	labor costs	**supplies**	**revenues**	**profit**
max	5480323	1036000	17649448	3600000
min	0	13000	-316000	-1023000
std.dev.	1591299	269607	5337812	855622
average	1678277	229762	3180056	520238

Table 1 Descriptive statistics of input and output variables

From Table 1 (and the data which can be given by authors) is seen that there is problem with three variables:

- labor costs - minimum is 0, so there is a problem with the zero value. More precisely, the DMU 11 has the labor costs equal to 0.
- revenues - minimum is negative, more precisely DMU 3 has the revenue equal to 0, DMU 11 has the revenue equal to -9000 and DMU 21 is equal to the minimum.
- profit - minimum is also negative. There are just two problematic DMUs, first is DMU 3 with the minimum value and DMU 21 with the value zero.

According to above information, for the first type of models (CCR_E and BCC_E), there are just 18 DMUs (DMU 3, DMU 11 and DMU 21 are excluded). For the rest of the models

(CCR_C and BCC_C), there are 21 DMUs (DMU 3, DMU 11 and DMU 21 are changed). Both cases are possible for the analysis (4 variables have to have at least 12 DMUs).

Table 2 shows the results and descriptive statistics of all models.

DMU	CCR	BCC	CCR	BCC
1	0.8743	1.0000	0.8528	1.0000
2	0.9728	1.0000	1.0000	1.0000
3			0.0260	0.2103
4	0.8168	0.8954	0.8818	0.8954
5	0.6369	0.9189	0.9175	0.9189
6	0.8866	1.0000	1.0000	1.0000
7	0.5622	0.7597	0.7587	0.7597
8	0.7420	1.0000	1.0000	1.0000
9	1.0000	1.0000	1.0000	1.0000
10	1.0000	1.0000	1.0000	1.0000
11			1.0000	1.0000
12	0.4049	0.6212	0.6100	0.6216
13	1.0000	1.0000	0.9962	1.0000
14	0.8678	0.9114	0.5376	0.9114
15	1.0000	1.0000	1.0000	1.0000
16	0.1452	0.2061	0.1649	0.1685
17	0.3523	0.4023	0.3310	0.3533
18	0.1467	0.4532	0.4437	0.4532
19	0.5514	0.5557	0.4215	0.5557
20	0.3000	1.0000	0.9884	1.0000
21			0.3540	0.4003
max	1.0000	1.0000	1.0000	1.0000
min	0.1452	0.2061	0.0260	0.1685
st.dev.	0.3033	0.2560	0.3214	0.2950
average	0.6811	0.8180	0.7278	0.7737

Table 2 Results and descriptive statistics of all models

Models with eliminated variables have similar results. From Table 2 it may be seen that there are more efficient variables for BCC model (9 efficient DMUs). The model CCR has just 4 efficient DMUs. This is according to the theoretical assumption. Also this mean, that we have chosen the proper model and method. The efficiency score for BCC model is higher then for CCR model.

Models with changed variables have also similar results. Again, from Table 2 it may be seen that there are more efficient variables for BCC model (10 efficient DMUs). The model CCR has just 7 efficient DMUs. So, this is also according to the theoretical assumption so we have chosen the proper model and method. The efficiency score for BCC model is higher then for CCR model.

Based on results from moth models, it is seen that for future analysis the BCC model should be better. Also, the background of SMEs in the hospitality branch in Ostrava is heterogenous so the variable return to scale is more proper.

From Table 2 it is seen that it is really important to include the variables into the analysis. As it is seen, all three excluded variables had different position in the analysis and their omission may have an impact on the analysis.

The three excluded variables has different position, it is the following:

- DMU 03 - CCR score is really low (0.0260) and BCC score is 0.2103, so we can conclude that is DMU is not efficient and actually it is one of the lowest/ worst one,
- DMU 11 - BCC (CCR) efficient,
- DMU 21 - CCR score is 0.3540 and BCC score is 0.4003, so we can conclude that is DMU is not efficient, but not the worst.

So it can conclude, that this provides much better picture on the problem. So generally speaking, it is important to have as much DMUs as it is possible to have.

Really interesting thing, from Table 2, is that if we compare the results of both BCC models, we may see that the score of model BCC_C has always equal or smaller sore then the BCC_E model.

Overall, we may say that it is important to look at all variables how do they interact together.

4 Conclusions

The micro, small and medium-sized enterprises (SMEs) are an important segment of every developed economy. The aim of this paper is to examined the efficiency of SMEs in the hospitality branch in Ostrava using data envelopment analysis (DEA). As this is the first research paper on this topic, the analysis had beec focused mainly on the chosen type of this model. The best model for this branch is probably the model with variable return to scale (model BCC) with all variables which may be transformed but not eliminated.

In future work, we would like to extend the data - in time and in DMUs. Probably, it would be good to make the panel analysis. Plus we would like to use different type of models of special DAE.

Acknowledgements

This article was supported by the Czech Science Foundation GACR 17-23495S.

References

Banker, R.D., Charnes, A. and Cooper, W.C. (1984). 'Some models for estimating technical and scale in efficiencies in data envelopment analysis'. *Management Science*, 30, pp. 1078-1092.

Charnes, A., Cooper, W. W. and Rhodes, E. (1978). 'Measuring the efficiency of decision making units'. *European Journal of Operational Research*, 2, pp. 429-444.

Charnes, A. et al. (1985). 'Foundations of data envelopment analysis for Pareto-Koopmans efficient empirical production functions'. *Journal of Econometrics*, 30, pp. 91-107. Charnes,

A., Cooper, W.W. and Li, S. (1989), 'Using Data Envelopment Analysis to evaluate Efficiency in the Economic Performance of Chinese Cities.' *Socio-Economic Planning Sciencies*, 23 (6), pp. 325-344.

Halme, M., Joro, T and Koivu, M. (2002), 'Dealing with interval scale data in data envelopment analysis.' *European Journal of Operational Research*, 137, pp. 22-27.

Pavelkova, D. and Knapkova, A. (2012). *Výkonnost podniku z pohledu finančního manažera*. Praha: Linde.

Production efficiency under uncertainty using the PROMETHEE method

František Zapletal [1]

Abstract. Efficiency is a desirable state of each production unit transforming inputs to outputs. Companies doing their business inefficiently in a long term can hardly succeed, or even survive. However, there are some barriers, which make a process of efficiency evaluation very tough in practice. These barriers are related with computational complexity of the evaluation process and also with limited possibilities of graphical presentation of the results. Over and above, managers are often sceptic due to simplifications, which are often done within a modelling process. Namely, uncertainty in data is often neglected, which can lead to distorted results. In this paper, I propose a new PROMETHEE based method for efficiency evaluation under uncertain input data. This method stems from the paper of Ishizaka et al. (2018) who have introduced a similar method under perfect information. Regardless a number of involved input and output factors, the results can always be presented graphically.

Keywords: efficiency, PROMETHEE, multi-criteria decision making, outranking.

JEL classification: C61

1 Introduction

If some quantitative method has a chance to succeed in practice, it should have as tractable algorithm as possible, provide graphical outputs and possibility to deal with uncertainty. The same applies for methods focused on efficiency evaluation. The PROMETHEE method is a popular method of multi-criteria decision making, which is very simple to use and understandable for practitioners. Originally, this method was used to get rankings of alternatives (units). Its original deterministic algorithm introduced by Mareschal et al. (1984) has also been extended with uncertain input data, see Geldermann et al. (2000), Goumas and Lygerou (2000). Recently, Ishizaka et al. (2018) came with an idea to use the PROMETHEE based algorithm to evaluate the technical efficiency of units. However, the proposed algorithm does not allow to deal with uncertain data. Therefore, this paper is focused on its extension. Namely, I introduce a novel PROMETHEE based method for efficiency evaluation in fuzzy environment. The new algorithm also provides graphical results of a problem.

The rest of the paper is organized as follows. The next section, Section 2, recalls the original PROMETHEE algorithm and its possible fuzzification. Section 3 brings a description how the efficiency of units should be evaluated when incorporating uncertainty. Section 4 deals with graphical representation of the results and a possible way how to interpret them. The results are summarised in Conclusions (Section 5), where I also present intended directions of the further research.

[1] VSB-Technical unversity of Ostrava, Faculty of Economics, Department of Systems Engineering, Sokolská 33, Ostrava, Czech Republic, frantisek.zapletal@vsb.cz

2 PROMETHEE algorithm and its fuzzification

The PROMETHEE method has been introduced by Mareschal et al. (1984) in effort to present a decision method for ranking alternative, which is user-friendly, computationally easy and easily tractable. Undisputably, this effort was successful with respect to the number of application of this method in practice, see Behzadian et al. (2010).

Considering a problem with s alternatives and k criteria. The algorithm of the PROMETHEE method for the complete ranking of alternatives can be summarised into the following five steps:

1) A preference function type for each criterion is chosen. The preference function assigns a preference degree to each value of the difference in performances of two alternatives. This preference degree expresses how strongly is the value of difference preferred. One can use a predefined type of preference function provided by Mareschal et al. (1984). By far the most popular type in literature is a linear one, see Fig. 1.
2) Preference degrees $P_i(A_x, A_y) = P_i(v_{i,x} - v_{i,y}) =\in [0, 1]$ is calculated for each pair of alternatives A_x, A_y with respect to criterion i, where $v_{i,x}$ is a value of performance of alternative x with respect to criterion i (in total, $s \times (s-1) \times k$ preference degrees are calculated).
3) Preference degrees are aggregated into preference indices expressing how much the decision maker prefers one alternative to another using the weights of criteria w. The preference indices are a part of (1) and (2), see the weighted sum of the preference degrees and the weights.
4) Preference indices are aggregated into positive and negative preference flows of alternatives (ϕ^+, ϕ^-). The positive flow of an alternative is a mean value of the preference indices comparing this alternative with the others (how much better is the alternative than the others). The other way around, the negative flow of an alternative is a mean value of the preference indices when comparing the remaining alternatives with the one under evaluation (how much worse is the alternative than the others), see (1) and (2).
5) Using the positive and negative flows for the ranking of alternatives does not guarantee a total order of the alternatives. Therefore, the partial flows are aggregated into net flows $\phi \in [-1, 1]$ of the alternatives using (3).

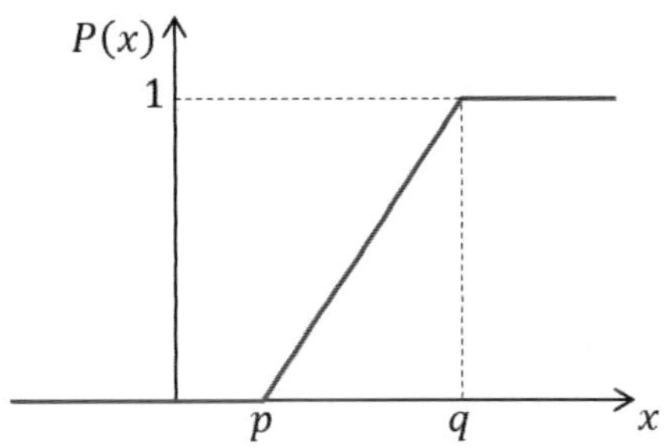

Figure 1 Linear shape of the preference function Mareschal et al. (1984)

$$\phi^+(A_t) = \frac{\sum_{j=1, j\neq t}^{s} \sum_{i=1}^{k} w_i \cdot P_i(v_{i,t} - v_{i,j})}{s-1}, \quad \forall t \qquad (1)$$

$$\phi^-(A_t) = \frac{\sum_{j=1, j\neq t}^{s} \sum_{i=1}^{k} w_i \cdot P_i(v_{i,j} - v_{i,t})}{s-1}, \quad \forall t \tag{2}$$

$$\phi(A_t) = \phi^+(A_t) - \phi^-(A_t), \quad \forall t \tag{3}$$

The original algorithm described above has been extended with fuzzy inputs by several authors, e.g., see Geldermann et al. (2000) and Goumas and Lygerou (2000). An extension introduced by Geldermann et al. (2000) is, in my opinion, the most natural one following the logic of the original algorithm. Therefore, I will work with this extension from now on. All the five steps of the original algorithm are done also in this extension, however, all of them must handle fuzzy quantities. For the sake of simplicity, one of the simplest fuzzy sets will be considered in this paper, i.e. triangular fuzzy numbers (TFNs), see Fig. 2. In the same figure, an α-cut of the displayed TFN is shown (i.e., $\left[[\tilde{a}]_\alpha^l, [\tilde{a}]_\alpha^r\right]$) TFNs are easy to handle and absolutely sufficient for practical use.

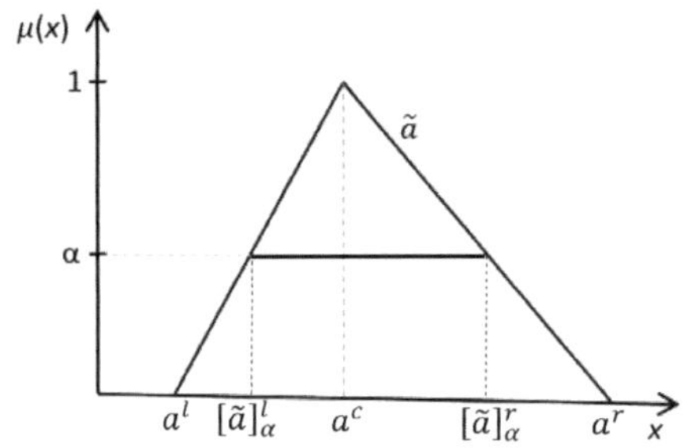

Figure 2 Triangular fuzzy number

In line with Geldermann et al. (2000), the fuzzy preference degrees are calculated as it is shown in Fig. 3 based on differences in fuzzy performances $\tilde{v}(i,j)$. These differences, as well as the preference flows, are calculated using a fuzzy extension of the original binary operation based on the Zadeh's extension principle. The fuzzy extensions of subtraction, addition and multiplication by a real number for TFNs are as follows (see Bector et al. (2005)):

$$\tilde{A} \oplus \tilde{B} = (a_l + b_l, a_c + b_c, a_r + b_r) \tag{4}$$

$$\tilde{A} \ominus \tilde{B} = (a_r - b_l, a_c - b_c, a_l - b_r) \tag{5}$$

$$k \odot \tilde{A} = (k \cdot a_l, k \cdot a_c, k \cdot a_r), \quad k \in \mathbb{R}^+ \tag{6}$$

where $\tilde{A}(a_l, a_c, a_r)$ and $\tilde{B}(b_l, b_c, b_r)$ are TFNs following the description in Fig. 2.

The fuzzified algorithm provides the values of the net flows expressed with TFNs ($\tilde{\phi}$).

3 Efficiency evaluation using Fuzzy PROMETHEE

As written above, this paper stems from the study by Ishizaka et al. (2018). These authors proposed to represent each alternative by two values - a net flow for inputs ϕ_{IN} and net flow for outputs ϕ_{OUT}. To get these values, the original set of k criteria must be split into two subsets: k_{IN} input criteria and k_{OUT} output criteria ($k_{\text{IN}} + k_{\text{OUT}} = k$). Each alternative can be easily represented as a point in the ($\phi_{\text{IN}}, \phi_{\text{OUT}}$)-plane, see Fig. 4. In order to keep the same logic and

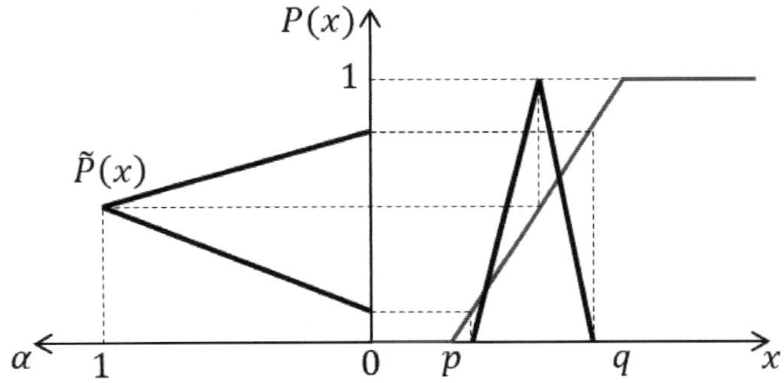

Figure 3 Fuzzy preference degrees Geldermann et al. (2000)

axis direction known from other similar analysis (like the Markowitz portfolio analysis), the net flows for inputs are reversed in the following way:

$$\phi'_{\mathrm{IN}}(A_t) = -\phi_{\mathrm{IN}}(A_t), \quad \forall t, \tag{7}$$

thus, the upper-right positions are preferred. An alternative is said to be technically efficient if it produces the maximum output (represented by ϕ_{OUT}) from the minimum quantity of inputs (represented by ϕ'_{IN}).

Fig. 4 shows the analysis of 8 alternatives. Four red points represent the efficient alternatives (they are on the efficient frontier). The remaining 4 (grey) alternatives are not efficient, since they are not on the efficient frontier (the Manhattan distance from the alternative to the efficient frontier (δ_{IN} and δ_{OUT}) is non-zero).

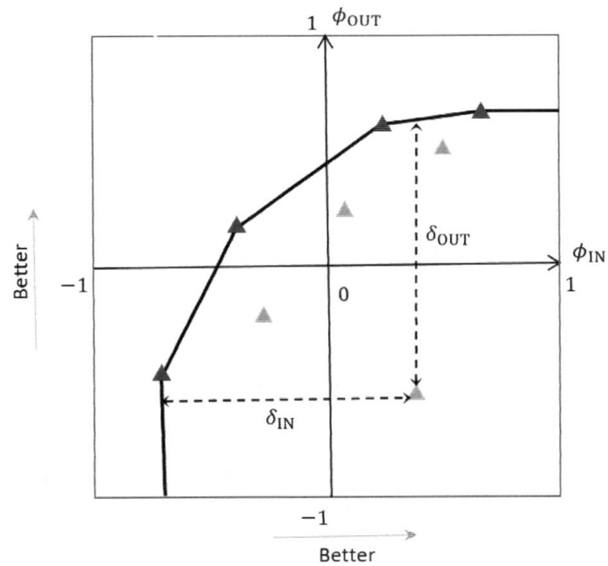

Figure 4 Efficiency evaluation with deterministic input data Ishizaka et al. (2018)

When switching into the uncertain environment, each alternative is again represented by two values of flows. But, using the extension of PROMETHEE by Geldermann et al. (2000), these two values are given by TFNs. In this case, each alternative can be visualised in 3-D space, where the axes provide the values of the net flow of inputs, net flow of outputs and membership degree, see Fig. 5. Thus, each alternative is visualised by a pyramid.

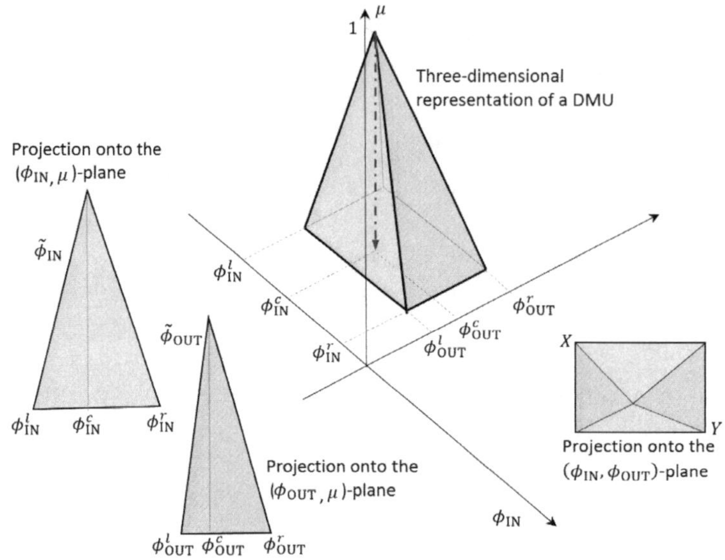

Figure 5 Graphical visualisation of an alternative based on the PROMETHEE flows in the fuzzy environment

However, the interpretation of results is not as easy as in the deterministic case because of the third dimension expressing the membership degree. One of possibilities how the results can be interpreted is presented in the next section and it is based on α-cuts.

4 Graphical representation of results and their interpretation

Despite it is possible, it is not recommended to visualise the final results using the 3-D graph like in Fig. 5. For many decision-makers, such presentation would be rather confusing and, for sure, almost impossible to interpret. Therefore, I prefer to use α-cuts of the polyhedra instead. If a pyramid representing an alternative is cut at some membership level, this alternative is visualised as a rectangle, which has increasing area with decreasing value of α. On the other hand, for $\alpha = 1$, the alternative is given only by a point, and the problem is identical with a deterministic case.

Fig. 6 shows an example with 6 alternatives (A_1-A_6). In this case, the pyramids are displayed from above, so that the rectangles correspond with the supports (bases) of the pyramids, and the edges and apex are also indicated there. For $\alpha = 1$, the efficient frontier is indicated by a black curve (i.e., A_3, A_4 and A_5 are efficient). For $\alpha < 1$, the interpretation is not so easy due to the uncertainty. Therefore, I distinguish 3 possible states:

- **an alternative A_x is surely efficient** - situation when, if A_x is represented by the worst values of ϕ_{IN} and ϕ_{OUT} (a lower right corner of the base) and all other alternatives are given by the best ϕ values (upper left corners of the bases), A_x is efficient.
- **an alternative A_x is possibly efficient** - situation when, if A_x is represented by the best values of ϕ_{IN} and ϕ_{OUT} (an upper left corner of the base) and all other alternatives are given by the worst ϕ values (lower right corners of the bases), A_x is efficient.

- **an alternative A_x is surely inefficient** - if an alternative A_x is not possibly efficient.

It is natural that each alternative, which id surely efficient is also possibly efficient.

In Fig. 6, A_3 is surely efficient, meanwhile A_6 is surely inefficient. The remaining 4 alternatives are possibly efficient.

The presented interpretation is natural, however, it evaluates the most of alternatives as 'possibly efficient', and, thus, decreases a distinguishing ability of the method. Therefore, it is better to make the evaluation above using not only the supports (bases), which represent the lowest membership degree α, but also different α values. Namely, based on the concept of possibility and necessity measures, see, e.g., Bector et al. (2005), the following interpretation can be done. Let A_x be an alternative under evaluation. This alternative is possibly efficient at α if and only if it is efficient when it is represented by the best possible values of ϕ's at α (i.e. the upper-left corner of the α-cut) while the remaining alternatives are represented by the worst possible values of ϕ's at α (i.e. the bottom-right corners of the α-cut). On the other hand, the same alternative A_x is efficient with certainty of $(1-\alpha)$ if and only if it is efficient when it is represented by the worst possible values of ϕ's at α (i.e. the bottom-right corner of the α-cut) while the remaining alternatives are represented by the best possible values of ϕ's at α (i.e. the upper-left corners of the α-cut).

Fig. 7 provides two sets of α-cuts of 6 alternatives from Fig. 6 (blue rectangles belong to $\alpha = 0.8$ and the orange ones to $\alpha = 0.1$). It can be seen that A_1 is possibly efficient at $\alpha = 0.1$ (red efficient frontier), but it is not efficient at $\alpha = 1 - 0.8 = 0.2$ certainty (blue efficient frontier).

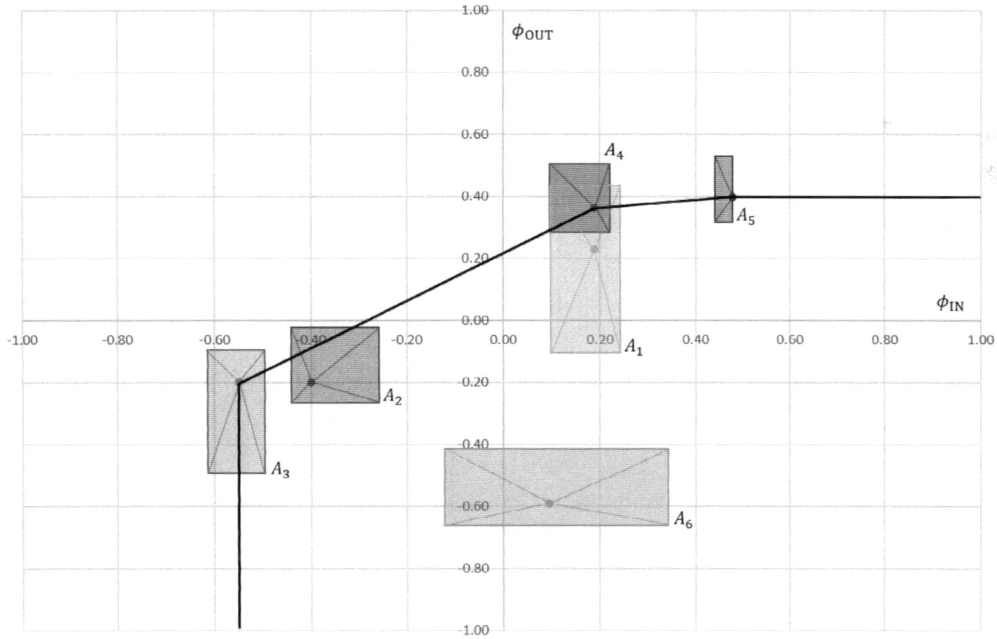

Figure 6 Graphical visualisation of the efficiency analysis (each alternative is displayed using the supports of ϕ's and the cores of ϕ's)

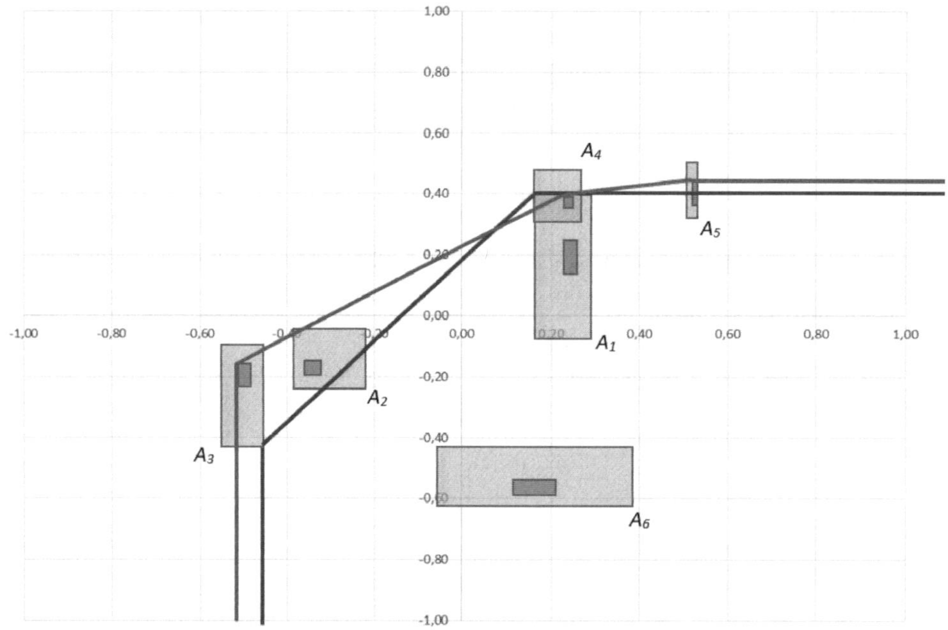

Figure 7 Graphical visualisation of the efficiency analysis - evaluation of A_1 under possibility of 0.1 (A_1 is efficient) and certainty of 0.8 (A_1 is not efficient).

5 Conclusions

In this paper, I have provided a new PROMETHEE based approach to evaluate production efficiency under uncertainty. The proposed approach has several advantages when comparing with other methods. First, the results can be displayed graphically regardless a number of criteria involved. Second, the algorithm is easily tractable and does not involve any complex mathematical programming problem. On the other hand, it is not always easy to choose a suitable shape of the preference function, which can significantly influence the results. The further research will be focused on how to get more information into the results. It would be very useful to assess not only if an alternative is efficient or not, but also how much it is inefficient. Therefore, I intend to find some efficiency measure to do this.

Acknowledgements

This work was supported the EU Operational Programme Education for Competitiveness Project [no. CZ.1.07/2.3.00/20.0296]. The support is greatly acknowledged.

References

Bector, C., Chandra, S., et al. (2005). *Fuzzy mathematical programming and fuzzy matrix games*, 169. Springer.

Behzadian, M., Kazemzadeh, R. B., Albadvi, A. and Aghdasi, M. (2010). 'Promethee: A comprehensive literature review on methodologies and applications'. *European journal of Operational research*, 200 (1), pp. 198-215.

Geldermann, J., Spengler, T. and Rentz, O. (2000). 'Fuzzy outranking for environmental assessment. case study: iron and steel making industry'. *Fuzzy sets and systems*, 115 (1), pp.

45-65.

Goumas, M. and Lygerou, V. (2000). 'An extension of the promethee method for decision making in fuzzy environment: Ranking of alternative energy exploitation projects'. *European Journal of Operational Research*, 123 (3), pp. 606-613.

Ishizaka, A., Resce, G. and Mareschal, B. (2018). 'Visual management of performance with promethee productivity analysis'. *Soft Computing*, 22 (22), pp. 7325-7338.

Mareschal, B., Brans, J. P., Vincke, P., et al. (1984). *Promethee: A new family of outranking methods in multicriteria analysis*. Technical report, ULB-Universite Libre de Bruxelles.

SECTION

C

CURRENT TRENDS AND ISSUES IN INFORMATION SYSTEMS DESIGN, MANAGEMENT AND SECURITY

A Comparison of the Efficiency of Czech Universities

Blanka Bazsova[1]

Abstract. The paper deals with the efficiency score of Czech universities obtained through calculations following the CCR and BCC DEA models. Both DEA models work with multiple inputs and outputs of homogeneous productive units. The efficiency score is the ratio between the inputs and outputs. The survey confirmed different results in the efficiency score. The efficiency scores were further compared. Seventeen universities were efficient according to the BCC DEA model while only seven universities were efficient according to the CCR DEA model.

Keywords: BCC model, CCR model, comparison, DEA, efficiency, universities.

JEL Classification: C44, I23

1 Introduction

The efficiency measurement is an important prerequisite for improving the behaviour of production units in a highly competitive environment. In today's world, university education is not a privilege but rather almost a standard expectation for a successful professional career (Gürdal et al, 2014). There are many aspects which also play an important role from the students' point of view. For example, the attractiveness of the field, reputation of the school and especially references from friends, classmates and others are important in choosing a school. The number of graduates in 2016 is shown in Figure 1.

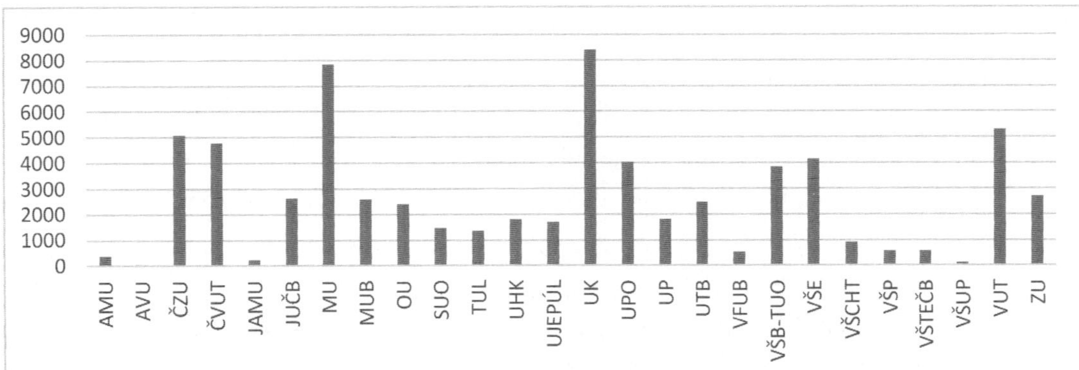

Figure 1 Number of graduates at public universities and high schools in 2016 [Own processing, data: MŠMT, 2016]

The DEA (data envelopment analysis) is the method which measures the efficiency of homogeneous productive units. DEA is used in many fields. Johnes (2006) states that DEA is a useful tool to express and quantify inputs and outputs. He implemented it in the efficiency measurement in higher education with a focus on the postgraduate and undergraduate English students. Hanclova (2016) proved the output DEA model by efficiency measurement in higher education. Also, Data Envelopment Analysis has been implemented in the banking industry a

[1] VŠB-Technical University of Ostrava/Department of Systems Engineering, 17.listopadu 2172/15, Ostrava-Poruba, 708 00, blanka.bazsova@vsb.cz

great deal. The efficiency of the banking system in the Czech Republic by using the CCR/I model was evaluated in a survey by Chytilova and Hanclova (2015).

Universities are homogenous units. They produce identical inputs and outputs and have similar organizational structure. They are managed by the Ministry of Education, Youth and Sport, and financed by the Ministry of Finance from the state budget. The amount of allocated money depends on the quality of its research, namely the volume of scientific papers, books and articles reported in the previous period. Apart from this, they have their own incomes which originates from the science activities. They receive money from the Grant Agency of the Czech Republic and Operational Programmes. This amount depends on the research and development projects.

It depends on the number of students and attractiveness of study courses at each university. It can be included as one of the risk indicators. Universities have the same inputs and outputs and similar organizational structure. Universities use the typical matrix structure, which is described and mentioned by Rehacek (2015). According to Wurmova (2012), studying at university brings many advantages for graduates. The goal of this paper is to compare the efficiency in public higher education by using two models – CCR and BCC.

Many authors have examined the possibility of measuring efficiency in higher education. Maryska and Doucek (2011) brought the comparison of the Czech and Austrian educational systems. They have done research in economic fields, focusing on the ICT education. If we look abroad, Abramo, Cicero and D´Angelo (2012) concerning their research on research productivity measurement methodology in 77 Italian universities. They conducted 183 hard research fields during the time period 2004-2008. DEA evaluations were conducted to compare the efficiency in public and private institutions of higher learning (Sav, 2012).

Sav (2012) used the stochastic frontier analysis and data envelopment analysis to estimate and compare the graduation rate efficiency and productivity across private and public universities. He worked with the data from 2005-2009. Ahnt, Charnes and Cooper (1988) used data envelopment analysis to estimate efficiency in public and private institutions.

The educational process in the Czech Republic has been researched in work by Denisov (2016). In his research, he involved every educational organization according to NACE distribution and implemented two-step cluster analysis. He used the variables such as: the number of employees, sales volume, number of jobs, number of activities, labour productivity. By using the Software SPSS he created cluster segments according to the number of employees and turnover.

The goal of this research is to compare results about efficiency, which will be calculated by the implementation of both approaches of the DEA method – the CCR model and BCC models. The research question is: How many differences in efficiency score are calculated using CCR and BCC model? The efficiency was measured in public high schools and universities in the Czech Republic from the point of view of their resources and number of graduate students.

2 Methods and materials

Data Envelopment Analysis (DEA) is one of the methods of the operations research. DEA was originally developed by Charnes, Cooper and Rhodes in 1978 (Charnes, Cooper and Rhodes, 1978). DEA is a non-parametric approach, which is based on the assessment of homogenous production units. DEA is a method of multi-criterion assessment for assessing the efficiency of production units (DMU – Decision Making Units), which use an identical input to produce an identical output (Toloo, 2015). Efficiency is based on a mathematical expression

$$Efficiency = \frac{output}{input}. \tag{1}$$

This method deals with multiple outputs and inputs (Johnes, 2005). Assume there are DMUs, which use a variety of inputs and produce different outputs. The efficiency is expressed as:

$$\theta = \frac{\sum weighted\ sum\ of\ outputs}{\sum weighted\ sum\ of\ inputs}. \tag{2}$$

If we indicate inputs as the variable $x_1, \ldots, x_m$ and outputs as the variable $y_1, \ldots y_n$, for DMUs whose amount is $j = 1, \ldots n$, then the calculation of the production units' efficiency is:

$$\theta_k = \frac{\sum_{j=1}^{n} u_j y_{jk}}{\sum_{i=1}^{m} v_i x_{ik}}. \tag{3}$$

Let us denote u and v as the weights of inputs and outputs, where k expresses the efficiency of the k-th DMU.

2.1 CCR model (Constant returns to scale)

Charnes, Cooper and Rhodes introduced the following input-oriented CCR model in 1978:

$$\max \theta = \sum_{r=1}^{s} u_r y_{r0} \tag{4}$$

$$\text{s.t. } \sum_{i=1}^{m} v_i x_{i0} = 1$$

$$\sum_{r=1}^{s} u_r \times y_{rj} - \sum_{i=1}^{m} v_i x_{ij} \leq 0, \text{ where } j = 1, \ldots, n.$$

We assume that the conditions of non-negativity apply for variables u and v are $v_i, \geq 0 \ i = 1, \ldots, m$ and $u_r \geq 0, \ r = 1, \ldots, s$. Variables u and v are unknown in this model, which values have calculated by means of the DEA CCR model. (Toloo, 2015). Efficiency score can reach values within the interval <0,1>. The production unit is efficient when $\theta = 1$. Efficient unit lays on the efficient frontier. The more the value approaches 0, the less the unit is efficient in its use of resources. Inefficient units can improve their efficiency in two ways: either increase their outputs or reduce their inputs.

2.2 BCC model

The BCC model has been designed by Banker, Charnes and Cooper in 1984. This model considers variable returns to scale. That means that in BCC models, the virtual unit is a convex combination of its sample units. The condition for the virtual unit H is that the λ for $k = 1, \ldots, p$

where $\lambda = 1$. This fact is the cause of more efficient units (Jablonsky and Dlouhy, 2015). Variable returns to scale can be decreasing, increasing or constant (Jablonsky and Dlouhy, 2004). The primary mathematical BCC model is defined as:

$$\max \theta_H = \sum_{r=1}^{s} u_r y_{r0} + \mu \tag{5}$$

$$\text{s.t} \sum_{i=1}^{m} v_i x_{i0} = 1$$

$$\sum_{r=1}^{s} u_r \times y_{rj} + \mu \leq \sum_{i=1}^{m} v_i x_{ij},$$

where $j = 1, ..., n$, $v_i, \geq 0$, $i = 1, \dots, m$, $u_r \geq 0$ $r = 1, \dots, s$, $\mu \in R$.

3 Data

This research uses 26 public universities and colleges in the Czech Republic. The research was carried out with four different variables, two inputs and two outputs. In particular, inputs are represented by total costs of each institution and labor costs (employees). Outputs are the number of graduates and total revenue. The authors involved considered inputs and outputs variables in this model:

x_1 – total costs
x_2 – labor costs
y_1 – number of graduates
y_2 – total revenue

DMU	Total costs	Labor costs	Number of graduates	Total revenues
Akademie múzických umění v Praze	461 070.16	17 947.95	367	72 030.67
Akademie výtvarných umění v Praze	93 657.67	300.57	50	2 943.32
Česká zemědělská univerzita v Praze	2 005 418.00	92 147.00	5 085	297 087.00
České vysoké učení technické v Praze	4 582 880.98	220 868.41	4 760	795 032.58
Janáčkova akademie múzických umění v Brně	230 874.46	485.66	216	3 790.17
Jihočeská univerzita v Českých Budějovicích	1 363 366.00	8 990.00	2 626	46 400.00
Masarykova univerzita	6 043 937.00	3 3497.00	7 824	142 123.00
Mendelova univerzita v Brně	1 557 956.82	91 948.15	2 574	381 706.49
Ostravská univerzita v Ostravě	852 661.00	4 049.00	2 372	10 616.00
Slezská univerzita v Opavě	548 340.09	1 850.00	1 469	1 1063.00
Technická univerzita v Liberci	1 065 317.94	2 7637.85	1 354	92 217.76
Univerzita Hradec Králové	545 484.00	1 354.00	1 785	3 445.00
Univerzita Jana Evangelisty Purkyně v Ústí nad Labem	722 869.00	9 029.00	1 681	39 069.00
Univerzita Karlova v Praze	9 535 930.03	68 267.08	8 387	352 257.31

Univerzita Palackého v Olomouci	3 415 357.00	16 515.00	4 031	62 709.00
Univerzita Pardubice	1 231 615.44	7 791.69	1 798	22 187.75
Univerzita Tomáše Bati ve Zlíně	1 088 036.00	9 504.00	2 440	45 798.00
Veterinární a farmaceutická univerzita Brno	868 895.77	50 617.40	518	256 882.61
Vysoká škola báňská - Technická univerzita Ostrava	2 550 776.00	49 433.00	3 854	173 931.00
Vysoká škola ekonomická v Praze	1 329 416.02	64 004.05	4 156	209 162.64
Vysoká škola chemicko-technologická v Praze	1 518 296.58	20 136.94	902	121 966.43
Vysoká škola polytechnická Jihlava	131 477.00	1 071.00	549	4 303.00
Vysoká škola technická a ekonomická v Č. Budějovicích	173 537.11	2 286.74	552	9 454.94
Vysoká škola umělecko-průmyslová v Praze	254 601.00	358.00	112	6 573.00
Vysoké učení technické v Brně	4 002 910.00	87 771.00	5 289	306 267.00
Západočeská univerzita v Plzni	2 161 290.64	14 160.28	2 685	82 920.68

Table 1 Input data in higher education [data: MŠMT, 2016]

4 Results

This research focused on public higher education – 26 universities or colleges and data in 2016. The total number of graduates was 67 436 students in 2016. The descriptive statistics of the input data is seen in Table 2 and Figure 3. Interestingly, the mean of the graduates was 2,085 and the median is higher than mean in 2016. We can state that 50% of universities have 2,593 graduates (Figure 3). The minimum number of graduates in 2016 was 50 (Akademie výtvarných umění) and maximum number was 8,387 (Univerzita Karlova).

Mean	**1 159 826**	**15 337.64**	**2 085**	**67 369.84**
St. dev.	2 160 341	48 715.3085	2 271.057	179 436.5
Min	93 657.67	300.57	50	2 943.323
max	9 535 930	220 868.41	8 387	795 032.6

Table 2 Input data and their descriptive statistics [Own calculation]

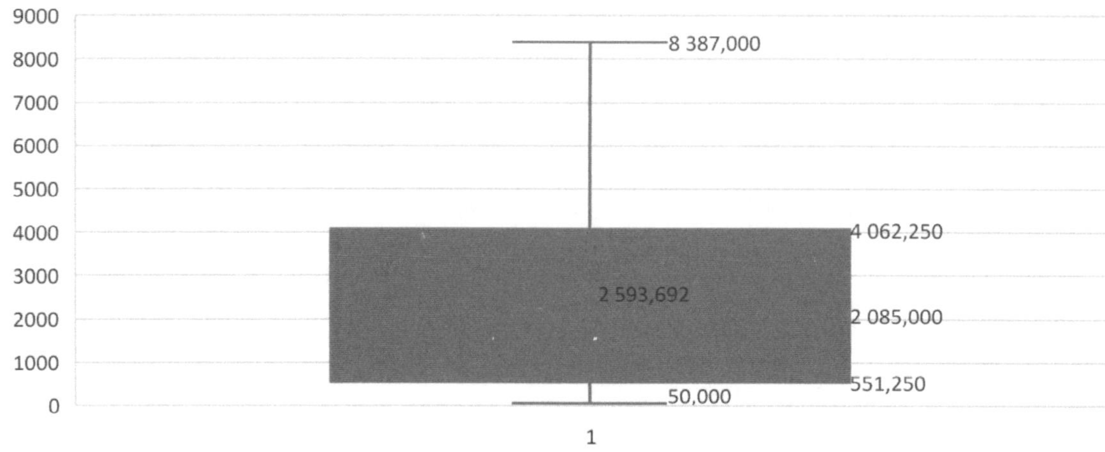

Figure 2 Boxplot of graduates in 2016. Own calculation

Universities' efficiency score calculated by both DEA models – CCR and BCC showed different results. Table 3 shows the efficiency score by using CCR and BCC method. When applying the CCR method there were only seven efficient universities (Mendelova univerzita, Slezská univerzita, Univerzita Hradec Králové, Vysoká škola ekonomická, VŠ polytechnická, Veterinární a farmaceutická univerzita Brno, Vysoká škola umělecko-průmyslová v Praze). When applying the BCC method, there were 17 universities: Akademie múzických umění, Akademie výtvarných umění, ČVUT, Jihočeská univerzita, Masarykova univerzita, Ostravská univerzita, Karlova univerzita, Univerzita Tomáše Bati, VŠCHT and Západočeská univerzita were added to the original list of universities. When comparing these results, the efficiency score increased by 39% (Table 3). When applying the CCR method, there were two inefficient units (Univerzita Pardubice and Palackého Universita Olomouc). When applying the BCC method there was only one inefficient university (Univerzita Pardubice).

	DMU	CCR	BCC
1	Akademie muzických umění v Praze	0.77845	0.77874
2	Akademie výtvarných umění v Praze	0.93705	1.00000
3	Česká zemědělská univerzita v Praze	0.89050	1.00000
4	České vysoké učení technické v Praze	0.72971	1.00000
5	Janáčkova akademie múzických umění v Brně	0.71320	0.83543
6	Jihočeská univerzita v Českých Budějovicích	0.87782	1.00000
7	Masarykova univerzita	0.66420	1.00000
8	Mendelova univerzita v Brně	1.00000	1.00000
9	Ostravská univerzita v Ostravě	0.76556	1.00000
10	Slezská univerzita v Opavě	1.00000	1.00000
11	Technická univerzita v Liberci	0.65276	0.66335
12	Univerzita Hradec Králové	1.00000	1.00000
13	Univerzita Jana Evangelisty Purkyně v Ústí nad Labem	0.85402	0.90178
14	Univerzita Karlova v Praze	0.76255	1.00000

15	Univerzita Palackého v Olomouci	0.58253	0.86805
16	Univerzita Pardubice	0.53273	0.57350
17	Univerzita Tomáše Bati ve Zlíně	0.89710	1.00000
18	Veterinární a farmaceutická univerzita Brno	1.00000	1.00000
19	Vysoká škola báňská - Technická univerzita Ostrava	0.68465	0.87973
20	Vysoká škola ekonomická v Praze	1.00000	1.00000
21	Vysoká škola chemicko-technologická v Praze	0.98890	1.00000
22	Vysoká škola polytechnická Jihlava	1.00000	1.00000
23	Vysoká škola technická a ekonomická v Č. Budějovicích	0.89466	0.89474
24	Vysoká škola umělecko-průmyslová v Praze	1.00000	1.00000
25	Vysoké učení technické v Brně	0.67465	0.90769
26	Západočeská univerzita v Plzni	0.87638	1.00000

Table 3 Results [Own calculation]

Table 4 provides descriptive statistic results. There are seven efficient DMUs – universities or colleges. The rest of the institutions are inefficient and they have been split into two intervals of inefficiency. When applying the BCC model there were 17 universities efficient. We got 10 differences in the efficiency score (Table 4).

	Number of units, where $\theta = 1$	**Number of units, where $0.6 \leq \theta < 1$**	**Number of units, where $0 \leq \theta < 0.6$**	**Mean**	**Std. dev.**	**Max**	**Min**
CCR	7 (26%)	17	2	0.8771	0.1475	0.5735	0.5327
BCC	17 (65%)	8	1	1	0.1134	1	0.5735

Table 4 Descriptive statistics of results [Own calculation]

The boxplots (Figure 3) have revealed that the CCR efficiency score is more scattered than the efficiency score BCC. Figure 4 shows that the median of the efficiency score obtained through the BCC method is higher than the median of the efficiency score of the CCR. The lowest value of efficiency is 0.57 (CCR efficiency). In comparison with BCC efficiency score it is lower than in the BCC. It is 0.8 in the BCC model.

Results at Masarykova Universita and České vysoké učení technické displayed in the bar chart (Figure 4) show the size of the difference. Identical results have been perceived on Masarykova univerzita v Brně, Slezská univerzita v Opavě, Univerzita Hradec Králové, VFUB, VŠE, VŠP and VŠUP.

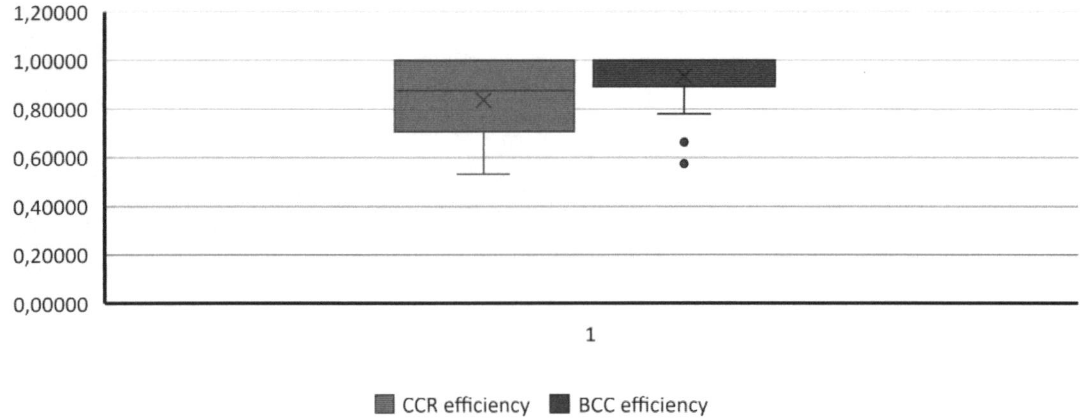

Figure 3 Boxplot – efficiency score by using both methods [Own calculation]

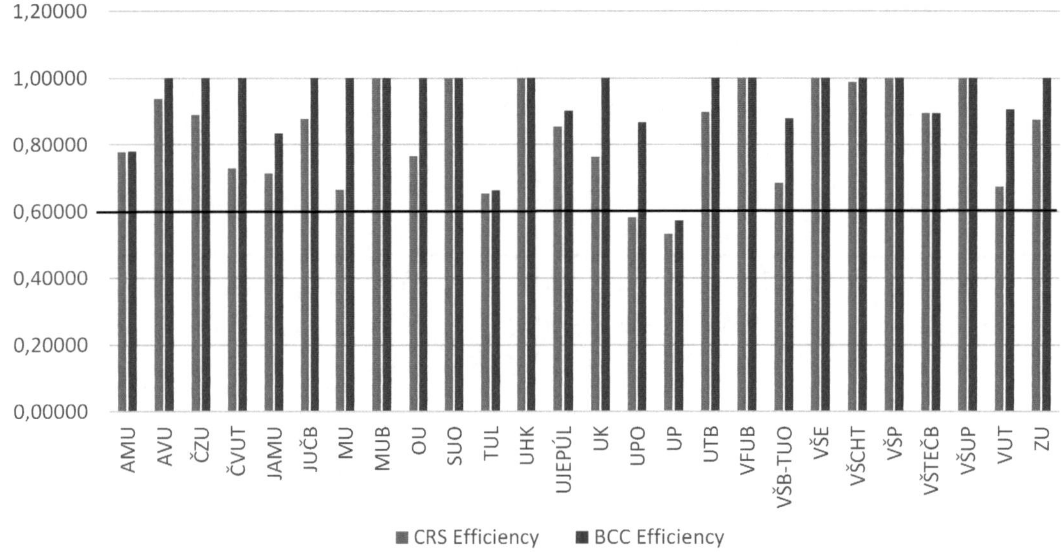

Figure 4 Efficiency of universities in 2016 by using both methods [Own calculation]

5 Conclusion

This paper focused on the efficiency score calculation in the higher education area. Results have been obtained by using the BCC and CCR models and compared by showing the differences in the efficiency score. Results obtained through the CCR model showed that 7 universities or colleges (Mendelova univerzita, Slezská univerzita, Univerzita Hradec Králové, Vysoká škola ekonomická, VŠ polytechnická, Veterinární a farmaceutická univerzita Brno, Vysoká škola umělecko-průmyslová v Praze) were efficient and two inefficient (Univerzita Palackého v Olomouci and Univerzita Pardubice). Results obtained through the BCC model showed that 17 universities were efficient Mendelova univerzita, Slezská univerzita v Opavě, Univerzita Hradec Králové, Vysoká škola ekonomická, VŠ polytechnická Jihlava, Veterinární a farmaceutická univerzita Brno, Vysoká škola umělecko-průmyslová v Praze, Akademie výtvarných umění, Česká zemědělská univerzita v Praze, ČVUT, Jihočeská univerzita v Českých Budějovicích, Masarykova univerzita, Ostravská univerzita, Karlova univerzita, Univerzita Tomáše Bati ve

Zlíně, VŠCHT and Západočeská univerzita v Plzni) and one university was inefficient (Univerzita Pardubice). Identical results (CCR and BCC model) have been perceived on Masarykova univerzita v Brně, Slezská univerzita v Opavě, Univerzita Hradec Králové, VFUB, VŠE, VŠP and VŠUP. The efficient score obtained through the CCR model is more scattered than the one obtained through the BCC model.

Acknowledgements

This paper was supported within Project SP2017/141 "Diskriminační analýza versus analýza datových obalů " and Operational Programme Education for Competitiveness – Project No. CZ.1.07/2.3.00/20.0296.

References

Abramo, G., Cicero, T. and D´Angelo, C.A. (2012). 'Revitising size effects in higher education research productivity'. *Higher Education*, 63 (6), pp. 701-717.

Ahnt, T., Charnes. A. and Cooper, WW (1988). 'Some statistical and DEA evaluations of relative efficiencies of public and private institutions of higher learning'. *Socio-Economic Planning Sciences*, 22 (6), pp. 259-269.

Denisov, I. (2016). 'Pattern of Organization Structure Develoopment The Case of Higher Education'. *Proceedings of the 13th International Conference on Efficiency and Responsibility in Education (ERIE 2016)*, Prague, Czech Republic, pp. 73-79.

Hanclova, J. (2016). 'Two-stage DEA Model for Comparing the Efficiency in Tertiary Education'. *Proceedings of the 13th International Conference on Efficiency and Responsibility in Education (ERIE 2016)*, Prague, Czech Republic, pp. 155-163.

Charnes, A., Cooper, W.W. and Rhodes, E. (1979). 'Measuring the efficiency of decision-making units'. *European Journal of Operational Research*, 3 (4), pp. 339-354.

Chytilova, L. and Hanclova, J. (2015). 'The impact of inclusion of non-traditional activities on efficiencies in European banking industry using the CCR-I model'. *Proceedings of the 11th International Conference Strategic management and its support by information systems (SMSIS2015)*, Uherske Hradiste, Czech Republic, pp. 208-220.

Jablonsky, J. and Dlouhy, M. (2004). *Modely hodnocení efektivnosti produkčních jednotek.* Praha: Professional Publishing.

Jablonsky, J. and Dlouhy, M. (2015). *Modely hodnocení efektivnosti a alokace zdrojů.* Praha: Professional Publishing.

Johnes, J. (2005). 'Measuring teaching efficiency in higher education: An application of Data Envelopment Analysis to economic graduates from UK Universities 1993'. *European Journal of Operational Research,* 174 (1), pp. 443-456.

Johnes, J. (2006). 'Data envelopment analysis and its application to the measurement of efficiency in higher education'. *Economic of Education Review*, 25 (3), pp. 273-288.

Maryska, M. and Doucek, P. (2011). 'Comparison of the Czech and Austria Education Systems'. *Proceedings of the 19th Interdisciplinary Information Management Talks (IDIMT 2011),* Jindrichuv Hradec, Czech Republic, pp. 23-34.

MŠMT. Výkonové ukazatele, [Online]. Available at: https://dsia.msmt.cz//vystupy/vu_vs.html [cited 2019-01-30].

Rehacek, P. (2015). 'Matrix Organization for Project Management' *Proceedings of the 11th International Conference on Strategic Management and its Support by Information Systems (SMSIS 2015)*, Uherske Hradiste, Czech Republic, pp. 160-165.

Sav, G. T. (2012) 'Frontier and envelopment evaluations of university graduation efficiencies and productivities: Elements for performance-based funding'. *Problems and Perspectives in Management*, 10 (4), pp. 71-79.

Toloo, M. (2015). *Data Envelopment Analysis*. Ostrava: VŠB-TU Ostrava.

Wurmova, N. (2012) Postavení vysokoškoláků a uplatnění absolventů vysokých škol na pracovním trhu 2010, Středisko vzdělávací politiky při Pedagogické fakultě UK, [Online]. Available at:http://www.strediskovzdelavacipolitiky.info/download/Absolventi_VS_2010.pdf [cited 2019-01-24].

Outliers in regression modelling: Influential vs. non-influential values and detection using information criteria

José Carlos Casas-Rosal[1], Julia Núñez-Tabales[2], José María Caridad y Ocerin[3], Petr Seďa[4]

Abstract. In the estimation of regression models in urban valuation, the detection of atypical values is of great importance to avoid possible spurious results, as a small subset of these observations, can exert a high influence in the parameters estimates. The Akaike Information Criterion is used to characterize multivariate outliers in non-robust regression modelling. The discriminating power to detect those outliers that are influential observations is analyzed, obtaining better results that with the classic methods available in well-known statistical packages in regression. This is of great importance in the construction of estimation models. A simulation modelling is performed to assess the validity of the proposed procedure in contrast with classical outlier detection methods in regression. The use of a Monte Carlo simulation study is motivated on the difficulties in the analysis of the sampling distribution of the AIC.

Keywords: Akaike Information Criteria, influential observations, outliers, non-robust regression models.

JEL Classification: C52, C59

1 Introduction

There are many studies in which the principal main is to identify atypical multivariate values in a set of data (Gumedze and Chatora, 2014; Pavlidou, Christoforos and Zioutas, 2018; Vakili and Schmitt, 2014). However, the proportion of them that focus their research on the detection of influential observations is not representative (Kaffine and Davis, 2017).

It is well established that outliers can be of great influence when estimating a non-robust regression model, so it is necessary to analyze the presence of outliers or atypical values in the sample data used (Caridad, 1998). A clear distinction ought to be made between values that are labeled as atypical but that do not have a clear influence on the final coefficient estimates from those that can modify in a significant way the results and their interpretation. For example, in a hedonic model in real estate market analysis, a large and high-priced property may be atypical but not influential if its price responds to these attributes in a similar way as the main bulk of data; on the other hand, a small size dwelling out-priced could greatly affect the estimated model. Such distinction between influential and non-influential outliers is of importance if a

[1] University of Cordoba, Department of Statistics and Econometrics, Plaza Nueva S/N, C.P. 14071 Córdoba, Spain, jcasas@uco.es
[2] University of Cordoba, Department of Statistics and Econometrics, Plaza Nueva S/N, C.P. 14071 Córdoba, Spain, es2nutaj@uco.es
[3] University of Cordoba, Department of Statistics and Econometrics, Plaza Nueva S/N, C.P. 14071 Córdoba, Spain, ccjm@uco.es
[4] VSB-Technical University of Ostrava, Faculty of Economics, Department of Mathematical Methods in Economics, Sokolská třída 33, 702 00 Ostrava 1, Czech Republic, petr.seda@vsb.cz

hedonic model is obtained using an automatic algorithm using a sample from a commercial real estate web (Casas-Rosal, 2017). The main statistical packages, such as IBM's SPSS provide several statistics to detect outliers (Belsley, Kuh &Welsch, 1980; Cook and Weisberg, 1982), but they fail to distinguish between influential and non-influential cases. The discrimination in both cases can be achieved in a more efficient way using the proposed methods based on likelihood-based measures.

The *AIC* (Akaike, 1973) and several related statistics have been widely used for model selection, and, to a lesser extent, in the identification of atypical values, Kitagawa and Akaike, 1998 and, more recently, Karagrigoriou, Mattheou and Vonta, 2011 and Alma, 2013. The broad idea is to study the variations in the AIC when 'suspect' data are taken away from the sample. Influential observations produce greater changes than non-influential outliers, so it is necessary to define procedures to determine when these variations are to be considered significant or not.

The use of a Monte Carlo simulation study is motivated on the difficulties in the analysis of the sampling distribution of the AIC. Two alternative methods are proposed and compared with the traditional approaches such as leverage of data, Bonferroni method, DfBetas, Cook's distance, DfFits and CovRatios measures.

These methods, although computationally expensive, show to be effective in identifying atypical values that are influential in the estimates of the regression coefficients.

2 Detection of outliers using AIC

Let's consider an univariate regression model such as $Y = m(x_1, x_2, \dots, x_k) + \varepsilon$ and a simple random sample of the endogenous variable with the corresponding controlled data for the exogenous variables $(y_j, x_{1i}, x_{2i}, \dots, x_{ki})$, $i = 1, 2, \dots, n$. The information criterion proposed by Akaike provides a measure of the relative loss of information when estimating a model with a sample rather than using the corresponding theoretical function. Its formula, for a model with k explanatory variables is

$$AIC = -2\ln L + 2(k + 1), \quad (1)$$

where L is the likelihood function of the variable $(Y_1, Y_2, \dots, Y_n)$. From the usual assumptions of the error distribution, $(\varepsilon_1, \varepsilon_2, \dots, \varepsilon_n)$ as a centred multivariate heteroskedastic and non-autocorrelated normal variables, and with non-random explanatory variables

$$AIC = n(\ln(2\pi) + 1 + \ln \sigma_\varepsilon^2) + 2(k + 1). \quad (2)$$

The *AIC* value is a measure of discrepancy between the goodness of fit performed and the theoretical adjustment, so that lower *AIC* values are related to a smaller discrepancy or loss of information, and, therefore, this criterion is used to compare models.

With a large enough sample, and considering the j data, $(y_j, x_{1j}, x_{2j}, \dots, x_{kj})$, is non-influential, if it is removed from the sample, it will be expected than non-significant changes will be observed in the parameter estimates. Also, the *AIC* value obtained with the corresponding n - 1 data, *AIC*(-*j*) should be like the *AIC* obtained with the full sample:

$$AIC(-j) = (n - 1)[(\ln(2\pi) + 1 + \ln \sigma_\varepsilon^2(-j)) + 2(k + 1) \quad (3)$$

being $\sigma_\varepsilon^2(-j)$ the residual variance obtained with n - 1 data points. Thus, the variation in the *AIC* due to removing the j point from the sample is

$$D_j = AIC - AIC(-j) = \ln(2\pi) + 1 + n\ln\sigma_\varepsilon^2 - (n-1)\ln\sigma_\varepsilon^2(-j) = \\ = \ln(2\pi) + 1 + \ln\sigma_\varepsilon^2(-j) + n\ln RATIO, \tag{4}$$

with $RATIO = \sigma_\varepsilon^2/\sigma_\varepsilon^2(-j)$. If $RATIO_j \approx 1$, then $D_j \approx \ln(2\pi) + 1 + \ln\sigma_\varepsilon^2(-j)$.

To avoid problems associated with the sample size, it is preferable to use the relative change of the *AIC*, that is

$$d_j = D_j/AIC. \tag{5}$$

Again, if the j-data is non-influential and $RATIO_j \approx 1$, then

$$d_j = \frac{\ln(2\pi) + 1 + \ln\sigma_\varepsilon^2(-j)}{n(\ln(2\pi) + 1 + \ln\sigma_\varepsilon^2) + 2(k+1)}. \tag{6}$$

When the sample size increases, it is observed that $d_j \to 0$. The residual variance is estimated using regression residuals by

$$\hat{\sigma}_\varepsilon^2 = \frac{1}{n-k-1}\sum_{i=1}^{n} e_i^2. \tag{7}$$

The Bayesian information criterion

$$BIC = n(\ln(2\pi) + 1 + \ln\sigma_\varepsilon^2)) + (k+1) + \ln n \tag{8}$$

can be also used. Its relative change when omitting an observation is

$$d_j^* = \frac{\ln(2\pi) + 1 + \ln\sigma_\varepsilon^2(-j)}{n(\ln(2\pi) + 1 + \ln\sigma_\varepsilon^2) + (k+1)\ln n}. \tag{9}$$

The *BIC* is less affected when the j data is omitted, and it can be shown that $d_j > d_j^*$.

3 Differences in the rate of change and coverage of the variance ratio

The parameter $RATIO_j = \sigma_\varepsilon^2/\sigma_\varepsilon^2(-j)$ tends to take values around one when the j data is non-influential, as is deduced with a simulation study, while for an influential outlier, this ratio tends to diverge from one. To show the likelihood of the results, a simple regression model, $Y = \alpha + \beta x + \varepsilon$ is used, although with general univariate models the results are similar. Taking different sample sizes, the influence of n can be assessed using different sets of random data, for different values of α, β, μ_x, R^2 and σ_ε. Several relations such as

$$\sigma_X^2 = \frac{R^2\sigma_\varepsilon^2}{\beta^2(1-R^2)}. \tag{10}$$

within the parameters provides the variance of the exogenous variable. A sensibility analysis is performed changing the initial set of control parameters α, β, μ_x, R^2 and σ_ε with reduced and non-significant changes in the results.

The design to simulate the random data is based on generating n - 1 data, and, later, adding the removed (j) point, both in the cases of being either an influential or a non- influential outlier:

- a normal centered white noise, ε, is obtained for n - 1 data, with several values of the coefficient such as $\beta = 10$, and with different levels of R^2;
- a sample of n - 1 values for the x variable is generated for different values of μ_x; its variance σ_x^2 depends on the determination coefficient, the β value and the error variance;
- then the endogenous variable data are calculated using the proposed model;
- AIC, $AIC(-j)$, BIC and $BIC(-j)$ and the residual variance $\sigma_\varepsilon^2(-j)$ are obtained;
- finally, the j-data is simulated: for the non-influential case it is centered at the medium point of x_{min} and x_{max}, and the response variable is generated for the model with the same random noise used previously;
- when this case is moved across the range of the exogenous variables, the results are similar. This procedure is repeated 1000 times for each specification;
- as output the ratios values and their changes are obtained.

In Table 1 some results are presented for $\alpha = 10$, $\beta = 10$, $R^2 = 0.7$ and $\sigma_\varepsilon = 1$.

n	Mean of the ratio	Standard deviation of the ratio	Relative change of the mean	Relative change of standard deviation
100	1.0004567	0.014226144	0.009904904	0.0048303067
500	0.9998525	0.002478247	0.001938958	0.0008680579
1000	1.0000485	0.001448631	0.001014361	0.0005079548

Table 1 Ratio and the proportion of change removing non-influential point

The mean value of the ratio is very close to one, and the difference decreases with larger sample sizes. Its standard deviation also decreases as n increases. Likewise, the mean of the rate of change tends to cero as the sample size increases, and its standard deviation also. This same study has been repeated for sample sizes between 100 and 5000, with increments of 100 with similar results as can be observed in the following figure. The statistic $RATIO(-j)$ tends to stabilize around one, even for not so large sample size; also, its standard deviation tends towards zero. Results are presented graphically in Figure 1 as well.

Similar results are presented for smaller samples, simulating data for values of n between 10 and 100. $RATIO(-j)$ show a decreasing trend and tends to stabilize around one from $n = 40$. However, the decrease in the rate of change is less pronounced with sample size and begins to stabilize for larger samples.

Several simulations are performed, introducing variations in the defined set of parameters, without noticeable changes in the results. Thus, it can be concluded that the proportion of change in the information criterion originated by eliminating a non-influential observation from the data set, is sufficiently small, and the ratio of its variances is close to unity for medium sample sizes.

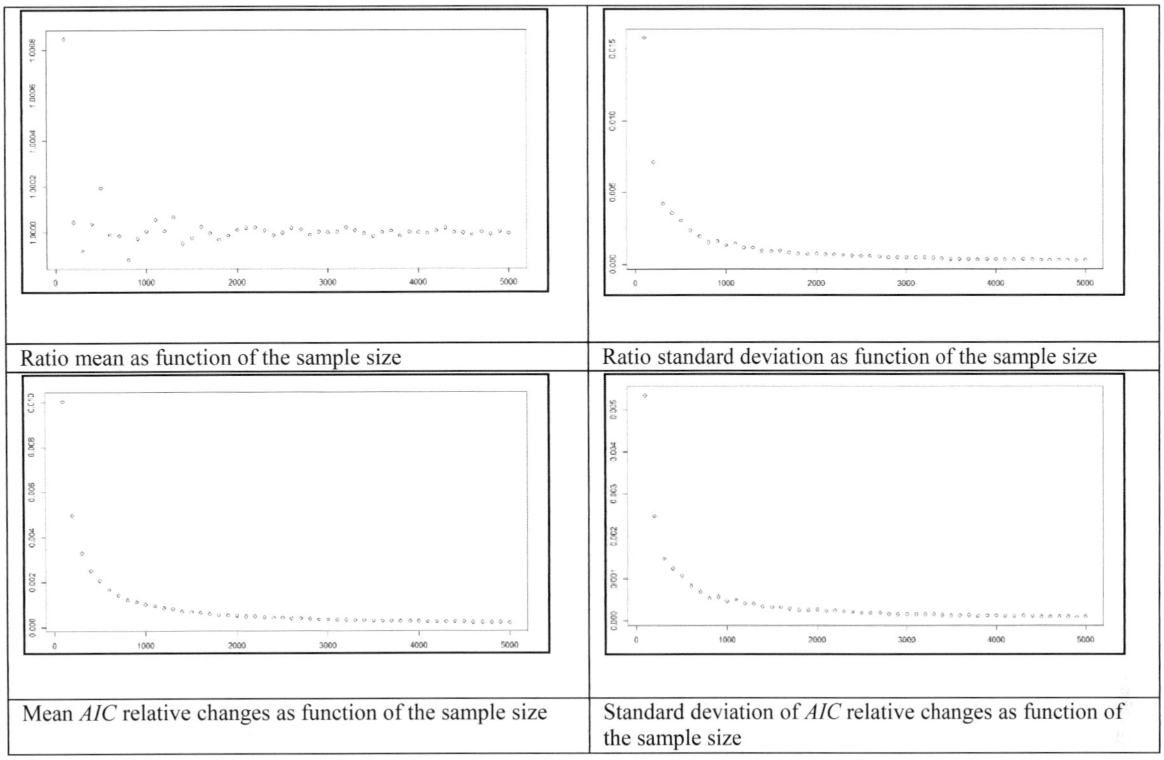

Figure 1 Evolution of the residual variances ratio and its relative changes

The problem that arises here is to determine the methodology to detect an observation that can be considered, with a reasonable degree of likelihood, as influential. Graphically, an observation is influential if the distance between the model and the point is significantly larger than the distance between some points estimated with the model and the rest of the points. The vertical distance to be considered cannot be used in absolute terms, since its magnitude depends both on the scale at which the points are measured, and of the shape of the data set, and, therefore, on the parameters chosen in the simulation.

For this reason, to increase the level of influence of an observation for a value located at midpoint of the exogenous variable range, it will be considered generated by

$$y_i^* = \hat{y}_i + \Delta\hat{y}_i \,, \tag{11}$$

been this point within the range of the endogenous variable Y. It is necessary to take into account that, for small values of β, this deviation from the model could not be significant; to avoid this situation, the value $\Delta\hat{y}_i$ should be positive and less than $max\{y_{max} - \hat{y}_i, x_{max} - x_i\}$. Then

$$y_i^* = \hat{y}_i + \frac{i}{m} k \cdot max\{y_{max} - \hat{y}_i, x_{max} - x_i\} \quad i = 1, \dots, m. \tag{12}$$

The parameter k is used to control the distance of the new point to the model. When k increases, the new case becomes 'more influential' in the estimation process, and this induces greater values both in the ratio of the residual variances and in the rate of change of the *AIC(-j)*. When the sample size is considered, the influence upon the considered ratio is clear. For example, for $n = 1000$, $\alpha = 10$, $\beta = 10$, $\mu_x = 5$, $R^2 = 0.7$ and $\sigma_\varepsilon = 1$, a uniform distribution of the exogenous data is used for $k = 1$, and the relations between the estimated values, $\hat{y}$ and the simulated values with the ratio of residual variances is presented in Figure 2.

When the point is moved away from the data set, that is, when it becomes 'more influential', the *RATIO* statistics increases, and, it becomes significantly different to one; its relative change also increases due to changes in the value of the information criterion. These results lead to justify that the rate of the change of *AIC(-j)* can detect the existence of influential observations. It should be noted that, as we will see below, this change is accelerated or not depending on some characteristics of the model. The results are similar when the atypical case is moved across the range of the exogenous variable; in this case the *RATIO* and the relative ratio increases at a higher pace with this point distance to the model.

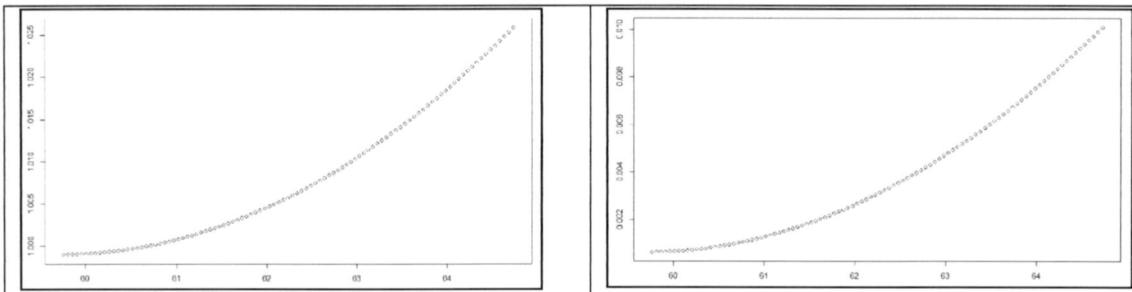

Ratio changes as the influential point is moved away of the rest of the sample scatter gram	Relative Ratio changes as the influential point is moved away of the rest of the sample scatter gram

Figure 2 Changes in ratios as a function of *k*

This allows us to identify the influential observations by comparing the *AIC* values of each of the models defined in different simulations, with the corresponding values obtained when a data point is removed, since the change produced by eliminating an influential observation will always be significantly higher than if this outlier is not influential. Thus, comparing different *AIC* values for different models, it is possible to identify which outliers are influential, as the variation is larger when an influential outlier is omitted comparing to the changes with an ordinary data or a non-influential is omitted from the sample.

n	**Mean: minima of y**	**Mean: maxima of y**	**Mean: minima of ratios**	**Mean: maxima of ratios**	**Mean: minima of ratio changes**	**Mean: maxima of ratio changes**
100	60.07276	64.63899	0.9900221	1.210896	0.0063179980	0.07115995
200	60.03600	64.91968	0.9950123	1.118325	0.0032062610	0.04218441
300	60.10896	65.23945	0.9966759	1.089146	0.0021400800	0.03232223
500	60.05560	65.53074	0.9980062	1.060134	0.0012908310	0.02204544
1000	60.01255	65.96450	0.9990037	1.035651	0.0006471602	0.01315847
2000	60.02617	66.21443	0.9995020	1.019248	0.0003240113	0.007166522
5000	60.07807	66.69190	0.9998009	1.008818	0.0001297429	0.003283337

Table 2 Mean values of the ratios and the ratios of change as a function of *n*

As k increases, its relationship with the ratio parameter is different to the relation with the rate of change, since the former maintains the behavior, but the rate of change stabilizes as expected by the nature of its definition.

The mean values obtained with 100 simulations are presented in Table 2; the minimum and maximum of Y, thus reflecting their distance, ratio and rate of change. The function that relates the distance with these, is strictly increasing, and the minimum and maximum values have been reached, in all the cases, for points to the minimum and maximum distance respectively.

As can be observed, the average ratio of the most influential observations decreases with sample size, since this is their general behavior, because the increase in sample size decreases the weight that a single observation has on the data set. The same situation is observed with the rates of change. However, their standard deviations also decrease as the sample size is larger, so there are always significant differences between the minimum and maximum values. The values of the deviations of the ratios and the exchange ratios are shown in the Table 3, as well as the p-values obtained when comparing their mean.

n	Ratios of minima deviations	Ratios of maxima deviations	Rate of change: minima deviations	Rate of change: maxima deviations	p-values for ratios	p-values for proportions
100	$8.0243\cdot10^{-6}$	0.08024300	0.00018486	0.02057711	$< 2.2\cdot10^{-16}$	$< 2.2\cdot10^{-16}$
200	$4.1459\cdot10^{-6}$	0.04145902	$6.1516\cdot10^{-5}$	0.01206736	$< 2.2\cdot10^{-16}$	$< 2.2\cdot10^{-16}$
300	$2.7786\cdot10^{-6}$	0.02778581	$3.2027\cdot10^{-5}$	0.00839610	$< 2.2\cdot10^{-16}$	$< 2.2\cdot10^{-16}$
500	$1.7632\cdot10^{-6}$	0.01763177	$1.5250\cdot10^{-5}$	0.00555527	$< 2.2\cdot10^{-16}$	$< 2.2\cdot10^{-16}$
1000	$7.3424\cdot10^{-7}$	0.00734200	$5.7636\cdot10^{-6}$	0.00249267	$< 2.2\cdot10^{-16}$	$< 2.2\cdot10^{-16}$
2000	$3.5540\cdot10^{-7}$	0.00355401	$1.8683\cdot10^{-6}$	0.00121097	$< 2.2\cdot10^{-16}$	$< 2.2\cdot10^{-16}$
5000	$1.8042\cdot10^{-7}$	0.00180418	$5.3523\cdot10^{-7}$	0.00062800	$< 2.2\cdot10^{-16}$	$< 2.2\cdot10^{-16}$

Table 3 Deviations and comparison of the ratios and the change ratios as a function of n

The statistics of the former tests do not decrease; when the sample size increases, the differences tend to be smaller, and the variability, maintaining significant differences. When the parameters used in the simulations are changed, the results tend to be stable; of course, the changes in the determination coefficient and in the variance of the errors is manifest for influential cases, and the proportions of change and the ratios increases with k.

4 Detection of influential observations using the AIC

Previously, changes in the AIC estimated on a simple regression model, have been proposed as a measure to discriminate between influential and non-influential outliers. The use with a general model using k exogenous variables is straightforward. Again, omitting the j observation form the sample, the $AIC(-j)$, for $j = 1, 2, \ldots, n$, their mean μ_{AIC} and sample standard deviation, σ_{AIC} the corresponding sample standard deviation, and their quartiles Q_1 and Q_3, show some characteristics related to the discrimination between different types of outliers.

In the absence of influential observations, the elements of this *AIC* set of values will be homogenous, since all of them are obtained from samples that differ only in one observation, which is supposed with no influence on the model estimates and using the same sample size. Also, the residuals of the n models are of the same order of magnitude. If *AIC(-j)* is considerable smaller than that of the rest, it shows an improvement of the goodness of fit with respect to the original model, and therefore the j observation can be considered influential.

Two heuristic criteria can be proposed to detect the potentially influential cases: an observation *j* will be considered influential either if

$$AIC(-j) < \mu_{AIC} - q\sigma_{AIC} \tag{13}$$

or if

$$AIC(-j) < Q_1 - q(Q_3 - Q_1) \tag{14}$$

for some a conveniently chosen q. The second criterion is more reliable as the quartiles are less influenced than the mean or the standard deviation, by extreme atypical values.

5 Comparison of different detection methods

To assess the reliability of the proposed criteria, and to compare the corresponding results with some well-known procedures available in statistical packages, a simulation study is employed. As an introduction, some results obtained with a simple linear model are presented. The values employed in this example are the following: $\alpha = 10$, $\beta = 10$, $\mu_x = 5$, $R^2 = 0.7$ and $\sigma_\varepsilon^2 = 5$, for different sample sizes, and changing the distance of the omitted data to the model. Different values of the former parameters have also been used. In Table 4 are enumerated the criteria that have been compared, including the two proposed in the previous section with the most widely used.

A sensibility analysis has been performed for every sample size considered, considering the variability in the distance of the potential atypical observation to the model.

Method based on	**Criteria**
Standardized *AIC*	$AIC(-i) < \mu_{AIC} - 3\sigma_{AIC(-)}$
AIC quartiles	$AIC(-i) < Q_1 - 3(Q_3 - Q_1)$
Studentized residuals	$\lvert\hat{\varepsilon}_{s_j}\rvert > 3\sigma_{\hat{\varepsilon}_{s_j}}$
Hat matrix	$h_j > \frac{3(k+1)}{n}$
Bonferroni test	$\alpha = 0.05$
Dffits	$\lvert Dffits_j\rvert > 3\sqrt{\frac{k+1}{n}}$
Dfbetas	$\lvert dfbeta_{ji}\rvert > \frac{3}{\sqrt{n}}$
Cook's distance	$CD_j > \frac{4}{n}$
Covratios	$\lvert COVratio_j - 1\rvert > 3\frac{k+1}{n}$

Table 4 Criteria for selecting atypical values

The corresponding sensibility is related to the detection method used, so for each of them, the 'critical distance values' are described, that is, the distances at which the outlier is marginally detected. The sample size influence on the outlier detection is considered in the simulations, as well as different sets of the model parameters. When a known influential case is introduced in the data set, it could or could not be detected, and some ordinary cases could also be mistakenly considered influential. All these situations are analyzed, as well as when there is more than one influential case. Another situation treated is when the potentially influential data is moved across the range of the exogenous variable, and even out of this range. As it will be seen, this is detected with the *AIC* variation criteria. Again, a sample size of $n = 1000$ is used as starting point.

The CovRatio method produces similar results to the 'Standardized *AIC*' and the '*AIC* quartiles' proposed criteria; at the margins of the scattergram all atypical points are detected. The Bonferroni test is more conservative, although if depends of the significance level used. The Hat matrix method only detects outliers when they are at the extremes of the range of the exogenous variable, without discriminating between influential and non-influential, and the DfBetas have less power to detect outliers depending of the values of the exogenous variables: it would detect outliers at the extremes but not within the range of the x values, unless they are quite separate from the rest of the observations; the Cook distance and the Dffits produce similar results: at the center of the exogenous variable range the minimum distance to detect outliers is larger than when the atypical point moves towards the extremes; Cook's distance sensibility is quite superior to Dffits's.

The mean values and standard deviations of the distances at which each of the methods first detect the influential case are tabulated, for the defined parameters, in a set of fifteen simulations, each of which 100 observations. Individually, for samples of size 1000, using atypical points at several positions within the range of the exogenous variable: x_{min}, $(x_{min} + x_{max})/2)$, x_{max} and in its quartiles. Result are presented in Table 5.

	x_{min}		Q_1		**Center**		Q_3		x_{max}	
Marginal dist	Mean dist	SD	Mean dist	SD	Mean dist	SD	Mean dist	SD	Mean dist	SD
Stand. *AIC*	5,2941	0,1755	5,2843	0,1207	5,2109	0,1541	5,2988	0,1386	5,2709	0,1367
AIC quartiles	5,1811	0,1546	5,1272	0,1598	5,1409	0,2165	5,1098	0,1456	5,1360	0,1804
Studentized residuals	6,8652	0,1903	6,9116	0,1773	6,8617	0,1677	6,8542	0,1516	6,8990	0,1708
Hat matrix	ALL	-	NONE	-	NONE	-	NONE	-	ALL	-
Bonfer. test	9,3056	0,2177	9,3332	0,2113	9,2258	0,1847	9,2821	0,1530	9,2932	0,1956
Dffits	2,9014	0,2157	8,1144	0,1699	9,3626	0,4216	8,0497	0,1224	3,0200	0,2537
Dfbetas	2,1430	0,1712	9,4568	0,3477	NONE	-	10,1010	0,3657	2,3019	0,1786
Cook's dist	1,9626	0,1435	5,4454	0,1451	6,3500	0,2499	5,3899	0,1146	2,0674	0,1597
CoVratios	ALL	-	5,0554	0,1301	4,9301	0,1401	5,0193	0,1177	ALL	-

Table 5 Mean and standard deviations of the marginal distance of detection an influential case

The two proposed methods produce better results than the classical procedures, and their behaviour is more consistent when the atypical value is displaced along the range of x values. Bonferroni and the studentized residual methods produce similar results along the range of the exogenous variable, but their sensibility is significantly lower than the proposed methods to detect influential and atypical data. The Hat matrix and DfBetas were not able to identify the influential case but at the extremes of the range of x values. The sensibility of the remaining methods is conditioned by the situation of the atypical value within the range of the explanatory variable.

The range of the y^* values is increased, and a new set of simulations is used to assess the sensibility of those methods that did not detect the influential data. In this case, the Dfbeta method could locate the outliers, at the center range at approximately 20 units, while de Hat method is not appropriate in this case.

Then some additional simulations were carried out with sample sizes of $n = 100$, 200 and 500. Each data set included 50 cases ordered at increasing distance from the model. There are not clear differences with previous results between the different methods, but in the Bonferroni's and in Dfbeta, the variability of these marginal distances is smaller in the two *AIC* and the CovRatio methods; also, when using the studentized residuals. The Dfbeta method detect the influential data in 3 to 5 simulations, for 20 replications of the experiment, while the Bonferroni test attain this objective in 90% of them.

From all the simulations performed, the Hat matrix and the DFbeta methods can be discarded. The first one is not detecting influential observations, unless they are located at one end of the cloud of points and the second primarily because of its reduced sensitivity, which could be solved by reducing the imposed limit value, and by its high variability in the detection process.

The Bonferroni method has identified, in some simulations, all observations as influential, which is, of course, erroneous, and has not identified any in other cases, under the same conditions in which it had previously done so. Therefore, it has a good behavior in general, but sometimes does not work correctly.

The methods based on the calculation of Dffits and Cook's distance, produce similar results with variable sensibility, and have achieved good and homogenous results in the detection of influential observations, but to a lesser extent than the CovRatios approach and the *AIC*'s based, and, also than the studentized residuals-based procedures. The first three provide similar results, and the fourth has a lower sensitivity.

However, the last parameter analyzed, the residual variance, has revealed to influence significantly the effectiveness of the proposed methods. This is not surprising because increasing the residual variance the cases are more dispersed, and, therefore the distance required to consider an influential observation will be larger. It shows the growth of the minimum detection distance as a function of the value of the residual variance, between 0.5 and 10. The increase experienced by the Bonferroni method is higher than the rest. The simulations were performed by shifting the influential observation to the extremes of the data set, where the hat matrix method began to detect observations from the minimum distance and including several influential observations simultaneously.

6 Conclusions

When the objective of the analysis is to detect atypical values that are influential, in the estimation of the non-robust regression model, some of the methods traditionally used by the statistical packages are not valid to discriminate between influential and the rest of the outliers.

The validation of AIC based methods has been made through numerous simulations that reveal that this information criterion, and its rate of change, when a suspected case is omitted from the sample, provides clear guidelines about the degree of influence of this observation on the estimation of the regression model.

The proposed methods, along with the method of the studentized residuals, have proved to be the best for the detection of influential observations, as their sensibility is homogenous at the whole range of the exogenous variable, their precision detecting outliers is more consistent and they can be used to discriminate between influential and non-influential cases.

The proposed results have been checked using both simple and multiple regression sets of simulated data, although the results presented here are mainly with the former. The leverage method can only detect outliers, without been able to distinguish if they are influential or not, at the extremes of the x values range. The DfBeta has the same shortcomings, even at different ranges of the exogenous variable values and its sensibility depends on these situations. Also, the procedures based on the DfFits, CoVratio and Cook's distances show a variability on their sensibility depending on the x values.

The minimum distance to detect atypical data with Bonferroni and with the standardized residuals methods, and with the AIC proposed procedure are invariant to the position of the atypical value in the scattergram. Bonferroni rate of errors is higher as it tends to mis categorize as influential some ordinary data, and it needs a larger distance to the rest of the data, to classify it as an outlier. Thus, as a brief conclusion, the AIC proposed method is considered superior to the alternatives in detecting outliers in regression models, and to classify some of these as influential.

References

Akaike, H. (1973). 'Information theory and an extension of the maximum likelihood principle'. *Proceedings of 2nd International Symposium on Information Theory*, Budapest, Hungary, pp. 267-281.

Alma, O. G. (2013). 'Performances Comparison of Information Criteria for Outlier Detection in Multiple Regression Models Having Multicollinearity Problems using Genetic Algorithms'. *Matematika*, 29 (2), pp. 119-131.

Belsley, D. A., Kuh, E. and Welsch, R. E. (1980). *Regression Diagnostics*. New York: Wiley.

Caridad, J. M. (1998). *Econometría: modelos econométricos y series temporales, vol 1.* Ed Reverté.

Casas-Rosal, J. C. (2017). *Métodos de valoración urbana*. Universidad de Córdoba.

Cook, R. D. and Weisberg, S. (1982). *Residuals and influence in regression*. New York: Chapman and Hall.

Gumedze, F. N. and Chatora, T. D. (2014). 'Detection of outliers in longitudinal count data via overdispersion'. *Computational Statistics & Data Analysis,* 79, pp. 192-202.

Kaffine, D. T. and Davis, G. A. (2017). 'A multi-row deletion diagnostic for influential observations in small-sample regressions'. *Computational Statistics & Data Analysis*, 108, pp. 133-145.

Karagrigoriou, A., Mattheou, K. and Vonta, I. (2011). 'On asymptotic properties of AIC variants with applications'. *Open Journal of Statistics*, 1 (2), pp. 105-109.

Kitagawa, G. and Akaike, H. (1982). 'A quasi Bayesian approach to outlier detection'. *Selected Papers of Hirotugu Akaike*, Springer, pp. 347-356.

Pavlidou, M., Christoforos B. and Zioutas, G. (2018). 'Outlier detection in skewed data'. *Simulation Modelling Practice and Theory*, 87, pp. 191-209.

Vakili, K. and Schmitt, E. (2014). 'Finding multivariate outliers with FastPCS'. *Computational Statistics & Data Analysis,* 69, pp. 54-66.

A note on statistical computing with long data streams

Michal Černý, Petr Štourač [1]

Abstract. We consider the row-by-row model for data streams. That is, data points are accessed one by one, and once a data point is touched, it is dropped forever. Furthermore, we assume that the available computer memory is polynomially bounded with respect to the dimension of data but is superpolynomially smaller than the length of the stream. We build on recent theory of statistical computing in such a restricted computational model (called stream data model) and define a class $\mathfrak{S}$ of functions efficiently computable in this model. We show how the computational restrictions affect L_p-norm estimators for linear regression. It follows that computing with data streams is, in a sense, substantially different from the traditional all-data-in-memory model. We also point out some challenges for further research.

Keywords: data streams; big data; regression; computational statistics.

JEL classification: C65

1 Introduction

Statistical processing of so-called Big Data is a hot topic in the current academic literature; we refer to (Tsai et al., 2015) as a representative of many survey papers. There is no generally accepted definition of the notion 'Big Data'. Practitioners often point out, informally, that 'Big Data' is an unstructured collection of data from multiple sources (such as transaction data, personal data, web and social network data, video data, commercial data etc.) where the lack of structure makes it difficult to perform analytics. This definition is, however, hard to handle formally. In this text we follow (Hastie et al., 2009) and simply understand a data set as a matrix of numbers. We give a specific meaning to the adjective 'Big': it refers to the size of the matrix related to the size of available computer memory.

We follow the recent paper (Černý, 2019) and elaborate on more details of the computational model designed therein. Then, we derive a consequence of the theory showing that L_p-norm estimators for linear regression (as a representative of a practically extremely useful statistical procedure) behave differently in the Big Data environment compared to the 'classical' case of 'small' data.

Statistical notions, used in this text without a reference, can be found e.g. in (Pesaran, 2015). Complexity theoretic notions can be found in (Arora and Barak, 2009). Generally, this text contributes to the area of complexity-theoretic treatment of statistical procedures; see e.g. (Černý and Hladík, 2014) for another example.

2 Computational model for Narrow Big Data

As outlined previously, we formalize a dataset as a matrix $A \in \mathbb{R}^{n \times p}$. Here, n stands for the number of observations and p stands for dimension.

[1]Bboth authors: University of Economics, Prague, Department of Econometrics, Winston Churchill Square 4, CZ13067 Prague, Czech Republic, cernym@vse.cz, petrstourac@seznam.cz.

Narrow ("long") datasets. A dataset is called *narrow* (or *long*) if n is significantly larger than p. Formally we will assume that n is superpolynomial with respect to p; that is,

$$\frac{p^k}{n} \to 0 \quad \text{for every fixed } k > 0. \tag{1}$$

Computational model for narrow datasets. We assume that a computer is equipped with memory cells, each of which is capable to store a single rational number and perform traditional arithmetic operations $+, -, \times, \div, \leq$ with them. The total size of memory is measured by the number M of memory cells. We assume that there exists a polynomial π of degree at least one such that

$$M \leq \pi(p). \tag{2}$$

That is, the memory is polynomially bounded with respect to the dimension of data, but *not* with respect to the length of the dataset. (See also (Kontorovich, 2012).)

How to access data. Assumptions (1) and (2) imply the main computational restriction: *the dataset A cannot be stored in memory.* Thus it is necessary to specify how a computer can access the data. Here, streaming comes into play.

A row of matrix A is called *data point*. We assume that data points are waiting in a queue. Only the top of the queue can be accessed by a special instruction which loads the data point into memory and deletes it from the queue. (Observe that M is large enough to store a single data point.) When the queue is empty, the special instruction outputs `END`.

The streaming model more formally. The informal description from the last paragraph captures the core intuition behind data streaming: the queue formalizes the stream, we can take data points from the top of the stream into the operational memory and process them, but the memory is too small to store the entire stream. When a data point is deleted from memory (to get new free space for processing following points in the stream), it is lost forever since it has been deleted from the queue.

A more formal definition can be given in terms of *one-way Turing machines*. We define a *streaming algorithm* as a Turing machine, where the input matrix A is written down on a separate tape, *the tape is read-only and one-way*. That is, the head can only move in a single direction. Then, the operational memory of size M is formalized by another tape with M cells, which is in the standard read-write and two-way regime. The model is depicted in Figure 1.

Why is this model natural. The main restriction is in the limited access to data points — a data point can be touched only once, then it is dropped and lost forever. This is exactly the property which captures processing of data streams.

This model can be also useful in other practical situations. Consider a huge dataset (i.e., A with huge n) which is stored on an external device (such as a cloud). The available memory is able to store only a block of size M. The costly operation is putting a block into memory. If a repeated access to the same block would be prohibitive, then we have essentially the same computational model: we can put the blocks into memory one-by-one, with no allowed repetitions. It follows that streaming algorithms, as defined before, are a natural computational model for the externally-stored Big Data, too.

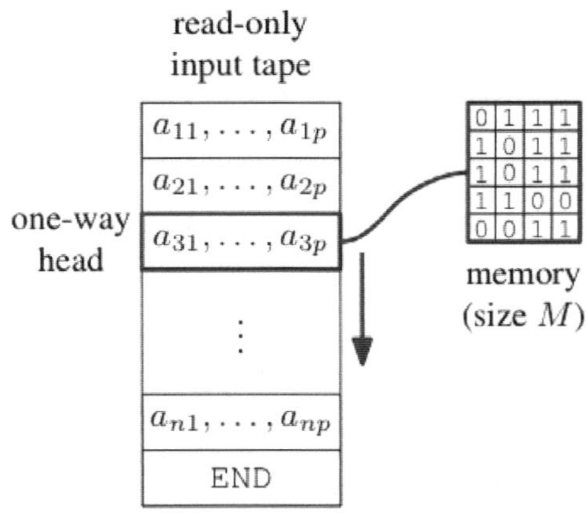

Figure 1 The stream model as a special Turing machine.

3 What can be computed in the stream data model: An easy example

Obviously, the computational model imposes serious restrictions on data analytic procedures. Some simple things are easy-to-compute. As a short example, let us assume a univariate dataset $A = (a_1, \ldots, a_n)^T$ and consider computation of the sample kurtosis

$$K = \frac{\frac{1}{n}\sum_{i=1}^{n}(a_i - \overline{a})^4}{(\frac{1}{n}\sum_{i=1}^{n}(a_i - \overline{a})^2)^2}, \tag{3}$$

where $\overline{a} = \frac{1}{n}\sum_{i=1}^{n} a_i$ is the sample arithmetic mean. This expression is not suitable for the stream model because we would need one round for computation of $\overline{a}$ and another round for computation of K (that is, each data point would have to be accessed twice and this is prohibited). But expansion of the polynomials results in an equivalent expression

$$K = \frac{s_4 - 4s_1^4 s_3 + 6s_1^2 s_2 - 3s_1^4}{(s_2 - s_1^2)^2}, \tag{4}$$

where $s_j = \frac{1}{n}\sum_{i=1}^{n} a_i^j$ with $j = 1, 2, 3, 4$. This results in a streaming algorithm in the following form:

{1} $i := 0$, $s_j := 0$ for $j = 1, 2, 3, 4$
{2} $a :=$ ReadDataPointFromStream
{3} **if** $a =$ END **then** output $\frac{s_4 - 4s_1^4 s_3 + 6s_1^2 s_2 - 3s_1^4}{(s_2 - s_1^2)^2}$ and stop
{4} $i := i + 1$
{5} $s_j := \frac{1}{i}[(i-1)s_j + a^j]$ for $j = 1, 2, 3, 4$
{6} **go to** {2}.

Remark. The structure of the algorithm resembles what is known in statistics as a *recursive procedure* (see e.g. (Cipra and Romera, 1991; Hendrych and Cipra, 2017)). However, in our case, the context is different: in recursive statistics, the task is to design new recursive procedures. Our question is: given a statistical procedure, can it be converted into a recursive procedure which produces exactly the same result?

4 Limits of computation: A surprising example

The previous section illustrated that some quantities, such as sample moments, can be easily computed by stream algorithms. The following theorem shows that some elementary quantities *cannot be computed at all.*

Theorem 1 ((Černý, 2019)). *There exists no streaming algorithm for computation of the sample median of a stream* $a_1, \ldots, a_n$.

The proof of Theorem 1 is based on Kolmogorov complexity, see (Li and Vitányi, 2008).

Theorem 1 gives an illustration of the fact that the combination of two limitations — restricted access to data $a_1, \ldots, a_n$ and restricted memory — has serious consequences. There exist some elementary quantities, such as sample quantiles, which cannot be computed *in principle.* This leads to the following definition.

Definition 1. (a) A function $f : A \mapsto \xi$, where A is a rational matrix and ξ is a rational number, is said to be *computable in stream* if there exists a streaming algorithm for f.
(b) $\mathfrak{S}$ is the class of functions computable in stream.

Comments on the definition. Formally, every statistical procedure can be formalized as a function mapping the input data A to a number ξ (which is the result of the procedure; it can be the value of a test statistic, it can be a descriptive statistic, it can be an estimate, it can be a YES/NO information whether a test rejects a hypothesis, or whatever a user can be interested in). Recall the example of sample kurtosis from Section 3, where algorithm $\{1\}$ – $\{6\}$ proved that $K \in \mathfrak{S}$. On the other hand, Theorem 1 implies that the sample median does not belong to $\mathfrak{S}$. More generally, it follows that the sample quantile function

$$Q(\alpha, a_1, \ldots, a_n) = \text{empirical } \alpha\text{-quantile of } a_1, \ldots, a_n$$

has also the property $Q \notin \mathfrak{S}$. The reason is that porоblem of computation of the sample median is a special case with $\alpha = 1/2$.

5 More on the class $\mathfrak{S}$: Regressions

We have seen that class $\mathfrak{S}$ — defined essentially by restrictions on the computational resources — is nontrivial from the statistical viewpoint, meaning that some natural functions, used commonly in data analysis, belong to $\mathfrak{S}$ and some do not. This question generalizes. So far we have considered elementary descriptive statistics only. What happens if we turn out attention to more "advanced" functions, such as regression estimators? Which of them belong to S and which do not?

Consider the traditional linear regression model (with folklore notation)

$$y_i = x_i^T\theta + \varepsilon_i, \quad i = 1, \ldots, n, \tag{5}$$

which is streamed "line-by-line", i.e.

$$A = \begin{pmatrix} x_1^T & y_1 \\ x_2^T & y_2 \\ \vdots & \vdots \\ x_n^T & y_n. \end{pmatrix}.$$

The L_2-norm (least-squares) estimator

$$\widehat{\theta}_{L_2} = \text{argmin}\,\|y - X\theta\|_2 = (X^TX)^{-1}X^Ty,$$

where X is the matrix with rows $x_1^T, \ldots, x_n^T$ and $y = (y_1, \ldots, y_n)^T$, can be computed in stream easily — the well-known Recursive Least Squares, updating $(X^TX)^{-1}$ by rank-one updates after arrival of a new data point from the stream, can be directly implemented by a stream algorithm. This shows $\widehat{\theta}_{L_2} \in \mathfrak{S}$.

But, conversely, L_1-norm estimates behave differently. Recall that the L_1-norm estimator (Least Absolute Deviations, LAD) minimizes the sum of absolute residuals:

$$\widehat{\theta}_{L_1} = \text{argmin}\,\|y - X\theta\|_1 = \text{argmin}\sum_{i=1}^{n}|y_i - x_i^T\theta|. \tag{6}$$

Theorem 2. $\widehat{\theta}_{L_1} \notin \mathfrak{S}$.

Proof. It suffices to consider the model of location

$$y_i = \theta + \varepsilon_i, \quad i = 1, \ldots, n.$$

Here, $\widehat{\theta}_{L_1}$ is the median of $y_1, \ldots, y_n$. If $\widehat{\theta}_{L_1} \in \mathfrak{S}$, then also median is in $\mathfrak{S}$. This contradicts Theorem 1. □

The stream model vs. full-memory-and-full-data-access model. Traditional approaches tacitly assume that the whole dataset can be stored in memory and that data points can be accessed repeatedly. Under such assumptions, L_1- and L_2-norm estimators for linear regression are equivalent from the complexity-theoretic viewpoint in the sense that both belong to the class $\mathfrak{P}$ of function computable in polynomial time. (Indeed, (6) can be formulated as a linear programming problem which is known to be polynomially solvable.)

Conversely, in the stream model, we have $\widehat{\theta}_{L_2} \in \mathfrak{S}$ but $\widehat{\theta}_{L_1} \notin \mathfrak{S}$. Although it might be tempting to regard $\mathfrak{S}$ as a stream analogy of $\mathfrak{P}$, we can see that the classes differ substantially.

More advanced procedures. In (Černý, 2019) it is shown that the class $\mathfrak{S}$ also contains functions formalizing "more advanced" statistical procedures, such as two-stage regressions. Generally, two-stage regressions are procedures working as follows:

(a) In the first stage, (5) is estimated using the L_2-norm estimator and residuals r are stored.
(b) In the second stage, an auxiliary dataset (X^*, y^*) is created from (X, y, r) and an auxiliary regression $y^* = X^*\theta^* + \varepsilon^*$ is estimated using the L_2-norm estimator. Then, a function of residuals from the auxiliary regression (such as the value of a goodness-of-fit statistic) is the output.

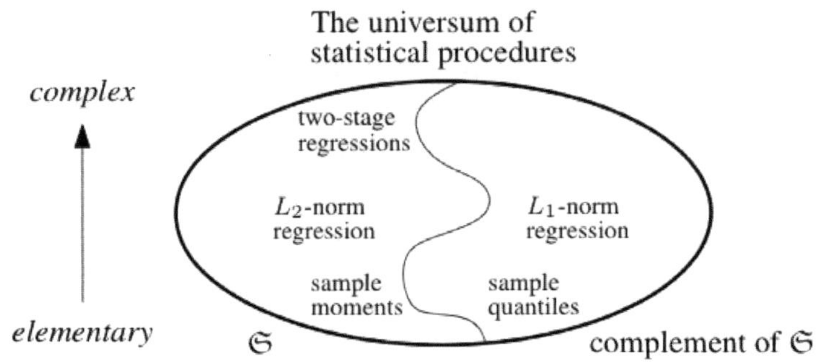

Figure 2 The universum of statistical procedures (i.e., the class of functions mapping data to rational numbers) and the class $\mathfrak{S}$.

Two important examples of two-stage regressions are White's heteroscedasticity test and Breush-Godfrey autocorrelation test, see (Pesaran, 2015).

Formulation of the problem indicates that one would need (i) to access data point multiple times (for example, data X, y enter both regressions) and (ii) one would also need memory of size proportional to n, the lenght of the stream. Indeed, just the storage of the residuals from (a) and (b) requires memory of size n. This is not allowed in the stream computing model.

Thus it might be surprising that we can overcome (i) and (ii) using a construction of a "clever" stream algorithm which requires only a small memory and works even if every data point in (X, y) is accessed only once. More formally:

Theorem 3. *((Černý, 2019)] Two-stage regressions are in* $\mathfrak{S}$.

Finally, we can summarize that the world of statistical procedures (i.e., the class of functions $A \mapsto \xi$) is split by the class $\mathfrak{S}$ into two nontrivial parts. Informally, this is visualized in Figure 2. There are two surprising facts: that the class $\mathfrak{S}$ contains complex procedures, such as two-stage regressions, and that its complement contains very elementary statistics, such as quantiles.

6 Conclusions and challenges

The question whether or not a given statistical procedure belongs to $\mathfrak{S}$ is of principial importance. Currently, there are many such procedures where the answer is unknown. For example, some max-type procedures (such as max-type changepoint tests, see (Černý, 2011) for example) seem to be too complex for stream computing. However, we do not have a formal proof. Similarly, procedures involving optimization techniques — such as maximum-likelihood methods or procedures involving linear programming (Mostafaee et al., 2016) — seem to be out of $\mathfrak{S}$, too.

A challenge is to reformulate the stream model for wide data or for big panel data. *Wide data* can be described as matrices $A \in \mathbb{R}^{n \times p}$ with $p \gg n$. Here, it is natural to assume that the matrix is supplied in a stream column-by-column. However, typical problems for such data sets, such as dimension reduction techniques, seem to be difficult for the stream data model. And panel data is a challenge even at a higher level: here, it makes sense to consider streaming in both dimensions, i.e. with respect to the time dimension and the dimension of panel units. And we could go further and consider, for example, spatial regressions (Formánek, 2019): here, the additional spatial dimension comes into play and we can study the effects of streaming in this new dimension.

Acknowledgements

The work of M. Černý was supported by the Czech Science Foundation within Project 19-02773S.

References

Arora, S. and Barak, B. (2009). *Computational Complexity: A Modern Approach.* Cambridge University Press.

Černý, M. (2011). 'Binary segmentation and Bonferroni-type bounds'. *Kybernetika*, 47 (1), pp. 38–49.

Černý, M. (2019). 'Narrow Big Data in streams: Computational limitations and regression'. *Information Sciences*, 486, pp. 379–392.

Černý, M. and Hladík, M. (2014). 'The complexity of computation and approximation of the t-ratio over one-dimensional interval data'. *Computational Statistics & Data Analysis*, 80, pp. 26–43.

Cipra, T. and Romera, R. (1991). 'Robust Kalman filter and its applications in time series analysis'. *Kybernetika*, 27, pp. 481–494.

Formánek, T. (2019). Semi-parametric spatio-temporal analysis of regional GDP growth with respect to renewable energy consumption levels. *Applied Stochastic Models in Business and Industry* (Online First), DOI:10.1002/asmb.2445.

Hastie, T., Tibshirani, R. and Friedman, J. (2009). *The Elements of Statistical Learning: Prediction, Inference and Data Mining.* Springer Verlag, New York.

Hendrych, R. and Cipra, T. (2017). 'Self-weighted recursive estimation of GARCH models'. *Communications in Statistics — Simulation and Computation*, 47 (2), pp. 315–328.

Kontorovich, L. (2012). 'Statistical estimation with bounded memory'. *Statistics & Computing*, 22 (5), pp. 1155–1164.

Li, M. and Vitányi, P. (2008). *An Introduction to Kolmogorov Complexity and Its Applications*. 3rd ed. Texts in Computer Science, Springer.

Mostafaee, A., Hladík, M. and Černý, M. (2016). 'Inverse linear programming with interval coefficients'. *Journal of Computational and Applied Mathematics*, 292, pp. 591–608.

Pesaran, M. H. (2015). *Time Series and Panel Data Econometrics.* Oxford University Press.

Tsai, C.-W., Lai, C.-F., Chao, H.-C. and Vasilakos, A. (2015). 'Big data analytics: a survey'. *Journal of Big Data*, 2 (21), pp. 1–32.

Process Petri Nets with Time Stamps and Their Subnets

Ivo Martiník[1]

Abstract. Process Petri nets with time stamps (PPNTS) are the newly introduced class of low-level Petri nets that extends the original concepts of workflow Petri nets with time stamps in the areas of modeling of generally parallel systems with the discrete time by deploying the new type of places called the resource places that is used for expressing conditions of a modeled process containing some initial resources. This article presents the definition and chosen properties of PPNTSs and in particular it introduces the concept and properties of their subnets that plays significant role in the area of analysis of static and dynamic properties of PPNTSs. With the support of these concepts the PPNTSs can be applied also in the area of the project management and the generalization of the CPM activities charts completed with the verification of their properties that is demonstrated in the simple example.

Keywords: Process Petri Nets with Time Stamps, Discrete Time, Subnet, Process Management, Proper-formed Net.

JEL Classification: C63, C88

1 Introduction

Petri nets (Diaz, 2009) is one of mathematical modeling languages for the description of all the kind of parallel systems and they represent a popular formalism connecting advantages of the graphic representation of a modeled system with the possibilities of its simulation and the formal analyzability. When studying distributed parallel programming systems, real-time systems, economic systems and many other types of systems, it plays a role modeling of the time variables associated with individual system events, the duration of the studied activities, the time history of the modeled system, and many other time characteristics. *Time Petri nets* and *timed Petri nets* (Popova-Zeugmann, 2013) are currently the two most important classes of low-level Petri nets that use the concept of discrete time in their definition. Other classes of low-level Petri nets with discrete time were introduced and discussed for instance in (Furia et al, 2012), (van Hee and Sidorova, 2013), (Martos-Salgado and Rosa-Velardo, 2014) and it can be stated that most of them use only the relative time variables usually related to the specific marking of the given Petri net. This fact can then cause difficulties, for example, in modeling complex time-synchronized distributed programming systems in which their individual components must be synchronized with the given external time source.

Workflow Petri nets (van der Alst and van Hee, 2004) were primarily introduced as the special subclass of classic low-level process Petri nets for their using in the area of workflow management. Workflow Petri Net is a continuous Petri net that includes within the set of all its places the unique input place and the unique output place. *Workflow Petri nets with time stamps* (Martiník, 2018) generalize the properties of WPN in the area of modeling of generally parallel

[1] VSB-Technical University of Ostrava, Faculty of Economics, Department of Applied Informatics, Sokolská třída 33, Ostrava, Czech Republic, ivo.martinik@vsb.cz.

systems with the discrete time. *Process Petri nets with time stamps* (PPNTS) extends the original concepts of workflow Petri nets with time stamps and their definition, introduction of the concept of their subnets and their properties are the main topics of this article.

The article is arranged into the following sections: in the section 2 the PPNTS and their main properties are described; section 3 explains the subnets of PPNTS, their selected properties are proved and the simple example of the presented concepts from the area of the project management is presented; section 5 then gives the conclusions of the research to conclude the article.

2 Process Petri nets with time stamps and their properties

Let $\boldsymbol{N}$ denotes the set of all natural numbers, $\boldsymbol{N} := \{1, 2, \ldots\}$; $\boldsymbol{N}_0$ denotes the set of all non-negative integer numbers, $\boldsymbol{N}_0 := \{0, 1, 2, \ldots\}$; $\varnothing$ denotes the empty set; $|A|$ denotes the cardinality of the given set A; $\mathscr{P}(A)$ denotes the family of all the subsets of the given set A; $A \times B := \{(x, y) \mid (x \in A) \wedge (y \in B)\}$ denotes the cartesian product of the sets A and B; $\neg$ denotes the logical negation operator; $\exists 1$ denotes "there exists at most one" statement; $f: A \rightarrow B$ denotes the function f with the domain A and the codomain B. Let $(A \subset \boldsymbol{N}_0) \wedge (\exists n \in \boldsymbol{N}: |A| = n) \wedge (A \neq \varnothing)$; then $max(A) := x$, where $(x \in A) \wedge (\forall y \in A: x \geq y)$.

Let A be the non-empty set. By the (non-empty finite) *sequence* σ over the set A we understand the function σ: $\{1, 2, \ldots, n\} \rightarrow A$, where $n \in \boldsymbol{N}$, that is denoted by $\sigma := <a_1, a_2, \ldots, a_n>$, where $a_i = \sigma(i)$ for $1 \leq i \leq n$. Function $\varepsilon: \varnothing \rightarrow A$ is called the *empty sequence* over the set A that is denoted by $\varepsilon := <>$.

Multiset M over the non-empty set S is a function $M: S \rightarrow \boldsymbol{N}_0$. The non-negative integer number $M(a) \in \boldsymbol{N}_0$, where $a \in S$, denotes the number of occurrences of the element a in the multiset M and we will say that $a \in M$ if $M(a) > 0$. The non-empty multiset M over a non-empty set S will be represented by the notation $M := [a^{M(a)}, b^{M(b)}, c^{M(c)}, \ldots]$, where $S := \{a, b, c, \ldots\}$, empty multiset M will be represented by the notation $M := \varnothing$. Notation S_{MS} then denotes the class of all the multisets over the set S.

Let $K, M \in S_{MS}$ be the multisets. Then the following is defined:

- addition of multisets: $K \oplus M := [s^{K(s) + M(s)} \mid s \in S]$;
- comparison of multisets: $K \leq M \Leftrightarrow \forall s \in S: K(s) \leq M(s)$;
- cardinality of multiset: $|M| := \sum_{s \in S} M(s)$;
- subtraction of multisets: if $K \leq M$ then $M \setminus K := [s^{M(s) - K(s)} \mid s \in S]$.

Definition 1. *Net NET* is an ordered triple $NET := (P, T, A)$, where P is finite non-empty set of the *places*, T is finite set of the *transitions*, $P \cap T = \varnothing$, and A is finite set of the *arcs*, $A \subseteq (P \times T) \cup (T \times P)$. □

Some commonly used notations for the nets are $\bullet y = \{x \mid (x, y) \in A\}$ for the *preset* and $y\bullet = \{x \mid (y, x) \in A\}$ for the *postset* of the net node y (i.e., place or transition). A *path* leading from the node x_1 to the node x_k of a net is a non-empty sequence $<x_1, x_2, \ldots, x_k>$ of net nodes, where $k \in \boldsymbol{N}$, which satisfies $(x_1, x_2), (x_2, x_3), \ldots, (x_{k-1}, x_k) \in A$. We will denote the set of all such paths of the given net NET leading from the node x_1 to the node x_k by $\boldsymbol{PATHS}_{NET}(x_1, x_k)$. Net NET is *connected* if $\boldsymbol{PATHS}_{NET}(x, y) \neq \varnothing$ for every of its pair of nodes x and y such that $x \neq y$.

Definition 2. *Process net with time stamps* (PNTS) *PNTS* is an ordered tuple *PNTS* := (*P*, *T*, *A*, *AF*, *TP*, *TI*, *IP*, *OP*, *RP*), where:

- (*P*, *T*, *A*) is the *connected net*, $\forall t \in T$: $(\bullet t \neq \emptyset) \wedge (t\bullet \neq \emptyset)$;
- *AF*: $(P \times T) \cup (T \times P) \rightarrow \mathbf{N}_0$ is the *arc function*, $AF(x, y) > 0 \Leftrightarrow (x, y) \in A$, $AF(x, y) = 0 \Leftrightarrow (x, y) \notin A$, where $x, y \in P \cup T$;
- *TP* is the *transition priority function*, *TP*: $T \rightarrow \mathbf{N}$;
- *TI*: $(T \times P) \rightarrow \mathbf{N}_0$ is the *time interval function*;
- *IP* is the *input place*, $(IP \in P) \wedge (\bullet IP = \emptyset) \wedge (\forall p \in (P \setminus \{IP\})$: $\bullet p \neq \emptyset)$;
- *OP* is the *output place*, $(OP \in P) \wedge (OP\bullet = \emptyset) \wedge (\forall p \in (P \setminus \{OP\})$: $p\bullet \neq \emptyset)$;
- *RP* is the finite set of *resource places*, $(RP \subseteq (P \setminus \{IP, OP\})) \wedge (\forall t \in T$: $\neg(\bullet t \subseteq RP))$.
- The class of all the PNTSs will be denoted by ***PNTS***. □

The connected PNTS *PNTS* contains the finite non-empty set *P* of the *places* that expresses the conditions of the modeled process and that are represented by the circles; the finite set *T* of the *transitions* that describes the changes in the modeled process and that are drawn by rectangles; the finite set *A* of the oriented *arcs* connecting the chosen place with the chosen transition or the chosen transition with the chosen place; the *arc function AF* that assigns with each arc the natural number (with the default value of 1, if not explicitly indicated in the PNTS diagram) that expresses the number of removed or added tokens from or to the place associated with that arc when firing the given transition; *transition priority function TP* that assigns with each transition the natural number that expresses its priority (with the default value of 1); the *time interval function TI* that assigns with each arc of the type (*transition*, *place*) the non-negative integer number *d* that expresses the minimum time interval during which the token has to remain in the *place* instead of being able to participate in the next firing of some transition (the value *d* associated with the respective arc is given in the format +*d* in the PNTS diagram with the default value of 0); the *input place IP* that is the only one place of the PNTS *PNTS* with no input arc(s); the *output place OP* that is the only one place of the PNTS *PNTS* with no output arc(s); the finite set *RP* of the *resource places* that is used for expressing conditions of a modeled process containing some initial resources and we use circles with the double line for their representation.

Definition 3. Let *PNTS* := (*P*, *T*, *A*, *AF*, *TP*, *TI*, *IP*, *OP*, *RP*) be the PNTS. Then:

1) *marking M* of the PNTS *PNTS* is the function *M*: $P \rightarrow (\mathbf{N}_0)_{\mathrm{MS}}$,
2) variable $\tau \in \mathbf{N}_0$ is the *net time* of the PNTS *PNTS*,
3) *state S* of the PNTS *PNTS* is an ordered pair $S := (M, \tau)$,
4) transition $t \in T$ is *enabled* in the state $S := (M, \tau)$ of the PNTS *PNTS* that is denoted by *t* **en** *S*, if $\forall p \in \bullet t\ \exists K \leq M(p)$: $(|K| = AF(p, t)) \wedge (\forall n \in K: n \leq \tau))$,
5) *firing of the transition* $t \in T$ results in changing the state $S := (M, \tau)$ of the PNTS *PNTS* into its state $S' := (M', \tau)$ that is denoted by $S\ [t\rangle\ S'$, where $\forall p \in P$: $M'(p) := (M(p) \setminus K) \oplus [(\tau + TI(t, p))^{AF(t, p)}]$,
6) *elapsing of time interval* $\delta \in \mathbf{N}$ results in changing the state $S := (M, \tau)$ of the PNTS *PNTS* into its state $S' := (M, \tau + \delta)$, where $\forall t \in T$: $\neg(t$ **en** $(M, \tau))$, that is denoted by $S\ [\delta\rangle\ S'$, so that: $(\forall t \in T\ \forall n \in \mathbf{N}, 1 \leq n < \delta$: $\neg(t$ **en** $(M, \tau + n))) \wedge (\exists t \in T$: t **en** $(M, \tau + \delta))$,

7) if $t_1, t_2, \ldots, t_n \in T$, $n \in \boldsymbol{N}$, are the transitions of the PNTS *PNTS* for which the following is valid in its state $S_1 := (M_1, \tau_1)$:
$\forall p \in (\bullet t_1 \cup \bullet t_2 \cup \ldots \cup \bullet t_n)\ \exists K \leq M(p)$: $(|K| = AF(p, t_1) + AF(p, t_2) + \ldots + AF(p, t_n))$
$\wedge\ (\forall n \in K: n \leq \tau))$,
we say that these transitions $t_1, t_2, \ldots, t_n \in T$ are *enabled in parallel* in the state S that is denoted by $\{t_1, t_2, \ldots, t_n\}$ ***en*** S,
8) finite non-empty sequence $\sigma := <t_1, t_2, \ldots, t_n>$ of the transitions $t_1, t_2, \ldots, t_n \in T$ for which the following is valid in the state $S_1 := (M_1, \tau_1)$ of the PNTS *PNTS*:
a) $(M_1, \tau_1)\ [t_1\rangle\ (M_2, \tau_1)\ [t_2\rangle \ldots [t_n\rangle\ (M_{n+1}, \tau_1)$,
b) $\forall t \in T: \neg(t\ \textbf{\textit{en}}\ (M_{n+1}, \tau_1))$,
is called *step* σ in the given state S_1 of the PNTS *PNTS* and it is denoted by
$(M_1, \tau_1)\ [\sigma\rangle\ (M_{n+1}, \tau_1)$,
9) finite non-empty sequence ρ of steps and time intervals elapsing that represents the following state changes
$(M_1, \tau_1)\ [\sigma_1\rangle\ (M_2, \tau_1)\ [\delta_1\rangle \ldots (M_{n+1}, \tau_n)\ [\delta_n\rangle\ (M_{n+1}, \tau_{n+1})$
of the PNTS *PNTS* is the sequence $\rho := <\sigma_1, \delta_1, \sigma_2, \delta_2, \ldots, \sigma_n, \delta_n>$ of the steps $\sigma_1, \sigma_2, \ldots, \sigma_n$ and the time intervals elapsing $\delta_1, \delta_2, \ldots, \delta_n$,
10) we say that the state S' of the PNTS *PNTS* is reachable from its state S if there exists the finite sequence $\rho := <\sigma_1, \delta_1, \sigma_2, \delta_2, \ldots, \sigma_n, \delta_n>$ of the steps $\sigma_1, \sigma_2, \ldots, \sigma_n$ and the time intervals elapsing $\delta_1, \delta_2, \ldots, \delta_n$ such that $S\ [\sigma_1\, \delta_1\, \sigma_2\, \delta_2 \ldots \sigma_n\, \delta_n\rangle\ S'$; the set of all the reachable states of the PNTS *PNTS* from its state S is denoted by $[S\rangle$; the set of all the finite sequences $\rho := <\sigma_1, \delta_1, \sigma_2, \delta_2, \ldots, \sigma_n, \delta_n>$ associated with all the reachable states $S' \in [S\rangle$ is denoted by $[S\rangle\rangle$, i.e.,
$[S\rangle\rangle := \{<\sigma_1, \delta_1, \sigma_2, \delta_2, \ldots, \sigma_n, \delta_n> \mid \exists S' \in [S\rangle: S\ [\sigma_1\, \delta_1\, \sigma_2\, \delta_2 \ldots \sigma_n\, \delta_n\rangle\ S', n \in \boldsymbol{N}\}$,
11) the set of all the states $S := (M, \tau)$ of the PNTS *PNTS* is denoted by $\boldsymbol{S}$,
12) the set of all the markings M associated with the set $\boldsymbol{S}$ of all the states of the PNTS *PNTS* is denoted by $\boldsymbol{M}$, i.e., $\boldsymbol{M} := \{M \mid (S = (M, \tau)) \wedge (S \in \boldsymbol{S})\}$,
13) *entry state* $S_e := (M_e, \tau_e)$ of the PNTS *PNTS* is every of its states where $(M_e(IP) \neq \emptyset) \wedge (\forall p \in (P \setminus (RP \cup \{IP\})): M_e(p) = \emptyset)$,
14) the set of all the entry states $S_e := (M_e, \tau_e)$ of the PNTS *PNTS* is denoted by $\boldsymbol{S_e}$,
15) *exit state* $S_x := (M_x, \tau_x)$ of the PNTS *PNTS* that is reachable from its entry state $S_e := (M_e, \tau_e)$ is every of its states where $(S_x \in [S_e\rangle\rangle) \wedge (|M_x(OP)| = |M_e(IP)|) \wedge (\forall p \in (P \setminus (RP \cup \{OP\})): (M_x(p) = \emptyset))$,
16) the set of all the exit states $S_x := (M_x, \tau_x)$ of the PNTS *PNTS* that are reachable from its entry state $S_e := (M_e, \tau_e)$ is denoted by $[S_e\rangle_x$,
17) the set of all the exit states S_x of the PNTS *PNTS* that are reachable from all its entry states $S_e \in \boldsymbol{S_e}$ is denoted by $\boldsymbol{S_x}$. □

Example 1. The above established concepts will be demonstrated on the simple example of the PNTS *PNT1* := (*P*, *T*, *A*, *AF*, *TP*, *TI*, *IP*, *OP*, *RP*) that is shown in Figure 1, where *P* := {**IP**, **P1**, **R1**, **OP**}; *T* := {**T1**, **T2**, **T3**}; *A* := {(**IP**, **T1**), (**IP**, **T2**), (**T1**, **P1**), (**T2**, **P1**), (**R1**, **T1**), (**T1**, **R1**), (**P1**, **T3**), (**T3**, **OP**)}; *AF* := {((**IP**, **T1**), 1), ((**IP**, **T2**), 1), ((**T1**, **P1**), 1), ((**T2**, **P1**), 1),

((**R1**, **T1**), 1), ((**T1**, **R1**), 1), ((**P1**, **T3**), 1), ((**T3**, **OP**), 1)}; TP := {(**T1**, 2), (**T2**, 1), (**T3**, 1)}; TI := {((**T1**, **P1**), 3), ((**T2**, **P1**), 3), ((**T1**, **R1**), 1), ((**T3**, **OP**), 6)}; IP := **IP**; OP := **OP**; RP := {**R1**}.

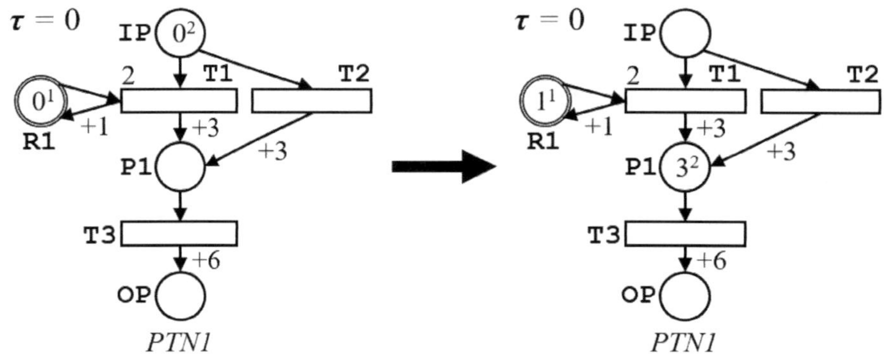

Figure 1 Firing of transitions **T1** and **T2** in PNTS *PTN1*

PNTS *PNT1* is in its entry state $S_e := (M_e, \tau_e)$, where marking $M_e := (M_e(\mathbf{IP}), M_e(\mathbf{P1}), M_e(\mathbf{R1}), M_e(\mathbf{OP})) = ([0^2], \varnothing, \varnothing, \varnothing)$, net time $\tau_e = 0$ (i.e., $\tau_e = \tau$). Marking M of any PNTS expresses the current time state of the modeled system using the time stamp associated with each of its anonymous token that occurs in any of its places in its state S. Individual values of the time stamps associated with the anonymous tokens, informally said, represent the values of the net time τ at which the respective token can first participate in the firing of selected enabled transition t of the given PNTS.

The transitions **T1** and **T2** are enabled in the entry state S_e of the PNTS *PNT1* because (see 4 of Definition 3):

- $(\mathbf{IP} \in \bullet\mathbf{T1} \wedge \exists K = [0^1] \leq [0^2] = M(\mathbf{IP})\text{: } (|[0^1]| = 1 = AF(\mathbf{IP}, \mathbf{T1})) \wedge ((\forall n \in [0^1]\text{: } n = 0 \leq 0 = \tau)) \wedge (\mathbf{R1} \in \bullet\mathbf{T1} \wedge \exists K = [0^1] \leq [0^1] = M(\mathbf{R1})\text{: } (|[0^1]| = 1 = AF(\mathbf{R1}, \mathbf{T1})) \wedge ((\forall n \in [0^1]\text{: } n = 0 \leq 0 = \tau))$;
- $\forall p \in \bullet\mathbf{T2}\ \exists K = [0^1] \leq [0^2] = M(\mathbf{IP})\text{: } (|[0^1]| = 1 = AF(\mathbf{IP}, \mathbf{T2})) \wedge ((\forall n \in [0^1]\text{: } n = 0 \leq 0 = \tau)$.

At the enabling of the transitions t_1 and t_2 of the given PNTS in its state S so called *conflict* occurs, if both transitions t_1 and t_2 have at least one common place in their presets, each of the transitions t_1 and t_2 is individually enabled in the state S, but the transitions t_1 and t_2 are not enabled in parallel in the state S (see 7 of Definition 3) and enabling of one of them will prevent enabling of the other (i.e., $(\bullet t_1 \cap \bullet t_2 \neq \varnothing) \wedge (t_1\ \textbf{\textit{en}}\ S) \wedge (t_2\ \textbf{\textit{en}}\ S) \wedge \neg(\{t_1, t_2\}\ \textbf{\textit{en}}\ S)$). The term of conflict can be obviously generalized for the case of the finite set $t_1, t_2, \ldots, t_n$, $n \in \boldsymbol{N}$, of the transitions of the given PNTS. When solving such conflict we will therefore follow the rule which determines, informally said, that from the set of transitions in conflict the one will be enabled whose value of the transition priority function TP is the highest. If such transition from the set of the transitions in conflict does not exist, the given conflict would have to be solved by other means. The same rule will be then applied for the case of the transitions $t_1, t_2, \ldots, t_n \in T$ that are enabled in parallel in the state S, i.e., if $\{t_1, t_2, \ldots, t_n\}\ \textbf{\textit{en}}\ S$ is fulfilled.

The transitions **T1** and **T2** in the entry state S_e of the PNTS *PNT1* are enabled in parallel, i.e., $\{\mathbf{T1}, \mathbf{T2}\}\ \textbf{\textit{en}}\ S_e$. When solving such case we will therefore follow the above rule. The transition **T1** is then enabled in the entry state S_e on the basis of that rule in our studied example because $TP(\mathbf{T1}) = 2 > 1 = TP(\mathbf{T2})$.

Firing of the transition **T1** changes the entry state $S_e := (M_e, \tau_e)$ of the PNTS *PNT1* into its state $S_1 := (M_1, \tau_e) = (([0^1], [3^1], [1^1], \varnothing), 0)$ (i.e., $S_e\ [\mathbf{T1}\rangle\ S_1$), where (see 5 of Definition 3):

- $M_1(\mathbf{IP}) = M_e(\mathbf{IP}) \setminus K = [0^2] \setminus [0^1] = [0^1]$;
- $M_1(\mathbf{P1}) = M_e(\mathbf{P1}) \oplus [(\tau_e + TI(\mathbf{T1}, \mathbf{P1}))^{AF(\mathbf{T1}, \mathbf{P1})}] = \varnothing \oplus [(0 + 3)^1] = [3^1]$;
- $M_1(\mathbf{R1}) = (M_e(\mathbf{R1}) \setminus K) \oplus [(\tau_e + TI(\mathbf{T1}, \mathbf{R1}))^{AF(\mathbf{T1}, \mathbf{R1})}] = ([0^1] \setminus [0^1]) \oplus [(0 + 1)^1] = [1^1]$.

Similarly, there is enabled transition **T2** in the state $S_1 := (M_1, \tau_e)$ and its firing changes the state S_1 of the PNTS *PNT1* into its state $S_2 := (M_2, \tau_e) = ((\varnothing, [3^2], [1^1], \varnothing), 0)$ (i.e., $S_1\ [\mathbf{T2}\rangle\ S_2$ - see Figure 1), where (see 5 of Definition 3):

- $M_1(\mathbf{IP}) = M_e(\mathbf{IP}) \setminus K = [0^1] \setminus [0^1] = \varnothing$;
- $M_1(\mathbf{P1}) = M_e(\mathbf{P1}) \oplus [(\tau_e + TI(\mathbf{T2}, \mathbf{P1}))^{AF(\mathbf{T2}, \mathbf{P1})}] = [3^1] \oplus [(0 + 3)^1] = [3^2]$.

There is no enabled transition in the state $S_2 := (M_2, \tau_e)$ because the tokens in the resource place **R1** can first participate in firing of the transition **T1** if the net time $\tau = 1$ and the tokens in the place **P2** can first participate in firing of the transition **T3** if the net time $\tau = 3$. So it is necessary to perform the time interval elapsing with the value of $\delta = 3$. This will change the state $S_2 := (M_2, \tau_e)$ into the state $S_3 := (M_2, \tau_1)$, where $\tau_1 := \tau_e + \delta = 3$ (i.e., $S_2\ [3\rangle\ S_3$). It can be easily verified that $S_2\ [\mathbf{T3}\rangle\ S_3$, where $S_3 := (M_3, \tau_1) = ((\varnothing, [3^1], [1^1], [9^1]), 3)$, and $S_3\ [\mathbf{T3}\rangle\ S_x$, where $S_x := (M_x, \tau_1) = ((\varnothing, \varnothing, [1^1], [9^2]), 3)$. There are no enabled transitions in the exit state $S_x := (M_x, \tau_1)$ of the PNTS *PNT1* that is reachable from its entry state $S_e := (M_e, \tau_e)$ (see 15 of Definition 3) and there is also no time interval elapsing value δ in the state S_x that enables any of the transitions.

Definition 4. Let $PNTS := (P, T, A, AF, TP, TI, IP, OP, RP)$ be the PNTS, $\boldsymbol{S_e}$ be the set of all of its entry states. Then *PNTS* is *proper-formed* PNTS if

$$\forall S_e \in \boldsymbol{S_e}: (\forall S \in [S_e\rangle\ \exists S_x \in [S_e\rangle_x: S_x \in [S\rangle) \wedge (\exists n \in \boldsymbol{N}: |[S_e\rangle\rangle| = n). \qquad \square$$

Example 2. It can be shown that the PNTS *PNT1* from Example 1 is the proper-formed PNTS. On the other hand the PNTS *PNT2* (that can be shown in Figure 2 in its entry state $S_e := (M_e, \tau_e)$) is not generally proper-formed PNTS. It is clear that the PNTS *PNT2* fulfills the condition that for any state S that is reachable from its any entry state S_e (i.e., $\forall S \in [S_e\rangle$) there exists an exit state $S_x \in [S_e\rangle_x$ such that S_x is reachable from the state S (i.e., $S_x \in [S\rangle$). In this case, however, the condition that the number of all the sequences of the states reachable from the entry state S_e is finite (i.e., $\exists n \in \boldsymbol{N}: |[S_e\rangle\rangle| = n$) is not fulfilled. It can be seen that, for instance, in the state $S \in [S_e\rangle$, $S := ((\varnothing, [1^1], \varnothing), 1)$ the sequence of the transitions **T2 T2** ... of any finite lengths can be fired and the number of all the sequences of the states that are reachable from the given entry state S_e is generally not final.

Definition 5. *Process Petri net with time stamps* (PPNTS) *PPNTS* is the ordered couple $PPNTS := (PNTS, S_e)$, where $PNTS := (P, T, A, AF, TP, TI, IP, OP, RP)$ is the PNTS and $S_e \in \boldsymbol{S_e}$ is the entry state of the PNTS *PNTS*. The class of all PPNTSs will be denoted by ***PPNTS***. $\square$

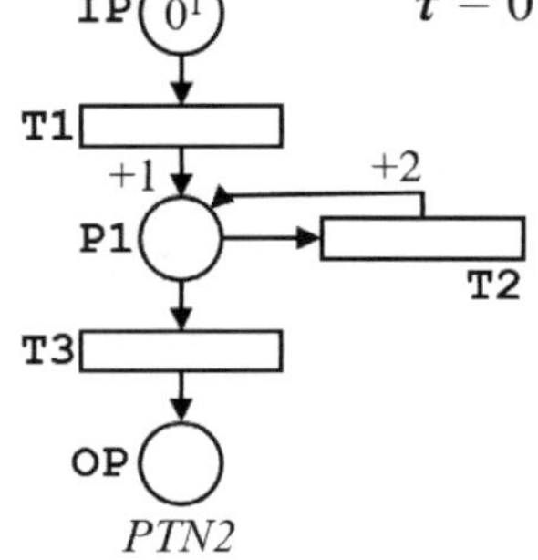

Figure 2 PNTS *PTN2*

3 Subnets of process Petri nets with time stamps and their properties

Formal introduction of the term *subnet* of a given PNTS is presented in the Definition 6.

Definition 6. Let $PNTS := (P, T, A, AF, TP, TI, IP, OP, RP)$ be the PNTS. Then we say that the PNTS $PNTS' := (P', T', A', AF', TP', TI', IP', OP', RP')$ is the subnet of the PNTS *PNTS* and we denote this fact by the statement $PNTS' :<: PNTS$ iff the PNTS *PNTS'* fulfills the following:

1) $(IP' \in P) \wedge (OP' \in P)$,
2) $((IP' \neq OP') \wedge (\forall t \in T: (IP', t) \in A) \vee (t, OP') \in A)) \Rightarrow t \in T'$,
3) $\forall t \in T': ((t, p) \in A) \vee (p, t) \in A) \Rightarrow p \in P'$,
4) $\forall p \in (P' \setminus \{IP', OP'\}): ((t, p) \in A) \vee (p, t) \in A) \Rightarrow t \in T'$,
5) $\forall (x, y) \in A: ((x \in P' \cup T') \wedge (y \in P' \cup T')) \Rightarrow (x, y) \in A'$,
6) $\forall a \in A': AF'(a) := AF(a)$,
7) $\forall t \in T': TP'(t) := TP(t)$,
8) $\forall a \in T' \times P': TI'(a) := TI(a)$. □

Remark 1. PNTS *PNTS'* is the, informally said, subnet of the PNTS *PNTS* (i.e., $PNTS' :<: PNTS$) iff the following applies:

1) the input place *IP'* and the output place *OP'* are both the elements of the set *P* of all the places of the PNTS *PNTS*,
2) if $IP' \neq OP'$ then all the transitions in the set $IP'\bullet$ within the PNTS *PNTS* and also all the transitions in the set $\bullet OP'$ within the PNTS *PNTS* are the elements of the set *T'* of all the transitions of the subnet *PNTS'*,
3) for all transitions *t* of the subnet *PNTS'* applies that all the places *p* contained within the sets $\bullet t$ and $t\bullet$ within the PNTS *PNTS* are also the elements of the set *P'* of all the places of the subnet *PNTS'*,
4) for all places *p* of the subnet *PNTS'* (with the exception of its input place *IP'* and output place *OP'*) applies that all the transitions *t* contained within the sets $\bullet p$ and $p\bullet$ within the PNTS *PNTS* are also elements of the set *T'* of all the transitions of the subnet *PNTS'*,
5) all the arcs of the PNTS *PNTS* connecting the places and transitions contained within the subnet *PNTS'* are also the arcs of the the subnet *PNTS'*,
6) all the values of the arc function *AF'* of all the arcs contained within the subnet *PNTS'* are equal to the values of the arc function *AF* of these arcs within the PNTS *PNTS*,

7) all the values of the transition priority function *TP'* of all the transitions contained within the subnet *PNTS'* are equal to the values of the transition priority function *TP* of these transitions within the PNTS *PNTS*,
8) all the values of the time interval function *TI'* of all the relevant arcs contained within the subnet *PNTS'* are equal to the values of the time interval function *TI* of these arcs within the PNTS *PNTS*.

Example 3. There are all the subnets of the PNTS *PTN1* from Example 1 in Figure 3.

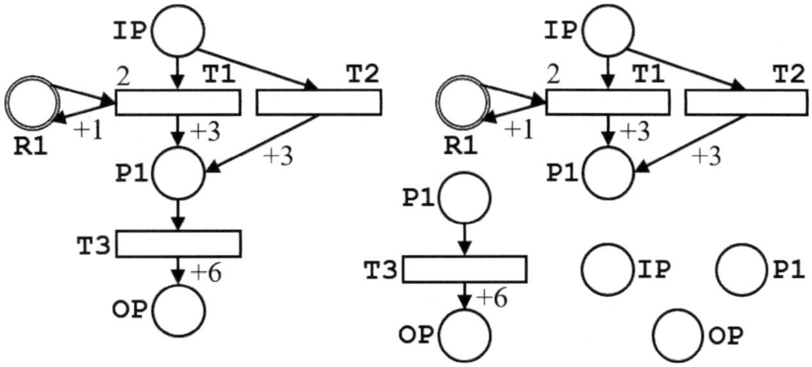

Figure 3 Subnets of PNTS *PTN1*

Lemma 1. Let $PNTS := (P, T, A, AF, TP, TI, IP, OP, RP)$ be the PNTS. Then:

1) $PNTS :<: PNTS$,
2) $\forall p \in (P \setminus RP)$: $PTSN' :<: PTSN$, where $PTSN' := (\{p\}, \emptyset, \emptyset, \emptyset, \emptyset, \emptyset, p, p, \emptyset)$; we will call such subnet *elementary*;
3) $\forall p \in (P \setminus RP)\ \forall q \in (P \setminus RP)\ \exists 1\ PNTS' :<: PNTS$: $PNTS' := (P', T', A', AF', TP', TI', p, q, RP')$; such subnet *PNTS'* will be denoted by the statement $PNTS<p, q>$.

Proof.

1) Clear, this proposition follows directly from Definition 6 and the fact that the PNTS *PNTS* is connected net (see Definition 2).
2) This proposition follows directly from Definition 6.
3) The proposition claims that there is at most one subnet *PNTS'* for any two places $p \in (P \setminus RP)$ and $q \in (P \setminus RP)$ whose input place is p and output place is q. If $p = q$ then the proposition follows directly from Definition 6. If $p \neq q$ and there exists such subnet *PNTS'* then it is necessary to prove that there does not exists another one subnet *PNTS''* with the input place p and the output place q such that $PNTS' \neq PNTS''$. We will then assume that there exist the place $r \in P''$ such that $r \notin P'$. Then, there must exist a path $<r, t_1, r_1, \ldots, r_n, t_{n+1}, p>$ within the *PNTS'* subnet. At the same time, however, $p \in P'$ (because it is the input place of the subnet *PNTS'*), $t_{n+1} \in T'$ (because $t_{n+1} \in \bullet p$), $((r_n, t_{n+1}) \in A') \vee ((t_{n+1}, p_n) \in A')$, …, $((r, t_1) \in A') \vee ((t_1, r) \in A')$, and therefore the place $r \in P'$, which is the contradiction with the assumption that $r \notin P'$. From these facts directly follows that $PNTS' = PNTS''$. □

Remark 2. There are non-elementary subnets *PTN1*<**`IP`**, **`OP`**>, *PTN1*<**`IP`**, **`P1`**>, *PTN1*<**`P1`**, **`OP`**> and elementary subnets *PTN1*<**`IP`**, **`IP`**>, *PTN1*<**`P1`**, **`P1`**>, *PTN1*<**`OP`**, **`OP`**> of the PNTS *PTN1* in Figure 3.

Lemma 2. Let *PNTS* := (*P*, *T*, *A*, *AF*, *TP*, *TI*, *IP*, *OP*, *RP*) be the PNTS, let the PNTS *PNTS'* := (*P'*, *T'*, *A'*, *AF'*, *TP'*, *TI'*, *IP'*, *OP'*, *RP'*) be any subnet of the PNTS *PNTS*, i.e., *PNTS'* :<: *PNTS*. Then

∀*PNTS'* :<: *PNTS*: *PNTS'* is proper-formed PNTS ⇒ *PNTS* is proper-formed PNTS.

Proof. Clear. From Lemma 1 directly follows that *PNTS* :<: *PNTS*. If applicable that ∀*PNTS'* :<: *PNTS*: *PNTS'* is proper-formed PNTS and at the same time we know that *PNTS* :<: *PNTS* then from these facts directly follows that *PNTS* is also proper-formed PNTS.

Remark 2. The opposite statement to Lemma 2 is not generally true, i.e., informally said, it is not true that if given *PNTS* is proper-formed PNTS then each of its subnet *PNTS'* is also proper-formed PNTS. There is proper-formed PNTS *PTN3* in Figure 4 (any token that is placed in any of its entry state S_e will always participate on the transition **`T1`** firing, because *TP*(**`T1`**) = 2, the transition **`T2`** will never be fired) whose subnet *PTN3'* := *PTN3*<**`P2`**, **`OP`**>is not proper-formed PNTS (see Example 2).

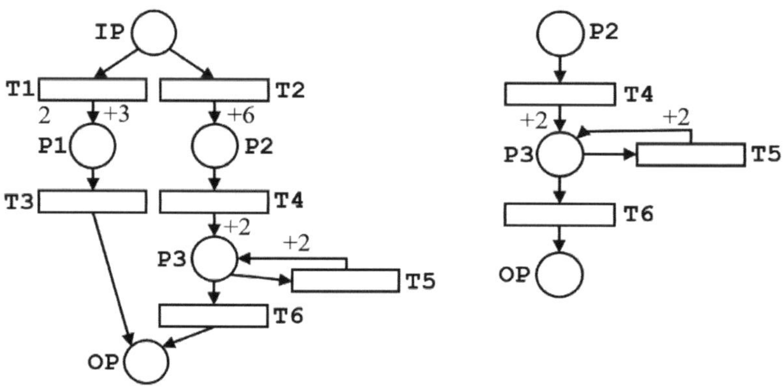

PTN3 *PTN3'*

Figure 4 PNTS *PTN3* and its subnet *PTN3'*

Example 4. Although the opposite statement to Lemma 2 is not generally true, it is often useful to analyze the properties of non-elementary subnets of the given PNTS, which is usually much less resource-intensive in the case of practical network analysis, and then prove the properties of the given PNTS as a whole that are based on the analysis of their simpler subnets. This fact will be demonstrated on the example from the project management area. Critical Path Method (CPM) is a method commonly used in project management for all the types of projects and it was developed at the end of 1950's (O'Brien and Plotnick, 2016). The CPM is designed to analyze the time-consuming of only projects where the duration of each of their activities including all their sub-activities is known (including the cases when it is uncertain). The basis for using CPM is to create a project model that includes the list of all its activities, the time duration of each activity that is constant and the dependencies between the project activities. The theory of PNTSs can be successfully applied especially to modeling processes and also determining their critical paths. An example of a simple process will be presented in the following paragraphs the property of proper-formed PNTS of which will be studied with using of the theory of PNTS subnets. The above mentioned process is described in the following table of its activities (see Table 1):

Activity	Duration time	Previous activities
A	8	-
B	1	F
C	3	-
D	3	C
E	2	A
F	5	G
G	6	B, D
H	4	C
I	9	G, H

Table 1 Table of activities, their time durations and dependencies of studied process

The PNTS *PTN4* that represents the process comprising the activities listed in Table 1 can be seen in Figure 5. The places **A**, **B**, **C**, **D**, **E**, **F**, **G**, **H** and **I** of the PNTS *PTN4* represent individual activities of the studied process, the appropriate values of the time interval function *TI* then express the time durations of relevant activities (i.e., for instance, the activity A is represented by the place **A** and its time duration is represented by the value of *TI*(**T1**, **A**) = 8, etc.). There are also presented all the non-elementary subnets of the PNTS *PTN4* in Figure 5, i.e., the subnets *PTN4*<**IP**, **OP**>, *PTN4*<**A**, **E**> and *PTN4*<**P1**, **I**>. It is clear that the subnet *PTN4*<**A**, **E**> is proper-formed PNTS. It is also immediately clear that the subnet *PTN4*<**P1**, **I**> is not proper-formed PNTS, because the transition **T2** will not be fired in any of its input states $S_e \in \boldsymbol{S_e}$ (because there will be no one token in the place **F** in any of its input states $S_e \in \boldsymbol{S_e}$). Based on these fact it is then trivial to show that the whole PNTS *PTN4* is also not proper-formed PNTS without the necessity of any detailed analysis of its properties.

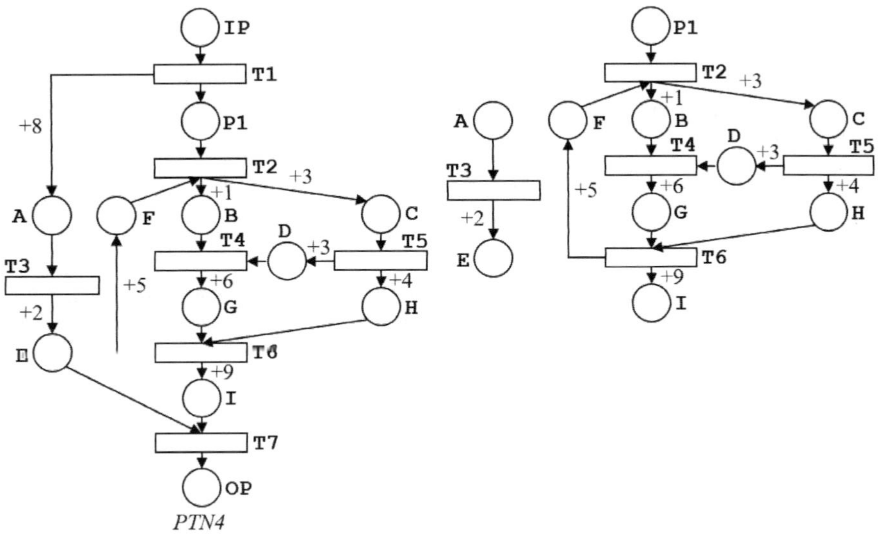

Figure 5 PNTS *PTN4* and its subnets *PTN4*<**A**, **E**> and *PTN4*<**P1**, **I**>

4 Conclusions

Further research in the field of PNTSs and their subnets is mainly focused into the area of PNTS synthesis with the support of *property-preserving Petri net process algebras* (PPPA) (Huang et al, 2012). PPPA does not need to verify composition of Petri net processes represented by PNTSs because all their algebraic operators preserve the specified set of the properties. Hence, if the source PNTSs satisfy the desirable properties, each of the composite PNTS, including the PNTS that models the resulting system itself, also satisfies these properties. These original PPPA can be then successfully generalized for the class of the PNTS (Martiník, 2018). When defining new types of PPPA unary, binary and *n*-ary algebraic operators above the PNTS class and proving their properties, the knowledge about subnets of PNTSs and their properties is strongly applied.

Acknowledgements

This paper was supported by SGS project No. SP2017/144 and also within Operational Programme Education for Competitiveness - Project No. CZ.1.07/2.3.00/20.0296.

References

van der Alst, W. and van Hee, K. (2004). *Workflow Management: Models, Methods and Systems*. Massachusetts: MIT Press.

Diaz, M. (2009). *Petri Nets: Fundamental Models, Verification and Applications*. London: John Willey & Sons.

Furia, C. A., Mandrioli, D., Morzenti, A. and Rossi, M. (2012). *Modeling Time in Computing*. Heidelberg: Springer-Verlag.

van Hee, K. and Sidorova, N. (2013). 'The Right Timing: Reflections on the Modeling and Analysis of Time'. *Application and Theory of Petri Nets and Concurrency 2013*, *Lecture Notes in Computer Science*, 7927, pp. 1-20.

Huang, H., Jiao, L., Cheung, T. and Mak, W., M. (2012). *Property-Preserving Petri Net Process Algebra In Software Engineering*. Singapore: World Scientific Publishing.

Martiník, I. (2018). 'Workflow Petri Nets with Time Stamps and Their Using in Project Management'. *Computer Information Systems and Industrial Management. Lecture Notes in Computer Science*, 11127. pp. 193-206.

Martos-Salgado, M. and Rosa-Velardo, F. (2014). 'Dynamic Networks of Timed Petri Nets'. Ciardo, G., Kindler, E. (eds.) *Application and Theory of Petri Nets and Concurrency 2014*, *Lecture Notes in Computer Science*, 8489, pp. 294-313.

O'Brien, J., J. and Plotnick, F., L. (2016). *CPM in Construction Management*. 8th ed. New York: McGraw-Hill.

Popova-Zeugmann, L. (2013). *Time and Petri Nets*. Heidelberg: Springer-Verlag.

Comparison of Selected Aspects of DAX and SQL

Vítězslav Novák[1]

Abstract. Data Analysis Expressions (DAX) and Structured Query Language (SQL) are not languages of the same type. SQL is a declarative language, whereas DAX is a functional language. They are not even used by the same tools. Yet many similar features can be found among them. For example, working with tables and their columns, the option of querying including features such as table join types or aggregation functions. The aim of this paper is not only to present a relatively young language – DAX, but primarily trying to compare it with SQL, which can help to clarify many interesting features of both languages.

Keywords: DAX, SQL, business intelligence, data model.

JEL Classification: A23, M15

1 Introduction

This paper aims to compare Data Analysis Expressions (DAX) and Structured Query Language (SQL) both in terms of the principles used by both languages and in terms of the speed of query execution over large amounts of data. Both languages use a data model consisting of tables and columns, so their comparison is possible. According to Microsoft (2019a), DAX is a library of functions and operators that can be combined to build formulas and expressions in Microsoft SQL Server Analysis Services, Power Pivot in Excel, and Power BI Desktop, especially in business intelligence solutions. According to Groff and Weinberg (2009), on the other hand, SQL is a tool for organizing, managing, and retrieving data from a relational database. SQL language has a much wider scope, which is obvious from the definition of both languages. The only purpose of DAX is to obtain data, whereas the purpose of SQL is also to organize and manage the data. To compare these languages, we will focus mainly on SELECT statement in SQL.

DAX is a relatively young language. As stated by Russo and Ferrari (2015), DAX appeared for the first time in 2010 with the first release of Power Pivot for Excel. Microsoft patented DAX as the US patent number 9,275,031 in 2009 (Dickerman, 2009), the second additional patent was filed in 2016 as the US patent number 9,665,555 (Dickerman, 2016). According to these patents DAX may empower people familiar with existing spreadsheet applications to perform multi-dimensional data analysis and data analysis with respect to relational data models (e.g., within existing spreadsheet applications). Unlike conventional spreadsheet formulae, a DAX beneficially is independent of particular cell ranges of the spreadsheet.

On the other hand, SQL is a relatively old language; its development started in the 1970s, but it is still not outdated. As written by Němec and Zapletal (2017), the traditional relational databases slowly lose their dominant place, mainly due to inherent limits in context of pro-

[1] VŠB - Technical university of Ostrava/Faculty of Economics, Department of Applied Informatics, Sokolská třída 33, 701 21 Ostrava 1, vitezslav.novak@vsb.cz.

cessing complex data that originate, nevertheless, SQL language stays as a still popular language for the data access and manipulation, even if we need to work with the unstructured content during the data analysis.

Because DAX and SQL serve a similar purpose, they have many similar features. Despite the fact that typology refers to SQL as a declarative language, whereas DAX is a functional programming language, according to Microsoft (2015), functional programming is only a form of declarative programming.

The most important common feature is, however, working with a data model consisting of tables and their columns, the option of querying even with large number of tables, including features such as table join types or aggregation functions. However, there is one significant difference here. SQL uses relational database schema, whereas data models used by DAX use a database engine called VertiPaq, which according to Russo and Ferrari (2015) is in-memory columnar database. Column databases rank according to Holubová, Kosek, Minařík and Novák (2015) among the NoSQL databases.

For these reasons, it may be interesting to compare similar features of these two languages, which may lead to their better understanding. The following chapters will introduce selected aspects of DAX and SQL and aim to compare them. A comparison of selected DAX and SQL features will be demonstrated on the following data model and data representing a very simple star diagram, where the Order table presents the fact table and the Date and Product tables represent dimension tables, see Figure 1.

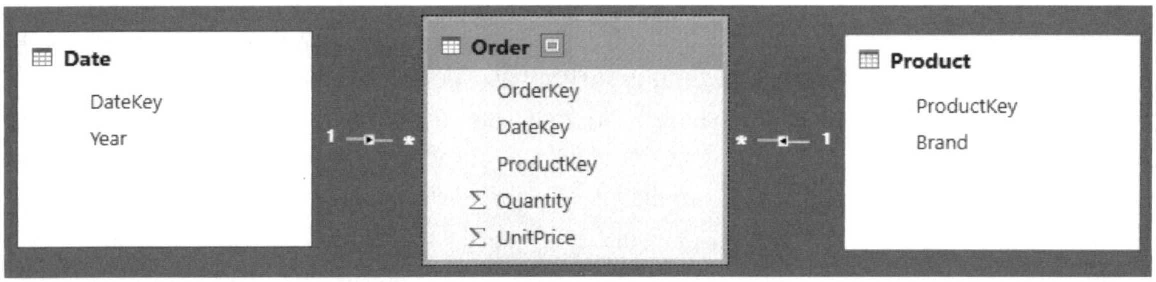

DateKey	Year
D1	2001
D2	2002
D3	2003
D4	2004

OrderKey	DateKey	ProductKey	Quantity	UnitPrice
O1	D1	P1	1	10 Kč
O2	D1	P2	2	20 Kč
O3	D2	P1	3	30 Kč
O4	D3	P3	4	40 Kč

ProductKey	Brand
P1	Apple
P2	Nokia
P3	Samsung
P4	Sony

Figure 1 Test data model and data

To demonstrate some of the DAX and SQL features, it should be noted that in the example above, not all records in dimension tables have related records in the fact table.

2 Relationships between tables

If the data model contains multiple tables, they are usually joined by relationships. In DAX, according to Russo and Ferrari (2017), relationships always have 1:N cardinality and, in addition to that, only consists of one column. The following chapters describe significant differences in the implementation of relationships in DAX and SQL.

2.1 Types of joins

According to the SQL standard for FROM clause of the SELECT statement, tables can be joined by one of several join types. INNER JOIN or LEFT OUTER JOIN are the most common ones. The difference in these two types of joins is that INNER JOIN selects from joined tables only those records with the same values in the joining columns. If a record in one table does not have a matching record in the joined table, it is not selected in the resulting set of records. LEFT OUTER JOIN, on the other hand, always selects all the records from the left table and their matching records from the right table.
According to Russo and Ferrari (2015), however, DAX only knows the LEFT OUTER JOIN. The following table compares SQL and DAX statements, which should determine the sum of quantities for each year while achieving the same result:

SQL

```
SELECT
    [Date].[Year],
    SUM([Order].[Quantity]) AS
SumOfQuantity
FROM
    [Date] LEFT OUTER JOIN [Order]
    ON [Date].[DateKey] = [Or-
der].[DateKey]
GROUP BY
    [Date].[Year]
```

	Year	SumOfQuantity
1	2001	3
2	2002	3
3	2003	4
4	2004	NULL

DAX

```
SumOfQuantity = SUMMARIZE(
    'Date';
    'Date'[Year];
    "SumOfQuantity";
    SUM('Order'[Quantity])
)
```

Year	SumOfQuantity
2001	3
2002	3
2003	4
2004	

Table 1 Example of table joins

According to Microsoft (1019b), the SUMMARIZE function in DAX used in the example above is a table function that returns a summary table for the required sums in group sets. DAX as well as SQL allows you to use both scalar (returning one value) and table (returning the entire table) functions.

As you can see in the example, the same result in both languages is achieved using the LEFT OUTER JOIN in SQL. Although the DAX expression above is made by calling the SUMMARIZE function (DAX is a functional language), there are many parts of the SQL SELECT statement such as an aggregated column or a column from the GROUP BY clause. What cannot be found here, however, is the explicit identification of table join – the primary and foreign key and the type of the join. Table names are mentioned in column names; relationships, including primary and foreign keys, are given by the data model; the only join type is LEFT OUTER JOIN, and this is why the type of join as well as the primary and foreign key are not needed to be (and even cannot be) explicitly stated in the DAX expressions.

However, if the data model contains tables without relationships, these tables can be joined using a function that replace the relationship. These functions include:

- NATURALINNERJOIN (requires a column of the same name and type in joined tables),
- NATURALLEFTOUTERJOIN (requires a column of the same name and type in the joined tables),
- CROSSJOIN – creates a Cartesian product of any two tables.

According to SQLBI (2019), an inner join, for example, can be created between non-relational tables and columns with the same name and data type, see Table 2 with an example of DAX equivalent in SQL:

SQL	DAX

`SELECT`
`    *`
`FROM`
`    [a] INNER JOIN [b]`
`    ON [a].[keyA] = [b].[keyB]`
	`FILTER (`
	`    CROSSJOIN (a, b),`
	`    a[key] = b[key]`
	`)`

Table 2 Example of creating an inner join using CROSSJOIN function

Such way of joining table is, however, not as effective as when relationships between tables are part of a data model.

2.2 Direction of a relationship

Unlike SQL, the DAX also addresses direction of the relationship. The direction determines the direction of filter propagation between tables. In the data model, the unidirectional relationship is graphically expressed by one arrow a and bidirectional relationship by a double arrow. The default direction of the relationship in DAX is unidirectional, always from the table on 1 side to the table on N side. This means that the filter is always propagated from the table on 1 side to the table on N side. It is not propagated from the table on N side to the table on 1 side, so if any field from this table is used in a pivot table, all its rows will be used. However, if the relationship is bidirectional, the filter is also propagated from the table on N side to the table on 1 side (see Table 2).

The direction of the relationship can be demonstrated on the example of a pivot table that should display the total quantity and number of brands per year.

Unidirectional relationship

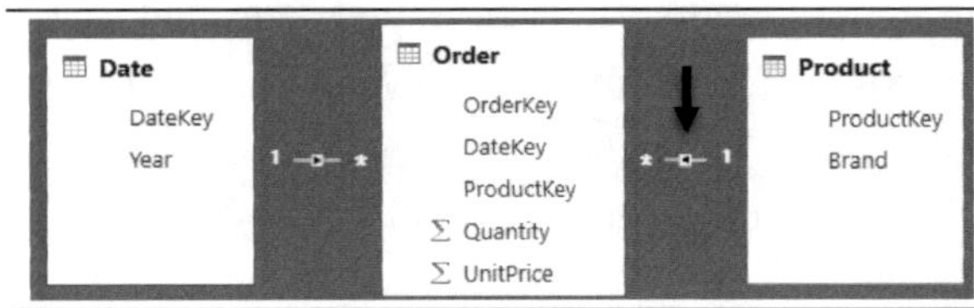

Year	Quantity	Počet pro: Brand
2001	3	4
2002	3	4
2003	4	4
2004		4
Celkem	**10**	**4**

Bidirectional relationship

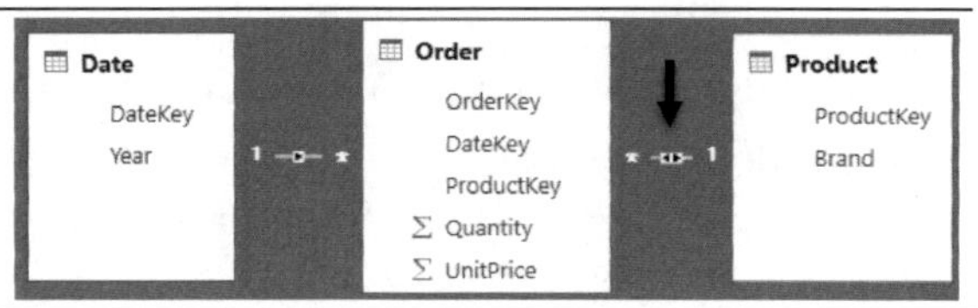

Year	Quantity	Počet pro: Brand
2001	3	2
2002	3	1
2003	4	1
Celkem	**10**	**4**

Table 3 Comparison of unidirectional and bidirectional relationship

In this example, data in rows is filtered by individual years. When using a unidirectional relationship between the Order and Product tables, the filter cannot be propagated against the direction of this relationship, so the number of product's brands is not filtered, and we see the total number of brands for each line. However, if the relationship is bidirectional, the filter may also be propagated in the direction to the Product table, so the number of products per year will be correct. In this sense, relationships in SQL appear to be bidirectional.

Power Pivot allows you to use only unidirectional relationships.

3 Calculations

If data is stored in normalized tables, they do not contain fields that can be calculated from other fields. The reason for that is both saving space on the storage medium and obtaining the actual calculated values from the input values without the need for changing the calculated values whenever the input values change. New columns can be so calculated from existing columns and aggregate values from values stored in multiple table rows.

3.1 Calculated fields

Referencing table fields is very similar in both SQL and DAX. Field names are in square brackets; the table names in SQL are also in square brackets, while in DAX they are in apostrophes, see the example of calculating order cost in the following table:

SQL	DAX
`[Order].[Quantity]*[Order].[UnitPrice] AS OrderPrice`	`OrderPrice = 'Order'[Quantity]*'Order'[UnitPrice]`

Table 4 Example of calculated field

In both languages, it is also true that both square brackets and apostrophes can be omitted if the name does not contain spaces or is not a reserved word of the language.

Although the calculated SQL and DAX fields are very similar, one concept is quite different. Calculated SQL values are computed at the time of query execution and are not stored, whereas calculated DAX values are computed at the time of table creation and are stored in memory, see Russo and Ferrari (2015). The advantage of this approach is faster execution of queries because there is no need to compute the calculated values when the query is executed.

3.2 Totals

The purpose of totals is to calculate an aggregate value from several values of one field. This is why aggregation functions are used. What is in SQL known as a total is in DAX called a measure. According to Laurenčík (2017), the term "measure" in DAX means the total used, for example, in Excel pivot table. The measures are implicit and explicit. The implicit measure is the total created in the above-mentioned pivot table by dragging a field to a values range. The subject of this paper is, however, explicit measures as they are created in DAX.

Aggregation functions of SQL and DAX are similar, but in DAX, it can be seen that its aggregation functions are more Excel-based, probably because they were first used in Power Pivot add-in for Excel. For example, instead of the SQL function of AVG it uses the AVERAGE function; the COUNT in SQL calculates the number of values in a column of any data type, whereas DAX COUNT, similarly to Excel, counts only the number of numeric values and like Excel uses the COUNTA function to count values in a column of any data type. Calculating the number of rows in a table is also solved in both languages: in SQL, the COUNT (*) expression must be used, whereas COUNTROWS is reserved for this purpose in DAX. The following table shows how to calculate the number of rows in a table using both SQL and DAX:

SQL	DAX

`SELECT`
`    COUNT(*) AS NumberOfRows`
`FROM`
`    [Order]`
	`NumberOfRows = COUNTROWS('Order')`

Table 5 Example of sum (measure)

If the SQL total needs to be divided into several groups, the GROUP BY clause is used for this purpose. There is no such thing in DAX. The breakdown of DAX measure into several groups will automatically occur in the pivot table, in which the measure is used. If the measure is placed in a range of values in the pivot table, and no field is placed in the row or column area, a single summary value is created for all rows of the table. However, if a field is added to a row or column area, the measure is automatically grouped into as many values as the field contains in the row or column area. Although the measure is the same expression in all cells of the pivot table, a filtering context is applied to this expression, which is given not only by fields in rows and columns areas, but also by the field in filters' area and the slicers used so that a different value may be in each cell of the pivot table.

DAX measures are always scalar. However, if the result of your query is not only an aggregate value but a table that contains aggregate values similar to using a SELECT SQL statement with aggregation functions, instead of measure, the appropriate table function such as the SUMMARIZE may be used in DAX (see example in Table 1).

4 Filtering

Filtering is a very important part of executing queries because we do not want to use all table records every time. The clause WHERE or HAVING is then used in the SQL SELECT statement, depending on whether filtering should occur before or after grouping rows.

As the DAX language is functional, functions are also used for filtering. The basic DAX function for filtering is FILTER. The FILTER function is a table function and is so often used as a parameter in other functions that require a table. Such table may again be the FILTER function, which leads to a nested function. The meaning of nesting can be the chaining of several filters using a logical product. The following table shows the filtering using two conditions associated with the logical sum. The logical sum of the two conditions can also be performed in the DAX using the AND function.

SQL	DAX

`SELECT`
`    *`
`FROM`
	`FILTER(`
	`    'Order';`
	`    AND(`

```
    [Order]
WHERE
    [Order].[UnitPrice]>10
AND
    [Order].[Quantity]<4
```

```
        'Order'[UnitPrice]>10;
        'Order'[Quantity]<4
    )
)
```

```
SELECT
    *
FROM
    (SELECT
        *
    FROM
        [Order]
    WHERE
        [Order].[UnitPrice]>10) AS
Filter1
WHERE
    [Filter1].[Quantity]<4
```

```
FILTER(
    FILTER(
        'Order';
        'Order'[UnitPrice]>10
    );
    'Order'[Quantity]<4
)
```

	OrderKey	DateKey	ProductKey	Quantity	UnitPrice
1	O2	D1	P2	2	20,00
2	O3	D2	P1	3	30,00

OrderKey	DateKey	ProductKey	Quantity	UnitPrice
O2	D1	P2	2	20 Kč
O3	D2	P1	3	30 Kč

Table 6 Example of filtering

As you can see from the example, filter nesting can also be understood as using SQL subqueries. However, all of the examples above return the same result. Using one or the other method of solution can only optimize the execution speed of filtering.

5 Query Performance Comparison

Due to the fact that DAX is used, among other things, over data stored in the in-memory columnar database, and calculated fields are computed and stored at the time of creating the table, while in SQL, the data is stored in relational database and calculated fields are computed at the time of query execution, it is hypothesized that a query executed over the same database will be performed much faster with DAX than with a SQL SELECT statement.

Query performance measurement was performed over a two-table data model: a dimension table with only 10 records and a fact table containing 1,000,000 records. The aim of the queries was to find out:

- total sum of values in the column of values in the fact table (query over one table),
- total sum of values obtained by calculating a field from fact and dimension tables for each value of the dimension table (query over two tables joined by relationship with calculated field).

Speed of the query execution was measured in Power Pivot (DAX) and SQL Server (SQL SELECT statement). It is clear from the measured results that if the queries do not use the joins of tables and calculated fields, the execution speed is similar in both of these languages. However, if a query uses table joins and computed fields using multiple tables to calculate fields, the execution speed of the SQL query begins to drop significantly, while the DAX query execution rate drops only slightly, which confirms the hypothesis defined above.

6 Conclusion

This paper aimed to compare the following two languages: SQL (namely its SELECT statement) and DAX. This comparison is possible because both languages in principle work with data models consisting of tables and their relationships, and it does not really matter that SQL uses a relational database schema whereas DAX a column database schema. It also does not matter much that SQL is a declarative while the DAX is a functional language. The paper shows that these languages share many similar features.

If there, however, is a question of which language knowledge it would be preferable to have first, then it would be the knowledge of SQL SELECT statement because DAX already uses all of its attributes in some way. These attributes include features such table joins, calculated fields or filtering. The DAX develops these attributes further, for example, both in the form of unidirectional relationships and the filtering context. In addition, as a functional language, DAX adds a tremendous amount of functions that performs both tasks usual in Excel such as new value calculation and tasks for less common functions such as data filtering or table joining.

Also, in the area of speed of queries processing over large amounts of data using multiple tables and calculated fields, DAX seems to greatly overcome the SELECT statement of SQL, which is mainly due to the used database scheme (in memory columnar database) and the storage of calculated fields in the DAX language.

We have, however, compared the DAX with only one SQL statement – SELECT. The SQL is much more elaborate language. Apart from the SELECT statement and data manipulation statements in general, SQL also includes data definition and transaction control statements. As far as these are concerned, SQL and DAX languages are, of course, incomparable because DAX does not cover them at all. DAX's purpose is to perform calculations in business intelligence solutions, so it focuses only on querying and related tasks.

References

Dickerman, H. J. et al. Pat. No. 9,275,031 United States, 2009.

Dickerman, H. J. et al. Pat. No. 9,665,555 United States, 2016.

Groff, J. R. and Weinberg, P. N. (2009). *SQL: The Complete Reference,* 3rd ed. New York: McGraw-Hill Education.

Holubová, I., Kosek, J., Minařík, K. and Novák, D. (2015). *Big Data a NoSQL databáze*. Praha: Grada.

Laurenčík, M. (2017). *Excel 2016: práce s databázemi a kontingenčními tabulkami*. Praha: Grada.

Microsoft (2015). Functional Programming vs. Imperative Programming, [Online]. Available at: https://docs.microsoft.com/en-us/dotnet/csharp/programming-guide/concepts/linq/functional-programming-vs-imperative-programming [cited 2019-03-15].

Microsoft (2019a). Data Analysis Expressions (DAX) Reference, [Online]. Available at: https://msdn.microsoft.com/en-us/query-bi/dax/data-analysis-expressions-dax-reference [cited 2019-03-01].

Microsoft (2019b). SUMMARIZE Function (DAX), [Online]. Available at: https://msdn.microsoft.com/en-us/query-bi/dax/summarize-function-dax [cited 2019-03-20].

Němec, R. and Zapletal, F. (2017). 'On the determination of query execution patterns of the application of the Anchor Data modeling method using machine-learning methods'. *Proceedings of the 12th International Conference on Strategic Management and its Support by Information Systems*, Ostrava, Czech Republic, pp. 55.

Russo, M. and Ferrari, A. (2015). *The Definitive Guide to DAX: Business Intelligence with Microsoft Excel, SQL Server Analysis Services and Power BI*. Redmond: Microsoft Press.

Russo, M. and Ferrari, A. (2017). *Analyzing Data with Microsoft Power BI and Power Pivot for Excel*. Redmond: Microsoft Press.

SQLBI (2019). From SQL to DAX: Joining Tables, [Online]. Available at: https://www.sqlbi.com/articles/from-sql-to-dax-joining-tables/ [cited 2019-04-15].

A comparison of technical efficiency between Spanish and Czech schools based on a stochastic meta-frontier production function

Petr Seďa[1], José Carlos Casas-Rosal [2], Rafaela Dios-Palomares [3], Carmen León-Mantero[4], Orlando Arencibia Montero [5], Juan Antonio Jimber del Río [6]

Abstract. The publication of the results of the last edition of the Programme for International Student Assessment report (PISA) in 2015 has underlined a great equality between the values obtained by Spain and the Czech Republic. However, while Spain slightly worsened in Science and improved in Mathematics and Reading, the Czech Republic, with traditionally better result, fell in all areas, balancing the results of both countries. The aim of the present paper is to examine the observed differences in students' test performance across Spain and Czech Republic schools. For this purpose, we consider that education is a multi-input production process subject to inefficient behaviour, which can be identified at school level using a parametric stochastic distance function approach. We use a two-step method. First, two stochastic frontier production functions are approached to estimate technical efficiency (TE) scores for schools in each country and second, a stochastic meta-frontier production function is approached to calculate comparable TE measures in order to estimate the gap between countries and the contributing factors.

Keywords: Czech Republic, Meta-frontier, PISA, Spain, Technical efficiency.

JEL Classification: D24, I20

1 Introduction

The Programme for International Student Assessment (PISA) evaluates the knowledge and skills in the areas of reading comprehension, mathematics and problem solving and comprehension of scientific texts, of international secondary students.

Various researches have analyzed the results obtained in different editions of this report. These studies showed that the aspects that influence our students performance are not only those related to school environment, but also personal and family environment (Cordero, Crespo and Pedraja, 2011; Dobrota, Jeremic and Bujajic, 2015; Mancebon, Calero and Choi, 2012). That

[1] VSB-Technical University of Ostrava, Faculty of Economics, Department of Mathematical Methods in Economics, Sokolská třída 33, 702 00 Ostrava 1, Czech Republic, petr.seda@vsb.cz
[2] University of Cordoba, Department of Statistics and Econometrics, C.P. 14002, Plaza Nueva S/N, 14071 Córdoba, Spain, jcasas@uco.es
[3] University of Cordoba, Department of Statistics and Econometrics, C.P. 14002, Plaza Nueva S/N, 14071 Córdoba, Spain, ma1dipar@uco.es
[4] University of Cordoba, Department of Mathematics, Avda. San Alberto Magno s/n, E-14071 Cordoba, Spain, cmleon@uco.es
[5] VSB-Technical University of Ostrava, Faculty of Economics, Department of Mathematical Methods in Economics, Sokolská třída 33, 702 00 Ostrava 1, Czech Republic, orlando.arencibia@vsb.cz
[6] University of Cordoba, Department of Agricultural Economics, C.P. 14002, Plaza Nueva S/N, 14071 Córdoba, Spain, jjimber@uco.es

is why, the PISA report also takes students' variables of social, cultural and economic context into account, as well as variables of the educational centers and the respective countries.

PISA studies have looked for factors that explain the results and contributing ideas for improvement. For example, Marchesi (2006) proposed to encourage aspects such as student confidence, a greater involvement of families in the educational process, inclusion of reading times or maintaining educational equity. Moreover, Martínez (2013) considered factors of incidence such as youth unemployment, high level of demand of the education system or the educational level of the family.

The review carried out by Cordero, Crespo and Pedraja (2013) determined that the research carried out in the area of the economics of education show that, independently of the analysis methodology used, variables of socioeconomic type, such as repetition of a course, concentration of immigrants or the socioeconomic level of families are factors that influence school performance.

The results obtained in the latest edition of PISA (2015) showed an improvement of Spanish students in Mathematics and Reading, and a slight drop in Science, equaling with students from the Czech Republic, whose results worsened in this last evaluation.

This paper has two main objectives. Firstly, to analyze the efficiency of the Spanish and Czech educational systems, as well as the factors on which they may depend, by estimating two stochastic production frontiers with output orientation and taking the result of PISA evaluation of 2015 (Aigner, Lovell and Smith, 1977; Meeusen and Van Den Broeck, 1977). Secondly, to study the existence of a gap between both systems through the estimation of a stochastic meta-frontier of production common to both (Huang, Huang and Liu, 2014).

Next, the Spanish and Czech educational systems will be briefly described. The following section will describe the methods used in the two phases of the work, based on the proposal by Huang, Huang, and Liu (2014). In the results section, the main results obtained will be shown, and, finally, some conclusions and comments will be delivered.

2 Educational Systems of Both Countries

In this section, the educational systems of Spain and Czech Republic will be briefly depicted. Our attention will be focused just on basic information about structures of educational system of the both countries.

2.1 Spanish educational system

The new educational legislation in Spain was completely introduced in Spain in 2016/2017 academic year (Organic Law 8/2013). This reform tries to supply the deficiencies detected in the previous model and cover the new needs that have arisen. The main objective of this improvement law is the efficiency of costs in education, teaching performance and educational offer improvement, school dropout reduction; scholarships in high school and university students' optimization; foreign language learning promotion and ICT etc.

Among the main characteristics of this educational system, we found the decentralization of educational competences. In this sense, although the central government regulates the general guidelines for the entire national territory, the regional ministries manage and administer the educational system in their autonomous region. On the other hand, schools, with the entire educational community participation, have their own capacity of organization, administration and concretion of the study program.

This is organized into stages, courses and levels of education that encompasses pre-school education (6 academic years, up to 6 years of age), primary (6 courses), compulsory secondary (4 courses), high school (2 courses), professional training, language, art, sports, adult and university education (Organic Law 2/2006). It is also a free system from the second cycle of infant education to the level that occupies us in this work, the compulsory secondary.

Together with primary education, this educational stage revolves around the development of key competences. It is intended that students:

- will reach basic knowledge in humanities, arts, sciences and technology fields;
- will acquire good study and work practices;
- will be prepared to access higher education and be able to face their obligations as citizens.

2.2 Czech educational system

The Ministry of Education, Youth and Sports is the responsible body for the education system administration. However, similar to the Spanish case, the regions and municipalities are responsible for administering secondary and basic schools, respectively, which provides them greater autonomy (Santiago et al., 2012).

The main achievements of the Czech education system are the high success rate among secondary school students and, therefore, the low school dropout rate. The high number of high school students enrolled in vocational specialization programs. Another important characteristic is that higher education is relatively cheap and administration and management of higher academic centers are autonomous. Likewise, the use of new technologies is promoted through the education legislation (Seďa, 2012).

Pre-primary education ranges from 3 to 6 years of age, with schooling from 5 to 14 years of age compulsory. Higher secondary education (from 15 to 19 years old) is offered in general and specialized high schools by vocational fields. Tertiary education, lasting three years, is taught in professional schools and institutions of higher education. Finally, higher education offers bachelor's degree, masters and doctoral programs (Santiago et al., 2012).

The Education Act of 2004 indicates as general objectives of secondary education, the acquisition of knowledge, skills, attitudes and values necessary for the full development of every citizen, both in the personal and civic area, which allow them to continue learning independently. In a similar way to the Spanish educational system, secondary education is based on the establishment of key competences: learning, problem solving, communication etc.

3 Methodology

The first part of this section will briefly explain the method applied to estimate the academic centers efficiency in both countries, as well as the existence of a technological gap in the education systems. In the second part, the used data will be analyzed and some previous results will be shown.

3.1 Formulation and estimation of the meta-frontier production function

We define the stochastic production frontier (SF) for the *i*-th school center of the *j*-th country as

$$Y_{ji} = f_j(X_{ji})e^{V_{ji}-U_{ji}} \tag{1}$$

where Y_{ji} denotes the output, in this case, it is the report PISA results, X_{ji} an inputs vector, V_{ji} represent statistical noise distributed independently and identically as $N(0,\sigma_{Vj}^2)$ and U_{ji} represents technical inefficiency and it is independent of V_{ji} and it is distributed as the truncated-normal distribution. Thus, the production technical efficiency is defined as

$$TE_{ji} = \frac{Y_{ji}}{f_j(X_{ji})e^{V_{ji}}} = e^{-U_{ji}}. \tag{2}$$

On the other hand, we define the meta-production frontier as the common border to all academic centers of the group of countries. It is denoted as, $f_M(X_{ji})$ and involves all the stochastic frontiers of the countries. It is expressed as:

$$f_j(X_{ji}) = f_M(X_{ji})e^{-U_{ji}^M}. \tag{3}$$

Thus, the technology gap ratio (TGR) is defined as

$$TGR_{ji} = \frac{f_j(X_{ji})}{f_M(X_{ji})} = e^{-U_{ji}^M} \tag{4}$$

i.e., the ratio of the *j*-th group's production frontier to the meta-frontier. Finally, the school's technical efficiency with respect to the meta-frontier production technology is defined as

$$MTE_{ji} = TGR_{ji} \cdot TE_{ji}. \tag{5}$$

The next method is proposed by Huang et al. (2014) to estimate TE_{ji} and TGR_{ji}. In the first step, the SF is estimated as

$$\ln Y_{ji} = lnf_j(X_{ji}) + V_{ji} - U_{ji}. \tag{6}$$

In the second step, the meta-frontier $f_M(X_{ji})$ is estimated as

$$\ln \hat{f}_j(X_{ji}) = lnf_M(X_{ji}) + V_{ji}^M - U_{jl}^M \tag{7}$$

where $\ln \hat{f}_j(X_{ji})$ is the estimate of the group-specific frontier from the first step. Since the estimates $\ln \hat{f}_j(X_{ji})$ are group-specific, the regression from the first step is estimated *J* times, one for each group. These estimates from all *J* groups are then pooled to estimate the meta-frontier in the second step (Figure 1).

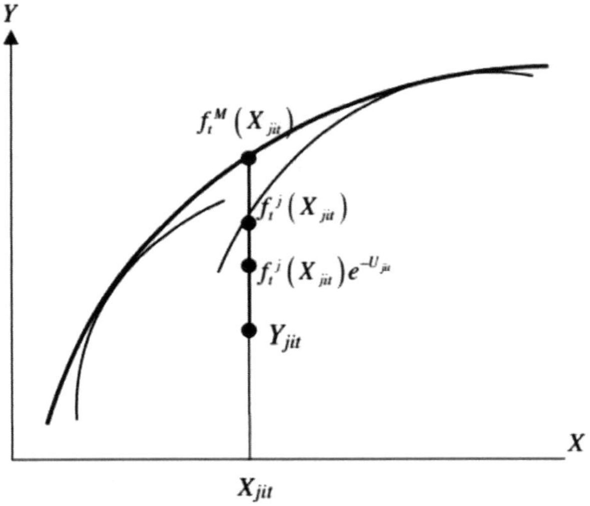

Figure 1 Stochastic meta-frontier [Huang et al., 2014]

3.2 Data sample description

The empirical study of this work has been carried out based on the 2015 PISA report results, in which an increasingly larger group of countries participate and whose main purpose is generating indicators on aspects of educational performance that allow actions for improvements.

The tests assess the understanding of concepts, the mastery of processes and the ability of students to cope in various situations. This is done in three areas: reading comprehension, science and mathematics. The evaluation is carried out through ten scores, so that possible measurement errors associated with factors that do not depend on the student, such as nervousness or poor health, can be controlled. The obtained values are normally distributed with mean 500 and standard deviation 100; and are called plausible values.

The used sample consists of 344 academic centers in the Czech Republic and 1177 in Spain. The proportion of private academic centers in the Czech Republic is 9.2% compared to 35.9% in Spain. The average values in the mathematics test are between 489.5 and 492.3 for Spanish students, while they are between 486.7 and 489.2 for Czech students. In reading comprehension, Spain obtains values between 498.3 and 500.9, and Czech between 481.7 and 484.2. In the discipline of Sciences, while Spanish centers score oscillates between 496 and 497.7; Czech score ranges between 489.1 and 489.9 (Table 1).

	Differences of means		***t*-statistics**		***p*-values**	
	Min	**Max**	**Min**	**Max**	**Min**	**Max**
Mathematics	0.292	5.653	0.264	1.378	0.169	0.792
Reading	14.034	19.163	3.326	4.571	7.10^{-6}	0.001
Science	6.130	8.854	1.573	2.265	0.024	0.117

Table 1 Comparison of the results of the PISA tests in Spain and Czech Republic

To analyse the results of the two countries, the average values of both countries have been compared from the 30 plausible values available for the three categories. The results show that there are no significant differences in the results of the mathematics tests (*p*-value between 0.169 and 0,792), the differences are not very clear for the science results (*p*-value between 0.024 and 0.117) and clear differences in the results in reading comprehension (*p*-value < 0.001), where the results reveal a lower score on this subject in the Czech Republic.

In this paper, we have selected at random one of the plausible values of reading comprehension, since they show the greatest differences between both countries. The study was carried out at the academic centre level, so the value used as an output of the academic centre production function is the average value obtained by all the students in the academic centre at this plausible value.

		Mean	Stand. Dev.	*t*-statistic	*p*-value
Number of computers per teacher	Czech Republic	41.027	31.719	1.474	0.141
	Spain	37.689	37.204		
Percentage of funds received by the government	Czech Republic	94.409	10.141	10.468	< 0.001
	Spain	85.468	21.619		
Percentage of students from socioeconomic disadvantaged homes	Czech Republic	13.964	18.237	-2.522	0.012
	Spain	17.188	18.904		
Class size	Czech Republic	23.495	5.205	-7.723	< 0.001
	Spain	26.478	8.743		
School size	Czech Republic	429.855	234.256	-15.016	< 0.001
	Spain	707.547	433.616		
Responsibility for resources	Czech Republic	1.383	1.325	23.656	< 0.001
	Spain	-0.356	0.596		
Percentage of teachers with ISCED level 6	Czech Republic	0.057	0.073	6.986	< 0.001
	Spain	0.028	0.041		
Shortage of educational material	Czech Republic	-0.088	0.821	-4.054	< 0.001
	Spain	0.139	1.138		
Interest	Czech Republic	-0.663	0.358	-36.819	< 0.001
	Spain	0.098	0.220		

Table 2 Used variables in the estimation of stochastic frontiers

Following the formulations described in the methodology, the stochastic frontiers of each country have been estimated. In this sense, the variables related to personal and material resources of the academic centre have been considered: number of professors with doctorate, number of computers per teacher and the index created by PISA that measures the level of shortage of materials. Those related to the independence of the entity are as follows: the degree of responsibility in the resources and the percentage of funds of the academic centre received by the government. Finally, the demographic characteristics of the academic centre have been considered: number of students per classroom, total number of students in the academic centre, their interest and the percentage of students who come from disadvantaged homes (Table 2).

4 Empirical Results

First, the results of both models are shown in Table 3. The LR variance nullity tests of U delivered p-value that is less than 0.001 for the Czech Republic and equal to 0.024 for Spain. It indicates the existence of significant differences in the technical efficiencies of the academic centres of each country.

The percentage of students from disadvantaged households reduces technical efficiency in both countries. However, while a greater responsibility in resources and a greater number of students in schools reduces the efficiency in the Czech Republic, the opposite is true in Spain.

	Czech Republic				Spain			
	Coeff.	**Std. Err.**	***Z*-stat.**	***p*-value**	**Coeff.**	**Std. Err.**	***Z*-stat.**	***p*-value**
Comp_Teach	0.023	0.013	1.71	0.087	0.001	0.003	0.31	0.007
Gov_Funds	-0.018	0.080	-0.22	0.825	-0.037	0.010	-3.66	< 0.001
Dis_Homes	-0.018	0.005	-3.90	< 0.001	-0.012	0.002	-6.44	< 0.001
Class_Numb	0.207	0.032	6.50	< 0.001	0.018	0.011	1.65	0.098
School_Numb	-0.045	0.014	-3.12	0.002	0.016	0.005	3.51	< 0.001
Resp_Resour	-0.017	0.008	-2.26	< 0.001	0.009	0.002	3.94	< 0.001
Teacher_PHD	0.051	0.009	5.53	< 0.001	0.015	0.004	4.07	< 0.001
Short_Mater	-0.016	0.007	-2.32	0.020	0.001	0.002	0.38	0.708
Interest	0.124	0.015	8.18	< 0.001	0.160	0.026	6.16	< 0.001
Constant	5.530	0.326	16.96	< 0.001	5.579	0.122	45.66	< 0.001
/lnsig2v	-7.937	0.779	-10.19	< 0.001	-6.283	0.193	-32.65	< 0.001
/lnsig2u	-3.409	0.138	-24.63	< 0.001	-5.891	0.372	-15.83	< 0.001
Sigma_v	0.019	0.007			0.043	0.004		
Sigma_u	0.182	0.013			0.053	0.010		
Sigma2	0.033	0.005			0.005	0.001		
Lambda	9.619	0.017			1.217	0.014		

Table 3 Results of the stochastic border estimations

On the other hand, the shortage of materials is not influential in the production function of the Spanish academic centres. Variables such as interest, teacher training, availability of computers for teachers and number of students per class have a direct relationship with the efficiency of the academic centres. The direct relationship between efficiency and number of students per class may seem incongruous. However, the regulation of education systems determines the number of students per class except in rural settings, where the shortage of students makes it difficult to complete the classes. The tests reveal that PISA evaluation results are significantly lower in these environments.

	Min	**Max**	**Mean**	**Std. Dev.**	**2-sample *t*-test**	***p*-value**
Czech Republic	0.548	0.992	0.871	0.090	-19.323	< 0.001
Spain	0.871	0.987	0.960	0.018		

Table 4 Summary of efficiency of the academic centers of both countries

Once the production frontiers have been estimated, the technical efficiency of the two countries has been calculated. The obtained results are shown in Table 4 and Figure 2. There are significant differences in the technical efficiency of the two countries so that Spanish schools are more efficient with the resources they have than the Czech academic centres.

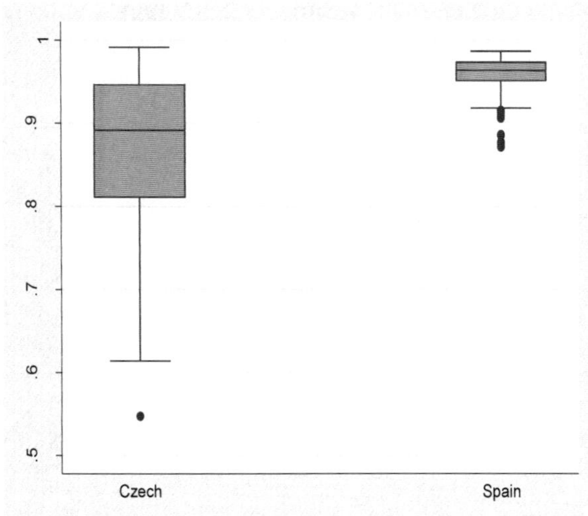

Figure 2 Boxplot of efficiency of the academic centers of both countries

Let's see now the results obtained in the second step of the study, in which the meta-frontier of production of both countries is estimated. The objective of study is the existence of a technological gap between both countries, so that the maximum levels of efficiency those aspiring to each academic centre differ significantly. To do this, equation (7) has been estimated with the environment variables that explain the existing gap.

Input variables	Coeff.	*Z*-stat.	*p*-value	Envir. variables	Coeff.	*Z*-stat.	*p*-value
Comp_Teach	0.007	3.78	< 0.001	Prof_Devel	0.002	1.12	0.264
Gov_Funds	-0.016	-2.54	0.011	Interest	0.080	9.59	< 0.001
Dis_Homes	-0.017	-17.94	< 0.001	Discipl_Clim	-0.027	-5.74	< 0.001
Class_Numb	0.177	10.11	< 0.001	Class_Numb	0.005	7.25	< 0.001
School_Numb	-0.005	-1.61	0.108	/lnsig2v	-6.685	-111.93	< 0.001
Resp_Resour	0.017	13.98	< 0.001	/lnsig2u	-2.452	-1.75	0.080
Teacher_PHD	0.037	17.93	< 0.001	Sigma_v	0.001	0.001	0.001
Short_Mater	-0.004	-2.88	0.004	Sigma_u	0.079	0.006	0.572
Interest	0.135	11.40	< 0.001	Sigma2	10^{-4}	-2.10^{-4}	< 0.001
Constant	5.251	73.44	< 0.001	Lambda	0.001	0.001	0.001

Table 5 Stochastic meta-frontier estimations

The results are shown in Table 5. The environment variables used are: level of professional development of the schools, interest of students, climate of discipline and, once again, size of the class, which makes reference to the distinction between urban and rural environments as indicated above.

As it can be seen, the climate of discipline, the size of the class and the interest of the students are fundamental to explain the efficiency in this case. In other words, the gap between the Czech

Republic and Spain. In Table 6 and Figure 3, the results show that the efficiency frontier of the Czech Republic is closer to the meta-frontier of global efficiency. Therefore, we can affirm that, although the Czech academic centres are less efficient with their available resources, the net efficiency level they can achieve is higher than in Spain.

	Min	Max	Mean	Std. Dev.	2-sample *t*-test	*p*-value
Czech Republic	0.900	0.999	0.979	0.197	-19.266	< 0.001
Spain	0.806	0.996	0.923	0.034		

Table 6 Summary of efficiency gap of each country to the meta-frontier

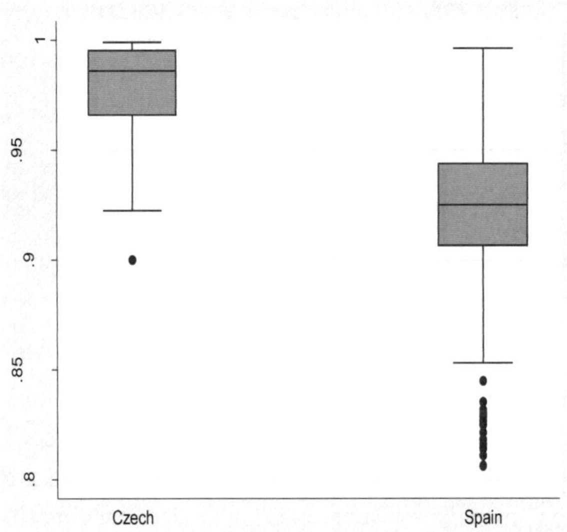

Figure 3 Boxplot of efficiency gap of each country to the meta-frontier

Conclusions

The results obtained for the estimation of the stochastic production frontiers reveal that the Spanish educational centers are more efficient than the Czech ones. It means that a more efficient usage of available resources is reflected in their students' results according to PISA's report. However, although Czech educational centers are less efficient with their resources, the maximum level of production they can achieve is higher than in Spain.

Therefore, the improvement of the Czech and Spanish education systems should be directed in two completely different ways, while Spain needs to contribute a greater amount of resources to the education of its citizens, the Czech Republic must make more efficient use of the resources available to it.

References

Act No. 561/2004 on Pre-school, Basic, Secondary, Tertiary Professional and Other Education 24. 9. 2004, [Online]. Available at: http://www.msmt.cz/uploads/soubory/IMzakon561ponovelach.pdf [cited 2019-01-20].

Aigner, D., Lovell, C. and Schmidt, P. (1977). ´Formulation and estimation of stochastic frontier production function models´. *Journal of Econometrics*, 6 (1), pp. 21-37.

Cordero, J. M., Crespo, E. and Pedraja, F. (2011). ´Exploring educational efficiency divergences across Spanish regions in PISA 2006´. *Revista de economía aplicada*, 19 (57), pp. 117-145.

Cordero, J. M., Crespo, E. and Pedraja, F. (2013). ´Rendimiento educativo y determinantes según PISA: una revisión de la literatura en España´. *Revista de Educación*, 362, pp. 273-297.

Dobrota, M., Jeremic, V. and Bulajic, M. (2015). ´Uncertainty and Sensitivity Analyses of PISA Efficiency: Distance Based Analysis Approach´. *Acta Polytechnica Hungarica*, 12 (3), pp. 41-58.

Huang, C. J., Huang, T. H. and Liu, N. H. (2014). ´A new approach to estimating the metafrontier production function based on a stochastic frontier framework´. *Journal of Productivity Analysis*, 42 (3), pp. 241-254.

Mancebon, M. J., Calero, J. and Choi, A. (2012). ´The efficiency of public and publicly subsidized high schools in Spain: Evidence from PISA-2006´. *Journal of the Operational Research Society*, 63 (11), pp. 1516-1533.

Marchesi, A. (2006). ´El informe PISA y la política educativa en España´. *Revista de Educación*, Número extraordinario, pp. 337-355.

Martínez, J. S. (2013). ´Fracaso escolar, PISA y la difícil ESO´. *RASE: revista de la Asociación de Sociología de la Educación*, 2 (1), pp. 56-85.

MECD (2013). ´Ley Orgánica 8/2013, de 9 de diciembre, para la mejora de la calidad educativa´. *BOE*, 295, pp. 97858-97921.

Meeusen W. and Van Den Broeck, J. (1977). ´Efficiency estimation from Cobb-Douglas production functions with composed error´. *International Economic Review*, 18 (2), pp. 435-444

Santiago, P., Gilmore, A. Nusche, D. and Sammons, P. (2012). *OECD Reviews of Evaluation and Assessment in Education: Czech Republic 2012*. OECD Publishing.

Seďa, P. (2012). ´Analysis of the Use of the Mathematica Software in the Mathematics in Economics e-learning Course´. *Proceedings of the 9th international conference Efficiency and Responsibility in Education*, Praha, Czech Republic, pp. 496-505.

Model of storage and shipping synchronisation in production warehouses

Dušan Teichmann[1], Michal Dorda[2], Denisa Mocková[3]

Abstract. Storages play an important role in logistical chains. There are many types of warehouses fulfilling different functions in the logistical chains. One type of the warehouses is a so-called production warehouse. We can meet with the production warehouses in production processes that are composed of the two following phases. The first phase is production of products themselves and the second phase is refinement of the products. The refinement process must be adapted in cases when the products do not meet requested quality standards after their producing. Refinement is typical for food industry. Many products of food industry must spend a certain time in the production warehouse – we can mention for example ripping cheese, dried meat and so on. The production processes of such foodstuffs require that their storing in the production warehouse must meet pre-defined conditions. Based on the conditions minimal times of storage are determined. In addition, it is not usually acceptable that there is a positive time delay between finishing the production phase and beginning the warehousing phase because such delay may spoil the products. And finally, some products must not be stored in the production warehouse longer than a pre-defined maximal time. All the mentioned factors may influence decisions of managers who plan the production processes. In the article we present a mathematical model of the production warehouse; the model coordinates storage in the warehouse and shipping from it so that the pre-defined minimal and maximal time the products must spend in the warehouse are met.

Keywords: production warehouse, refinement, production planning, linear programming.

JEL Classification: C61

1 Introduction – our motivation to deal with the problem

Warehousing plays an important role in many logistical chains. Warehouses usually have a balance function. That means they balance differences between supply and demand over time. Based on the balance function one may state that the warehouses are passive elements of the logistical chains. However, there are examples when the warehouses can play an active role. It usually happens for products for which it is typical that their production process ends with a refinement phase. During the refinement phase the products are placed in a warehouse where the products undergo desired changes in their quality to meet demands of customers. More specifically, some examples of the refinement processes are ripening, fermentation, drying and so on. The warehouses that are designated for refinement of the products are according to

[1] VSB – Technical University of Ostrava, Faculty of Mechanical Engineering, Institute of Transport, Ostrava – Poruba, 17. listopadu 15/2172, 708 33, Czech Republic, dusan.teichmann@vsb.cz.
[2] VSB – Technical University of Ostrava, Faculty of Mechanical Engineering, Institute of Transport, Ostrava – Poruba, 17. listopadu 15/2172, 708 33, Czech Republic, michal.dorda@vsb.cz.
[3] Czech Technical University in Prague/Faculty of Transportation Sciences, Department of Logistics and Management of Transport, Horská 3, Prague 2, 128 03, Czech Republic, mockova@fd.cvut.cz

Schulte (1994) called the production warehouses and storing the products in such warehouses is named warehousing connected with the production process.

Suppose a producer receives a further contract to produce a certain volume of production. Because the producer has already received other contracts and the contracts are in progress, a certain percentage of the production capacity and of the production warehouse capacity is occupied by the current contracts and, therefore, the occupied capacities are not available for the new contract – only the free production capacity (if any) can be used for the new contract. Therefore, managers of the producer must decide about the new contract in terms of time. That means they decide how the free production capacity should be used to fulfil the new contract. Let us consider that satisfying the new contract is not possible from current production (production made to satisfy the older contracts). This is for example because a time schedule of deliveries within the older contracts is defined and cannot be changed. That means the producer is not able to execute the new contract from the current volume of production. Another reason why the new contract cannot be executed is the producer does not overproduce. That means the producer has no produce in reserve and, therefore, cannot execute the new contracts from the existing reserve.

The managers deal with the problem of deciding about increasing the volume of production to satisfy the new contract. Let us assume that such increasing is possible, there is a free production capacity (including the capacity of the production warehouse) available for the new contract. Besides planning the production phase itself, other processes which are connected with the refinement phase in the production warehouse must be taken into account. In the production warehouse two basic processes are done – storage the products in the warehouse and consequent shipping the refined products to the customer. A feasible time schedule of both processes must obey the time limits given for the refinement phase. If the production warehouse were not taken into account in the planning process, it could easily happen that the produced products cannot be stored under prescribed conditions. It means the refinement process is not done in a correct way which may lead to spoilage of the products. Therefore, it is necessary to synchronise the free production capacity with the capacity of the distribution warehouse. The production warehouse is not only limited by its capacity but also by the shipping capacity. In addition, it is desirable to plan the shipping process as effective as possible. That means a minimal number of the vehicles should be used for shipping the products. Using the minimal number of the vehicles brings their maximal utilisation.

In the article an approach for dealing with the problem based on the linear programming methods is presented. The total number of the vehicles used for shipping the refined products represents an optimisation criterion in the model, main constraints of the model result from the free production capacity and the production warehouse (the storage and the shipping capacity). In addition, it is also requested that the products must spend the pre-defined time in the production warehouse, the time is given by its minimum and maximum. The presented model can be applied also in cases when no limits for the time the products must spend in the production warehouse are defined. In such cases the minimal time equals to 0 and the maximal time tends to an arbitrarily chosen high value. Instead of the arbitrarily chosen high value the time when the new contract must be fulfilled can be used.

2 State of the art

The model presented in the article can be incorporated into a group of optimisation approaches devoted to production planning, warehousing and distribution. Many articles have been published in the past. From the latest review articles, we can mention for example an article written by Andersson et al (2010). To solve the problem many optimisation approaches are applied. We can point out linear programming models presented by Catalá et al (2013) or a metaheuristic method based on Tabu search strategy developed by Rusdiansyah and Tsao (2005). An important piece of work is presented in Keizer et al (2017), the article deals with design of a logistical network for distribution of perishable products. An integrated planning of production and distribution in a three-level supply chain (several external suppliers – a single manufacturer – a multi-retailer) is discussed in Niknamfar (2015). Other alternative approaches for solving the problems relating to synchronisation of production and distribution can be found for example in (Tang, 2008) or (Rizk, Martel, and D´Amours, 2008).

3 Problem formulation and mathematical model

Let a planning period be given, within the planning period a certain volume of production Q must be produced and shipped to a customer. The planning period is divided into n time intervals (we drew inspiration from discretisation of time usually done in mathematical models in renewal theory). For each time interval $i = 1, \dots, n$ the volume of production that it is possible to deliver to the production warehouse (the volume of production is limited by the free production capacity a_i) is known. In addition, a loading capacity CN_i and a production warehouse capacity CS_i must be given (both capacities are always estimated at the beginning of each time interval). A minimal time $MINIM$ and a maximal time $MAXIM$ the products must spend in the production warehouse are known. Let us assume that both values are constant during the whole planning period. The products made for the new contract are delivered to the single customer and we assume that the products are shipped by the vehicles of the same type with a capacity K. Our task is to decide about the volumes of additional production in the individual time intervals so that the products are delivered to the customer with the minimal number of the vehicles.

With respect to the minimal time the products must spend in the production warehouse it is obvious that the capacities a_i must be determined only for $i = 1, \dots, n - MINIM$. If the minimal time the products must spend in the warehouse $MINIM = 0$, then the new contract can be realised in any time interval of the planning period.

Let us further assume that the production warehouse must be empty (with zero reserve) from the point of view of the additionally planned volume of production at the beginning and at the end of the planning period. The zero reserve at the beginning of the planning period ensures that no free volume of production is available in order to execute the new contract. On the other hand, the zero reserve at the end of the planning period means there is no free volume of production in the warehouse, such free volume of production could be used for executing new contracts concluded after terminating the planning period. However, it would be possible to modify a model presented in the article if we assumed a nonzero reserve in the production warehouse.

In order to model our task, we must define following groups of variables:

x_i... the volume of production coming to the warehouse in the time interval $i = 1, \dots, n - MINIM$

y_j... the number of the vehicles shipping the products in the time interval $j = 1 + MINIM, \dots, n$

w_i... the volume of production found in the warehouse in the time interval $i = 0, \dots, n$ (the volume of production which is shipped in the consequent time interval $i = 1, \dots, n$ is excluded)

z_{ij}...the volume of production coming to the warehouse in the time interval $i = 1, \dots, n - MINIM$ and shipping in the time interval $j = 1 + MINIM, \dots, n$

The mathematical model of the task can be defined in the following form:

$$\min f(x, y, z, w) = \sum_{j=1+MINIM}^{n} y_j \tag{1}$$

subject to:

$$\sum_{i=1}^{n-MINIM} x_i = Q \tag{2}$$

$$x_i \leq a_i \qquad i = 1, \dots, n - MINIM \tag{3}$$

$$x_i = \sum_{j=i+MINIM}^{i+MAXIM} z_{ij} \qquad i = 1, \dots, n - MAXIM \tag{4}$$

$$x_i = \sum_{j=i+MINIM}^{n} z_{ij} \qquad i = n - MAXIM + 1 \dots n - MINIM \tag{5}$$

$$\sum_{i=1}^{j-MINIM} z_{ij} \leq K y_j \qquad j = 1 + MINIM, \dots, 1 + MAXIM \tag{6}$$

$$\sum_{i=j-MAXIM}^{n-MINIM} z_{ij} \leq K y_j \qquad j = 2 + MAXIM, \dots, n \tag{7}$$

$$w_0 = 0 \tag{8}$$

$$w_n = 0 \tag{9}$$

$$w_j = w_{j-1} + x_j \qquad j = 1..MINIM \tag{10}$$

$$w_j = w_{j-1} + x_j - \sum_{i=1}^{j-MINIM} z_{ij} \qquad j = MINIM + 1, \dots, MAXIM \tag{11}$$

$$w_j = w_{j-1} + x_j - \sum_{i=j-MAXIM}^{j-MINIM} z_{ij} \qquad j = MAXIM + 1, \dots, n - MINIM \tag{12}$$

$$w_j = w_{j-1} - \sum_{i=j-MAXIM}^{j-MINIM} z_{ij} \qquad j = n - MINIM, \dots, n \tag{13}$$

$$w_i \leq CS_i \qquad i = 1, \dots, n \tag{14}$$

$$y_j \leq CN_j \qquad j = 1 + MINIM, \dots, n \tag{15}$$

$$x_i \geq 0 \qquad i = 1, \dots, n - MINIM \tag{16}$$

$$y_j \in Z_0^+ \qquad i = 1 + MINIM, \dots, n \tag{17}$$

$$w_i \geq 0 \qquad i = 0, \dots, n \tag{18}$$

$$z_{ij} \geq 0 \qquad i = 1, \dots, n - MINIM \quad j = 1 + MINIM, \dots, n \tag{19}$$

Function (1) represents the optimisation criterion of the model – the total number of the vehicles that transport the products to the customer after the refinement phase of the production process. Constraint (2) ensures that the volume of production which is requested by the new customer will be produced in the planning period. A group of constraints (3) models that the volumes of production coming to the productive warehouse in the individual time intervals do not exceed the free production capacity. Groups of constraints (4) and (5) ensure realisation of the refinement process. That means the constraints model that the volume of production will be spread out in the time intervals according to the minimal and the maximal time the products must spend in the production warehouse. Groups of constraints (6) and (7) recalculate the volumes of shipped production in the individual time intervals to the numbers of the vehicles that deliver the products to the customer. Constraints (8) and (9) ensure that there is an available capacity (reserve) of the production warehouse at the beginning and the end of the planning period; the available capacity can be used for meeting exceptional requests. In our case we do not assume a positive available capacity, it is equal to 0 in both constraints. If the positive available capacity were requested, they would be substituted in the right sides of both constraints. Groups of constraints (10) – (13) preserve continuity in the stock volume for the individual time periods. A group of constraints (14) ensures that the free capacity of the production warehouse is not exceeded. A group of constraints (15) ensures that the shipping capacity of the production warehouse is not exceeded. Groups of constraints (16) – (19) define domains of definition for all the variables used in the model.

4 Calculation experiment with the proposed model

To test the proposed mathematical model some calculation experiments were carried out. We tested the model on a simple example – it is necessary to produce $Q = 200$ units of production, the planning period consists of $n = 8$ consecutive time intervals and a length of the refinement process is given by $MINIM = 3$ time intervals and $MAXIM = 4$ time intervals. The vehicles that transport the refined products have their capacity equal to $K =$

100 units of production. The available production capacities, production warehouse capacities and loading capacities are summarised in Table 1 for the individual time intervals.

Time interval i	**1**	**2**	**3**	**4**	**5**	**6**	**7**	**8**
a_i	130	20	20	20	50	40	0	90
CS_i	200	110	140	100	100	150	150	60
CN_j	3	0	2	4	4	4	1	4

Table 1 Available production capacities, production warehouse capacities and shipping capacities

Our task is to decide how many products should come to the production warehouse and how many products should be shipped in the individual time intervals so that the free production capacity, production warehouse capacity and shipping capacity are not exceeded in the individual time intervals, the time the products must spend in the production warehouse are satisfied and the total number of the vehicles used for shipping the products to the customer is as minimal as possible.

Solving the model with the presented inputs was carried out using optimisation software Xpress-IVE. Results of the optimisation calculation are summarised in Table 2. The first column of the table corresponds to the individual time intervals 1 up to 8. In the second column information how many products should come to the production warehouse is provided for the individual time periods. The values in the remaining columns give information how many products should be shipped from the production warehouse in the individual time periods. By summing the shipped volumes of production in the individual rows, we get the values of x_i. In Table 2 one can also see that the minimal and the maximal time for storing the products in the production warehouse are satisfied. That means for example that the products coming to the production warehouse in the first time interval leave the warehouse in the fourth or the fifth time period.

Time interval i	x_i	z_{i1}	z_{i2}	z_{i3}	z_{i4}	z_{i5}	z_{i6}	z_{i7}	z_{i8}
1	110	0	0	0	50	60	0	0	0
2	0	0	0	0	0	0	0	0	0
3	0	0	0	0	0	0	0	0	0
4	40	0	0	0	0	0	0	0	40
5	50	0	0	0	0	0	0	0	50
6	0	0	0	0	0	0	0	0	0
7	0	0	0	0	0	0	0	0	0
8	0	0	0	0	0	0	0	0	0

Table 2 The results of the calculation experiment – the production volumes coming to the production warehouse and shipping from the warehouse in the individual time intervals

By checking the results one can verify that neither the free production capacity nor the free capacity of the production warehouse is exceeded – see Table 3.

Time interval i	**1**	**2**	**3**	**4**	**5**	**6**	**7**	**8**
a_i	130	20	20	20	50	40	0	90
x_i	110	0	0	40	50	0	0	0
CS_i	200	110	140	100	100	150	150	60
w_i	110	110	110	100	90	90	90	0
CN_j	3	0	2	4	4	4	1	4
y_j	0	0	0	1	1	0	0	1

Table 3 Checking not exceeding the available production capacities, capacities of the production warehouse and shipping capacities

We can see in Table 3 that no capacity limitation is exceeded. To ship the products 3 vehicles are used. Regarding the shipped volumes of production in the individual time intervals, it happens that the vehicles are not fully loaded. More precisely, their utilisation is 50%, 60% and 90%. Such utilisation of the vehicles (especially the first and the second value) is problematic, especially in the case when the vehicle is transporting the products loaded with 50% of its capacity only and leaves 60 products that can be shipped in the production warehouse. The vehicle would be fully loaded if another 50 products were loaded. However, if loading the first vehicle were 100%, then loading the vehicle departing the production warehouse in the fifth period would be only 10%. Postponement of shipping the remaining 10 products, which were produced in the first period, to the last time interval is not possible because the products can spend maximally 4 time intervals in the production warehouse. On the other hand, postponement of production of the remaining 10 products is not possible as well because the last time interval, when the products can be produced regarding the free production capacity, is the fourth interval. If the 10 products were produced in the fourth time interval, the latest time interval they should be shipped would be the eighth time interval.

The problems presented in the previous paragraph are caused by the optimisation criterion which may be considered unsuitable after discussion of the results of the calculation experiment. We stated that the minimal number of the vehicles used for shipping the products brings their maximal utilisation. On the other hand, we must point out that based on the free production capacities the minimal number of the vehicles is always 3. That means by increasing utilisation of the vehicles we are not able to reduce the number of the vehicles below 3.

5 Conclusions

The presented article dealt with optimisation of storage and shipping the products in the production warehouse. The production warehouse is used for refinement the products. In the article, optimisation of the processes is done by using the linear mathematical model. The planning period is divided into the consecutive time intervals and for each time interval the volume of production coming to the production warehouse and shipping from it is calculated. The calculation experiment was carried out with the proposed mathematical model to test its solvability. The experiment was done in optimisation software Xpress-IVE.

Within our further research activities, we would like to improve the model. We believe that its applicability is broader than it is presented in the article. The model can be supplemented with a heterogenous vehicle fleet (several types of the vehicles differing in their capacity) or more than one customer can be considered. It is also possible to apply different optimisation criterions, we can mention for example the total warehousing costs or the total costs of the system which incorporate the warehousing, shipping and transportation costs in a single optimisation criterion. And finally, optimisation calculations are necessary to carry out for bigger tasks to test the model for solving real problems.

Acknowledgements

The article has been supported by The Ministry of Education, Youth and Sports of the Czech Republic from the Specific Research Project (SP2019/101).

References

Andersson, H.; Hoff, A., Christiansen, M., Hasle, G. and Løkketangen, A. (2010). 'Industrial aspects and literature survey: Combined inventory management and routing'. *Computers & Operations Research, 37 (9)*, pp. 1515 – 1536.

Catalá, L. P., Moreno, M. S., Durand, G. A., Blanco, A. M. and Bandoni, A. (2013). 'Optimal Production Planing of Concentrated Apple and Pear Juice Plants'. *Iberoamerican Journal of Industrial Engineering*, 5 (10), pp. 172 – 187.

Keizer, M., Akkerman, R., Grunow, M., Bloemhof, J. M., Haijema, R. and Vorst, J. G. A. J. (2017). 'Logistics network design for perishable products with heterogeneous quality decay'. *European Journal of Operational Research*, 262 (2), pp. 535 – 549.

Niknamfar, A. H. (2015). 'Multi-objective production-distribution planning based on vendor-managed inventory strategy in a supply chain'. *Industrial Management & Data Systems*, 115 (6), pp. 1086 – 1112.

Tang., J., Yung, K., Ip, A. W. H. and Liu, S. (2008). 'Synchronized Production and Transportation Planning Using Subcontracted Vehicles in a Production-Distribution Network'. *Transportation Planning and Technology*, 30 (2-3), pp. 113 – 146.

Rizk, N., Martel, A. and D´Amours, S. (2008). 'Synchronized production-distribution planning in a single-plant multi-destination network'. *Journal of the Operational Research Society*, 2008, 59 (1), pp. 90 – 104.

Rusdiansyah, A., Tsao, D (2005). 'An integrated model for the periodic delivery problems for vending-machine supply chains'. *Journal of Food Engineering*, 70, pp. 421 – 434.

Schulte, Ch. (1991). *Logistik.* Munchen: Verlag Vahlen.

Testing Approach Suitable for Big Data

Jaroslav Zacek[1], Marek Malina[2]

Abstract. There are a lot of enterprise systems having problems with unsustainable source code and limited documentation. However, these systems are still in production and must be maintained. That fact arises a significant risk of data inconsistency caused by additional changes in business logic during maintaining or refactoring process.
We propose a new concept to record and test large production databases which can be useful for developers that have to understand how the part or whole application works and later to change the source code of the specific legacy component. To prove our concept, we have developed a framework called QACheck. The framework is hooked up in the system for capturing all data streams for developers before the maintenance process. Later, it is able to create a reversible SQL script to revert all data changes generated during the test phase. To verify our approach, we successfully tried the procedure on the production system in a typical business case.

Keywords: enterprise systems, SQL, quality assurance, testing, database consistency.

JEL Classification: JEL L86, JEL C88

1 Introduction and motivation

During our practical experiences with legacy systems, we have challenged the situation that we knew nothing about the architecture and the size of the data source is significantly big. There are also a lot of legacy projects that need to be transferred between developer units (main motivation could be outsourcing or moving branches to other countries). These legacy projects often have limited documentation and quality of the source code is not according to the latest standards. Also, the very often complication is the data source itself. Sometimes it is distributed and heavy transaction-based sometimes the database is very big and cannot be replicated for testing purposes. In most of these cases, the data model is unknown as well. The goal of the new team is to understand the software components of the whole application or even the solution. Unit tests or any other kind of tests are usually not presented at all. We've tried to search for some suitable approaches (Alexandrov 2013, Abidin 2016) but none of them are suitable for legacy enterprise systems.
Our goal is to design a new testing approach that developer can use to record current data that flows in the system, create a bijection data sets and apply these data sets to production database when operations are not reversible. You can see our typical legacy n-layer backend application in Figure 1. Usually, in big corporations (telecommunications, banking), these systems are not isolated. They are part of the broader integrated corporate information system connected by the enterprise service bus. We are aiming our approach to the Big Data from a volume point of view. Our typical example is a database with 6 million transactions that increases every day and

[1] University of Ostrava, department of Informatics and Computers, 30. Dubna 22, Ostrava, CZ, Jaroslav.zacek@osu.cz.
[2] University of Ostrava, department of Informatics and Computers, 30. Dubna 22, Ostrava, CZ, marek.malina@osu.cz.

cannot be easily duplicated. The input for that database is data stream loaded every day by close of business.

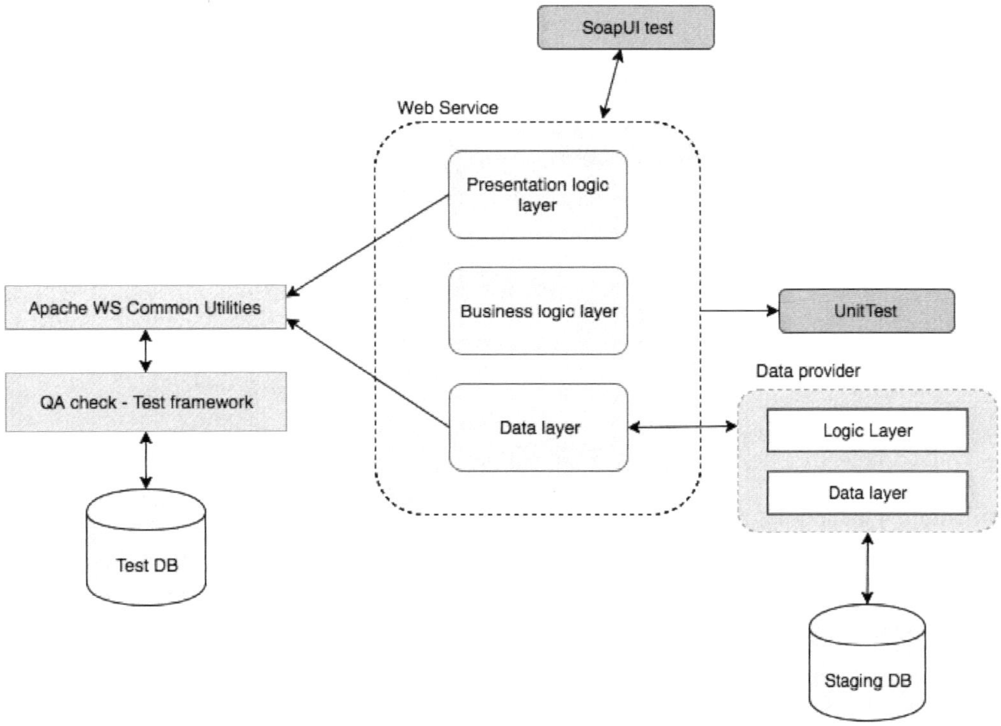

Figure 1 Our typical n-layer legacy application

2 Designing new test approach

Our framework is called QACheck, and it consists of multiple modules. The first module isolates a specific part of the application as a "black box". Let's state that every program starts at a specific point (catching button click event, calling web services, etc.) and we can pass input parameter through that point. By calling that specific point, some logic is performed (calling other methods, communication with the database) and some data could be retrieved as a return reference. This method will be considered as a primary testing method for us where we can start to collect and later mock the data stream. The core of the framework is placed between the UI and the database layer, and it is component oriented. Therefore, the framework is applicable as an integration testing tool.

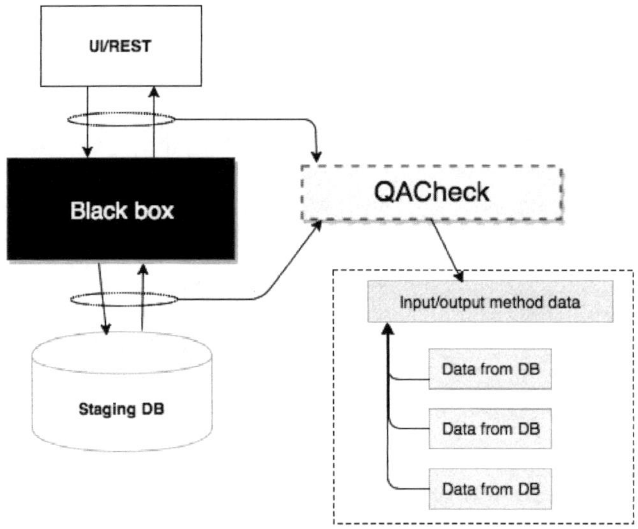

Figure 2 QACheck architecture

From our testing framework point of view, the tested method looks like a black box, and it covers just inputs and outputs of the current data stream. The framework does not care about business logic. It only records all its input and output data and all database calls that has been performed inside the body of the tested method. Later, we will use this recorded data to test that method after refactoring.

Because we applied the closure principle, there are only two points in the application (input and output of the tested method, database calls). Everything in between is a logic which represents the black box for the QACheck framework (see Figure 2).

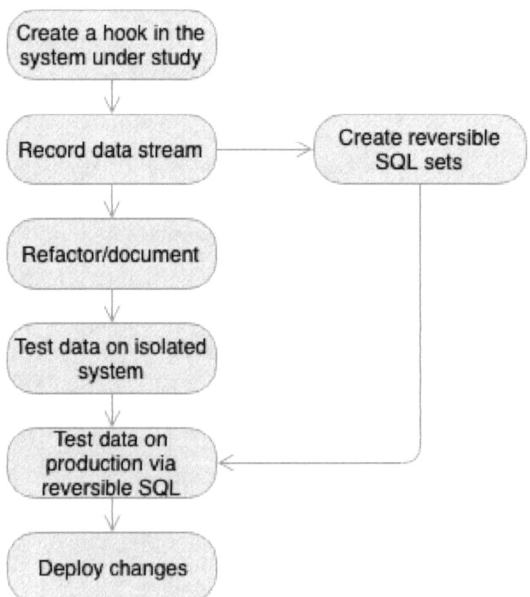

Figure 3 QACheck methodology

Complete workflow of QACheck shows Figure 3. The first step is to create a hook in the cur-rent system to capture all data streams. At first, we have to fulfill the principle that tested method has been run, and the database has replied to the tested method. Then we do not have to care if the call was originally initiated by the external system, and tested method communicates with the staging database or if the call was performed by unit test and tested method communicates with the testing database.

The second step is to record all data streams to cover every possible scenario. We can use (and it is recommended) production data of the current system. Based on the recorded data and database calls, QACheck framework can state that tested method works in the same way with the same result as before any changes.

It is evident that recorded data have a hierarchical structure - one call of the tested method creates one dataset that consists of 0 to N records in the database. If we re-run the tested method again, multiple datasets will be created.

Because of that principle, we can run any method (and record data) with any input data to cover all user scenarios. If the framework detects same data in the input and output, it automatically stores new one and removes older one to omit all duplicities in the database.

After these steps, we can start the refactoring process. Later, when the modifications are done, we check them on the isolated system utilizing our previous data records.

3 Reversible SQL

Even thou we have the system fully tested with our record, we cannot be sure that new solution works without any problems. We can increase the percentage of success by testing our solution on the production database. However, that also contains a big risk in case of any bugs that possibly can influence our data stream. We can create a reversible SQL data sets and close them into one transaction to fix potentially irreversible changes (most of the operations classified under DML). We have to state a transition function for all keywords that modifies data:

- INSERT;
- UPDATE;
- DELETE.

In theory, we are searching for bijection function all keywords to state reversible operations. Practically we have to combine multiple steps for every keyword to create a data snapshot that can be used later to revert changes in the production database.

Typical INSERT command consists of two keywords followed by the name of the table and values that should be inserted:

INSERT INTO *table_name* (*column1*, *column2*, *column3*, ...)

During the insertion process, we have to ensure that we can later identify those rows in the data table. This condition is very hard to achieve if we are working with legacy systems based on direct SQLs. Most of the enterprise systems use object-relation mapping (ORM), so we can use the fact that every ORM framework uses unique row identifier (UID). We have to collect them and create a reversible set of DELETE commands to revert initial state. All steps of the process represent Figure 4.

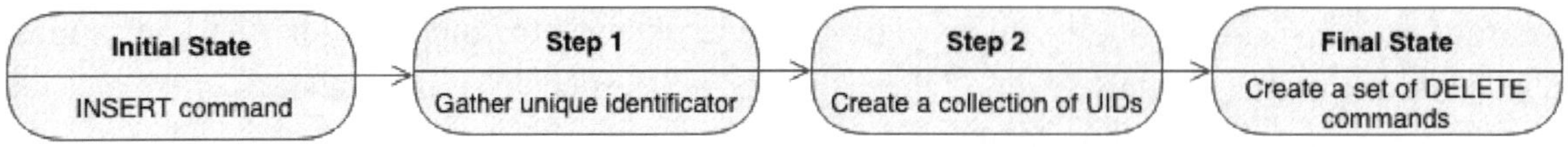

Figure 4 Reversible INSERT workflow

The second of DML set is the UPDATE command. Transformation of that command is easier than insert, because the part of the UPDATE syntax is selection:

UPDATE *table_name* SET *column1* = *value1*, *column2* = *value2*, ... WHERE *condition*;

WHERE section is followed by conditions typical for data query language (DQL) and we can also use the name of the table at the beginning of the statement. We will create a SELECT statement by combing these two components and perform them in the database to record the data sample. After we record the data, it can be easily modified to set of UPDATE commands that will be used later to revert the original state of the production database. All steps are shown in Figure 5.

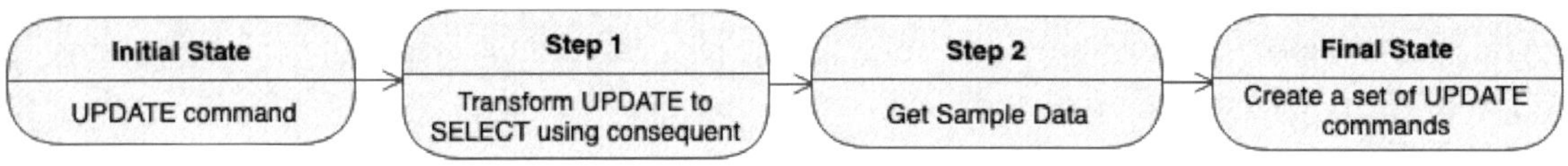

Figure 5 Reversible UPDATE workflow

The last part of DML queries is DELETE command. This situation is analogy of previous example, because the syntax of DELETE command is simpler than update:

DELETE FROM *table_name* WHERE *condition*;

As in the previous example, we will use WHERE section from the consequent of the query to sate our conditions for SELECT query. When the data set is a recorder, we will create a set of INSERT command that will be a reversible operation to DELETE command. The workflow is shown in Figure 6.

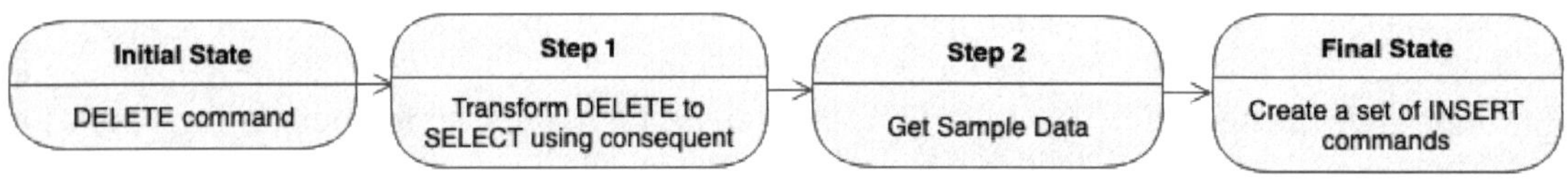

Figure 6 Reversible DELETE workflow

4 Verification

We have performed verification on an older .NET legacy project with no documentation. We have chosen one user scenario - create a report, and we have added QACheck as a hook for CreateReport method call. The first step was to record necessary testing data, so we have just run the method, and Test Manager logged every output data into our testing database (as seen in Figure 3). We have recorded one call that was a composite of three inner calls. After the process was finished, we have got one data set in our testing database mapped to one input data set. All these steps were covered by the transaction. Reversible SQL commands must be created on the fly step by step. Otherwise, we are not able to ensure data consistency.

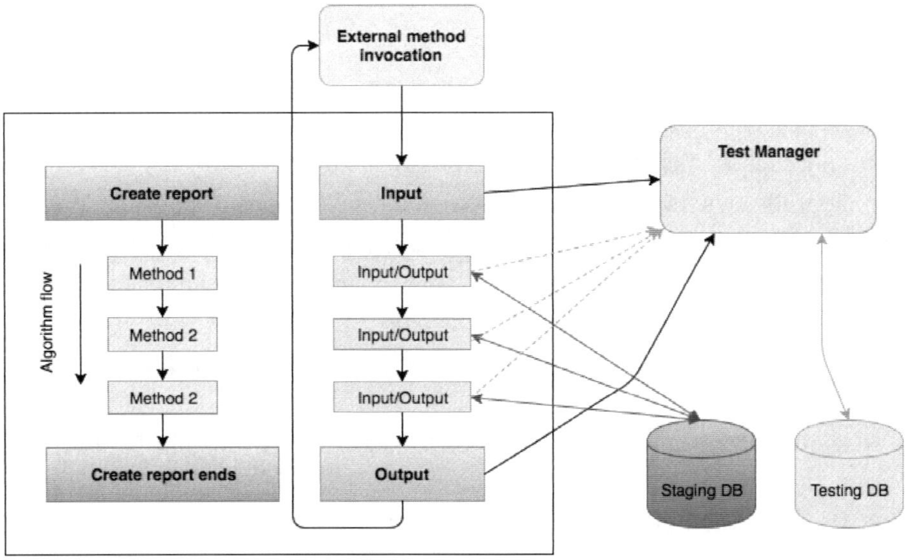

Figure 7 Recording

Later, we had a detached staging database and started refactoring process (Figure 8). We had re-run CreateReport method after every small change and checked if the output data matches with original data recorded from the staging database. During the testing process, we were sure we did not break anything, and we did not alter anything from the staging database. The whole process can be automated through some typical continuous integration tool (such as Jenkins, Travis, etc.).

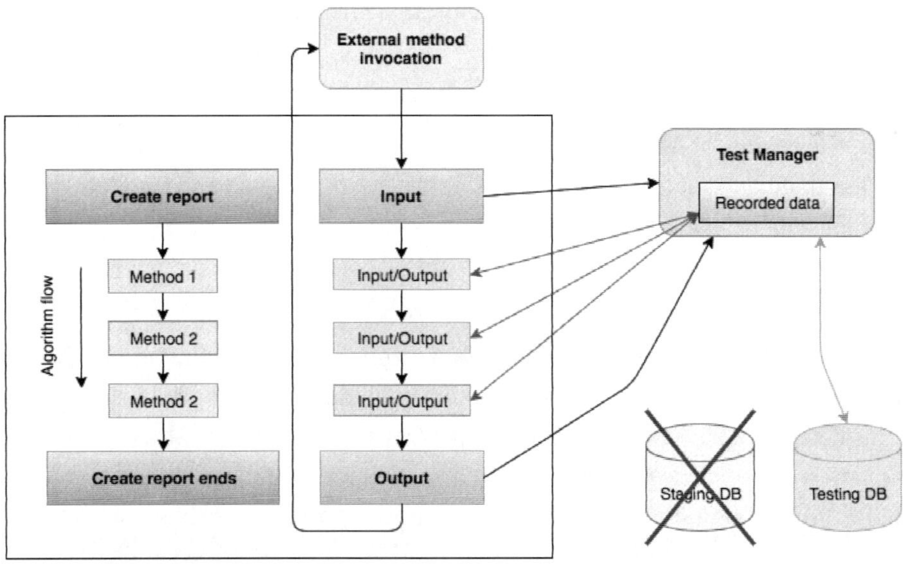

Figure 8 Testing mode after refactoring process

If the process is successful, we can reconnect the production database and rerun the test. When the test suite is complete, we can assert our values and then apply our reversible SQL sets to get the database to the state before testing. We have created a transaction during the recording process, so now we can perform reversible SQL backward.

5 Preconditions and Limitations

- Developer must be able to alter the source code of the tested method (or the application). Otherwise, he is not able to use it.
- Test approach is meant to be used in serial communication. If a developer wants to use it in a parallel way some modifications must be applied.
- Proposed test approach relies on the fact that there is exactly one place in the application, where tested method (black box) communicates with a database (external interfaces) utilizing "dynamic" data layer (there are no hard relationships, and we can record data flow). If there is no data layer, a developer must add an extra data layer into the application.
- Our testing approach supposes only one input point into the testing method and one output to communicate with the external world (database). For that reason, the testing data are stored in a master-slave structure. If another structure if necessary (e.g., instead of DB we have to communicate with the other external system), this logic and data structure must be altered.
- Testing data are stored for different names of companies and different versions. If the application is developed as a single product (one solution) or it has just one version, some specific default name must be set (nonblank text).
- The data source should not be replicate or distributed. If the source is replicated, we might increase the size of the database. If the data source is distributed, we can lose data consistency between nodes.
- The data model must be strict without any business logic (PL/SQL, T-SQL, etc.) and stored procedures.
- The data model cannot have any internal triggers.

For now, filesystem or Microsoft SQL server could be used as a testing database. If we want to use another database such as MySQL or Oracle, we have to add some DataProvider class that manages other concurrent connections.

6 Conclusion

This paper aimed to show that we can test even large data sets on the production database. This approach is not very suitable for hard-wired complex data models, for example, heavy business logic in the database or many references between tables. On the other hand, the approach is very handy if we are working with big data in the form of data streams. We have tried our approach on typical business case – create a simple report. Concerning the limitations stated in chapter 5, it can be used widely in current enterprise information systems.

References

Abidin, A., Lal, D., Garg, N. and Deep, V. (2016). 'Comparative analysis on techniques for big data testing'. *Proceedings of Information Technology (InCITe)-The Next Generation IT Summit on the Theme-Internet of Things: Connect your Worlds, International Conference*, Nioda, India, pp. 219-223.

Alexandrov, A., Brücke, C. and Markl, V. (2013, June). ‘Issues in big data testing and benchmarking‘. *Proceedings of the Sixth International Workshop on Testing Database Systems,* New York, USA, pp. 1-5.

Andrews, R. and Boyne, G. A. (2010). ‘Capacity, leadership, and organizational performance: Testing the black box model of public management‘. *Public Administration Review*, 70 (3), pp. 443-454.

Bau, J., Bursztein, E., Gupta, D. and Mitchell, J. (2010). ‘State of the art: Automated black-box web application vulnerability testing‘. *Proceedings of Security and Privacy,* Berleley/Oakland, California, USA, pp. 332-345.

Haviv, Y. A., Kalman, D., Pikus, D., Tripp, O. and Weisman, O. (2015). U.S. Patent No. 9,032,528. Washington, DC: U.S. Patent and Trademark Office.

Herzig, K., Greiler, M., Czerwonka, J. and Murphy, B. (2015). ‘The art of testing less without sacrificing quality‘. *Proceedings of the 37th International Conference on Software Engineering-Volume,* New York, USA, pp. 483-493.

Kochhar, P. S., Thung, F., Nagappan, N., Zimmermann, T. and Lo, D. (2015). ‘Understanding the test automation culture of app developers‘. *Proceedings of Software Testing, Verification and Validation,* Singapore, pp. 1-10.

Lübke, D. and van Lessen, T. (2016). ‘Modeling test cases in BPMN for behavior-driven development‘. *IEEE software*, 33 (5), pp. 15-21.

Ministr, J., Stevko, M. and Fiala, J. (2009). ‘The IT Service Continuity Management Principles Implementation by Method A2‘. *Proceedings of 17th Interdisciplinary Information Management Talks: IDIMT-2009: System and Humans, a Complex Relationship*, Jindrichuv Hradec, Czech Republic, pp. 131-140.

Noguchi, T., Washizaki, H., Fukazawa, Y., Sato, A. and Ota, K. (2015). ‘History-based test case prioritization for black box testing using ant colony optimization‘. *Proceedings of Software Testing, Verification and Validation,* Graz, Austria, pp. 1-2.

Rahman, M. and Gao, J. (2015, March). ‘A reusable automated acceptance testing architecture for microservices in behavior-driven development‘. *Proceeding of Service-Oriented System Engineering* Washington, USA, pp. 321-325.

Shahbaz, M. and Groz, R. (2014). ‘Analysis and testing of black-box component-based systems by inferring partial models‘. *Software Testing, Verification and Reliability*, 24 (4), pp.253-288.

Vale, T., Crnkovic, I., De Almeida, E. S., Neto, P. A. D. M. S., Cavalcanti, Y. C. and de Lemos Meira, S. R. (2016). ‘Twenty-eight years of component-based software engineering‘. *Journal of Systems and Software*, 111, pp. 128-148.

A Comparison of Selected Regions in the Czech Republic from Perspectives of Digitalization and Industry 4.0

Martina Žwaková[1]

Abstract. Digitalization is present in many aspects of business as mentioned for example by Vogelsang (2010) and can be considered as a part of business environment. In this paper, regions in the Czech Republic have been chosen as a level of detail as an environment, where companies are situated and also have interactions.

These environments can be assessed according to supportiveness of conditions for digitalization and Industry 4.0. There can be many factors identified which have impacts on digitalization. In this paper, it is assessed from the perspective of supportive conditions or stimuli more than from the view of technical aspects.

As more indicators are used to compare the regions, multivariate approach of Analytic hierarchy process has been used. Beforehand the comparison regions in the Czech Republic have been divided into groups and the comparison has been applied on one selected group of regions.

Keywords: Supportive factors for digitalization and Industry 4.0, AHP, Cluster analysis, Regions.

JEL Classification: C38, D80, O30, L16

1 Introduction

Aim of this paper is to compare Moravian-Silesian region with comparable regions in the Czech Republic in terms of supportive environment for digitalization and Industry 4.0 expansion. Digitalization as described by Vogelsang (1010, p. 3) is based on interpretation of data in the specific form of binary code which can be processed by machines, therefore the technical view is highlighted. Industry 4.0 is perceived as widening and deepening of collaboration between persons and advanced technologies and devices (Mařík et al., 2016, p. 21). Various indexes are used for a purpose of a comparison at the level of states. From a very complex index created by World Economic Forum (Baller Silja, Dutta Soumitra and Bruno Lanvin, 2017) or the DESI indicator (European Commission, 2019) to indicators, that are focused more on a technical area as an index designed by Roland Berger Consultants (Soldatos et al. (2016, p. 166) or Mařík et al. (2016, p. 167).

In this paper, focus is on supportive factors which can help to develop suitable environments for digitalization. Ten indicators have been used for the assessment. These indicators are divided into three groups: users of technologies (consumers), education for ICT development and resources in and for ICT. Based on these indicators, cluster analysis has been applied to identify a group of regions with characteristics which can be assumed as similar in comparison with Moravian-Silesian region. Identified regions are then compared from the perspective of the ten indicators using analytic hierarchy process. Quantitative data is used for the comparison of regions. Weights for the indicators and groups of indicators are calculated based on averages of

[1] VŠB – Technical University of Ostrava, Faculty of Economics, Sokolská třída 33, 702 00 Ostrava, Department of Business administration, martina.zwakova@vsb.cz

values obtained from questioning, where importance of each indicator has been evaluated from four perspectives.

2 Methodology and data

Based on the selected indicators, cluster analysis has been applied to identify a group of regions with characteristics which can be assumed as similar in comparison with Moravian-Silesian region. Identified regions are then compared from the perspective of the ten indicators using analytic hierarchy process. Data from Czech Statistical Office (Český statistický úřad) has been used to obtain values for indicators which are listed in Appendix 1, table 1, assessed year is 2016. These values are used as a basis for Cluster analysis, also this quantitative data is used for the comparison of regions. Weights for the indicators and groups of indicators are calculated based on averages of values obtained from questioning, where importance of each indicator has been evaluated from four perspectives.

2.1 Cluster analysis

Cluster analysis which is described by several authors as Ward (1963), Lance a Williams (1967), Everitt (2011), Mirkin (2013), Xu and Wunsch (2009), Hebák et al. (2005), Řezanková, Húsek and Snášel (2009), Pielou (c1984) and many others, is used to identify group of objects (regions) based on levels of similarities in their characteristics measured by their distances, more approaches to distance calculation can be used paired with different clustering algorithms. There is Ward clustering method and Euclidean distance (1) described for example by Zhang (2008, p. 74) used in this paper

$$D_E(X,Y)=\sqrt{\sum_{k=1}^{n}\left(x_k-y_k\right)^2} \tag{1}$$

where $D_E(X,Y)$ represents overall distance between region X and Y, k represents number of indicators and x_k and y_k represents value for k^{th} indicator for region X and Y.

Ward method is based on Ward criterion used for merging objects, minimising increase (squared) distance weighted by numbers of objects in clusters, into clusters Ward (1963). Based on this criterion two objects (regions in this paper) with least distance are merged to the first cluster. The procedure is described e.g. by Mirkin (2013, p. 137-138) or Xu and Wunsch (2009, p. 32-33). After each merge of clusters distances have to be recalculated and the procedure of merging clusters ends in the cluster including all objects is created (Mirkin, 2013, p. 137-139). For recalculation of distances, equation (2) is used as follows

$$D\left(C_t,\left(C_i,C_j\right)\right)=\frac{n_i+n_t}{n_i+n_j+n_t}\cdot D(C_t,C_i)+\frac{n_j+n_t}{n_i+n_j+n_t}\cdot D\left(C_t,C_j\right)-\frac{n_t}{n_i+n_j+n_t}\cdot D\left(C_i,C_j\right) \tag{2}$$

newly merged clusters' distance is marked as $D(C_i, C_j)$. The distances between newly established cluster and other clusters (with t^{th} order) is marked as $D(C_t,(C_i, C_j))$. Distance of ith cluster and t^{th} cluster is presented as $D(C_t, C_i)$ and correspondingly distance from j^{th} cluster as $D(C_t, C_j)$. Distances are recalculated with regards to number of entities represented by n in the each cluster. This procedure is described by Xu and Wunsch (2009, p. 34).

Identified clusters can be graphically represented by dendograms as mentioned by Hebák et al. (2005, p. 11). Group of analysed regions has been derived from dendogram, which is presented in Appendix 3. The R program is used for calculations related to clustering (R Core Team, 2017).

2.2 Analytic hierarchy process

Application of the process is based on pair comparison of object according to each indicator used for an analysis and also on pair comparison of indicators themselves. From pair comparison, importance or weights are derived for assessed objects and also for indicators. (Fotr, Ševcová a kol., 2016, Saaty, 2006). Indicators for comparison are structured in a form of hierarchy, where main goal is divided into sub-categories and at the level of specific indicators. (Saaty, 2006, p. 107).

For a comparison n x n types of matrices are used, where objects in the rows are compared to objects in the columns. If a matrix is marked as A (3), it can be represented in the following form

$$A = (a_{ij}), (i, j = 1, 2, 3, \ldots, n) \tag{3}$$

where a_{ij} represents pair comparisons of ith and j^{th} object (variant of indicator depending of the assessed level of hierarchy), (Saaty, 2006, p. 47). Scales recommended by Saaty (2006, p. 73) are used for an evaluation, however quantitative data can be also used instead of scales (Fotr, Ševcová et al., 2016, p. 196).

After calculation or assignments of ratios to the matrix, weights representing importance or level of achievement for the variant or indicator, as eigenvalues of the rows in the matrix, eigenvalues can be substituted by geometric means (Saaty, 2006, p. 80). For the lowest level of the hierarchy for variants assessed from a perspective of an indicator. This procedure is applied in the paper, where also distributive approach is used, based on normalization to sums of geometric means as described by Saaty (2006, p. 16-21). Weights calculation (4), as described by Saaty (2006, p. 16 - 21), symbols adjusted for purposes of the paper, are calculated as follows for v^{th} variant from the perspective of ith indicator

$$w_{vi} = \frac{GM_{vi}}{\sum_{v=1}^{n} GM_{vi}} \tag{4}$$

where GM_{vi} represents geometric mean for v^{th} variant which is divided by a sum of geometric means for all assessed variants from a view of specific indicator. In the paper, regions are considered as variants.

Analogically, weights for indicators at the local level, where wl_i is local weight of ith indicator, is calculated as in equation 2.5 using local geometric means for the indicators GML_i. Also weights for groups of indicators are calculate using equivalent procedure, weight for j^{th} group of indicators is represented by w_j, global weights are obtained as local weights in a group multiplied by weight of the specific group (Saaty, 2006, p. 16). In case of different number of indicators included to the group m_j, where m_j represents number of indicators in j^{th} group, global weights are influenced. To decrease these impacts a recalculated weights are used (5) as follows

$$wg_i = wl_i * \frac{w_j * \frac{m_j}{\sum_{j=1}^{k} m_j}}{\sum_{j=1}^{k} w_j * \frac{m_j}{\sum_{j=1}^{k} m_j}} \tag{5}$$

where wg_i is global weight of ith indicator, where local weight wl_i is multiplied by w_j adjusted by a ratio of indicators in j^{th} group of indicators to all indicators in k groups of indicators and normalized by a sum of all adjusted weights w_j. This adjustments calculation is presented based on the procedure described by Saaty (2006, p. 16 and 121 - 122), used symbols are adjusted to purposes of this paper. Overall ranking of the variant (region) is calculated as sum of w_{vi} multiplied by adjusted global weights wg_i as the procedure is described by Saaty (2006, p. 115 - 116).

2.3 Indicators for assessment and data used

Ten selected indicators, which can be considered as supportive factors for enlargement of usage and implementation of digitalization with emphasis more on indicators from area of supportive factors than on indicators of technical character and also three sub-areas which have been used can be seen in the diagram in the Figure 1. Names of indicators can be abbreviated in the tables or texts, full description of used indicators and measures are presented in Appendix 1, table 1.

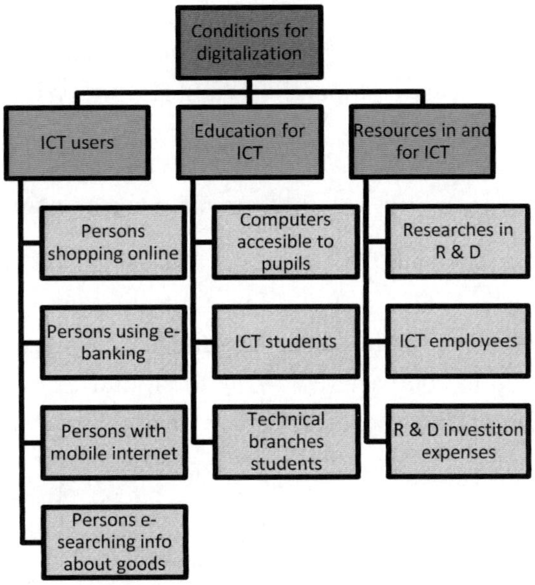

Figure 1 Structure of indicators [Author's processing, source of indicators – Český statistický úřad, 2018]

At first Users of ICT, where focus is on work of users (population) with ICT, as Mařík et al. (2016, p. 162, 164) mentions development of usage of digital technologies and Industry 4.0 is also influence by abilities to work with them on a side of potential users, as it is affected by capacity to adopt digital technologies in a form of products and services. The second area is Education for ICT, where not only number of students of ICT (educated professional are important for development of digitalization ((Mařík et al., 2016, p. 162)), but also educated professionals are essential (Mařík et al., 2016, p. 166 – 167) same as development of skills important for usage of ICT taught from primary schools (Mařík et al., 2016, p. 164, 185). Third area is Resources in and for ICT, either financial resources in a form of investments to Research

& Development whose importance is mentioned Mařík et al. (2016, p. 73-102) or human resources, employees in R & D or employees in ICT branch, also mentioned as important by Mařík et al. (2016, p. 162).

Adjustments and testing of data

The indicators have been selected based on conditions of accessibility of data and their completeness and a condition of quantitative character of data. Condition of accessibility of data has a significant importance in selection of indicators. To sustain comparability of regions from perspectives of indicators, the indicators in a form of ratio, either percentage or calculated to one unit have been used. To apply this approach, particular indicators had to be obtained by additional calculations. Indicators obtained by additional calculations are marked with * in Appendix 1, table 1.

As indicators with different measures are used, it is needed to transform data to minimize an influence of different measurements used for purposes of cluster analysis. In this paper, an approach of normalization of data – transformation to scales with standard deviation 1 and average 0 is applied as described by (Hebák et al. 2004, p. 106 - 107), (Řezanková, Húsek and Snášel 2007, p. 29-32). Řezanková, Húsek and Snášel (2009, p. 27-28) also mention appropriateness of usage indicators without presence of strong multicollinearity. Data was tested for presence of multicollinearity using VIF (variance inflation factor), where values greater than 10 indicates strong multicollinearity (Kennedy, c2003, p. 213). For indicators used in this paper values lower than 10 are achieved as can be seen in Appendix 1, table 2. For AHP values in former measures are used.

3 Results of the applied analyses and comparison of selected regions

At first all regions in the Czech Republic (and capital city Prague) have been divided into groups based on application of cluster analysis. From four identified groups one group of regions has been selected for further analysis. As the focus is on Moravian-Silesian region, group including this region has been selected to compare regions with similar characteristics. This group consists of four regions: Moravian-Silesian, Zlín, Pardubice and Karlovy Vary. These regions have been then compared using analytic hierarchy process.

3.1 Cluster analysis

The procedure of clustering is applied in this paper to filter data by identification of smaller groups of regions, when a group including Moravian-Silesian region is selected for further analysis and assessment. A structure of identified groups of regions is presented in Appendix 3, figure 2. Four main objects can be identified on the selected level of detail, three groups and one object which consists only of capital city Prague and has specific conditions from a view of supportive factors for digitalization. A graph with values for ten indicators used for the analysis for each of the four regions and group average values is presented in Appendix 3, figure 1, following descriptions are based on this graph and values for specific regions and indicators from Czech Statistical Office.

In the text a term group is used, if it is not defined differently, it represents group of analyzed regions. Overall average is defined as an average of all regions including Prague (14 objects) – due to normalization, overall average for all indicators is 0 (also in the graph in Appendix 3, figure 1), group average is calculated from values for four regions: Moravian-Silesian Zlín, Plzeň and Karlovy Vary region. Standard deviations in the group and for all regions have been compared for all indicators. For all indicators, standard deviations have been lower in case of identified group compared to all regions (fourteen regions including Prague).

For the easier presentation normalised values are used complemented by original values. Source of the values for specific regions and for calculations of average values is Czech Statistical Office (Český statistický úřad, 2018). If the focus is on comparison of group averages and overall average of indicators, this group as a whole can be characterised by focus on perspective of education in technical branches (indicator of students in technical branches - 19,29 % compared to overall average 17,98 % and indicator of computers accessible to pupils). Group average for indicator ICT students (4,40 %) is below overall average (4,93 %). In case of indicators in area of ICT users values are close to the overall average, for indicator of persons shopping online, indicator of persons using internet banking and indicator of persons using mobile internet above average and in case of indicator of persons searching information about goods and services online below average. When whole group is assessed, indicators included in the area of resources for ICT, for all indicators, values are below overall average.

When attention is paid to particular regions in the group and their specifics, values lower than overall average are achieved in case of indicator of research and development investment expenses in private sector and in case of indicator of researcher in R & D in Karlovy Vary region. Values above overall average are achieved in case of Karlovy Vary region also in case of indicator of persons shopping online (51,7 % compared with 45,74 %) and indicator of persons using internet in mobile phones (47,8 % compared with 42,07 %), in contrast, ratio of persons searching information about goods and services online (59,7 %) is above overall average (65,58 %) in Karlovy Vary region. Above overall average value is identified also in Plzeň region for indicator of persons with mobile internet. Higher value in comparison with overall average is achieved in Moravian-Silesian region for indicator of computers accessible to pupils at first stages at primary schools. High values (compared to overall average) of indicator of students of technical branches are achieved in Moravian-Silesian and Zlín region.

Moravian-Silesian region can be characterized by values lower than overall averages and close to the group averages in case of indicators included in the area of resources in ITC, except of the indicator of employees in ICT, where the value is close to the overall average is identified. Values higher than group averages are achieved in case of all indicators incorporated in the area of education for ICT, in case of indicator of students of technical branches and indicator of computers accessible to pupils at first stages at primary schools values higher than overall average are achieved. If the perspective of users of ICT is assessed in Moravian-Silesian region, values below group and also overall averages are identified in case of indicator of persons shopping online, indicator of persons using internet in mobile phones and indicator of persons using internet banking. Value lower than overall average, but higher than group average, is achieved for the indicator of persons searching information about goods online. Based on this analysis, perspective of education for ICT can be assumed as strength for Moravian-Silesian region.

3.2 Analytic hierarchy process (AHP)

Analytic hierarchy process has been realized using identical indicator as used in cluster analysis with the hierarchy displayed in figure 3.1. Differently from the approach used for the cluster analysis values of indicators haven't been used in the normalized form, but using original measures. As regions evaluated as regions with similar features according to the cluster analysis, big differences between regions in the assessed group can't be expected. The aim of Analytical hierarchy process application is to identify a position of Moravian-Silesian region among the regions included in the group. At first a pair comparison of regions for each of the indicator is realized and partial weights are achieved. These weights are presented in Appendix 2, table 1.

As different importance of indicators is assumed, weights for these indicators are also calculated using procedure previously described in the paper. Pair comparison of the indicators is based on subjective assessment (questionnaire) realized by five respondents, author and four other respondents from the academic area. Each indicator has been evaluated from four perspectives to assess its importance in further details. The perspectives are: Current support, Support for future/ sustainability, Positive influence on development of business environment – competitiveness and Positive influence on abilities and usage of elements of digitalization. Simultaneously importance of three groups of indicators, Users of ICT, Education for ICT and Resources in and for ICT has been evaluated.

Value from 1 to 5 has been assigned to each indicator assessed from specific perspective, where the biggest importance is represented by number 5. Values obtained from all respondents are used for calculation of averages for each combination indicator/perspective. A table including average evaluation for each indicator from all four perspectives is presented in Appendix 2, table 2. Average values of importance of groups of indicators and indicators themselves have been calculated from partial average values in four perspectives for each specific indicator. These average values are used for calculation of global weights of indicators. Calculated weights for indicators are also displayed in table 1

Persons shopping online	**Persons using e-banking**	**Persons with mobile internet**	**Persons info about goods online**	**Computers for pupils**	**ICT students**	**Tech. branches students**	**Researches in R & D**	**ICT em-ployees**	**R & D invest.**
0.097	0.0902	0.102	0.103	0.096	0.112	0.102	0.084	0.110	0.104

Table 1 Weights for indicators based on four perspective assessment [Calculated by author based on data from questionnaire]

where it can be seen that indicators of ICT employees and of ICT students can be assumed as indicators with higher impact. The indicator with the lowest impact from all assessed indicator is indicator of researchers in research and development in private sector. Overall values (weights) of assessed regions identified based on the cluster analysis are displayed in the table 2 with their ranking.

Region	Overall value	Ranking
Plzeň	0.271095	1
Karlovy Vary	0.202476	4
Zlín	0.262763	3
Moravian-Silesian	0.263666	2

Table 2 Ranking of regions based on weighted indicators [Calculated by author based on data from Český statistický úřad, 2018]

As it can be seen in the table 2, Moravian-Silesian region is placed at the second position in the ranking with very similar value compared to Zlín region which is placed at third position. The most suitable conditions in the business environment from the view of supportive factors for expansion of Industry 4.0 and wider usage of digitalization among the analyzed group of regions are identified in Plzeň region. If achieved values (weights) of regions (before multiplication by weights of indicators) in Moravian-Silesian region are compared to the average values calculated from values (weights) for all four regions for each indicator, it can be observed, that in case of six indicators, values above average are achieved, mainly in case of indicator of employees in ICT and computers accessible to pupils at first stages at primary schools as it can be also seen in Appendix 3, figure 1.

4 Conclusion

This paper has been focused on the comparison of regions from the view of the suitability of conditions or supportive factors for expansion and usage of elements of digitalization based on the ten selected indicators. The regions have been sorted to clusters using cluster analysis to obtain groups with similar conditions from the view of supportive factors for digitalization. Four objects have been identified, three groups and Prague with specific conditions as the cluster itself. One of the clusters including Moravian-Silesian, Zlín, Pardubice and Karlovy Vary region has been selected for further analysis as the aim is to assess Moravian-Silesian region and comparable regions.

Basic characteristics of this group have been described in comparison with overall averages for all regions; specifics of particular regions have been similarly outlined. Focus is also on Moravian-Silesian region, where its features are summarized and compared with overall and also group averages, these findings are represented also in Appendix 3, figure 2. Analytic hierarchy process has been used for comparison of included regions using an approach of different weights for indicators. Weights of the indicators are calculated based on questioning and assessment from four perspectives to include importance of the indicators. Ranking of the four regions have been calculated. Moravian-Silesian region has the second position in the ranking with the overall value close to the Zlín region which is on the third place.

Acknowledgement

This research was financially supported by the Moravian-Silesian region within the program „Podpora vědy a výzkumu v Moravskoslezském kraji 2017" (RRC/10/2017).

References

Baller, S., Dutta, S. and Lanvin, B. (2016). The global Information Technology Report 2016, [Online]. Geneva: World Economic Forum and INSEAD. Available at: www.weforum.org/reports/the-global-information-technology-report-2016 [cited 2018-11-15].

Český statistický úřad, (2018). Český statistický úřad, [Online], Available at: https://www.czso.cz/; https://www.czso.cz/csu/czso/podminky_pro_vyuzivani_a_dalsi_zverejnovani_statistickych_udaju_csu [cited 2018-12-18].

European commision. (2019). Digital single market: DESI by components, [Online]. Available at: https://digital-agenda-data.eu/charts/desi-components#chart={%22indicator%22:%22DESI%22,%22breakdown-group%22:%22DESI%22,%22unit-measure%22:%22pc_DESI%22,%22time-period%22:%222018%22}. [cited 2019-01-04].

Everitt B. et al. (2011). *Cluster analysis,* 5th ed. Chichester, West Sussex, U.K.: Wiley.

Fotr, J. and Švecová, L.. (2016). *Manažerské rozhodování: postupy, metody a nástroje,* 3rd ed. Praha: Ekopress.

Hebák, P. et al. (2004). *Vícerozměrné statistické metody. (1).* Praha: Informatorium.

Hebák, P. et al. (2005). *Vícerozměrné statistické metody. (3).* Praha: Informatorium.

Kennedy, P. (c2003). *A guide to econometrics,* 5th ed. Cambridge: The MIT Press.

Lance, G. N. and Williams, W. T. (1967). 'A general theory of classificatory sorting strategies 1. Hierarchical systems'. *The Computer Journal*, 9 (4), pp. 373-380.

Mařík, V. et al. (2016). *Průmysl 4.0: výzva pro Českou republiku.* Praha: Management Press.

Mirkin, B. (2013). *Clustering – A Data Recovery Approach 2nd edition.* Boca Raton: CRC Press and Taylor & Francis group.

Pielou, E. C. (c1984). *The Interpretation of Ecological Data – A Primer on Classification and Ordination.* New York: John Wiley & Sons.

R Core Team. (2017). R: A language and environment for statistical computing. R Foundation for Statistical Computing, Vienna, Austria, https://www.R-project.org/.

Řezanková, H., Húsek and Snášel, V. (2009). *Shluková analýza dat*, 2nd ed. Praha: Professional Publishing.

Saaty, T. L. (2006). *Fundamentals of decision making and priority theory with the analytic hierarchy process.* Pittsburgh, PA: RWS Publications.

Vogelsang, M. (2010). *Digitalization in Open Economies – Theory and Policy Implications.* Heidelberg: Physica-Verlag Heidelberg.

Xu, R., Wunsch, D. C. (2009). *Clustering.* Hoboken: Wiley.

Ward, J. H., Jr. (1963). 'Hierarchical grouping to optimise an objective function'. *Journal of the American Statistical Association*, 58, pp. 236-244.

Zhang, J. (c2008). *Visualization for Information Retrieval.* Berlin: Springer-Verlag Berlin Heidelberg.

Appendix 1 – List of indicators and testing of multicollinearity

Indicator	Measurement
Persons using internet for shopping	% from population older than 16 years
Persons using internet for internet banking	% from population older than 16 years
Persons using mobile internet	% from population older than 16 years
Persons using internet for searching information about goods and services	% from population older than 16 years
Students of ICT at state or private universities (according to permanent residence)	% from overall number of students at state or private universities (according to permanent residence)
Researches in R & D in private sector*	% of full time equivalent from employed population
Computers accessible to pupils at the first stage of primary schools	Number of computers per 100 pupils
Students of technical branches at state or private universities (according to permanent residence)	% from overall number of students at state or private universities (according to permanent residence)
R & D investment expenses – private sector *	Mil. Kč per 1 business unit
Employment in information and communication branches *	% from employed population

Table 1 Indicators used for assessment regions from a perspective of expansion of digitalization [Author's processing, source of indicators and measurements – Český statistický úřad, 2018]

Multicollinearity matrix

	Persons shopping online	Persons using e-banking	Persons with mobile internet	Persons searching info about goods online	Computers accessible to pupils at the first stage of primary schools	ICT students	Technical branches students	Researches in R & D	ICT employees	R & D investment expenses
Persons shopping online	8.224549	-5.79497	-1.0618	-4.10011	4.395657	0.387035	-3.22347	5.094754	2.426179	0.071758
Persons using e-banking	-5.79497	7.237101	-0.54755	0.388951	-4.48618	-2.07	3.331996	-5.31875	-1.16171	2.730218
Persons with mobile internet	-1.0618	-0.54755	3.384644	0.719775	1.21114	1.062314	1.094057	0.719336	0.281637	-2.09798
Persons searching info about goods online	-4.10011	0.388951	0.719775	7.371656	-2.20045	1.814814	-0.61467	-1.2886	-3.99135	-3.65191
Computers accessible at the first stage of primary schools	4.395657	-4.48618	1.21114	-2.20045	5.382474	0.333747	-2.02446	5.244383	2.248034	-0.75662
ICT students	0.387035	-2.07	1.062314	1.814814	0.333747	4.760212	-1.04417	-0.10425	-1.59715	-5.21349
Technical branches students	-3.22347	3.331996	1.094057	-0.61467	-2.02446	-1.04417	4.726707	-3.72347	0.233469	1.980582
Researches in R & D – private sector	5.094754	-5.31875	0.719336	-1.2886	5.244383	-0.10425	-3.72347	7.845238	2.08991	-0.04035
ICT employees	2.426179	-1.16171	0.281637	-3.99135	2.248034	-1.59715	0.233469	2.08991	3.907187	2.073365
R & D investment expenses – private sector	0.071758	2.730218	-2.09798	-3.65191	-0.75662	-5.21349	1.980582	-0.04035	2.073365	8.27609

Table 2 Multicollinearity matrix [Author's calculations based on data from Český statistický úřad, 2018]

Appendix 2 – AHP, weights of variants (regions) and importance (weights) of indicators

	Persons shopping online	Persons using e-banking	Persons with mobile internet	Persons searching info about goods online	Computers accessible to pupils at the first stage of primary schools	ICT students	Technical branches students	Researches in R & D – private sector	ICT employees	R & D investment expenses - private sector
Weight of the indicator	0.097200	0.09015	0.102164	0.102543	0.095739	0.111966	0.10223	0.084287	0.109874	0.103853
Plzeň region	0.246170	0.25758	0.275862	0.256291	0.242021	0.245741	0.234078	0.334475	0.229502	0.399222
Karlovy Vary region	0.273112	0.25311	0.274713	0.231127	0.230053	0.244539	0.230348	0.079746	0.146019	0.054194
Zlín region	0.248811	0.25411	0.227012	0.26055	0.256649	0.251299	0.27436	0.32139	0.230275	0.314069
Moravian-Silesian region	0.231907	0.23521	0.222414	0.252032	0.271277	0.258422	0.261215	0.26439	0.394205	0.232515

Table 1 Calculation of the weights based on pair comparison [Author's calculations based on data from Český statistický úřad, 2018]

Indicators/Perspectives	Current support	Support for future/ sustainability	Positive influence on development of business environment - competitiveness	Positive influence on abilities and usage of elements of digitalization	Average
Users of ICT	4.2	3.4	3.2	4	3.7
Education for ICT	2.6	4.6	3.8	4.6	3.9
Resources in and for ICT	4.2	3.8	3.6	3.4	3.75
Persons shopping online	4.2	2.8	3.6	2.8	3.35
Persons using e-banking	2.8	2.4	3.4	3.4	3
Persons with mobile internet	3.4	3.4	3.2	3.6	3.4
Persons searching info about goods online	3.4	3.4	3.8	3	3.4
Computers at the first stage of primary schools	2.2	3.8	2	3.8	2.95
ICT students	2.8	4.2	3	3.8	3.45
Technical branches students	2.6	3.6	3	3.4	3.15
Researches in R & D – private sector	3	3.4	2.8	2	2.8
ICT employees	3.8	4.2	3.2	3.4	3.65
R & D investment expenses – private sector	3.4	4.6	3.8	2	3.45

Table 2 Assessment of indicators based on four perspectives – scale 1-5. 5 - highest impact [Author's processing based on questioning. backgrounds for selection of perspectives - literature resources as Mařík, 2016]

Appendix 3 – Structure of clusters and graph of normalized values of indicators

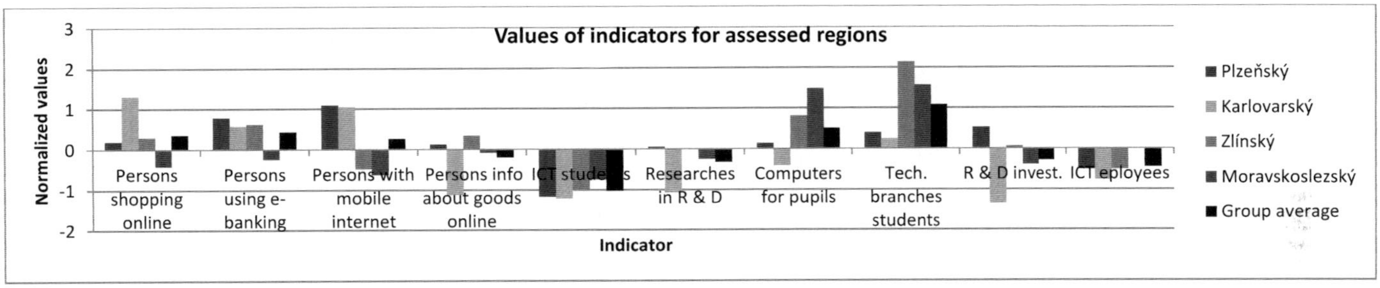

Figure 1 Graph with values of indicators for four analyzed regions [Author's calculations based on data from Český statistický úřad, 2018]

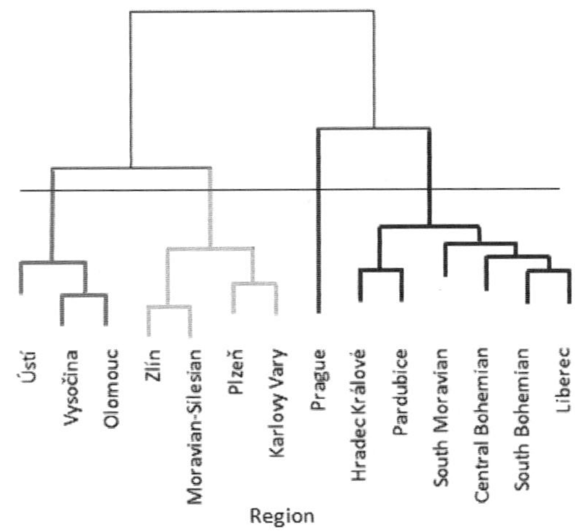

Figure 2 Structure of groups of regions based on 10 indicators [Author's calculations based on data from Český statistický úřad, 2018]

SECTION

D

APPLICATIONS OF NEW MEDIA AND INTELLIGENT TOOLS IN THE DIGITAL ECONOMY AND MODELLING

Non-stationary time series prediction based on empirical mode decomposition and artificial neural networks

Lun Gao[1], Huanyu Li[2]

Abstract. Non-stationary time series prediction has always been a problem. Traditional models are often difficult to predict accurately due to cumulative errors. The EMD model commonly used in vibration and sound signal processing can separate signals according to frequency to reduce the error caused by signals of different frequency. This idea can be applied to high-frequency data processing in finance. This article uses empirical mode decomposition (EMD) techniques to decompose non-stationary time series into a series of intrinsic mode functions (*IMFs*) and one residual (*r*) . Then, by constructing a neural network model for each *IMF* and r, thereby achieving a combined prediction of the original time series. Using the Prague trading market data to verify the effectiveness of the method, The results show that this method has higher prediction accuracy than the backpropagation artificial neural network model. The empirical results of the paper show that the EMD combination prediction can effectively solve the non-stationary problem, and the prediction accuracy achieves good results.

Keywords: Combined Forecast, EMD, Backpropagation, Artificial Neural Network.

JEL Classification: G17, G11, G24

1 Introduction

Financial time series signals are the carriers of all information in the market. Signal acquisition and time-frequency analysis are important contents in the field of financial forecasting. However, signals obtained from the market are subject to various influences, and inevitably carry noise with limited accuracy. However, the noise spectrum will inevitably carry a certain amount of information that cannot be discarded. Therefore, the decomposition of time series signals has become the first step in time series analysis and prediction. Empirical mode decomposition, referred to as EMD is an adaptive decomposition method， the method is well known (Huang, 1998). The signal decomposition result consists of several intrinsic mode functions (*IMF*) arranged in order from high frequency to low frequency. For time-series signals, the noise is concentrated on the high-frequency *IMF* component, and the *IMF* can be predicted separately to reduce noise interference. The stock market plays a decisive role in today's economic activities. It is a barometer of the economy of a country or region. Studying the stock market trend helps countries, companies and even individuals to effectively avoid financial risks where Zhu et al. (2013) provide the solution.

Experts and scholars have done a lot of research on time series fluctuations and predictions. For example, Tully and Lucey (2007) pointed that the APGARCH model can better describe the price fluctuation of gold than the GARCH model based on normal distribution. However

[1] Technical University of Ostrava / Faculty of Economics, Department of Finance, lun.gao@vsb.cz
[2] Technical University of Ostrava / Faculty of Economics, Department of Finance, huanyu.li@vsb.cz

although the APGARCH model can describe the long memory of financial time series, the traditional statistical models and economic models are based on the assumption that the data is linear. It is difficult to capture nonlinear patterns hidden in time series, and usually cannot obtain accurate prediction results where this solution already exists (Zhang et al., 2008).

In order to overcome the limitations of traditional models, computational intelligence methods such as artificial neural networks (ANN) and support vector machines (SVM) are applied to time series prediction for example Parisi et al (2008) applied recursive neural network models in gold price prediction. Experimental results show that the prediction accuracy of these methods is better than the traditional model.

The main goal of this paper is to use EMD to decompose the original signal, and then predict the decomposed data, and finally obtain the predicted value that reduces the cumulative error. With the help of empirical mode decomposition technique in the field of digital signal processing and artificial neural network model. This paper models and predicts the data series of the Prague stock exchange market based on EMD and BP-ANN. So far, few scholars have used EMD and ANN to predict the stock market. The stock market index data is a non-stationary time series because it has trends and periodicity (mean and variance changes with time). The article uses EMD to decompose the time series into several *IMFs*, each of which is a time series signal. These time signals have a distinct pattern relative to the original signal that can be mined, using neural networks to predict these signal sequences separately. The empirical results of the article show that the model works well.

This paper is divided into four parts. The first part is Introduction, which is a brief introduction to the article; the second part is to describe the model used in the article and list its formula; The third part is the empirical analysis part. The model cited in the second part will be used to predict the data from the Prague stock exchange market, and the results will be analyzed. Finally, in the fourth part, it is concluded that the composite model based on the EMD model is significantly better than the single traditional model.

2 EMD combined forecasting model Introduction

2.1 Theory of Empirical mode decomposition (EMD)

The idea of EMD decomposition is to decompose the signal into several relatively stationary, uncorrelated intrinsic mode functions (*IMFs*). An intrinsic mode functions function should satisfy the following two conditions. The solution already exists (Cui et al., 2015):

1) In the entire data sequence, the number of extreme points should be equal to the number of zero-crossing points, or at most one difference.
2) At any point in time, the local mean defined by the local maxima and local minima of the signal should be zero.

Briefly, *IMF* is a time series with a mean close to zero and no obvious trend. The nature of *IMF* is exactly in line with the needs of traditional time series analysis, so non-stationary time series can be decomposed by EMD to obtain a series of *IMFs*, and then to analyzed. Meanwhile, for non-stationary time series, the residual amount produced by EMD decomposition generally contains a certain trend, so it called trend term. The trend term reflects the overall trend of the original time series, the problem is well-known (Zhu et al., 2013) which eliminates minor events and short-term effects.

The EMD method first needs to find the local pole of the signal $x(t)$ to get the upper and lower envelopes by interpolation and then calculate the mean of the upper and lower envelopes. Rao et al. (2015) had denoted as $m1$. *It* calculates by equation (1):

$$d(t) = x(t) - m1. \tag{1}$$

Repeat the steps until the obtained $d(t)$ satisfies the condition of the intrinsic mode function. Then get $d(t)$ as the first intrinsic mode function which is recorded as: $IMF1 = c(t)$. Then replace $x(t)$ with the residual $r(t) = x(t) - d(t)$. The i-th *IMF* is usually expressed as $c_i(t)$. If $d(t)$ is not an *IMF*, use $d(t)$ instead of $x(t)$ to calculate. Cycling above steps until the residuals meet certain termination screening conditions.

After that all intrinsic mode functions $IMFn$ and residual $r(t)$ will finally get from the signal $x(t)$. The original signal can be expressed as:

$$x(t) = \sum_{i=1}^{n} c_i(t) + r(t) \tag{2}$$

where n is the number of *IMFs* and $r(n)$ is the trend term.

The EMD decomposition is based on three assumptions: 1) any signal can be decomposed into several *IMF* components; 2) each *IMF* component could be linear or non-linear, the number of local zero and extreme points are the same, and the upper and lower envelopes are locally symmetric about the time axis; 3) a signal can contain several *IMF* components. When the sequence extreme points are not obvious, it is necessary to find the extreme points by several differences where Liu et al (2018) pointed out.

2.2 The Back-Propagation neural networks

In this paper, the neural networks and Back-Propagation will be used to predict the PX Index. After the Empirical mode decomposition applied, the original data will be divided into several intrinsic mode functions (*IMFs*) and a residual data. These decomposed signals include the features of original data, so the Neural networks will be built to predict the *IMFs* and trend term.

Xu and Ju (2000) proved The Back-Propagation is a sensible approach to enabling the adaptation of each weight.We try to minimize the error between each target output and the output actually computed by the network. At the output layer, the weight update rule is very simple. And through the investigation, the neural networks have three hidden layers' sigmoid can reach any Nonlinear functions with finite discontinuity points.

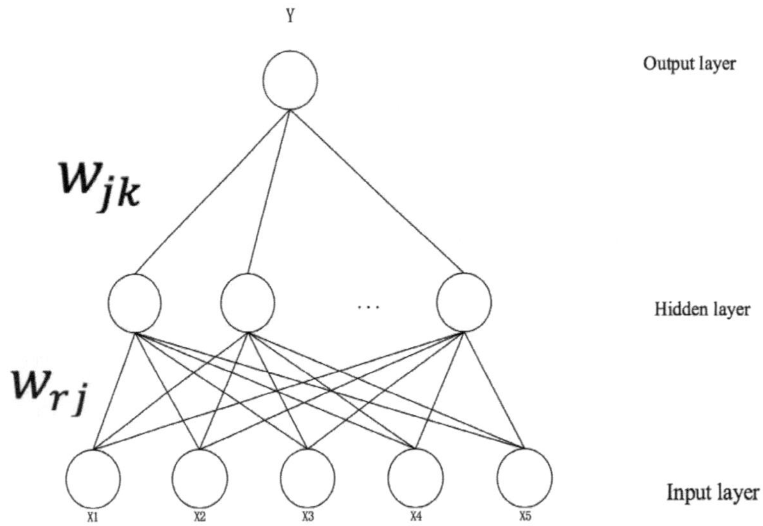

Figure 1 Back-Propagation Learning Three-layer feed-forward network [Word print]

From the chart before, it is obviously seen the neural networks have three-layer networks, and every node in each layer just responsible for the layer before and put the information to the next layer. And set we have n sample (X_n, Y_n) (n=1,2,3...n), the weight between the input layer and hidden layer is w_{rj}, and the weight between the hidden layer and the output layer is w_{jk}, besides the threshold value of the hidden layer and output layer are θ_j, θ_k D, where D. Marcek and D.M. Marcek (2006) improved the method.

Now the function can be get from the hidden layer, which is:

$$X_j = f\left(\sum_{i=1}^{n} w_{rj} \cdot x_i + \theta_j\right) j = 1,2,3...,n \tag{3}$$

The function of the output layer is:

$$Y_1 = f\left(\sum_{j=1}^{m} w_{jk} + \theta_k\right) k = 1,2,3...,m \tag{4}$$

And the $f(\mu)$ is the sigmoid function, the form show below:

$$f(\mu) = \frac{1}{1+e^{-\mu}} \tag{5}$$

But the Back-Propagation method need data to learning, set the input data have n sample, $A_1, A_2, A_3, ..., A_n$, and these data response to $Y_1, Y_2, Y_3, ..., Y_n$, but the results are different from neural networks' output. The Back-Propagation will depend on the real output $\hat{y}_1, \hat{y}_2, \hat{y}_3, ..., \hat{y}_n$, use the error between the teaching data and real data to modify the weight and threshold. If we use the square function to measure the error, for the n sample, have:

$$E = \frac{1}{2} \cdot \sum_{i=1}^{n} \sum_{i=1}^{m} (Y_1^i - \hat{y}_1^i) \tag{6}$$

And in this function, the $\hat{y}_1^i$ is the real output by the first sample, and Y_1^i is the responsible output (teaching output), and Hertz et al. (1991) and Bishop (1995) proved that for the given learning accuracy ϵ, if the $E < \epsilon$ we stop learning.

Moreover, even though the database did not be simplified, the neural network will also study the data set, but if it is needed to improve the learning efficiency and accelerate the convergence speed, the data should be simplified by the function below:

$$x_i' = \frac{x_i - \min(x)}{\max(x) - \min(x)}, i = 1,2,3, \ldots \quad (7)$$

3 The prediction of Prague stock exchange Index based one Empirical mode decomposition

3.1 Data source and method

In this paper, data from the Prague Stock Exchange will be cited, from 07/11/2017 to 07/02/2019 (total 312 data), the last close of PX Index as the research object. We use the neutral networks to predict the PX index, for evaluating our results, we use B-P learning to predict the empirical mode decomposition data and original data. In this paper, all results are calculated by MATLAB and Eviews.

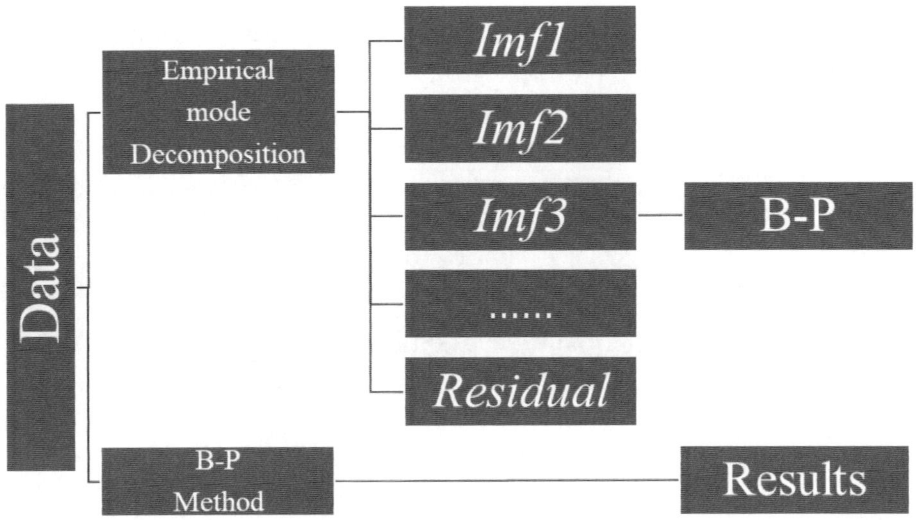

Figure 2 Modeling process

3.2 Description of data

From the 312 data, the max data is 1140.01, and the minimum data is 977.91 and other statistical indicators seen in table 1, and first, it is necessary to perform Augment Dickey-Fuller (ADF) test see in Figure 3 on the data to verify that the data is non-stationarity.

	MAX	MIN	AVE	SD	MEDIAN	KURT	SKEW
DATA	1140.01	977.91	1080.84	33.1662	1081.19	0.2179	-0.6273

Table 1 PX Index statistic description [MATLAB]

Null Hypothesis: SIGNAL has a unit root
Exogenous: Constant
Lag Length: 0 (Automatic - based on SIC, maxlag=15)

		t-Statistic	Prob.*
Augmented Dickey-Fuller test statistic		-1.803899	0.3783
Test critical values:	1% level	-3.451214	
	5% level	-2.870621	
	10% level	-2.571679	

*MacKinnon (1996) one-sided p-values.

Figure 3 ADF test of signal data [Eviews]

It can be clearly seen from the Figure 3 that the t-statistic is 1.804 and the P-value is 0.3783. Based on this, the data signal is non-stationary. The following can perform empirical mode decomposition on the original signal data.

3.3 Empirical mode decomposition

Based on the algorithm's settings, empirical mode decomposition will automatically decomposes the signal data and arrange the *IMFs* from high to low according to frequency. See in Figure 4 to Figure 6.

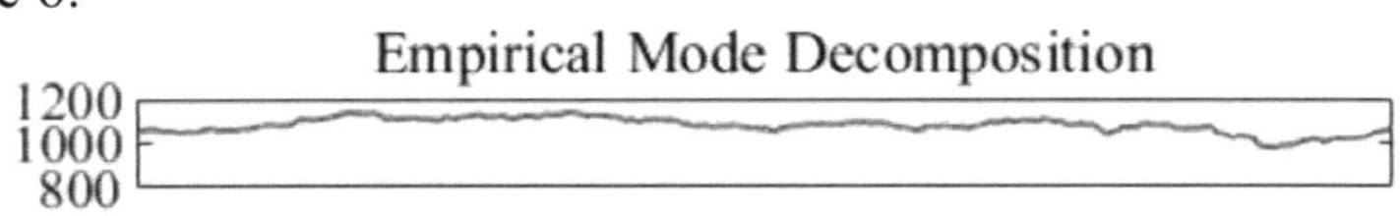

Figure 4 Original signal [Matlab print]

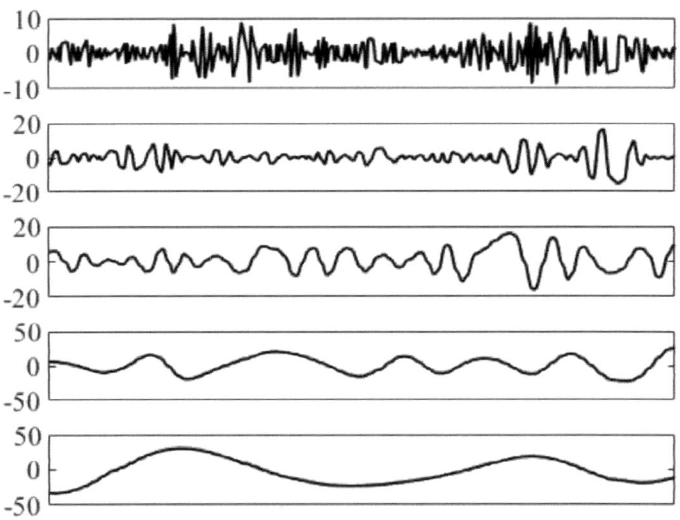

Figure 5 IMF1-5 [Matlab]

Figure 6 Residual [Matlab]

	PCCs	Var	Var (%)	Max	min	Median
IMF1	0.120356	11.50276	1.03%	8.816625	-8.87996	-0.05749
IMF2	0.124345	16.41069	1.47%	16.45531	-15.3168	-0.08493
IMF3	0.22602	37.21889	3.34%	16.12771	-15.7305	1.136634
IMF4	0.423452	132.7634	11.90%	24.82698	-22.6367	0.986932
IMF5	0.533911	317.5178	28.46%	30.44799	-33.1106	-6.02323
Residual	0.719324	526.1348	47.17%	1106.367	1037.331	1088.59
Observe	null	1115.506	100%	null	null	null

Table 2 Statistic description of EMD data

After EMD decomposition of the data signal, 5 *IMF*s and a trend term are generated. Each of the *IMF* component curves exhibits an oscillating form that is substantially symmetric around the zero mean line, the local maximum and the local minimum. The period of the five *IMF* components is from short to long, that is, the frequency is from high to low. The trend term reflects the non-stationarity of the original sequence to some extent and the trend is oscillating, which is consistent with the observation of the original sequence.

After the calculation of each components the Pearson correlation coefficient (PCCs), variance, the contribution of variance, the maximum, the minimum and the median will be got. In the table 2, it can see the results get from calculation. In 95% confidence interval, the *IMF4*, the *IMF5* and the residual have higher linear correlation with raw signal data, and their variance contribution are also higher, which means the main information of the original signal data is reflected in the *IMF4*, the *IMF5* and the residual. In the field of signal analysis, vibration and noise reduction, high frequency signals can be discarded as noise. However, in financial time series analysis, any loss of signal can cause huge errors, so all *IMFs* need to be predicted.

3.4 Model Results and comparison

In this paper, 312 time points are considered in our calculation, and B-P method will take the closest 30 data as the test set. Author set the parameters when use the neural networks. Author divided the 312 data into 10 group, as the training data, the second group is the target as the first group and so forth. The model set the input layer, neurons are 30, the hidden layer, there are 10 neurons, and output layer has 30. Training will set threshold as 0.0005, the Purelin function.

Many standards can be used to measure results, like the mean absolute distance *(MAD),* sum of squared error *(SSE),* mean square error*(MSE)*and root mean squared error*(RMSE).* In this paper, author take the MSE and RMSE as evaluating indictors.

In many financial trades, analytic solutions cannot be got, so the prediction of the future trend is same significant as the results. The times- series can go up and go down in the nest epoch, we ignore the conditions two results are same. When the current index is higher than last index, we call it up trend, otherwise, it is the down trend. The table below show the B-P and EMD prediction results.

	MSE	RMSE	Trend prediction
B-P(EMD)	269.779	16.425	75%
B-P (non-EMD)	902.603	30.043	70%

Table 3 Predict results From EMD and B-P [Source: calculation based on MATLAB]

In the table 3, it demonstrates two comparisons, one is B-P with EMD, other is B-P without EMD. From the table, regardless of the EMD method, the neural networks show great prediction accuracy, the trends are 75% and 70%. And in other way, the empirical mode decomposition shows great function in reducing the accumulative errors, the accuracy increased nearly 50%. The RMSE of B-P model with using EMD is 16.425, however without using the EMD, the results increased to 30.043. This means that the model's error is significantly reduced after using the EMD model. Use the help of the model, empirical mode decomposition doesn't affect the trend but has significant promotion in the accuracy. After the empirical mode decomposition, the data are more regular to analysis, is better for neural networks to predict.

	Less 1%	1%-2%	2%-5%	Over 5%
B-P (EMD)	54.17%	29.17%	12.50%	4.17%
B-P (non-EMD)	20.83%	25.00%	33.33%	20.83%

Table 4 The absolutely rate of the neural networks with EMD and without EMD

From the table 4, the same results are shown with the table 3. After the empirical mode decomposition, the neural networks can increase the accuracy obviously. The upper table show that after the empirical mode composition, the neural networks can decrease the error, there is 4.17% predict index over 5%, so the model is very accuracy.

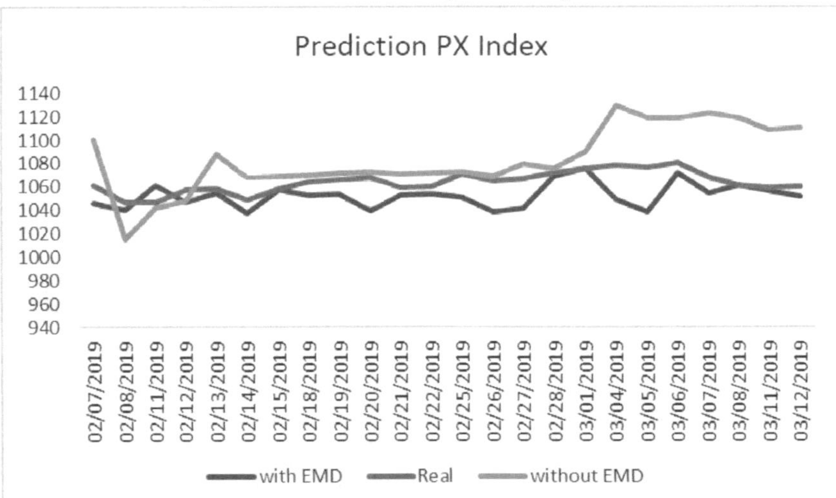

Figure 7 Prediction PX Index comparisons [Excel print]

4 Conclusion

With the help of empirical mode decomposition, the non-stationary time series will be decomposed into *IMFs* and residuals. Use the *IMFs* to construct the neural networks to predict the PX Index, the results from calculation demonstrate the EMD has significant effect in non-stationary time series data. The RMSE and MSE is obvious less than the B-P without EMD model. And in the B-P EMD model, we can see the RMSE is 16.425, the predict accuracy is very high, however without the EMD, we can see the RMSE is 30.043, it is very high, it means day error is 30 average. This paper shows the empirical mode decomposition can be used in financial analysis, can eliminate errors and increase the accuracy in prediction.

Acknowledgements

Thanks to Ms. Huimin Chen from Nanjing University for giving technical guidance to this paper.

References

Arnold,T. (2014). *A Pragmatic guide to Real Options*. New York: Palgrave Macmillan.

Bishop, Ch. M. (1995). *Neural Networks for Pattern Recognition*. New York: Oxford University Press.

Cui,B. B., Chen,X. Y. and Song,R. (2015). 'The EMD Threshold Filtering applied in Fiber Optic Gyro Drift Signal Denoising (EMD 阈值滤波在光纤陀螺漂移信号去噪中的应用)'. *Acta Optica Sinica*, 2, pp. 61-66.

Hertz,J. A., Krogh,A.S. and Palmer, R. G. (1991). *Introduction to the Theory of Neural Computation*. Mass, USA: Addison-Wesley.

Huang, N. E. et.al. (1998). 'The empirical mode decomposition and the Hilbert spectrum for nonlinear and non-stationary time series analysis'. *Proceedings of the Royal Society A*, pp. 903-993.

Liu,H. J., Liu,S. G. and Li, M. (2018). 'EMD and Wavelet Threshold Denoising Method of Gear-shift Acceleration Signals' *Noise and vibration control,* 38 (20), pp.198-203.

Marcek, D. and Marcek, D. M. (2006). *Neural Networks and Their applications*. Zilina: University of Zilina Press (in Slovak).

Parisi, A., Parisi, F. and Diaz,D. (2008). 'Forecasting Gold Price Changes: Rolling and Recursive Neural Network Models'. *Journal of Multinational Financial management,* 18 (5), pp. 477-487.

Rao, Y. Z., Wang, L., Rao, R., Shao, Y. J. and Liu, J. (2015). 'A method for blasting vibration signal de-noising based on empirical mode decomposition wavelet threshold'. *Journal of Fuzhou University (Natural Science Edition),* 43 (2), pp. 271-277

Tully, E. and Lucey, B. M. (2007). 'A Power GARCH Examination of the Gold Market'. *Research in International Business and Finance,* 21 (2), pp.316-325.

Zhang, X., Lai, K. K. and Shou, Y. W. (2008). 'A New Approach for Crude oil Price Analysis Based on Empirical Mod Decomposition'. *Energy Economics,* 30 (3), pp. 905-918.

Zhu, J. P., Zhang, N. X. and Zhu, W. Z. (2013). 'The EMD combined prediction and application in non-stationary time series (非平稳时间序列的 EMD 组合预测及其应用)' . *Statistics & Decision*, 15, pp. 4-8.

Xu, JZ. and Ju, JX. (2000) 'Application of B-P Neural Network in Economic Forecast of Data Communication Business (BP 神经网络在数据通信业务经济预测中的应用)' *Forecasting,* 6, pp. 60-64.

Stock Value and Currency Exchange Rate Prediction Using an Artificial Neural Network Trained By a Genetic Algorithm

Martin Maděra [1] , Dušan Marček [2]

Abstract. Prediction of a stock value or a currency exchange rate is a complex problem which has benefited from recent advancements and research in machine learning. Very popular model for the predictions are deep neural networks. This paper discusses two training algorithms for the feedforward neural networks the backpropagation algorithm and a genetic algorithm. Although the backpropagation algorithm is a reliable way to train a neural network, it can be very demanding on computational resources for lager datasets which are common in some types of trading. Heuristics like the genetic algorithms can help to lower the demands of the training process. The discussed genetic algorithm is an implementation of a classical genetic algorithm with Rank selection of parents for crossover and genes represented as a real number. The accuracy of predictions made by the network trained using this algorithm is then compared to the network trained by backpropagation.

Keywords: Genetic algorithm, Neural network, Time series prediction, Exchange rate prediction.

JEL classification: C63, C61, C53

1 Introduction

The stock values or currency exchange rates can be precisely predicted using ARIMA models (autoregressive integrated moving average models) which work well in situations when the users are not strictly time-constrained. Creating an ARIMA model can be very demanding on computational resources and time especially when a large data set is used for making the model. The process of creating an ARIMA model is also hard to parallelize which means it cannot fully use the computational potential of nowadays computers.

Artificial neural networks are mathematical models which can approximate every math function (Hornik, Stinchcombe, and White 1989) including an ARIMA model and can be developed (trained) using machine learning algorithms. This paper discusses a genetic algorithm for training a neural network and compares it to backpropagation. Backpropagation is an algorithm based on computing an error a neural net made and computing which parameters of the net affected the error. (Basheer and Hamjeer 2000) For larger networks, especially the deep neural networks which have more than three layers, this leads to computing many partial derivatives which can be rather demanding on nowadays computers. Genetic algorithms on the other hand generally do not have this issue however since they are heuristic algorithms, they can give an imperfect result.

The goal of this paper is to find a genetic algorithm for training an artificial neural network so that the network trained by this algorithm gives essentially the same results for prediction as

[1]Technical University of Ostrava, Faculty of Economics, Ostrava, Czech Republic, Department of Applied Informatics, martin.madera@vsb.cz

[2]Technical University of Ostrava, Faculty of Economics, Ostrava, Czech Republic, Department of Applied Informatics, dusan.marcek@vsb.cz

a neural network trained by backpropagation.

The chosen data set for prediction is high frequency trading data representing a currency exchange rate between Czech Koruna (CZK) and Euro (EUR) for the 1st week of December 2018. The data were analysed, pre-processed and an AR prediction model was created. Two neural networks were trained, one using backpropagation and one using the chosen genetic algorithm. The genetic algorithm was refined so that the networks give statistically the same result which was validated using a t-test.

2 Used data

The data used for research discussed in this paper were published by GAIN Capital company and are freely available at http://ratedata.gaincapital.com/.

2.1 Data description

The data comes in CSV (Comma Separated Values) format and data for exchange rate of CZK (Czech Koruna) to EUR (Euro) for the 1st week of December 2018 was used.

Date Time	Bid Rate
02/12/2018 18:29	25.9402
02/12/2018 18:30	25.938
02/12/2018 18:31	25.9377
02/12/2018 18:32	25.947
02/12/2018 18:33	25.9486
02/12/2018 18:34	25.9486
02/12/2018 18:35	25.9508
02/12/2018 18:36	25.9498
02/12/2018 18:37	25.9498
02/12/2018 18:38	25.9516

Table 1 Preview of used data, source: http://ratedata.gaincapital.com/

The data set starts at the 2nd December 2018 17:02:14 and ends at the 17th December 2018 16:59:55. It contains 60586 values. It should have 1-minute time resolution however some values are duplicate, some are missing. Table 1 shows a preview of the data.

2.2 Data pre-processing

For creating a prediction model for a time series, the series must be free of duplicate values and the values must be evenly spaced in time. The STATA software was used for this. After removal of duplicates and interpolating the missing values, the time series showed a declining trend, see Figure 1.

For successful usage of the Box-Jenkins method for creating an ARIMA (autoregressive integrated moving average) model, the data should be stationary. If the time series is log transformed and differentiated, the trend disappears, see Figures 2 and 3. (Marček 2013)

The pre-processed data were saved to a CSV file which was later used for training and evaluating the neural networks.

2.3 Box-Jenkins, ARIMA model

On 99% confidence, both the autocorrelogram and the partial autocorrelogram show autocorrelations up to 10th value, see Figure 4 and Figure 5. According to the Box-Jenkins method, the ARIMA (10, 1, 10) model can be used. The parameters for the model were found using STATA software, see Figure 5. This model can be approximated using artificial neural networks (Marček 2013).

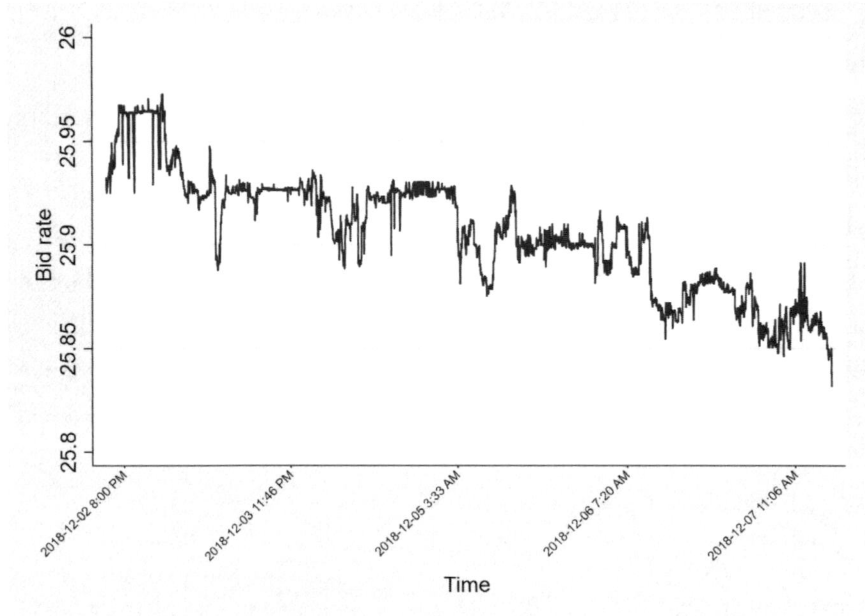

Figure 1 Original time series, CZK/EUR exchange rate.

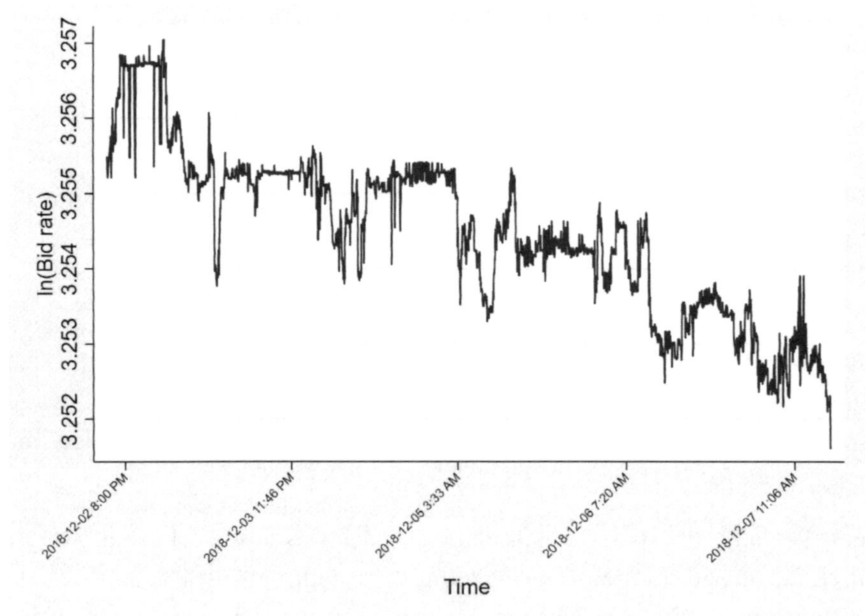

Figure 2 Exchange rate, log transformed.

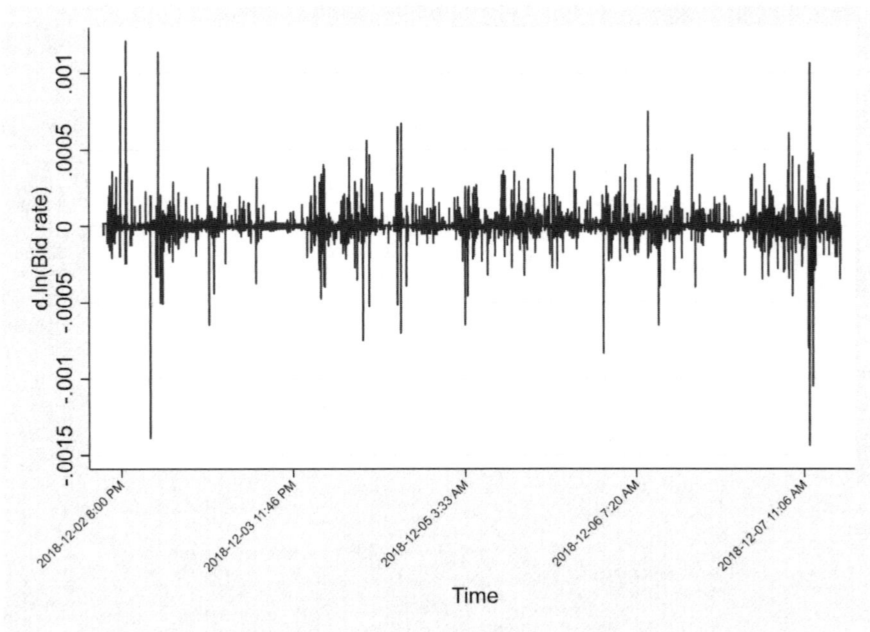

Figure 3 Exchange rate, log transformed and differentiated.

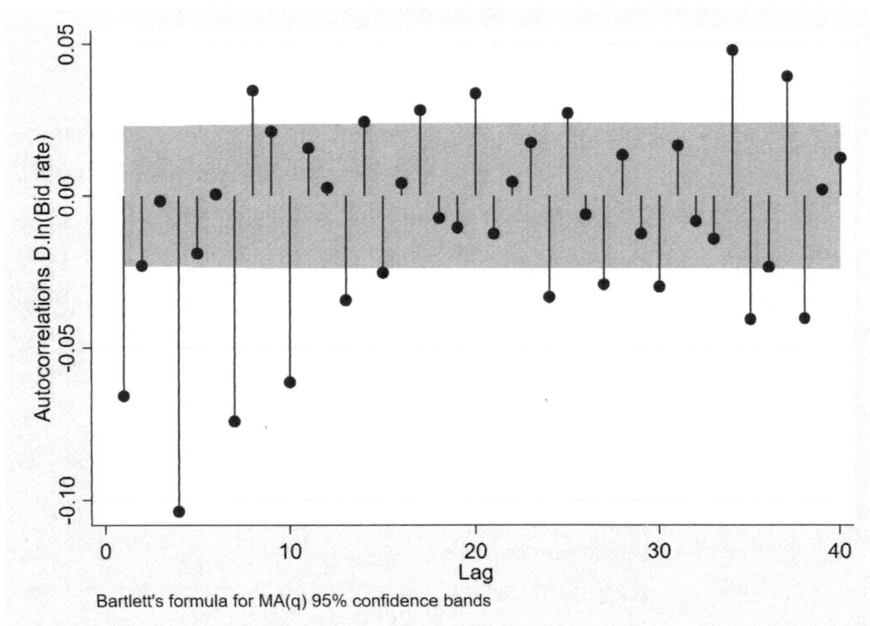

Figure 4 Autocorrelogram of differentiated and log transformed exchange rate

3 Neural network trained by backpropagation

Although the goal is to develop a genetic algorithm for training neural networks, a baseline for comparison is needed. Based on author's experience in commercial software development, there are several options currently available for use in commercial software. One of the commercial-grade libraries is Deeplearning4j (https://deeplearning4j.org/), a deep learning and vector/matrix library for the Java platform. Since the author is the most experienced with Java and has experience with Deeplearning4j from commercial software development (although

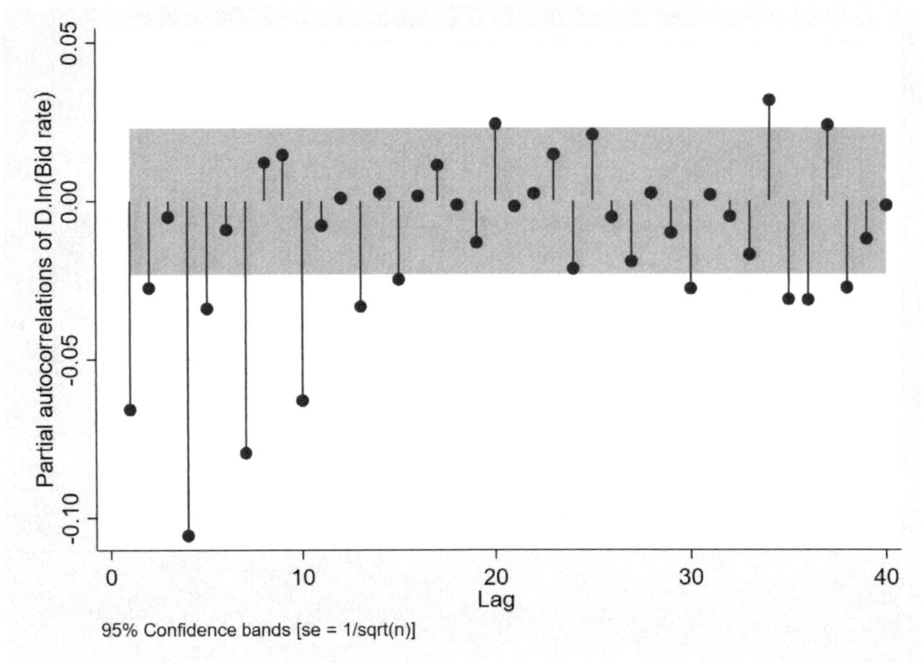

Figure 5 Partial autocorrelogram of differentiated and log transformed exchange rate

limited to the matrix operations), this one was chosen as the baseline.

Deeplearning4j defines an API (application programming interface) for defining multi-layer neural networks to be trained using the backpropagation algorithm. This algorithm is dependent on vector and matrix operations, which are optimized for currently available computers or computer clusters and the mathematical operations can be run on either CPUs (central processing units) or GPUs (graphical processing units) if CUDA (library for C programming language created by the NVidia company allowing software to perform parallel computations on their graphical cards) is available. The author's computer does not have a GPU supporting CUDA, therefore only the CPU was used for computations. The author's computer has a CPU with 6 independent cores supporting the Hyper-Threading technology.

The API of the Deeplearning4j library allows for easy creation of multi-layered neural networks and allows for defining many parameters of layers. However, defining custom activation functions, loss functions or even training algorithms, though technically possible, is rather inconvenient. This library was not meant to be extended. The needs of this project were to define a three-layer neural network with bias, hidden layer with sigmoid activation function, output layer with linear activation function (or identity function) and Mean Squared Error loss function. Deeplearning4j already provides optimized implementations of these things so extending it was not needed for this case.

3.1 Shape of the network

The ARIMA model for predicting this time series is based on 10 auto-regressive and 10 moving average values, as shown in section 2.3. Therefore, the network should have 20 neurons in the input layer. The Deeplearning4j implementation of neural networks uses a neuron with no input wired to each other neurons as a bias. It is crucial that the values of (input + bias) are rather small, because sigmoid function is used as an activation function of the one hidden layer. The last, output layer has the identity function the activation function and has only 1 output neuron. Based on empirical experience the good size of the hidden layer is 25 neurons. Larger size did not provide better results while smaller provided worse.

The resulting shape of the network was three layers, having 20 - 25 - 1 neurons each. This network can be used for approximating the above mentioned ARIMA model, predicting a value for 1 time unit (1 minute in this case) in the future from 10 past values (10 minutes from the past) and 10 past error terms of the moving average part of the ARIMA model.

3.2 Training the network

The network was trained using Stochastic Gradient Descent algorithm with learning rate of 0.25 (this value was based on empirical experience) and the loss function was Mean Squared Error. Their implementations were provided by the Deeplearning4j library.

The time series data was split into training and evaluation data so the training data consist of 90% of the original series. The training data were split into mini-batches of 1000 samples. Parameters of the network were changed after each mini-batch. After passing through all the original data, Mean Squared Error (MSE) was computed for evaluation data. When the MSE for evaluation data started to raise, the training was stopped because this is a usual sign of overfitting and overtraining.

Predictions for the evaluation data was then calculated using the trained network and stored into a CSV file for further analysis.

3.3 Performance evaluation

For the size of input data, training of the network took on average roughly 20s on the author's computer and average CPU load was 77% on 6-core CPU with Hyper-Threading.

4 Neural network trained by genetic algorithm

Since Deeplearning4j does not allow custom training algorithms (in the time of writing this article), a custom implementation of both genetic algorithm and neural networks was used. Since the author has experience with implementing machine learning algorithms in LISP language, which was traditionally popular in machine learning and artificial intelligence, Clojure language was chosen for this implementation. Clojure is a modern dialect of LISP language, dynamically compiled to the Java bytecode (https://clojure.org/). Although it does not support all features of Common Lisp, all the libraries and frameworks used in Java can be seamlessly used form Clojure as well (and Clojure libraries can be used from Java)

4.1 Neural network implementation

Neural networks are represented as a collection of matrices of weights and biases. Clojure is a functional programming language, not object oriented - therefore there is no benefit in defining classes or interfaces (these features exist in Clojure mainly for interop with Java).

Each layer of the network is represented by a matrix of weights and vector of biases.

$$\begin{pmatrix} w_{11} & \cdots & w_{1n} \\ \vdots & \ddots & \vdots \\ w_{m1} & \cdots & w_{mn} \end{pmatrix} \times \begin{bmatrix} a_1 \\ \vdots \\ a_m \end{bmatrix} + \begin{bmatrix} b_1 \\ \vdots \\ b_m \end{bmatrix} = \begin{bmatrix} z_1 \\ \vdots \\ z_m \end{bmatrix} \tag{1}$$

$$W^L \times A^{L-1} + B^L = Z^L \tag{2}$$

$$A^L = \sigma(Z^L) \tag{3}$$

Where:

W	is a matrix of weights,
W^L	is a matrix of weights in the present layer (L and $L-1$ are indices, not powers),
A^{L-1}	is a column vector of activations of the previous layer,
B^L	is a column vector of biases of the present layer,
Z^L	is a column vector of weighted input (sometimes referred to as potentials) of the present layer,
σ	is the activation function (here: sigmoid or identity).

Equations 1 and 2 show the weighted input (z) of each layer in both expanded matrix form and using capital letters as matrices. This can be viewed as a vector of potentials of neurons in the layer. Note that weight matrix (W) is transposed compared to the most literature sources. This way it is easier to work with it in code. So $w_1 1$ is the weight of the synapse from the 1st neuron of the previous layer to the 1st neuron of the current layer, $w_2 1$ is the weight of the synapse from 1st neuron of previous layer to the 2nd neuron of the current layer. $\sigma(Z^L)$ is a simplified notation for applying an activation function to each element of Z vector, creating A vector. These equations are based on (Nielsen 2015).

4.2 Genetic algorithm implementation

Genetic algorithms traditionally work with genes either 0 or 1. For this application, this is inadequate, because this algorithm need to find weights and biases of a neural network, which can be an arbitrary floating point decimal numbers. On the other hand, for genetic algorithms to be efficient, the state space needs to be limited. Therefore, each parameter is transformed into interval [0, 1]. An individual for the genetic algorithm then consists of floating point numbers from [0, 1] interval and count of parameters in intervals equals to count of all weights and biases of the network. Each individual consist of 550 genes which is the number of parameter (count of all weights and biases) in the neural network.

$$i = \frac{P - P_{min}}{|P_{max} - P_{min}|}$$
$$I = (i_1 \ldots i_n) \tag{4}$$

Where:

P is a parameter of the network (either weight or bias),

i is a gene

I is an individual expressed as a list of genes.

Genetic algorithms work with populations of individuals, which are then evolved using crossover, mutation and selection. Equation 4 shows the way an individual is constructed in this case. The individuals in each generation are crossed using single crossover point technique and mutation randomly mutates a gene, generating a new floating point number from interval [0, 1].

Selecting individuals for crossover uses a rank-selection technique (Saini 2017). From a technical point of view, a linked-list is constructed and the worst individual is added once, second worst twice etc. Therefore the best individual in population consisting of 300 individuals is 300x more likely to be chosen than the worst. In contrast to technique based solely on a loss function value, if one individual is much better than others, it does not prevent others from being chosen for cross breeding. The rank selection helps preventing a loss of diversity in population.

Loss function of this algorithm reconstructs a neural network from each individual and uses the training data to compute predictions. Predictions are compared to expected (correct) values and Mean Squared Error is computed for each individual. This is the result of a loss function. The lower, the better (some genetic algorithms use vitality function - the higher, the better).

Next generation consist of elites which are preserved, crossed individuals, mutated individuals and couple of newly generated individuals. Table 2 shows the empirically chosen parameters of the genetic algorithm for training this neural network. The genetic algorithm is created as a library therefore it can have more general use in the future.

Since computing the loss function for an individual does not affect the other individuals, its call is parallelized. The genetic algorithm does not define the loss function, it only defines a callback keeping it general. It is up to the calling code to ensure its thread-safety.

Parameter	**Value**
Population	300
Elites	1 individual
Crossbreds	145 pairs
Mutants	1% chance either elite or crossbred
Randoms	300 - (elites + crossbreds + mutants)

Table 2 Genetic algorithm parameters

5 Performance evaluation

For the size of input data, training of the network took on average roughly 40s on the author's computer and average CPU load was 85% on 6-core CPU with Hyper-Threading. The predictions based on validation data were stored into a CSV file for further analysis.

Compared to the Deeplearning4j's backpropagation algorithm, this one is slower but the average CPU load is higher. This is due to good optimization techniques used in Deeplearning4j. The algorithm was analysed using VisualVM profiler for Java Virtual Machine. Further optimizations for the genetic algorithm are possible:

- More efficient rank selection. Currently, there is a rather naive implementation and the profiler showed rather high CPU time.
- More efficient usage of memory. Although Clojure immutable data structures are rather well optimized (Clojure was created for usage in processing of large volume of data), some of the functions for its processing produce temporal structures which are immediately garbage collected. Merging more collection operations together (e.g. using Clojure transducers https://clojure.org/reference/transducers) can be beneficial.
- Using another matrix library. Clojure in its core library (equivalent to standard libraries of other programming languages) defines an API for vector and matrix operations, but its default implementation is pure Clojure/Java. On the other hand, Deeplearning4j uses Intel MKL library which is hand-optimized assembler implementation, making it faster for numerical computations.

6 Results

Each value from the prediction results of both networks was compared to the actual value and a difference was calculated. Two data sets were created, one for each network, containing these differences. Variance ratio test was performed (see Figure 6) showing that both result sets have statistically equal variances. A t-test with equal variances was performed (see Figure 7) showing that the mean of the result sets is statistically equal. It was therefore concluded, that there is no statistically significant difference between predictions made by each of the neural networks.

```
Variance ratio test
------------------------------------------------------------------------------
   Group |     Obs        Mean    Std. Err.   Std. Dev.   [95% Conf. Interval]
---------+--------------------------------------------------------------------
Backprop |     500    .0019818    .0001624    .0036317    .0016627    .0023009
 Genetic |     500    .0021717    .0001653    .0036958     .001847    .0024964
---------+--------------------------------------------------------------------
combined |   1,000    .0020768    .0001158    .0036633    .0018494    .0023041
------------------------------------------------------------------------------
    ratio = sd(Backprop) / sd(Genetic)                            f =   0.9656
Ho: ratio = 1                                    degrees of freedom = 499, 499

    Ha: ratio < 1               Ha: ratio != 1                 Ha: ratio > 1
  Pr(F < f) = 0.3480         2*Pr(F < f) = 0.6961          Pr(F > f) = 0.6520
```

Figure 6 Screenshot of a STATA output: Variance ratio test between results

```
Two-sample t test with equal variances

   Group |     Obs        Mean    Std. Err.   Std. Dev.   [95% Conf. Interval]
---------+--------------------------------------------------------------------
Backprop |     500    .0019818    .0001624    .0036317    .0016627    .0023009
 Genetic |     500    .0021717    .0001653    .0036958     .001847    .0024964
---------+--------------------------------------------------------------------
combined |   1,000    .0020768    .0001158    .0036633    .0018494    .0023041
---------+--------------------------------------------------------------------
    diff |           -.0001899    .0002317               -.0006446    .0002649
------------------------------------------------------------------------------
    diff = mean(Backprop) - mean(Genetic)                         t =  -0.8193
Ho: diff = 0                                     degrees of freedom =      998

    Ha: diff < 0                 Ha: diff != 0                 Ha: diff > 0
 Pr(T < t) = 0.2064         Pr(|T| > |t|) = 0.4128          Pr(T > t) = 0.7936
```

Figure 7 Screenshot of a STATA output: T test between results

7 Conclusion

It was shown that the genetic algorithm mentioned in section 4 can be used to train a neural network to approximate an ARIMA model for predicting currency exchange rates. Although the implementation of the algorithm has room for improvement, the shortcomings can be addressed as mentioned in section 5.

Acknowledgement

This article was created with the financial support of the Student grant competition EkF, VŠB-TU Ostrava as a part of the project SP2019/81.

References

Basheer, I. A. and Hamjeer, N. (2000). 'Artificial neural networks: fundamentals, computing, design, and application'. *Journal of Microbiological Methods*, 43 (1), pp. 3-31.

Hornik, K., Stinchcombe, M. and White, H. (1989). 'Multilayer feedforward networks are universal approximators'. *Neural Networks*, 2 (5), pp. 359-366.

Marček, D. (2013). *Pravdepodobnostn modelovanie a soft computing v ekonomike*. VŠB-TU, Ostrava, 2013.

Nielsen, M. A. (2015). *Neural Networks and Deep Learning*, [Online]. Determination Press, 2015. Available at: http://neuralnetworksanddeeplearning.com/.

Saini, N. (2017). 'Review of Selection Methods in Genetic Algorithms'. *International Journal of Engineering And Computer Science*, 6 (12), pp. 261-263.

Comparison of quantitative approaches for paper web break prediction

Jan Manďák[1]

Abstract: This paper deals with a frequent predictive maintenance use case in pulp-and-paper manufacturing industry – prediction of a paper web break. From the analytics perspective it is an early classification problem. The input features are time series measurements from sensors. First and second differences along with original centered variables are used to predict paper break 4 minutes before their occurrence. L1 regularization and correlation to response were used from feature selection methods and PCA from the dimension reduction methods was also tested. Logistic regression, random forest and gradient boosting classifiers were trained using data with original class distribution and also with minority class oversampled using SMOTE. All models achieved highest performance with features selected based on correlation to response. The oversampling by SMOTE has significantly improved recall at the cost of decreased precision. If the company was to select model which predicts as much paper breaks as possible, gradient boosting model with recall 0.888 on the test would be the option. Random forest model represents an option with good trade-off between recall (0.794) and precision (0.692).

Keywords: Paper break, early classification, PCA, L1 regularization, precision, recall.

JEL Classification: C38, L73

1 Introduction

The manufacturing industry nowadays face the challenge to cut costs and streamline its production processes. New technologies such as *big data*, *internet of things (IoT)* or *machine learning* bring great possibilities to make manufacturing sector more efficient. It is common in manufacturing processes to have several interconnected sensors collecting the data over time. These data, usually multivariate time series, are stored in various types of databases and can be subsequently analyzed for various purposes. *Predictive maintenance* is probably the best known use case of these data. The aim of predictive maintenance is to predict the outage of a machine before it occurs and therefore create cost savings for a manufacturer.

One example of predictive maintenance use case for pulp-and-paper manufacturing industry, which is deeply analyzed in this paper, is prediction of a situation when a paper breaks. Let us describe the paper manufacturing process a little bit. A paper machine, usually several meters long, ingests raw material at one end and produces reels of paper. Several sensors measuring both raw materials (e.g. amount of pulp, fiber, chemicals) and process variables (e.g. blade type, couch vacuum, rotor speed) are placed in different parts of the machine. Sometimes the paper breaks in this continuous rolling process, which causes stopping of the machine and process. Theses stops are of course costly for the mill and it is necessary predict in advance such paper breaks (Ranjan et al, 2018). Ranjan et al (2018) also states that even 5% reduction of the number of break events will give a significant cost saving for a mill.

[1] Stora Enso Ostrava, 28. října 3348/65, 702 00 Moravská Ostrava a Přívoz, jan.mandak@storaenso.com

Paper web break prediction has already been studied mainly by Pietro Patrone Bonissone, Yu-To Chen or Syed Amaz Imtiaz. Bonissone and Goebel (2002) used sensor readings and further analyzed the data using principal components analysis (PCA), adaptive neural fuzzy-inference system and trend analysis. They achieved root mean squared error (RMSE) 0.0975 on the test data set. Imtiaz et al (2006) also used PCA and a combined index based on the Hoteling's T2 and Q-statistics to develop a sheet-break predictor. Their overall fault prediction rate was 63 %. Prediction of a paper web break was also a subject of some patents. Bonissone et al (1999) created a patent which uses a neural network to predict web break tendencies from sensor measurements taken from the paper machine. They also used an induction tree model to isolate the root cause of the predicted web break tendencies. Chen and Bonissone (2002) created another patent for web break prediction based on principal components analysis, neuro-fuzzy systems and trending analysis.

The aim of the paper lies in a comprehensive comparison of various techniques for the web break prediction, which takes into account selected feature selection methods (L1 regularization, correlation to response variable), dimension reduction methods (PCA), class balancing methods (SMOTE) and classifiers (logistic regression, gradient boosting, random forest).

2 Data description

The dataset is provided by Ranjan et al (2018), who made accessible data collected from the network of sensors in a mill along with the unwanted events of paper breaks. Here is a brief information about the data set:

- it has 18,398 records,
- the frequency of the data is two minutes,
- time is the timestamp of the row,
- y is the binary dependent variable,
- x1-x61 are the predictors; all of them are continuous except of x61 (binary variable) and x28 (categorical variable),
- all predictors are centered.

The objective of this task is to predict paper break before it occurs. We could also consider this problem as an early classification problem. Probably the most challenging is the fact that this classification task is highly unbalanced – the paper break occurred only 124 times out of 18,398 records. Ranjan et al (2018) proposed a straightforward approach for an early classification – simply move binary response variable up by k rows. They recommend that k should not be higher than 2. In this paper we moved y up by 2 rows and therefore we predict the event two period (4 minutes) ahead.

Feature engineering is typically important in this type of classification problem. Schfer and Leser (2017) have proposed a first difference of the predictors, representing a gradual change in a variable. However, the first derivative may not necessarily trigger the event. A second difference of a variable representing sudden change should be also tried. Besides the first and second differences Ranjan et al (2018) also suggested to create change of the level of the categorical variable x28, instead of the actual value. A binary variable x28change was created and is equal to 1 when the level of variable x28 in time *t* is different from the level in time *t-1* and otherwise 0.

3 Description of applied quantitative approaches

Four scenarios are tested for original distribution of response variable and four scenarios are tested for increased number of response variable by SMOTE. The scenarios are the following:

1) all variables without correlated variables,
2) only variables selected by L1 regularization in logistic regression,
3) variables highly correlated with response,
4) principal components created using PCA.

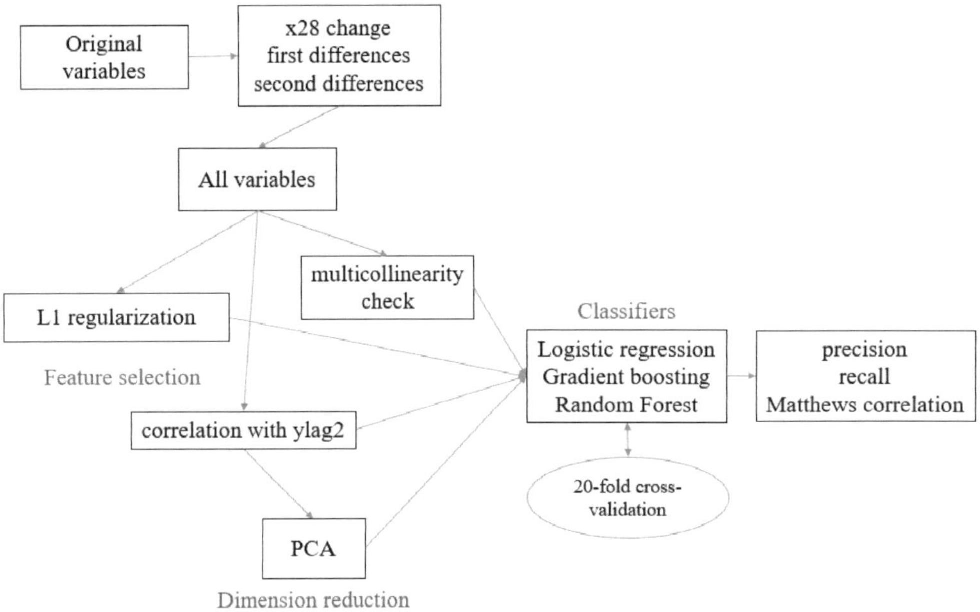

Figure 1 Schema of the quantitative approaches

3.1 Feature selection

Because of the fact that besides original 61 variables also first and second differences of these variables were created, there are about 180 variables. It is quite a big number and feature selection methods need to be applied to prevent models from overfitting. Two methods were tested - L1 regularization for logistic regression and selection of top 20 variables highly correlated with response variable.

L1 regularization (The Lasso) is a regularization method, whose biggest advantage over L2 regularization (ridge regression) is that regression coefficients of unimportant variables can be set to 0. Thanks to this L1 regularization can be added to the cost function of various types of regression models and can serve as a feature selection method. The L1 regularization has the following form (Raschka, 2016):

$$L1: \|w\|_1 = \sum_{j=1}^{m} |w_j| \quad (1)$$

The second method used as a feature selection method is the selection of variables most correlated with response variable. The *Pearson correlation coefficient* is used:

$$r_{xy} = \frac{\sum_{i=1}^{n}(x_i - \bar{x})(y_i - \bar{y})}{\sqrt{\sum_{i=1}^{n}(x_i - \bar{x})^2}\sqrt{\sum_{i=1}^{n}(y_i - \bar{y})^2}}. \tag{2}$$

The selected variables are further analyzed for the presence of multicollinearity. If the absolute value of correlation between two selected predictors is higher than 0.5, than variable with lower correlation towards target is removed.

3.2 Dimension reduction

Principal component analysis (PCA) is an unsupervised linear transformation technique. The reduction of dimensions suppresses the noise in the data and tries to preserve the information, but only up to a certain threshold. In case of exceeding this threshold the useful information in the data is suppressed (Vantuch et al, 2016). The aim of PCA is to find the directions of maximum variance in high-dimensional data and projects it onto a new subspace with equal or fewer dimensions that the original one (Raschka, 2016, p. 128). The advantage is that the principal components are uncorrelated, so we do not have to take care about multicollinearity. It should be noted that PCA is highly sensitive to data scaling so all features have to be standardized prior to PCA.

3.3 Class balancing

Class balancing appears frequently in natural or industrial systems not measured in laboratory conditions which has been handled in many previous studies (Mišák et al, 2017; Mišák et al, 2018). The *SMOTE* (Synthetic Minority Over-sampling Technique) algorithm was used to increase the number of minority class examples (Chawla et al, 2002). The minority class is over-sampled by taking each minority class sample and introducing synthetic examples along the line segments joining any/all of the k minority class nearest neighbors (Chawla et al, 2002, p. 328). Synthetic samples are created the following way:

1) Compute difference between the feature vector of observation in minority class and its *k* nearest neighbors (*k* depends on the amount of over-sampling, e.g. *k*=2 for 200 %).
2) Multiply this difference by a random number between 0 and 1, and add it to the feature vector under consideration.

This approach effectively makes the decision region of the minority class more general.

3.4 Classifiers

Logistic regression is member of a class of models called *generalized linear models* (Zumel and Mount, 2014). The aim of generalized linear models for a binary dependent variable and linear regression models for a continuous variable is to estimate a regression equation that relates the expected value of the dependent variable *y* to one or more predictor variables, denoted by ***x*** (Heeringa et al., 2010). The logistic function takes the following form:

$$log\left(\frac{\pi(x)}{1-\pi(x)}\right) = \beta_0 + \beta_1 x_1 + \cdots + \beta_p x_p, \tag{3}$$

where the left-hand side is called the logit or log odds. The unknown regression coefficients $\boldsymbol{\beta} = (\beta_1, \beta_2, .. \beta_p)$ in equation (7) have to be estimated based on training data. The method used for estimation is called *maximum likelihood* (James et al., 2013).

Random forests are frequently used machine learning models based on ensembles of decision trees. The bagging procedure means taking repeated *random samples with replacement* from the training data set. Random forests further enhance the bagging by randomizing the set of variables that each tree is allowed to use. This should lead to de-correlating the trees. The process of building a random forest model is the following (Zumel and Mount, 2014):

1) Draw a bootstrapped sample from the training data
2) For each sample, create a decision tree, and at each node of the tree
   - Randomly select a subset of *mtry* variables from the *p* total features (typically, the number of candidate predictors is $m \approx \sqrt{p}$)
   - Pick the best variable and the best split from that set of *mtry* variables
3) Continue until the tree is fully grown

Gradient boosting technique produces a prediction model which is and ensemble of weak models. The weak models are typically decision trees. A final single strong learner combines weak learners in an iterative fashion. Let's describe the steps of *gradient boosting*. The goal is to find a model $\boldsymbol{F}$ to predict values of the form $\hat{y} = F(x)$ by minimizing some cost function. At each stage *m*, it is assumed that there is some weak learner F_m, which is improved by constructing a new model *h*. Formally we can define it as:

$$F_{m+1}(x) = F_m(x) + h(x). \tag{4}$$

The model *h* is fitted to the residual $y - F_m(x)$ and therefore each F_{m+1} tries to correct the errors of its predecessor F_m.

3.5 Predictive performance measures

Assessment of predictive accuracy was done using three performance metrics – *precision*, *recall* and *Matthews's correlation*. As it was already mentioned the data set is highly imbalanced and therefore accuracy is not a suitable metric for assessment of predictive power of models. The *precision* measures what portion of predictions that a paper should break are correct. It is computed as:

$$precision = \frac{TP}{TP+FP}. \tag{1}$$

Another important metric is *recall*. The recall tells us what portion of paper breaks was a model able to predict. The calculation is as follows:

$$recall = \frac{TP}{TP+FN}. \tag{1}$$

The Matthews correlation coefficient (MCC) is used in machine learning as a measure of the quality of binary and multiclass classifications. It takes into account true and false positives and negatives and is generally regarded as a balanced measure which can be used even if the classes are of very different sizes. The MCC is in essence a correlation coefficient value between -1 and +1. A coefficient of +1 represents a perfect prediction, 0 an average random prediction and -1 an inverse prediction. The formula for calculation of MCC is as follows:

$$MCC = \frac{TP \cdot TN - FP \cdot FN}{\sqrt{(TP+FP) \cdot (TP+FN) \cdot (TN+FP) \cdot (TN+FN)}}. \quad (3)$$

4 Predictive results

Predictive performance measures described in the previous section – precision, recall and MCC are compared in various scenarios. Stratified 20-fold cross-validation was used to deeply test the abilities of the selected approaches and models. Mean values as well as standard deviations across folds were computed. Several approaches were tested using response variable with *original class distribution* (see Section 4.1) and also using minority class *oversampled using SMOTE* (see Section 4.2). The data were prepared using *Python* package *numpy* (Oliphant, 2006 and McKinney 2010), models were estimated with the *scikit-learn* package (Pedregosa et al, 2011) and *matplotlib* package was used to visualize results (Hunter, 2007).

4.1 Original class distribution

The whole dataset was used for the first three (gradient boosting, logistic regression and random forest) models. 117 variables out of 180 original ones were removed because of multicollinearity (Pearson correlation coefficient > 0.5), 63 variables remained in the data set. The variable with higher correlation to response was retained when deciding of which variable to remove. See mean values of performance metrics along with their standard deviations in Tab. 1 and Fig. 2. Confidence intervals for metrics are represented by vertical black line.

The best model seems to be gradient boosting with mean recall 0.375 an mean precision 0.389. Random forest model achieved higher precision, but was not able to successfully predict as many paper breaks as gradient boosting model.

classifier	precision	recall	Matthews
gradient boosting	0.389 (0.327)	0.375 (0.267)	0.344 (0.244)
logistic regression	0.405 (0.473)	0.117 (0.112)	0.203 (0.216)
random forest	0.778 (0.411)	0.217 (0.153)	0.399 (0.224)

Table 1 Performance metrics for models with 63 variables

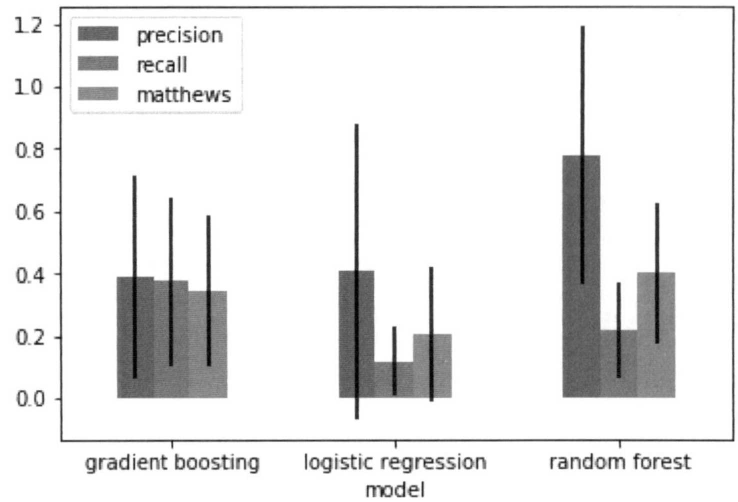

Figure 2 Performance metrics for models with 63 variables

In the second phase of modelling 45 features out of 180 were selected using L1 regularization for logistic regression. The regression coefficients of 135 variables were equal to zero and these variables were therefore removed and new models were trained using only 45 variables with non-zero coefficients (see Tab. 2 and Fig. 3 for performance metrics). This approach seems not to be suitable for this use case, performance of all models decreased.

classifier	precision	recall	Matthews
gradient boosting	0.313 (0.347)	0.248 (0.236)	0.255 (0.256)
logistic regression	0.005 (0.010)	0.153 (0.286)	-0.006 (0.041)
random forest	0.654 (0.472)	0.212 (0.156)	0.349 (0.260)

Table 2 Performance metrics for models with features selected using L1

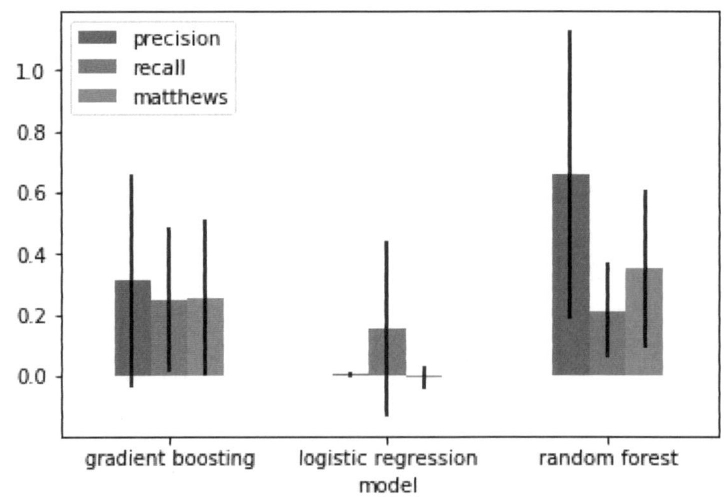

Figure 3 Performance metrics for models with features selected using L1

In the third scenario top 20 variables with highest correlation to response were selected, 14 of them were second differences, 2 first differences and 4 original values. 8 variables were further removed because of multicollinearity (correlation higher than 0.5). High number of second differences is in line with the assumption of Ranjan et al (2018) that second differences (sudden changes) can have an impact on web breaks. This approach seems to have the best performance, see Tab. 3 and Fig. 4.

classifier	precision	recall	Matthews
gradient boosting	0.775 (0.235)	0.560 (0.285)	0.623 (0.187)
logistic regression	0.790 (0.297)	0.371 (0.234)	0.522 (0.222)
random forest	0.948 (0.125)	0.592 (0.212)	0.732 (0.130)

Table 3 Performance metrics for variables correlated with response

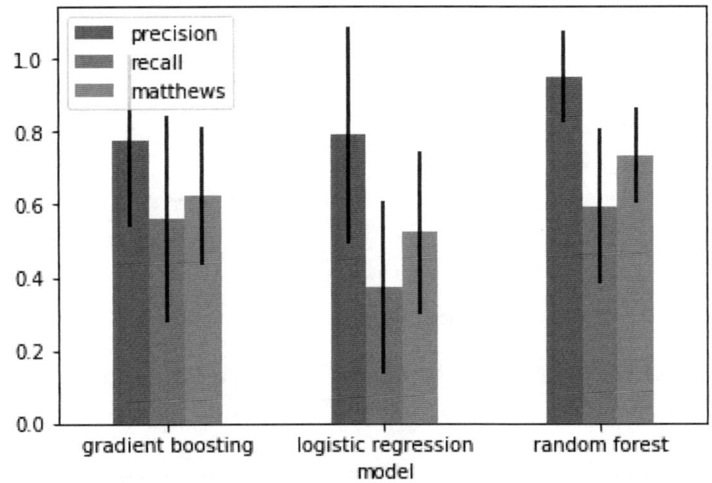

Figure 4 Performance metrics for variables correlated with response

In the last scenario not feature selection method, but *dimension reduction method PCA* was done with variables selected in previous approach. PCA was tested also with original 180 variables, but all models suffered from low precisions and recalls and high standard deviations. 8 principal components were selected for creation of predictive models, because they covers 80 % of variance in the data set (see. Fig. 5).

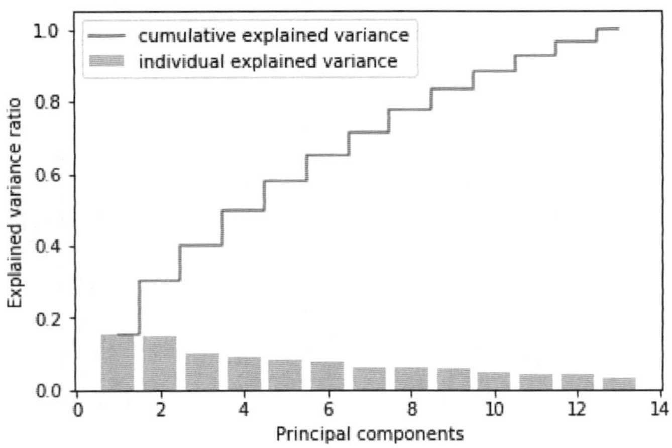

Figure 5 Explained variance ratio

The first two principal components which covers the highest portion of variance in the data are plotted in scatter plot (see Fig. 6). Observations representing paper breaks are colored by green color, observations representing smooth state are colored by red color. We can see that the classes are quite well separated, but some observations are overlapping and therefore another principal components need to be used for classification.

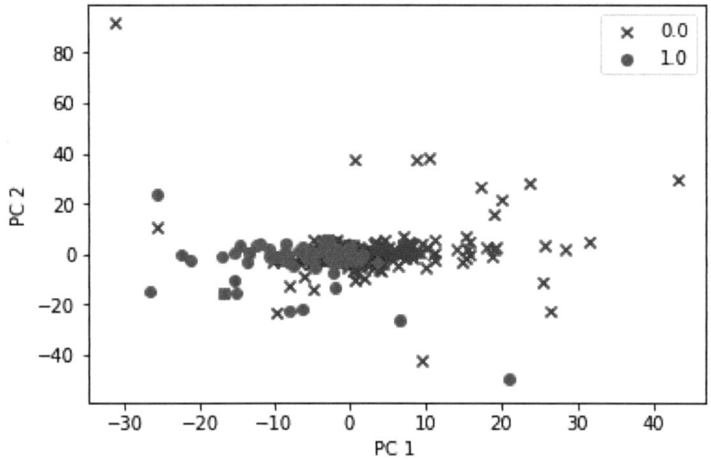

Figure 6 The first two principal components

As it is clear from Tab. 4 and Fig. 7, dimension reduction outperformed L1 regularization and the approach with original variables, but approach with variables selected by correlation to target remains the best one.

classifier	precision	recall	Matthews
gradient boosting	0.513 (0.279)	0.345 (0.232)	0.394 (0.181)
logistic regression	0.685 (0.346)	0.374 (0.273)	0.475 (0.233)
random forest	0.818 (0.289)	0.400 (0.268)	0.541 (0.213)

Table 4 Performance metrics for PCA approach

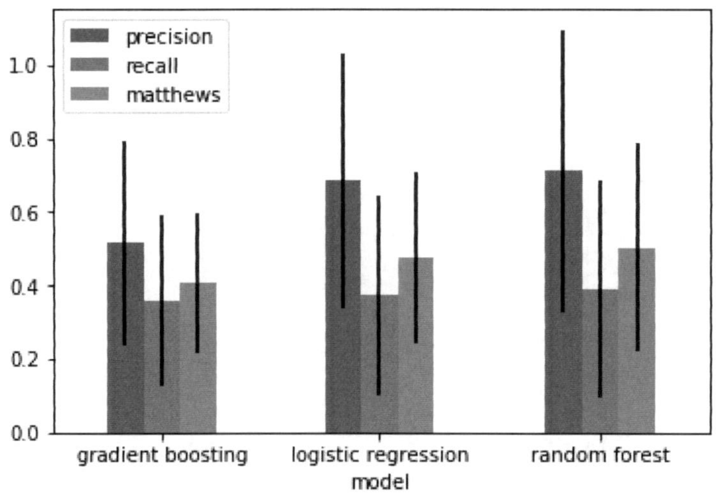

Figure 7 Performance metrics for PCA approach

4.2 Class balancing using SMOTE

As it was already mentioned, the dataset we have at hand is strongly unbalanced. Class balancing methods could therefore improve the classification ability of models. According to Blagus and Lusa (2013) it is preferred to perform balancing the data set after feature selection, because most variable selection methods assume that the samples are independent which is not the case of oversampling the minority class. The variables selected in previous scenarios are kept and SMOTE is subsequently applied only in folds used for training, in folds used for testing original data were preserved. The approach with features selected using L1 regularization was not tested here because of poor results in the previous phase with original class distribution.

The Tab. 5 shows, that SMOTE helped to improve predictive performance. The highest improvement is visible at gradient boosting – mean recall has increased from 0.375 to 0.725.

classifier	precision	recall	Matthews
gradient boosting	0.431 (0.297)	0.725 (0.207)	0.518 (0.198)
logistic regression	0.034 (0.060)	0.550 (0.289)	0.082 (0.105)
random forest	0.795 (0.303)	0.410 (0.205)	0.548 (0.194)

Table 5 Performance metrics for models with 63 variables (SMOTE)

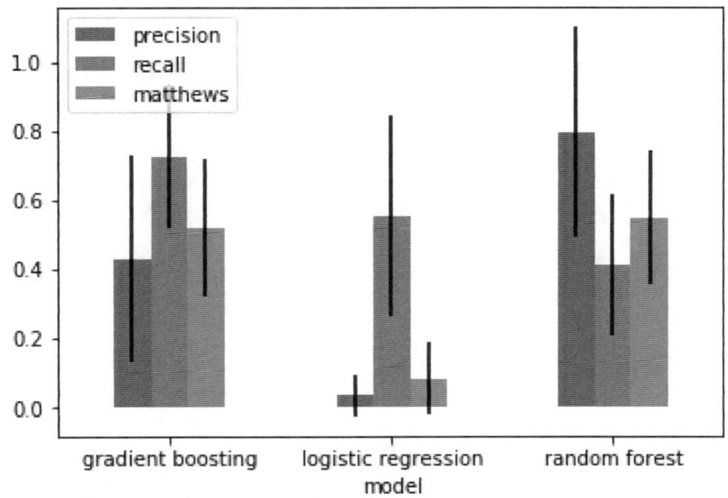

Figure 8 Performance metrics for models with 63 variables (SMOTE)

Next, variables mostly correlated with response were taken into account together with SMOTE oversampling. Mean recall of all models has increased, but precision has decreased significantly (see Tab. 6 and Fig. 9). The best models seems to be the random forest model with good trade-off between precision (0.836) and recall (0.683). Random forest model has also the highest Matthews correlation coefficient (0.739).

classifier	precision	recall	Matthews
gradient boosting	0.494 (0.177)	0.748 (0.219)	0.593 (0.158)
logistic regression	0.133 (0.091)	0.668 (0.276)	0.275 (0.145)
random forest	0.836 (0.180)	0.683 (0.217)	0.739 (0.150)

Table 6 Performance metrics for variables correlated with response (SMOTE)

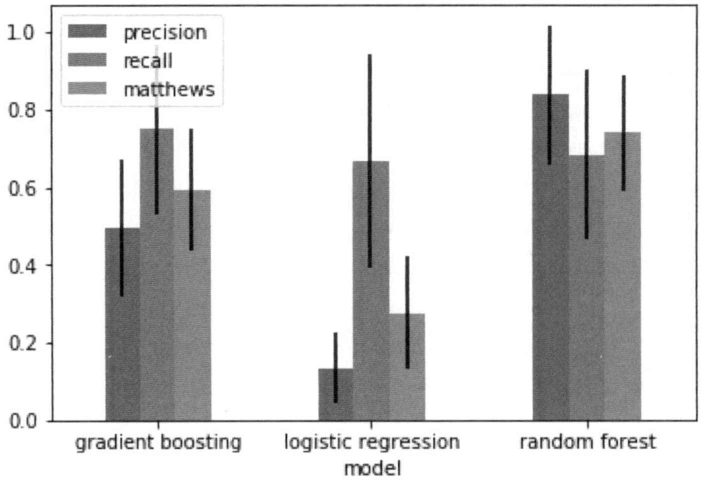

Figure 9 Performance metrics for variables correlated with response (SMOTE)

A similar pattern as in the previous approaches appeared with the use of PCA and SMOTE. Mean recall values of all models has increased, but precision has decreased. The decrease is obvious – mean values of precision for gradient boosting and logistic regression don't reach even 10 % (see Tab. 7 and Fig. 10).

classifier	precision	recall	Matthews
gradient boosting	0.009 (0.060)	0.653 (0.231)	0.227 (0.106)
logistic regression	0.080 (0.055)	0.693 (0.287)	0.214 (0.113)
random forest	0.317 (0.176)	0.565 (0.244)	0.410 (0.190)

Table 7 Performance metrics for PCA approach (SMOTE)

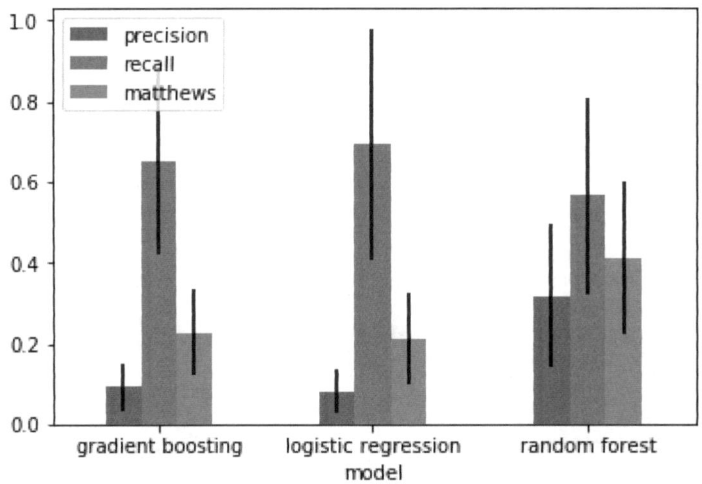

Figure 10 Performance metrics for PCA approach (SMOTE)

4.3 Predictive performance on the test set

The best results were achieved using features selected based on correlation with response. These features were used with original class distribution as well as with minority class oversampled using SMOTE to train models on the whole training data set (80 % of the data). The remaining 20 % of the data was used to test the predictive ability on unseen data. It should be noted that the minority class was oversampled only in the training data set, not in the testing data set. The results are shown in the Tab. 8.

	classifier	precision	recall	Matthews
original class distribution	gradient boosting	0.666	0.412	0.521
	logistic regression	0.273	0.265	0.262
	random forest	0.812	0.265	0.463
SMOTE	gradient boosting	0.526	0.888	0.678
	logistic regression	0.047	0.559	0.139
	random forest	0.692	0.794	0.739

Table 8 Performance metrics computed on the test data set

The best classifier from the point of view of predicting paper breaks is gradient boosting model trained with the help of SMOTE oversampling. This model was able to catch 88.8 % of such paper breaks, but with relatively higher portion of false positives (47.4 % of predictions to paper break). Random forest model represents an option with good trade-off between recall (0.794) and precision (0.692). Logistic regression could be a good model to explain the effect of individual predictors, but from the predictive performance point of view is the weakest one.

5 Conclusions

Several quantitative approaches were tried to predict paper web breaks 4 minutes before they occur, including feature selection using L1 regularization and correlation to response, dimension reduction using PCA, oversampling minority class using SMOTE and classifiers logistic regression, random forest and gradient boosting. The main finding from the feature engineering perspective is that the second differences representing sudden changes are very useful. In terms of selection of features an approach based on correlation to response with removal of correlated features seems to be the best one. Oversampling using SMOTE helped to increase recall of all models, but at the cost of decreased precision. The highest recall on the test set was achieved by gradient boosting model trained with the help of SMOTE oversampling (88.8 % of paper breaks were correctly predicted). On the other hand, this model had relatively higher portion of false positives (47.4 % of predictions to paper break). Random forest model represents an option with good trade-off between recall (0.794) and precision (0.692).

There are two main directions which will be further tested to expand the analysis. The first one is the use of another methods for feature selection, class balancing and classification. The second one is based on totally different viewpoint on this problem – to look at it as an anomaly detection rather than an early classification.

References

Blagus, R. and Lusa, L. (2013). 'SMOTE for high-dimensional class-imbalanced data'. *BMC Bioinformatics*, 14 (106).

Bonissone P., Chen, Y.T. and Khedkar P. (1999). 'System and method for predicting a web break in a paper machine'. US Patent 5, 942, 689, August, 1999.

Chawla, N. V., Bowyer, K. W., Hall, L. O. and Kegelmeyer, W. P. (2002). 'SMOTE: synthetic minority over-sampling technique'. *Journal of artificial intelligence research*, 16, pp. 321-357.

Chen, Y.T. and Bonissone, P. (2002). 'System and method for paper web time-break prediction'. US Patent 6, 405, 140, June, 2002.

Hunter, J. D. (2007). 'Matplotlib: A 2D Graphics Environment'. *Computing in Science & Engineering*, 9, pp. 90-95.

James, G., Witten. D., Hastie, T. and Tibshirani, R. (2013). *An introduction to statistical learning: with applications in R*. New York: Springer. Springer texts in statistics, 103.

Wikimedia Foundation (2001). Matthew's correlation coefficient, [Online]. Available at: https://en.wikipedia.org/wiki/Matthews_correlation_coefficient [cited 2019-01-03].

McKinney, W. (2010). 'Data Structures for Statistical Computing in Python'. *Proceedings of the 9th Python in Science Conference*, pp. 51-56.

Mišák, S., Fulnecek, J., Vantuch, T., Buriánek, T. and Jezowicz, T. (2017). 'A complex classification approach of partial discharges from covered conductors in real environment'. *IEEE Transactions on Dielectrics and Electrical Insulation*, 24 (2), pp. 1097-1104.

Mišák, S., Ježowicz, T., Fulneček, J., Vantuch, T., and Buriánek, T. (2016). 'A novel approach of partial discharges detection in a real environment'. *Environment and Electrical Engineering (EEEIC), 2016 IEEE 16th International Conference on,* pp. 1-5.

Pedregosa et al (2011). 'Scikit-learn: Machine Learning in Python'. *Journal of Machine Learning Research*, 12, pp. 2825-2830.

Ranjan, Ch., Mustonen, M., Paynabar, K. and Pourak, K. (2018). 'Dataset: Rare Event Classification in Multivariate Time Series'. *arXiv preprint arXiv:1809.1071v2.*

Schfer, P., and Leser, U. (2017). 'Multivariate time series classification with weasel+ muse'. *arXiv preprint arXiv:1711.11343.*

Travis, E, Oliphant (2006). *A guide to NumPy*. USA: Trelgol Publishing.

Vantuch, T., Snasel, V., and Zelinka, I. (2016). 'Dimensionality Reduction Method's Comparison Based on Statistical Dependencies'. *Procedia Computer Science*, 83, pp. 1025-1031.

Applying the IoT in the Area of Determining the Locations of Persons and Equipment

Milos Maryska[1] , Petr Doucek[2], Lea Nedomova[2]

Abstract. This article presents an application of Internet of Things (IoT) technology in the field of safety – specifically the verification of the presence and movements of employees in a selected locality. The foundation for our choice of application to present here is an extensive analysis of the opportunities that exist for the application of the IoT towards the area of safety. One application opportunity that is viewed with great expectations by companies that struggle with significant risks caused by external factors concerns the need to unambiguously identify persons' presence in specific places or spaces. This article includes a proposal for the technical execution of precisely such an IoT application. In addition to outlining the proposed solution's equipment and execution, the article's discussion portion also evaluates its financial effectiveness. Here we have concluded that the deployment of a passive approach toward reporting the locations of persons or equipment using RFID chips and long-range readers of these chips is very effective and financially advantageous relative to comparable reporting prepared manually or semi-automatically. We see a fully automated solution based on IoT technologies as very financially efficient.

Keywords: Internet of Things, safety, security, access systems.

JEL Classification: O332, L63, D23.

1 Introduction

The potential of the applications grouped under the term "Internet of Things" (IoT) has developed quite gradually. The earliest utilization of the IoT was in beverage distribution: it provided monitoring of drinks' cooling levels (Foote, 2018). This was soon followed by the application of the IoT via various applications based on systems using Radio-Frequency Identification (RFID) technologies. This development continued up to the state we see today, wherein IoT technologies and their deployment has found a place among the important parts of the world of information and communication technologies (ICT). In terms of recent history, specifically 2013, the IoT has developed into a system that joins together within itself many different technologies with different functional focuses that utilize a variety of communication protocols. We can give as examples of applications with different protocols the following: sensors, GPS/mobile devices, devices for tracking equipment movements, devices for tracking employee movements and positions, etc. The last two years have seen general acceptance for the definition of the IoT as a dynamic global network infrastructure with self-configuring abilities that is based on standard, interoperable communication protocols. These protocols' foundation lies in two

[1] University of Economics, Prague, Department of Information Technologies, W. Churchill sq. 1938/4, Prague, Czech Republic, milos.maryska@vse.cz

[2] University of Economics, Prague, Department of System Analysis, W. Churchill sq. 1938/4, Prague, Czech Republic, doucek@vse.cz, nedomova@vse.cz

traits: within them, physical and virtual "Things" are identified by physical attributes, and virtual individuals utilize an intelligent interface and are integrated into a broad information network (Kranenburg, 2008).

Another area into which IoT technologies are rightfully classified is that of industrial innovation – i.e. Industry 4.0. Here they are conceptually bound with the term "Industrial Internet of Things" (IIoT). The application of IIoT technologies is connected with two main areas – 1) cyber-risks, connected primarily with questions of the wireless transmission of data among production sites and the monitoring equipment that will be used to implement the Industrial Internet of Things (IIoT), and 2) issues of personal data protection (Aserkar, Seetharaman, Chu, Jadhav and Inamdar, 2017). These two main areas, IIoT vs. data, have very different natures. While secure IIoT communication is a topic for new research and the application of new technologies, personal data security (Novák and Doucek, 2017) tends more to be connected with process management and modeling (Basl and Doucek, 2019).

Another area where IoT technologies are used both inside and outside of the IIoT is that of safety. In this area, we have performed research into the applicability – both technological and financial (Maryska et al, 2018) – of individual solutions. For this article, we are constraining ourselves to a single application opportunity: verifying, and in this case specifically detecting, the presence of employees in a selected location (Leyh et al, 2016). The ability to unambiguously determine the presence – or better yet, the locations – of employees at selected sites amounts to a significant factor in, above all, extreme situations such as cave-ins, landslides, tsunamis, etc.

Various technical solutions for monitoring employees' positions all help to reduce the risk of loss of life.

This application opportunity makes use of RFID sensor chips, with the sensor determining whether a certain known RFID device has been detected within the sensor's perimeter or not. When it is detected, information on this fact is recorded into a database. The purpose when determining the locations of persons, equipment, or other things is real-time monitoring of their locations in case it becomes necessary to deal with exceptional events threatening the safety of persons or of equipment or other things.

This topic area is being addressed by not only academic institutions, but also private companies, which are trying out, for example, the use of RFID chips as part of their employee equipment, etc. (Montanika z.s., 2019).

2 Problem Formulation

The utilization of the IoT in industry is a very current topic. One important application is in monitoring the locations of employees and equipment, with the goal of reducing the risks connected with exceptional or critical situations. This article's goal is to analyze and propose possibilities for utilizing IoT solutions to monitor the locations of employees or equipment.

A similar basic approach can then also be applied in other areas where information on employee movements is also processed. This topic is also addressed in projects drafted for the

Technology Agency of the Czech Republic by the nation's ministries, e.g. the Ministry of Interior.

3 Methodology

The basic data obtained for this article primarily comes from an extensive survey among experts in the Czech energy industry. This survey was conducted among roughly 50 experts from a variety of businesses as well as the academic sphere in the 2016/2017 winter season.

To obtain the relevant data, over 67 workshops were held; these took place in two rounds. 50 workshops were held in the first round. The workshops had a structured form and were accompanied with questionnaire support. Our questionnaires for asking questions and identifying technologies for IoT and business opportunities were based on the technique of guided questioning, with the use of open and closed questions (Řezanková, 2010).

After the holding of all 50 workshops, we processed and evaluated the questionnaire data, which enabled us to merge all the duplicate application opportunities that were identified and create a set of unique application opportunities.

In the second round, containing 17 workshops, 124 unique application opportunities were identified by the experts and academics, and solution priorities in a range from 1 to 3 were then assigned to them, with 1 being the most important and 3 the least important in terms of implementation. Let us add here that:

- The list of identified application opportunities can always vary, due to both workshop attendance composition and changes in the IT fields within the IoT.
- The information identified continues to be expanded with the arrival of further analyses and research into the literature, as well as consultations with experts in further areas of research – e.g. ethics or psychology.

4 Results

A comprehensive overview of the outputs of the entire study is provided in detail and commented upon in the article named (Maryska et al, 2018). Here let us simply state that in priority 1, we identified 16 application opportunities, while priority 2 was assigned to 20 opportunities, and priority 3 has been identified for 25 application opportunities. For the remaining 63 application opportunities, no priority was set in light of certain of their factors – such as their importance, costs, implementation speed, or benefits for society – having non-uniform evaluations.

As stated above, within this article we are focusing on one of the application opportunities with a priority of 1. Specifically, this is a system for determining the locations of employees and pieces of equipment.

The overall problem area of systematically addressing the identification of employee and equipment location determination can be divided up into the following five steps:

- Technical solution;
- Sensors;
- Communication in the IoT network;

- Work with data before its transmission;
- Power supply;
- Data processing.

4.1 Technical Solution – Description

There are basically two possible technical solutions, depending on the type of the given application.

- Method A can be used for open spaces and is based on monitoring locations using GPS sensors.
- Method B can be used for both open and closed spaces and is based on monitoring location using ID readers with a modem (these readers can be powered via either a battery or the power grid).

Device operation requirements are an important prerequisite for each of the two methods:

- For method A, in light of GPS power consumption, there is the requirement that a given device work for at least 168 hours on one battery charge.
- For method B, the minimum required length of operation for one battery charge is 2 years.

Due to how the system works, no large data-transfer volumes are needed, and so a low-cost, low-energy IoT network can be used for both methods.

The technical solution must include the development, and then implementation, of software that enables the following:

- Identifying the locations of defined employees;
- Raising an alarm if no system message on activity by the monitored employee arrives during a defined period of time.

4.2 Sensors

By "sensor" here, we mean a general device that can be used to determine the location of a person or a piece of equipment and that enables the sending of information to a central node.

For determining locations, two types of sensors can be used. In case A, where location tracking is being handled using GPS, a "sensor" is any device that has available both a GPS chip and a chip for communicating with a selected transmission network. An employee's business phone is one typical example. GPS trackers are another; while they do not have advanced features like a phone does, they can be used effectively in determining current locations. GPS satellite visibility is a prerequisite in order for this approach to be usable. Thus for e.g. mining, the deployment of these technologies is not worth considering. Its effectiveness is also reduced if a tracked person or piece of equipment is underwater or is covered by a landslide.

In case B, where location tracking is handled using ID chips, the sensor is the reader of the chips or of the cards that are assigned to each employee or piece of equipment. This device must be able to "read" a device equipped with a corresponding ID card/chip at up to a defined distance, and by reading this data, information on the location of the employee or piece of equipment is obtained – as well as, simultaneously, information on the employees or on the equipment that is present in the defined area.

In case A, where mobile phones are used for transmission, traditional GSM protocols – with which phones can communicate natively – can be used.

For case B, a network such as SIGFOX is suggested as the IoT network to use, because tests have shown SIGFOX to be significantly more jamming-resistant than other low-energy IoT networks and to simultaneously have a sufficient nationwide reach.

4.3 Communication within the IoT network

In IoT networks, devices do not perform any network registration when transmitting data (with the exception of the mentioned phone access in case A). At the moment of creation of a data transmission request, the device sends out a message. Generally, no post-message verification of each message's acceptance is performed within the IoT network. Instead, robustness and guaranteed message delivery are achieved through the following mechanisms:

- The message is typically sent three times in a row. In this way, the risk of non-delivery is reduced;
- When IoT networks are designed, care is generally taken to ensure that, in as many cases as possible, multiple base stations can accept a transmitted message;
- Every message has a unique ID number automatically implemented for it within the modem by the protocol; this ID is incremented automatically and thus, should a message go undelivered, this fact can be discovered quickly and automatically. In this kind of situation, the receiving device can generate a defined event and inform the user of data loss;
- If no message is received from a given end device after a defined period, the system that would normally receive its data can, once again, generate an event and pass it on to the user in a standardized way.

Both systems must be defined in such a way as to make it possible not only to proactively provide information on the location of a person or piece of equipment upon request, but also to send information on an entity's last known location to a center at defined intervals such as 1/5/10 minutes.

4.4 Work with Data before Its Transmission

One frequent discussion here is whether the data needs to be processed in some way before it is transmitted.

For this type of message, it is not necessary to pre-process the data in any fundamental way. The data is transmitted in the form of a message containing information on a location and a subject.

In case A, the subject's ID and its GPS location are transmitted.

In case B, the subject's ID and the ID of the sensor at which the subject was identified are transmitted. The information on the sensor's location is known, since this information is a pre-defined item, in light of the sensor's being stationary.

4.5 Power Supply

The power supply method is another important parameter for IoT solutions. This parameter has a significant influence on the overall economic efficiency of the proposed solution. For both of the identified approaches, it is a battery, which, in light of the method of use, has an assumed charge lifetime of at least 7 days for the GPS sensor and at least 2 years for the chip.

The equipment is designed to be have low energy requirements, due to its not being dependent on an external energy source.

4.6 Data Processing

The data is stored in a standard relational structure in a relational database. The solution is independent of the specific platform used.

The actual data processing can be performed by anyone who has the needed knowledge of SQL and who also knows the solution's data model – which is very simple. A number of applications can then be applied to the data obtained; these will then analyze this data, using both Big Data processing principles and those of data mining, or various statistical methods.

5 Discussion

Within our discussion, we focus primarily on case B, wherein the locations of persons or pieces of equipment are determined using stationary readers and ID chips.

Through brief research into sensor manufacturers, we determined that the price of an IoT device that is able to read ID chips within a 20m perimeter is about 5,000 CZK apiece. A chip that will be read in a defined perimeter at a defined sensor type costs a few dozen crowns. Let us assume e.g. 50 CZK apiece. Installation costs and the costs for operating the device within a given IoT network must be figured in alongside these costs.

Any question of costs is always connected with questions of benefits, yields, or reductions to other, related costs.

Within the context of monitoring the locations of persons, we see the main benefit as coming in connection with legislative requirements for monitoring said persons, e.g. in mines, high-risk operations, etc. In all of these cases, requirements exist today for keeping records – which may be kept in various forms. The solution we propose makes the entire record-keeping process significantly simpler. The level of precision depends solely on how numerous the readers deployed within the tracked space are.

Let us imagine here the example of applying the above-mentioned solution towards monitoring the locations of persons in mines. With this solution, if a cave-in occurs, we know with 100% certainty who is in the mine, and we know with high precision where each given person or piece of equipment is located. The level of precision depends solely on the above-mentioned sensor count. Rescue operations can then be managed and organized better on the basis of this information.

Assigning a value to this aspect of IoT technologies' benefits is difficult, and with our knowledge, impossible. Assigning a value to this aspect was not even possible for the survey respondents with whom we discussed the given subject area.

Assigning a value to the first benefit – automating compliance with legislative requirements – is connected primarily with saving the human labor that is in turn connected with preparing reports to meet the legislative requirements. If we are to assume that the IoT solution will be replacing e.g. record-keeping on paper, then the savings can be extremely large, and the return on investment can come in mere days or months, depending on the number of devices installed. Individual employees will similarly save time, as automatic reporting will eliminate their need for manual reporting. Increased reporting precision, as well as the possibility of using the recorded data for analytical purposes, are other value factors.

The actual reliability of a solution based on RFID chips is also a strongly important value factor. If they are deployed, for example, in employees' helmets, then when a helmet is damaged and a replacement helmet is used, the solution's "overview" value is lost – and thus so is its main benefit. For this reason, it is appropriate to consider a multi-chip solution, wherein an employee will have an RFID chip placed e.g. within their lamp, their helmet, and their entry card, and the receipt of a signal from at least 50% of their RFID chips will suffice for correct registration of their location. This will prevent not only problem situations caused when an employee borrows a piece of equipment short-term, but also those caused when equipment is damaged and replacement equipment is used for a certain amount of time. Meanwhile, the use of a larger number of RFID chips will increase the reliability of the whole solution.

If we are to look briefly at case A, that is, the determination of locations using devices with GPS support: these devices can be used easily in every situation where it is necessary to know not only current locations, but also ongoing locations. The monitoring of automotive transportation is a traditional example of this application. Examples for the energy industry may include transfers among an enterprise's individual operations, transfers connected with energy readings, and also the positions of persons or pieces of equipment e.g. in electrical companies' sites of operation.

6 Conclusions

There are many IoT devices that can be applied in various areas of human activity. These can be IoT devices for sensing vehicle movements to prevent unnecessary trips, devices for tracking parking-lot vacancy levels, devices for sensing that noise limits have been exceeded, and much more.

In this article, we focused on one specific application opportunity: the use of IoT sensors for monitoring the locations of persons or pieces of equipment. There are two basic types of IoT equipment sets for determining location; the first is active equipment in the form of GPS sensors, and the second is sensors in the form of RFID chips and stationary readers for them. They can be used both for monitoring entry into restricted spaces, and for monitoring movements within defined areas. Remote RFID-chip sensors with a detection perimeter of up to 20 meters can serve this goal.

One example of a use for the passive-measurement approach can be found in the monitoring of the positions of persons and pieces of equipment in mines, where precision depends on the number of sensors etc. that is used.

In the context of our article, RFID-chip sensors are connected to a server via a SIGFOX network. On this server, data is processed and stored in a relational database.

We can consider the following to be such solutions' main benefits:

- Immediate identification of the location of persons or pieces of equipment with high precision;
- Easy installation;
- Low operating costs;
- Low investment costs.

Meanwhile we see the following as negative factors: limited device lifetimes in connection with battery life, the limited reach of RFID-chip readers for the passive determination method; the limited reach of GPS signals for the active determination method.

Acknowledgements

This paper has been written with the support of the Czech Science Foundation project GAČR 17-02509S and with contribution of long term institutional support of research activities by Faculty of Informatics and Statistics, University of Economics, Prague IP400040.

References

Aserkar, R., Seetharaman, A., Chu, J., Jadhav, V. and Inamdar, S. (2017). 'Impact of personal data protection (PDP) regulations on operations workflow'. *Human Systems Management*, 36 (1), pp. 41-56, DOI: http://dx.doi.org/10.3233/HSM-161631.

Basl J. and Doucek, P. (2019). 'Informatic, Metamodel of Indexes and Maturity Models for Company's Industry 4.0 Readiness'. *Informatic*, in press.

Foote, K., D. (2018). *A Brief History of the Internet of Things, Data Education for Business and IT Professionals*, [Online]. Available at: http://www.dataversity.net/brief-history-internet-things/ [cited 2019-01-11].

Leyh, Ch., Schaffer, T., Bley, K., Forstenhausler, S. (2016). 'SIMMI 4.0 – A Maturity Model for Classifying the Enterprise-wide IT and Software Landscape Focusing on Industry 4.0'. *Proceedings of the Federated Conference on Computer Science and Information Systems (FEDCSIS),* New York, USA, pp. 1297-1302, DOI: 10.15439/2016F478.

Maryska, M., Doucek, P., Nedomova, L. and Sládek, P. (2018). The Energy Industry in the Czech Republic: On the Way to the Internet of Things. *Economies*, 6 (2), pp. 1-13, DOI: 10.3390/economies6020036

Montanika z.s., (2019). *Důlní služby*, [Online]. Available at: http://montanika.cz/dulni-sluzby/ [cited 2019-01-11].

Novák, L. and Doucek, P. (2017). 'Regulation of Cyber Security in the Banking Sector'. *IDIMT-2017 Digitalization in Management, Society and Economy,* Czech Republic, pp. 49-54.

Řezanková, H. (2010). *Analýza dat z dotazníkových šetření*. 2nd ed. Praha: Professional Publishing.

van Kranenburg, R. (2008) *The Internet of Things: A Critique of Ambient Technology and the All-Seeing Network of RFID,* Amsterdam, Netherlands.

Information support of daily scrum meetings

Jan Ministr[1], Tomas Pitner[2], Roman Danel[3], Vyacheslav Chaplyha[4]

Abstract. The vast majority of the software developers use the agile framework for project management. Agile approach provides more flexibility and adaption to the changes against classic software development approach. The key methodology of agile approach represents the scrum. The core of scrum management forms sprint, which represents a time shift activity and envelops all other events of scrum. The outcome of the sprint should be the increment in development of the project, which is possible to submit to the customers or the users.

The paper maps the possibilities of visualization of the course of individual sprints at everyday meetings of the research team (stand up meetings), which have a decisive influence on the quality of communication of the research team and the overall success of the project.

Keywords: agile development, scrum, sprint, daily stand-up, scrum board, backlog, Kanban.

JEL Classification: D83, L15, L85

1 Introduction

Scrum is process framework used primarily for creating, delivering and maintaining of software products. Scrum assumes that software development is too complex and unpredictable to accurately plan. The agile scrum framework is set on the philosophy of empiricism, which says that all knowledge comes from the experience and based on that all decisions are made in advance. This requires empirical process control to ensure visibility, control and adaptation of all scrum activities. This is achieved through an iterative and incremental development process shown in Fig. 1. The scrum stands on three main principles:

1) ***Transparency*** says that all participants should possess all the data needed for making adequate and well-grounded decisions. Information has to be clear and expressed by the common language so everyone is able to understand. Any discrepancy requires immediate discussion and resolution.
2) ***Inspections*** identifies the potential issues, which may occur in the scrum process. Not only it helps the team to check the progress towards the sprint goal but it also serves as a detection of unwanted variances.
3) ***Adaption*** goes hand in hand with the inspection. Once the undesirable variance is detected the whole process needs to be adjusted as soon as possible to minimize the implications.

[1] VSB – Technical University of Ostrava, Faculty of Economics, Department of Applied Informatics, 17. Listopadu 2172/15, 70800 Ostrava-Poruba. Czech Republic, jan,ministr@vsb.cz.

[2] Masaryk University, Faculty of Informatics, Department of Computer Systems and Communications, Botanická 68a, Brno Czech Republic, tomp@fi.muni.cz.

[3] Technical and Economic University in České Budějovice, Faculty of Technology, Department of Civil Engineering, Okružní 517/10, 370 01 České Budějovice, Czech Republic, rdanel@mail.vstecb.cz.

[4] Lviv National Agrarian University, Department Automatic Control and Computer-integrated Technologies, 1, V. Velykoho Str., Dublyany, Lviv region, 80381, Ukraine, 4vyach@gmail.com.

Scrum is a framework helping the teams to organize their work. It allows the teams to adjust the scrum based on their needs. Nevertheless, it has also defined several keystones. Main of them are events, artifacts and roles, which are associated to the each team member.

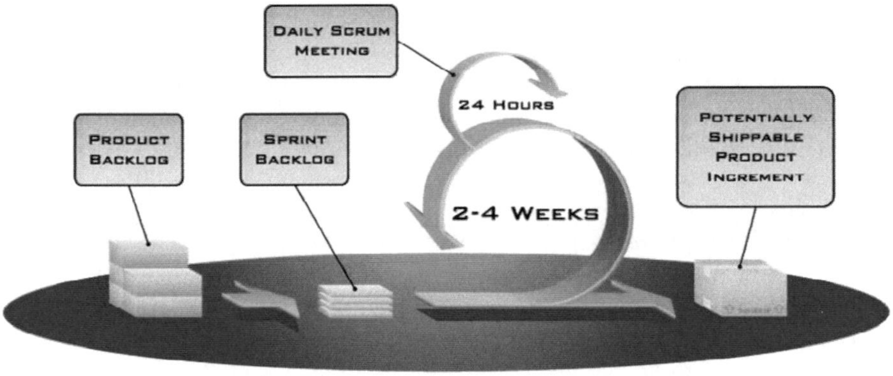

Figure 1 Scrum process Overview [Rubin, 2012]

1.1 Scrum process description

Scrum project starts with a vision of the system to be developed as shown Fig. 1.
The software development process according to the scrum method can be divided into three basic development phases:

1) ***Pregame*** in which scrum project starts with a vision of the system to be developed. Then a Product Backlog list is created, a rough plan of the project and the first design of the architecture. The Product Backlog is prioritized and divided into proposed releases.
2) ***Game*** when all the work is done in Sprints, which represents iterations lasting 1 to 4 weeks. Processing sprint itself can be divided into the following four steps:
   a) A Sprint is initiated with a Sprint planning meeting, where the Product Owner and Team get together to agree upon Product Backlog items to be implemented over the next Sprint.
   b) After deciding what has to be done in the next Sprint, the Team develops the Sprint Backlog, i.e., a list of tasks that must be performed to the end of the Sprint. The tasks in the list emerge should be divided so that each takes roughly 4 to 16 hours.
   c) Every day the Team gets together for a 15-minute meeting called a Daily Scrum. The purpose of the meeting is to synchronize the work of all Team members. At the Daily Scrum, each Team member answers three questions:
      - *What have you done on this project since the last Daily Scrum meeting?*
      - *What will you do before the next meeting?*
      - *Do you have any obstacles?*
   d) At the end of the Sprint, a Sprint review meeting is held at which the Team presents what was developed during the Sprint to the Product Owner and any other stakeholders who want to attend. After the Sprint review and prior to the next Sprint planning meeting, the Scrum Master also holds a Sprint retrospective meeting in order to encourage the Team to revise, within the Scrum process framework, its development process to make it more effective and enjoyable for the next Sprint.
3) ***Postgame****,* which represents the preparation of the project for its final delivery, including documentation, integration and testing.

2 Usage status of scrum in software companies

The VersionOne report (VersionOne, 2018) states that the most widely used agile software development tool in year 2017 was the Daily Standup, which is used by 90 percent of software companies in the whole.

As main reasons of adopting agile approach states the next five findings:

- Accelerate software delivery (75%)
- Manage changing priorities (65%)
- Increase productivity (55%)
- Better business/IT alignment (49%)
- Increased software quality (46%)

As main benefits of adopting agile approach states the next five findings

- Manage changing priorities (71%)
- Project visibility (66%)
- Better business/IT alignment (75%)
- Delivery speed/Time to market (62%)
- Team productivity (61%)

VSB - Technical university of Ostrava realized scrum research in Czech Republic, which was attended by three thousand eight hundred eighty respondents.

As main reasons for adopting scrum were reported:

- Consistency of processes and procedures (70%)
- Implementation of a common tool across development teams (60%)
- Use of agile consultants or coaches (58%)

As main benefits for adopting were reported:

- Possibility of manage changing priorities (73%)
- Increase of team productivity (65%)
- Project visibility (71%)

In all of the above findings, lead to conclusion that"

- The level of scrum usage in the Czech Republic and the world is no different
- Scrum and agile approach help software companies around the world to improve their work

3 Scrum performance monitoring

The ensure of continuous monitoring of the scrum development process through appropriate set of measures is crucial to visibility, inspection, and adaptation. The following measures of progress are usually used (Chlopecký et al. 2015):

1) ***The actual velocity*** represents gradually the amount of work accomplished in each Sprint. The planned velocity was estimated by the Scrum team at the beginning of each Sprint and the actual velocity is calculated at the end of the Sprint. The goal of the team is to keep as little difference as possible between these variables so that the planned velocity should be estimated considering the actual velocity of previous Sprints and there should be no changes in development team in the middle of the project.

2) ***The Sprint burndown*** *chart* represents the amount of work remaining that needs to be accomplished till the end of the Sprint.

As an additional indicator is sometimes used EVM (Earned value Management) that provides the values of schedule performance index (SPI) and cost performance index (CPI) on a daily basis, thus enabling immediate response in the case of deviation from the plan, which can be especially useful when longer Sprints are used. Computation of SPI and CPI requires collection of only one additional base measure, i.e., the number of hours spent on each task between two consecutive Daily Scrum meetings (Mahnic and Vrana, 2007).

4 Scrum tools

Daily Scrum meetings serve as a means of empirical process control in order to ensure visibility, inspection, and adaptation (Matula et al, 2016). They represent one of the most important Scrum practices providing continuous insight into project activities and serving as a means for immediate detection and resolution of possible impediments (Adisa et al., 2010). The meetings must not be for reporting to the Scrum Master, but for the team members to inform each other about the current state of the project. Well performed daily scrum should meet these objectives (Yip, 2016):

- commitment is shared;
- each member's status is expressed to the team and all spectators;
- all current impediments are addressed and remove steps are initiated;
- team members are supportive to each other which leads to the strong team;
- sprint focus is adapted and next direction is established.

4.1 Scrum board

During the sprint period the team needs to know, how the sprint runs and what they are able to deliver in the current increment. For these purposes is used scrum board. Scrum board is graphical representation of the state of the current sprint which helps the team make sprint backlog items visible. It is the central place where the whole team can see and record the progress towards the sprint goal. The board can be visualizing as a table containing set of columns and user stories. Each story is divided into multiple tasks which represent the actual sprint backlog. Tasks are visualized as a yellow cards as shown Fig. 2. Cards are movable among the columns which analogically changes their state. At the beginning of the sprint all the work is not started therefore it is placed in the 'To do' column. As the sprint goes, cards are sequentially moved from the left to the right based on the work progress. Each column represents specific state which is assigned to the cards inside of it. Mostly the common default state are [SCRM-study, 2016):

- *'To Do'* - for not started work,
- *'In progress'* - for work which has been started but not finished,
- *'Testing'* - for work which has been done but is currently being tested,
- *'Done' - for completed work.*

From the quick look it should be clear which work is finished and what is left, who is currently working on specific tasks and if the team is able to finish the work in the sprint and deliver the increment (Šochová, 2013). The content of the board is not strict and should be adjusted based on the team needs in order to visually display all the valid information related to the team work.

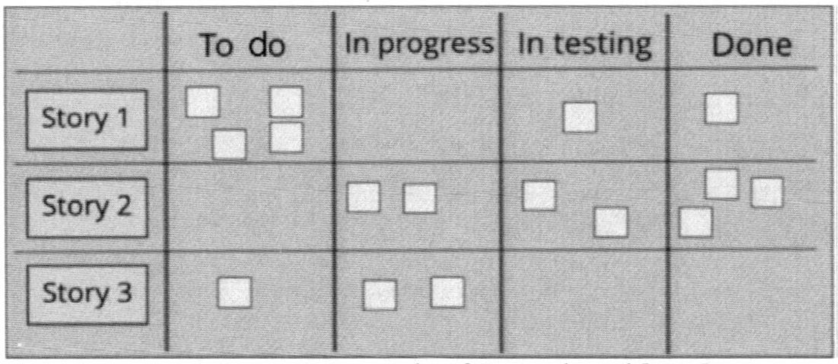

Figure 2 Example of Scrum board [own]

In practice there is a trend where scrum teams adopt some key Kanban principles in their project when dealing with the work visualization (Planview, 2018). Kanban is like scrum methodology used for managing the work (Rozehnal and Novak, 2017). While in scrum the work is always planned and executed in the time intervals called Sprints, there is no such a thing as a sprint in Kanban (Kniberg nad Skarin, 2010). Instead, Kanban uses explicit limits which are applied on the different states of the workflow. These limits restrict the maximum amount of work entering the state which allows the teams to optimize their capacity. One of the main features enhancing the scrum process is making the flow of work more visual as shown Fig 3.

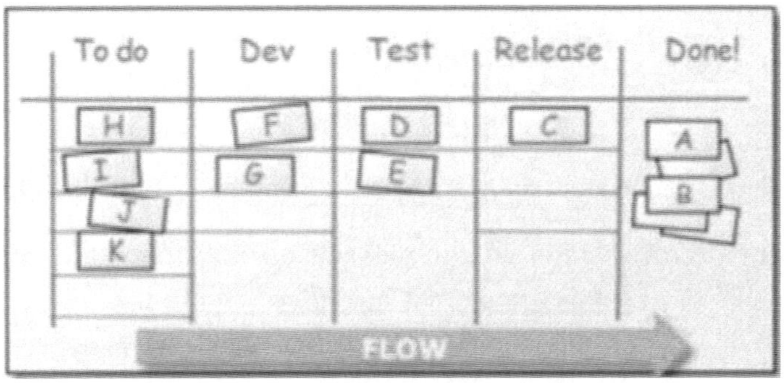

Figure 3 Example of Kanban board [own]

4.2 Physical type of board

One of the original approaches of scrum board visualization is using physical board. This technique includes all forms from crafting own paper-based board to reusing wall, window or even magnetic whiteboard. One of the greatest advantage is their high customization. Physical scrum boards are able to convey all the information team might need, because it depends only up to the human creativity. The board is mostly located in the team's room. This may serve as a good referencing point so everybody is on the same page with the current sprint status. The board is updated by the team members and reviewed regularly on daily scrum meetings. One of the main flaws of this type of scrum board is its availability (Ministr and Stevko, 2009). It expects the whole team to be located at the same location, otherwise it might be difficult for some members to reach and update it remotely.

4.3 Digital type of board

If is development team geographically distributed is appropriate to use digital type of board which in most cases can run in the internet browser therefore are available from the different locations in the world (Beley and Chaplyha, 2017). These type of boards serve as an emulators of the physical boards. The main principle is to copy the look and feel of the physical boards. Instead of physical cards moving between the columns the mouse or keyboard is used to move the virtual cards on the screen.

Figure 4 Magic Quadrant for Enterprise Agile Planning Tools. [Gartner, 2018]

Not all digital scrum boards are standalone. In most cases they are part of complex agile tool. The most popular software scrum tools are shown in Fig. 4.

5 Conclusion

The use of Scrum improves the communication among the Team members and maximizes co-operation. A key factor in the success of such a managed project is the good management of sprints through everyday meetings (stand ups). The quality of these meetings is strongly influenced by the way and the visualization of the project. The successful management of individual Sprint is usually supported by physical or digital boards. The choice of using this tool depends on the possibilities of the development team generally going to the digital boards that usually are integrated into the complex Enterprise agile planning Tools.

Appropriate visualization helps to organize work of team by considering its preferences and special knowledge. From the Product Owner's and Scrum Master's point of view it is most important that the software development process becomes visible, controllable, and manageable. All problems are immediately detected during Daily Scrum meetings and can be removed as soon as they emerge.

Acknowledgements

This paper was supported within Operational programme Education for Competitiveness -project No. CZ.1.07./2.3.00//20/0296.

References

Adisa., Schubert, P, Sudzina, F. and Johanson, B. (2010). 'Living Requirements Space An open access tool for enterprise resource planning systems requirements gathering'. *Online Information Review,* 34 (4), pp. 540-564.

Beley, O. and Chaplyha, V. (2017), 'The Application of Neural Networks for the Intelligent Analysis of Multidimensional Data'. *Proceedings of 4th International Scientific-Practical Conference Problems of Infocommunications. Science and Technology (PIC S&T)*, Kharkiv, Ukraine, pp. 400-404.

Chlopecký, J., Rolčíková, M. and Kratochvíl, M. (2015). 'Decision making influence of some macroeconomic factors concerning prospective sales of fine silicon carbide'. *Proceedings of 15th International Multidisciplinary Scientific GeoConference SGEM*, Albena, Bulgaria, pp. 171-178.

Kniberg, H. and Skarin, M. (2010). *Kanban and Scrum making the most of both.* USA: C4Media.

Mahnic, V. and Vrana, I. (2007). 'Using stakeholder-driven process performance measurement for monitoring the performance of a Scrum-based software development process'. *Elektrotehniski vestnik*, 74 (5), 241–247.

Matula, J., Zacek, J. and Hunka, F. (2016). 'Relevant user stories by using DEMO analysis'. *Proceedings of the 11th Scientific Conference Internet in the Information Society*, Dabrowa Gornicza, Poland, pp. 21-30.

Ministr, J. and Stevko, M. (2009). 'The IT Service Continuity Management Principles Implementation by Method A2'. *Proceedings of 17th Interdisciplinary Information Management Talks*, Jindrichuv Hradec, Czech Republic, pp. 131-140.

Planview LeanKit. (2018). Kanban vs. Scrum: Jaké jsou rozdíly?, [Online]. Available at: https://leankit.com/learn/kanban/kanban-vs-scrum/ [cited 2019-01-15].

Rozehnal, P. and Novak, V. (2017). 'Process, Function, Service - What is What in It Governance'. *Proceedings of 25th Digitalization in Management, Society and Economy Conference*, Podebrady, Czech Republic, pp. 351-358.

Rubin, K. S. (2012). *Essential Scrum: A Practical Guide to the Most Popular Agile Process,* An Arbor: Addison-Wesley Professional.

SCRMstudy, (2016). *A Guide to the Scrum Body of Knowledge (SBOK Guide).* Phoenix: VMEdu, Inc.

Šochová, Zuzana. (2013). Jak vypadá Scrum Board, [Online]. Available at: https://soch.cz/blog/management/agile/scrum-management/jak-vypada-scrum-board/.

VersionOne. (2018). 12th annual state of agile report, [Online]. Available at: https://explore.versionone.com/state-of-agile/versionone-12th-annual-state-of-agile-report [cited 2019-01-22].

Yip, J. (2016). It's not just standing up: Patterns for daily standup meetings, [Online]. Available at: https://www.martinfowler.com/articles/itsNotJustStandingUp.html [cited 2019-01-24].

Cybersecurity Qualifications for Industry 4.0 Era

Jan Ministr[1], Tomáš Pitner[2], Nikola Šimková[3]

Abstract. Cybersecurity plays important role in the digital economy, namely in the coming Industry 4.0 era. In the operational technology (OT) area, the lack of workforce knowledgeable in cybersecurity is even more appealing than in IT. In this paper, we describe existing frameworks and identify a need for national qualification framework for the Czech Republic with the focus at the needs of industry in this respect.

Keywords: Industry 4.0, cybersecurity, qualifications.

JEL Classification: C61

1 Introduction

With the advent of coming Industry 4.0, we see a gradual merge of information and operational technology in many industrial fields and virtually all critical infrastructures. It means the digital economy will only be sustainable if there is knowledgeable and skilled cybersecurity workforce (NICE, 2016). This vision should also be fulfilled thanks to the mission of the National Initiative for Cybersecurity Education (NICE). The NICE tries "to energize and promote a robust network and an ecosystem of cybersecurity education, training, and workforce development".

This motivation led us to examine existing cybersecurity frameworks and identify what kind of qualification framework should be suitable for a new Era – Industry 4.0. To fulfill this aim, we describe Industry 4.0 Era and cybersecurity as its important challenge in Section 1. Section 2 deals with an overview of what improvements in cybersecurity education can help to fill the gap in the labor market. In association with this aspect, it is important to describe existing frameworks in this area and provide a critical summary of the presented frameworks (Section 3). Based on the research, we identify a need for a national qualification framework in Section 4. Finally, we conclude with the summary in Section 5.

1.1 Industry 4.0 Era

The Industry 4.0 means both incremental technological development in overwhelming automation and optimization of manufacturing and supply chain but brings also disruptive concepts present never before affecting all production phases, i.e. design, simulation, production, test, delivery, and maintenance. It includes the abilities and scenarios such as (Hermann, Pentek & Otto, 2016):

- *Interconnection* – the machines, devices, sensors, and people are able to communicate with each other;
- *Information transparency* – the technology enables decision making based on availability of information from the whole manufacturing process;
- *Technical assistance* – helping people by removing unsafe, exhausting, or repetitive work and helping informed decision by visualization of comprehensive data;

[1] VŠB-Technical University of Ostrava, Faculty of Economics, Czechia, jan.ministr@vsb.cz
[2] Masaryk University, Faculty of Informatics, Czechia, tomp@fi.muni.cz
[3] Masaryk University, Faculty of Informatics, Czechia, simkova@fi.muni.cz

- *Decentralized decision* – cyber-physical systems can make as autonomous decisions as possible since the intelligence and data availability is present in a distributed way.

The technological areas enabling Industry 4.0 bring opportunities but also numerous challenges. Rüßmann et al (2015) names a couple of them, specifically pointing out cybersecurity as one issue:

- Big Data and Analytics
- Autonomous Robots
- Simulation
- Horizontal and Vertical System Integration
- The Industrial Internet of Things
- *Cybersecurity*
- The Cloud
- Additive Manufacturing
- Augmented Reality

1.2 Cybersecurity

In order to facilitate cybersecurity education for Industry 4.0, it is necessary to define the term of cybersecurity. The Joint Task Force on Cybersecurity Education (JTF) (2017) defines cybersecurity as "computing-based discipline involving technology, people, information, and processes to enable assured operations. It involves the *creation, operation, analysis, and testing* of secure computer systems. It is an *interdisciplinary course of study, including aspects of law, policy, human factors, ethics, and risk management* in the context of adversaries." The work CSEC2017 by JTF advances cybersecurity as a new computing discipline, but it does not forget to emphasize its character of multidisciplinary.

1.3 Cybersecurity Risks in Industry 4.0

The nature of Industry 4.0 brings numerous inherent risks that must be avoided or mitigated in order to make the transition to Industry 4.0 viable. We can name a couple of them:

- Risk of *cyber-espionage of industrial intellectual property* such as documentation for construction (CAD files), business process descriptions, or other business documents that cannot be kept in a safe but must be (partially) shared in the supply chain.
- Risks caused by *blurred security perimeter* in contrast to traditional environment with clear borders.
- *Big-data specific risks* including *Internet of Things* systems and privacy issues.
- Risks arising from growing transition from on-premise to *cloud system operations* in the so-called *cloud manufacturing* including virtualization.

All together according to Thames and Schaefer (2017) *"Industry 4.0 will face traditional cybersecurity issues along with its very own unique security and privacy challenges. If these challenges are not appropriately addressed, the true potential of Industry 4.0 may never be achieved."*

2 Need for a qualified workforce

2.1 Lack of cybersecurity workforce

Another important feature of cybersecurity is a serious lack of workforce that may worsen. The European Commission (EC) (2015) states that "demand for skilled workers with digital skills *increases by approximately 4% each year*. Unless decisive action is taken, the shortage of ICT professionals in the EU could worsen to *825,000 vacant posts* by 2020." The EC (2017) also claims that effective cybersecurity is based largely on the skills of the relevant staff. However, *350,000 cybersecurity experts* are missing in Europe in the private sector by 2022.

At the same time, the president of the Australian Computer Society (ACS) stated that *"Australia will need an estimated 100,000 more ICT specialists by 2020 but a mere 4000 IT graduates are produced at tertiary level each year."* Another report from Australia states: *".... The demand for skilled ICT workers will increase from 638K today to 695K by 2020 with ICT university graduates meeting only 1% of this demand. Additionally, there has been a 35% drop in enrolment rates for ICT subjects at universities since 2001."*

2.2 Main areas

Caelli and Liu (2018) identified the following significant gaps in cybersecurity education in Australia that might be relevant in other, such as European and Industry 4.0 contexts, too:

- *"vertical" vs. "horizontal" subject areas*, e.g. healthcare requirements, etc. including appropriate national and international standards;
- an understanding of the *history of the subject*, its present status and likely future trends, e.g. the IS 7498-2 security standard for the OSI model networks, USA "Orange Book" / UK ITSEC;
- *contemporary computing security requirements, including Internet-of-Things (IoT),* cloud;
- systems and *security of virtualization/container* technologies;
- a layered, "*security architecture*" analysis and development approach from hardware to operating systems to network stacks to middleware to applications, etc. and
- *trusted/trustworthy computer systems and their evaluation*, e.g. the "Common Criteria";
- *national and international legal/regulatory arrangements* in cybersecurity/cyber conflict, response to attacks/penetration, etc.

2.3 Summary of main challenges

Thus, main improvements in cybersecurity education can be done in the following areas:

- Approaching vertical subject areas for specific domains, eg. healthcare and critical infrastructures – needs to educate capabilities to see the big picture from multiple viewpoints;
- Keeping pace with contemporary computing security requirements imposed by (Industrial-)IoT and cloud technologies – the Industry 4.0 is backed by modern computer infrastructures such as clouds and communication technology;
- Learn design and implementation of secure architectures following security-by-design – goes hand-in-hand with the "vertical" view, required as the systems get more complex,

it needs appropriate means for verification, validation, and certification of the whole solutions/systems/infrastructures rather than particular isolated items;

- Studying (inter)national regulatory arrangements – since the advent of globalization, Industry 4.0 only rarely operates exclusively on a factory, enterprise, or national scale. Rather, the supply chains almost always cross boundaries of single enterprises and countries;
- Trusted computer systems and its certification – to create common markets for secure Industry 4.0 products and systems, there is an urgent need for (supra-)national systems for certification.

In this complex context, an immediate question arises: How to cope with the described lack of professionals? It is necessary to identify where and what is missing. There are some areas where cybersecurity is essential. Examples are critical sectors and infrastructures, as well as key businesses. As is clear from the definition, cybersecurity is a term that involves several aspects. Therefore, we need a taxonomy and framework for cybersecurity. At the same time, it is important to recognize the urgent priorities. There should be found a way to help resolve the unwanted status quo.

3 Existing frameworks

3.1 European e-competence framework

European e-competence framework (e-CF) (2014) is a common European framework for ICT professionals in all industry sectors. The four dimensions reflect different levels of business and human resource planning requirements in addition to job proficiency guidelines:

1) 5 e-Competence areas: Plan, Build, Run, Enable and Manage;
2) 40 competences with a generic description;
3) 5 proficiency levels (e-1 to e-5), which are related to European Qualifications Framework (EQF) levels 3-8;
4) samples of knowledge and skills relate to 40 competences.

3.2 NICE Cybersecurity Workforce Framework

NICE Cybersecurity Workforce Framework (2017) is a national focused resource that categorizes and describes cybersecurity work in the US. It establishes a taxonomy and common lexicon for public, private, and academic sectors. It comprised of the components:

1) 7 categories – a high-level grouping of cybersecurity functions (Figure 1);
2) 33 specialty areas – distinct areas of cybersecurity work;
3) 52 work roles – the most detailed groupings of specific knowledge, skills, and abilities required to perform tasks in a work role.

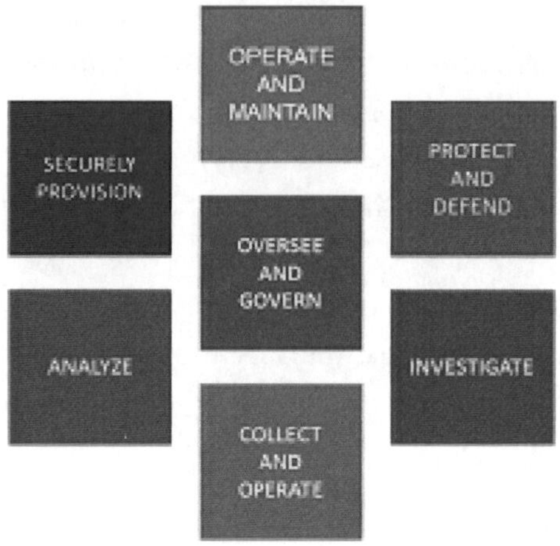

Figure 1 Seven categories of NICE framework [NICE Cybersecurity Workforce Framework, 2017]

3.3 JTF Cybersecurity curricula

The JTF has developed comprehensive curricular guidance in cybersecurity education. To define *Cybersecurity curricula (CSEC2017 JTF)* multiparty effort is required in the form of collaboration between major international computing societies (JTF, 2017):

- Association for Computing Machinery (ACM);
- IEEE Computer Society (IEEE CS);
- Association for Information Systems Special Interest Group on Security (AIS SIGSEC);
- International Federation for Information Processing Technical Committee on Information Security Education (IFIP WG 11.8).

Cybersecurity Curricula (2017) states in the introduction that "both government and non-government sources project nearly *1.8 million* cybersecurity-related positions going unfilled by 2022". The acute, immediate, and growing workforce demand requires establishing new cybersecurity programs or courses of study within existing programs. The institutions responsible for study programs need curricular guidance based on a comprehensive view of the cybersecurity field, the specific demands, and the relationship between the curriculum and cybersecurity workforce frameworks. Therefore, the Curriculum guidelines for post-secondary degree programs in cybersecurity was created.

The CSEC2017 JTF defines the audiences for this cybersecurity guidance:

- Faculty members in computing-based disciplines at academic institutions;
- Industry members who will assist with cybersecurity program development;
- Training and professional development providers;
- Faculty members in non-computing based disciplines;
- Academic administrators with oversight for program development;
- Workforce framework developers (government and non-government);
- Policymakers;
- Members of the K-12 educational community.

The CSEC2017 JTF thought model has three dimensions: 8 knowledge areas, 6 crosscutting concepts, and disciplinary lenses. We can see the model in Figure 2.

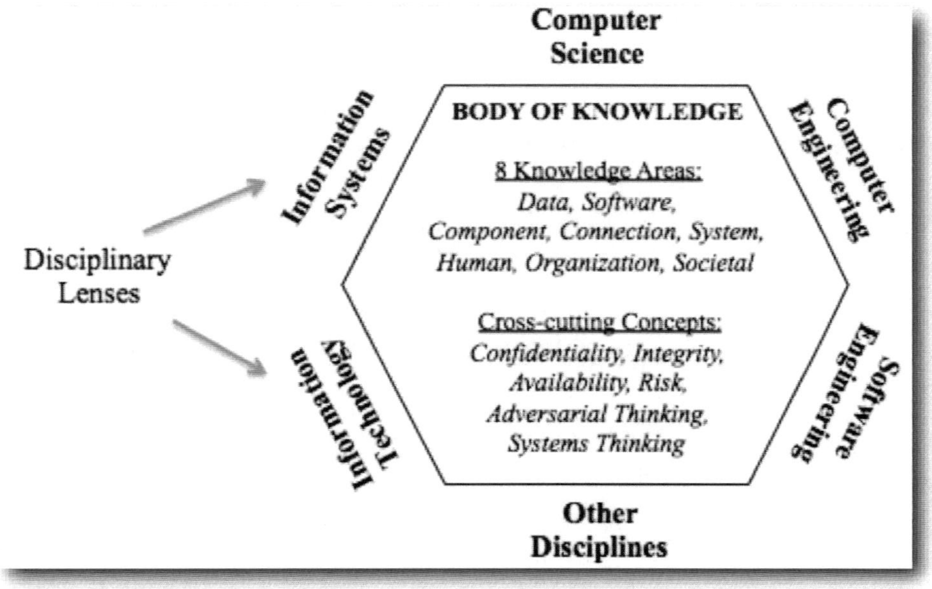

Figure 2 CSEC thought model [CSEC2017 JTF, 2017, p. 20]

3.4 Critical summary

After studying the existing frameworks, we provide a summary of the presented frameworks (**Chyba! Nenalezen zdroj odkazů.**). As we can see, the European e-competence framework generally focuses on ICT, but there are also two frameworks deals with cybersecurity. Another important aspect is the structure of the frameworks. The frameworks for work include at least knowledge and skills, while the JTF Cybersecurity curricula contains only knowledge. However, the knowledge is associated with learning outcomes, what is relevant for curriculum guidelines. In addition, the frameworks are designed for different locations.

Framework	**European e-competence framework**	**NICE Cybersecurity Workforce Framework**	**JTF Cybersecurity curricula**
Locations	Europe	US	international
Focus	ICT competences	cybersecurity work	cybersecurity education
Sectors	industry	public, private and academic	public, private and academic
Dimensions	4	3	3
Evaluation	+ based on competences rather than job profiles	+ taxonomy for all sectors	+ curriculum guidelines
	- generally focuses on ICT, no cybersecurity	+ deals with cybersecurity	+ deals with cybersecurity
	- general for Europe	- focuses on the national level, but the US	- general for the World
	- only knowledge and skills	+ detailed structure (knowledge, skills, and abilities)	- only knowledge

Table 1 Summary of the existing frameworks

4 Czech National qualification framework

As mentioned, cybersecurity frameworks appear in the world, but the general all-catch framework for the Czech Republic is missing. It is necessary to take into account the specifics of the Czech environment. Cybersecurity is intermixed within ICT professions. For this reason, the Masaryk University, Faculty of Informatics is engaged in the preparation of students for their career in the area of cybersecurity. One specialization of the new IT Management program is Information technology security (described in Pitner and Ministr, 2017). Although it should appear rather in secondary or upper-secondary education than at the university level, thanks to that we have a reference framework and starting point for National qualification framework in cybersecurity.

Several efforts have emerged in this area, but none with significant impact. To establish the national qualification framework collaboration of responsible bodies is required, such as NÚKIB - National Cybersecurity Agency, Ministries of Defense, Interior, Police, and Critical infrastructure operators. Moreover, strong academic coordination can help to incorporate the interdisciplinary nature of cybersecurity into the framework. Experts in the IT, law, sociology/politology areas should be involved. The framework should bound to new accreditation system (self-governed "institutional" or national one). We can also be inspired by the conclusions of the study (Cabaj et al., 2018) where 21 cybersecurity master programs of universities belonging to the top 700 universities (according to the 2017 ranking of QS World Ranking of Universities) were analyzed and reviewed.

5 Conclusion

As the number and impact of cyberattacks are becoming more and more serious, the importance of cyber security is growing. The problem is a significant lack of qualified workforce that may worsen. To meet workforce demand has been establishing new cybersecurity programs or courses of study. Frameworks, such as European e-competence framework (e-CF), NICE Cybersecurity Workforce Framework and Cybersecurity curricula (CSEC2017 JTF), help to create them. We identified and described a need for national qualification framework in cybersecurity for the Czech Republic. In the future, we will make efforts to create a framework.

Acknowledgements

This paper was supported within Operational programme Education for Competitiveness -project No. CZ.1.07./2.3.00//20/0296.

References

Cabaj, K., Domingos, D., Kotulski, Z. and Respício, A. (2018). ‘Cybersecurity education: Evolution of the discipline and analysis of master programs‘. *Computers & Security*, 75, pp. 24-35.

Cybersecurity Curricula (CSEC2017 JTF) (2017). Curriculum Guidelines for Post-Secondary Degree Programs in Cybersecurity, [Online]. Available at: https://cybered.hosting.acm.org/wp-content/uploads/2018/02/newcover_csec2017.pdf.

European Commission (EC) (2015). A Digital Single Market Strategy for Europe COM/2015/0192 final, [Online]. Available at: https://eur-lex.europa.eu/legal-content/EN/TXT/?uri=COM%3A2015%3A192%3AFIN [cited 15 Sep., 2018].

European Commission (EC) (2017). Resilience, Deterrence and Defence: Building strong cybersecurity for the EU JOIN/2017/0450 final, [Online]. Available at: https://publications.europa.eu/en/publication-detail/-/publication/794f8627-985b-11e7-b92d-01aa75ed71a1 [cited 15 Sep, 2018].

European e-Competence Framework (e-CF) (2014). A common European framework for ICT Professionals in all industry sectors, [Online]. Available at: http://www.ecompetences.eu/wp-content/uploads/2014/02/European-e-Competence-Framework-3.0_CEN_CWA_16234-1_2014.pdf.

Herman, M., Pentek, T. and Otto, B. (2016). 'Design Principles for Industrie 4.0 Scenarios'. *49th Hawaii International Conference on System Sciences (HICSS),* Koloa (HI), USA.

Joint Task Force on Cybersecurity Education (JTF) (2017). *Cybersecurity Curricular Guidelines. CSEC 2017*, [Online]. Available at: http://cybered.acm.org/ [cited 15 Sep, 2018].

Ministr, J., Pitner, T. and Šimková, N. (2018) 'Cybersecurity Qualifications', *Proceedings of 21st International Conference Information Technology for Practice 2018*, Ostrava, pp. 141-146.

National Initiative for Cybersecurity Education (NICE) (2016). Strategic Plan, [Online], Available at: https://www.nist.gov/sites/default/files/documents/2018/01/16/nice_strategicplan_011218_web.pdf.

NICE Cybersecurity Workforce Framework (2017), [Online]. Available at: https://www.nist.gov/itl/applied-cybersecurity/nice/resources/nice-cybersecurity-workforce-framework [cited 15 Sep 2018].

Pitner, T. and Ministr, J. (2017). 'Cybersecurity within IT Management Studies'. *Proceedings of 20th International Conference Information Technology for Practice 2017*, Ostrava, Czech Republic, pp. 159-165.

Rüßmann, M., Lorenz, M., Gerbert, P., Waldner, M., Justus, J., Engel, P. and Harnisch, M. (2015). 'Industry 4.0: The future of productivity and growth in manufacturing industries'. *Boston Consulting Group*, 9.

Thames, J. and Schaefer, D. (2017). *Cybersecurity for Industry 4.0 -Analysis for Design and Manufacturing*. Cham: Springer.

SQL Query Similarity Using Graph-theoretic Approach

Radek Němec[1], František Zapletal[2]

Abstract. In this paper, we investigate possibility of representing a SQL query using an undirected graph, and use such representation to determine similarity, much like in a way regular text documents are examined during the classification process, e.g., for the purpose of sentiment analysis, etc.
We analyze use of two possible approaches with two graph similarity metrics to measure similarity between certain query graph and a super graph that represents certain class of queries. The results indicate possible applicability of the idea, but also revealed several pitfalls and limitations.

Keywords: query graph, graph theory, Anchor Data Modeling, graph similarity.

1 Introduction

Although the current situation in the field of databases and data warehousing favors NoSQL technologies, the relational database modelling paradigm is not forgotten at all, as stated by Poleto, de Carvalho and Costa (2015). In fact, majority of companies still use relational databases as a platform for their business-process-performance management effort (through usage of data warehouse as a key data source). The changes in the business world, however, happen despite the technology used and they influence also data transformation and storage needs. And despite tehe fact that cloud providers promote use of In this paper, we focus on the study of a data modelling technique called Anchor Data Modelling (ADM) (Regardt et al, 2009), which is applied in the data mart design and implementation field. The technique is supposed to offer agile data modelling features, through implicit logical data model decomposition (the 5th or 6th normal form). Agile modeling is useful in the business world, although the usefulness and benefits of "agile-anything" must be first studied thoroughly.

In our previous paper (Němec and Zapletal, 2017), we tried to apply a clustering technique using several aggregated features of sample SQL queries (e.g., amount of large dimension's attribute used in a query, etc.), which were run within the database schema built using the ADM technique. The results were, however, not sufficiently pointing out which features are related to the benefits of using the technique, i.e. better query execution time (QET) results in comparison with the classic star schema (i.e. using the 3rd normal form based relational tables for the dimension instead of highly normalized relations for each property of the dimension).

We already know exact differences of each query's execution time (as compared to the execution of its counterpart, using the classical star schema), and we know that certain queries executed much faster than others which executed much slower. The effort of using aggregated features failed. One question then still remains unanswered: what query content can we associate (with a certain precision) with the faster execution of the given query, when the ADM based schema is used as the base approach for the design of the underlying data mart's data

[1] VŠB-Technical University of Ostrava, Department of Systems Engineering, Sokolská 33, Ostrava, radek.nemec@vsb.cz.
[2] VŠB-Technical University of Ostrava, Department of Systems Engineering, Sokolská 33, Ostrava, frantisek.zapletal@vsb.cz.

model. And to this question we try to find answer using a different approach than in the former study.

Given a growing popularity of text analysis methods, and especially graph-theoretic approaches to the representation of the content of a certain document (i.e. paragraph of text, etc. – see Violos et. al (2016), Sonawane and Kulkarni (2014)), we came up with an idea of a novel approach. We may study the query execution features through the analysis of query text from a graph-similarity point of view. Certain structure of a query statement is likely to yield positive QET difference results and certain structure should imply rather negative outcomes in terms of query execution times (as evident from our previous research). The results might be useful also for the field of Big-Data related query composition, because the SQL is still one of the most used languages for writing queries despite the fact, that the data might reside in a NoSQL database environment, and that the SQL query must be first translated into a particular NoSQL data storage environment's native form (e.g., most Hadoop-related data stores have an abstraction layer that can convert SQL queries into programming code, e.g. in Pig language).

The goal of the paper is to apply this approach and compare two possible variants, how to measure the similarity between undirected graphs representing each query, using two possible metrics of graph similarity.

The rest of the paper is divided into 3 sections. In the first section, we describe briefly the ADM method, and in more detail the idea of the graph representation of a query. In the following section, we describe the methodology of an experiment in which we would like to show how the approach can be beneficial for classification purposes. In the last section, we describe and conclude the results.

2 Anchor Data Modeling and graph representation of a query

In this section, we first briefly summarize fundamental facts about the ADM method. Next, we describe in more detail the idea of representing query statement content using an undirected graph.

2.1 Brief overview of the Anchor Data Modelling technique

The ADM technique is based on the usage of several distinctive conceptual constructors. These are convertible into logical objects and physical relational tables, at the end of the data modelling process. Each attribute of any entity is defined separately and represented as a single relation (the *Attribute*), with only 2 attributes, i.e. a composite key attribute and an actual value of the entity's property. Attributes in the anchor data model are connected through the *Anchor* relation, which is a source of business keys for related *Attributes*. Anchors are then connected through *Tie* constructors, which represent *M*-to-*N* relationships between entities by default.

The overall structure of the resulting database schema is normalized and in the 5th normal form by design, i.e. relations cannot be further decomposed without losing certain information value of the entity. The database schema can be also in the 6th normal form (Date, Darwen and Lorentzos, 2003), in which the primary key of at least one relation includes additional attributes indicating validity of store values in time. The database schema representing a dimensional data model used in this paper was designed and constructed using a hybrid ADM approach, described in Němec and Zapletal (2014a).

The aspect of the high degree of normalization itself is the one that is linked with potential query execution performance benefits, as mentioned in the original paper by Regardt et al. (2009). This paper, however, provides a rather small body of evidence for the justification of query execution benefits within the traditional data warehouse database schema (i.e. the schema in the 3rd normal form). Golov and Rönnbäck (2015) brought evidence that the ADM use is beneficial even when processing of Big Data is desired, with superior query execution results obtained in favor of the ADM. There are, however, no other works discussing the differences between ADM and the traditional data modelling, or the use in special cases, like OLAP, etc. In our ongoing work, we strive to create such body of evidence, and mainly to assess the potential usefulness of this approach for OLAP purposes.

We studied the query-execution-performance benefits in Němec and Zapletal (2014a,b), focusing on the business-reporting field and the environment of a sample data mart so far. In addition, similar results were obtained when the ADM-method based database schema was used within several Business Intelligence software tools (Němec, 2015). Again, the results showed superiority of processing queries, if the ADM-based schema was selected in test reports in most of the tools in the test suite. In Němec and Zapletal (2017), we tried to apply clustering machine-learning method to cluster queries using aggregated query content features, but with not very satisfying results. In this paper, we try to open a new track and adopt traits of an approach that stems from the field of text data analysis.

2.2 Graph-theory based representation of a SQL query statement

A graph G is an ordered pair $G = (V, E)$ where V is a set of vertices (also called nodes) and E represents sets of labelled/unlabelled, or weighted edges between a subset or between the vertices in V. The direction of paths between vertices can be of concern, so the graph G can be either directed or undirected (whether paths or only associations between nodes are to be studied).

As for the objective of our study, we decided to represent SQL queries by undirected graphs, in which every set of vertices V represents a set of query text components that can be found also in other (similar) queries. To be able to compare a certain query graph with a larger set of query graphs, the set V can include vertices representing one of the following options (Fig. 1 shows a picture of an undirected graph of a hypothetical SQL query statement):

- labels of certain SQL query statement clauses, i.e. "Select" and "Order By" (other are omitted because queries in the dataset does not contain any complicated joins and also the "Group By" clause is tied with use of aggregation function and the physical demands of rows grouping during query execution optimization are usually negligible in comparison with demands of joins and table scans (Němec and Zapletal (2014b));
- labels of table columns listed within "Select", "Order By", or the "Where" part of the statement (these can be common for multiple graphs);
- labels of filtering conditions within the "Where" part (these can be reused).

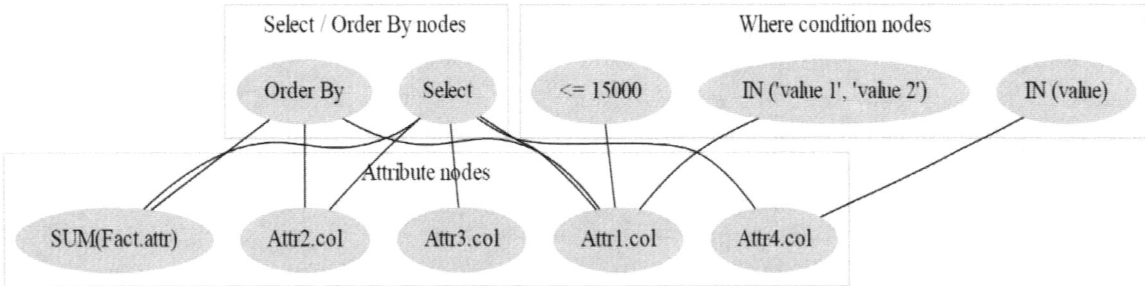

Figure 1 Undirected graph representing content of a hypothetical SQL query statement

The graph based representation has one important trait: the graph matching can be done using a much smaller dataset in comparison with the eventual comparison using the whole query statement text, in which we would need to construct a large matrix of all features (words in a query statement). Such approach, however, would not preserve enough semantics of relationships within the query, which is important to us since we look for actual associations of query content artifacts with their contribution to the query execution efficiency.

3 Experiment methodology

The input dataset contains 290 query texts with query number (*QNO*) and actual QET difference values, associated with each of the queries in the dataset. Every query's text was converted into a query graph $G_{QNO} = (V_{QNO}, E_{QNO})$ where labelled vertices in the set V_{QNO} represent one of query statement's parts, i.e.:

- "Select" clause label,
- "Order By" clause label,
- "Column name" or "Aggregated column name" label,
- "Filtering condition" description.

Each edge in the set E_{QNO} represents one of these associations:

- "Select" – "Column name",
- "Select" – "Aggregated column name",
- "Order By" – "Column name",
- "Order By" – "Aggregated column name",
- "Column name" – "Filtering condition",
- "Aggregated column name" – "Filtering condition".

It is desired to determine similarity of each graph G_{QNO} to a class super graph $G_S^{(C)}$, i.e. a graph of all query graphs corresponding with certain class $c = \{1, -1\}$, joined into one graph using a certain rule. Two approaches, related to the mentioned rules will be studied and then impact of use of two metrics will be analysed.

The first approach is to treat each class super graph $G_S^{(C)}$ as a collection of all graphs, for which the corresponding queries performed either with QET difference within range: $(\min(QET)\,;\,0)$ (class $c = -1$), or within range: $<0\,;\,\max(QET))$ (class $c = 1$). So, in other words, super graph $G_S^{(1)}$ will contain nodes and vertices related to queries that performed better, or the same using the ADM-based schema, while $G_S^{(-1)}$ will contain the opposite cases.

The second approach differs from the first one in the fact that only 30 best- and 30 worst-performing queries (as given by values of QET differences)[3] will be selected for construction of each class super graph. Such potential outlier cases might be important for us, because they may contain clues on what statement content composition is extremely beneficial to the query execution efficiency.

As for the metrics, we will use graph-size based similarity metrics. The first metric, which was used by Violos et al. (2016) within the sentiment analysis task to compute similarity between N-gram word graphs, stems from the idea that certain edges (i.e. associations between words), or vertices (i.e. words) should be common to both the graph of an actual document (optionally pre-classified with certain polarity class), and a "gold standard" graph, which is a graph representing all/selected documents with content corresponding with only one polarity class (i.e. with negative, positive or neutral content in terms of the sentiment expression). The edge-based Containment Similarity (CS) the authors used, will be computed similarly in our case (see equation 1):

$$CS\left(G_{QNO}, G_S^{(C)}\right) = \frac{\sum_{e \in G_{QNO}} \mu\left(e, G_S^{(C)}\right)}{\min\left(\left|G_{QNO}\right|, \left|G_S^{(C)}\right|\right)}, \qquad (1)$$

where e is total count of common edges in either of graphs, and $\left|G_S^{(C)}\right|$ are the sizes of matched query- and class super graph (given by the total count of edges).

Alternatively, we will compute a metric based on a ratio between total count of common edges and the size of the class super graph, which should partially mitigate the fact that queries might not be long enough to represent the whole class super graph. Therefore, the Containment Ratio (CR) metric will be computed according to the equation 2:

$$CR\left(G_{QNO}, G_S^{(C)}\right) = \frac{\sum_{e \in G_{QNO}} \mu\left(e, G_S^{(C)}\right)}{\left|G_S^{(C)}\right|}. \qquad (2)$$

In the final step, a computation of query classification precision, using a vector of similarities as predictors and a class label c as a response variable will be carried out using the Support Vector Machine (SVM) algorithm, to prove that this approach can be used to classify new queries arriving into the dataset – Aggarwal & Zhai (2012) recommend SVM algorithm for text classification problems.

4 Experiment results

With the current size of the input query dataset, the construction of each graph took several milliseconds. The query graph is not very large so the approaches are constrained only by the total amount of the compared graphs. The SVM classifier accuracy was determined using the 80:20 rule (80% of cases as train cases and 20% of test cases) and the linear kernel was used to

[3] 30 queries equals roughly 10% of the dataset size and 30 is also a generally acknowledged minimal amount of cases, for which we can assume normal distribution of values in the dataset

make the classification more efficient. The results in Table 1 show accuracy of the SVM classifier using similarities vectors, based on the graph similarity metrics and class super graph construction approaches.

Graph similarity metric	Class super graph construction approach	
	All queries	**Top and bottom 30**
CS	74% (st. dev. 0.054)	74% (st. dev. 0.052)
CR	76% (st. dev. 0.046) (216 queries for the class $c = -1$ and 74 queries for the class $c = 1$)	73% (st. dev. 0.058)

Table 1 SVM classifier accuracy results (average of 10 runs of the classifier)

As shown, the average accuracy in 10 runs of the SVM classifier was quite high (73% to 76%) and the *CR* metric gives the highest accuracy for eventual classification, if the graph was constructed using all queries relevant to a certain class. The *CS* performed also quite well, but there is one possible pitfall in using the *CS* metric. The larger is the query dataset, the more likely it is that the query is similar to both class super graphs, resulting in distorted results. Queries are usually not too long in comparison with all class-relevant queries combined, and the amount of nodes/edges in the matched graph can be equal to the amount of common nodes/edges. Queries in the dataset were not the same although some of them were quite similar.

When we look at average similarities for each metric and class super graph construction approach (Fig. 2), we can see that the potential problem with the *CS* metric is quite evident there (the similarities are, on average, almost the same for both classes). The *CR* metric values are, however, also quite close (but much lower). As we can see, the use of 30-query sample to construct class super graphs proved to be beneficial to a certain degree (the average similarity is more different and standard deviation raised a bit).

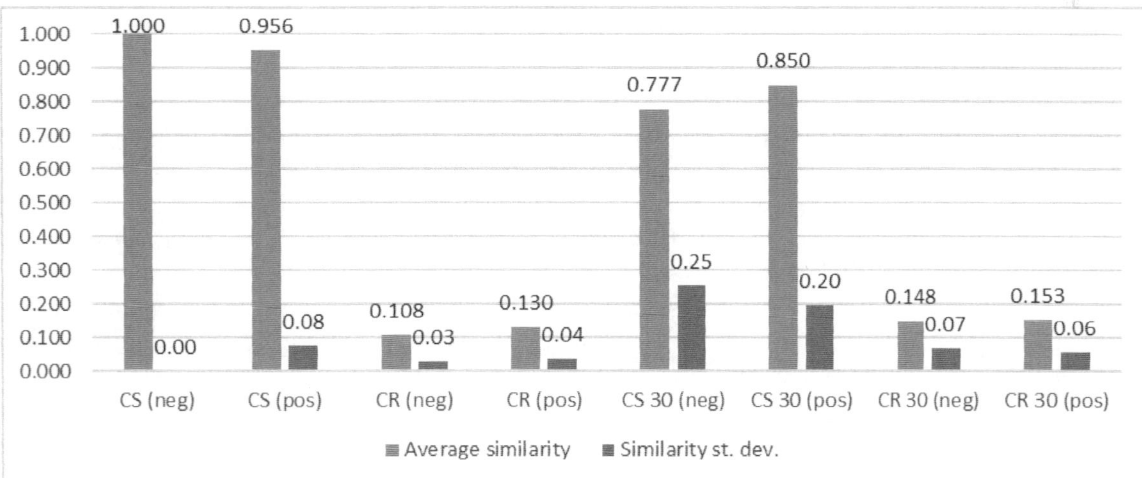

Figure 2 Average similarities by each approach variant and similarity metric

There are several limitations of the approach. First, the accuracy is not very high and there are some issues with the actual similarity values (mostly same for the *CS* metric). Second, the dataset size is not very extensive so adding much more queries might help to improve the potential usefulness of the approach as a whole. Third, the two-class limitation might be too strict because there might be several query processing profiles present. Thus, analysis of multiple levels of query execution time differences might yield better results. The last limitation is that the edges were not weighted at all, which might be desirable if we consider different physical processing needs of certain operations, like table scans or joins[4]. This might also help to determine more precisely how would the query execution environment behave, if such a query was eventually executed for the first time by the user.

5 Conclusion

The graph-theoretic approach we analysed in this paper, to compare query graph with a class-relevant super graph proved to be quite useful, with test classification accuracy above 70%. The adopted text classification approach seems promising but there are, however, several issues considering the metrics and approach variants we used in this paper and which we would like to explore in more detail in our future work.

Acknowledgements

This paper was made with financial support of the European Social Fund within the project CZ.1.07/2.3.00/20.0296 and the Student Grant Competition project SP2018/146 "Evaluation of comparison applications using cognitive analysis and the Data Envelopment Analysis method".

References

Aggarwal, C. C. and Zhai, C. (2012). 'A Survey of Text Classification Algorithms'. *Mining Text Data.* New York: Springer, pp. 163-222.

Date, C. J., Darwen, H. and Lorentzos, N. A. (2003). *Temporal Data and the Relational Model: A Detailed Investigation into the Application of Interval and Relation Theory to the Problem of Temporal Database Management.* Oxford: Elsevier.

Němec, R. and Zapletal, F. (2014a). 'The Design of Multidimensional Data Model Using Principles of the Anchor Data Modeling: An Assessment of Experimental Approach Based on Query Execution Performance'. *WSEAS Transactions on Computers*, 13, pp. 177-194.

Němec, R. and Zapletal, F. (2014b). 'Analysis of Query Execution Performance Factors in the Anchor Multidimensional Database Schema Environment'. *Selected Paper of the MEKON 2014 Conference*, Ostrava, pp. 481-491.

Němec, R. and Zapletal, F. (2015). 'Application of selected classification and clustering methods on the database query categorization'. *Proceedings of the 11th international conference Strategic Management and its Support by Information Systems 2015*, Ostrava, pp. 439-446.

Němec, R. and Zapletal, F. (2017). 'On the determination of query execution patterns of the application of the Anchor Data modeling method using machine-learning methods'. *Proceedings of the 12th International Conference on Strategic Management and its Support by Information Systems 2017*, Ostrava, pp. 434-444.

Němec, R. (2015). 'Assessment of query execution performance using selected Business Intelligence tools and experimental agile oriented data modeling approach'. *Proceedings of the 2015 Federated Conference on Computer Science and Information Systems*, Warsaw, Poland, pp. 1327-1333.

Poleto, T., de Carvalho, V. D. H. and Costa, A. P. C. S. (2015). 'The Roles of Big Data in the Decision-Support Process: An Empirical Investigation'. *Proceedings of the 1st International Conference ICDSST 2015 (Lecture Notes in Business Information Processing 216).* Belgrade, Serbia, pp. 10-21

[4] More complex ADM-schema based queries typically include as many joins as there are columns selected from Attribute relational tables, or used within the Where condition part of the statement

Violos, J., Tserpes, K., Psomakelis, E., Psychas, K. and Varvarigou, T. (2016). ‘Sentiment Analysis Using Word-Graphs’. *Proceedings of the 6th International Conference on Web Intelligence, Mining and Semantics*, Nimes, France.

Sonawe, S. S. and Kulkarni, P. A. (2014). ‘Graph Based Representation and Analysis of Text Document: A Survey of Techniques’. *International Journal of Computer Applications*, 96 (19), pp. 1-8.

Collecting and systematizing "smart solutions" for residential real estate, especially in Central and Eastern Europe, with special regard to the Visegrad countries

Daniel Orosz[1]

Abstract. The first smart home controller computer or program was designed in the second half of the 60s, it was far ahead of its time and was not commercialized. More than five decades had to wait more significant spreading of these systems, which thanks for the internet widespread availability and reliability. While in just a fragment of the traditional property real estate owners have been using the smart apps, in the case of newly built real estate, it is almost essential to have some clever features. The benefits are clear, in the long run, initial surplus investments are likely to return, the overhead costs of housing may be reduced, their comfort levels and their viability can be significantly improved. It is likely that in almost all residences in the future there will be some clever function. I would like to give a brief overview of what we mean by smart city and smart home terms and illustrate the situation in some of the cities in the Central and Eastern European region, what is the situation of becoming a smart home in this area.

Keywords: smart city, smart home, smart solutions, Visegrad countries.

JEL Classification: R11, O18, O33

1 Introduction

Urban development increasingly requires the use of advanced technologies, with a particular focus on the range of tasks to be solved. In developing countries, the problems identified by the rapidly growing population are dominant, while in developed countries, whose populations are mostly aging, they are more focused on improving quality of life, reducing social inequalities and developing sustainable structures. These problems can be solved by applying the smart city concept in cities, as the rapid development of technology offers new development paths for cities that can handle the problems, the challenges of competitive and sustainable cities at the same time. In this paper, I would like to give a brief overview of what we mean by smart city and smart home terms and illustrate the situation in some of the cities in the Central and Eastern European region, what is the situation of becoming a smart home in this area.

2 Smart City concept

The smart city concept appeared in the 1980s and '90s, thanks to the widespread use of information and communication technologies (ICT). In the 2000s, the increasing use of the internet made it possible for cities to make more and more electronic services available to their citizens (e-government, e-learning, etc.), while nowadays the revolution of intelligent wireless sensors is taking place (Bizjan, 2014).

[1] University of Miskolc/ Institute of World – and Regional Economics, Department of Regional Economics, 3515 Miskolc-Egyetemváros, Hungary, regorosz@uni-miskolc.hu

The term "smart city" is used more and more often, but there is no uniform concept for this, often there are unique solutions per settlement. In recent years, many definitions have been formulated for the "smart city" - but yet there is no uniform, universally accepted definition - and I will quote some of them.

- A Smart City performs outstandingly in the following six areas: economy, people, governance, mobility, environment, living conditions. (Giffinger et al., 2007),
- a smart community is a community that makes conscious efforts to use information technology to make life and work in the area significant and essential is, rather than as ancillary. (California Institute, 2001)
- "The concept of smart city, where citizens, objects, utilities, etc. are perfectly interconnected with the use of everyday technologies to significantly improve the experience of a 21st century urban environment" (Northstream, 2010).
- The smart city is the product of a combination of the digital city and the 'Internet of Things' (Su et al., 2011),
- The smart city monitors and integrates all critical infrastructures (including roads, bridges, tunnels, railways, subways, airports, harbors, communications, water, energy, and major buildings) to optimize its resources, plan its activities with respect to safety while maximizing services for the population. (Hall, 2000).

2.1 Measuring the performance of smart cities

The ISO is an international standardization organization, has identified factors that can measure the performance of a smart city. A smart city index is a summary of many indicators, and the city's 'intelligence' is characterized by a number of different practices. Smart cities can be compared based on these indices. I briefly introduce two indexes, because with these rankings I will select the cities that I will examine in a later chapter in terms of which level they are in the process of becoming a smart home (Bakonyi P. et al. 2018).

2.2 Global Cities Index

The Global Cities Index is a smart city index that examines the performance of cities around the world in 27 terms, in five categories: business activity, human resources, information exchange, culture, policy (ATKearney 2016).

Components of the Global Index examining the current situation and their weights:

- business activity (30%): capital flows, market dynamics, presence of major companies;
- human resources (30%): quality of education;
- cultural experience (15%): access to major sporting events, museums and other exhibitions;
- political situation (10%): political events, prominent thinkers, embassies.
- information exchange (15%): access to information through internet and other media sources

Components of the Global Index for Future Situation:

- personal well-being (25%): security, health, social tensions, environmental protection;
- economy (25%): long-term investment and GDP;

- innovation (25%): proportion of patent-based businesses, non-governmental investments, incubation, startups;
- Governability (25%): transparency, quality of bureaucracy, simplicity of business

2.3 European Smart Cities Index

Five aspects of Europe's medium-sized cities and their evaluation factors are the follows:

- Smart economy: innovation ability, entrepreneurial ability, external thinking of the economy, productivity, flexibility of the workforce, integration into the international world, ability to transform.
- Intelligent population: level of education, attitudes to lifelong learning, social and ethnic plurality, flexibility, creativity, openness, participation in public life.
- Intelligent urban management: participation in decision-making, public and social services, transparent city management, forward-looking strategies, sustainable, innovative and secure transport system, availability of info-communication infrastructure, availability of local and international access.
- Intelligent environment: environmental protection, low pollution, sustainable resource management, attractive natural conditions.
- Quality of life: cultural facilities, conditionality of health care, safety of individuals, housing conditions, educational infrastructure, attractiveness of tourism, social cohesion

European cities perform excellently in many areas, such as traffic management, emissions, culture. (smart-cities.eu, 2014)

3 Definition of Smart Home

Smart Home does not have a general definition yet, there are many different definitions, and there some expressions in the literature, which only partly covers or is similar to Smart Home for example: remote home, home automation system, automated home, home energy management system, etc. While the concept of a smart home or smart house is already well-known to most people, but there is no unified definition yet available.

In the following, I cite some "smart home" definition:

- "Smart home" or "smart house" is a home that includes advanced automation systems to provide the public with sophisticated supervision and control over building functions. For example, a smart home can control lighting, temperature, multimedia, security, window and door, and many other features (smarthomeenergy.co.uk, 2017).
- "Smart home" is a home equipped with lighting, heating and electronic devices that can be controlled remotely from a smartphone or computer: our smart home can be tracked over the Internet to ensure, for example, that central heating is on or the gas stove is turned on by the time we get home (oxforddictionaries.com 2017).
- "Smart Home is a private home with many home automation tools, consumer electronics, and more. Networking these tools provides new services and benefits to residents" (H. Strese, U. Seidel, T. Knape, and A. Botthof, 2010).
- "The controllable and intelligent home, where every system, including heating and lighting, communicates with each other, and can be controlled from anywhere, anytime

from a phone, tablet or computer, for the main goal for energy efficiency" (honeywell.com, 2016).

3.1 A general introduction to Smart Home systems

A smart home consists of three main parts. These are the following:

- communication channel: wired, wireless,
- peripheral devices: sensors, actuators,
- central control unit.

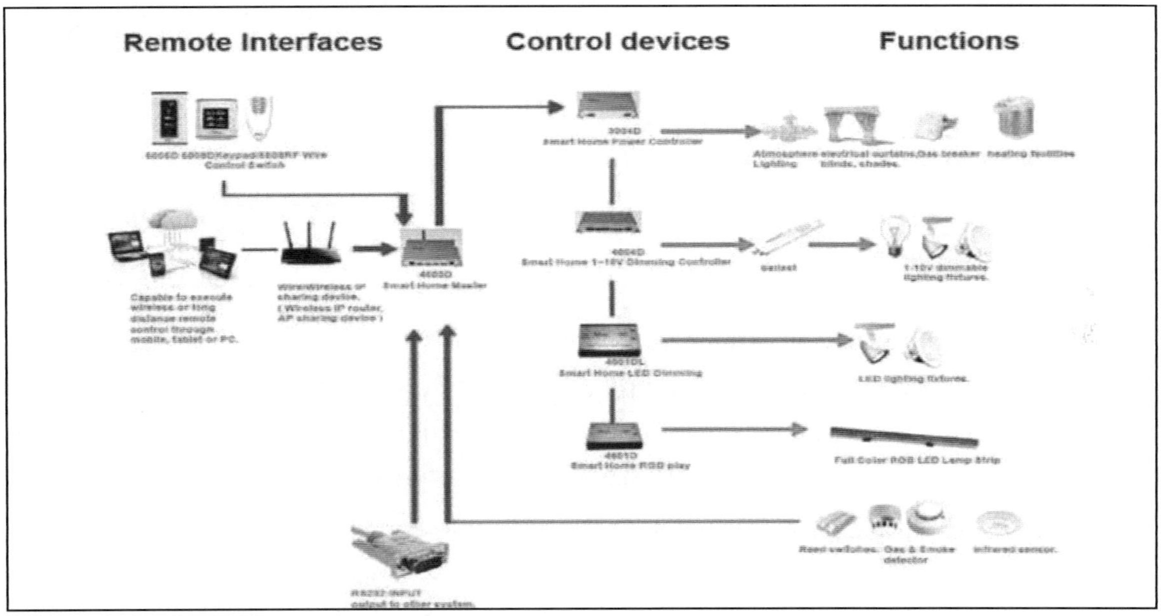

Figure 1 Typical structure of Smart Home systems [G. Chong et al. (2011)]

Usually, among the main benefits of "smart homes", three are highlighted. In the first place, optimized energy use is usually included, as the system can be taught according to our habits, so we can easily control, for example, the heating or cooling of our apartment, which can greatly reduce our costs.

In second place, there is the convenience feature, as the learned features let the system know exactly when and what device to turn on.

The third major benefit is security, as we can remotely observe our home and control our smart tools. Other benefits include monitoring your health.

Among the drawbacks are the high cost of systems, and the fact that there is not enough experience for users in this area, so they are afraid to start building a smart home system. This is also due to the fact that the whole system itself is very complex (incompatibility between the devices of different manufacturers, it is worth to choose a complex system of one manufacturer), and it involves significant risks if used without expertise.

The benefits and disadvantages of "smart home" are summarized in the following table:

Advantages	Disadvantages (possible barriers)
Optimized energy consumption	Relatively expensive
Real Estate Value Added Effect	Lack of experience
Increased sense of security	Hacker danger
Quality of life increasing effect	Complexity
Saving (time, money, energy)	Any damage to the interconnections can disrupt the system
Possibility of convenience features	The technology takes time to learn and get used to. Some people believe it makes life too complicated.

Table 1 The possible advantages and disadvantages of "smart homes" [Mussab A., et al. (2017), K. Hanly (2017), D. Mocrii et al. (2018), Biljana L. et al. (2017), own edition]

4 Popular companies of smart home systems and good practices for the 'smart home' developments in the Visegrad countries

4.1 Popular companies of smart home systems

I have examined the situation of the smart home market in the Visegrad countries. I've been examined the ten most popular companies by google rank and I wanted to know what services they offer (table 2), for what price, where can we buy the products.

Each of the companies has a complex system, which means that there is a central control unit that can be connected to various smart home devices. Most of the companies offer similar services, such as: control light, temperature, security, entertainment and shadow. Only two companies were found which offer healthcare or solar energy products related to smart home systems.

Firm	Light control	Heat/cool control	Security	Entertainment	Health monitoring	Shadow technique	Solar energy	Complex system
FIBARO	x	x	x	x		x		x
Chameleon	x	x	x	x		x		x
Quantum - Studio	x	x	x	x		x	x	x
Somfy	x	x	x			x		x
INELS	x	x		x				x
INCELOR	x	x	x	x		x		x
Legrand	x	x	x	x	x	x		x
iSTYLE	x	x	x	x				x
Xiaomishop	x	x	x	x		x		x
Conrad	x	x	x	x		x		x

Table 2 Popular Smart Home companies in the Visegrad countries [own edition]

I was categorized by price and subdivided into four groups: low (0-850 EUR), medium (850 to 1600 EUR), high (1600 to 3300 EUR) and overpriced over 3300 EUR. Products usually can be purchased online, but one or two companies have their own shop. The companies are advertising themselves mostly online, in one case we found traces of TV commercial.

4.2 Good practices for the 'smart home' developments

In the **Global Cities Index 2018** ranking of Prague (47th), Warsaw (54th) and Budapest (62nd) are included, so I was looking for examples of smart home developments in these cities and I would like to present the following good practices.

4.2.1 Prague

The Smart Home Care pilot project in Prague was approved by the mayor in 2017. This project is part of the European Union project, called 'Triangulum', in which Prague is actively involved. The whole project is linked to the Smart City concept, based on ICT infrastructure. The main goal of the Prague project is to test a smart system implemented in Prague's 7th District using the LYSE BLINK video communication tools (triangulum-project.eu, 2017).

Many other companies in the city are also installing smart home systems. One of the most well-known is the Domat Control System, which focuses on energy efficiency, but T-Mobile also has such a system in the city (domat-int.com, 2018).

4.2.2 Budapest

In Budapest, many companies have recognized the business potential of smart homes, and many of them have developed their own systems. Such companies include Cordia, FIBARO, iNELS, Innospot, Chameleon Smart Home… etc. Cordia has completed the biggest smart home development project:

"The development of 1500 new smart homes has been announced by Cordia, which is one of the largest real estate developments in the period since the change of regime. New projects were planned for 8 different locations in Budapest. According to the analysis of the company, there is now a significant demand for new homes, which the supply cannot keep up to now" (portfolio.hu, 2016).

In 2014, the **Europen Smart Cities Index** ranked several cities in the Visegrad countries. These are: Plzen (50th), Usti nad laben (51st), Banska Bystrica (54th), Rzeszow (55th), Szczecin (56th), Nitra (59th), Kosice (60th), Bydgoszcz (62nd), Győr (63rd), Pécs (64th), Bialystok (66th), Kielce (68th), Miskolc (69th), Suwalki (70th).
In the above-mentioned cities, I also looked for examples of smart home improvements, some of which are highlighted in the next section.

4.2.3 Kielce

A conference was held in April 2018 - How will the homes of the future look like in smart Kielce, and the company FIBARO, which deals with smart home developments, took part in it. In the framework of this, it was examined how much the city residents spend on heating for a year and concluded that using smart thermostats could reduce their costs by up to 42%. This will also be taken into account in the future for residential developments in the city (fibaro.com, 2017).

4.2.4 Kosice

"Since October 3, 2018, a successful Smart Project is supported also by SmartHome Lab, which Fpt Slovakia decided to open. The lab will allow you to simulate use of various common household devices in Smart Home environment, thanks to the interaction of IT specialists with the system, it will be possible to improve existing smart household features. The bonus of the system's practical use in the lab will also be the possibility of adding new features or commands that will further enhance the comfort of a "smart" user." (fpt.sk, 2018)

Conclusion

Based on the Global Cities Index and the European Smart Cities Index examined, the cities of the Visegrad region are not among the European leaders in the process of becoming a smart city, but they have recognized the potential of this in several cities. In the study, I examined a small part of the smart city concept and what smart home initiatives have been in the cities of the Visegrad region which are ranked in one of the examined indexes. In recent years, several such smart home projects have been launched in the region, one of the largest in Budapest, where demand for smart homes is such that supply cannot keep pace. I have also examined the smart home systems market in the Visegrad countries, and I highlighted ten companies. Each of the companies has a complex system and various services.

Acknowledgements

This research was supported by the project nr. EFOP-3.6.2-16-2017-00007, titled Aspects on the development of intelligent, sustainable and inclusive society: social, technological, innovation networks in employment and digital economy. The project has been supported by the European Union, co-financed by the European Social Fund and the budget of Hungary.

References

Bakonyi P. et al (2018). *Az okos város (Smart City)*. Dialóg Campus Kiadó: Budapest.

Stojkoska B. L. R. and Trivodaliev, K. V. (2017). 'A review of Internet of Things for smart home: Challenges and solutions'. *Journal of Cleaner Production*, 140, pp. 1454-1464.

Bizjan, B. (2014), 'Smart cities in Europe An overview of existing projects and good practices', *Smart Cities Conference.*

California Institute (2001), [Online]. Available at: http://smartcommunities.org/concept.php [cited 2019-01-12].

Chong, G., Zhihao, L. and Yifeng, Y. (2011). 'The research and implement of smart home system based on Internet of Things'. *Proceedings of International Conference on Electronics, Communications and Control (ICECC),* Ningbo, China.

domat-int.com (2018), [Online]. Available at: https://domat-int.com/en/references/case-studies/smarthome-prague-family-house [cited 2019-02-22].

fibaro.com (2017), [Online]. Available at: www.newsroom.fibaro.com [cited 2019-01-12].

fpt.sk (2018), [Online]. Available at: https://www.fpt.sk/en/najviac-inteligentnych-zariadeni-do-domacnosti-najdete-v-kosickom-fpt/ [cited 2019-02-24].

Giffinger, R., Fertner, Ch., Kramar, H. and Meijers, E. (2007). *Smart cities. Ranking of European medium-sized cities*. Vienna: University of Technology.

Hall, R. E. (2000). 'The vision of a smart city'. *Proceedings of the 2nd International Life Extension Technology Workshop*, Paris, France.

Hanly, K. (2017). 'Costs, advantages and disadvantages of smart homes', *Digital Journal.*

honeywell.com (2016), [Online]. Available at: www.intelligensotthon-tudastar.hu/egy-smart-home-rendszer-altalanos-felepitese/ [cited 2019-03-01].

Kearney, A. T. (2016). *Global Cities 2016. Which Global Cities performing best today, which have the best long-term potential, and what makes a "smart city"?* Korea: A.T. Kearney.

Mocrii, D. et al (2018). 'IoT-based smart homes: A review of system architecture, software, communications, privacy and security'. *Internet of Things*, 1-2.

Mussab A., et al (2017). 'A review of smart home applications based on Internet of Things'. *Journal of Network and Computer Applications,* 97.

Northstream (2010), [Online]. *White paper on revenue opportunities*, Available at: http://northstream.se/ [cited 2019-01-10].

oxforddictionaries.com (2017), [Online]. Available at: https://en.oxforddictionaries.com/definition/smart_home [cited 2019-01-14].

portfolio.hu (2016), [Online]. Available at: www.portfolio.hu/ingatlan/lakas/ezekben-a-keruletekben-epul-fel-az-1500-uj-okos otthon.230983.html [cited 2019-02-10].

smart-cities.eu (2014), [Online]. Available at: http://www.smart-cities.eu/?cid=01&ver=3 [cited 2019-03-02].

smarthomeenergy.co.uk (2017), [Online]. Available at: http://smarthomeenergy.co.uk/what-smart-home [cited 2019-02-10].

Strese, H., Seidel, U., Knape, T. and Botthof, A. (2010). *Smart Home in Deutschland, Berlin*. VDI/VDE-IT

Su, K., Li, J. and Fu, H. (2011). 'Smart city and the applications'. *IEEE International Conference on Electronics, Communications and Control (ICECC)*, pp. 1028–1031.

triangulum-project.eu (2017), [Online]. Available at: https://www.triangulum-project.eu/?page_id=2344 [cited 2019-01-30].

Possibilities of ITIL and PCF Mapping

Petr Rozehnal[1], Roman Danel[2]

Abstract. The paper deals with the issue of parallel deployment of frameworks supporting management in organizations. The possible mapping between the ITIL framework, which is used to manage IT services, and the Process Classification Framework used to support process management (including, but not limited to, information technology) is also discussed. Both frameworks are process-based, but their concepts are different in many ways. However, their parallel deployment has not been sufficiently analyzed in the literature.

Keywords: Information technology, frameworks, process, ITIL, PCF.

JEL Classification: M15, O31, O32

1 Introduction

As the information technology (IT) plays more significant role in business, management requirements growth. There are several frameworks that support the IT management. Moreover, we can also mention standards that affect management in IT. With regard to the diversity of business environments, frameworks are not worked out as a solution description but mostly as best practices. Their approach brings the source of knowledge and experience presented in a logical way. The possibilities of their implementation are individual, unique in each company.

We can find several important IT frameworks that differ in their focus. In this paper, we deal with ITIL, dominant process-oriented framework for IT service management, and Process Classification Framework (PCF), leading framework for benchmarking, performance improvement and managing content, which was developed by APQC in 1992.

ITIL and Process Classification Framework are process oriented and cover the area of information technology (Note: PCF is not specialized only for IT management area but for all main function areas in an organization); they are both worldwide known, leaders in their specializations with a long history.

We are aware of the fact that the discussed frameworks have a different focus. While ITIL is used for IT/ICT services management, PCF is typically used for benchmarking, process performance improvement and content management. The way of how these frameworks are described is also different. ITIL has extensive documentation and description is realized in the form of books (Note: ITIL is a commercial product, and its books are not publicly available). It is not just a description of processes since ITIL explains IT service as a management approach. The PCF description is brief, and the processes are hierarchically structured. More detailed information and case studies are available to APQC members only.

The goal of the paper is to support the possibility of their parallel deployment and to discuss the compatibility of both frameworks. In the next part, we argue the reasons for frame-

[1] VSB Technical University of Ostrava, Faculty of Economics, Department of Applied Informatics, Sokolská tř. 33, Ostrava, petr.rozehnal@vsb.cz.

[2] Institute of Technology and Businesses in České Budějovice, Faculty of Technology, Department of Mechanical Engineering, Okružní 517/10, 370 01 České Budějovice, rdanel@mail.vstecb.cz.

work mapping. Part 3 describes methodological approach, and in part 4 we analyze several typical ITIL issues and how they are addressed in the PFC. The last part discusses main conclusions.

2 Methodology

To study the common elements of the mentioned frameworks, PCF and ITIL, we started with a short analysis of their terminology. A common element is a process, which both frameworks understand in the same way (AXELOS, 2011; APQC, 2018), Both frameworks use a bit different terminology in relation to the area of focus. ITIL, for example, deals with services and functions meanwhile APQC PCF with services and solutions. ITIL is focused on services while the PCF's focus is much broader. PCF does not sufficiently distinguish the terminology that is important in ITIL such as incident, request or event.

PCF brings a comprehensive taxonomy of processes; the aim of the PCF implementation is to avoid process modelling mistakes. Identification of processes is essential for understanding their value. PCF is designed as a generic framework of business processes that can be applied to multiple industries and sectors. PCF framework has five levels: category – process group – process – activity (a key step performed to execute a process) – task (an element of work that goes into executing an activity) and describes more than 1,000 processes and activities. For the analysis of the PCF APQC framework, we focused on the category 8.0 ("Manage Information Technology") that addresses the IT management. We analyzed dependencies and structure of PCF for IT management and compared it with the structure of ITIL processes. We used the documentation from APQC's Process Classification Framework 7.2.1 and ITIL version 3 (2011 release).

With regard to the scope of the paper, we decided not to analyze the complete mapping between ITIL and PCF. We have selected important issues from ITIL framework and compared them with the PCF approach.

Note: There are several versions of the APQC PCF framework. When studying the framework, be aware of the fact that there is a significant change in numbering of processes between the version 6 and 7. In this paper, we use the latest version of PCF.

3 Simultaneous use of different frameworks

We are aware of the differences between frameworks, mainly their different purpose. On the other hand, there are cases when it is necessary to deal with the parallel implementation of the frameworks, and then they need to be aligned. Cater-Steel et al. (2006) analyze the multiple application of IT frameworks in enterprises. Pereira and da Silva (2012) claim problems with IT governance implementation due to complexity and overlapping of IT frameworks.

Cowan (2010) states the necessary to develop unique approach that supports situations with multiple frameworks (such as PCF, Cobit, ITIL, BPM, or SCOR). Frameworks are conceptually based as best practices, so the implementation teams must find their own way of applying and using them. The information about compatibility of frameworks, their overlapping and mapping of individual parts can support their deployment. We may find a lot of resources where these issues are discussed (Open Group, 2007; ITGI & OGC, 2005; ITGI &

OGC, 2008; Meijer et al., 2011). The frameworks also contain information about relationships to other frameworks (e.g. Cobit). Marrone and Kolbe (2011) summarize conclusions of several studies in their study. Furthermore, processes should be supported by software tools in practice. In this way, the software affects processes (and vice versa). Tiganoaia, Cercel & Pavlicek (2017) state the need for interoperability to integrate functional area processes with the processes within the organization.

As mentioned above, PCF is not an IT framework. PCF covers the most important functions and emphasizes the process approach. There are six categories of processes: 1.0 Develop Vision and Strategy, 2.0 Develop and Manage Products and Services, 3.0 Market and Sell Products and Services, 4.0 Deliver Physical Products, 5.0 Deliver Services, 6.0 Manage Customer Service. In addition to that, the PCF describes seven management and support services categories: 7.0 Develop and Manage Human Capital, 8.0 Manage Information Technology, 9.0 Manage Financial Resources, 10.0 Acquire, Construct, and Manage Assets, 11.0 Manage Enterprise Risk, Compliance, Remediation, and Resiliency, 12.0 Manage External Relationships, 13.0 Develop and Manage Business Capabilities.

APQC claims the PCF framework as a world authority for areas such as process benchmarking and performance improvement. The reasons for multiple frameworks application may be caused outside the IT management when the IT department uses another framework. This is different in comparison to the situation when multiple IT frameworks are used. Figure 1 illustrates the scope of frameworks. For example, PCF category 8.0 Manage Information Technology plays an important role for IT management area and is crucial to IT frameworks overlapping. Next category, 9.0 Manage financial resources, has strong relationship to the area of financial management. Both categories support main operating processes that deal with outputs creation (category 1.0 to 6.0). Moreover, the category 1.0 Develop Vision and Strategy is important as it is a starting point for the entire organization. Tesmer and Varney (2011) compare and classify frameworks according to different types (functional, enterprise) and branch of industry (industry, cross-industry). It is necessary to understand the nature of each framework (Ministr & Pitner, 2017) to apply it in an effective way. They analyze use of Cobit to support information security area.

The process management activities like process improvement/optimization or process reengineering based on PCF framework may be in conflict with IT management approach based on ITIL with ITIL process classification.

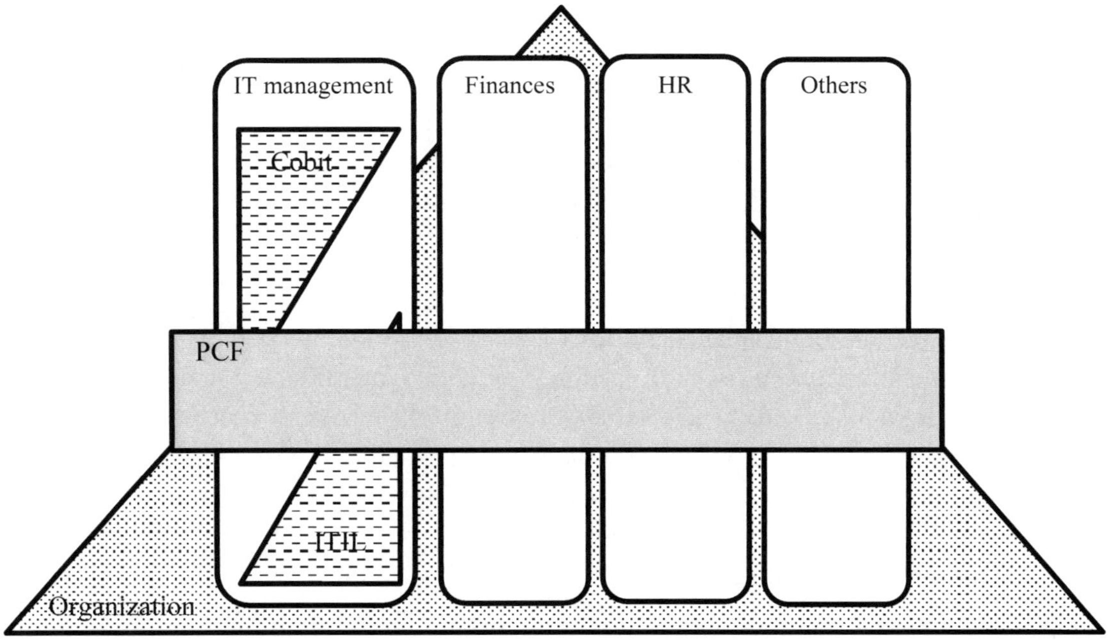

Figure 1 Relationship between PCF and other management areas

4 Examples of mapping between frameworks

First of all, it is worth to note that PCF defines processes in a hierarchical way using several levels (as stated above). The process categories are grouped by a function approach. There is no sequential arrangement used. The elements numbering doesn't imply a certain order. This aspect is important in comparison to IT frameworks where the emphasis is on the process continuity.

When PCF and ITIL are interconnected, initially, PCF section eight mapping seems to be essential. However, a more detailed analysis and published case study reveals that process mapping is a more complex task across the entire PCF structure.

4.1 Study of Strategy processes mapping

Top-down management approach considers the term strategy as an important element that is a starting point for other activities. Both ITIL and PCF operate with the term. The main differences between the frameworks are 1) in scope 2) in focus and 3) in details.

The scope of ITIL covers the area of IT service management, managing standardization of IT processes, mapping computer assets to process activities etc. However, its strategy applies only to IT services. ITIL discusses IT services in the context of business needs satisfaction by the supplier and understands the service as a means of delivering a value. PCF is process-oriented, it defines internal processes that support organization management. ITIL's strategic goal is to define the portfolio of services offered to customers. PCF's process approach aligns different functions of strategic processes and main strategy of the organization.

For comparison, it would be useful to use PCF process 8.2.4 Define IT service management strategy, which is similar to the ITIL process Strategy management for IT service. Nevertheless, it is not possible to simply link this ITIL process to the PCF process 8.2.4.

PCF defines seven activities in the process 8.2.4 Define IT service management strategy. Only one of them represents real tasks for IT service management strategy. Others are more concerned with setting up a service management system than with creating a strategy. This does not mean that in other categories and processes there are no processes/activities that are relevant for the service strategy.

ITIL process of Strategy management for IT service has three main subprocesses (strategic assessment, generation, execution) and feedback activities measurement and evaluation (AXELOS, 2011, fig. 4.3, p. 138). There is also a strong link to others processes from Service Design phase (such as Service portfolio or Demand management) as well as to some processes from other phases. From the recommended activities, it is obvious that ITIL respects the context of service deployment. In Strategic assessment there are, for example, analyses of internal and external environment, definition of market, or industry factor analysis. Many inputs (partial analysis) that are respected in ITIL when considering Service strategy are realized in PCF framework processes/activities but outside the IT area. The suggested ITIL and PCF mapping is as follows:

ITIL, Strategic Assessment	PCF 1.1.1, 1.1.2, 1.1.3, 8.1.1, 8.1.2,
ITIL, Strategy Generation	PCF 1.1.4, 8.1.3, 8.2,1, 8.2.2, 8.2.4, 8.3.1, 8.5.1,
ITIL, Strategy Execution	PCF 8.6.1, 8.7.1, 8.7.2, 8.7.4

On the other hand, ITIL does not address many of the areas processed under the PCF process group 8.2 Develop and manage IT business strategy. For example:

- PCF process 8.2.1 Define Business Technology and Governance Strategy defines "the need of technology in business and systematic implementation of IT investments" (APQC, 2019). This part of the strategy definition corresponds rather to Cobit framework.
- PCF process 8.2.2 Manage IT Portfolio Strategy is responsible for "systematic management of IT investments, projects and activities" (APQC, 2019) and analyzes the value from IT portfolio and resource allocation. These activities are much wider and with different focus than ITIL portfolio management.
- PCF process 8.2.3 Define and Maintain Enterprise Architecture belongs to Enterprise architecture area (EA) which is mentioned in Cobit and generally in frameworks like TOGAF or Zachman. ITIL does not deal with EA.

4.2 Examples of outsourced processes mapping

We can explain ITIL "Service Operation" mapping to PCF on the following example. If an IT company uses internal (in-house) services and external (outsourcing) services, ITIL does not distinguish these processes in the "Service Operation". PCF distinguishes between service delivery (towards customers; services represents the outputs of core business) and between IT services, which it understands as operating inside an organization (internally or externally). The suggested mapping is as follows:

ITIL Service Operation	PCF 5.2.2, 5.2.3, 5.3
ITIL Continual Service Improvement	PCF 2.1.2, 2.2.x

In comparison to IT service processes, e.g.:

ITIL Request Fulfilment	PCF 8.1.6, 8.7.5, 8.7.6, 8.7.7, 8.7.8
ITIL Incident Management	PCF 8.7.5, 8.7.6, 8.7.7, 8.7.8

ITIL versus PCF mapping must respect different approach of both frameworks.

PCF Section 8.0 maps well on to the ITIL framework at the process level. For in-house and outsourcing processes, the processes are replicated or needs to be divided in two in some cases. PCF classifies the outsourcing also in category five "Deliver Services", so this mapping should also be used. However, duplication of processes should be avoided. It is necessary to understand what additional activities are required to realize the delivery of work as a result of the outsourced relationship.

ITIL "Continual Service Improvement" (CSI) aims to continually improve the effectiveness and efficiency of IT processes and services. CSI also deals with innovation of services, and outsourcing is one of the possible innovations (Dumas at all, 2013). PCF category two "Develop and Manage Products and Services" should have been also used for the mapping of processes delivered as outsourcing.

5 Conclusion

We may summarize main differences that influenced mapping between frameworks:

- scope of enterprise functional areas - general enterprise processes versus IT service management area;
- focus on core enterprise entity - process versus IT service (solved by IT processes);
- level of description details - general versus detailed;
- method of description, terminology - brief versus descriptive.

It is helpful to understand and accept these differences before the process of mapping is started. Meaning of key terms such as process and service must be harmonized. The mapping between both frameworks is limited by above mentioned differences. In part four we have described links between processes, but these are strongly influenced due to fact that PCF is a list of processes without their sequence.

Although ITIL at first glance appears to be a framework that can be used exclusively in an IT/ICT environment, it provides recommendations for service lifecycle management, which is generally applicable in any environment where process management is applied. Both from the supplier and customer perspective.

PCF should be applied as a starting point to develop a classification of major process areas. A company that wants to create a process architecture can use PCF as a reference framework. One of the possible scenarios of its use may look as follows. At the beginning it is necessary to check each category and decide if it is relevant. The next step is to replace generic term in PCF with terms that are common within the company. Third step is providing a standardized vocabulary of terms (e.g. what is an “implementation”? – it could be implementation of software but also implementation of new regulations in the organization).

The paper deals with two issues in the IT service area. The service strategy and service delivery were discussed. ITIL discusses the processes of strategy management only in the scope of IT services but in a very complex way. Such approach is important for holistic understanding of service concept and necessary to respect business perspectives of IT services. PCF covers processes that support strategy development in a broader context. As a result, there are a lot of processes/activities that support general strategy design (not only IT service strategy). Moreover, these processes/activities are structured with respect to functional and not sequential aspects. With regard to its complex focus, the PCF framework is more suitable for mapping with a similarly focused IT framework. In the IT strategy area, we can mention for example Cobit, which is often seen as an umbrella for IT frameworks deployment. Cobit that is focused on IT management conceives the term “strategy” in a much wider context.

The service delivery area illustrates other differences in approach between the both frameworks. It is important to distinguish the nature of the objects to which a framework is applied. In PCF, IT services are addressed in category 8, while services for customers in category 5. The PCF specializes in process definition and description. Despite being process oriented, ITIL is more descriptive and applies management philosophy approach.

The purpose of PCF is to categorize, unify terminology and create process definitions that can then be applied to other process management methodologies. The ITIL implementation can be based on this process definition. Parallel, simultaneous implementation of PCF and ITIL (or other IT methods) can support a unified process management approach across the organization.

References

APQC. (2018). *Glossary pf process and performance excellence terms*, [Online]. Available at: https://www.apqc.org/knowledge-base/download/317732 [cited 2019-01-11].

AXELOS. (2011). *ITIL® Service Strategy*. 2nd ed. London: TSO.

Cater-Steel, A., Tan, WG. and Toleman, M. (2006). Challenge of adopting multiple process improvement frameworks. *The 14 the European conference on information systems (ECIS 2006)*, Gothenburg, Sweden, pp. 1-12.

Pereira, R. and da Silva, M. M. (2012). ‘Literature Review: Guidelines and Contingency Factors for IT Governance’. *The European, Mediterranean & Middle Eastern Conference on Information Systems 2012 (EMCIS2012)*, Munich, Germany, pp. 342-360.

Marrone, M. and Kolbe. L. M. (2011). ‘Impact of IT Service Management Frameworks on the IT Organization‘. *Business & Information Systems Engineering,* 3 (1), pp. 5-18.

Cowan, M. (2010). Aligning by Process across a Large Enterprise, [Online]. Available at: https://www.apqc.org/knowledge-base/download/37250/AligningbyProcessAcrossaLargeEnterprise%5B1%5D.pdf [cited 2019-01-24].

Machteld M., Smalley, M., Taylor, S. and Dunwoodie, C. (2011). *ITIL® V3 and BiSL: Sound guidance for business IT alignment from a business perspective*. The Stationery Office.

Open Group. (2007). Mapping of TOGAF 8.1 with COBIT 4.0 (Part I).

ITGI & OGC, (2005). Aligning Cobit, ITIL and ISO 17799 for Business Benefit: Management Summary.

ITGI & OGC. (2008). Aligning CobiT® 4.1, ITIL® V3 and ISO/IEC 27002 for Business Benefit.

APQC. (2019). APQC Process Classification Framework (PCF) - Cross Industry - Excel Version 7.2.1, [Online]. Available at: https://www.apqc.org/knowledge-base/collections/apqcs-process-classification-framework-pcf-cross-industry-and-industry-sp [cited 2019-01-15].

Tesmer, J. and Varney, J. (2011). Using Process Frameworks to Get Real Work Done. APQC,

[Online]. Available at: https://www.apqc.org/sites/default/files/files/Tesmer,%20John%20-%20Using%20Process%20Frameworks%20to%20Get%20Real%20Work%20Done-1.pdf [cited 2019-01-10].

Dumas, M., LaRosa, M., Mendling, J. and Reijers, H. (2013). *Fundamental of Business Process Management*. 2nd edition. Springer.

Ministr, J. and Pitner, T. (2017). 'Process Support of Information Security according to COBIT (R) 5'. *Proceedings of the International Conference on Strategic Management and its Support by Information Systems 2017*. Ostrava, Czech Republic, pp. 418-424.

Tiganoaia, B., Cercel, C. and Pavlícek, A. (2017). 'Some Risk Management Software Tools – An Exploratory Study'. *The European Proceedings of Social & Behavioural Sciences*. Barcelona, Spain, pp. 23-32.

Word-Graph vs. Bag-of-Words Feature Extraction for Solving Author Identification Problem

Miloš Švaňa [1]

Abstract. In this paper we examine multiple methods for solving the problem of text vectorization in context of text classification. We compare two variants of a traditional Bag-of-Words technique to a newly proposed Word-Graph approach based on graph representation of a text document and measuring similarities between graph structures. We further propose modifications to the Word-Graph method potentially improving classification accuracy. Results of experiments performed while solving an author identification problem on a dataset consisting of speeches made during meetings of Slovak National Parliament show that the Word-Graph approach offers similar levels of accuracy as traditional methods. Proposed modifications significantly improve the performance in case of imbalanced number of documents for each class in the training set.

Keywords: Machine Learning, Natural Language Processing, Word-Graph, Bag-of-Words, Classification.

JEL classification: C88

1 Introduction

Both researchers and businesses are interested in understanding documents written in human languages. Such texts represent a significant source of data to support decision making. Additionally long-term visions of many technological companies include the idea of natural communication between humans and computers (Google Assistant, Cortana, Siri).

One of the most important tasks performed on natural language text documents is classification. Its practical applications include sentiment analysis, topic modeling, spam filtering, automatic language detection or author identification.

Generally speaking classification algorithms can process only objects described by numerical features. Therefore one of the main challenges in text classification is extracting such features from text documents. Bag-of-Words is a traditional approach to this problem. In its basic form it transforms the text document into a vector of word frequencies. Although intuitive, this method has some significant disadvantages: resulting feature vectors are high-dimensional, sparse and ignore context of the words.

In this paper we are investigating an alternative Word-Graph approach used previously by Castillo et al. (2015) and Violos et al. (2016). This method represents text documents as directed graphs and uses graph similarity metrics to extract features. In their paper the authors test the approach on a tweet sentiment analysis task examining different similarity measurements.

We are applying this method in context of author identification, which is characterized by long text documents (opposed to limited length tweets) and large amount of classes. Our aim is to compare method's classification accuracy with the traditional Bag-of-Words approach.

[1] VŠB - Technical University of Ostrava, Faculty of Economics, milos.svana.st@vsb.cz

Furthermore, we intend to examine how the algorithm behaves, when the number of documents is similar for each class and when there are notable differences.

If the algorithm potentially underperforms we aim at proposing and examining additional modifications increasing classification performance.

The paper is structured as follows: Section 2 provides an overview of text vectorization algorithms, namely variants of the Bag-of-Words approach and the Word-Graph technique. Section 3 proposes modifications to the Word-Graph method potentially improving classification accuracy. Experiment methodology is explained in section 4, results of the experiments are discussed in section 5. Finally, in section 6 we summarize the main findings and propose directions of further research.

2 Text Vectorization Fundamentals

As mentioned in introduction, most classification algorithms are capable of processing only numerical features. Therefore, text documents have to be transformed into such representation. This process is often called *vectorization*.

Bag-of-Words is a traditional approach used to solve the problem. Raschka (2015) describes it as a two-step process:

1) Construction of a vocabulary of unique tokens (words) from the whole corpora (set of text documents),
2) Transforming documents into feature vectors containing numbers of occurrences of each token in given document.

This naive approach comes with an issue: it ignores token relevancy (how useful a token is when distinguishing between multiple classes). Ramos (2015) describes how this problem can be solved by replacing token frequencies with the *term frequency - inverse-document frequency* metric. For a word w in document d is it calculated as follows:

$$w_d = f_{w,d} \cdot log\frac{n_d}{1 + f_{D,w}} \tag{1}$$

In equation 1:

- $f_{w,d}$ represents the frequency of the word w in document d,
- n_d is the total number of documents in the training set,
- and $f_{D,w}$ is the inverse frequency - number of documents containing word w.

Although *term frequency - inverse document frequency* removes the problem of word relevancy, Bag-of-Words methods still have other unresolved issues - most notably they ignore meaning and context of the words.

Word-graph representation partially addresses the problem of context. The approach used by Violos et al. (2016) can be again divided into multiple steps:

1) Construction of a word-graph for each document.
2) Construction of a word-graph for each class by merging graphs of documents belonging to the given class. A node or an edge is a part of the class word-graph if it is present in at least in one of the document graphs.

3) Calculation of similarity between all document graph and class graph combinations.

In a Word-Graph each word is represented by a node. There is a directed edge connecting two words if in the target word can be found in n or less positions after the origin word. Such a graph is illustrated by figure 1

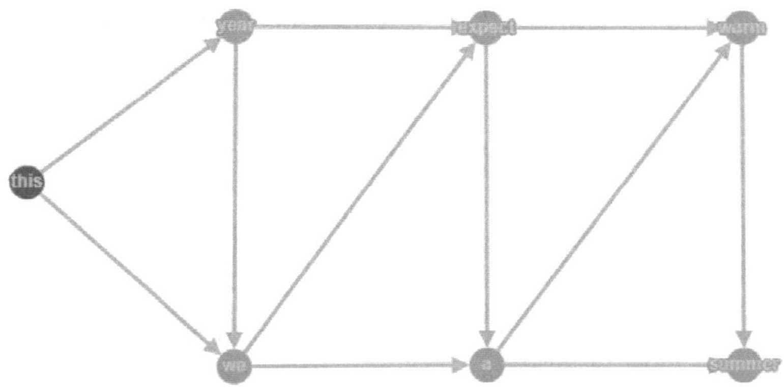

Figure 1 Word-Graph for document "This year we can expect a warm summer" and $n = 2$

Violos et al. (2016) proposes multiple metrics for measuring similarity, all based on comparing graphs' edges. The results show only small differences in classification accuracy. In this paper we are using the *containment similarity* metric calculated as the number of common edges divided by number of edges in the smaller graph:

$$CS(G_T, G_C) = \frac{\sum_{e \in G_T} \mu(e, G_C)}{min(|G_T|, |G_C|)} \tag{2}$$

Function $\mu(e, G)$ in equation 2 is a membership function returning 1 if the edge e can be found in graph G and 0 otherwise.

Intuitively, during classification one can simply select the class having the highest value of the similarity metric. Violos et al. (2016) proposes an alternative approach: calculate the similarity metric for each *document graph - class graph* pairing and use the results to train a classifier using well known approaches such as Support Vector Machines.

For comparison, Castillo et al. (2015) utilize the Word-Graph differently, selecting top 100 most important nodes (words) as ranked by centrality measures and then building a vector of word frequencies similarly to the Bag-of-Word approach. This method is not further studied in this paper.

Both Castillo et al. (2015) and Violos et al. (2016) use a word as a basic unit for graph construction. It is worthy to mention an alternative approach examined by Aisopos et al. (2016). Authors use character groups of fixed length instead of words. Slightly worse results are reported in their paper.

3 Proposed Word-Graph Modifications

We further propose a set of modifications potentially improving the accuracy of the Word-Graph approach. These modifications are tested on the same classification problem and the results compared to the original algorithm.

3.1 Edge weights

As mentioned by Violos et al. (2016), one of the directions worth examining is adding weights to the Word-Graph edges. We test a simple approach inspired by the Bag-of-Words techniques; we define the weight of each edge as the number of occurrences of the word pair. This leads to a modified similarity metric:

$$CS(G_T, G_C) = \frac{\sum_{e \in G_T} min(w_{e,G_T}, w_{e,G_C})}{min(|G_T|, |G_C|)} \tag{3}$$

In equation 3 $w_{e,G}$ represents the weight of the edge e inside graph G. As shown in equation 4 size of a graph $|G|$ is calculated as the sum of all its edge weights:

$$|G| = \sum_{e \in G} w_{e,G} \tag{4}$$

3.2 Feature scaling

When calculating the similarity metric as defined by equation 3 for the training set at least one value in the feature vector will be 1 (similarity between the document and the class the document belongs to). This is generally not the case when calculating similarities for unknown samples afterwards. In other words, the training set does not accurately represent unseen data which might cause issues for the classifier. To solve this problem we propose to normalize the feature vectors or to scale them to the $[0; 1]$ interval. Both options are examined during experiments.

3.3 Recurrent edges

Another modification inspired by Bag-of-Words methods is adding recurrent edges the graph (edges leading to the same word). Combined with edge weights and similarity metric as defined above, recurrent edges add information about number of occurrences of each word as a separate token to the graph.

3.4 Weighted classes

Similarity metric as defined in section 3.1 can potentially favor classes having larger amount of documents in the training set. The class graph will be bigger (in terms of edge count) and contain more unique words. As a potential solution, we propose to modify the similarity metric to account for the number of documents in the training set for given class:

$$CS(G_T, G_C)^* = CS(G_T, G_C) \cdot ln(n_C) \tag{5}$$

In equation 5 we propose the use of the natural logarithm of the number of documents in given class n_C. The idea is based on the assumption that with growing number of documents fewer previously unseen words are added to the vocabulary. This hypothesis should be validated by further research.

4 Experiment methodology

Goal of the experiments is to compare the accuracy of the Bag-of-Words approach (both word count and term frequency - inverse document frequency variants) and the Word-Graph representation when solving an author identification problem.

A set of speeches made during meetings of Slovak national parliament is used as training data. To examine the problem in a reasonable time the amount of classes in the dataset is reduced to 10. Length of a single speech has to be at least 150 characters.

Two different subsets of speeches fulfilling these requirements are tested. First one consists of classes having similar number of documents - ranging from 300 to 400. The second subset represents a situation where the number of documents in each class is not balanced - first 10 classes having 250 documents or more are selected.

Scikit-learn implementations of Bag-of-Words methods were chosen for testing. Transformation of text documents and similarity metric calculation is implemented "from scratch" using Python. This custom implementation is made compatible with other parts of the Scikit-learn[1] framework, allowing for automated hyper-parameter tuning using Grid Search.

Each grid search configuration is tested using 5-fold cross-validation. Best performing configuration is then used on a training set comprising of 10% of available documents.

As mentioned in section 1, Bag-of-Words approach produces high-dimensional feature vectors. To reduce the number of dimensions only up to 1000 most relevant words are selected to train the classification model. These words are chosen by Scikit-Learn *SelectKBest* feature selector which uses Anova *F-value* to rate features.

Linear Support Vector Machine is chosen to perform the final phase of classification using either Bag-of-Words vectors or Word-Graph similarities as input. This method is one of the recommended techniques for solving text classification problems (Aggarwal and Zhai, 2012) and according to Violos et al. (2016) it was one of the best performing techniques when dealing with the sentiment analysis problem presented in the paper.

5 Results

Figure 2 shows the accuracy results of the balanced classes experiment. Modifications proposed in section 3 slightly improve the performance of the Word-Graph method compared to the original one. Accuracy of the modified method sits between the naive Bag-of-Words (CountVectorizer) and the TfIdf approach.

The test was repeated multiple times and in some instances the modified Word-Graph method outperformed the TfIdf vectorizer. This behavior might be caused by random 5-fold splitting and selection of the test sample.

The difference in accuracy between the original and modified versions of the Word-Graph vectorization is fully visible in Figure 3 displaying the results for the case of imbalanced classes[2]. Original technique wasn't able to provide higher then 90% accuracy while the per-

[1] https://scikit-learn.org/stable/

[2] Largest class having 1701 documents, the smallest one 252 documents

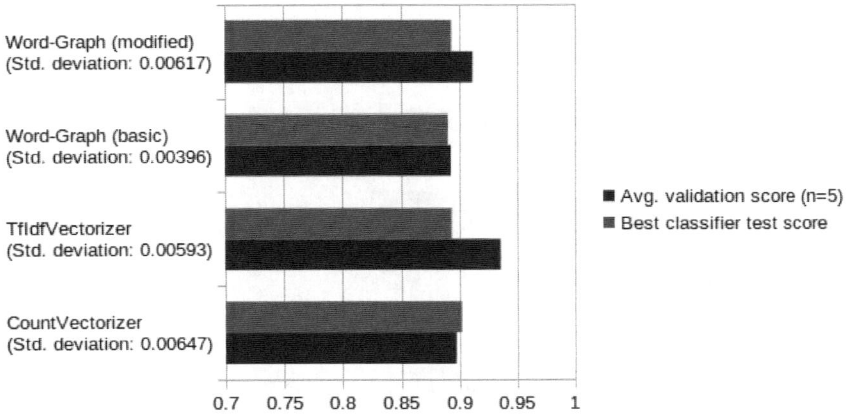

Figure 2 Accuracy of different vectorization methods given a dataset with balanced classes

formance of the modified version is still placed between CountVectorizer and TfIdfVectorizer.

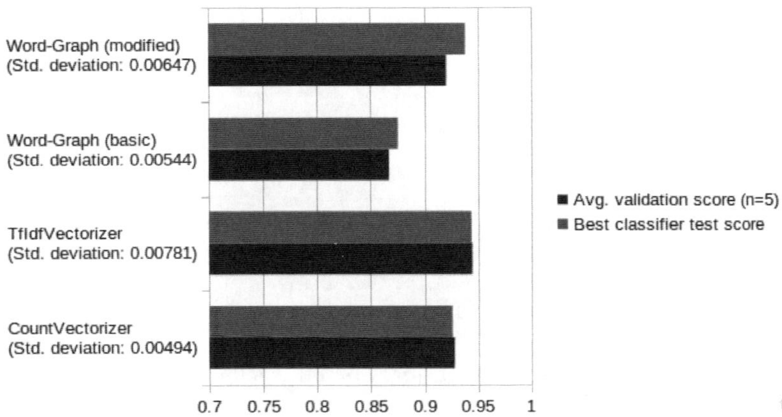

Figure 3 Accuracy of different vectorization methods given a dataset with imbalanced classes

Taking modifications described in section 3 into account separately, most significant improvement is observed after adding recurrent edges. Figure 4 also shows that using scaling or weighted classes separately actually causes the accuracy to fall. When it comes to scaling, the chart shows results for normalization which performed significantly better than the $[0; 1]$ range scaler. It is important to note that the scaling validation score has high variance compared to other modifications.

Another discovered finding is the fact, that best performance was provided when setting the window size for word graph to $n = 2$ (only the edges to the following word and the word itself are created). Accuracy of the algorithm falls down with increasing window size as illustrated in Figure 5.

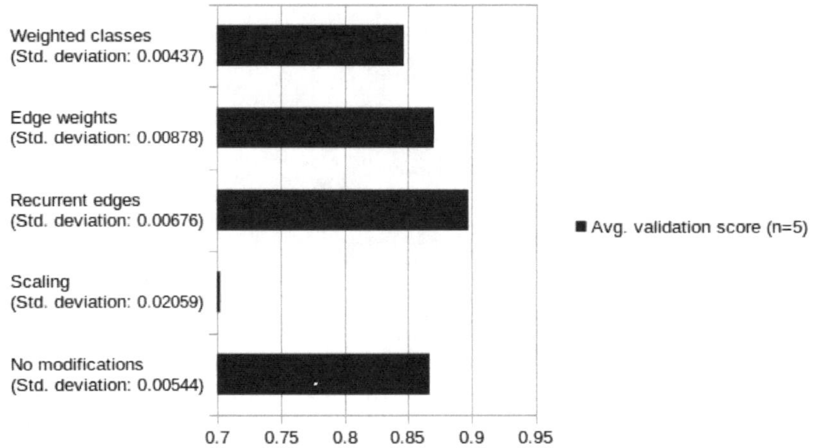

Figure 4 Influence of separate Word-Graph modifications on classification accuracy

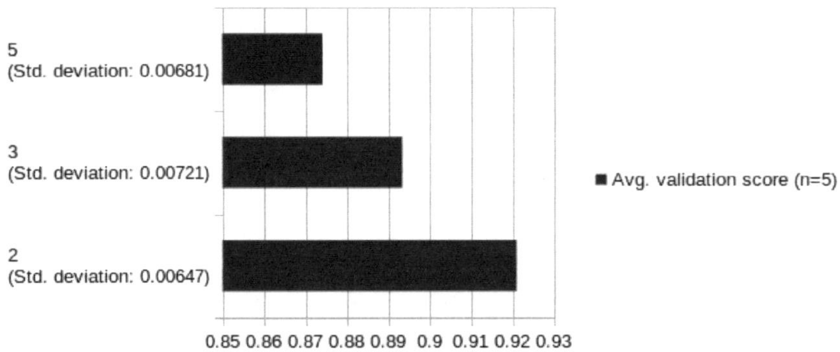

Figure 5 Classification accuracy for different window sizes

Training score (obtained from testing the classifier on the same data as it was trained on) was 1.0 or very close to 1.0 for each Word-Graph experiment.This significant difference between the training and test scores is, according to Raschka (2015), a sign of overfitting.

6 Conclusion

Results of comparison of multiple approaches to text vectorization show that the Word-Graph technique provides accuracy comparable to more traditional Bag-of-Words approaches. Application of proposed modifications, recurrent edges in particular, helps improving model's accuracy especially in the case of imbalanced number of documents belonging to different classes.

The Word-Graph approach to text classification will be further examined focusing namely on comparing different similarity metrics, edge weight definitions, types of classifiers and solving problems with higher number of classes. Overfitting is another relevant issue of the Word-Graph model that needs to be addressed.

Additionally, best performing configuration uses a small window and many Bag-of-Words inspired modifications. This might might signal that the model simply mimics Bag-of-Words approaches without adding any value when solving text classification problems. This hypothesis should also be examined.

7 Acknowledgments

This article was created with the financial support of the Student grant competition EkF, VŠB-TU Ostrava as a part of project SP2019/81.

References

Aggarwal, C. C. and Zhai, C. (2012). *Mining Text Data*. Springier, New York.

Aisopos, F., Tzannetos, D., Violos, J. and Varvarigou, T. (2016). 'Using n-gram graphs for sentiment analysis: an extended study on Twitter'. *2016 IEEE Second International Conference on Big Data Computing Service and Applications*, pp. 44-51.

Castillo, E., Cervantes, O., Vilariño, D., Báez, D. and Sánchez A. (2015). 'UDLAP: Sentiment Analysis Using a Graph Based Representation'. *Proceedings of the 9th International Workshop on Semantic Evaluation*, pp. 556-560.

Ramos, J.E. (2003). 'Using TF-IDF to Determine Word Relevance in Document Queries'. *Proceedings of the First Instructional Conference on Machine Learning*, Born, Germeny, pp. 1-4.

Raschka, S. (2015). *Python Machine Learning*. Birmingham: Packt Publishing.

Violos, J., Tserpes, K., Psomakelis, E., Psychas, K. and Varvarigou, T. (2016). 'Sentiment Analysis Using Word-Graphs'. *Proceedings of the 6th International Conference on Web Intelligence, Mining and Semantics*, Nimes, France.

Authors	Collective of authors
Editors	Radek Nemec, Lucie Chytilova
Department	Department of Systems Engineering
Title	Proceedings of the 13th International Conference on Strategic Management and its Support by Information Systems
Place, Year, Edition	Ostrava, 2019, 1st ed.
Number of pages	425
Publisher	VŠB-Technical University of Ostrava, Faculty of Economics, Czech Republic
Publication form	1) Electronic, distributed on a USB pen drive 2) On-line, published on a publicly accessible website
Production	Department of Systems Engineering

VŠB - Technical University of Ostrava
17. Listopadu 15/2172
708 33 Ostrava - Poruba
Czech Republic

ISBN 978-1-5108-8872-2

9 781510 888722

CURRAN ASSOCIATES INC.
proceedings.com